MW01629090

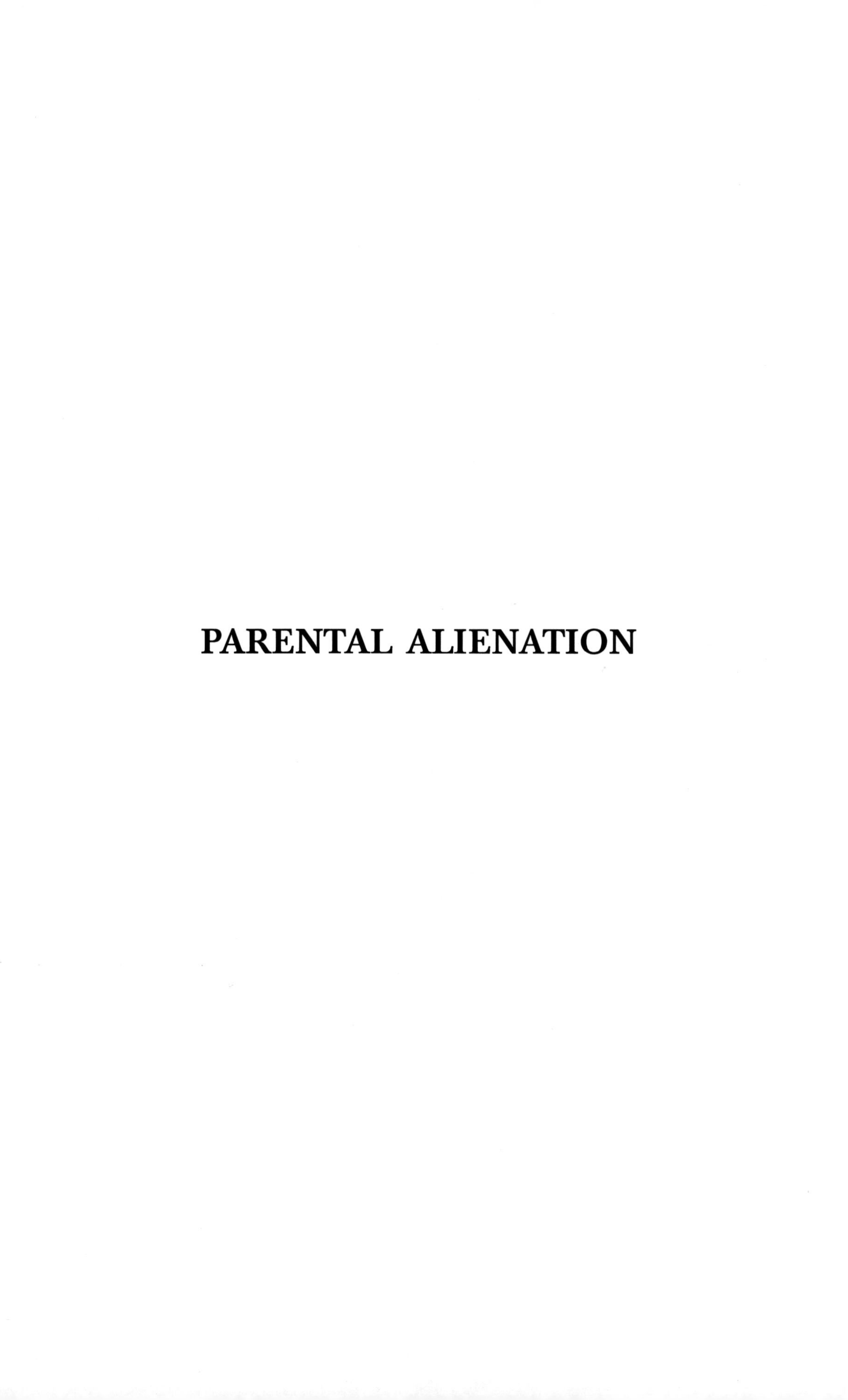

PARENTAL ALIENATION

Publication Number 1116

AMERICAN SERIES
IN
BEHAVIORAL SCIENCE AND LAW

Edited by

RALPH SLOVENKO, B.E., LL.B., M.A., PH.D.

Professor of Law and Psychiatry
Wayne State University
Law School
Detroit, Michigan

PARENTAL ALIENATION

The Handbook for Mental Health and Legal Professionals

Edited by

DEMOSTHENES LORANDOS

WILLIAM BERNET

and

S. RICHARD SAUBER

(With 11 Other Contributors)

CHARLES C THOMAS • PUBLISHER, LTD.
Springfield • Illinois • U.S.A.

Published and Distributed Throughout the World by

CHARLES C THOMAS • PUBLISHER, LTD.
2600 South First Street
Springfield, Illinois 62704

ISBN 978-0-398-08881-1 (hard)
ISBN 978-0-398-08750-0 (ebook)

Library of Congress Catalog Card Number: 2013011346

With THOMAS BOOKS *careful attention is given to all details of manufacturing and design. It is the Publisher's desire to present books that are satisfactory as to their physical qualities and artistic possibilities and appropriate for their particular use.* THOMAS BOOKS *will be true to those laws of quality that assure a good name and good will.*

Printed in the United States of America
MM-R-3

Library of Congress Cataloging-in-Publication Data

Parental alienation : the handbook for mental health and legal professionals / edited by Demosthenes Lorandos, William Bernet, and S. Richard Sauber ; (with 11 other contributors).
pages cm. -- (Behavioral science & law ; 1116)
Includes bibliographical references and index.
ISBN 978-0-398-08881-1 (hard) -- ISBN 978-0-398-08750-0 (ebook)
1. Parental alienation syndrome--Handbooks, manuals, etc. 2. Mental health laws--Handbooks, manuals, etc. I. Lorandos, Demosthenes, 1946– editor of compilation. II. Bernet, William, editor of compilation. III. Sauber, S. Richard, editor of compilation. IV. Title: Handbook for mental health and legal professionals.

RJ506.P27P38 2013
618.92'89--dc23

2013011346

CONTRIBUTORS

Amy Baker has a doctorate in developmental psychology from Teachers College of Columbia University and has twenty-five years' experience conducting applied research on children and families. She is the author of *Adult Children of Parental Alienation Syndrome: Breaking the Ties That Bind* (W. W. Norton); the author or coauthor of over seventy peer reviewed academic articles; the coeditor of the forthcoming *Working With Alienated Children and Families: A Clinical Guidebook* (Routledge Press) and a coauthor of the forthcoming *Co-Parenting Under Fire: Protecting Your Child From Loyalty Conflicts and Alienation* (New Harbinger Publications).

R. Christopher Barden is a psychologist/lawyer/scientist trained at Harvard, Stanford, U.C. Berkeley, and the University of Minnesota. He is a nationally recognized litigator, licensed clinical psychologist, and national award-winning research scientist in psychology. He serves as an expert witness, attorney, and/or litigation consultant in family, civil, and criminal cases. He has won many dozens of parental alienation cases in over thirty states. Dr. Barden has published in the leading science and professional journals and texts in child psychology, social psychology, clinical psychology, psychiatry, surgery, pediatrics, and law. Contact Dr. Barden at rcbarden@mac.com.

William Bernet, M.D., a graduate of Harvard Medical School, is professor emeritus at Vanderbilt University. He is board certified in general psychiatry, child psychiatry, and forensic psychiatry. Dr. Bernet has testified as an expert in eighteen states. He has published articles and chapters regarding group and individual therapy with children and adolescents, humor in psychotherapy, forensic child psychiatry, child maltreatment, true and false allegations of abuse, satanic ritual abuse, child custody, parental alienation, and testimony regarding behavioral genomics. Dr. Bernet and Judge Don Ash published *Children of Divorce* (2007). He edited *Parental Alienation, DSM-5, and ICD-11* (2010).

Tamara Brockhausen graduated from the PUC University in São Paulo and earned a master's degree in clinical psychology from São Paulo University with a thesis on Parental Alienation and Psychoanalysis. She is a mediator, clinical specialist, and the former mediator for the Bar of Santana, São Paulo. She is a practicing psychoanalyst, and works in forensic psychology as a technical and psychotherapeutic assistant in cases of parental alienation, child abuse, and custody disputes. She is also an author, researcher, and speaker on Parental Alienation, child sex abuse, and differential diagnosis. She was a contributor to *Parental Alienation, DSM-5, and ICD-11.*

Terence W. Campbell, Ph.D., is board certified in forensic psychology by the American Board of Professional Psychology. He was one of the first Michigan psychologists to regularly undertake child custody evaluations. The Michigan Supreme Court recognized Dr. Campbell's work in its *Fletcher* decision, finding that attempts at inferring parental fitness from impressions of moral fitness are contraindicated by peer-reviewed data. Dr. Campbell's published exchanges with Dr. Richard Gardner prompted a more sophisticated, empirically driven conceptualization of parental alienation. Dr. Campbell is the author, or coauthor, of seven different books. His peer-reviewed articles have appeared in many scientific and professional journals.

Doug Darnall, Ph.D., is an Ohio psychologist in practice since 1979. He worked as a court psychologist for Trumbull County Family Court for twenty-one years and is currently CEO at PsyCare. He has published *Divorce Casualties: Protecting Your Children from Parental Alienation* and *Divorce Casualties: Understanding Parental Alienation.* He has appeared in court on over one hundred cases in twelve states involving custody, parental alienation, and other forensic matters. He has appeared on the Montel Show and Court TV. He has given presentations for the Missouri State Bar, North Dakota State Bar Associations, AFCC, Children's Rights Council, and local and state bar associations.

Christian T. Dum, Ph.D., studied psychology, computer science, and physics at the University of Vienna, the Vienna University of Technology, and the Massachusetts Institute of Technology. He was a member of the physics faculty at Cornell University and did research in space physics. He currently heads a registered nonprofit organization in Germany that informs on the psychological and legal aspects of child custody (www.beideeltern.de). He has contributed to this organization since 1997, with parental alienation an early and continuing important topic.

Bradley W. Freeman, M.D., is a board-certified general, child & adolescent, and forensic psychiatrist. Clinically, he works closely with the eating disorders population but also practices child and adolescent inpatient psychiatry, which covers a broad range of acute psychiatric conditions. In his forensic work, Dr. Freeman performs a variety of criminal and civil assessments such as parenting time evaluations, parental fitness assessments, competency to stand trial, sexual abuse evaluations, and malpractice. He also works with a team of mental health professionals who give guidance and perform evaluations for children and adolescents who are in the custody of the state.

Demosthenes Lorandos, Ph.D., J.D., is a first-generation American of Greek and Australian descent. After graduating from San Francisco State he studied science at the New School for Social Research. He has been a clinical and forensic psychologist for four decades. He trained in law with the Jesuits at the University of Detroit and has been a litigator for two decades. He is a senior partner at *Lorandos Joshi,* a litigation firm with offices in New York, Washington, DC, and Ann Arbor. He has been involved in parental alienation cases all over the United States for more than thirty years.

Michele Lowrance has been a domestic relations judge in Cook County since 1995. She is the author of *The Good Karma Divorce* (2010) and coauthor of *Parental Alienation 911 Workbook.* She's a regular contributor to the Huffington Post and serves on the Cook County Advisory Board for Marriage and Family Counseling Service. She has been a guest on Good Morning America, the CBS Morning Show, ABC, and CNN and cohosts Family Matters Radio with Jill Egizii. She has been a presenter on parental alienation for Illinois Judicial Education, the Cook County Child Representatives Program, and the Association of Family and Conciliation Courts.

Deirdre C. Rand, Ph.D., is a psychologist in private practice who is well-known for her articles on the spectrum of parental alienation syndrome (PAS), including a follow-up study of interventions and a social psychology perspective on the views expressed by parental alienation critics. She helped to develop the Family Bridges Workshop for severely alienated children, an educationally oriented program designed to help families in which the court has determined that the rejected parent should have sole custody. Dr. Rand's articles are the basis of an online CE course on parental alienation, offered through the Zur Institute.

S. Richard Sauber, Ph.D., is a Board-Certified Diplomate in Clinical and Family Psychology, ABPP. He has a national family forensic practice from his office in Boca Raton, Florida. He has conducted forensic evaluations in sixteen counties within the State of Florida, fourteen other U.S. states, and several provinces in Canada, where he also holds a license. Formerly, he was Professor of Psychology in the Departments of Psychiatry in the Medical Schools of Brown, Columbia, and the University of Pennsylvania. He has authored or edited sixteen professional books and has served as the editor of the *American Journal of Family Therapy* editor since 1976.

Richard A. Warshak, Ph.D., is a clinical, research, and consulting psychologist and Clinical Professor at the UT Southwestern Medical Center. Dr. Warshak's groundbreaking research has made him one the world's most respected authorities on divorce, custody, and the psychology of alienated children. His work appears in 13 books, 65 articles, and more than 100 presentations in North America, Europe, and the Middle East. His book, *Divorce Poison,* is the classic guide to parental alienation. Dr. Warshak was a White House consultant on child custody. He appears in a PBS documentary and in *Welcome Back Pluto: Understanding, Preventing, and Overcoming Parental Alienation.*

Abe Worenklein, M.Sc., Ph.D., is a clinical/forensic psychologist and family mediator in private practice in Montreal, professor at Dawson College, and lecturer at Concordia University. Dr. Worenklein has been declared an expert witness in Superior Court and Youth Court several hundred times primarily in Canada and has been cited in many Canadian judgments on parental alienation. He has presented on this topic at many professional conferences in Canada and the United States. Dr. Worenklein is on the committee to have parental alienation accepted into *DSM-5* and *ICD-11* and on the International Editorial Board of the *American Journal of Family Therapy.*

PREFACE

Each of us has authored and edited many professional textbooks. This book, because of its complexity, has taken more time and commitment than any other writing project. During the last two years, focused devotion was needed to bring this book to completion and finally publication. The easiest part was in the naming the text: *Parental Alienation: The Handbook for Mental Health and Legal Professionals.*

It all began in early 2011, when the publisher of *The International Handbook of Parental Alienation Syndrome: Conceptual, Clinical and Legal Issues* contacted Dr. Demosthenes Lorandos. Publisher Charles C Thomas requested an updated and new book offering a comprehensive text on what has been happening in the field of parental alienation. *The International Handbook* consisted of thirty-four chapters, which were invited and edited by Richard A. Gardner, M.D., S. Richard Sauber, Ph.D., and Demosthenes Lorandos, Ph.D., J.D. A telephone conference between Drs. Lorandos and Sauber took place to discuss the writing project, which resulted in their consideration and commitment to the publisher's request. In February of 2011 Dr. Lorandos and Dr. Sauber invited William Bernet, M.D., to join this editorial challenge. Dr. Bernet is a well-known child and forensic psychiatrist with expertise in parental alienation. His most recent contribution was editing *Parental Alienation, DSM-5, and ICD-11.* He is professor emeritus in the Department of Psychiatry at Vanderbilt University.

The three of us began either weekly, biweekly, or monthly telephone conferences to plan the text. The frequency of our conferences varied according to how much work was required between conference calls. The selection of contributors consisted of careful scrutiny in terms of experts with scientific credibility and fieldwork expertise in clinical and forensic practice in order to obtain an immediate practical perspective as to what was happening in this subspecialty. These cases required a family specialization in order to address clinically and legally the journey of alienated children and their siblings and what was happening to the mothers and fathers assuming such positions of the alienating parent or target parent. Once the contributors were invited to submit a draft chapter in their specialty, each of the three editors reviewed and communicated with each of the authors to revise and further revise their chapter. The three editors of this text were each responsible for one third of the chapters while reading and critiquing every chapter. The chapter contributors were delighted when they finally received word from the editors that their chapters were accepted to be published in this edition. The book editors were not spared the ordeal of having their chapters critiqued and having themselves to revise their own chapters, often consisting of major rewrites.

The conventions of syntax and standardization of language in this text required major discussion in order that this text would define mild, moderate, and severe alienation. Clarification is offered in terms of the concepts of parental alienation and parental alienation syndrome. Vignettes were used to offer practical significance throughout many chapters to complement the theoretical presentations; actual cases were used in the vignettes, although the authors disguised the real identities of the families described in this book. After reviewing hundreds of references describing the parties in alienation cases from around the world and after a great deal of discussion concerning nomenclature, the editors adopted the convention of "alienating parent" and "target parent" for this project. One contributor requested alternate terminology ("favored parent" and "rejected parent") so as to be consistent with that author's previous writings in the field.

Dr. Lorandos was the executive editor and conducted the meetings during each of the ongoing telephone conferences. One could only imagine what it was like to have three chief chefs in the kitchen at one time, three leaders as professors and practitioners in the field, simultaneously speaking to provide input into the project. In August 2012, the three editors met for two days of intensive work in reviewing and concluding most of the project while residing and dining at the home of Dr. Sauber.

We wish to acknowledge the patience and tolerance of the contributors for participating in this ordeal, some of whom had more or less experience in professional writing, as well as other contributors to be named for their assistance in this project. Early on, the litigation firm *Lorandos Joshi* made a commitment to this project that involved hundreds of staff hours in research, editing, and logistics. The editors would like to acknowledge and thank Sarah B. Vasquez, MPH, for her tireless editorial and research help. Ms. Vasquez is the senior researcher at *Lorandos Joshi* and is a Ph.D. student in forensic psychology. Bruce D. Bielawa, J.D., D.M.A., is an associate attorney at *Lorandos Joshi* and his efforts in research and the compilation of material for the supplement took many hours. Researcher Gabriel H. Hinman, B.A. (Philosophy) spent countless hours tracking down research citations from around the world and changing them into APA format. The editors would also like to thank Dr. Lorandos' editor Ms. Sheani Chanmugam, a Principal Attorney Editor at Thomson Reuters Westlaw. Ms Chanmugam and Thomson Reuters were supportive and helpful in the two years of extended research that went into this text. Bradley W. Freeman, M.D., a forensic child psychiatrist at Vanderbilt University, created the name index for this handbook.

The *Supplemental Reference Guide* was a later idea of Dr. Sauber, given that Dr. Lorandos compiled and annotated 485 PA cased in the United States and in Canada and Dr. Bernet had accumulated the beginning of a major bibliography of scientific and clinical references to parental alienation as cited in his recent book on parental alienation and the *DSM-5* and *ICD-11*. This material should not be omitted from this effort as it went beyond that which could be included in the primary text. Thus, a *Supplemental Reference Guide* was created and expanded with additional new cases in the litigation citations and new journal articles, public media presentations, and books which were added to the current references in the bibliography. This *Supplemental Reference Guide* is intended to be updated every few years as the standard reference source for the subspecialty of parental alienation. It will be accessible and useful for mental health and legal professionals as well as for the family members and victims of parental alienation.

Thus, *Parental Alienation: The Handbook for Mental Health and Legal Professionals* is published as a one-volume hard copy and the *Supplemental Reference Guide* is published on a CD as a sleeve inside the back cover. Also, it will be published as an e-book with both the text and *Supplemental Reference Guide* included. The three sections of the *Supplemental Reference Guide* include sample motions, noteworthy legal case citations in the United States and Canada, and a master bibliography of professional references in the field. The *Handbook* and the *Supplemental Reference Guide* offer the reader the most up-to-date coverage available on the subject of parental alienation from a mental health and legal perspective as well as from a clinical and forensic approach to helping the family of the alienated child(ren), the alienating parent and the target parent.

DL, WB, and SRS
January, 2013

CONTENTS

SECTION II: FOUNDATIONS OF PARENTAL ALIENATION: HISTORICAL, SCIENTIFIC, AND LEGAL

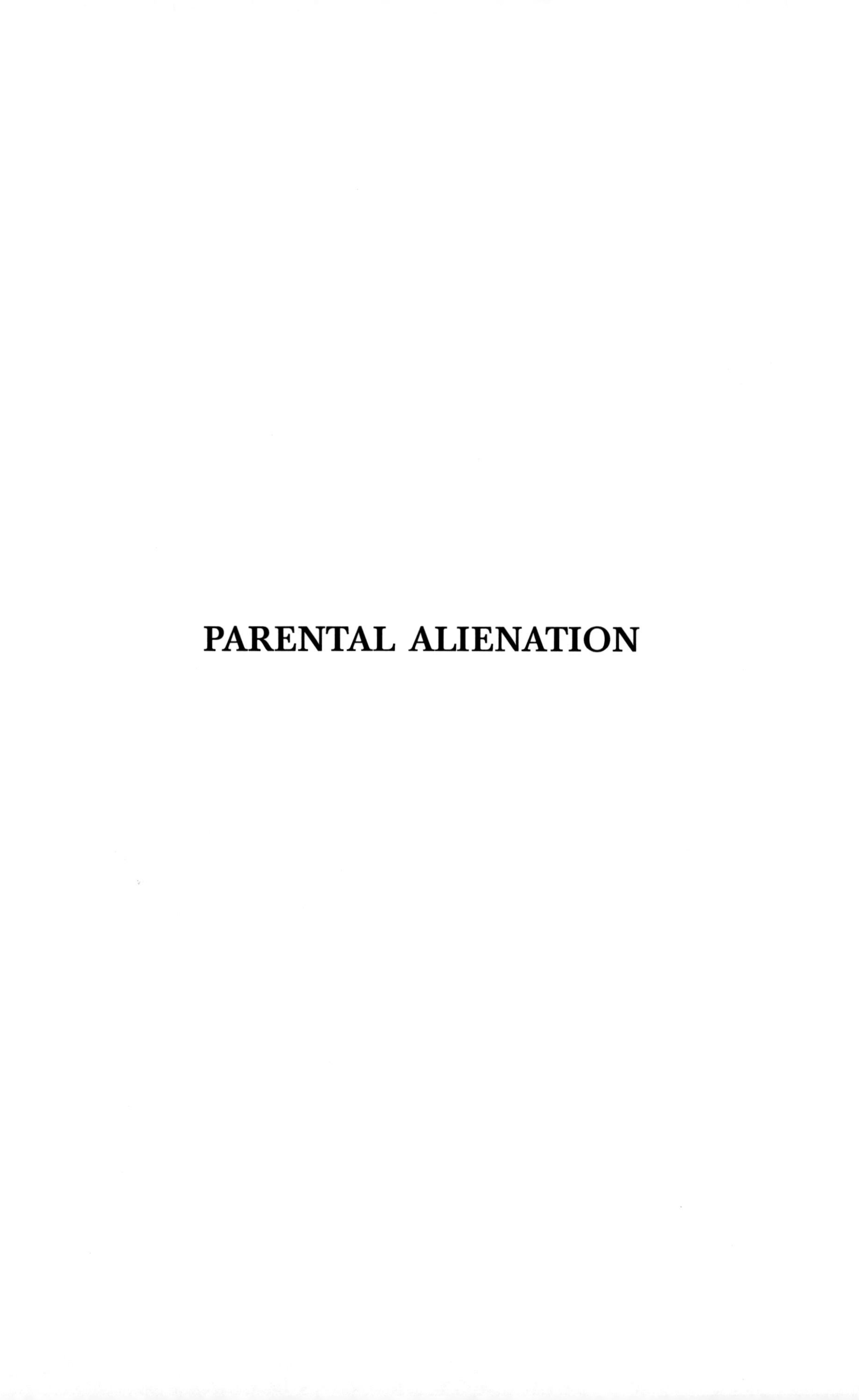

PARENTAL ALIENATION

Section I

Strategies for Mental Health and Legal Professionals

Chapter 1

OVERVIEW OF PARENTAL ALIENATION

DEMOSTHENES LORANDOS, WILLIAM BERNET, AND S. RICHARD SAUBER

Parental alienation (PA) is a serious mental condition that affects hundreds of thousands of children and families in the United States and comparable numbers in other countries. Mental health professionals (MHPs), family law attorneys, and everyday citizens observe PA on a regular basis, even if they do not know that the phenomenon has a name, where it comes from, or what to do about it. PA is not new. PA has been observed for many decades and has been described and discussed in the scientific literature of MHPs, in legal literature and precedents, and in popular literature, although the condition has been called a variety of names other than "parental alienation."

PA is a mental condition in which a child–usually one whose parents are engaged in a high-conflict separation or divorce–allies himself or herself strongly with an alienating parent and rejects a relationship with the "target" parent without legitimate justification.

Several features of the definition should be noted. PA can be conceptualized as a mental condition of the child (e.g., the child has a false belief that the rejected or target parent is evil, dangerous, or not worthy of love) or an aberration in the relationship between the child and the rejected, target parent (e.g., absence of communication and camaraderie between child and parent even though they previously enjoyed a loving, nurturing relationship). We refer to "separation or divorce" because PA often occurs prior to legal divorce and in families in which the parents were never married in the first place. PA may occur in high-conflict marriages when the parents are still living in the same household. It is essential to recognize that the child's rejection of the target parent is without legitimate justification. If a parent was abusive or severely neglectful, the child's rejection of that parent is understandable or legitimate and does not constitute PA. It is best to follow the convention of most writers, who use "estrangement" to refer to warranted rejection of a parent and "alienation" to refer to unwarranted rejection. Finally, we realize that the target parent may not be a typically "perfect" mother or father and that the target parent may have contributed in some way to the child's dislike of him or her. However, the essential feature of PA is that the child's rejection of the target parent is far out of proportion to anything that parent has done to justify the rejection.

ALTERNATIVE NAMES FOR THE SAME PHENOMENON

In the last eight decades, various authors have described the phenomenon of PA but have provided different names for it. For example, Wilhelm Reich (1945) wrote that many divorced parents defend themselves against what he called "narcissistic" injury by fighting for custody of their children. He found that parents who experienced narcissistic injury often defamed each other and did so in front of the children. Louise Despert (1953) said, "It is a sharp temptation for the parent who remains with the child to break down their love for the one who has gone" (p. 52). Westman, Cline, Swift, and Kramer (1970) wrote that a "pattern is found in which one parent and a child team up to provide an effect on the other parent. . . . In these cases one parent appears to deliberately undermine the other through a child."

Since the 1980s, many MHPs and legal professionals in the United States and other countries have identified, described, discussed, and named the condition that we are calling parental alienation. The proliferation of names has led to confusion and, at times, disagreement among professional colleagues. Here are some examples in chronological order.

Johnston, Campbell, and Mayes (1985) reported the "distress and symptomatic behavior of 44 children . . . who were the subject of post-separation and divorce disputes over their custody and care." The authors described six primary responses of these children to their parents: "strong alliance," "alignment," "loyalty conflict," "shifting allegiances," "acceptance of both" with "avoidance of preferences," and "rejection of both." Their definition of strong alliance was "a strong, consistent, overt (publicly stated) verbal and behavioral preference for one parent together with rejection and denigration of the other. It is accompanied by affect that is clearly hostile, negative and unambivalent." They wrote, "The child consistently denigrated and rejected the other parent. Often, this was accompanied by an adamant refusal to visit, communicate, or have anything to do with the rejected parent."

Child psychiatrist Richard Gardner (1985) introduced the concept of "parental alienation syndrome" (PAS):

> [Parental alienation syndrome refers] to a disturbance in which children are obsessed with deprecation and criticism of a parent–denigration that is unjustified and/or exaggerated. . . . The concept of the parental alienation syndrome includes the brainwashing component but is much more inclusive. It includes not only conscious but subconscious and unconscious factors within the parent that contribute to the child's alienation. Furthermore (and this is extremely important), it includes factors that arise within the child–independent of the parental contributions–that contribute to the development of the syndrome. (p. 3)

Although Gardner never named the condition after himself, PAS has been called "Zespół Gardnera" or "Gardner Syndrome" in Poland.

Wallerstein and Blakeslee (1989) suggested that some mothers could be "entangled with Medea-like rage." Thus, the "Medea syndrome," referring to the Greek myth in which Medea avenged the betrayal of her husband Jason by killing their two children.

Stanley Clawar, a sociologist, and Brynne Rivlin, a social worker, published their monumental study, which had been commissioned by the American Bar Association (Clawar & Rivlin, 1991). They used the terms "programming" and "brainwashing" to describe the attitudes and behavior that cause PA. They said,

> [One parent may] hinder the relationship of the child with the other parent due to jealousy, or draw the child closer to the communicating parent due to loneliness or a desire to obtain an ally. These techniques may also be employed to control or distort information the child provides to a lawyer, judge, conciliator, relatives, friends, or others, as in abuse cases. (p. 15)

Wallerstein, Kelly, Blakeslee, Johnston, Gardner, Clawar, and Rivlin were writing about the same children and the same clinical phenomenon. When Johnston wrote about the impact of polarizing parents in high conflict cases, she noted that "strong alignments are probably most closely related to the behavioral phenomena Gardner referred to as parental alienation syndrome" (1993). Kelly and Johnston (2001) subsequently renamed the condition "the alienated child" to focus clinical attention on the child rather than on the activities of the parents. In 1994, Ira Turkat argued that custodial parents engage in a variety of direct and indirect behaviors designed to alienate children from the nonresidential parent. Turkat argued that the result was that the children became preoccupied with unjustified criticism and hatred of the nonresidential parent (Turkat, 1994). He called the process "malicious parent syndrome" (Turkat, 1999). Warshak (2006) defined "pathological alienation" as

> a disturbance in which children, usually in the context of sharing a parent's negative attitudes, suffer unreasonable aversion to a person or persons with whom they formerly enjoyed normal relations or with whom they would normally develop affectionate relations. (p. 361)

VARIOUS MEANINGS OF PARENTAL ALIENATION

There are two sources of confusion regarding the definition of PA. The first is that various authors have used different terms and phrases for the phenomenon that we call PA. Second, various authors use the term parental alienation to identify different, but related, behaviors.

For example, some authors use parental alienation to name the indoctrinating and brainwashing maneuvers of the alienating parent and "parental alienation syndrome" to name the resulting mental condition of the child. Douglas Darnall (2010), for instance, wrote that a definition of PA is

> A parent's purposeful campaign of vilification characterized by anger, resistant and inconsistent compliance with court orders, conscious or unconscious denigration of the child's other parent, and interference with the other parent/child relationship. (pp. 5–6)

Gardner (2006) made a different distinction between parental alienation and parental alienation syndrome. He said that parental alienation referred to all types of impaired relationship between parent and child:

> [Parental alienation] can be caused by parental physical abuse, verbal abuse, emotional abuse, mental abuse, sexual abuse, abandonment, and neglect. . . . A child can also be programmed by one parent to be alienated from another. That particular category of parental alienation is generally referred to as parental alienation syndrome. (p. 6)

Gardner (2002) also criticized the use of parental alienation in court testimony as a watered-down synonym for parental alienation syndrome. Garrity and Baris (1994) used parental alienation and parental alienation syndrome synonymously. They wrote,

> Parental alienation is very real. It occurs when one parent convinces the children that the other parent is not trustworthy, lovable, or caring–in short, not a good parent. This persuasion may be consciously malicious and intended to destroy the children's relationship with the other parent. Or it may take a more insidious, even unconscious form arising from the personality issues as yet unresolved in the childhood of one parent. (p. 66)

CAUSES OF PARENTAL ALIENATION

There are several psychosocial pathways to PA. The most common is that the alienating parent indoctrinates the child to dislike and/or fear the target parent. Although PA most often arises in the context of a dispute between the parents over the child's custody, it can arise during the course of other types of conflicts, such as a dispute between a parent and a grandparent. Other family members–such as stepparents or grandparents–may contribute to the creation of PA. On occasion, other individuals–such as therapists and child protection workers–may cause PA to occur by encouraging or supporting the child's refusal to have contact with the alienated parent (Hellblom Sjögren, 2012).

PA almost always arises in the context of intense conflict between the target parent and somebody else. In circumstances of persistent, passionate conflict, it is possible that a child may develop a mild level of PA even without active brain-washing by one of the parents. That is, "parental alienation without indoctrination" can occur when the child gravitates to one parent and shuns the other parent in order to remove himself from the "war zone of parental battles" (Bernet, 1995, pp. 41–46). However, a common characteristic of severe levels of PA is "intentionality." As Sauber repeatedly asserts, it is never unintentional, accidental, or naïve behavior by the alienating parent that leads to a full-blown case of severe PA (Sauber, 2006).

We agree with Kelly and Johnston (2001) that PA may be caused by an interaction of several psychosocial processes. The target parent may contribute in some way to the child's rejection. For example, the target parent may lack an involved, warm style of nurturance. He or she may have devoted insufficient time to parenting activities. For the diagnosis of PA, however, the intensity and duration of the child's refusal to have contact with the target parent is far out of proportion to the relatively minor weaknesses in that person's parenting skills.

DEFINITION OF HIGH CONFLICT

Because PA usually occurs in the context of high-conflict separation or divorce, it is important to have an understanding of the meaning of high conflict. That topic was extensively reviewed by Glenn Gilmour (2004) in a background paper, "High-conflict Separation and Divorce: Options for Consideration," that he prepared for the Canadian Department of Justice. Gilmour summarized,

> In short, the literature indicates that parental conflict is a major source of harm to children, whether the children are in intact families or their parents have separated or divorced. Children whose parents have separated or divorced where there is a high level of conflict between the parents display greater behavioural problems than children from low- or medium-conflict divorced families. (p. 16)

Gilmour sought to arrive at a behavioral or operational definition of "high-conflict separation or divorce." He reviewed several articles and book chapters that identified external markers of high conflict, including *In the Name of the Child,* a book by Johnston, Roseby, and Kuehnle (now in its second edition, 2009); *Caught in the Middle,* a book by Garrity and Baris (1994); and *The Early Identification and Streaming of Cases of High-Conflict Separation and Divorce* (2001), a review by Ron Stewart. The features of high-conflict separation and divorce listed in Box 1.1 are based on those references.

CHARACTERISTICS OF ALIENATING PARENTS

Many alienating parents have demonstrable difficulties in their psychosocial functioning. As long ago as 1985, Benedek and Schetky reported that in high conflict custody cases, overly anxious parents tended to act out their mistrust for their former spouses. They wrote that anxious parents may transmit their anxiety to their child, causing the child to feel that he or she will not be safe visiting the other parent. Blush and Ross (1987) described cases of PA in which the personality of the alienating parent served as the force driving the alienation. In some of those situations, Blush and Ross described a pattern they termed the justified vindicator. They wrote,

> In this instance, a hostile, emotionally expansive, and dominant female has directly appealed to "experts" in both the mental health and legal communities. She frequently becomes insistent that formal, punitive legal measures be taken via prosecution before reasonable proofs have been demonstrated.

BOX 1.1
EXTERNAL MARKERS OF HIGH-CONFLICT SEPARATION OR DIVORCE

PA typically occurs when a child is exposed to a pathogenic environment: a high degree of conflict between his or her parents. Although there may be variation in the manifestations of high-conflict separation or divorce, the following behaviors or external markers are commonly observed:

- Verbal acts, such as abusive language, threatening violence
- Physical acts, such as slamming doors, throwing things, endangering each other
- Actual or alleged domestic violence
- Actual or alleged child sexual abuse
- Child experiencing emotional endangerment
- A history of access denial
- Family dysfunction, such as substance abuse, severe psychopathology
- Involvement of child welfare agencies in the dispute
- Several or frequent changes in attorneys
- The unusual number of times the case goes to court
- The length of time it takes for the case to be settled
- The large number of documents, such as diaries and affidavits, that have been collected

This list is based on Garrity and Baris (1994); Gilmour (2004); Johnston, Roseby, and Kuehnle (2009); and Stewart (2001).

> One of the accompanying phenomena with this type of female parent is that she frequently has concurrent criminal action pending with her domestic legal action.

Many researchers explain that alienating parents tend to be rigidly defended and moralistic. These alienators perceive themselves to be flawless, and virtuous, and they externalize responsibility onto others. They lack insight into their own behavior and the impact their behavior has on others (Bagby, Nicholson, Buis, Radovanovic & Fidler, 1999; Bathurst, Gottfried & Gottfried, 1997; Siegel, 1996). Research literature consistently documents that psychopathology and personality disorders are present in a significant proportion of high-conflict parents litigating over custody or access (Friedman, 2004; Siegel & Langford, 1998). Psychological disturbance–including histrionic, paranoid, borderline, and narcissistic personality disorders or characteristics as well as psychosis, suicidal behavior, and substance abuse—are common among alienating parents (Johnston, Walters & Olesen, 2005; Rand, 1997a, 1997b; Turkat 1999; Warshak, 2010a).

Two groups of researchers found that the maladaptive personality traits of alienating parents were consistently identified through objective psychological evaluation materials. Concerning the Minnesota Multiphasic Personality Inventory®-2 (MMPI®-2), Siegel and Langford (1998) wrote, "The present study is an attempt to gain understanding of parents who engage in alienating tactics through a statistical examination of their MMPI-2 validity scales." They tested sixteen female subjects who met the criteria for classification as PAS parents; eighteen female subjects were considered non-PAS parents. The authors concluded,

> The hypothesis was confirmed for K and F scales, indicating that PAS parents are more likely to complete MMPI-2 questions in a defensive manner, striving to appear as flawless as possible. It was concluded that parents who engage in alienating behaviors are more likely than other parents to use the psychological defenses of denial and projection, which are associated with this validity scale pattern.

Gordon, Stoffey, and Bottinelli (2008) examined the MMPI-2 data of seventy-six cases where PA was found and eight-two custody cases (controls) where PA did not operate. They found that mothers and fathers who were alienators had much higher scores on measures of psychological dysfunction; that is, test scores that indicated primitive defenses such as splitting and projective identification. Two different MMPI-2 indexes were used to measure these primitive defenses: L + K – F and (L + Pa + Sc) – (Hy + Pt). The first index (L + K – F) identifies persistent defensiveness. Elevations on this index would be expected in those cases of parents viewing themselves as an "all good parent" while condemning the former spouse as an "all bad parent." The second index ([L + Pa + Sc] - [Hy + Pt]) is the Goldberg Index (Goldberg, 1965). The Goldberg Index is a regression equation score that is the T score of (Lie + Paranoia + Schizophrenia) – (Hysteria + Psychasthenia). Those high pathology scores were much more prevalent in the alienator group; the scores for the target parents were most like the scores of the control parents. Gordon and colleagues (2008) concluded that their overall study strongly supported the definitions Gardner put forward with respect to PAS.

METHODS FOR CAUSING PARENTAL ALIENATION

Many authors have described the specific behaviors that an alienating parent might use to induce PA in the child. Gardner (1992) gave many examples of alienating strategies he had observed in conducting child custody evaluations. Gardner said that mothers alienated children against their fathers by repeatedly vilifying the father with derogatory names, destroying every item in the house that might remind the children of the father's existence, frequently complaining about how little money the father provided, exaggerating the father's minor psychological problems, and interfering with the father's visitation schedule (pp. 83–91). Gardner said that fathers alienated children against their mothers by failing to encourage the children to spend time with the mother; physically protecting the child from the imagined dangers associated with the mother; concocting a sex-abuse allegation against the mother's live-in boyfriend; seductive maneuvers, such as frequently cuddling and hugging the children; criticizing the mother for "never working a day in her life"; and developing secret codes with the children that were used in the service of hurting the mother (pp. 107–112).

After reviewing 700 cases of family counseling, mediation, and forensic evaluation, Clawar and Rivlin (1991) identified and described the following techniques in the PA context they termed brainwashing: denying and not acknowledging the social existence of the other parent; attacking something about the character, lifestyle, past, present, or future of the target parent; discussing visitation arrangements with the child, thus pressuring the child to make a choice; failing to inform the other parent of educational, social, and religious functions, thus communicating that the other parent lacks importance; creating or exaggerating differences between themselves and the other parent in front of the children; asking the children to ally their sympathies and support with the alienating parent; making moral judgments regarding the target parent's values, lifestyle, friends, and so on; implicitly or explicitly threatening to withdraw affection if the child expresses a desire to be with the other parent; creating the belief that the other parent is not sincere in his or her love for the child; creating the belief that the other parent is unable to properly care for the child; and convincing the child to doubt his or her ability to perceive reality (pp. 15–36).

Amy Baker (2007a) studied adults who said they had been alienated from one of their parents as children. She asked the subjects to describe the strategies that the alienating parent had used to bring about the PA. Baker said that 40 percent or more of her adult subjects reported the following alienating strategies when they were children: general bad-mouthing of the target parent by the alienating parent; limiting contact with the target parent; anger and withdrawal of love following visitation with the target parent; telling the child the target parent does not love him or her; forcing the child to choose one parent over the other; bad-mouthing specifically to create the impression that the target parent is dangerous; and confiding in the child about adult relationships (p. 64).

Gulotta, Cavedon, and Liberatore (2008) in Italy conducted psycholinguistic analyses of the statements of alienated children and the dialogue between the children and the alienating parents. They provided many examples of the subtle and not-so-subtle messages that an alienating parent might communicate to a child.

In some cases, one or both parents make false allegations of physical or sexual abuse in order to prevent the other parent from obtaining custody or access to the children. These cases usually involve several reports to child protection authorities and the police about the alleged abuse. In some cases, both parents make allegations of abuse against each other, but more frequently it is only one parent who makes a false claim of sexual or physical abuse of a child.

PARENTAL ALIENATION AND DOMESTIC VIOLENCE

Although domestic violence typically includes physical aggression or assault, such as hitting, kicking, shoving, and slapping, it may also involve sexual abuse, emotional abuse, severe neglect, and economic deprivation. Whatever the manifestation of domestic violence, the underlying theme is that the perpetrator controls and dominates his or her victim. In addition to controlling the spouse or domestic partner, the perpetrator of domestic violence often endeavors to control the children also. After the couple separates or divorces, the perpetrator may continue to control the children and alienate them from the former partner as a way to punish him or her.

Jaffe, Johnston, Crooks, and Bala (2008) have been most active in pointing out that aspect of PA. They wrote,

> Abusive ex-partners are likely to attempt to alienate the children from the other parent's affection (by asserting blame for the dissolution of the family and telling negative stories), sabotage family plans (by continuing criticism or competitive bribes), and undermine parental authority (by explicitly instructing the children not to listen or obey).

Also, Warshak (2010b) described a pattern he observed in families that featured coercive control and domination; in other words, a parent continues harassing and controlling the ex-partner by manipulating the children to turn against the victim parent.

CAUSING PARENTAL ALIENATION IS CHILD ABUSE

Authors in many countries have explained how a person who induces a child to experience PA is perpetrating child abuse. For example, Gardner (1998) wrote, "Whether such parents are aware of the negative impact on the child, these behaviors of the aligned parent (and his or her supporters) constitute emotional abuse of the child." Janet Johnston and Joan Kelly (2004) agreed on the issue of alienation as abuse, referring to PA as "an insidious form of emotional abuse of children that can be inflicted by divorced parents."

A professional organization of child neurologists and psychiatrists in Italy offered the following:

> Psychological abuse includes: acts of rejection, psychological terrorism, exploitation, isolation and removal of the child from the social context. . . . A further form of psychological abuse may be the alienation of a parent figure by the other parent . . . in "Parental Alienation Syndrome." (Società Italiana di Neuropsichiatria dell'Infanzia e dell'Adolescenza, 2007, p. 10)

A psychologist in the Republic of South Africa wrote:

> Involvement of mental health professionals who have no insight into PAS may exacerbate matters. The longer the time spent with the alienating parent, the more likely the process of alienation will be consolidated. It is suggested that PAS be recognized as a form of child abuse; accordingly custody may be awarded to the innocent party, with sanctions potentially applied against the alienating party. (Szabo, 2002)

CRITERIA FOR DIAGNOSIS OF PARENTAL ALIENATION

The most widely accepted criteria for the diagnosis of PAS were originally published by Gardner (1985, 1992), who wrote that children with PAS manifested some or all of eight characteristic behaviors. We have adapted Gardner's eight criteria for the diagnosis of PA, as we use the term in this book (see Text 1.2). It is important to emphasize that the diagnosis of PA is based upon the *level of symptoms in the child,* not on the symptom level of the alienating parent.

It should be noted that some children are more susceptible than others to the indoctrination promulgated by the alienating parent because of both external and internal factors. That is, a child may be more vulnerable because of stressful such external factors as: the shared parenting arrangements;

a new intimate partner of their parent; changes in the child's residence, peers, and school system; and economic factors causing the child to adjust to a new home in a less expensive neighborhood and attending a new school. Also, the intensity and duration of the child's symptoms depend on internal factors such as the child's temperament, which affects the child's susceptibility to influence by others. A child low in susceptibility may rebuff a parent's attempt to "poison" the child against the other parent, whereas a highly susceptible child is likely to internalize and believe the false propaganda intentionally programmed by the alienating parent. (*See* Chapter 7, "Reunification Planning and Therapy," for a more detailed discussion of the child's "vulnerability" due to external circumstances and the child's "susceptibility" due to personality and temperamental factors, especially in regard to reunification.)

Some researchers have studied the frequency with which the eight criteria occur in individual cases of PA or PAS. For example, Baker and Darnall (2007) collected information from sixty-eight parents whose children were severely alienated from them. They used a questionnaire to determine how often the eight symptoms of PAS listed by Gardner had been observed by their subjects. The authors found "general support for the presence of the eight symptoms of PAS." In this research, 88 percent of the target parents said that the alienated child "always" or "often" denigrated, rejected, or belittled them. Also, 98 percent of the target parents said that the alienated child "completely" or "mostly" gave weak, frivolous, or absurd reasons for rejecting them.

Future research will likely show that some of the eight criteria are more important than others. It may be that some criteria will be dropped or modified. It may be that new criteria will be identified and added. The criteria for many psychological disorders–including well-known conditions such as autism and attention-deficit/hyperactivity disorder–have evolved based on the results of extensive field trials and ongoing research.

SYMPTOMS IN CHILDREN, VICTIMS OF PARENTAL ALIENATION

The child's symptoms that define PA–refusal to see one of the parents, a campaign of denigration, hatred that is unjustified and disproportionate to the circumstances, and so on–are usually just the tip of an iceberg of maladaptive attitudes and destructive behaviors. PA is a powerful psychosocial force that leads the child to develop comorbid emotional problems, troublesome and often deviant behaviors, and impaired interpersonal relationships.

BOX 1.2
CRITERIA FOR THE DIAGNOSIS OF PARENTAL ALIENATION

For the diagnosis of PA, the child must manifest the following two behaviors:

- **Campaign of denigration against the target parent**. The child often presents complaints in a litany, some trivial, many false or irrational. The child often denies ever having experienced good times with the target parent when that is clearly not the case. Alienated children are likely to eschew the potential for reconciliation.
- **Frivolous rationalizations for the child's criticism of the target parent**. The child's reactions of hatred or disdain are unjustified and disproportionate to the circumstances they describe. They may claim to be fearful, but they do so easily and without typical fear reactions.

Also, the child must manifest two or more of the following six attitudes and behaviors:

- **Lack of ambivalence**. The child manifests all-or-none thinking, idealizing the alienating parent and devaluing the target parent.
- **Independent-thinker phenomenon**. The child proudly states the decision to reject the target parent is his or her own, not influenced by the alienating parent.
- **Reflexive support of the alienating parent against the target parent**. The child immediately and automatically takes the alienating parent's side in a disagreement.
- **Absence of guilt over exploitation and mistreatment of the target parent**. The child may be oppositional, rude, disrespectful, and even violent toward the target parent and shows little or no remorse for those behaviors.
- **Borrowed scenarios**. The child makes rehearsed statements that are identical to those made by the alienating parent. Younger siblings may mimic what they have heard their older sibling say. They usually are unable to elaborate on the details of the events they allege.
- **Spread of the child's animosity toward the target parent's extended family**. Expressed feelings and hatred often include the extended family or friends of the target parent, even when the child has had little or no contact with them. Occasionally, the child's hatred extends to pets of the target parent.

Mental diagnoses often are identified in alienated children, including conduct disorders, mood disorders, substance abuse, and personality disturbances.

Johnston, Walters, and Olesen (2005) found that "alienated children had more emotional and behavioral problems of clinically significant proportions compared to their nonalienated counterparts." Johnston (2005) said that alienated children "are likely to be more troubled–more emotionally dependent, less socially competent, have problematic self-esteem (either low or defensively high), poor reality testing, lack the capacity for ambivalence, and are prone to enmeshment or splitting in relations with others." She also noted,

> Severely alienated children also are likely to manifest serious conduct disorders and can behave very inappropriately, at least in the presence of the rejected parent. Extreme expressions of hatred, rage, contempt, and hostility can be acted out in rudeness, swearing, and cursing, hanging up the phone, spitting at or striking a parent, sabotaging or destroying property, stealing, lying, and spying on the rejected parent.

Summarizing a great deal of the research, Fidler and Bala (2010) explained that data consistently show that alienated children are at risk for emotional distress and adjustment difficulties and are at much greater risk than children from litigating families who are not alienated. They reported that clinical observations, case reviews, and both qualitative and empirical studies uniformly indicate that alienated children may exhibit poor reality testing; illogical cognitive operations; simplistic and rigid information processing; inaccurate or distorted interpersonal perceptions; disturbed and compromised interpersonal functioning; self-hatred; low self-esteem, or inflated self-esteem, or omnipotence; pseudomaturity; gender-identity problems, poor differentiation of self or enmeshed relationships; aggression and conduct disorders; disregard for social norms and authority; poor impulse control; emotional constriction, passivity, or dependency; and lack of remorse or guilt.

LONG-TERM CONSEQUENCES OF PARENTAL ALIENATION

The principle that family-of-origin relations influence future relationships and life adjustment is the foundation of several schools of developmental psychology. There are many studies that document long-term psychological damage associated with alienation and estrangement. Wallerstein and Blakeslee (1989) exclaimed that they had "seen a great deal of evidence that

Medea-like anger severely injures children at every age." They added,

> When one or both parents act the Medea role, children are affected for years to come. Some grow up with warped consciences, having learned how to manipulate people as the result of their parents' behavior. Some grow up with enormous rage, having understood that they were used as weapons. Some grow up guilty, with low self-esteem and recurrent depression. (p. 196)

Several researchers have commented on the long-term, deleterious effects of PA. Kenneth Waldron and David Joanis (1996) argued that in the context of PA children learn that "hostile, obnoxious behavior is acceptable in relationships and that deceit and manipulation are a normal part of relationships." Philip Stahl (2003) reported the following:

> When children are caught up in the midst of this conflict and become alienated, the emotional response can be devastating to the child's development. The degree of damage to the child's psyche will vary depending on the intensity of the alienation and the age and vulnerability of the child. However, the impact is never benign because of the fact of the child's distortions and confusions.

Amy Baker (2005, 2007a) studied adults who had experienced PA as children. This was a retrospective, qualitative study in which she conducted semi-structured interviews of thirty-eight adults who had been child victims of PA. She identified several problematic areas in these subjects: high rates of low self-esteem to a point of self-hatred, significant episodes of depression in 70 percent of the subjects, a lack of trust in themselves and in other people, and alienation from their own children in 50 percent of the subjects, which suggests that PA is multigenerational. Approximately one third of the sample reported having had serious problems with drugs or alcohol during adolescence, using such substances to cope with painful feelings arising from loss and parental conflict. Baker found that these adults, victimized as children, had difficulty trusting that anyone would ever love them; two thirds had been divorced once and one quarter more than once. Baker's respondents reported that they became angry and resentful about being emotionally manipulated and controlled, and their anger and resentment negatively affected their relationship with the alienating parent. About half of Baker's sample reported that they had become alienated from their own children. Baker reported that although most of the adults distinctly recalled claiming during childhood that they hated or feared the target parent and on some level did have negative feelings, they did not want that parent to walk away from them and secretly hoped someone would realize that they did not mean what they said.

With regard to the long-term consequences of PA, Canadian Justice Martinson (2010) wrote from the perspective of the courts:

> While professionals may not agree on the exact nature of alienation or on what the best responses should be, it is crystal clear that in alienation and other high conflict cases the stakes for children are extremely high. They can be seriously harmed. The longer the problem continues, the more harmful the situation can become and the more difficult it will be to resolve. . . . There are also long term adverse consequences for children including but not limited to difficulty forming and maintaining healthy relationships, depression, suicide, substance abuse, antisocial behavior, enmeshment, and low self-esteem.

PREVALENCE OF PARENTAL ALIENATION

Estimates of the incidence and prevalence of PA in high-conflict cases vary from study to study. For example, Johnston and her colleagues reported the prevalence of alienation in several studies. Johnston and Campbell (1988) said that alienation was seen in as many as 40 percent of high-conflict cases. Johnston (1993) reported that 7 percent of the children in one study and 27 percent of the children in a second study had strong alignment with one parent and rejection of the other parent. In 2003, Johnston reported on an alignment study. She defined alignment as the "child's behavioral and verbal preference for one parent with varying degrees of overt or covert negativity toward other parent." She found that 15 percent of children in a community sample of divorcing families and 21 percent in contested custody cases experienced either "some" or "much" alignment with one parent or the other. In 2005, Johnston, Walters, and Olesen reported rates of PA of about one fifth of high-conflict populations.

Clawar and Rivlin (1991) found that in about 80 percent of 700 counseling cases, there was some element of parental programming in an effort to implant false and negative ideas about the other parent with the intention of turning the child against that other parent. Their work focused on emotional issues, persistent programming, and brainwashing, which sometimes resulted in severe PA. Leona Kopetski, Deirdre Rand, and Randy Rand (2006) identified PA in 20 percent of the 413 families they evaluated between 1976 and 1990. Sandra Berns (2001) reported on a study of divorce judgments from 1995 to 2000 in Brisbane, Australia, where PA was found to be present in 29 percent of reviewed cases.

Hetherington and Kelly (2002), in discussing findings from the Virginia Longitudinal Study of Divorce and Remarriage, wrote,

> As obviously destructive as conflict is to all involved in this dilemma, it was surprising to discover that six years after divorce, 20 to 25 percent of our couples were engaged in just such conflictual behavior; former spouses would make nasty comments about each other, seek to undermine each other's relationship with the child, and fight openly in front of the child. Aside from being damaging, constant put-downs of the other parent may backfire, producing resentment and a spirited defense of the criticized parent by the child. . . . Conflictual co-parenting distresses children and undermines their well-being, and it makes parents unhappy, too. (p. 138)

Amy Baker (2007b) reported research wherein she surveyed 106 MHPs who conducted custody evaluations. The respondents reported that PAS occurred in as many as 55 percent of their cases. An average rate over all respondents, whether skilled or unskilled in the differential diagnosis of PAS, was 11.2 percent (SD = 13). Baker found that the evaluators who identified PAS more frequently were more familiar with the concept of PAS, were more likely to assess for PAS, were more likely to believe that one parent can turn a child against the other parent, and were more confident in their evaluations. In 2009, Bow, Gould, and Flens (2009) reported on their survey of 448 mental health and legal professionals who were experienced with parental alienation. They wrote, "When respondents were asked [in] what percentage of child custody cases was parental alienation an issue, the mean reported was 26%."

The great disparity in these results reflects varying definitions of PA, different populations being studied, and different levels of experience in identifying PA. We conclude that some degree of PA (that is, mild, moderate, or severe) occurs in approximately 20 to 30 percent of high-conflict separations and divorces.

OTHER CAUSES OF CONTACT REFUSAL

"Contact refusal" refers to the behavior of a child who avoids spending time with one of his parents. There are many reasons that children may not want to see a parent after separation or divorce. Most authors make a distinction between "estrangement" and "alienation." Estrangement refers to a child's rejection of a parent that is justified "as a consequence of the rejected parent's history of family violence, abuse and neglect" (Johnston, 2005). In contrast, alienation refers to a child's rejection of a parent that is unjustified, in other words, "unreasonable negative feelings and beliefs . . . that are significantly disproportionate to the child's actual experience with that parent" (Johnston, 2005). With that distinction in mind, estrangement is not a diagnosable mental condition because it is normal behavior. Alienation, on the other hand, is an abnormal mental condition because is consists of maladaptive behavior (refusal to see a loving parent) that is driven by a false or illogical belief (that the target parent is evil, dangerous, or not worthy of love).

The differential diagnosis of contact refusal includes a child's normal preferences for one parent over the other or one household over the other. The differential diagnosis also includes mental disorders such as separation anxiety disorder or oppositional defiant disorder. The child might properly refuse to visit a parent who has been abusive or very neglectful. The child might be manifesting PA, which could have been brought about by the child's removing himself or herself from the battle scene by gravitating to one parent and shunning the other, by the accidental indoctrination of a naïve alienator, by the purposeful indoctrination of an active or obsessed alienator, or perhaps because of a shared psychotic disorder with the alienating parent. (*See* Chapter 2, "The Psychosocial Assessment of Contact Refusal," for a fuller discussion of this topic.)

LEVELS OF SEVERITY

There are two ways to think about the severity of the symptoms or behaviors that are manifested in cases of PA. First, one can consider the *level of symptoms manifested by the child* who is the victim of PA. The child's symptoms can be classified as mild, moderate, or severe, depending on the intensity of the child's refusal to see the target or alienated parent. Box 1.3 provides the definitions of mild, moderate, and severe PA. Second, one can consider the *level of alienating behaviors manifested by the parent* who is inducing PA in the child. Box 1.4 supplies descriptions of mild, moderate, and severe degrees of alienating behaviors. The activities and attitudes of the preferred or alienating parent have also been called naïve, active, and obsessed, respectively (Darnall, 1998).

It is important to keep in mind that the diagnosis of PA is based on the symptoms and behaviors manifested by the child and the severity of PA is based on the intensity of the symptoms and behaviors manifested by the child. Although generally a child who is subjected to more severe degrees of a parent's alienating behaviors is likely to manifest a more severe level of PA, that is not always the case. It is possible for a parent who is moderately alienating to induce only a mild degree of PA in a child, for example, if the child previously enjoyed an unusually strong bond with the target parent. On the other hand, it is possible for a parent who is moderately alienating to induce a severe degree of PA in a child, for example, if the child was already somewhat fearful and insecure.

BOX 1.3
LEVELS OF SEVERITY OF PARENTAL ALIENATION AND TYPICAL TREATMENT APPROACHES

Mild PA means that the child resists contact with the target parent but enjoys the relationship with that parent once parenting time is underway. A typical intervention for mild PA is strongly worded instruction or psychoeducation. For example, a judge might clearly order the parents to stop exposing their child to conflict and stop undermining the child's relationship with the other parent, as well as instructing the child to cooperate with the parenting plan and follow the schedule that has been ordered. A parenting coordinator might meet with the parents regularly to help them communicate in a constructive manner and advise them regarding the child's activities with the target parent. (*See* Chapter 3 for a case vignette and additional details.)

Moderate PA means that the child strongly resists contact and is persistently oppositional during parenting time with the target parent. The treatment of moderate PA usually focuses on changing the behavior of the parents, reducing the amount of conflict and improving communication, for example. A parenting coordinator works with the parents together, and individual counseling is frequently arranged for the alienating parent (to help the parent stop indoctrinating the child against the target parent), the target parent (to help the parent be less frustrated and improve parenting skills, as needed), and the child (to help the child avoid the parents' battles and have a healthy relationship with both parents. (*See* Chapter 4 for more information.)

Severe PA means that the child persistently and adamantly refuses contact and may hide or run away to avoid being with the target parent. When the child manifests a severe level of PA, the alienating parent is usually obsessed with the goal of destroying the child's relationship with the target parent. The alienating parent has little or no insight and is convinced of the righteousness of his or her behavior. It is usually necessary to protect the child from the influence of the alienating parent by removing the child from his or her custody, greatly reducing the parenting time with that parent, and requiring the parenting time to be supervised. (*See* Chapter 5 for more information.)

TREATMENT OF PARENTAL ALIENATION

Experienced clinicians have proposed a number of treatments or interventions for PA. As is true for most psychiatric disorders, the appropriate treatment depends on the severity of the condition. (*See* Box 1.3 for the definitions of mild, moderate, and severe PA and a brief explanation of the interventions to consider for each level of severity.) Although the choice of treatment depends primarily on the level of symptoms in the child, it may also depend on the intensity of the indoctrination and the attitude of the alienating parent. The various treatment approaches tailored to the specific intensity of the PA are described in detail in Chapter 3 (mild PA), Chapter 4 (moderate PA), and Chapter 5 (severe PA).

If PA is so severe that the relationship between the child and the target parent has been totally interrupted for an extended period of time and is characterized by intense anger, fear, frustration, and mutual distrust, a higher level of intervention is called for. This is often called "reunification therapy." To be successful, reunification therapy is likely to require court sanctions in order to stabilize the relationship between the child and target parent from the ongoing malicious behavior of the alienating parent. Reunification therapy is defined later in this chapter and discussed in detail in Chapter 7.

Prevention and early intervention of PA is also very important. Katherine Andre and Amy Baker (2009) published a prevention approach called *I Don't Want to Choose: How Middle School Kids Can Avoid Choosing One Parent over the Other.* It is a structured program for group discussions with children of divorced parents, that can be implemented by school counselors.

BOX 1.4
LEVELS OF SEVERITY OF ALIENATING BEHAVIORS

Mild degree of alienating behavior: Naïve alienators make negative comments about the other parent of that parent's household but without serious intentions of harming the child's relationship with that parent. For example, a father might say, "If you get scared at Mommy's house, call my cell phone. I'll come and pick you up."

Moderate degree of alienating behavior: Active alienators intentionally desire to criticize and undermine the target parent. They realize that what they are doing is wrong and potentially harmful to the child. For example, a father might say, "I don't trust Mommy's new boyfriend. When you visited them last weekend, did he look at you in the bathroom or try to touch your private parts?"

Severe degree of alienating behavior: Obsessed alienators are determined to destroy the child's relationship with the target parent. For example, a father might say, "I'm pretty sure that Mommy's boyfriend is a sexual pervert. If he does anything that makes you uncomfortable, call 911 and say he molested you."

Early intervention refers to identifying children and families who are at risk for developing PA and who are manifesting some signs and symptoms of that disorder. For example, it is likely that very early cases of PA come to the attention of therapists in private practice and mental health centers who work with children of parents who are headed toward divorce. As PA becomes better understood by frontline clinicians, they will be able to intervene with parent counseling and psychoeducation at a time when the condition is mild and more treatable.

CONTROVERSY REGARDING PARENTAL ALIENATION SYNDROME

Between 1990 and 2010 there was considerable discussion and debate regarding PA and PAS in the mental health and legal professional literature. Most of the disagreement related to PAS as it was conceptualized and defined by Richard Gardner, as well as Gardner's recommendation that cases of severe alienation should be treated by transferring custody of the child from the alienating parent to the target parent. For example, Gardner was criticized by Faller (1998, 2000), Faller and DeVoe (1995), Bruch (2001), and Hoult (2006). In 2001, Kelly and Johnston critiqued Gardner's definition of PAS (which they felt focused too much on the role of the alienating parent) and proposed a reformulation of the phenomenon as "the alienated child" (which focuses more on the feelings and behavior of the child). (*See* Chapter 10, "The History of Parental Alienation from Early Days to Modern Times," and Chapter 13, "Parental Alienation Initiatives around the World," for a more complete discussion of the controversies regarding PA and PAS.)

GENERAL ACCEPTANCE OF PARENTAL ALIENATION CONCEPT

In 2000, Elizabeth Ellis published her text *Divorce Wars: Interventions with Families in Conflict.* Ellis explained that by the year 2000, the concept of PA had "come to be accepted by clinicians working with families involved in post divorce conflict." She went on to point out, "Definitions for PAS have been unclear, because clinicians still confuse a child's symptoms with the parent's behavior and the qualities of the relationship between the child and the alienating parent" (p. 227). Ellis offered a brief review of *folie à deux* and suggested that it involved striking similarities to PAS. In *folie à deux,* the primary individual who is dominant in the relationship gradually imposes his or her delusional system on the more passive, initially healthy, second person (p. 218).

In 2010, Joan Kelly pointed out that there was "broad consensus among the mental health and family law community that the risk of child alienation is increased in highly conflicted separations accompanied by protracted adversarial child custody disputes" (Kelly, 2010). She commented that although case analysis and research improved our understanding with respect to PA, there existed ample frustration about the "surprisingly little progress made by courts in successfully dealing with these cases in the past 30 years."

Although some MHPs and attorneys reject the concept of PAS as defined by Gardner, almost all MHPs and legal professionals accept the general definition of PA used in this book. That is, almost all MHPs and legal professionals agree that some children whose parents are engaged in a high-conflict separation or divorce ally themselves strongly with one parent and reject a relationship with the other parent without legitimate justification. In an informal poll of members of the Association of Family and Conciliation Courts conducted in 2010, 98 percent of the 300 respondents agreed with the question, "Do you think that some children are manipulated by one parent to irrationally and unjustifiably reject the other parent?" (Baker, Jaffee, Bernet & Johnston, 2011).

Although the great majority of MHPs and legal professionals agree that some children of divorced parents manifest PA–as we use the term–there has not been agreement on whether PA should be a formal diagnosis for use by MHPs. The proposal that PA become an official diagnosis was published in *Parental Alienation, DSM-5, and ICD-11* (Bernet, 2010). (*See* Chapter 15 of this book for an account of the development and submission of proposals that PA be included as a diagnosis in *DSM-5* and *ICD-11*.)

ROLE OF MENTAL HEALTH PROFESSIONALS

MHPs sometimes find themselves involved in cases of PA involuntarily and perhaps unwittingly. For example, a social worker might already be the therapist for a parent who then divorces and becomes either the alienating or the target parent as the family sinks into an alienation scenario. A school counselor might be working with an overly anxious child who takes a turn for the worse when his parents divorce and he forms a strong alliance with one parent and rejects the other. On the other hand, MHPs also become involved in PA cases in a voluntary, knowing manner. A psychiatrist might agree to conduct a custody evaluation although she realizes that one of the parents has alleged that the child is manifesting PA. A psychologist might agree to help a child and his mother re-establish a healthy relationship after being alienated from each other for several years.

Many MHPs are reluctant to become more than superficially involved in these difficult cases because each parent's attorney will challenge them unless they support that parent's position. Advocacy for one parent leads opposing counsel to attempt to discredit them, disregard their evaluation, or present their work as inadequate in an effort to remove them from the case. However, some MHPs make the opposite mistake of becoming overly involved in PA situations; for example, trying to be both the child's therapist and the custody evaluator. It is almost always risky and hazardous for a MHP to take on multiple roles. It may constitute an ethical violation, which could be brought to the attention of the state licensing board. Fidler and Bala (2010) explain that it is very difficult for one MHP to achieve desired objectives and meet the various, complex, and often competing needs of different family members. Trouble and headaches will certainly be encountered when a MHP assumes dual roles of therapist and decision maker (Bernet, 1983; Bone & Sauber, 2012; Greenberg, Gould, Schnider, Gould-Saltman & Martindale, 2003; Kirkland & Kirkland, 2006; Sullivan, 2004).

In this chapter, we briefly discuss the various roles MHPs occupy in high-conflict custody cases: evaluator, therapist, parenting coordinator, reunification specialist, and mental health consultant. *See* Chapter 2 for a more complete explanation of the evaluation process and Chapters 3, 4, and 5 for a discussion of the treatment of mild, moderate, and severe cases of PA. For additional information regarding reunification therapy, *see* Chapter 7. MHPs and legal professionals also try to influence courts and legislatures in shaping social policy, which is discussed in Chapter 9.

Custody Evaluator

In high-conflict custody cases, attempting to aid the court in its determination of the best interests of the children can be a rewarding, frustrating, and/or thankless task. Evaluators must be cognizant of the interacting dynamics between the parents, between each parent and the children, between the children and their siblings, between the parents and the children's network of social support (stepparents, grandparents, friends, parents of friends, school personnel, etc.), and between the parents and their communities. The use of multiple interviews among the interested parties as well as collateral interviews is essential. Repeated interviews of the children with significant members of their social support network may be very important. In high-conflict cases, the children's sense of themselves and their histories–the stories they tell about themselves–must be carefully scrutinized. Sauber and Worenklein (2012) have addressed the pertinent and unique issues involved in conducting a custody evaluation in alienation cases, particularly the need to dispel false allegations with credible evidence.

Regarding rumors, evaluators must be careful to trace ideas, stories, and allegations back to their origins. Rumors may have their origins in real or imagined happenings. The evaluator considering them must be careful lest they be co-opted into serving an alienator's purposes. MHPs who perpetuate false information without checking the facts may unwittingly contribute to, rather than alleviate, a family's distress. In so doing, they become part of the problem (Greenberg, Gould, Gould-Saltman & Stahl, 2003; Stahl, 2003).

When PA has occurred, the relationship between the parents can be complex and perplexing. Hobbs (2006) reminds us that alienators can be parents of either gender. Also, that evaluators must remember:

> [Allegations in the context of PA] comprise severe provocation to the recipient partner. Those allegations are intended to hurt the target parent and to manipulate key others to effect their removal from their children, and these allegations will precipitate anger in response. In fact, they may be expressly designed in order to precipitate an angry response so that the alienating parent can present that successfully provoked anger as further evidence against the target parent. (p. 78)

Psychological testing can be very helpful in child custody evaluation when PA is suspected. Bricklin and Elliot (2006) have spent decades scrutinizing children's sense of their relationships with others. Their diligent work with their Perceptions of Relations Test (PORT) and Bricklin Perceptual Scales (BPS) provides a detailed and ever expanding database of children caught in high-conflict custody combat. Objective psychological measures such as the ubiquitous MMPI-2 have immediate utility in high-conflict custody evaluations. Siegel and Langford (1998) and Gordon and colleagues (2008) have shown that alienating parents have MMPI-2 profiles that distinguish them from target parents and from parents in custody disputes that do not involve PA.

Perhaps the circumstance in which children's perceptions of relations, multiple interviews, and the use of psychological measures are put to the strictest test is in the evaluation of child sexual abuse allegations in the context of a child custody dispute. One of the earliest reviews of sexual abuse allegations related to custody and visitation disputes was reported by Blush and Ross (1987). Those authors tracked complaints and motions brought to the court by high-conflict parents, and they learned to identify what issues provoked parental disputes between the parties and when those disputes originated. They described the "sexual allegations in divorce" (SAID) syndrome. Blush and Ross directed evaluators to carefully assess the background and history of a couple before any allegations of sexual abuse developed, which may explain how escalating exchanges between the disputing parents triggered the sexual abuse allegations. In a similar vein, Wakefield and Underwager (1991) suggest understanding the "natural history" of an allegation, paying close attention to the origin, nature, and timing of the allegation, as essential in evaluating its validity and reliability. For a more complete discussion of this topic, *see* Chapter 6, "Sexual Abuse Allegations in the Context of Custody and Visitation Disputes."

Therapist for Family Members

The Association for Family and Conciliation Courts (AFCC) published a document entitled *Guidelines for Court-Involved Therapy* (2010) that defines and outlines court-ordered therapy as different and distinct from traditional psychotherapy. The *Guidelines* were intended to serve several purposes: to assist members of AFCC and others who provide treatment to court-involved children and families, to assist those who depend on mental health services or on the opinions of MHPs in promoting effective treatment and assessing the quality of treatment services, and to assist the courts to develop clear and effective court orders and parenting plans (p. 1).

In a comprehensive overview of the literature on alienation and MHP intervention, Fidler and Bala (2010) concluded that "counseling or psychotherapy tend to be suitable for mild and some moderate cases." Facing the taxonomic three levels of PA–mild, moderate, and severe–Birnbaum and Radovanovic (1999) and Warshak (2010a) argue for several tiered options of court-ordered therapy. Conventional therapy, they say, is most likely to be effective in early stages with less severe problems and when the alienating parent and child are likely to cooperate.

In any of these levels of severity, MHPs must be prepared for what they will hear from the alienators. Kopetski and colleagues (2006) listed the primary justification for alienation in each case they studied. They identified nineteen different justifications, including separation anxiety, the child's being fearful of the other parent, the child not needing a father, child abuse, spousal abuse, and the child being older and having a right to refuse visits. Some cases involved allegations of child abuse along with other kinds of justifications, such as the mother alleging separation anxiety and sex abuse or the father alleging that the mother was emotionally unstable and neglected the children. There were several cases in which more than one type of child abuse was alleged.

Rumors seemed to occur in every case that Kopetski and colleagues studied. Rosnow and Foster (2005) explained, "People have a tendency to spread rumors that they perceive as credible (even the most ridiculous stories), although when anxieties are intense, rumormongers are less likely to monitor the logic or plausibility of what they pass on to others." Although rumors are usually untrustworthy and are not ordinarily passed on, Rosnow and Foster found that they are virulent when the person who repeats them "is motivated by some ulterior or devious personal objective."

MHPs who treat children of divorced parents must remember that many children who participate in court-ordered therapy do so with overt resistance and reluctance. Parents who support or accept their children's rejection of the other parent usually lack motivation to participate in therapy when the professed goal is to heal the damaged parent-child relationship. Also, therapists are often persuaded by alienated children's compelling borrowed scenarios. Therapists must understand the power of the alienating parent in economically controlling the continuation of the therapy. An alienating parent may abruptly cease treatment due to spurious reasons, for example, saying the child did not feel comfortable with the therapist. The therapist must be careful to assess false allegations that appear to be justified.

MHPs who begin this work must also be ready to stop it as well. Donner (2006) explained that family therapy, co-parenting counseling, parent education, and cognitive-behavioral therapy may be insufficient to modify the complex behavior of alienating parents. Donner wrote that these parents are unable to think beyond their own needs and may harbor unconscious desires to hurt their children.

Fidler and Bala (2010) argued that the goals of therapy should include not only reunification with the target parent, but also facilitating global healthy child adjustment and coping mechanisms. This includes correcting the child's distorted and polarized views and replacing them with more realistic views of each parent; improving the child's healthy relationships with *both* parents; addressing divorce-related stress, boundaries, and age-appropriate autonomy; and restoring adequate parenting, co-parenting and parent-child roles. They argued that it is impossible to predict with certainty how any child will react to firm attempts to repair a damaged relationship with a target parent.

Parenting Coordinator

Parenting coordination was a concept introduced in 2001 through the AFCC. The concept was developed by AFCC task forces and resulted in

Model Standards of Parenting Coordination and finally the *Guidelines for Parenting Coordination* in 2005. The overall objective of the parenting coordinator is to assist high-conflict parents to implement their parenting plan; to monitor compliance with the details of the plan; to resolve conflicts regarding their children and the parenting plan in a timely manner; and to protect and sustain safe, healthy, and meaningful parent-child relationships (AFCC, 2005). Essentially, it is an alternative dispute resolution process to help conflicting parents make parenting decisions and comply with parenting agreements and orders.

Parenting coordinators in high-conflict custody cases are always faced with tension. In this tug of war, Sullivan and Kelly (2001) offered the following:

> Single days or weekend visits often do not provide sufficient time for rejected parents and children to have a productive experience free of the influence of aligned parents. Children most often arrive emotionally shut down and suspicious and generally become more guarded and hostile as they anticipate going back to the aligned parents at the end of the visit.

Sauber (2006) suggested that the PAS-trained parenting coordinator does not need to tiptoe around in his or her treatment of the child and his or her requests of the parents. The court appointment, access to the judge, and credibility with the court provide the power necessary to recommend and follow up with changes that need to be implemented within the family system. Sauber cautioned that if the child or parent does not fully understand that the parenting coordinator has the power to recommend or change or influence the parenting time schedule, the therapeutic efforts to implement parenting time or repair the family relationships will be seriously compromised. The parents and the court should not confuse the role of an assessor or evaluator with a parenting coordinator's mission when confronted with the question: Is it in the child's best interests to have contact with the target parent? Strong, explicit court orders and solid guidelines are the only way out of answering this query. This dilemma should be addressed either before the parent coordination begins or during this process by another MHP.

Reunification Specialist

Discussions in the social science literature describe few options for children who suffer severe and unreasonable alienation from a parent and highlight the ineffectiveness of available remedies. For example, Rand, Rand, and Kopetski (2005) reported the failure of traditional psychotherapy in their follow-up study of the forty-five children from twenty-five families Kopetski had studied over twenty years starting in 1976. A range of moderate to severe

PAS characterized those cases. Alienation was interrupted by judicial action for twenty children from twelve families where there was enforced visitation or a change of custody. For those in the treatment group for whom there were only orders for therapy and gradually increased access, however, alienation remained uninterrupted and in some cases became worse.

Qualitative case studies and experienced clinicians have found that traditional psychotherapy as the primary intervention simply does not work in severe and even in some moderate alienation cases (Clawar & Rivlin, 1991; Dunne & Hedrick, 1994; Gardner, 2001; Kopetski, 1998a, 1998b; Kopetski et al., 2006; Lampel, 1996; Lowenstein, 2006; Lund, 1995; Rand, 1997b; Rand et al., 2005). Fidler and Bala (2010) concluded that "all severe and some moderate cases of alienation . . . are likely to require a different and more intrusive approach if the relationship with the rejected parent is not to be abandoned and the alienation is to be successfully corrected."

A reunification option, short of reversing custody, is for the court to order a prolonged period of residence with the target parent, such as during the summer or an extended vacation, coupled with counseling and temporarily restricted or suspended contact with the alienating parent. This arrangement, which in the long run provides less disruption and greater continuity of care, may in some cases be more appropriate than reversing custody permanently. This period of prolonged residence affords the child and target parent the uninterrupted time and space needed to repair and rebuild their relationship, assuming that the alienating parent either relinquishes his or her malicious efforts or gives up trying to destroy the target parent's relationship with the alienated child.

Warshak (2010b) and Warshak and Otis (2010) offered an alternative approach called Family Bridges, in which the target parent and the alienated child travel to a program site–a family home, hotel, or vacation resort–for four consecutive days. The alienated children and the target parent share their experiences with one another and re-examine their assumed, indoctrinated false beliefs to which the children have become accustomed. In commenting on Family Bridges, Kelly (2010) wrote that the daily structure and other program components were guided by well-established evidence-based principles and incorporated multimedia learning, positive learning environment, focused lessons addressing relevant concepts, and learning materials providing assistance with integration of materials. She noted that the lessons and materials were drawn from universally accepted research in social, cognitive, and child developmental psychology, sociology, and social neuroscience. Another important feature of Family Bridges, wrote Kelly (2010), is the safe atmosphere created by the program leaders from the very beginning. She saw this as an essential feature of the program that promotes more willing participation and active learning. *See* Chapter 5 for a more complete discussion of Family Bridges.

Another approach to bringing the alienated child back into a relationship with the target parent is the development of a comprehensive reunification plan. Reunification therapy is generally a one-time opportunity, so it needs to be done correctly from start to finish. Usually, the alienated child is resistant and must be "forced" to meet with the target parent. Also, the alienating parent may publically support the idea of reunification but will privately engage the child, and often alienation allies as well, to sabotage and undermine the therapeutic effort. Thus, the likelihood of success becomes minimal without good planning. Frequently, it is helpful for the court to appoint an independent expert or an expert retained by the target parent to conduct a study and formulate a well-developed plan or blueprint for all the parties to follow. The reunification planner may be a different MHP than the reunification therapist.

Most MHPs acknowledge that they have neither the training nor the experience to work as a reunification specialist. Generally, the reunification specialist is contacted by a "selection committee," which may be comprised of the clients and/or their attorneys. The selection committee should consider the competence of the prospective therapist, her or his level of experience, and her or his willingness to adhere to a well-developed reunification plan developed by an independent evaluator or at least participate in the formulation of an effective approach to reunification as the process unfolds. (*See* Chapter 7 for a further discussion of reunification therapy.)

Mental Health Consultant

Systemic issues in family law create "points of slippage" when the judge is vulnerable to being misled, which is related to the court's bias toward the protection of children, the unmatched discretion and latitude of the family trial judge, and the fact that psychological matters are being decided by someone unlikely to be trained in psychology. Also, attorney representation by its very nature consists of advocating by another non-psychology professional. Alienation cases are confusing, highly conflictual, and replete with false allegations and questions of credibility. It takes a skillful MHP to assist the attorney in a consultative role, much like an attorney may rely on a forensic accountant. A mental health consultant should serve in a nonvisible but active role with both the client and the attorney, never testifying or blurring the roles of therapy and evaluation.

During the initial phase of the consultation, the MHP must determine whether the case involves PA or simply estrangement that resulted from abuse by the rejected parent. If it is a case of estrangement, we recommend that the mental health consultant offer the client rehabilitative advice and then withdraw from the case. On the other hand, if it is a case of PA, the mental health consultant as a team member assists in developing an effective strategy from the chronology of the case to the conflicting findings and opinions throughout the case, whether presented in court proceedings, depositions, or collateral contacts. The role of the consultant includes advising the attorney how to challenge therapists, evaluators, guardians ad litem (GALs), parenting coordinators, and other lay witnesses and experts involved in the case. The mental health consultant's role is confined to "consultation" rather than "collaboration," the latter term meaning shared authority in making decisions (Bone & Sauber, 2012).

ROLE OF THE ATTORNEY

It is easy to identify various levels of PA in mental health settings, in a variety of legal contexts; and in the everyday lives of neighbors, friends, and relatives. Attorneys may have several roles in cases that involve PA, but the most common is serving as the lawyer for one of the parents. Attorneys may also serve as a GAL for the child or as a "best interest" attorney representing the child. Litigating cases involving PA requires a skill set and knowledge of legal procedures that go beyond those used in less complex family law scenarios.

When the attorney represents the target parent, it is essential to ask the client to carefully document past events. Every moment in the child's life prior to the onset of PA must be documented and potential exhibits and witnesses identified. Lorandos (2011) recommends a method by which a master chronology file and a master document are created that ultimately includes every file, document, photograph, video, and witness statement or transcript. The database includes a complete list of all witnesses with contact information and citations to relevant places in the master document and chronology file. Organization of this material is critical to help the judge understand what has happened and what can be done about it.

The attorney for the target parent must demonstrate how the behavior of the alienating parent contributed to the development of PA, and whether it is in the early stage of mild PA or in the more advanced stage of moderate or severe PA, when the campaign of denigration, emotional poisoning, and brainwashing have escalated (Sauber, 2006). Sauber also instructs that the attorney should be mindful that the client will be anxious, angry and depressed. It is the attorney's challenge to carefully explain to the judge how this came about, assign appropriate responsibility, and offer expert recommendations to ameliorate the condition. After gaining the client's trust, the attorney must advise the client with regard to appropriate behavior and management of his or her emotions. The attorney must aid the client to be steady, truthful, and direct in testimony about being a victim but "at the same time present[ing] to the judge examples, facts, and detailed descriptions of the particulars that are taking place" (Sauber, 2006, p.13). The attorney for the target parent also has the responsibility of carefully selecting an expert either by mutual agreement with opposing counsel or without it. An expert who does not know the research will not qualify under the *Frye, Daubert,* or Canadian *Mohan* standards.

An attorney always has the option of retaining a mental health consultant as a member of his litigation team. A mental health consultant assists the attorney and the target parent in organizing files such as e-mails between the parties, proof that the false allegations are fabricated, preparing questions for the direct and cross-examination of various witnesses, pointing out the strengths and weaknesses of the case findings and opinions of the therapist and evaluators, screening collateral contacts, and other ways of helping the attorney represent the "unpopular" position of the target parent (Bone & Sauber, 2012).

On the other hand, the attorney may represent the preferred parent in a case in which the child has refused contact with the rejected parent. There are several possible causes of contact refusal including alienation, estrangement, and other mental conditions. (*See* Chapter 2 for a discussion of the differential diagnosis of contact refusal.) In addition to conducting her or his own assessment, the attorney may want to arrange for a comprehensive evaluation of the family. That could be accomplished through an agreed order with opposing counsel or a motion to the court. If the attorney determines that her or his client is actively indoctrinating the child against the target parent, she or he is confronted by an ethical dilemma; in other words, whether to zealously advocate for a parent who is perpetrating psychological child abuse.

We recommend that the attorney for the alienating parent avoid contributing to child abuse by adopting the following strategies: (1) The attorney should advise the parent to cease his or her alienating activities and find a way to encourage the child to have a good relationship with the other parent. The attorney should point out that a collaborative approach to child rearing is likely to benefit both the parent and the child in the long run. That approach may work with naïve and some active alienators but not with obsessed alienators. (2) The attorney should advise the parent to accept a parenting plan and a parenting time schedule that allows both parents to be involved in raising the child. Unfortunately, an obsessed alienator is unlikely to accept that advice. (3) If the alienating parent is unable to understand or follow the attorney's advice, the attorney should resign from the case.

Also, an attorney may be appointed by the court to serve as the child's GAL. It is the duty of the GAL to identify and serve the best interests of the child, which is not necessarily what the child consciously wants or explicitly requests. If the child is experiencing PA and his or her adamant desire is never to see the target parent again in his or her life, the GAL should not support the child's demands, usually driven by a false belief that the target parent is evil or dangerous. When presented with a situation like this, the GAL should educate himself regarding the various causes of contact refusal. The GAL may request to have the child and the parents evaluated by a competent MHP who could help the parents, the GAL, and the other legal personnel understand the basis for the child's contact refusal, whether it is PA or some other explanation.

Finally, the court may appoint a "best interests" attorney to represent the child and to make legal decisions for the child, such as whether or not to testify in court,whether or not to submit to a psychological evaluation, and whether or not to agree to the release of medical records. These considerations are often based on the child's credibility, harmfulness to the child, and long-term intended and unintended consequences of participation in court procedures. Everyone involved in a case should keep in mind that alienated children offer compelling testimony that is convincing to the child's attorney and to the judge, although it is based on fabricated statements that the child often comes to believe are true. Both the GAL and the attorney representing the child should be familiar with PA and avoid the traps and land mines that are created for them by the alienating parent. Further, in some cases alienated children should be restricted from testifying by the very fact that they are alienated and unable to express their true opinions and preferences (Sauber, 2006).

For a more complete discussion of the activities of the attorney in these difficult cases, *see* Chapter 8, "Legal Interventions in Cases of Parental Alienation."

ROLE OF THE COURT

Whereas the behavioral sciences have been concerned with PA for the last 70 years, PA has been identified in legal proceedings for more than 200 years. Stephens (2009) documented cases of PA all the way back to the eighteen century in England. There has been much criticism for many years regarding the handling of PA cases in court, with the criticism ranging from the adversarial nature of law itself to the rules and policies of many courts to the behavior of individual judges. Many mental health and legal writers have expressed concern regarding: absence of active case management, legal disputes that continue for months and years, litigation that unnecessarily escalates conflict, litigation that encourages the children to gravitate to one parent and shun the other parent, and repeated violations of orders going unpunished so parents make a mockery of the court's authority.

Several judges in the United States and Canada have been outspoken in their suggestions for how to reduce the trauma of PA. For example, Judge Michele Lowrance (2010) of Chicago stresses the corrosive power of anger in these circumstances and works to redirect it. Justice Donna Martinson (2010) of British Columbia argued that "several steps are necessary in order to maintain the focus on the best interests of the children and move the case to a resolution in a just, timely and affordable way," including early identification of the high-conflict cases; setting, right at the start, firm rules about the expected conduct of the parents toward the litigation, the children, and each other; setting a time frame within which the case must be concluded; and setting a schedule within the time frame for all the steps that must be taken before a solution can be reached, including any necessary psychological or other assessments.

In cases involving PA, case management is important. Bala, Fidler, Goldberg, and Houston (2007) wrote,

> It is important for judges to take control of alienation cases, to limit the possibility of manipulating the court process by the parents, and to ensure a firm and quick response to violations of court orders. These are cases for which judicial case management is especially appropriate.

In cases involving PA, therapeutic jurisprudence may be very effective. Sauber (2006) pointed out that the court has the power and the influence–even more than the psychologist, psychiatrist, mental health counselor, social worker, or family therapist–to moderate or alleviate PA. Fidler and Bala (2010) wrote, "In many alienation cases, the education, coaching, and threats or encouragement of a judge can be a prime motivator for change. Many times in these circumstances, we see children adapt to firm court orders."

In cases involving PA it is important to set limits, which may require extreme measures. That may take the form of contempt citations, imposed supervised contact, a reversal of custodial arrangements, and suspension of visitations with the indoctrinating parent. Sauber (2006) wrote, "It takes 'guts' for a judge to order this reversal even if the evidence is compelling, knowing how much the children will 'hate' and protest living with the 'despised' parent" (p. 15).

In cases involving PA, environmental changes may be very effective in helping children overcome unreasonable negative attitudes. Several authors describing their qualitative research using case studies have reported on the benefits of changing custody or enforced parenting time in severe alienation cases. For example, Clawar and Rivlin (1991) reported an improvement in children's relationships with rejected parents in 90 percent of 400 cases in which an increase in the child's contact with the target parent was court ordered. They wrote,

> Children may say, "I hate her. I'll never speak with her if you make me go see her," "I'll run away," or "I'll kill myself if he comes to see me." However, in some cases, children were told to say these things by the programming and brainwashing parent. . . . It is not uncommon to see these threats disintegrate after court orders change. (p. 144)

Today, there is general recognition that a reversal of custody may be warranted in severe cases (Drozd & Olesen, 2009; Johnston & Goldman, 2010; Johnston et al., 2009; Warshak, 2010b).

PARENTAL ALIENATION AROUND THE WORLD

There is a vast international literature regarding PA that mental health and legal professionals in the United States know almost nothing about. PA has been identified and described in the professional literature of at least thirty countries on six continents. The phenomenon of PA transcends politics, culture, and religion. It has been identified in Malta (a tiny country that is almost completely Roman Catholic) and Malaysia (a large country that is almost completely Islamic). The legislatures of Brazil and of two states in Mexico have made it illegal for a parent or any other person to induce PA in a child. *See* Chapter 14 for a discussion of the precedential legislation in Brazil and how it came about. *See* Chapter 13, "Parental Alienation Initiatives around the World," for an overview of international research regarding PA and how it has been recognized by legislatures and courts in many countries.

One way to conceptualize PA is to consider it a violation of one of the fundamental rights of children: to have a meaningful relationship with both of their parents. Mental health writers and legal authorities in Europe have emphasized how the rights of children–as expressed by supranational organizations such as the United Nations and the European Court of Human Rights–have been violated when they experience PA.

For example, in 1924, the General Assembly of the League of Nations created a document, the Declaration of the Rights of the Child, which consisted of five principles. The General Assembly of the United Nations developed a more comprehensive document and kept the same name (United Nations, 1959). Principle 6 of the 1959 document stated

> The child, for the full and harmonious development of his personality, needs love and understanding. He shall, wherever possible, grow up in the care and under the responsibility of his parents and, in any case, in an atmosphere of affection and of moral and material security.

In 1989, the United Nations established the Convention on the Rights of the Child (CRC), which consists of fifty-four sections or articles. The CRC was designed to establish that children have rights and to ensure that adults and their governments protect them. For example, the CRC (United Nations, 1989) provides that "In all actions concerning children . . . the best interests of the child shall be a primary consideration" (Article 3) *and* "States Parties shall undertake all appropriate legislative, administrative, and other measures for the implementation of the rights recognized in the present Convention" (Article 4) *and* "States Parties shall use their best efforts to ensure recognition of the principle that both parents have common responsibilities for the upbringing and development of the child" (Article 18). It is ironic that of all the countries in the United Nations, only the United States and the lawless land of Somalia have failed to ratify the CRC.

Editors' Notes

- In this book, parental alienation (PA) refers to a mental condition in which a child–usually one whose parents are engaged in a high-conflict separation or divorce–allies himself or herself strongly with one parent (the alienating parent) and rejects a relationship with the other parent (the target parent) without legitimate justification.
- The most common cause of PA is indoctrination of the child by the alienating parent to dislike or fear the target parent. Parents have been characterized as: *mildly alienating* (making negative comments about the other parent but without a serious intention of undermining the child's relationship with that parent), *moderately alienating* (having a conscious intention to undermine the targeted parent, knowing it is wrong and possibly harmful to the child), and *severely alienating* (determined to destroy the child's relationship with the other parent).

- The eight criteria for the diagnosis of PA are the child's *campaign of denigration* against the target parent, *frivolous rationalizations* for the child's criticisms, *lack of ambivalence,* the *independent-thinker* phenomenon, *reflexive support* of the alienating parent, *absence of guilt* over exploitation of the target parent, *borrowed scenarios,* and *spread of the child's animosity* toward the target parent's extended family.
- There are many treatments for PA. The choice of treatment depends on whether the level of PA in the child is *mild* (the child resists contact with the target parent but enjoys the relationship once parenting time is underway), *moderate* (the child strongly resists contact and is persistently oppositional during parenting time with the target parent), or *severe* (the child persistently and adamantly refuses contact with the target parent).

REFERENCES

Association of Family and Conciliation Courts (AFCC). (2005). *Guidelines for parenting coordination.* Madison, WI: Association of Family and Conciliation Courts.

Association of Family and Conciliation Courts (AFCC). (2010). *Guidelines for court involved therapy.* Madison, WI: Association of Family and Conciliation Courts.

Andre, K., & Baker, A. J. L. (2009). *I don't want to choose: How middle school kids can avoid choosing one parent over the other.* New York: The Vincent J. Fontana Center for Child Protection.

Bagby, R. M., Nicholson, R. A., Buis, T., Radovanovic, H., & Fidler, B. J. (1999). Defensive responding on the MMPI-2 in family custody and access evaluations. *Psychological Assessment, 11,* 24–28.

Baker, A. J. L. (2005a). The long-term effects of parental alienation on adult children: A qualitative research study. *American Journal of Family Therapy, 33,* 289–302.

Baker, A. J. L. (2007a). *Adult children of parental alienation syndrome: Breaking the ties that bind.* New York: W.W. Norton & Co.

Baker, A. J. L. (2007b). Knowledge and attitudes about the parental alienation syndrome: A survey of custody evaluators. *American Journal of Family Therapy, 35*(1), 1–19.

Baker, A. J. L., & Darnall, D. (2007). A construct study of the eight symptoms of severe parental alienation syndrome: A survey of parental experiences. *Journal of Divorce & Remarriage, 47*(1/2), 55–75.

Baker, A. J. L., Jaffee, P. G., Bernet, W., & Johnston, J. R. (2011). Brief report on parental alienation survey. *The Association of Family and Conciliation Courts eNEWS, 30*(2).

Bala, N., Fidler, B. J., Goldberg, D., & Houston, C. (2007). Alienated children and parental separation: Legal responses in Canada's family courts. *Queen's Law Journal, 33,* 79–138.

Bathurst, K., Gottfried, A. W., & Gottfried, A. E. (1997). Normative data for the MMPI-2 in child custody litigation. *Psychological Assessment, 9,* 205– 211.

Benedek, E. P., & Schetky, D. H. (1985). Custody and visitation: Problems and perspectives. *Psychiatric Clinics of North America, 8*(4), 857–873.

Bernet W. (1983). The therapist's role in child custody disputes. *Journal of Child Psychiatry, 22,* 180–183.

Bernet, W. (1995). *Children of divorce: A practical guide for parents, attorneys, and therapists.* New York: Vantage.

Bernet, W. (2010). *Parental alienation, DSM-5, and ICD-11.* Springfield, IL: Charles C Thomas Publisher.

Berns, S. S. (2001). Parents behaving badly: Parental alienation syndrome in the family court–Magic bullet or poisoned chalice. *Australian Journal of Family Law, 15*(3), 191–214.

Birnbaum, R., & Radovanovic, H. (1999). Brief intervention model for access-based postseparation disputes: Family and court outcomes. *Family and Conciliation Courts Review, 37,* 504.

Blush, G. J., & Ross, K. L. (1987). Sexual allegations in divorce: The SAID syndrome. *Conciliation Courts Review, 25*(1), 1–11.

Bone, J. M. & Sauber, S. R. (2012). The essential role of the mental health consultant in cases of parental alienation. In A. J. L. Baker & S. R. Sauber (Eds.), *Working with alienated children and families: A clinical guidebook* (pp. 71–89). New York: Routledge.

Bow, J. N., Gould, J. W., & Flens, J. R. (2009). Examining parental alienation in child custody cases: A survey of mental health and legal professionals. *American Journal of Family Therapy, 37*(2), 127–145.

Bricklin, B. & Elliot, G. (2006). Psychological test-assisted detection of parental alienation syndrome. In R. A. Gardner, S. R. Sauber & D. Lorandos (Eds.), *The international handbook of parental alienation syndrome: Conceptual, clinical and legal considerations* (pp. 264–275). Springfield, IL: Charles C Thomas Publisher.

Bruch, C. (2001). Parental alienation syndrome and parental alienation: Getting it wrong in child custody. *Family Law Quarterly, 35,* 527.

Clawar, S. S., & Rivlin, B. V. (1991). *Children held hostage: Dealing with programmed and brainwashed children.* Washington, DC: American Bar Association Section of Family Law.

Darnall, D. (1998). *Divorce casualties: Protecting your children from parental alienation.* Lanham, MD: Taylor Publishing Co.

Darnall, D. (2010). *Beyond divorce casualties: Reunifying the alienated family.* Lanham, MD: Taylor Trade Publishing.

Despert, J. L. (1953). *Children of divorce.* New York: Doubleday.

Donner, M. B. (2006). Tearing the child apart: The contributions of narcissism, envy, and perverse modes of thought to child custody wars. *Psychoanalytic Psychology, 23,* 542–551.

Drozd, L. M., & Olesen, N. W. (2009). *When a child rejects a parent.* Paper presented at the 46th Annual Conference of the Association of Family and Conciliation Courts.

Dunne, J., & Hedrick, M. (1994). The parental alienation syndrome: An analysis of sixteen selected cases. *Journal of Divorce and Remarriage, 21*(3/4), 21–38.

Ellis, E. M. (2000). *Divorce wars: Interventions with families in conflict.* Washington, DC: American Psychological Association.

Faller, K. (1998). The parental alienation syndrome: What is it and what data support it? *Child Maltreatment, 3*(2), 100–115.

Faller, K. (2000). Child maltreatment and endangerment in the context of divorce. *University of Arkansas Little Rock Law Review, 22,* 429–444.

Faller, K., & DeVoe, E. (1995). Allegations of sexual abuse in divorce. *Journal of Child Sexual Abuse, 4*(4), 1–25.

Fidler, B. J., & Bala, N. (2010). Children resisting post-separation contact with a parent: Concepts, controversies, and conundrums. *Family Court Review, 48*(1), 10–47.

Friedman, M. (2004). The so-called high-conflict couple: A closer look. *American Journal of Family Therapy, 32*(2), 101–117.

Gardner, R. A. (1985). Recent trends in divorce and custody litigation. *Academy Forum, 29*(2), 3–7.

Gardner, R. A. (1992). *The parental alienation syndrome: A guide for mental health and legal professionals.* Cresskill, NJ: Creative Therapeutics.

Gardner, R. A. (1998). *The parental alienation syndrome: A guide for mental health and legal professionals* (2nd ed.). Cresskill, NJ: Creative Therapeutics, Inc.

Gardner, R. A. (2001). Should courts order PAS children to visit/reside with the alienated parent? A follow-up study. *American Journal of Forensic Psychology, 19*(3), 61–106.

Gardner, R. A. (2002). PAS vs. PA: Which diagnosis should evaluators use in child custody disputes? *Amerian Journal of Family Therapy, 30*(2), 93–116.

Gardner, R. A. (2006). Introduction. In R. A. Gardner, S. R. Sauber & D. Lorandos (Eds.), *The international handbook of parental alienation syndrome: Conceptual, clinical and legal considerations* (pp. 5–11). Springfield, IL: Charles C Thomas Publisher.

Garrity, C., & Baris, M. (1994). *Caught in the middle: Protecting the children of high-conflict divorce.* Toronto, ON: Maxwell Macmillan Canada, Inc.

Gilmour, G. A. (2004). *High-conflict separation and divorce: Options for consideration.* Ottawa: Department of Justice Canada (2004-FCY-1E).

Goldberg, L. R. (1965). Diagnosticians vs. diagnostic signs: The diagnosis of psychosis vs neurosis from the MMPI. *Psychological Monographs: General and Applied, 79*(9), 1–28.

Gordon, R. M., Stoffey, R., & Bottinelli, J. (2008). MMPI-2 findings of primitive defenses in alienating parents. *American Journal of Family Therapy, 36*(3), 211–228.

Greenburg, L. R., Gould, J. W., Gould-Saltman, D. J., & Stahl, P. M. (2003). Is the child's therapist part of the problem? *Family Law Quarterly, 37,* 241–265.

Greenburg, L. R., Gould, J. W., Schnider, R. A., Gould-Saltman, D. J., & Martindale, D. A. (2003). Effective intervention with high-conflict families: How judges can promote and recognize competent treatment in family court. *Journal of the Center for Families, Children and the Courts, 4,* 49–65.

Gulotta, G., Cavedon, A., & Liberatore, M. (2008). *La Sindrome di Alienazione Parentale (PAS): Lavaggio del cervello e programmazione dei figli in danno dell'altro genitore.* [The Parental Alienation Syndrome (PAS): Brainwashing and Programming of Children to the Detriment of the Other Parent] [Italian]. Milan, Italy: Giuffrè.

Hellblom Sjögren, L. (2012). Barnet avskiljs från sina föräldar, omhändertas jml LVU och påverkas att ta avstånd från dem båda [The child is separated from its parents, taken into forced custody and is influenced to reject them both] [Swedish]. In: *Barnets rätt till familjeliv: 25 svenska fallstudier av föräldraalienation* [*The Child's Right to Family Life: 25 Swedish Case Studies of Parental Alienation*] (pp. 339–376). Lund, Sweden: Studentilleratur.

Hetherington, E. M., & Kelly, J. (2002). *For better or for worse: Divorce reconsidered.* New York: W.W. Norton & Co.

Hobbs, T. (2006). PAS in the United Kingdom: Problems in recognition and management. In R. A. Gardner, S. R. Sauber, & D. Lorandos (Eds.), *The international handbook of parental alienation syndrome: Conceptual, clinical and legal considerations* (pp. 71–89). Springfield, IL: Charles C Thomas Publisher.

Hoult, J. (2006). The evidentiary admissibility of parental alienation syndrome: Science, law and policy. *Children's Legal Rights Journal, 26*(1): 1–61.

Jaffe, P. G., Johnston, J. R., Crooks, C. V., & Bala, N. (2008). Custody disputes involving allegations of domestic violence: Toward a differential approach to parenting plans. *Family Court Review, 46*(3), 500–523.

Johnston, J. R. (1993). Children of divorce who refuse visitation. In C. E. Depner & J. H. Bray (Eds.), *Non-residential parenting: New vistas in family living* (pp. 109–135). Newbury Park, CA: Sage Publishing.

Johnston, J. R. (2003). Parental alignments and rejection: An empirical study of alienation in children of divorce. *Journal of the American Academy of Psychiatry and the Law, 31*(2), 158–170.

Johnston, J. R. (2005). Children of divorce who reject a parent and refuse visitation: Recent research and policy implications for the alienated child. *Family Law Quarterly, 38,* 757–775.

Johnston, J. R., & Campbell, L. E. (1988). *Impasses of divorce: The dynamics and resolution of family conflict.* New York: The Free Press.

Johnston, J. R., Campbell, L. E. G., & Mayes, S. S. (1985). Latency children in post-separation and divorce disputes. *Journal of the American Academy of Child Psychiatry, 24*(5), 563–574.

Johnston, J. R., & Goldman, J. R. (2010). Outcomes of family counseling interventions with children who resist visitation: An addendum to Friedlander and Walters. *Family Court Review, 48,* 112–115.

Johnston, J. R., & Kelly, J. B. (2004). Rejoinder to Gardner's "Commentary on Kelly and Johnston's 'The alienated child: A reformulation of Parental Alienation Syndrome.'" *Family Court Review, 42,* 622–628.

Johnston, J. R., Roseby, V., & Kuehnle, K. (2009). *In the name of the child: A developmental approach to understanding and helping children of conflicted and violent divorce* (2nd ed.). New York: Springer.

Johnston, J. R., Walters, M. G., & Olesen, N. W. (2005). The psychological functioning of alienated children in custody disputing families: An exploratory study. *American Journal of Forensic Psychology, 23*(3), 39–64.

Kelly, J. B. (2010). Commentary on "Family bridges: Using insights from social science to reconnect parents and alienated children" [Warshak 2010]. *Family Court Review, 48*(1), 81–90.

Kelly, J. B., & Johnston, J. R. (2001). The alienated child: A reformulation of parental alienation syndrome. *Family Court Review, 39,* 249–266.

Kirkland, K., & Kirkland, K. E. (2006). Risk management and aspirational ethics for parenting coordinators. *Journal of Child Custody, 3*(2), 23–43.

Kopetski, L. (1998a). Identifying cases of parental alienation syndrome, Part I. *Colorado Lawyer, 27*(2), 65–68.

Kopetski, L. (1998b). Identifying cases of parental alienation syndrome, Part II. *Colorado Lawyer, 27*(3), 61–64.

Kopetski, L. M., Rand, D. C., & Rand, R. (2006). Incidence, gender, and false allegations of child abuse: Data on 84 parental alienation syndrome cases. In R. A. Gardner, S. R. Sauber, & D. Lorandos (Eds.), *The international handbook of parental alienation syndrome: Conceptual, clinical and legal considerations* (pp. 65–70). Springfield, IL: Charles C Thomas Publisher.

Lampel, A. (1996). Child's alignment with parents in highly conflicted custody cases. *Family and Conciliation Courts Review, 34,* 232–235.

Lorandos, D. (2011). Saving Tonya Craft: An integration of science and law. *Champion, 35,* 24–29.

Lowenstein, L. F. (2006). The psychological effects and treatment of the parental alienation syndrome worldwide. In R. A. Gardner, S. R. Sauber, & D. Lorandos (Eds.), *The international handbook of parental alienation syndrome: Conceptual, clinical and legal considerations* (pp. 292–301). Springfield, IL: Charles C Thomas Publisher.

Lowrance, M. (2010). *The good karma divorce.* New York: Harper Collins.

Lund, M. (1995). A therapist's view of parental alienation syndrome. *Family and Conciliation Courts Review, 33,* 308–316.

Martinson, D. J. (2010). One case–one specialized judge: Why courts have an obligation to manage alienation and other high-conflict cases. *Family Court Review, 48*(1), 180–189.

Rand, D. (1997a). The spectrum of parental alienation syndrome, Part I. *American Journal of Forensic Psychology, 15*(3), 23–52.

Rand, D. (1997b). The spectrum of parental alienation syndrome, Part II. *American Journal of Forensic Psychology, 15*(4), 39–92.

Rand, D. C., Rand, R., & Kopetski, L. (2005). The spectrum of parental alienation syndrome, Part III: The Kopetski follow-up study. *American Journal of Forensic Psychology, 23*(1), 15–43.

Reich, W. (1945, 2006). *Charakteranalyse* [Character Analysis] [German] (8th ed.). Cologne, Germany: Kiepenheuer & Witsch.

Rosnow, R. L., & Foster, E. K. (2005). Rumor and gossip research. *Psychological Science Agenda, 19*(4).

Sauber, S. R. (2006). PAS as a family tragedy: Roles of family members, professionals, and the justice system. In R. A. Gardner, S. R. Sauber, & D. Lorandos (Eds.), *The international handbook of parental alienation syndrome: Conceptual, clinical and legal considerations* (pp. 12–32). Springfield, IL: Charles C Thomas Publisher.

Sauber, S. R., & Worenklein, A. (2012). Custody evaluations in alienation cases. In A. J. L. Baker and S. R. Sauber (Eds.), *Working with alienated children and ramilies: A clinical guidebook.* New York: Routledge.

Siegel, J. (1996). Traditional MMPI-2 validity indicators and initial presentation in custody evaluations. *American Journal of Forensic Psychology, 13*(3), 55–63.

Siegel, J., & Langford, J. (1998). MMPI-2 validity scales and suspected parental alienation syndrome. *American Journal of Forensic Psychology, 16*(4), 5–14.

Società Italiana di Neuropsichiatria dell'Infanzia e dell'Adolescenza (SINPIA) (Italian Society of Child and Adolescent Neuropsychiatry) (2007). *Linee guida in tema di abuso sui minori* [Guidelines on the subject of child abuse] [Italian]. Trento, Italy: Edizioni Centro Studi Erickson. Retrieved from http://www.sinpia.eu/atom/allegato/154.pdf

Stahl, P. M. (2003). Understanding and evaluating alienation in high-conflict custody cases. *Wisconsin Journal of Family Law, 24*(1), 20–26.

Stephens, R. (2009). *A historical perspective on parental alienation and child custody disputes: 1760–present.* Unpublished manuscript.

Stewart, R. (2001). *The early identification and streaming of cases of high-conflict separation and eivorce: A review.* Ottawa: Department of Justice Canada (2001-FCY-7E/7F).

Sullivan, M. J. (2004). Ethical, legal, and professional practice issues involved in acting as a psychologist parent coordinator in child custody cases. *Family Court Review, 42,* 576–582.

Sullivan, M. J., & Kelly, J. B. (2001). Legal and psychological management of cases with an alienated child. *Family Court Review, 39,* 299.

Szabo, C. P. (2002). Parental alienation syndrome. *South African Psychiatry Review, 5*(3), 1.

Turkat, I. D. (1994). Child visitation interference in divorce. *Clinical Psychology Review, 14*(8), 737–742.

Turkat, I. D. (1999). Divorce-related malicious parent syndrome. *Journal of Family Violence, 14,* 95–97.

United Nations (1959). Declaration of the rights of the child. Retrieved from http://www.un.org/cyberschoolbus/humanrights/resources/child.asp

United Nations (1989). Convention on the rights of the child. Retrieved from http://www.ohclr.org/EN/ProfessionalInterest/Pages/CRC.aspx

Wakefield, H., & Underwager, R. (1991). Sexual allegations in divorce and custody disputes. *Behavioral Sciences and the Law, 9,* 451.
Waldron, K. H., & Joanis, D. E. (1996). Understanding and collaboratively treating parental alienation syndrome. *American Journal of Family Law, 10*(3), 121–133.
Wallerstein, J. S., & Blakeslee, S. (1989). *Second chances: Men, women, and children a decade after divorce.* New York: Ticknor & Fields.
Warshak, R. A. (2006). Social science and parental alienation: Examining the disputes and the evidence. In R. A. Gardner, S. R. Sauber, & D. Lorandos (Eds.), *The international handbook of parental alienation syndrome: Conceptual, clinical and legal considerations* (pp. 352–371). Springfield, IL: Charles C Thomas Publisher.
Warshak, R. A. (2010a). Alienating audiences from innovation: The perils of polemics, ideology, and innuendo. *Family Court Review, 48*(1), 153–163.
Warshak, R. A. (2010b). Family bridges: Using insights from social science to reconnect parents and alienated children. *Family Court Review, 48,* 48–80.
Warshak, R. A., & Otis, M. R. (2010). Helping alienated children with family bridges: Practice, research, and the pursuit of "humbition." *Family Court Review, 48*(1), 91–97.
Westman, J. C., Cline, D. W., Swift, W. J., & Kramer, D. A. (1970). Role of child psychiatry in divorce. *Archives of General Psychiatry, 23*(5), 416–420.

Chapter 2

THE PSYCHOSOCIAL ASSESSMENT OF CONTACT REFUSAL

WILLIAM BERNET AND BRADLEY W. FREEMAN

When parents separate or divorce, there are many possible outcomes for the parents as well as for the children. In the most general terms, divorce might be beneficial for one or both of the parents or it might be harmful or injurious. Parental divorce might be beneficial in some ways for the children or it might be damaging. Since there are various circumstances that could affect a divorce, the family relationships may play out through a multitude of scenarios.

Ideally, of course, the divorcing parties are not overly angry or purposefully hurtful to each other. Ideally, divorcing parents are able to communicate with each other in a constructive manner and share the joys and challenges of raising their children. Ideally, the children continue to enjoy satisfying and rewarding relationships with both of their parents. In some divorced families however, the children do not enjoy seeing both parents and may actively avoid spending time with either the mother or the father.

We use the term contact refusal for the behavior of a child or adolescent who avoids spending time with one of his or her parents. Contact refusal is a general term for a behavior or symptom that has a number of possible underlying causes. The concept of contact refusal is similar to the concept of school refusal, which is a behavior that is sometimes manifested by children and teenagers. Just as there are a number of possible causes for a child's school refusal, there are several possible causes or explanations for contact refusal.

In this chapter, we explain how a mental health professional (MHP) should assess a child whose primary symptom is contact refusal. In the first part of this chapter, we define and discuss possible explanations for a child's avoidance of one parent, which we refer to as the differential diagnosis of contact refusal. The phrase differential diagnosis is a medical term that refers to the process of examining the various potential causes of a behavior or symptom. In the second part of this chapter, we explain the typical procedure for conducting an assessment of the child and his or her family.

DIFFERENTIAL DIAGNOSIS

In both clinical and forensic settings, the evaluator develops a differential diagnosis based on all the available data, such as an account of the child's behavioral and psychological symptoms, the psychosocial history of the child and family, interviews of the child and parents, information from collaterals, review of records, and psychological testing. Several authors have published their versions of the differential diagnosis of contact refusal; they are discussed here in chronological order.

Johnston (1993) identified several themes among children who were reluctant to visit one of the parents: normal separation anxiety in young children; the child's limited cognitive ability to understand both parents' opposing viewpoints, so that alignment with one parent resolves painful loyalty conflict; the child's inability to extricate his feelings and thoughts from those of an emotionally distressed parent; the child's exposure to emotional abuse and physical violence between the parents; and the child's sense of counter-rejection by the rejected parent.

Drozd and Olesen (2004) developed a decision tree that focused "on the differential analysis of allegations of alienation and allegations of spousal abuse." Their evaluation protocol considers three general topics or hypotheses: exploring the normal developmental processes, exploring the poor parenting hypothesis, and exploring the abuse hypothesis. Those authors made a distinction between alienating behavior (an example of poor parenting "when one parent says negative and disparaging things about the other parent to the child") and sabotaging behavior (a phenomenon in the context of an abusive family, when the aggressor parent "engage[s] in behavior designed to sabotage the child's relationship with the victim parent").

Bernet (2006) listed the following factors that might cause a child to resist or refuse visitation: maltreated child, purposeful indoctrination, accidental indoctrination, parental alienation syndrome (PAS), worried child, stubborn child, and child escaping conflict.

The formal proposal that parental alienation (PA) be included in *DSM-5* and *ICD-11* (Bernet, Boch-Galhau, Baker & Morrison, 2010) listed specific conditions and diagnoses that should be considered in the differential diagnoses of contact refusal: loyalty conflicts, physical abuse of child, sexual abuse of child, shared psychotic disorder, separation anxiety disorder, specific phobia, oppositional defiant disorder, adjustment disorder, parent-child relational problem, and PA disorder.

Cavedon and Magro (2010), Italian psychologists, recently published a book regarding the evaluation of PA. They described the possible relationships between a child and his or her divorced parents: a positive relationship with both parents; a greater attachment to one of the parents; having an alliance with one parent but still having feelings of affection toward the other parent; the "estranged" child, who has experienced violence, sexual abuse, or psychological maltreatment by a parent; and the "alienated" child, who rejects the target parent, with no apparent sense of guilt or ambivalence and persists in refusing all contact with that parent (pp. 45–46).

Freeman (2011) classified contact refusal as "pathologic purposeful" (related to child abuse, parental substance abuse, PA, and purposeful indoctrination) and "nonpathologic accidental" (such as anxiety on the part of the child or parent, environmental factors, and accidental indoctrination).

THE CONTEXT OF CONTACT REFUSAL

There are several situations in which an MHP might encounter contact refusal. For the readers of this book, the most obvious one is the circumstance in which parents are divorced and the child prefers to be with one parent and avoids or resists spending time with the other parent. However, there are other occasions when a child might manifest contact refusal. For instance, a child might run away from home and resist being returned to his or her parents' household. Also, a child might be placed with foster parents and resist transitioning back to her or his parents' care. In this chapter, we will focus on the differential diagnosis of contact refusal by children of parents who are separated or divorced.

MHPs might come upon an instance of contact refusal when conducting an evaluation of a new client or patient. In evaluating a child, most MHPs collect information about the child's family, such as the names and occupations of the parents, whether they are married, the names and ages of siblings, and the names of significant members of the child's extended family. It is standard practice to assess the relationships among those family members. Of course, if the parents are not living together, the evaluator would ask about parenting time arrangements.

In seeing a new client, the evaluator must ask questions to achieve a clear and complete picture of the family relationships. For example, the custodial parent and the child may have decided long ago that there is no need or desire for the child to spend time with the child's noncustodial parent. That is not the reason the child has been brought to see the MHP, and the custodial parent and child might have no interest in volunteering any information regarding the parent who is absent from the child's life. It is up to the evaluator to find out who that missing parent is, where he or she is, and the reasons why the child no longer has a relationship with that parent.

In other circumstances, the child's refusal to visit the noncustodial parent may be the "chief complaint" or the primary reason why the child has been brought for evaluation and, perhaps, treatment. In that case, it is obvious that the child's contact refusal will need to be assessed. In another scenario, the child is already in treatment or counseling with an MHP when the parents divorce and the child develops a new behavior: contact refusal. Of course, another possibility is that a MHP may be conducting a custody and visitation evaluation and learns that contact refusal is one of the features of that divorced family. Finally, a therapist may be meeting with a divorced couple to facilitate coparenting and contact refusal may come up in that context.

Every MHP who works with divorced parents and the children of divorced parents will have many opportunities to hear about both isolated instances and continuing patterns of contact refusal. In conducting an assessment of the situation, the first step is to avoid arriving at a conclusion before considering all the possible underlying reasons why contact refusal is occurring in the family. The same advice applies to legal professionals, who are likely to encounter instances of contact refusal in family law cases. The problem is that the custodial parent (who is likely the parent who has brought the child to the MHP) and the attorney's client (who has hired the attorney to represent his or her interests) will have already formed their opinions as to why the child refuses to see one of the parents. The therapist (who only hears the version of one parent) and the attorney (who only represents one parent) should try to keep an open mind as to why the child is resisting and avoiding a relationship with the rejected parent. The therapist and the attorney should consider the differential diagnosis of contact refusal that is presented in this chapter.

The differential diagnosis of contact refusal includes a normal, understandable preference the child might have for one parent over the other; loyalty conflict, when the child attempts to love both parents; avoiding a loyalty conflict by gravitating to one parent and shunning the other; being worried or depressed, such as experiencing separation anxiety; being overly stubborn or oppositional; estrangement due to previous maltreatment; accidental indoctrination of child against a parent, leading to PA; purposeful indoctrination leading to PA; and shared delusional disorder. In this chapter, each of these parent-child relationships is illustrated with a brief clinical vignette.

NORMAL PREFERENCES

In considering the differential diagnosis of contact refusal, the most benign explanation is that the child is simply expressing a normal, understandable preference. Typical children in intact families may have a more comfortable and stronger relationship with one parent and prefer to engage in activities with that parent rather than the less-favored parent. To some extent, there are developmental factors that affect the child's preference. For example, a young child might have a stronger attachment to his mother if she was the primary caregiver during his early years. On the other hand, a preadolescent boy might indentify with his father and prefer to spend time with him kicking a soccer ball or studying astronomy together.

When parents divorce, the child may express a desire to spend more time in the household of the parent who is preferred at that time and may try to avoid spending time with the other parent. That may occur because the less-preferred parent has deficits in his or her parenting skills. For example, the less preferred parent may be less demonstrative in his or her affection, less nurturing, less energetic, or simply not particularly fun to be with. Also, there may be activities or events that the child enjoys at one household. For instance, perhaps the child enjoys building model airplanes and has an extensive collection of models at the father's household, so he prefers to spend his weekends there. Perhaps the child knows that her next door neighbor at her mother's household is having a sleepover, so she wants to spend a particular weekend with her mother.

It is a normal attitude for a child to feel closer to Parent A at times and perhaps closer to Parent B at other times. It is normal for teenagers to want to hang out with friends rather than spend much time with parents. Those attitudes do not constitute a mental disorder and should not be labeled as such. Mothers and fathers who are successful at coparenting deal with such preferences on a day-to-day basis. They encourage the child to enjoy activities with both parents. They collaborate with each other in deciding whether to adjust the parenting time schedule to accommodate the child's preferences.

Vignette

Jimmy, age six, loved both his parents, who were divorced, but he felt more secure with his mother. Jimmy's father was a kind, responsible parent, but had a less-nurturing style than his mother had. During the summer, Jimmy alternated weeks between the parents' households. Jimmy required surgery for an inguinal hernia, which happened to be scheduled for one of the weeks of his father's parenting time. When the time came for the boy to transfer from his mother's home to his father's, Jimmy refused to go. He strongly wanted to be in his mother's care when he went to the hospital for the surgery. His parents talked to each other, and they readily agreed to that change in the parenting time arrangements. Jimmy's parents were supportive and nobody was irritated at his insistence on deviating from the usual routine.

LOYALTY CONFLICTS

Although divorcing parents may be angry and hostile toward each other, the child may retain affection and good feelings toward both mother and father. When she has parenting time with her mother, she misses her father; when she is in the father's household, she misses her mother. Having a low level of divided loyalty is not problematic for the child and is not a mental disorder. It is also normal for a child to feel bad about neglecting a parent, to worry about the absent parent, to miss the absent parent, and even to feel a little inappropriate guilt about the divorce.

However, a child with a high level of divided loyalty may develop a mental disorder if, for example, either parent or both parents expect the child to support that parent's side in the daily and weekly disagreements that occur. If Mom expects the child to agree with her, the child feels guilty at not siding with Dad; if Dad pressures the child to be on his side, the child feels distressed in rejecting Mom. Since the child's devotion toward Mom competes with her allegiance with Dad, the child experiences a high level of divided loyalty that is problematic because the child persistently feels uncomfortable.

A child who experiences significant loyalty conflict over a period of time is likely to develop emotional or behavioral symptoms such as sadness, worrying, somatic symptoms, and oppositionality. It is extremely uncomfortable to be caught in an unending battle that features external conflict (between the two parents) and internal conflict (the child's affection for Mom versus her affection for Dad). Occasionally, children who feel torn between warring parents may become dangerous to themselves and require a safety plan such as emergency hospitalization. The psychiatric diagnosis for a child who is symptomatic as a result of severe loyalty conflict would typically be an adjustment disorder, for example, an adjustment disorder with depressed mood or an adjustment disorder with mixed disturbance of emotions and conduct.

Vignette

The most common psychosomatic symptoms that occur in children are headaches and stomachaches, and Stephanie, age eleven, had both. Stephanie had a good relationship with both of her parents prior to their divorce. After the divorce, she lived most of the time with Mom but had considerable parenting time with Dad. The parents divided their responsibilities. With regard to homework, Mom focused on arithmetic and science, whereas Dad helped Stephanie with spelling tests and geography. The problem was that the parents endlessly bickered with each other and frequently argued when Stephanie transitioned from one household to the other. Stephanie dreaded the "switching hours" and developed anticipatory physical symptoms including abdominal pain and vomiting. The headaches and stomachaches vanished when the parents firmly resolved to stop disagreeing in front of Stephanie.

CHILDREN'S ACTS TO AVOID CONFLICT

A child who experiences severe loyalty conflict for an extended period of time may devise a solution that removes her from the battleground between the parents. The child may avoid conflict–or escape from ongoing conflict–by gravitating to one side of the dispute and forming a strong alliance with that parent. That solution requires the child to reject the other parent, even though she previously enjoyed a loving, mutually satisfying relationship with that parent. That is, the child experienced cognitive dissonance, which she resolved by aligning with one parent and rejecting the other. Klosinski (1993) described that process long ago. He said that when a child is caught in loyalty conflicts and can no longer bear the feelings of guilt, "A frequently observed defensive reaction of the child is a sudden and exaggerated taking of sides with one parent and a turning against the other."

Cognitive dissonance is a well-known mental phenomenon that has been extensively studied by psychologists (Festinger, 1957; Mills & Harmon-Jones, 1999). Cognitive dissonance is an uncomfortable feeling or tension that is caused by holding conflicting ideas simultaneously. People are highly motivated to reduce or eliminate the tension or stress caused by cognitive dissonance. There are a number of ways to reduce dissonance, such as totally adopting one attitude or belief and totally rejecting the opposing attitude or belief. In the case of a child with a severe loyalty conflict, the child experiences cognitive dissonance because it is very stressful to love Mom and to love Dad at the same time that Mom and Dad seem to despise each other. The child may resolve the tension by aligning closely with one parent and rejecting the other parent. Since the child rejects a relationship with one parent and the rejection goes well beyond anything justified by the rejected parent's behavior, that is an example of PA. Thus, it is possible for PA to occur during a high-conflict divorce even though no one has actively indoctrinated the child against the rejected parent.

Vignette

Bailey was a nine-year-old boy whose parents divorced after months of loud arguing and mutual recriminations. Bailey lived with his mother, and several weeks after the divorce she took him for a mental health evaluation because he had problems sleeping and had not been eating well. His behavior at school had deteriorated. Before the divorce, the family saw Bailey as a "chip off the old block" because he was very attached to his father. Following the divorce, Bailey refused to visit his father. Bailey believed that the divorce happened because his father had done something bad. He told the guidance counselor at school he was mad at his father and never wanted to see him.[1]

WORRIED OR DEPRESSED CHILDREN

Parental divorce is one of the most stressful and frightening events that a child might experience. It has both short-term and long-term consequences (Huurre, Junkkari & Aro, 2006; Mustonen, Huurre, Kiviruusu, Haukkala & Aro, 2011; Wallerstein, Lewis & Blakeslee, 2001). A high-conflict divorce–when parents recruit their children for endless warfare–may be more stressful and damaging than a parent's death (Gardner, 1979). In such a situation, a child may become very anxious or depressed and develop a mental disorder, which causes the child to reject a relationship with one of the parents.

For example, suppose that even before the parents' separation and divorce, a child already had a stronger and more comfortable attachment to the custodial parent. When the parents separated, the child was frightened

1. In this chapter, three vignettes–pertaining to Bailey, Colby, and Heather–are adapted from Freeman, B. W. (2011). The differential diagnosis of contact refusal. *Child and Adolescent Psychiatric Clinics of North America, 20,* 467–477; used by permission of Elsevier, Inc.

and worried that more bad things might happen. After the departure and loss of the noncustodial parent, she worried that she might lose the custodial parent as well. She worried that something might happen to the custodial parent, and she resisted leaving that parent, had nightmares, and had severe anxiety when the custodial parent left her with a babysitter. The psychiatric diagnosis for the child would probably be separation anxiety disorder (Bagnell, 2011; Connolly, Suarez & Sylvester, 2011; Suveg, Aschenbrand & Kendall, 2005). Orgilés Amorós, Espada Sánchez, & Méndez Carrillo (2008) found that Spanish children whose parents were divorced had higher levels of separation anxiety than did the children whose parents were together.

Vignette

Sally, age ten, tended to be a worrier even under the best of circumstances before her parents separated and divorced. After the divorce occurred, Sally turned down invitations to sleep over at friends' homes and at times slept in her mother's bed. Her mother had a chronic medical condition and Sally worried excessively about her mother's health. Sally enjoyed having parenting time with her father and she readily engaged in activities with him. She became anxious at bedtime, however, and had recurrent panic attacks when she was expected to spend the night at her father's home. She refused to stay in her father's home after dinner was completed. A psychologist diagnosed Sally with separation anxiety disorder and treated her with cognitive behavioral therapy.

STUBBORN CHILDREN

Many children have a stubborn streak to their personalities that does not necessarily rise to the level of a mental disorder. For example, a child who is not resilient and flexible may become irritable and angry when plans change unexpectedly. A child who is overly indulged may become entitled in his interactions with his parents and other adults. A child with oppositional tendencies may react poorly to the stresses that arise when his parents separate and divorce. He may blame the noncustodial parent for messing up his life and refuse to see that parent.

Rather than gracefully accommodate to the inconvenient, court-imposed schedule of transitioning between two households, the child may sullenly dig in his heels and refuse to participate in the parenting plan ordered by the court. He may manifest the behavioral symptom of contact refusal. The child's oppositional behavior is likely to frustrate the parents, and their responses may aggravate the problem even further. If that pattern is persistent and impairs the child's day-to-day functioning, the psychiatric diagnosis is likely to be oppositional defiant disorder (Hamilton & Armando, 2008; Maughan, Rowe, Messer, Goodman & Meltzer, 2004).

Vignette

Howard, age ten, had always been strong-willed. When his father said it was time for dinner, Howard insisted on finishing a videogame. When his mother told him to wear a jacket to school because it was a cold morning, he ran to the school bus without the coat. His parents had learned to warn him ahead of time when an unusual event was about to occur. At times, they cajoled and negotiated with Howard to induce him to follow their expectations. When his parents informed the children of their plan to separate, Howard cried. Later, he became angry and blamed his parents for ruining his life. The custodial parent was his mother, and when it was time to visit his father, Howard yelled, "I won't go! I won't go! I won't go!" With time and with the gentle encouragement of both parents, Howard gradually gave in and enjoyed spending time with both his mother and his father.

MALTREATED CHILDREN

In some divorced families the child is abused, neglected, or disliked by one of the parents. If that is the case, it is understandable that a child would not want to spend time with or have a relationship with a parent who treated him badly. It is understandable that the child would protest loudly, be highly oppositional, and even threaten to run away if plans were made for him to visit an abusive parent. That would also be true if the child had been treated badly by the current boyfriend or girlfriend of a parent. Substance abuse by a parent or stepparent–which is frequently associated with neglect or abuse–may be a legitimate reason for a child to resist visiting that household.

It is not a mental disorder for a child to refuse to spend time with an abusive caregiver. That is normal behavior. In that regard, most authors make a distinction between estrangement and alienation. *Estrangement* refers to a child's rejection of a parent that is justified "as a consequence of the rejected parent's history of family violence, abuse and neglect" (Johnston, 2005). In contrast, *alienation* refers to a child's rejection of a parent that is unjustified, in other words, unreasonable negative feelings and beliefs . . . that are significantly disproportionate to the child's actual experience with that parent" (Johnston, 2005). With that distinction in mind, estrangement is not a diagnosable mental condition because it is normal behavior. Alienation, on the other hand, is an abnormal mental condition because it is consists of maladaptive behavior (refusal to see a loving parent) that is driven by a false or illogical belief (that the rejected parent is evil, dangerous, or not worthy of love). Gardner (1999) suggested criteria for differentiating PAS from abuse and neglect.

Vignette

Colby was a seven-year-old boy whose parents recently divorced. They were married for twelve years before his mother filed for divorce after learning of the father's infidelity. After the divorce, Colby had scheduled visitation with his father every other weekend. After about a year, he began to have difficulty transitioning back to his mother's home. He began crying and begging his father to not take him back. Colby told his father that his mother's boyfriend hurt him and he was afraid of him. Colby's father spoke with his ex-wife about what Colby had said, and she stated that it could not be true. She also said that Colby had never approached her about being hurt. When Colby arrived for the next visit with his father, he had obvious bruises on his back and legs. After his mother could not explain the injuries, an investigation ensued, which revealed that the mother's boyfriend had been teasing and physically abusing Colby.

ACCIDENTAL INDOCTRINATION

Some parents indoctrinate their children to fear or dislike the other parent, but they do not do it purposefully. Perhaps the custodial parent–the mother, for example–is an overly anxious individual who worries most of the day and communicates her anxiety to the child. Mom may start crying or be visibly upset when she sends the child to visit the father, so the child starts to believe that there is something fearful about visiting Dad. Perhaps Mom continues to be very angry at Dad and expresses her anger when the child can hear her, so the child rapidly figures out it is in his interest to imitate Mom's attitude and reject a relationship with Dad. Accidental indoctrination can lead to PA, in that the child refuses contact with the target parent without legitimate justification. However, accidental indoctrination typically results in a mild degree of PA because the alienating behaviors of the favored parent are sporadic, not persistent and relentless. Also, those cases are usually treatable because the alienating parent readily stops his or her inappropriate behaviors when they are pointed out.

Vignette

Heather was a six-year-old girl with exercise-induced asthma. Her parents recently divorced, and her mother was the primary residential parent. Before the divorce, Heather had a close relationship with her father. Their relationship slowly deteriorated after the divorce to the point that Heather refused to visit her father and clung to her mother during the scheduled exchanges. Beginning when the parents separated, Heather's mother cried at the transition times and repetitively told Heather, "I love you. I miss you. I can't wait for you to come back." During her time with her father, the mother telephoned Heather repeatedly asking if she was all right and then said, "I miss you so much. I can't wait for you to come home." When Heather returned to her mother, her mother ran to her, became tearful, and said, "I'm so happy you're back. I've been worried sick about you. I don't know what to do when you're gone." The father noticed that Heather gravitated away from him. Just before Heather began to refuse visitation with her father, she told him, "Stop being so mean to Mommy. I hate you."

PURPOSEFUL INDOCTRINATION

It is easy to see how an angry, spiteful, vengeful parent might purposefully brainwash or systematically indoctrinate a child against the other parent. For example, the indoctrinating parent might repeatedly emphasize his or her own affection for the child and repeatedly comment on actual, perceived, or fabricated deficiencies in the other parent. The anger of the alienating parent may have been justified at some time in the past, for example, because of the target parent's infidelity during their marriage. On the other hand, the intense resentment of the alienating parent may be driven by his or her maladaptive personality traits, such as those seen in individuals with narcissistic and borderline personality disorders. There are hundreds of published examples of purposeful indoctrination in psychology, psychiatry, and legal publications. The classic citations include *Children Held Hostage: Dealing with Programmed and Brainwashed Children* (Clawar & Rivlin, 1991) and *The Parental Alienation Syndrome: A Guide for Mental Health and Legal Professionals* (Gardner, 1992).

Persistent, relentless criticism of the target parent may cause the child to develop PA and reject that parent. That type of indoctrination usually continues for a long time–months to years–and typically results in moderate and severe levels of PA. Cases that have reached a severe level of PA may be intractable and particularly difficult to treat. It is advantageous, of course, to identify PA earlier when it is much more likely to be treatable.

Vignette

There are several examples of PA caused by purposeful indoctrination in Chapters 4 and 5 of this book. A fictional example was related in *The Look of Love,* a book by Jill Egizii (2010). In the book, Anna Reinhardt's children, Betsy and Andrew, abruptly turned against her after she moved out of the family home. Their father, Erik Reinhardt–wealthy and politically powerful–easily alienated the children against Anna. A dramatic moment occurs near the end of the book when the children are expected to testify in open court before the judge who will determine their custody. Without spoiling the story, we will say that the book has a happy ending.

SHARED DELUSIONAL DISORDER

The term *folie à deux,* introduced by Lasègue and Falret in the nineteenth century (1877), refers to a syndrome in which two individuals with a close, long-lasting relationship share the same delusional belief. Generally the older or more dominant person has an established delusion that is "shared" with a younger or more passive person. In *DSM-IV-TR,* that condition was called "shared psychotic disorder." In *DSM-5,* the diagnosis of shared psychotic disorder has been removed and the condition is considered a type of delusional disorder. Perhaps the most accurate terminology is used by *ICD-10,* "induced psychotic disorder."

For example, a parent with paranoid schizophrenia or delusional disorder might have a fixed, false belief that the FBI has been tapping the family's telephone and following them in unmarked vehicles. The parent talks about the delusion so much that the child adopts the same false belief and starts monitoring the neighborhood for FBI agents. Typically, if the child's relationship with the delusional parent is interrupted, the child's delusional beliefs diminish or disappear. Several authors have commented that severe cases of parental alienation resemble a shared delusional disorder. For instance, Gardner (1999) said:

> When paranoia fuels PAS, the victim of the paranoid delusional system is often limited to the denigrated spouse–at least, this is the case in the early phases. With ongoing litigation, the paranoia may expand to all the people who provide support to the targeted parent. Typically, the paranoid system becomes illogical and preposterous; for example, that the targeted parent would perpetrate abusive behavior–and even sexual molestation–in front of court-ordered supervisors. Often the PAS parent and the programmed child

> jointly entertain the same delusion. . . . In such cases the DSM-IV diagnosis of shared psychotic delusion (folie à deux) is warranted.

Ellis (2000) wrote regarding *folie à deux:* "Little known and very rarely seen, this quaint term is now referred to . . . as shared psychotic disorder. A brief review of what is known about *folie à deux* reveals striking similarities to PAS" (p. 218).

Vignette

Angela's mother had multiple delusions. She thought the CIA was tracking her movements; she thought her own parents sexually abused her in satanic rituals; she thought her ex-husband was videotaping his sexual activities with Angela. Angela's father sought a change in custody on the basis of a substantial change in circumstances. When the court-appointed evaluator interviewed Angela, she said that her father, who lived in another state, came into her bedroom every night and photographed her nude.

CONTACT REFUSAL RESULTING FROM A COMBINATION OF CAUSES

Human behavior is complex and often there are multiple underlying causes for a person's actions. Although we have discussed nine different causes of contact refusal in this chapter, there are no doubt other causes or combinations of causes of contact refusal that have occurred in some families. When a person has two mental conditions at the same time–such as major depressive disorder and posttraumatic stress disorder–they are said to be comorbid. Thus, comorbidity refers to the simultaneous appearance of two or more psychiatric or physical illnesses. If a child or adolescent is manifesting contact refusal, there may be two or more underlying causes that are prompting that behavior to occur.

Separation Anxiety and Accidental Indoctrination Together

Anxious parents frequently have anxious children, which is the result of a genetic predisposition as well as learned behavior, because the child senses the parent's worries and adopts them as her own. Suppose a father has generalized anxiety disorder, so he tends to catastrophize and worry endlessly when his daughter visits her mother. He gives the child too many admonitions and instructions, such as "I'm going to worry myself to death when you're at your mom's house," and "If you have a bad dream tonight, call me on my cell phone." Although the father is not intentionally undermining the child's relationship with her mother, he is accidentally indoctrinating the child to be fearful during the mother's parenting time. If the child internalizes her father's worries and generates her own system of worries, she may develop separation anxiety disorder. Her contact refusal is a result of an internal process (separation anxiety disorder) and external factors (accidental indoctrination by her father).

Estrangement and Alienation Together

As Kelly and Johnston (2001) wrote, "Children who are realistically estranged from one of their parents as a consequence of that parent's history of family violence, abuse, or neglect need to be clearly distinguished from alienated children." It is possible for child maltreatment and PA to occur together, however. For example, suppose that Parent A–under the influence of alcohol–was physically abusive to the child on one or two occasions. Then Parent A made a commitment to abstain from alcohol and became an attentive, nurturing parent. Parent B, however, made a very big deal of the abuse incidents and indoctrinated the child against Parent A. Because the child's rejection of Parent A was out of proportion to anything Parent A had done, the child manifested PA. Although this combination may be unusual, PA and a history of child abuse can coexist.

Purposeful Indoctrination, Normal Preferences, and Cognitive Dissonance Together

Consider the following complicated set of circumstances: the parents divorced because Dad had an affair with another woman, whom he ultimately married. Mom was devastated and enraged by Dad's infidelity, and she took every opportunity to criticize him to their two sons (purposeful indoctrination). The boys accused their father of being an alcoholic and a sex addict. Also, they greatly disliked their new stepmother, an imperious woman who nagged at the boys to improve their table manners, so the boys avoided having meals at the Dad's home (normal preferences). Finally, there was incessant arguing between Mom and Dad, which occurred during almost every transition from one household to the other. It was impossible for the children to align with both Mom and Dad at the same time, so they gravitated to Mom's side of the argument and rejected Dad (cognitive dissonance).

This book is about PA, not simply contact refusal. It is important, however, to understand that PA occurs in a larger context. If the primary symptom of the child is refusal to have visitation with the noncustodial parent, there are several possible explanations to consider and the evaluator should not jump to the conclusion that it is a case of PA. Just as there are several possible causes of contact refusal, there are several possible causes of PA. Evaluators should consider those possibilities before arriving at a conclusion, such as a formal diagnosis, and devising a treatment plan.

AN OVERALL STRATEGY TO ASSESS CONTACT REFUSAL

The MHP's general plan should be to conduct an assessment in such a way as to determine if contact refusal is occurring and, if that is the case, to identify the most likely etiology. The ultimate reason for conducting the evaluation in that manner is to recommend specific interventions that should be helpful to the particular child. There is no generic treatment for all children who manifest contact refusal. The treatment for a particular child depends on the underlying cause of that child's behavior.

The assessment of contact refusal is best approached in an organized fashion, which helps the examiner maintain an unbiased approach and remain mindful of the various hypotheses that must be considered for a thorough and robust opinion. The assessment typically begins as any other mental health assessment. As information is collected, the examiner is better able to determine whether contact refusal is present, the particular cause of the contact refusal, and the preferred treatment or intervention.

The overall approach described in this chapter was not created specifically for the assessment of contact refusal but is the methodology generally used by MHPs in seeing a new patient, client, or evaluee. In the encyclopedic *Handbook of Child and Adolescent Psychiatry,* Dulcan (1998) wrote

> Every clinical assessment should yield a formulation in which the clinician integrates possible etiologic factors, considers the differential diagnosis, and identifies both targets to be addressed in treatment and areas in which further evaluation is needed. (p. 5)

In general, the initial assessment of a new client by a MHP proceeds through the following steps:

1. **Identify the chief complaint or the primary symptoms that prompted the child's parents to seek professional consultation**. Sometimes, the chief complaint is obvious, as when the father says, "I'm divorced and my son says he hates his mother and refuses to stay at her house." Some-

times, there are several presenting symptoms that must be considered together, such as "My daughter has gotten very rebellious and cussed out her teacher in the sixth grade," and "I'm divorced. My daughter refuses to eat dinner with my new wife and me," and "My daughter says she hates her mother and refuses to stay at her house."

This step in the process sometimes occurs during the phone call when the parent contacts the MHP to set up an appointment. If not then, this step occurs during the first part of the MHP's first interview with the parent or parents. The examiner will need to ask each parent about the time they spend with the child and how the child behaves during the transition period between the two homes. Learning about contact refusal is not always straightforward. One parent may attempt to cover up the contact refusal or the child may give inaccurate details about the situation. Usually, clarity is achieved as more data are collected during the course of the evaluation.

2. **Develop a differential diagnosis for the chief complaint.** As a starting point, the evaluator should keep in mind the different possibilities for the child's problematic behavior or mental condition. Some of those possibilities are reasonable and normal; others are pathological. Although a parent may present his or her own understanding of the behavior, it is the responsibility of examiners to arrive at their own conclusions through an unbiased evaluation of the data available. If the chief complaint is contact refusal, the differential diagnosis includes all the conditions discussed in the first half of this chapter: the child has a normal preference, has a loyalty conflict, is dealing with continual fighting between the parents, is worried or depressed, is being stubborn, has been abused, has compromised reality testing, and PA.

3. **Collect enough general information to narrow down the full differential diagnosis to a short list of two or three possibilities.** Usually, this step occurs during the MHP's first interview with one or both of the child's parents. During that interview, the MHP develops a complete account of the child's presenting problem by asking suitable questions. The MHP also collects information about the child's relationships with the parents and other family members, the developmental history, the child's experiences in school and with peers, and medical information. That is the standard historical information that the MHP is likely to collect during the initial assessment of any new client or patient. During this step of the evaluation process, the MHP is able to rule out the less likely causes of the child's contact refusal after considering and testing various possibilities before arriving at a firm conclusion. For example, the MHP might be able to rule out the following in a hypothetical case: the benign situation of a child simply stating a normal preference to avoid visiting a parent (because the pattern of behavior is very intense and persistent), the child's contact refusal is the result of

severe anxiety or depression (because the child is apparently happy and functions well in almost every aspect of life), and estrangement due to child abuse (because neither the preferred parent nor the child report abuse).

4. **Collect additional detailed information to identify the specific cause of the child's contact refusal.** The procedure and the questioning is largely the same during the first part of most evaluations. However, the procedure and the questioning may become very specialized during the latter part of mental health evaluations, because the MHP tries to confirm whether a particular mental condition is the cause of the child's problematic behavior. For example, if the MHP strongly suspects that the child's contact refusal is driven by separation anxiety, the evaluator may arrange for the youngster to take a standardized psychological test such as the child version of the Child Behavior Checklist. If the MHP strongly suspects that the child suffers shared psychotic disorder, the evaluator may seek permission to talk with the parent's own mental health provider.

There is no absolute set of rules for how an evaluation should be conducted when the chief complaint is contact refusal. The typical evaluation consists of the following interviews, however, first, a preliminary joint meeting with both parents together. The purposes of that meeting are to make sure the parents and the MHP agree on the reasons for the evaluation, to explain to the parents how the evaluation will be conducted, and to schedule all the subsequent meetings. Second, individual meetings with both parents are held to collect their respective observations and opinions regarding the child and other family members. Third, two interviews of the child in which she is brought to the first interview by one parent and then to the second interview by the other parent. This is designed to decrease bias and also to provide an opportunity to observe the parenting styles of each parent and the child's relationship with each parent. The child is interviewed individually during the first part of the session, and then the parent is invited into the meeting. The parent and child are asked to do a standard activity together and their interactions are observed. Fourth, there may be interviews with important collateral parties, such as stepparents and grandparents.

In addition to the face-to-face interviews, the MHP may want to have telephone conversations with other informants, such as the child's teacher, the pediatrician, other family members, family friends, and the psychotherapists who have worked with the child and the parents. Depending on the circumstances of the particular case, the MHP may want to send for documents and records such as school records, medical records, and legal records related to the parents' separation and divorce. Depending on the way the differential diagnosis is developing, the MHP may want to arrange for psychological testing of the child and/or the parents. Typically, the mother and father

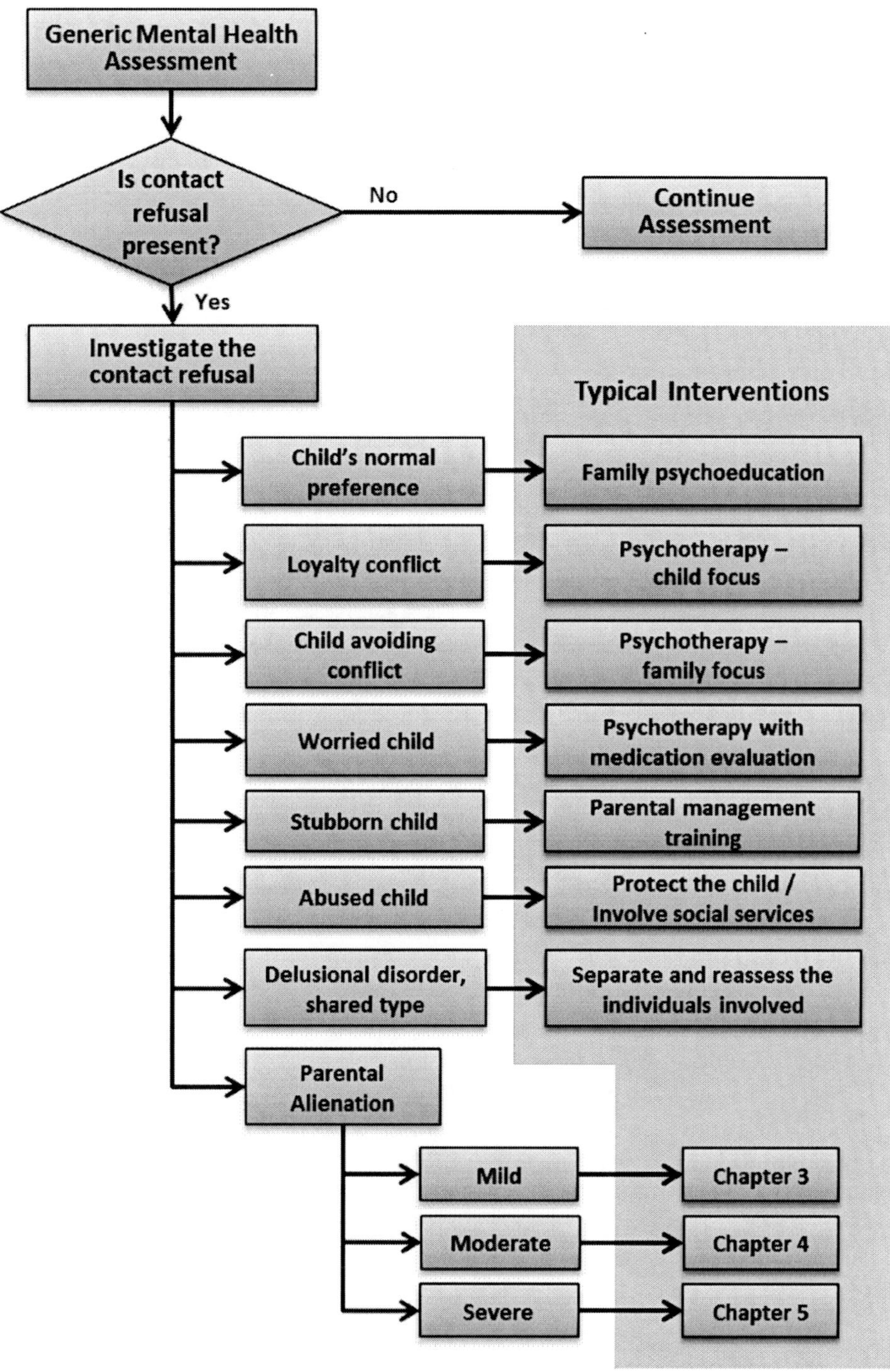

Figure 2.1. Typical Assessment Procedure for Contact Refusal.

are given the same tests. For example, if there is reason to administer personality testing to one parent, the same tests are given to both parents.

The general approach described is similar to the procedure for a child custody evaluation or parenting time evaluation. In fact, the phenomenon of contact refusal should be addressed in every custody evaluation and commented upon in some fashion in the report. If the examiner has determined that contact refusal is not present, then she should note that as a pertinent negative finding. On the other hand, if contact refusal is found, an orderly investigation should ensue to determine the underlying reason for that behavior.

TREATMENT RECOMMENDATIONS FOR CONTACT REFUSAL

First, the evaluator considers the entire range of possible explanations for the contact refusal. Then, the evaluator narrows down the list to two or three leading possibilities. Finally, the evaluator identifies the cause that fits the particular facts and circumstances of the case most precisely, and that leads to treatment recommendations. Here are eight examples for how that process would flow.

1. **The child's normal preference**. The relationship that children have with their parents is dynamic. The relationship can change abruptly or slowly as each person grows and has new experiences. A child who was once close with his mother during the formative years may develop a stronger relationship with his father as he approaches adulthood. There are natural and reasonable preferences that children and adolescents develop throughout their life. The MHP must determine if contact refusal is part of this normal developmental process. If the child does not exhibit animosity toward a parent and has few problems before and following the transitions between households, it is likely that this is a normal process.

The intervention for that type of contact refusal is focused on the parents. Psychoeducation about human development will help remedy their concern or anxiety about the situation and encourage both parents to work in concert in maintaining healthy relationships with the child. In contentious situations, however, the parents may not be amendable to that intervention and attempt to persuade the examiner of his or her point of view. In that case, it is critical for the MHP to have strong supporting evidence for her or his opinion. She or he may want to recommend counseling for one or both parents to discuss their own anxieties.

2. **Loyalty conflict**. In some instances, a child who previously had a secure attachment to both parents is now dealing with repeated separations.

A sense of guilt and sadness for the other parent is normal as the child transitions between his mother and father. Those feelings typically resolve as the child adjusts to the new situation and the parents are supportive. Unfortunately, some children are unable to adjust for various reasons and the conflict they feel evolves into a more significant and prolonged state of psychological distress. The loyalty conflict may be driven by both intrapsychic processes (e.g., the child feels guilty about loving both parents) and conflict in the child's external world (e.g., the battle between the parents). The child may be able to describe what she is experiencing: "I really miss Mom," or "I miss Dad when I'm not there," or "Dad seems lonely when I'm not there, so I better stay with him." The child may try to resolve the distress by allying with one parent and rejecting the other parent, but the child still feels uncomfortable and guilty in making that choice.

To aid the child who is struggling with a significant loyalty conflict, it may be helpful for her to see a therapist. The involvement of the parents in the therapy is ideal as long as they do not have a contentious relationship. The child and parents work together in therapy to help the child adjust to their new living arrangements. Psychotropic medication may be useful depending on the clinical picture, for example, if the child is extremely anxious or depressed.

3. **Child avoiding conflict between the parents.** It is painful for the child when parents argue over the child, in front of the child, and through the child. A child in that situation may initially love both parents but eventually get out of the battle zone by siding with one parent and rejecting the other. Although that maneuver might alleviate the child's anxiety, it is an unhealthy long-term solution because of the disruption of the child's relationship with one of the parents.

The child with a loyalty conflict feels uncomfortable or somewhat guilty in supporting one parent and rejecting the other. On the other hand, the child who resolves cognitive dissonance by totally aligning with one parent and totally rejecting the other parent no longer feels guilty; he simply feels he is doing the right thing. The child might say to himself, "I have no interest in seeing Mom ever again. She didn't give me the birthday present I wanted. I want to totally stay with Dad." The MHP should determine the nature of the child's relationship prior to the separation and then seek information about how the rejection started and what the response was from the parents. A child escaping external parental conflict may have experienced mood symptoms and anxiety prior to the rejection, and that has since resolved, at least superficially. Obtaining clear evidence to support that etiology is crucial because children in abusive relationships can behave in a similar fashion.

When the child is reacting to the high-conflict relationship between the parents, the intervention should involve family therapy. The parent who is not being rejected by the child should support the child's relationship with the other parent. Perhaps the most difficult aspect of the intervention is that the parents should be cordial with one another and be willing to support the child's relationship with the other parent. As with children who have loyalty conflicts, medication may be a warranted component of the treatment plan as well.

4. **Worried or depressed child**. Children are dependent on their parents. They rely on their parents to meet their basic needs and to provide them with healthy experiences. When an intact family is disrupted by parental separation, the children naturally experience an unhealthy stress. Fortunately, children tend to be resilient, and they can tolerate change and can adapt to new situations. Some children, however, have tremendous difficulty making this adjustment and anxiety ensues. The outcome largely depends on the relationship between the parents after the divorce. A high-conflict postdivorce parental relationship can be very damaging to the mental health of a child. The MHP should explore the relationship between the parents and how that relationship affects the feelings and behavior of the child. A very anxious child might say, "I don't like going back and forth between my parents. I don't think either of them really wants me around. They might think I don't love them."

If the child's contact refusal is driven by a high level of anxiety or depression, there are two distinct prongs for intervention. First, the child should be considered for both psychotherapy interventions and medication. Second, the parents should be educated about their impact on the child and perhaps involve themselves in their own therapy to help alleviate, or at least control, their own emotions when around the child. If interventions are recommended only for the child, the chance of long-term resolution to the contact refusal is poor.

5. **Stubborn child**. Most children are resistant to change. Some undergo a period of adjustment before settling into a new routine, but others will act out for long periods of time in the face of change. Occasionally, the acting out includes contact refusal. The MHP should explore the parents' perception of the child and what they do to encourage a healthy relationship with the other parent. If the parents are acting appropriately and making reasonable decisions, the focus should turn to the child. The MHP should attempt to determine if the child has been abnormally defiant or oppositional in the past with either parent and, if so, how the parents responded. In considering this etiology for contact refusal, the MHP should be careful not to blame the child but rather the circumstances surrounding the child. An

oppositional child might say, "Everybody says I need to spend time with my mom but I'm not going to. She and I don't get along. She tries to boss me around too much. My dad understands me better."

In this case, unless a psychological illness is suspected, psychotherapy and medication may not be especially useful. An intervention to consider is psychoeducation for the parents in which they learn how to set limits and reinforce realistic consequences with their child together as well as focus on rewarding positive behavior. This type of intervention requires that the parents work closely together in parenting their child. Oftentimes, this is not practical. Reconsider the diagnosis if the parents are unable to work together because there might be another reason that accounts for the contact refusal.

6. **Abused child**. There are situations in which the child is being abused by one or, perhaps, both parents. If a child refuses to spend time with an abusive parent, that is normal behavior. The MHP should certainly explore the child's safety with both parents. For example, perhaps both parents are abusive but the mother is less abusive so the child sides with her.

Questioning the parents about abuse is difficult in these cases because they are acutely aware of how their responses might affect the evaluator's opinion. It is useful to ask parents how they discipline the children and why they get disciplined. The MHP should gauge the threshold that each parent has for disciplining the child and how the parent tailors the punishment to the behavior. Some parents believe in corporal punishment; others do not. The act of corporal punishment does not mean the parent is abusive, but that must be explored. The MHP should continue to probe regarding abuse if, for example, a father might say, "If she doesn't clean up the dinner table then she knows she going to get a whopping." That statement alone does not indicate abuse. The MHP should ask the parent more specific questions about punishments. If the father then stated, "Well, I usually just give her a spanking but if she continues to give me a hard time, I use my belt," the MHP should directly and indirectly ask about the intensity of the punishment and whether the child was ever physically injured.

Nonaccidental injury to the child is often enough to substantiate the presence of physical abuse. In that circumstance, the contact refusal is legitimate and the safety of the child is paramount. The MHP must comply with jurisdictional mandates for reporting child abuse. Typically, the MHP should involve child protective services (CPS), and the possibility of their involvement needs to be discussed at the outset of the assessment. Although the MHP may have extensive experience with child abuse evaluations, she should defer further abuse investigation to CPS or another entity in order to maintain an unbiased role as much as possible in the parenting evaluation.

7. **Shared delusional disorder**. On rare occasions, a parent may develop a pathological perspective about the other parent, which the child begins to incorporate into her own belief system. The MHP should explore those beliefs with the parent and the child separately. The MHP should assess how those thoughts started but not dismiss them as delusional unless they are either bizarre or they cannot be realistically substantiated. The parent might say, "My ex-wife is evil. She is determined to destroy my life and everything I care about. She gets inside my head, like she knows what I'm thinking. She never leaves me alone," and the child might say, "I hate how mean Mom is. She's trying to control us and make us poor. I don't like how evil she is to us." The MHP may consider arranging for the parent and the child to have psychological testing to help clarify the diagnosis.

If the most likely explanation for contact refusal is shared psychotic disorder, the intervention is fairly straightforward. Separating the delusional parent from the affected child is usually enough to treat the child. The parent will need his or her own psychological evaluation with consideration of psychotherapy and perhaps medication. By definition, delusions are fixed and resolution for that type of situation may not be possible. The child may still be able to have contact with the delusional parent as long as he is supported and there are individuals who remain vigilant in case the child begins to incorporate the delusion again. That is more likely with younger children and less bizarre delusions.

8. **Parental alienation**. Some parents indoctrinate their children against the other parent, either accidentally or intentionally. In order to make the diagnosis of PA, the MHP must collect detailed information about the child's experiences with both parents; for example, has the preferred parent repeatedly tried to "protect" the child from the rejected parent without good cause? Frequently, the best source of information is the preferred parent's own explanations for why he or she has restricted or discouraged contact with the rejected parent. Also, has the rejected parent behaved in a way to justify the child's rejection? It may be necessary to interview collateral informants and review medical and legal records to answer that question. Finally, the MHP should assess whether the child manifests symptoms typical of PA, such as persistent denigration of the rejected parent, rejection of that parent's extended family without good reason, and lack of ambivalence (total support of one parent and total rejection of the other parent). Because of the complexity of those situations, it is helpful to categorize PA as mild, moderate, or severe. Chapters 3, 4, and 5 provide guidance on both the evaluation and the interventions for the varying degrees of PA.

Editors' Notes

- The differential diagnosis of contact refusal includes the child's normal preferences for one parent over the other; adjustment disorder; separation anxiety disorder; oppositional defiant disorder; child maltreatment; PA caused by indoctrination, either accidental or purposeful; PA without indoctrination; and shared psychotic disorder.
- Alienation refers to a child's refusal to spend time with one of the parents without a reasonable explanation; estrangement refers to a child's refusal to spend time with one of the parents based on a reasonable cause, such as a history of child maltreatment.
- Frequently, two or more of the factors discussed in this chapter contribute to the child's contact refusal. For example, a child might be experiencing separation anxiety and accidental indoctrination at the same time.
- In a typical assessment of contact refusal, the MHP should initially consider the entire differential diagnosis for the presenting problem or chief complaint. As the evaluation progresses, the MHP is able to narrow down the possibilities and determine the underlying cause of the contact refusal.

REFERENCES

Bagnell, A. L. (2011). Anxiety and separation disorders. *Pediatrics in Review, 32*(10), 440–445.

Bernet, W. (2006). Sexual abuse allegations in the context of child custody disputes. In R. A. Gardner, S. R. Sauber, & D. Lorandos (Eds.), *The international handbook of parental alienation syndrome: Conceptual, clinical and legal considerations* (pp. 242–263). Springfield, IL: Charles C Thomas.

Bernet, W., Boch-Galhau, W. V., Baker, A. J. L., & Morrison, S. L. (2010). Parental alienation, DSM-V, and ICD-11. *American Journal of Family Therapy, 38*(2), 76–187.

Cavedon, A., & Magro, T. (2010). *Dalla separazione all'alienazione parentale. Come giungere a una valutazione paritale [From separation to parental alienation. How to arrive at an expert evaluation]* [Italian]. Milan, Italy: FrancoAngeli.

Clawar, S. S., & Rivlin, B. V. (1991). *Children held hostage: Dealing with programmed and brainwashed children.* Chicago, IL: American Bar Association.

Connolly, S. D., Suarez, L., & Sylvester, C. (2011). Assessment and treatment of anxiety disorders in children and adolescents. *Current Psychiatry Reports, 13*(2), 99–110.

Drozd, L. M., & Olesen, N. W. (2004). Is it abuse, alienation, and/or estrangement? A decision tree. *Journal of Child Custody, 1*(3), 65–106.

Dulcan, M. K. (1998). Types and goals of clinical assessment. In J. D. Noshpitz, S. I. Harrison, & S. Eth (Eds.), *Handbook of child and adolescent psychiatry* (pp. 3–9). New York: John Wiley & Sons.

Egizii, J. (2010). *The look of love.* Santa Ana, CA: Seven Locks Press.

Ellis, E. M. (2000). *Divorce wars: Interventions with families in conflict.* Washington, DC: American Psychological Association.

Festinger, L. (1957). *A theory of cognitive dissonance.* Stanford, CA: Stanford University Press.

Freeman, B. W. (2011). Children of divorce: the differential diagnosis of contact refusal. *Child and Adolescent Psychiatric Clinics of North America, 20*(3), 467–477.

Gardner, R. A. (1979). Death of a parent. In J. D. Noshpitz (Ed.), *Basic handbook of child psychiatry* (pp. 270–283). New York: Basic Books.

Gardner, R. A. (1992). *The parental alienation syndrome: A guide for mental health and legal professionals.* Cresskill, NJ: Creative Therapeutics.

Gardner, R. A. (1999). Differentiating between parental alienation syndrome and bona fide abuse-neglect. *American Journal of Family Therapy, 27*(2), 97–107.

Hamilton, S. S. & Armando, J. (2008). Oppositional defiant disorder. *American Family Physician, 78*(7), 861–866.

Huurre, T., Junkkari, H., & Aro, H. (2006). Long-term psychosocial effects of parental divorce: a follow-up study from adolescence to adulthood. *European Archives of Psychiatry and Clinical Neuroscience, 256*(4), 256–263.

Johnston, J. R. (1993). Children of divorce who refuse visitation. In C. Depner & J. H. Bray (Eds.), *Non-residential parenting: New vistas in family living* (pp. 109–135). Newbury Park, CA: Sage.

Johnston, J. R. (2005). Children of divorce who reject a parent and refuse visitation: Recent research and social policy implications for the alienated child. *Family Law Quarterly, 38,* 757–775.

Kelly, J. B., & Johnston, J. R. (2001). The alienated child: A reformulation of parental alienation syndrome. *Family Court Review, 39*(3), 249–266.

Klosinski, G. (1993). Psychological maltreatment in the context of separation and divorce. *Child Abuse & Neglect, 17*(4), 557–563.

Lasègue, C., & Falret, J. (1877). La folie à deux ou folie communiquée [A madness shared by two or communicated insanity] [French]. *Annales medico-psychologiques, 18,* 321–355.

Maughan, B., Rowe, R., Messer, J., Goodman, R., & Meltzer, H. (2004). Conduct disorder and oppositional defiant disorder in a national sample: Developmental epidemiology. *Journal of Child Psychology and Psychiatry, 45*(3), 609–621.

Mills, J., & Harmon-Jones, E. (1999). *Cognitive dissonance: Progress on a pivotal theory in social psychology.* Washington, DC: American Psychological Association.

Mustonen, U., Huurre, T., Kiviruusu, O., Haukkala, A., & Aro, H. (2011). Long-term impact of parental divorce on intimate relationship quality in adulthood and the mediating role of psychosocial resources. *Journal of Family Psychology, 25*(4), 615–619.

Orgilés Amorós, M., Espada Sánchez, J. P., & Méndez Carrillo, X. (2008). Trastorno de ansiedad por separación en hijos de padres divorciados [Separation anxiety disorder in a sample of children of divorce] [Spanish]. *Psicothema, 20*(3), 383–388.

Suveg, C., Aschenbrand, S. G., & Kendall, P. C. (2005). Separation anxiety disorder, panic disorder, and school refusal. *Child and Adolescent Psychiatric Clinics of North America, 14*(4), 773–795.

Wallerstein, J. S., Lewis, J. M., & Blakeslee, S. (2001). *The unexpected legacy of divorce: A 25 year landmark study.* New York: Hyperion.

Chapter 3

MILD CASES OF PARENTAL ALIENATION

DOUGLAS C. DARNALL

Vignette

Sara and John finally split after three years of fights with no resolutions. John walked out after learning that Sara accused him of verbal abuse and threatened to call the police because she said she was afraid and believed it was only a matter of time until he would physically assault her and their daughter Becky, age 14. John felt that he needed to protect himself from her making a false allegation. Sara in turn wanted to protect Becky from her father's abuse. She later admitted on the witness stand that John never assaulted their child but expressed the opinion that it was only a matter of time until he would physically abuse her. Sara would say that Becky needed a relationship with her father but felt that protecting their child outweighed his having time alone with her. Sara wanted his time with their child to be supervised. She also complained about his lax parenting skills, such as his failure to monitor the child's television viewing and ignoring her scheduled bedtime. Sara knew she should temper her fear, but her attitude toward John was permeated with cautionary comments to the child. Her attitude was apparent to the child because of the angry tone in her voice when mentioning John. She began finding excuses why Becky could not go for her parenting time, refusing to give John the schedule of their child's social activities and subtly listening in on Becky's phone calls for any sign of verbal abuse. Sara tried to strengthen her relationship with her daughter by using her as a confidant. She stated that her daughter was her best friend. She frequently called Becky when she was with her father to be sure she was safe. "After all, isn't that what a good mother is to do?"

Sara and John have put their daughter Becky in the middle of their hostilities. Becky in particular feels the stress about not knowing how to align her allegiances. She loves her father but does not want to disappoint her mother. She feels pressured to reject her father when she is in her mother's presence. Sometimes Becky is protective of her father because she sees the pain in his face. At the same time, Becky risks losing her mother's affection if she expresses any desire to spend time with her father. Becky tries to temper her anxiety by withdrawing and emotionally shutting down when the subject of her father comes up. Her face turns blank and her voice softens when she is in the presence of both parents. Sometimes the anxiety becomes so severe that she refuses to see her father, even knowing how much that hurts him. Becky sees no way out. She is very alone with her feelings. Once a visit takes place, whether frequent or infrequent, however she no longer feels this disconnect emotion or conflict.

CHILDREN ARE THE VICTIMS

DEFINITION. This chapter is about mild parental alienation (PA), which refers to situations in which the child objects to and criticizes the target parent but yet enjoys the presence of the target parent once time passes or the location is no longer in close proximity to the alienating parent.

Becky's reaction to her mother's alienating behavior is expected. Alienation hurts children. Becky is expected to align with one parent to the detriment of the other. Children similar to Becky learn quickly that to emotionally survive, they must withhold any public displays of affection and resist any pronouncements that they want to spend more time with the target parent. Many alienated children feel pressured to reject what was once a loving, caring parent.

Usually, parents in the throes of a divorce may sense early on that something is beginning to go very wrong with their child. They may not be able to identify the problem but sense the change in their child's attitude. That is because the inception of alienation may be very subtle; it may begin with a disapproving frown at the mention of the other parent's name, refusal to acquiesce to the child's request for additional time, refusal to give the child private time for phone calls, or irrational criticism about the target parent's parenting skills. The child exposed to the alienation activities senses tension when the subject of the target parent is raised. The child, like Becky, is torn between divided loyalties.

Children want to love both parents without being hampered by a self-serving alienating parent. Even children who are mistreated will seek the inept parent's approval and love. Most often, children exposed to mild alienating strategies can let denigrating comments go in one ear and out the other, making excuses for the target parent and continuing to seek his or her approval. Over time, if the child is emotionally beaten down by the persistent alienating behavior, he or she begins to put up a wall against the target parent.

Parents feeling targeted will argue that their child is being brainwashed (Clawar & Rivlin, 1991). The child is trapped in the middle, with nowhere to go. The child may begin to question her or his own reality about what is true and not true. During the course of mild alienation, the child may begin appearing rather distant, overly critical, and nonresponsive to loving gestures from the target parent, especially in the alienating parent's presence. A common defense for a child caught in mild alienation is saying, "I don't want to see you this weekend." This is a parent's worst nightmare: the thought that "my child doesn't want to spend time with me." The target parent will question, "What have I done to deserve my child's rejection?" The target parent will search for answers because the rejection is out of character and contrary to his or her experiences with the child. The target parent will question, "Is my ex-spouse turning the children against me?"

Alienation is a very subtle process that can begin years before a separation or divorce. Becky had seen the subtle changes in her mother's attitude toward her father. She felt the tension grow between her parents with casual critical comments. There are warning signs that alienation is on the horizon. The number of signs or symptoms of alienation are infinite. During the inception of alienation, the target parent may begin hearing from the children denigrating comments about him or her made by the alienating parent. The comments can sound innocent enough, such as, "Let me do that, your father doesn't know what he's doing," "Your mother is acting like a bitch and won't let me do anything for fun," or "You don't have to listen to your mother." Becky may dismiss her mother's comments, although in time her mother's persistence may take a toll on Becky's feelings toward her father. Sometimes children exposed to mild alienating behavior are not very affected by these comments but will typically react more to their parent's emotional intensity than the words. If children are habitually exposed to denigrating comments, they become confused about how they perceive or feel about the target parent. Their personal history with the target parent may be rewritten by the alienating parent's behavior. The children may talk to a trusted family member about how they are feeling, looking for some affirmation that the feelings are rational. One risk for the child looking for affirmation occurs when the confidant is aligned with the alienating parent and reinforces in the child's mind that the alienation is justified. Frequently, extended family members such as grandparents and new significant others are a powerful source of alienation.

Children want to avoid conflict between their parents. Rather than take a side, most children, even exposed to alienation strategies, prefer to keep quiet. A child's lack of emotional expression is not an indictment toward either parent. This is the child's way of coping with an uncomfortable situation. A parent respecting a child's right to draw their own opinions and feelings from their own personal experience will not push his or her opinions or history of past events onto the child. This only confuses him or her. Children have a right to develop their own history with a parent founded on personal experience rather than on what they are told. Although mildly alienated children may keep their opinions to themselves, they are usually able to judge for themselves about the target parent's behavior without feeling compelled to agree with the alienating parent. Both parents allow differences of opinion about events.

All children get angry with their parents. One minute the child hates the parent and the next minute she or he climbs onto the parent's lap. A difference with a child exposed to mild alienation behavior is the ability to forgive and allow his or her anger to heal. Alienated children hold on to their anger and use the anger to rationalize and perpetuate the hatred. If a child's anger appears to be out of proportion to the offense and the healing never happens, one has to ask who or what is preventing the healing from occurring. The source is usually an alienating parent.

Children value their relationships with extended family members. Their bond may be stronger with some members than others because of their experiences with particular family members. Children can usually give good reasons about why they feel a stronger bond with one family member compared to others, such as geographic distance, time spent together, or how comfortable the child feels with the family member. Severely alienated children's reasons for their animosity are often irrational and frequently influenced by the alienating parent's attitude to the family member. The child's animosity and rejection will extend to all family members (Sauber, 2006).

ANTECEDENTS TO ALIENATION

When parents divorce, the rules for how to relate with each other will change. The changes often lead to misunderstanding and animosity that will bring about an attack of denigrating comments between the parents, often in the presence of the children. The parents may not intend to expose the children to their animosity, but the effect on the children can be a precursor for mild alienation. A child exposed to unregulated emotions is frightened and confused about where to turn for comfort and security. The child may unconsciously gravitate to his or her mother's arms to be soothed in her warmth. The father then feels rejected and perhaps jealous of the attention that the mother receives.

There are different motivations for why a parent would engage in mild alienating behaviors. Frequently, the alienating behavior is accidental and without malicious intent. The alienating behavior can take the form of denigrating comments, unfair comparisons with the ex-spouse, or inquisitive questions about the other parent's activities that are none of the questioning parent's business. The behavior denotes a negative judgment to the child about the target parent. Becky may not be able to verbalize the exact reasons for her feelings, except that she is witness to her mother's attitude anytime her father's name comes up in the conversation. She has learned to keep quiet and noncommittal.

Anger and betrayal are powerful motivators that can incite alienating behavior. Angry parents know better than to incite alienation, but the stress of single parenthood will at times cause the most well-meaning parent to explode with a diatribe of slanderous comments and passionate reasons for refusing parenting time. A new significant other is a frequent stimulus that incites alienation. When the parent regains self-control, the mildly alienating parent may repent with soft-spoken apologies to the child and occasionally to the target parent. This is in contrast to the moderately alienating parent, who will either rationalize his or her behavior or try to avoid the issue all together. Both the mildly and moderately alienating parent are capable of feeling guilty. This is never true for a severely alienating parent.

EARLY SIGNS OF ALIENATION

When discussing mild alienation, there are two aspects that must be addressed. The first aspect is identifying alienating behaviors. Typically, parents engaging in mildly alienating behavior are not in need of therapy but instead can benefit from education. The second aspect the parents must understand is how damaging alienating behavior is for the children. Identifying the early signs of alienation is a precursor to preventing moderate to severe alienating behavior from occurring. Sometimes alienating parents will get defensive if they are made to feel they are to blame for their behavior, but parents engaged in mild alienation are typically receptive to education once the behavior is pointed out to them in a supportive and gentle manner. A number of studies (Darnall, 2008; Baker & Chambers, 2011) have identified the more frequent alienating behaviors. Here is a description of the more common signs of alienation with interventions to help parents avoid more serious alienation and concurrently strengthen their relationship with their children.

Denigrating comments directed toward the target parent in the children's presence. Parents need to learn to monitor what they say in the children's presence. Most children have heard one parent making a denigrating comment about the other parent. Comments such as, "Your father is so stupid, he doesn't know what he is talking about" or "Your mother is such a bitch." There probably is not a child who has not heard a parent making a denigrating comment about the other parent. Alienation occurs if the comments persist and children are made to feel that they have to agree with the offending parent. This is Becky's struggle.

Interference with parenting time. Parenting time is the "booty" in high-conflict divorces. The parent who says "no" and refuses access to the children will ignite anger and bitterness in the target parent. A parent or child saying "no" has the power, not the target parent. This is the most common reason why parents return to court with a contempt motion.

Interfering with communication between the children and the target parent. Interfering with communication can take many forms: intercepting letters, e-mails, and text messages; not allowing privacy during phone calls; and scheduling activities when a phone call is scheduled. Children, like anyone else, have a right to privacy. Many mental health professionals (MHPs) argue that parents should not read their children's private e-mails, letters, or text messages or intrude in their children's conversations with the other parent. Children should be warned that what they write on Facebook or Twitter is not private and can haunt them for years.

Scheduling competing activities. Court orders are the law and must be respected by both the parents and the children. There are special circumstances that can arise that will interfere with scheduled parenting time. This should occur rarely and be coordinated with the other parent. If changes in parenting time occur too often, the target parent will begin to distrust the other parent and may become resentful. Proposed changes in parenting time should be coordinated and agreed upon before the children become involved. After the parents agree, only then should the children be involved. The children should never be given the impression that the other parent is preventing them from some special activity. A reality that parents and the children must accept is that they cannot always have everything they want. Hearing a "no" is a fact of life.

Asking the child to spy on the other parent. Each divorced parent has a right to privacy. In most respects, what goes on in the other household is none of the other parent's business. Children should never hear "Don't tell your mother" or "Would you find out how your father can afford a new car when he says he doesn't have the money to buy you a Kindle?" These are examples of spying, which places the child between both parents and potentially requires the child to lie. This is not a lesson a parent should want to teach her or his children. Nothing should ever occur in either household that should be a secret when the children are present that should be a secret.

Getting upset when the child displays affections toward the other parent. Children do not want to hurt either parent unless they are severely alienated. Both parents should tell children that it is okay to show affection toward the other parent.

This list of alienating behaviors is not all inclusive. Becky is exposed to her mother's denigrating comments, senses her mother's fear when in her father's presence, and hears her mother's displeasure if she expresses any affection or desire to spend time with her father. Becky and her father are paying the emotional price of Sara's alienating behavior.

DIFFERENTIATING BETWEEN MILD AND MODERATE ALIENATION

The distinction between the behavior of the mildly and moderately alienating parent is important because the interventions are different. The naïve or mildly alienating parent responds well to education whereas the moderately alienating parent benefits from professional help (Darnall 2008). One reason is that the moderately alienating parent continues to struggle with betrayal or the inability to heal from a contentious divorce. He or she may feel threatened when the children are introduced to the target parent's new significant other. Moderately alienating parents have moments when they are triggered into rages, spewing venomous tirades toward the children. Unresolved ex-spousal issues are usually what motivate the alienating parent's rants. Usually, they will accept professional help to learn how to temper their emotions and heal the pain because they know that their behavior is hurtful to the children and themselves. They are capable of feeling remorse about their behavior and admit to the harm they are causing the children. When they are more rational, they support the value for the children of having a loving relationship with the target parent.

INTERVENTIONS

How to respond to alienating behavior depends on the perspective of the parties involved in the case. The court will hear arguments alleging alienation and make a judgment about how to respond with a court order intended to help the parents reduce their hostilities and support a more amicable environment for the children. Parents engaged in mild alienating behaviors are receptive to changing their behavior when their problem behavior is brought to their attention. The difficulty they encounter is being able to sit back and objectively look at how they are behaving. For example, an alienating parent can learn to discriminate between ex-spousal and parental issues without much difficulty. On the other hand, parents may not be able to understand how symbolic communication contributes to the tensions between them without some therapeutic intervention. Education for the mildly alienating parent can come from many sources. The resources should have knowledge of alienation, be politically neutral, and have ample professional experience in family law, family therapy, alienation, and recent literature on reunification therapy.

THE COURT'S INTERVENTION

Target parents facing the fear of losing their child's affection and time together to an alienating parent need help. A source of help can come from a trusted therapist, an attorney, and even a judge who can offer guidance at the conclusion of a legal proceeding. Guidance must begin by understanding the motivation and dynamics of the alienation. Most often, a therapist is in a better position to make this assessment.

The court should explain one parent should not be quick to blame the other parent for the problems that he or she is having with the child. Alienation is only one possible explanation for a parent-child problem. The target parent could be contributing to his or her own problems because of an overly punitive parenting style, failure to bond, or perhaps a mental or substance abuse disorder. A qualified therapist may be necessary to make these distinctions regarding the reasons for the parent-child problem and recommend appropriate intervention.

The court is able to order a mental health intervention when the judge or magistrate recognizes the likelihood of alienation or estrangement. Ordering the child to counseling is very common but rarely helps reduce alienating behavior for many reasons. To begin with, children typically do not like counseling and will blame the target parent for forcing it on them. Forced counseling may broaden the chasm between the children and target parent. Secondly, there is the possibility that ordering the children to counseling may imply to them that the problems between their parents are their fault and, even more irrationally, suggest to the children that they are responsible for fixing the hostilities between the parents. The alternative is to order counseling for both parents while giving the therapist access to the children and significant others if they are a party to alienating behavior. The court order should include a statement about who is responsible for payment, monitoring the parents' compliance to the court order, and sanctions for failing to comply. Both parents should be aware that private insurance will typically not pay for this kind of counseling because insurance only pays for the treatment of a mental disorder and requires a mental health diagnosis for payment. Under these circumstances, neither parent will want a diagnosis. Sara and John would probably be receptive to court ordered counseling if they were told that the purpose of the counseling was to help Becky and the children's adjustment to the divorce rather than blaming a parent for alienation. If a parent is made to feel defensive, he or she will be less inclined to cooperate.

PARENT INTERVENTIONS

Most parents going through separation and divorce appreciate the importance of their children having a loving relationship with both parents. Most divorcing parents try to protect children from the trauma caused by the breakup of the family. During the heat of the separation and divorce, parents will occasionally lose self-control and words are said in the children's presence that they later regret. Parents must not forget that they are a reflection of their children's reality and how the children will perceive interpersonal relationships, particularly between loved ones. Sometimes parents need to be reminded of this point. Children learn vicariously or by example displayed by their parents. They learn how to express their anger and affections and how to resolve interpersonal conflicts by observing their parents. Parents not engaged in alienation understand this.

Most often a goal of divorcing parents is helping the children avoid trauma during the course of the separation. Becky needs loving support from both parents. Exposing the children to unregulated emotional turmoil, verbal denigration of the other parent, withholding access of parenting time, and a hostile atmosphere can instill fear and anxiety in a child who has very little resilience. Children are usually helpless victims of the parents' animosities. Some children are more resilient than others. Younger children may cry or get angry, defending the target parent with comments like, "Daddy is not a drunk" or "Mommy is smart." Over time the child may feel beaten down with the denigration and appear stoic or unresponsive to the comments. Older children may appear stoic while seething beneath their apathetic façade. Observing that the child appears indifferent gives the parent the false impression that the child is adjusting well to the divorce. Becky has learned this lesson well. Children who are emotionally beaten down will often dissociate themselves from the turmoil, appear unresponsive, and have a blank look on their face. This blank expression says that the child is stressed. Trauma can and should be avoided, beginning with recognizing how alienation can harm the children if left unchecked.

Parents desperate for answers will search for answers. They frequently turn to the Internet or popular books (Baker, 2007; Darnall, 2008, 2010; Warshak, 2010) and come across Gardner's (1998) symptoms of parental alienation syndrome (PAS). Reading the symptoms, desperate parents will do a mental inventory of their child's behavior and compare what they experience with Gardner's criteria. They may feel despair after reading that reversing their children's alienation is difficult but not impossible. The lessons learned from the target parent's search are twofold: learn how to prevent mildly alienating behavior from becoming severe and secondly find hope that alienation is reversible. For the most part, children exposed to mild alienation, such as Becky, will not display the typical symptoms of parental alienation. What target parents may observe in their children are mild examples of alienation that are similar to parental alienation but to a significantly lesser degree.

When parents recognize that they are a target of the other parent's alienating behavior, there are three concurrent strategies they can implement. The first strategy is to learn the symptoms of alienation and learn how to intervene. The second strategy, similar to the first, is recognizing the symptoms of alienation so the target parent will resist or avoid the temptation to retaliate with his or her own alienating behavior toward the other parent. As frustrated as target parents may feel, they cannot sit back and wait for the alienating parent to somehow spontaneously change her or his behavior. It is true that how the alienating parent behaves will be influenced by the target parent's behavior. The target parent is not helpless. The third strategy is to focus energy to strengthen the relationship with the children.

Parents become role models when they display resilience in the face of trauma and pain. Parents accomplish this task by regulating their emotions, displaying a strong sense of security, and assuring children of the value of maintaining a loving relationship with both parents. Parents under the stress of divorce will have their transgressions. Naïve or mildly alienating parents may not always be conscious of their transgressions or alienating behavior. The intervention for the naïve, mildly alienating parent is parent education that begins with learning the signs and symptoms of alienation, proceeding with honest introspection, self-monitoring, and learning more effective strategies on how to express their hurt or frustration in the children's presence. Concurrently, both parents must be cognizant of how their behavior can jeopardize the children's emotional attachment with both parents (Siegel & McIntosh, 2011). If alienation progresses to the extent that Sara becomes obsessed with her desire to destroy the relationship between the children and John, the damage to the children and the extended family could be irreversible.

Alienating parents frequently argue that they are only trying to protect the children from the emotional or physical damage caused by the target parent. What they do not understand is that their behavior and rigidity can be more damaging to the children because they are teaching the children not to trust their instincts. They are told either subtly or overtly not to trust the emotional bond and love they feel toward the other parent.

Experience teaches that parents can avoid the damage caused by alienating behavior if they understand and learn how to avoid blaming, make the distinction between ex-spousal and parental issues, and rebuild their life as a single parent. Target parents must recognize that they cannot control the other parent's alienating behavior and instead focus their energy on keeping their relationship with their children strong. They must be told to not retaliate with their own alienating behavior.

Parents should learn that blaming does nothing more than cause the parent to feel helpless and bitter. The assumption with blame is that circumstances will not change unless the other parent changes his or her behavior or attitude. So, the blaming parent sits and waits. This is irrational and rarely, if ever, works. Instead, the parent should first learn to recognize blaming statements and learn to restate what they want to say. Therapists can teach blaming parents to make "I statements" rather than "you statements." Just a slight change in language can have a dramatic effect on how a message is received by the other parent.

Some parents going through a separation or divorce feel isolated and alone with their feelings because they are faced with family rejection. These parents may use the child as a confidant for emotional support. Although doing so is understandable, this practice will cause the child considerable distress because the implication is that the child should side with the disclosing parent. This is a common and subtle form of alienation. Both parents should learn the distinction between parental and ex-spousal issues. Ex-spousal issues are emotionally charged issues that relate to personal issues between the parents, such as who had the affair or the reasons for the divorce, and have nothing to do with how the children should be raised. Parental issues focus on concerns about raising children, such as improving school grades and scheduling extracurricular activities or topics that directly involve the children. Children can be part of the conversations dealing with parental issues but should not hear or be engaged in conversations about ex-spousal issues. After parents are educated about parental and ex-spousal issues, they will hopefully learn to monitor their behavior.

Parents must be told that sharing ex-spousal issues with the children puts the children right in the middle between the two parents' hostilities. The children will be stressed and may even be embarrassed by what they hear. Some parents will argue that they are only being honest with the children. They will share court papers and give intimate reasons for the divorce. This should never occur. The offending parent should be specifically told to stop this practice. Doing so is nothing more than a veiled behavior designed to alienate the children from the target parent. Sharing ex-spousal issues with the children will not enhance the relationship with the other parent. The motivation is more sinister. Parents like Sara should learn to understand and respect the boundaries between what children are entitled to know and what should be private between the two parents. Reasonable parents understand and respect these boundaries once these concerns are brought to their attention.

Sara may think she meant well when using her daughter as a confidant, but she was actually alienating her daughter from her father if she expected her daughter's allegiance. She is also blurring boundaries between being a parent and a buddy. This is not effective parenting. Sara needs to be told the risk of using her daughter as a confident and the potential harm she is causing her daughter. Someone that Sara trusts has to tell her to stop confiding ex-spousal issues to her daughter.

Parents can do a lot for children by learning to take better care of them. The stress from separation and divorce can endure for months and sometimes years. During this transition, parents should be reminded to take care of themselves and not obsess over the divorce. There is much that parents can do to re-energize themselves:

- Build a new social network.
- Find or learn new fun activities.
- Accept that change is a part of life and can be filled with new opportunities.
- Take time to think about new personal goals that do not just involve being a parent. Participate in an exercise program, volunteer work, or a self-help endeavor.
- Avoid new life stresses. Avoid making major decisions until the stress level is under control. Move very slowly in making new significant relationships.

- Consciously force oneself to find what is positive in life. Learn how mood is influenced by positive rather than negative self-talk.
- Get professional help if one continues to obsess about the divorce and fails to heal.

John's best defense against Sara's alienating behavior is to focus on strengthening the bond between himself, Becky, and the siblings. Sometimes the court will stop a parent's parenting time to allow the tensions between the target parent and the children to subside. The judge may recommend waiting until the child is ready to spend time with the target parent. This rarely works because children by their very nature want to avoid anything that causes them to feel uncomfortable. They will not tell an alienating parent they want to see the target parent if they know that will upset their mother or father. To repair the damage caused by either estrangement or alienating behavior, the target parent must have access to the children. There may be conditions under which the access has to be supervised if there are questions or allegations of abuse or excessive discipline.

When interacting with the children, a target parent may be asked how to respond to a situation that comes up and they do not know what to do. Usually, the best answer for the parent is to do what will reduce the children's anxiety. What the target parent wants to do is to help the child feel comfortable during their time together. Ways of reducing the anxiety include not disparaging the other parent, avoiding discussing the divorce, engaging in physical and fun activities, having longer parenting time with fewer exchanges, and resisting interrogating the children.

THERAPEUTIC INTERVENTION

Doing therapy with an alienating parent and child victim of parental alienation is very challenging. The challenge comes from a bias that therapists have, which is believing that our clients are always truthful. A therapist can be taken in by the persuasive arguments from an alienating parent. Therapists must recognize their vulnerability and consciously remain objective and remind themselves there are two sides to the story. An alienating parent, particularly moderate and severely alienating parents, will attempt to enmesh the therapist as an ally to their cause. The therapist must resist the ruse.

Most children exposed to alienating behavior may not require psychotherapy, unless efforts to get the parent to change the alienating behavior have failed. If the child's coping skills and mood deteriorate, he or she may require a personal therapist. The therapist has to monitor the child's adjustment, listening or watching for depression, behavioral problems, or a drop in school grades.

An obvious example of an alienating behavior is showing the children the court papers. This should never occur. Often, the confiding parent has little to say about the other parent that is good. He or she will use the court papers to point out all that is wrong with the other parent. The offending parent should be specifically told to stop this practice. Some parents are unable to be sufficiently introspective to gain insight about how this behavior will adversely affect the children. This is the example illustrating how a trained professional will learn a lot by observing how a parent thinks and interacts with the other parent and their children. The therapist will recognize behaviors that can escalate to more severe forms of alienation or high conflict and then empathically point out the behaviors and damaging thinking and suggest more constructive ways to think or behave. The therapist should not be afraid to be direct with the parent. Most parents are very receptive to improving their behavior, providing they are not made to feel defensive. While learning new ways of thinking, the naïve or mildly alienating parent should never feel blamed or denigrated, but instead the therapist should be help the parent understand that we could all improve our communication.

A question needing an answer is, what will motivate Sara to change her attitude and behavior? An answer is the realization that her persistent behavior will have lasting negative consequences for Becky (Emery, 1982; Johnston, Kline & Tschann, 1989). On balance, if Sara does not stop disrespecting the boundaries between herself and her daughter and stop the denigrating comments, she will continue hurting her daughter. The damage is not just to the relationship that Becky has with her father, and the damage can continue for years to come. Becky's relationship with John's extended family may be jeopardized as well as her mental health. For that reason, the alienation must stop. Having a library of journal articles available that a therapist can show the doubtful parent is very helpful. Education rather than confrontation is a more effective way of working through a parent's resistance. Education from resources other than the therapist or attorney is safer and less threatening for a defensive parent. There are many well-written books on this topic available to parents (Baker, 2007; Darnall, 1998, 2008, 2010; Warshak, 2010). Suggesting to the parent that they first read one of the popular books on PA before beginning therapy can be helpful and save time and money for the mildly alienating parent as well as the target parent.

Parents should learn that alienation can occur without spoken words. Children as well as adults can be influenced by the emotional energy or intensity that a parent emits. Becky would know this. We have all had the experience of emotionally reacting to a person because of their energy rather than the words spoken. Sometimes we like or dislike someone simply because of how we feel toward them with no rational reason. Becky is no different, particularly when reacting to her mother's negative energy toward her father. The energy that divorcing parents emit is typically grounded in past resentments and a sense of betrayal that they carry forward. Parents may not understand the strength of their feelings but they must learn to identify these feelings and begin monitoring and tempering their negative emotions. The angry parent needs to consciously try to convey a more amicable attitude toward the second parent. The first parent must also understand that their child is a witness and an innocent victim of the negative energy. The alienated child could learn to fear the target parent, not because of what they have personally experienced but instead because of what they hear and see or the hostile energy that radiates from the alienating parent. An impartial and trusted attorney or a MHP can bring this to the parent's attention. One technique for helping the parent recognize his or her negative energy is to use an example with a family pet. Pets can sense a person's energy and respond with either affection or aggression. We have all met people we immediately either liked or disliked. Questions for a parent to answer are, "What kind of energy do you convey to the other parent?" and "Is it possible that the hostility you are feeling from the other parent is a response to your own negative energy?"

There is a risk that mild alienating behavior is a precursor to more severe forms of alienation. Parents who are motivated by fear are afraid that if they do not disparage the target parent, their relationship with the children will be imperiled. They may feel they must strengthen the bond with the children at the other parent's expense. Alienating behavior is more deliberate, void of any excuses or rationalizations. Alienating parents are quick to blame the other parent for the reason the alienation is deserved. Those on the outside may align with the alienating parent, buying into the reasons why the target parent deserves to be persecuted. Although the behavior may be subtle, a trained evaluator or MHP should be able to predict the progression to a more severe form of alienation by looking at the parent's history of alienation behavior, assessing for a personality disorder, and taking into consideration the depth of the parent's hurt or anger.

The target parent may not know where to turn for help. He or she may seek answers from the Internet or from a trusted friend. The target parent may initially blame himself or herself or think that what he or she is feeling is only his or her imagination. Initially, it may be inconceivable that the children could turn against him or her. "How could I think that my child that I have loved for years would just turn against me?" Becky likely senses her father's consternation, particularly when both parents are together during an exchange. Becky has learned that she must contain her affection for her father unless they are alone.

CONFUSING SYMBOLS

The source of many conflicts between warring parents is their lack of understanding about the role that symbols play in their hostilities. "Symbols" in this context are any objects or acts that take on a value greater than their original intrinsic value. An example is a divorced father walking into his ex-wife's home uninvited to get a soda from the refrigerator. The act may have little intrinsic value, but symbolically the act represents a lack of respect and a violation of boundaries. The offender may resent the other parent's enforcing the boundary, especially if the wife continues to live in the marital home. The wife resents the intrusion and disregard of her space. The parent's resentments are fertile ground for alienation and can be avoided if each parent understands the symbolic significance of the behavior and learns to respect each other's boundaries. Therapists should help parents understand that symbols can be irrational and resistant to change and will sometimes evoke irrational feelings. In this example, someone must tell the father that his behavior is wrong and that he should respect his ex-wife's boundaries. Both parents would benefit from learning about symbols and how they apply to their new role as divorced parents. Education is a great deterrent for these misunderstandings.

FAMILY CULTURE

In calmer times, parents will acknowledge the differences in the way they parent. One parent may be perceived as a pushover, whereas the other parent is more of the disciplinarian. These differences in parenting rarely cause significant problems to the children because they learn to discriminate how they behave with each parent. After a separation or divorce, these differences can become exaggerated, and one parent may believe that he or she must assert influence on how the other parent should set rules, convey family values, and discipline. This places the children squarely in the middle. This creates fertile ground for mild alienation when one parent begins to criticize the other parent's parenting skills in the child's presence. This practice must stop. The critical parent should be reminded that the other parent has a right to do whatever they want with the child, providing that the parenting is consistent with court orders, the child's basic needs are met, and his or her behavior is lawful. The critical parent may not like what he or she is being told, but once the parent accepts this reality, much of the tension and risk of alienation will subside. The parent's attorney can be of great help by explaining the new rules and boundaries to her or his client now that she or he is separated.

A common conflict among family cultures has to do with parental rules for children. Sara is offended because she does not like John's lack of restrictions on their daughter's television viewing. She should learn that the father can have his own rules, providing they are consistent with court orders and community standards. Sometimes the differences between the parents' family culture/values become very complex. One example can be that a parent has strong religious values that differ from the other parent's. If one parent refuses to comply with the other parent's values, they may have to go to mediation or court. Until then, the offended parent has to live with the other parent's failure to cooperate. One parent does not have the right to assert his or her values on the other parent. Forcing the child to comply with the first parent's rule while with the other parent will cause the children to feel tense, disloyal to one parent, or worse, encourage the child to lie. Having the child live with the different values is less damaging than putting the child in the middle. Children can learn to adjust to different family culture/values. Children make these adjustments with different teachers at school with few problems. In fact, learning to negotiate between different value sets is a skill taken into adulthood.

MIND READING

Mind reading, theorizing, and hypothesizing are the same for our purposes. Humans by our very nature are nosy and want to understand what we do not know. Consequently, parents will theorize or conjecture about what they do not know or understand about the other parent's behavior. A trap can be that parents will emotionally react to their theory as if the theory were true. Theorizing can stir very strong feelings and lead to serious misunderstanding. Theorizing can lead to alienating behavior on the part of both parents and be very confusing to the children. Avoiding the risk of alienation from theorizing begins with instructing the parent on the relationship between one's thinking, self-talk, or beliefs and one's emotions. Once these relationships are understood, the parent must learn to monitor his or her thinking or beliefs and recognize the difference between their theory and reality. The mother may theorize by saying, "Your father does not care about you. If he did, he would buy you a computer." The reality may be that the father cannot afford the computer. One way to distinguish between a theory and reality is to turn a declarative sentence into a question directed toward the other person. For example, the mother may ask the father, "Are you able to afford a new computer?" or "How can we work together in getting the computer?" Asking the questions and calmly listening and discussing the concern will minimize the risk of alienation.

Sara has strong feelings about John because her theory is that Becky's safety is at risk when she is with her father. She lacks the insight to recognize how her behavior and attitude are harming Becky. Sara does not understand how her self-talk incites her intense feelings which are conveyed to Becky. She is teaching Becky to fear her father by her attitude and negative energy. She needs to recognize what she is doing because she is harming her daughter for her own selfish agenda.

INTRODUCING A NEW SIGNIFICANT OTHER

Introducing the children to a new significant other is frequently the trigger that ignites alienating behavior. This is true for both mothers and fathers. A wise confidant will warn the unsuspecting parent about the risk of alienation when the other parent learns of a new romantic interest or the children are introduced to the new interest too soon. The naive or mildly alienating parent cannot use the argument that, "I have a life too," and expect everyone to be happy. The new significant other may remind the other parent of the betrayal she or he suffered or cause the children anxiety because they do not know how to divide their loyalties. Parents should learn to move very slowly when introducing a new significant other and do so only when they feel assured that the relationship with the children is strong.

RESPONDING TO ALIENATING BEHAVIOR

Much can be said about a parent's alienating behavior. The target parent is the other side of the equation. Parents and children each have their own perception of alienating behavior. Alienating parents are usually naïve and fail to recognize their subtle alienation. Initially, they only feel that something is wrong. A parent may get defensive when his or her behavior is pointed out. The other parent's alienating behavior may surprise the target parent. The children are caught in the middle, not knowing where to place their allegiance. The children, depending on their cognitive development and sensitivities, may completely ignore the behavior or become confused and nervous anytime the parents are together for either an exchange or a conversation. Children live by a simple rule: "When uncomfortable, avoid." Avoiding may be an emotional shutdown that can be seen on the child's face. Sometimes a parent has to make a decision that can affect the children and does not know what to do. The best answer is to do what will reduce the child's anxiety. That advice is rarely wrong.

It is imperative for the target parent to not get defensive when feeling victimized by alienation. The educator needs to be supportive and function like a mentor or educator rather than make indictments. The target parent must be told not to retaliate with his or her own alienating behavior. Name-calling, verbal attacks, and intense emotions only make the situation worse. The target parent needs to be reassured that the best defense is anxiety-calming behavior, focusing on strengthening the relationship with the children rather than on retaliation. Secondly, both parents should be reminded that they should not behave in a manner that could cause their attorney to have to defend those behaviors. This can be a serious distraction in the courtroom.

STRENGTHENING THE BOND

The best response by the target parent to minimize the damage caused by mild alienating is to focus on strengthening the bond with the children (Darnall, 2010). It is true that mildly alienating parents can benefit from education, but the alienating parent may not be receptive to learning how to avoid alienation behavior. Someone who is trusted, knowledgeable, and politically neutral should give the education.

Strengthening the bond between a target parent and the children is very dependent upon the child's developmental needs and age. Here are some general concepts that can be helpful regardless of the child's age.

Positive pathogenesis. It is easy to feel frustrated and angry with an oppositional child. Parents sometimes have to be reminded that their ability to influence their child's values and behavior comes from their power to build the child's self-esteem or self-worth. Parents gain power to influence their child's behavior when most of the interaction between the two is positive and reinforcing. This is positive pathogenesis. A parent may need to be reminded, or perhaps given "homework," to make it a point to say at least three positive statements each day to his or her child. Doing so strengthens the bond. A corollary for a parent taking a child to the other parent is to always end parenting time on a positive note. Discipline should be completed, and the parent should make an assertive effort to make up and forgive before the exchange. Unless agreed upon in advance, one parent should never expect the other parent to continue with the discipline or punishment during his or her parenting time.

Sharing fun and memorable activities. During the family breakup, it is more important than ever for the nonresidential parent to consciously have fun or initiate new memorable activities with the children. Parents should be told to listen to the children to find out what is fun for them or how they would like to spend some of their parenting time together. Sitting in a restaurant looking quietly at each other, waiting for the other to talk can be uncomfortable. Instead, physical activity will help reduce anxiety and is usually more pleasurable for everyone. This is not meant to suggest that children should not be disciplined or corrected. Parents have to make demands on children. As a parent, the goal is for the child to comply with a demand rather than the child always feeling happy, but sharing fun activities should be a priority.

Positive mentoring. Children as well as parents are in strange territory when facing the family's breakup. The children frequently do not know how to feel or react to these unique circumstances. They question, "Where do I place my loyalties? Whose rules do I follow? Can I love both parents?" These questions offer parents an opportunity to mentor their sons or daughters. Mentoring and calmly educating the children will enhance the emotional closeness and help to deter the damaging effects of divorce or alienation. The mentoring parent should listen to the children's concerns, offer support, avoid any temptation to alienate, and strive to reduce the children's anxiety. Parents may benefit from professional help to learn how to mentor. The positive mentoring parent must understand that he or she has minimal or no control over how the alienating parent behaves. She or he only has control over how he or she behaves or responds to the child. Once the target parent realizes this, he or she can stop blaming the other parent and move on to spending constructive time with the children.

Learning forgiveness. Parents sometimes have to be reminded that they are role models. Children will vicariously learn from watching their parents about how to express anger, hurt, and betrayal. Parents need to be asked what they want their children to learn from their behavior. Do they want their children to learn forgiveness and compassion or retaliation and bitterness?

Controlling emotions. Parents feeling the heat of a divorce battle must be taught to control their emotions and passions. Self-regulation of emotions is imperative. Maybe the anger and hurt is justified, but the hostile outbursts only make matters worse for the children. This is especially true in the courtroom. If the parent hopes to win his or her argument and gain the judge's support, he or she must appear likeable. Otherwise, the anger will be used against the parent, supporting the other parent's argument that the out-of-control parent is not fit to parent.

CONCLUSION

Children learn from their parents how to speak to others and behave. Children have the formidable task of learning how to relate to the adult world. Parents are the primary role models for good and bad behavior. Children vicariously learn from observation. This includes appropriate expressions of anger, displays of affection, and how people resolve disputes. Alienating parents must stop and think about what they are teaching their children by how they behave. Are they teaching love and forgiveness or hate and retribution? Children cannot make that choice for their alienating parent.

Vignette

Becky cannot be expected to resolve her mother's anger toward her father and stop the alienating behaviors. She needs help from others, a counselor or family friend, to bring her mother's alienating behaviors to her mother's attention. With supportive education, Sara will learn about the risk of violating boundaries, using Becky as a confidant, and projecting her fears for Becky's safety to rationalize her excessive need to rescue her from imaginary threats. Sara would be instructed to monitor her tone of voice and her language. Her motivation for change must be the realization that her behavior is not protecting Becky but instead is hurting her and her long-term relationship with her father. Becky and John are the beneficiaries of Sara's change in behavior and her attitude. The ability to make changes with instruction from either a counselor, trusted friend, or popular literature is what separates a mild alienating parent from a parent who is obsessed or determined to destroy what was once a loving relationship between a target parent and the children.

Editors' Notes

- Dr. Darnall explains mild alienation as a condition in which the child objects to having any kind of contact with the target parent while denigrating this parent in such a way that the faults seem unreasonable or irrational. However, time sharing with the target parent often leads to a positive experience for the mildly alienated child because they are able to either forget or distance themselves from the other parent's disparaging comments about the target parent.

- Dr. Darnall points out that it is the children who are the victims of the alienating behavior. For example, the demanding parent criticizes and blames the other parent for what could be considered "almost anything."
- Dr. Darnall brings to the reader's attention the harm that the alienating parent does and the potential damaging effects on the child. This behavior can be changed as the angry, alienating parent becomes more aware of his or her denigrating comments or as the therapist is helpful in bringing about this recognition of his or her projection, displacement, or naiveté.
- Dr. Darnall explains the various ways that therapists can be helpful in familiarizing themselves with parental alienation and then using psychoeducational approaches such as homework or therapeutic reading or including the alienating parent and the target parent together in a joint session to resolve their animosity.

REFERENCES

Baker, A. J. L. (2007). *Adult children of parental alienation syndrome: Breaking the ties that bind.* New York: The Norton Professional Book.

Baker, A. J. L., & Chambers, J. (2011). Adult recall of childhood exposure to parental conflict: Unpacking the Black Box of Parental Alienation. *Journal of Divorce & Remarriage, 52*(1), 55–76.

Clawar, S. S., & Rivlin, B.V . (1991). *Children held hostage: Dealing with programmed and brainwashed children.* Chicago, IL: American Bar Association.

Darnall, D. C. (1998). *Divorce casualties: Protecting your children from parental alienation.* Dallas, TX: Taylor Publishing Company.

Darnall, D. C. (2008). *Divorce casualties: Understanding parental alienation.* Dallas, TX: Taylor Publishing Company.

Darnall, D. C. (2010). *Beyond divorce casualties: Reunifying the alienated family.* Dallas, TX: Taylor Publishing Company.

Emery, R. E. (1982). Interparental conflict and the children of discord and divorce. *Psychological Bulletin, 92*(2), 310–330.

Gardner, R. A. (1998). *The parental alienation syndrome: A guide for mental health and legal professionals* (2nd ed.). Cresskill, NJ: Creative Therapeutics, Inc.

Johnston. J. R., Kline, M., & Tschann, J. M. (1989). Ongoing postdivorce conflict: Effects on children of joint custody and frequent access. *American Orthopsychiatric Association, 59*(4), 576–592.

Sauber, S. R. (2006). PAS as a family tragedy: Roles of family members, professionals, and the justice system. In R. Gardner, S. Sauber, & D. Lorandos (Eds.), *The international handbook of parental alienation syndrome: Conceptual, clinical, and legal consideration* (pp. 12–32). Springfield, IL: Charles C Thomas Publisher.

Siegel, D. & McIntosh, J. (2011). Family law and the neuroscience of attachment, Part II. *Family Court Review, 49*(3), 513–520.

Warshak, R.A. (2010). *Divorce poison new and updated edition: How to protect your family from bad-mouthing and brainwashing.* New York: Harper Collins Publishing.

Chapter 4

MODERATE CASES OF PARENTAL ALIENATION

ABE WORENKLEIN

Vignette

Jonathan, age twelve, and Samantha, age nine, have been living with their mother, Mrs. Edna Smith, in Montreal since their parents' separation two years ago. They reportedly had a good relationship with their father, Mr. John Smith, who, although quite busy at work, would attend all parent-teacher meetings and school events and go to both of the children's athletic events when he was able. The communication between Mr. and Mrs. Smith was open for the first year after the separation, and they shared information regarding the children by telephone and through the Our Family Wizard® website (www.ourfamilywizard.com).

The situation changed once the children's mother began dating a gentleman from Vancouver approximately one year after the separation, and she and her live-in boyfriend became engaged to get married once the divorce was finalized. Mr. Smith reported that he began experiencing significant difficulty in reaching the children by telephone and that the children's previous attitude toward him was less enthusiastic. Initially, he attributed this to the fact that the children were adjusting to their mother's new relationship. However, the children began coming up with excuses why they could not see their father, generally attributing their inability to do so to previous engagements or schoolwork. Such excuses had never been previously presented. He also expressed concerns that the children began referring to their mother's fiancé as "Daddy Bob." Also, the children were upset with Mr. Smith because he did not attend a parent-teacher meeting, which Mr. Smith was not aware of and which was attended by their mother and her fiancé. Mr. Smith reported as well that the children were very preoccupied with what their soon-to-be stepfather was doing with them, for example, shopping for a variety of toys, games, and clothing; doing their homework; and even taking them to the dentist, while "remembering" events from the past when their father would refuse to spend time with them because of his work commitments. Mr. Smith reported as well that the children began talking increasingly about their being excited to engage in activities with their soon-to-be stepfather, while providing excuses to cancel scheduled time with their father, which they insisted was their own decision. What was particularly disturbing to Mr. Smith was that when he asked the school secretary why recently he had not received an e-mail from the school, she informed him that the only numbers listed at the school, that were also to be used for emergency purposes, were the home and cell numbers of Ms. Smith and her fiancé.

Mr. Smith contacted his attorney after discovering that his name was removed, maintaining that the children were being alienated from him. Although Mr. Smith recognized that the children enjoyed spending time with their soon-to-be stepfather, he became very upset and raised his voice at the children's mother when she suggested that she and the children would like to relocate to Vancouver, British Columbia, the location of her fiancé's home office. Mr. Smith was quite clear that he would not permit such a move, and he subsequently reported noticing an even greater deterioration in the children's relationship with him. He reported that the children had attempted to argue with him regarding the proposed move to Vancouver, even accusing him of never having cared about their happiness despite concrete evidence to the contrary in videos, pictures, and so on. They often used the word "we" when discussing their mother's desire to relocate to Vancouver.

Not only were the children initially very negative with Mr. Smith at the time of transitions from their mother, they adamantly refused to spend time with him unless he would take them shopping or to the arcade, like their soon to be stepfather did. In fact, the children argued with him and attempted to convince him that it was their wish not to be with him and that they had "rights." Once the children finally agreed to go with him, they often questioned him about what was taking place in court and why he was upset at their mother for putting their soon-to-be stepfather's name and phone number on the school emergency list, and they also accused him of breaking down the marriage. They expressed concern as to why their father believed that their mother and her fiancé were influencing them, since, in fact, it was they who did not want to spend time with him. They also were clear with him that they did not want to live in a "joint custody" situation because they wanted to "relocate" to Vancouver. Mr. Smith was also greatly concerned by the fact that John, who had difficulty reading and spelling and who had been diagnosed with dyslexia, would periodically send him very vulgar e-mails with impeccable spelling regarding his father's not having been as involved in their lives as was their mother's fiancé.

At the same time, Mr. Smith was told that the children did not want to visit the paternal grandparents or their uncles and aunts, nor did they want to associate with their paternal cousins. Mrs. Smith maintained that the children had a better relationship with her fiancé than with their own father. Their father had reportedly prioritized his work over the children and was less attuned to the children's needs than their soon-to-be stepfather.

Mr. Smith, on the other hand, reported that he has always had an excellent relationship with the children, that he had spent a significant amount of quality time with them until the children began to be alienated from him. He recognized that prior to the divorce, Mrs. Smith had a healthy psychological bond with the children but that subsequent to the divorce, her anger and her preoccupation with moving clouded her judgment. Mr. Smith said that this led to the alignment of the children with her and to their becoming alienated from him and anything having to do with him or his family.

INTRODUCTION

Warshak and Otis (2010) have recognized that "working in an emerging area of practice requires a delicate balance of courage and caution–courage to pursue new paths, caution to ensure the well-being of those we serve." Many questions remain in terms of how to best help children who can be classified as having a moderate degree of parental alienation (PA). Warshak and Otis (2010) use the term "humbition" to express a needed balance and fusion of humility and ambition. Although MHPs are eager to intervene and to help parents and children normalize their relationship with each other, it is very clear that there are many challenges that must be confronted. Furthermore, one needs to maintain a balanced perspective of the dynamics of alienation as well as the needs that are being satisfied through the alienation by children as well as their parents. One must also recognize that moderate PA does differ significantly from mild PA while having some characteristics that are less extreme than those of severe alienation.

DESCRIPTION OF MODERATE PARENTAL ALIENATION

In moderate PA, "all eight of the primary manifestations are likely to be present, and each is more advanced than one sees in mild cases, but less pervasive than one sees in the severe type" (Gardner, 1998, p. 121). When looking at the eight symptoms of PA proposed by Gardner, one notes that children who fall into this category will ultimately go with the target parent after expressing and demonstrating significant reluctance to do so. Moderately or severely alienated children will express consistent negative feelings regarding the target parent whether or not in the alienating parent's company, in the examiner's office, in their school setting or on the playground with their friends, or in any other environment when the topic of parenting arises. Unlike in severe cases, however, the children may come to enjoy themselves during the time that they spend together with the target parent, although not admitting this when the alienating parent is present.

A child who manifests symptoms of moderate PA is involved in a significant campaign of denigration, particularly at transition times. Their deprecation of the target parent is not as extreme as it is for children in the severe category, however. Severely alienated children also have numerous rationalizations for the vilification of the target parent that are more frivolous and nonsensical than in the moderate cases. At the same time, there is a lack of ambivalence, and these moderately alienated children view the target parent as being all bad and the alienating parent is seen as being all good. Such children support the alienating parent in a reflexive manner and maintain that their negative feelings toward the target parent were not promoted or originated by sources other than themselves. Such children appear to be very insensitive to the emotional pain of the target parent, do not show any remorse or guilt, and will use "borrowed scenarios." Finally, such children will generalize their dislike to extended family and will express reluctance to spend time with them. Unlike children in the severe form of PA, children in the moderate range generally will quiet down and involve themselves with the target parent. Visitation is possible in that there is an absence of destruction of property, persistent vilification, and continuous agitating behavior, as is present in the severe form of PA.

Baker (2006, 2007) is quite clear that causing PA is an extremely serious form of emotional abuse and that the child is rejected, isolated, terrorized, corrupted, verbally assaulted, and threatened with abandonment. This is particularly the case in situations of moderate to severe alienation. Furthermore, the child is told that the target parent does not love or has never loved the child, and the target parent is unworthy of the child's love. At the same time, personal details are shared with the child, who does not have the cognitive or emotional capacity to fully understand such information. The child is frequently made to feel responsible for the alienating parent's well-being. Baker (2007) reports that many of the these children have low self-esteem as adults not only as a result of internalizing the negative characterizations of the target parent, but also as a result of blaming themselves and feeling guilty for abandoning younger siblings.

EVALUATION OF MODERATE PARENTAL ALIENATION

In any case in which PA is being alleged, it is imperative for the evaluator to rule out estrangement as being the cause of the child's reluctance to spend time with the target parent. The evaluator must also assess the presence of a campaign of denigration and other behaviors symptomatic of PA. Furthermore, the evaluator must ensure that a thorough evaluation is conducted, including the use of a variety of assessment techniques and instruments, interviewing of collateral sources, observation of parent-child interactions, and interviewing and observing the behavior of the alienated child in the presence and in the absence of other siblings. The evaluator must also rule out any variables that may be instrumental in the child's refusal/ reluctance to spend time with the target parent and to ensure that the child's refusal is not the result of realistic estrangement (Sauber, 2006).

A proper evaluation must take into account the large number of themes used by an alienating parent in aligning the child with that parent and in distancing and making the child increasingly antagonistic to spending time with the target parent. Clawar and Rivlin (1991) have identified twenty-five detection factors used by alienators to distance children from the target parent. Careful and thorough interviews must be done with alienated children as well as with any nonalienated siblings to uncover strategies as well as the themes that were used in distancing the children from the target parent. For example, the dynamics behind alienation may be explained by the children's being subjected to particular techniques imposed by the alienating parent. These may include the threat of withdrawal of love, inculcation of the belief that only the parent who cares for them full time really loves them and can be depended upon, and that the other parent poses a real danger to them. The evaluator must be aware of the existence of what may be considered "hybrid" situations in which there are understandable and justified reasons why a child may be reluctant to spend time with a parent in addition to the identification of alienating behaviors carefully placed in motion by the alienating parent.

It is imperative for the evaluator to include a variety of assessment tools in order not only to develop a complete understanding of whether there is moderate alienation, but also to understand the dynamics of how the alienation was put into place. A comprehensive evaluation must take into account different assessment techniques including interviews, standardized instruments, parenting and personality assessments, collateral sources, observations of parent-child interaction, review of documents, family histories, and so on, as well as new instruments that are being developed for PA screening, such as those by Baker (2012) and Sauber and Worenklein (2012).

The evaluator should consider the variety of motivational factors that often influence the beliefs and the behavior of the alienating parent. The evaluator must devise relevant questions to ascertain whether these motivational factors are present based on what the children report during the interviews, as well as answers to questions from the alienating parent. The most common motivational factors for parents who alienate their children, according to the research of Clawar and Rivlin (1991) are

- revenge
- self-righteousness
- fear of losing the child
- sense of past history
- proprietary perspective
- jealousy
- child support
- loss of identity
- out of sight, out of mind
- self-protection
- maintaining the marital/adult relationship through conflict
- power, influence, control and domination

Although Gardner spent a great deal of time describing the dynamics of PA and the behavior of the alienating parent, it is generally accepted that each of the parents as well as the affected child can also play a significant role in the alienation (Kelly & Johnston, 2001; Johnston, 2003). Kelly and Johnston (2001), for example, maintain that one should be aware that the child's developmental stage and the "vulnerabilities of the child to alienation" must be considered in the dynamics of PA. They report that the child's temperament and personality vulnerabilities, including anxiety, fear, passivity, dependency, poor reality testing, fear of rejection, poor self-esteem as well as cognitive limitations and the absence of critical analytic and problem-solving abilities, increase the child's vulnerability to alienation. The child may also have a closer bond with one parent because of similar temperaments, greater time spent with that parent, shared interests, and same gender (Kelly & Johnston, 2001).

Kelly and Johnston also maintain that the child's moral and cognitive development, as well as the child's feeling abandoned by the target parent or spending minimal time with the target parent, increase the likelihood of the child's becoming alienated. They point out that as the child matures from being concrete in thinking to being increasingly able to entertain contradictory perspectives, the child may shift allegiances. At a certain point, it may become too onerous for the child to alternately align herself or himself with one parent while with that parent. As a result, the child may entrench himself or herself with an allegiance to one parent so that he or she does not have to deal with reconciling contradictory information or deal with the resulting stress (Johnston & Roseby, 1997).

Kelly and Johnston (2001) point out that often the target parent contributes to alienation in a significant manner, although such behaviors by themselves should not lead to the extreme behaviors demonstrated by alienated children. One often finds personality disorders and psychopathology present in high-conflict parents who are focused on litigation and who perceive themselves as being virtuous and free of responsibility. Such parents lack insight into the potential effects of their behavior on the children. Kelly and Johnston (2001) point to a lack of empathy and the presence of rigidity and harshness in parenting style that, although not being emotionally or physically abusive, may lead the alienated child to reject the parent based on such parenting tendencies. In addition, they point out that at times a target parent's withdrawing in the face of the high conflict only reinforces messages that may be communicated by the alienating parent, namely, that the target parent was not a devoted parent and did not care much about the child.

Although it is true that a child's personality may play a significant role in giving in to the alienating parents' efforts to distance the child from the target parent, one must also consider the role that the child's perception of conditional love by the alienating parent plays in the dynamic. Children may actually feel more secure with the target parent and more insecure with the alienating parent. They may feel the target parent will always be there unconditionally, and therefore it is necessary to concentrate on pleasing the alienating parent. This is particularly problematic in situations in which the child is placed in a very strong conflict of loyalty between the two parents.

The criteria used to determine the presence or absence of alienation should be considered by having the evaluator develop questions that tap into the many themes utilized by an alienating parent to align the child with him or her. As described earlier, Clawar and Rivlin (1991) provide twenty-five detection factors as well as possible questions corresponding to these detection factors. Clawar and Rivlin also provide possible responses by children that can be used to detect brainwashing and programming while ensuring that the questions are not socially and/or emotionally laden or judgmental but rather "intentionally neutral enough to promote an openness and willingness to communicate" (p. 95). Rohrbaugh (2008) uses the twenty-five detection factors that Clawar and Rivlin cite and provides examples of questions that can uncover the presence and the modalities of PA (pp. 420–426). The questions are asked by an evaluator, therapist, or judge.

Question	Child's Answer
1. **Restrictions on permission to love both parents** • Do you feel free in your heart to love both of your parents? • Is there anything that you are really afraid of that could happen because of the divorce?	• Dad said that if I go to live with Mom, I'll never see him again.
2. **Inappropriate and unnecessary information** • Is Mom/Dad upset about anything special that you know of? • You seemed very angry when you mentioned Mom. Do you know why you feel angry at her?	• My Dad was having an affair while my Mom was having me in the hospital. • Mom never wanted me to be born. Dad said she wanted an abortion, but he wouldn't let her do it.
3. **Presents one parent as a martyr** • Is there something that you think could happen that would make the family situation better now?	• Mom destroyed our family with this divorce. Dad always says that he still loves her and that she can come back.
4. **Contradictory statements** • How do you feel about your Mom/Dad?	• Daddy's a bad man. I never want to see him again. But I really love him. I'd miss him a lot.
5. **Use of indirect statements quoting brainwashing parent?** • How did this weekend go? Does Mom/Dad have an opinion about the time you spend at Dad's/Mom's?	• When I get home, Mom says things like, "Too bad you had to go with your Dad this week-end–you missed a great ski trip. I bet you only watched TV, as usual." Mom's right, he's boring.

Question	Child's Answer
6. **Character assault on target parent** • What do you like about being at Mom's?	• Mommy has lots of boyfriends who sleep over. Daddy says she's a whore because the Bible says so.
7. **Anxiety arousal** • Are there things that are upsetting to you now?	• Mom and Dad [the stepfather is called "Dad"] have to listen when Steve [biological father] telephones us because if he finds out where we live, he might kidnap us.
8. **Good parent versus bad parent** • How do you feel about Mom at this point? • How do you know this?	• I know Mom is bad. • Because Daddy says so, and I believe everything he says. My Dad never lies to me.
9. **Collusion or one-sided alliance** • Sometimes children think things may be unfair. Is there anything that you think is unfair?	• Dad just bought a new car but Mom's poor–he should have given us the money.
10. **Scripted views** • You said you were confused about the fight and what really happened. What does Mom/Dad think happened?	• I really thought I saw Dad's girlfriend hit Mom first but Dad says he saw Mom start it. I'm confused now.
11. **Radically changed and dysfunctional behavior outside family** • I heard you've become a really good student–even better than before. Why do you think this has happened?	• My grades have really improved since Mom and Dad decided to split. I figured out it's because school is the only place where I can escape.

continued

Question	Child's Answer
• At the time when you have your headaches or stomach-aches, do you remember any particular thing in your mind?	• I really get terrible headaches and stomachaches. I wish my parents would leave me alone. I feel like I'm in the middle, and they're both pulling my arms off.
12. **Guilt about own role in family or custody dispute** • Is there anything that you feel guilty about since this whole family change started?	• I testified against my Mom in court, and I lied to the judge.
13. **Nonverbal messages** • People can send messages with words and with gestures. Does Mom/Dad use gestures? How?	• I know Dad doesn't want to hear anything about Mom. If we did something special with her, and we're still excited when we see him, he acts (looks away as if to imitate Dad) like he doesn't care.
14. **Child as spy or conduit of information** • Is there anything that you've done during your parents' separation that makes you feel not as good as you'd like about yourself?	• I brought Mom some of Dad's business receipts to help her in court because he says he has no money.
15. **Age-inappropriate statements** • When you talk about your father, you use the word "father," but when you talk about your stepfather, you use the word "Dad." Could you tell me why you use different names?	• Anyone can be a father, but it takes someone special to be a Dad.

Question	Child's Answer
16. **Colludes in secret-keeping** • Are there secrets that are bothering you about this whole custody problem?	• Dad told me to keep this a secret, but we're running away if he loses in court.

In situations in which there is a moderate degree of PA, there are a variety of themes used by the alienating parent that clearly affect the child in a significant way. Clawar and Rivlin (1991) discuss many such themes, the following are among them:

Denial of Existence. This is when the alienating parent never talks about the other parent, destroys photographs of the other parent, sometimes even cutting out the face of the target parent from family pictures; does not allow the child to have a picture of the other parent in the child's room; does not relay messages or provide letters or presents sent by the target parent. The alienating parent does not acknowledge the presence of the other parent at school events or sporting events. Professionals working with an alienated child often find that the child reinterprets positive events into negative events based on the "spin" that the alienating parent put on it. Furthermore, the alienating parent will often sidetrack a child from discussing positive interactions with the other parent and will not inform the other parent of important dates and events, leading the child to believe that the other parent does not care about him. Not providing the school with the target parent's phone numbers or address is not uncommon.

Indirect Attacks. These can originate from the alienating parent or his other family toward the target parent's extended family, the career of the target parent, the target parent's living arrangements and travel, as well as his or her activities and associates.

Middle Man Syndrome. Often the alienating parent discusses issues with the child that ordinarily should only be discussed with the other parent. For example, the alienating parent may ask the child, "Do you want to spend more time with me during the summer?" This results in a great deal of pressure being placed on the child to make a choice and to have the child state that the time with one parent is better than the time with the other parent. This creates a conflict of loyalty and can close down communication.

"I Don't Know What's Wrong With Him" Syndrome. Generally, what takes place with this theme is that an initial phase of discussion goes well until the alienating parent pushes a trigger to incite the target parent.

This leads to the alienating parent's making a comment on the inability of the target parent to control his or her temper. In fact, this could explain why many alienated children do not want to have their parents in close physical proximity of each other at a sports or school event out of fear that there could be a blowup between them.

Ally Syndrome. In such scenarios, the alienating parent attempts to get the alienated child to side with him or her against the other parent. This is often done with questions such as "What do you think *we* should do?" Other questions include "What would you do if you were me?" or "Do you think it is fair for your father to want to have the whole spring vacation?" In fact, questions sometimes go as far, according to Clawar and Rivlin (1991), as "Do you think we should ask for sole custody?" or "Do you see what I've had to live with for the past 10 years?" Clearly, the alienating parent asks the child such questions in order to gain the child's sympathy and support.

Morality Syndrome. Very frequently, the alienating parent provides moral opinions and judgments about the target parent. For example, after an early elementary school child was told by his mother "Your father is the son of Satan," the child was asked by this professional how he felt about the statement. The child replied that he felt terrible because it would mean that he was the grandson of Satan. Similarly, statements such as "*We* don't believe in cheating the government out of taxes" or "*We* believe in getting married before living together" have the same effect of presenting the other parent in a negative light. In fact, during a PA evaluation, an eight-year-old boy reported that his father had told him, "Your mother gave every guy on the block a blow job." The boy was asked what was meant by a blow job and the boy responded that he has no idea what it means but that it must have been something really bad because his father was very red in the face when he said it and because she did it to every man on the block.

In order to increase the likelihood of successfully normalizing the relationship between the child and the target parent, it is important for the evaluator to recommend and for the judge to impose a court order that is explicit in stating that it is in the best interest of the alienated child to be reunified and resume contact with the previously target parent. Interventions must be specified. Furthermore, the consequences of not following the court order should also be specified. Warshak, in his book *Divorce Poison* (2010), points out that

> Despite their vehement protests, children and teens welcome the sense of protection and control that comes when adults exert appropriate authority to keep children on the right track. Children who have been drafted in a war against a parent welcomed the release that comes when the court rescues them from the burden of choosing one parent over the other. Just as rapid-

> ly as children seem to abandon their love for a parent, they reclaim that heritage under the proper circumstances when it is safe to do so and when we offer them a face-saving way to do it. We do not build a relationship from scratch; we uncover what has always been there. (p. 304)

It should be noted that, unfortunately, postseparation religious conflicts often lead to moderate (and severe) alienating behaviors. The court is sometimes faced with serious dilemmas when one parent may have alienated the child from the other parent as a result of religious differences. In such cases, the alienating parent reports that the child refuses to go with the target parent because of significant differences in their values, which the child cannot accept. Unfortunately, sometimes religious leaders become enmeshed in the conflict and become supportive, along with the rest of the religious community of the alienating parent, without fully appreciating the dynamics of PA and its consequences

TREATMENT AND INTERVENTIONS

To begin therapy in a haphazard manner with families in which there is a child displaying symptoms of moderate PA "is a prescription for stalemate or disaster" (Johnston, Walters & Friedlander, 2001). Such children require a family based intervention plan that includes not only the alienated child but also siblings, both the alienating and target parents, and other family members who may be contributing to the dynamics of the alienation. Too often the alienating parent is not involved in the therapeutic process, nor is the alienating parent expected or encouraged to participate in normalizing the child's relationship with the target parent. Although some may believe that isolating or punishing the alienating parent will disempower them, such methods often make the alienating parent more anxious. This may then further exacerbate the intensity of the dynamics, leading to a greater degree of anxiety and a resulting increase in alienation (Johnston et al., 2001). A therapist in this circumstance should build a therapeutic alliance with the alienating parent in order to ensure progress in reunifying and normalizing the child with the target parent. At the same time, there should be no giving up on the part of the target parent in situations of moderate alienation. The target parent's "throwing in the towel" will only reinforce the alienated child's beliefs and the alienating parent's statements and innuendos to the child (Gardner, 1999).

It is imperative that the treating professional establish a plan of treatment that considers the goals of the intervention as well as the modalities thereof. The treating professional may adjust such plans, depending on what arises during the treatment. The interventions should be tailored to the particular circumstances of each situation, however. The age of the alienated children in terms of their ability to apply critical analysis of information that may have been presented to them by the alienating parent should also be taken into account. When there is a hybrid form of alienation–that is, when there are some elements of estrangement as well as significant elements of alienation–one needs to deal with both, not only in the alienated children but also in the parents. Therapists should be open to the possibility of estrangement as well as alienation and should be equipped to deal with each. Clearly, the cooperation of each parent and their cooperation and resistance need to be dealt with whether there are court orders for the parents' collaboration or not.

The involvement of a mediator is contraindicated because mediators, for the most part, do not have the training necessary for dealing with alienation cases. Moreover, Vestal (1999) was quite clear that mediating such cases can provide a forum for one parent to "espouse" hurtful views, which can cause pain to the other parent. Because one parent often sees the other parent as being completely wrong and as being malicious, it is highly unlikely, particularly in cases of moderate or severe alienation, that an agreement can be reached. Even if an agreement can be reached between the parents, one still has to deal with interventions for the alienated child. Vestal (1999) also points out that because of the pathology often found in an alienating parent, mediation may not be an appropriate avenue for intervention.

It is essential to recognize that cases entering family court that involve an alienated child require intensive and coordinated case management to intervene effectively (Sullivan & Kelly, 2001). Treatment will be facilitated by having only one judge assigned to the file. This would not only ensure continuity but also prevent delays in legal interventions that would likely occur if a different judge needed to become familiar with the case.

One needs to ensure that the goal in therapy is to convert the child's distorted, unjustified, and rigidly held view of the target parent as being "all bad" and the alienating parent as being "all good" into a more realistic view of each parent based on all of the aligned child's experiences with both parents. At the same time, the alienating parent needs to understand the potential effects of PA on the child both in the present and in the future as an adult (Baker, 2006, 2007). In addition, one needs to ensure that the parenting arrangement enables the child to have "conflict-free access to the good parts or the positive attributes of both parents in ways that promote the child's healthy psychological development" (Johnston et al., 2001).

It is also important to recognize and accept that interventions to combat PA are extremely difficult to put into place when there is minimal or no contact between the child and the target parent. Although some of the methods used to normalize the relationship between the alienated child and the target parent may initially seem extreme or coercive, one should recognize that the potential effects of alienation on a child in the short and long term require such measures in the child's best interests. The court must specify in an unequivocal manner the need for full cooperation from both parents and the children along with consequences for not abiding by the court's order. Although the therapist may at times be accused of being too rigid in the manner of implementing change, such extreme situations require firmness, reason and emotion at the same time to demonstrate to the child the potential effects on the child of continuing to view the target parent negatively (Lowenstein, 2005).

According to Gardner (1999, p. 197), what is required is "the need for an authoritarian and even dictatorial approach" to the alienating parent and the alienated children. Furthermore, he believed that all parties involved need to deal with one therapist because "fractionalization" will lead to a breakdown of communication as well as an intensification of the pathological interactions that lead to and perpetuate parental alienation syndrome (PAS). Therapists who often see children alone are left with the belief that the children, even in cases of alienation, have been estranged from the target parent rather than having been alienated. Such children, notwithstanding their having been exposed to and subjected to the irrational and unjustifiable negativity regarding the target parent, often are quite convincing when they state that their complaints about and perspectives of the target parent are justified. As a result, such children are often reinforced for their perceptions rather than being empowered to critically analyze them.

In some situations, treatment progress can be greatly assisted by having the parent referred to a parenting course or coach with experience in high-conflict divorces who understands their effects on children who are enmeshed in the conflict. Such a professional can assist the target parent to deal with behaviors that contribute to PA, including the target parent's rejecting the child as a result of that parent's anger, frustration, and humiliation. In addition, alienation is sometimes found when the target parent prioritizes his or her needs ahead of the child's during the marriage and following the separation.

In view of the fact that one often finds personality disorders and psychopathology present in a large percentage of high-conflict parents who are focused on litigation and who perceive themselves as being virtuous and free of responsibility, one may need to ensure that the treating professional has experience working with personality disorders.

It is also important that target parents receive help in terms of coping with their children's rejection and help them develop "thick skins." It is very important to provide target parents with an understanding as to why and how the child who formerly had a close and loving relationship with the target parent could, within a short period of time, turn against them. Such parents need to recognize that often the most significant difficulty takes place during the transition from one parent to the other, to the extent that after an initial short period of time, the children allow themselves to enjoy their time with the target parent. When the child continues a negative diatribe and displays anger throughout the visit, the parent needs to be encouraged to see that she or he should not personalize the rejection (if there are no behaviors by the target parent that could explain the change in the child's attitude). Rather, she or he should understand it as being a reflection of the efforts of the alienating parent.

It is also beneficial for the target parent to recognize that the mood and behavior of the child may fluctuate during the visit, especially in the case of moderate alienation. Often such demonstrations "relieve" the child because, at least initially, the child is doing what is expected of him or her by the alienating parent. This allows the child to subsequently tell the alienating parent that he or she was reluctant to be with the target parent during the access. Such fluctuations are exacerbated by contact with the alienating parent, and particularly if the alienating parent is allowed to have telephone or physical contact with the child during the time that the child is with the target parent. Otherwise, the alienating parent is likely, for example, to call the child to make sure that the child is "okay," thereby providing a reminder that the alienating parent is concerned about the child's safety and security when the child is in the presence of the target parent. It is also common for the alienating parent to provide the child with money for the child to pay for snacks, the movies, and so on to ensure that the child is not given the opportunity to appreciate something concrete provided by the target parent. The underlying message communicated by the alienating parent is often lost on the young child unless clarified during the therapy.

Although it is extremely tempting for the target parent to spend a large amount of time discussing the child's allegations or concerns with the child, it is far more beneficial for the target parent to have an enjoyable time with the child by engaging in activities or discussions that disprove some of the child's allegations and accusations. It is also extremely important for the target parent to recognize that an alienated child is concerned about rejecting the alienating parent, particularly when the child expresses affection for the target parent. The target parent should encourage the child to express any emotion, positive or negative, at which occurrence the child will recognize contrasts with what takes place when he or she is with the alienating parent. The child is thereby more likely to recognize the significant difference in the parents' respective acceptances of the child, and the child is thereby more likely to appreciate the time that he or she spends with the target parent.

The target parent should be taught to recognize that although the situation is an extremely difficult one to deal with, it is also extremely difficult for the child to deal with. The target parent should be helped to recognize that the situation could be worse, as in the case of severe alienation, in which the child adamantly refuses to go with the target parent. Furthermore, the target parent should recognize that if the child really did not want to go with her or him, the child could make it impossible for the target parent to see her or him. Gardner (1999) was quite clear that the target parent should get some solace from this.

It is also commonly observed that when there are several siblings, one sibling may mimic the words and behaviors of the others so that the child is not placed under pressure by the other siblings. At times, the other alienated siblings may put an intense amount of pressure on a nonalienated child to keep a united front. It is common for older siblings to become allies with the alienating parent in ensuring that a nonalienated child follows the other children. In this way, the older children become accomplices to pressure the younger children to also reject the target parent. Consequently, treatment should ensure that children are seen individually as well as together, especially in such situations.

One needs to recognize as well that, although children may refuse overtly to spend time with the target parent, being forced by the therapist or by the court to visit with the target parent allows the children to say to the alienating parent that they had no choice. Often the children will describe the therapist as being mean and stupid and as not understanding them. Gardner (1999) maintained that many alienated children often want to see the target parent and need the excuse that they are being forced to, thereby removing them from extremely strong loyalty conflicts.

Although in most cases, alienators in the moderate category of alienation are not receptive to insight-oriented therapeutic intervention, one can present the potential short-term and long-term effects on children in terms of problematic behavior and relationships. Issues of jealousy, rejection, rage, abandonment fears, and potential loss of identity in the alienating parent, however, may fuel the fire so that logic and reason are often rejected. At times, it is important to validate some of the fears and anxieties of the alienating parent. At the same time, the therapist must provide constructive recommendations regarding going on with life and living life to the fullest. Also important are discussions of the potential consequences of alienation. Such strategies may help alienating parents to defocus from the target parent and focus more on themselves in a positive fashion. In some cases, anger management and stress reduction techniques may be useful in the event that the alienating parent can come to understand the potential effects on the alienated child.

Because the symptoms of moderate PA are more apparent than those in cases of mild alienation, the therapist can greatly benefit from cognizance of the answers that the child may have provided to the evaluator's questions that reveal the existence of programming and brainwashing. For example, answers to "Why do you think that your mother is trying so hard to have more time with you?" or "Are you aware of anything that your mother and father are upset about?" allow the therapist to have a window on why the child is reluctant to spend time with the target parent. Discussing the answers and doing reality testing in a nonconfrontational manner can allow the child to do his or her own reality testing and to come to reality-based answers. Many alienated children often do not use critical reasoning when presented with statements, questions, innuendos, and so on about the target parent. Encouraging them to think for themselves is very helpful in getting children to have a more realistic view of their parents. Often, the use of pictures and videos in combination with discussion of positive events and interactions with the target parent and the target parent's extended family can be quite beneficial in normalizing the child's relationship with the target parent.

Promoting reality testing with the child in a safe and nonconfrontational environment, where the child is encouraged to "say it as it is," allows the child to negate three key messages often communicated by the alienating parent to the child (Baker, 2007):

- The alienating parent is the only one who cares,
- The alienating parent is needed in order for the child feel safe and good about himself or herself,
- The target parent, who is dangerous and does not love the child anyway, must be disallowed in order to maintain the love and approval of the alienating parent.

As a result of learning about these messages, the child is more likely to recognize that the alienating parent's love is conditional.

It is absolutely critical for the court and the therapist to recognize that the "mission of alienating the child" is greatly assisted and enhanced by the passage of time in which there is no or very limited movement to normalize the child's relationship with the target parent. The passage of time is the greatest ally of the alienating parent. It has been noted that the alienating parent "never misses an opportunity to miss an opportunity," especially when there are no changes implemented in the court or effected in the context of therapy. One should recognize that situations involving a child's reluctance or refusal to spend time with the target parent often become more entrenched with time, especially after the child is exposed to half-hearted or unsuccessful interventions that are not well thought-out.

RECOMMENDATIONS FOR INTERVENTION

Once a child has been identified as having been alienated, particularly in moderate and severe alienation situations, the recommendations of Sullivan and Kelly (2001) can be quite helpful with family court. They point to the following principles that need to be seriously considered:

Continuity and Case Management. Due to the fact that there may be termination not only of parent-child relationships but also of relationships among therapists, attorneys, extended family, and family court personnel, it is imperative that the MHPs and legal professionals have the roles clearly defined and protected as part of the court order. Doing so will ensure that there is case continuity, which is critical in order to provide effective interventions.

Evaluators can recommend the types of interventions, the professional qualifications of individuals who can provide such interventions, and the conditions under which professionals can be withdrawn from the case. In addition, there need to be modalities in place for the evaluator to communicate the findings of the evaluation to the professionals who will be providing the interventions. Furthermore, the modalities by which the professionals are able to communicate with each other need to be in place.

Clear, Detailed, and Enforceable Orders. Due to the fact that such cases involve a great deal of conflict between the two parents, the court order needs to contain detailed and clear parameters as to where and when visits occur, the length of time, the location where the child will be picked up and dropped off, and the fact that the visits are not negotiable. The court order as well should specify that the target parent needs to be informed of important education, health, and social/activity information about the child and that neither parent should make unilateral decisions regarding the child's health, education, or extracurricular activities that could interfere with the other parent's access to the child. The use of the Our Family Wizard® website (www.ourfamilywizard.com) can assist parents in communicating effectively with each other and keep each parent informed of important information regarding the child(ren).

Conflict Management. Due to the fact that the alienated child may perceive conflict as reflecting negatively on the target parent and positively on the alienating parent (who may be perceived as having been victimized) one should attempt to ensure that the parents are disengaged, that transitions do not involve face-to-face contact, and that parents alternate attendance at the child's activities.

Continuity of Contact Between the Child and the Target Parent. Experience has shown that generally when there is no access between the child and the target parent, the child demonstrates a greater resistance to reinstitute contact with the target parent. The child will often interpret the lack of contact with the target parent as being due to the target parent's lack of motivation or rejection of the child. It is extremely important that, in the event there is a problem with the access, the situation be addressed as soon as possible as an urgent matter in court. One needs to recognize as well that the alienated child may more vigorously object to the visits with the target parent while the case is waiting to go to court. Furthermore, one should not be misled about the presence of alienation despite a child's appearing more receptive to visits with the target parent just prior to a court hearing.

Heightened resistance by the child should not be the rationale for contact to be modified, however. Having an individual monitor visits between the target parent and the alienated child can provide valuable information regarding the degree of comfort of the child throughout the access. The behavior of the target parent when the child may become oppositional, as well as the behavior of the alienating parent at the time of the transfer, in addition to the manner in which the target parent handles the rejection and is supportive and validating of the child, can also be quite useful.

Despite a child's verbal statements that she or he refuses to have anything to do with the target parent, the child's actual behavior in the presence of the target parent may be totally different, particularly if such interaction is observed through closed-circuit television.

Shared Responsibility for the Resolution of the Alienation. It is imperative that both parents clearly understand that in order for progress to occur, they are both responsible for ensuring that the child has a meaningful relationship with each of them. This could include the requirement that both parents are responsible for paying for reunification therapy or for supervised visits along with the threat of court sanctions if alienating behavior continues. Such sanctions can include fines or conditional judgments regarding custody. It is critical that the professionals who are working with the child are able to communicate with each other and that they not work at cross-purposes.

Case Management. Situations being heard in the family court system with allegations of PA require intensive, coordinated, and continuous case management in order to ensure effective interventions and judgments. It is generally accepted that the therapist should be court appointed and that the judge dealing with such a situation needs to remain on the case so that there is one judge who knows all of the details and intricacies of the situation and to ensure continuity and consistent interventions. Gardner (1998) maintained that in situations of moderate PA, the "hard-nosed" court-appointed therapist can be quite crucial in the treatment, and clearly, such a therapist should have a thorough understanding of the manifestations as well as the techniques and themes used by the alienating parent in alienating the child. Furthermore, the therapist should know to what extent the therapist has the court's support and to what extent the therapist can threaten the alienating parent with sanctions and other consequences.

Professional Independence. The therapist must maintain professional independence and not be controlled by the alienating parent into slowing down the normalization of the alienated child with the target parent, nor by the target parent, who may pressure the therapist into proceeding too quickly. The therapist should recognize that the longer the litigation goes on, the less likely the treatment will be successful. Consequently, it is extremely important for there to be a court judgment as soon as possible, thereby reducing the need for the children to behave in a negative manner with the target parent.

Both Parents Should Be Seen. The court-appointed therapist should see both parents and the child who has been alienated, even if the alienating parent has his or her own therapist. Although alienating parents may refuse treatment, they sometimes will manipulate the therapist into believing that they will be fully cooperative and are very interested in doing whatever they can do to help the child. One needs to be alert to the possibility that such parents will be "economical with the truth" and ultimately do what they can to sabotage therapy. Gardner (1999) reported that such parents "can create a façade of wanting peace and cooperation, while covertly continuing the campaign of aggression and sabotage." In such an event, the therapist should inform the court that the alienating parent is sabotaging the therapy by his or her lack of active and genuine involvement and by the lack of effort with the child.

Use of Collateral Contacts. Gardner also believed that sometimes an "insider" on the alienator's side of the family can be productive in defusing the situation when such an individual is aware that the alienator has gone too far because of animosity, jealousy, fear of abandonment, the presence of a new companion for the alienated parent, and so on. At times, such an individual can bring reality into the picture by presenting to the alienating parent how the children are being affected and the possible future effects on the alienated children.

Role Clarity. As a result, when the therapist becomes involved, the therapist should consider the role that each of the parties play. One should note as well that at times, an alienator may not even realize the potential effects on a child of robbing the child of his or her childhood and how the child's future relationships as well as the child's present sense of identity can be so adversely affected (Baker, 2007). In the vignette presented earlier, when John was questioned regarding his impeccable spelling, the adolescent reported that his mother had proofread his e-mail before he sent it to his father. The mother was confronted with this declaration in the report and she subsequently called the evaluator, stating that she was "not thinking." Although she thanked the evaluator for "pushing her to her senses" and for helping her realize her mistake, she was subsequently charged with contempt of court for not ensuring that the court order was followed regarding access to the children's father.

Impaired Insight. Many alienating parents in this category have their judgment clouded by their feelings, so that they have difficulty in not only recognizing the present and future effects of their campaign of denigration on the alienated children, but also seeming oblivious to the potential impact on their own future relationship with the children.

THERAPEUTIC CONSIDERATIONS

The therapist should help parents separate their thoughts and feelings from the child and learn how to ensure that the child does not become enmeshed in the conflict. It would be helpful for the alienating parent to understand not only the short-term consequences, but also the long-term consequences (Baker, 2007, 2012), as well as the value to the child of maintaining the relationship with the target parent. At the same time, the target parent may need help in developing empathy for the child and in setting reasonable limits. Therapy for the child should include activities and discussion on reducing rigid black-or-white thinking, separating the child's feelings from those of the parents, and providing opportunities for the child to practice critical thinking. As can be seen, there should be a combination of both therapy and education in order for successful intervention.

It is important to ensure that the benefits of an ongoing relationship among the children and the target parent are established. As a result of all family members reinforcing the fact that the child has more to benefit by having a positive relationship even by disputing it, the alienated child is able to focus more on reestablishing the relationship that the child had with the target parent previously. In addition, it is important to establish the modalities and the structure of the contact initially, although they may become less structured and more a function of the arrangements that the target parent and the alienated child agree on.

It is necessary that the alienating parent and the target parent receive professional intervention for their respective views. Interventions with the target parent, however, may need to include how to deal with his feelings of rejection and possibly anger when in the presence of the child. Different strategies for being patient should be addressed with the target parent, including the importance of being persistent and not giving up. It is important to ensure certain commitments are made by the target parent in order to encourage the relationship of the child with the target parent and to reinforce with the child that the target parent is not a bad person and that it would be to the child's benefit to have a meaningful and significant relationship with the target parent. At the same time, if the target parent did something that is unacceptable, it should not be whitewashed. In addition, the treating MHPs may need to provide emotional support to the target parent as well as to the alienating parent and the child. At times, the alienating parent as well needs to receive emotional support when she or he recognizes the harm that may have been caused by PA as well as the loss of the child's having had a good relationship with the target parent.

Friedlander and Walters (2010) describe Multi-Modal Family Intervention. This program includes "understanding and addressing how the stress of the parental separation and divorce process have affected the child; teaching the child coping strategies; changing the child's distorted 'good/bad' views and polarized feelings towards both parents into more realistic ones; and restoring appropriate co-parental and parent-child roles in the family."

It is vital that therapists recognize that, similar to Clawar and Rivlin who found that 80 percent of alienated children wanted the alienation to stop and wanted people to recognize that there was alienation taking place, Baker found that alienated children did not want their parents to walk away from them and similarly hoped that someone would realize that they did not mean what they said. These findings are extremely important because, unfortunately, professionals representing or treating children with moderate or severe PA often give great weight to the children's verbal statements, believing that children mean what they say. It is unfortunate that in Canada, for example, the child's attorney represents the child's wishes versus what is in the child's best interest, in the same way that an attorney represents an adult's wishes. Frequently, the child in such situations is empowered and the court may not get the sense that such children have been manipulated.

It is also important for therapists to recognize that alienated children and adolescents need to feel that the therapist is not talking down to them. The results of a study by Johnston and Goldman (2010) suggests that teenagers whose autonomy is respected and who feel empowered are more likely to subsequently initiate contact with the target parent and are better able to distance themselves from the ongoing high conflict within the family. They report that almost all of the youth who had actively resisted or refused visitation subsequently reinitiated contact with the target parent, often after reaching the age of emancipation at eighteen years old. Some expressed remorse and regret for their totally negative stance; others did not offer any explanation for their having rejected a parent.

Another very interesting finding was that "resistant offspring who had been forced by court orders to see a successive array of therapists for reunification counselling were, as young adults, contemptuous and blamed the court or rejected parent for putting them through this ordeal" (Johnston & Goldman, 2010). They furthermore found that long-term alienation starting during the early teenage years is unlikely to happen, although situations in which a teenager is alienated during the early teenage years in most cases range from a few months to a couple of years and are a common hazard in highly conflicted family situations.

The importance of early intervention is especially important, and therapists need to recognize that some target parents may be more difficult to work with than others. Johnston and Goldman (2010) found that in situations of earlier, more chronic family dysfunction and more reality-based concerns by the child, there is likely to be an enduring rejection of the parent. They also report that successful outcomes are more likely with proactive measures and early intervention "before the child's stance and family dynamics become immutable and bogged down in litigation." They found that positive outcomes can occur in situations in which target parents have parenting limitations in the context of a chronically conflicted family when the children are able to achieve what they feel to be a safe distance from the more difficult parent and when the contact is limited to structured or mutually enjoyable activities. On the other hand, poor outcomes generally involved a target parent with significant parenting deficits, often one who is short tempered and one who continues litigation. One should question whether, in fact, Johnston and Goldman are referring to alienation, estrangement or a hybrid form of the two.

Qualitative and empirical studies, together with case studies and clinical observations, indicate that alienated children have significant difficulties in many areas. In fact, child protection agencies in the United States and Canada are increasingly finding that such children are in need of protection. Although child protection agencies may be more focused on issues of physical abuse, physical neglect, and sexual abuse, some agencies are increasingly training personnel to differentiate estrangement from alienation and to recognize the different themes and manifestations of PA. Thankfully, judges are increasingly aware of the potential impact of alienation on the child's present and future development, especially in cases of at least moderate alienation in which there is clear evidence that the alienation is not justified and that there are multiple indications of the efforts of the alienating parent to distance and alienate the child from the target parent. On the other hand, many judges rotate in and out of family court and should be educated about PA rather than become indoctrinated themselves by the alienating parents and by their attorney's convincing arguments, compelling fabrications, and false allegations against the target parents.

Vignette

The vignette presented earlier demonstrates some of the tactics used by alienating parents as well as the manifestations in the children. The judge concluded that there was enough evidence, based on the testimonies heard in court, of the existence of moderate PA. The judge ordered that no major decisions regarding the children's health, education, and general welfare were to be made without the father's involvement. In addition, Ms. Smith was told by the court that a move some 2300 miles away was not in the children's best interest and that such a move would only entrench the children further in their being distanced, literally and figuratively, from their father. Family therapy with a professional experienced in working with alienated children was ordered for the family. This psychologist met with Jonathan and Samantha on a regular basis as well as with each of the parents, individually and together. In addition, the psychologist met with each of the children individually and together at times with the target parent. The use of videos of summer vacations and photographs was useful in the interventions, because the children could not deny that they did previously enjoy being with their father, notwithstanding their vehement denial of this during the custody evaluation and even in the early stages of the intervention.

Mr. Smith was also given significant time by the court, including extended weekends starting from Thursday night and extending to Monday morning every second weekend as well as an overnight in the alternating week from Thursday after school to Friday morning. The access was to be extended an additional day in the event of statutory holidays or school professional days with no physical contact allowed between the children and their mother or soon to be stepfather or their extended families during such times that they were with their father. Each of the parents was strongly encouraged to be actively involved in the therapy, and the judge kept the family file, because the judge felt it was important to have the same judge follow the file in view of its complexities and the size.

Editors' Notes

- Dr. Worenklein provides the differences between mild, moderate, and severe alienation. He defines moderate PA as when the child consistently complains and rejects the unwanted visits but will ultimately go with the target parent after expressing and demonstrating significant reluctance to do so. Moderately alienated children will express consistent negative feelings regarding the target parent whether or not in the alienating parent's company, in the examiner's office, in their school setting or on the playground with their friends, or under any circumstances in which the topic of parenting arises or when parenting inquiries are made.
- Dr. Worenklein describes an example of moderate PA with two children, Jonathan and Samantha, age 12 and 9, respectively. They reportedly had a good relationship with their father, who was very involved in the children's academic and recreational events in the past, before their parents separated. Although the communication between the parents was open in the first year after the separation, the situation changed with the commencement of a new relationship between the children's mother and another man. The children became increasingly reluctant to spend time with their father although they did agree to spend time with him if he would take them shopping or to the arcade, as they said their stepfather did. The children furthermore attempted to argue with their father to allow them to move with their mother to Vancouver, where their soon-to-be stepfather lived. In addition to difficulties in seeing the children, Mr. Smith discovered that his name was removed from the emergency list of telephone numbers at the children's school. Although Mr. Smith began experiencing difficulty in reaching his children by phone, he attributed this to the fact that the children were adjusting to their mother's new relationship. However, he soon realized that the children were being alienated from him in that they came up with excuses as to why they could not see him, generally attributing their inability to do so to previous engagements or to school work. Mr. Smith reported that although the children were reluctant to spend time with him, they did begin to relax with him after 15 to 20 minutes even if they did not go shopping or to the arcade. Yet, the children reported to their mother that they had a boring time with their father and wished they could spend less time with him.
- Dr. Worenklein explains how interview questions and themes will uncover PA. There are specific methods of evaluating PA that include determining whether the symptoms identified by Gardner were present and

to what extent they persisted. Additionally, observation of the target parent-child relationship and interviews with the alienated child would demonstrate the presence of restrictions on permission to express love to both parents, inappropriate information conveyed to the child, presentation of one parent as the martyr, the child's being exploited as a spy, or not wanting to associate with the alienated parent's support network.

- Dr. Worenklein offers guidelines for successful intervention for moderate alienation cases. These include therapeutic techniques such as exercises in critical thinking, the need for an experienced therapist to confront the alienated children as well as the alienating parent, the use of pictures illustrating the target parent sharing activities with the children, thereby contradicting the child's assertions, and supportive therapy to the target parent. There is the need for continuity among the judges such that one judge presides per case regardless of occasion and timing. Access and time sharing with the alienated child and the target parent are essential despite efforts and excuses by the child and alienating parent to avoid this responsibility to enforce the court's order.

REFERENCES

Baker, A. J. L. (2006). Patterns of parental alienation syndrome: A qualitative study of adults who were alienated from a parent as a child. *The American Journal of Family Therapy, 34*(1), 63–78.

Baker, A. J. L. (2007). *Adult children of parental alienation syndrome: Breaking the ties that bind.* New York: W. W. Norton.

Baker, A. J. L. (2012). Differentiating alienated from not alienated children: A pilot study. *Journal of Divorce and Remarriage, 53*(3), 178–193.

Clawar, S. S., & Rivlin, B. V. (1991). *Children held hostage: Dealing with programmed and brainwashed children.* Washington, DC: American Bar Association Section of Family Law.

Friedlander, S., & Walters, M. G. (2010). When a child rejects a parent: Tailoring the intervention to fit the problem. *Family Court Review, 48*(1), 98–111.

Gardner, R. A. (1998). *The parental alienation syndrome: Guide for mental health and legal professionals* (2nd ed.). Cresskill, NJ: Creative Therapeutics.

Gardner, R. A. (1999). Family therapy of the moderate type of parental alienation syndrome. *The American Journal of Family Therapy, 27*(3), 195–212.

Johnston, J. R. (2003). Parental alignments and rejection: An imperial cult study of alienation and children of divorce. *Journal of the American Academy of Psychiatry and Law, 31*(2), 158–170.

Johnston, J. R., & Roseby, V. (1997). *In the name of the child: A developmental approach to understanding and helping children of high conflict and violent families.* New York: Free Press.

Johnston, J. R., Walters, M. G., & Friedlander, S. (2001). Therapeutic work with alienated children and their families. *Family Court Review, 39*(3), 316–333.

Johnston, J. R., & Goldman, J. R. (2010). Outcomes of family counselling interventions with children who resist visitation: An addendum to Friedlander and Walters. *Family Court Review, 48*(1), 112–115.

Kelly, J. B., & Johnston, J. R. (2001). The alienated child: A reformulation of parental alienation syndrome. *Family Court Review, 39,* 249–266.

Lowenstein, L. F. (2005). *Signs of parental alienation syndrome and how to counteract its effects.* Southern England Psychological Services. Available: http://www.parental-alienation.info/publications/24-sigofparalisynandhowtocouitseff.htm

Rohrbaugh, J. B. (2008). *A comprehensive guide to child custody evaluation: Mental health and legal perspectives.* New York: Springer.

Sauber, S. R. (2006). PAS as a family tragedy: Roles of family members, professionals, and the justice system. In R. Gardner, S. Sauber, & D. Lorandos (Eds.), *The international handbook of parental alienation syndrome* (pp. 12–32). Springfield, IL: Charles C Thomas Publisher.

Sauber, S. R., & Worenklein, A. (2012). Custody evaluation in alienation cases. In A. J. L. Baker & S. Richard Sauber, (Eds.), *Working with alienated children and families: A clinical guidebook* (pp. 47–70). New York: Routledge

Sullivan, M., & Kelly, J. B. (2001) Legal and psychological management of cases with an alienated child. *Family Court Review, 39*(3), 299–315.

Vestal, A. (1999). Mediation and parental alienation syndrome: Considerations for an intervention model. *Family and Conciliation Courts Review, 37*(4), 487–503.

Warshak, R. A. (2010). *Divorce poison: how to protect your family from badmouthing and brainwashing.* New York: Harper.

Warshak, R. A., & Otis, M. R. (2010). Helping alienated children with family bridges: Practice, research and the pursuit of "humbition." *Family Court Review, 48*(1), 91–97.

Chapter 5

SEVERE CASES OF PARENTAL ALIENATION

Richard A. Warshak

Vignette

Bradley Beecher is twelve years old and a favorite of his teachers, coaches, and friends' parents. He rarely strays past the limits at school and on the soccer field. His quick, clever wisecracks leave his teachers unsuccessfully suppressing their smiles. His parents beam when fielding compliments from other adults about Brad's good behavior, charm, and manners. People would be shocked, however, to see how he treats his mother behind closed doors.

Before his mother filed for divorce a year earlier, Brad and Mom enjoyed a close, loving, better than normal relationship. A former middle school teacher, Vicki Beecher intuitively knew how to greet Brad's friends, lay out healthy snacks, and then retreat from the game room. This made their home the favorite center for peer activity and sleepovers. Brad's closest friends found Vicki easy to talk to and confided in her when facing problems with parents and peers. They called her their second mother.

The news of his parents' divorce hit Brad hard. He became more needy, wanting his mother to linger in his room at bedtime. A week after his father moved out, Brad spent his first weekend in his dad's new apartment. Brad returned to his mother Sunday evening. She would later say that he came back to her "a different person." Surly, nearly snarling, he walked right past his mother with no greeting, went to his room, and slammed the door. Later that night he yelled at her, "It's all your fault Dad moved out. You care only about yourself. I hate you and I hate living here. When I'm twelve, the law says I get to decide where I live, and I'm moving in with Dad."

Vicki had no idea what brought this on. She wracked her brain wondering what she said or did wrong. "It was probably a normal reaction to the family transition," she thought. "It will pass."

Rather than pass, Brad's hostility escalated during the next month. Seemingly overnight he transformed from a compliant, loving child to a disobedient, disrespectful brat. He constantly berated her cooking, her mannerisms, her very existence. He vacillated between ignoring her and cussing at her. Brad stopped inviting his friends to the house.

Vicki wanted professional help for Brad, but the temporary court orders required Brad's dad to consent and he did not "believe in therapy." When Brad's outbursts–they reminded Vicki of a toddler's tantrums–began to include threats to her physical safety and prized possessions, she hired Brad's favorite cousin, Carson, to help her manage. Carson was beginning his junior year in college majoring in psychology.

Things improved for a while. Brad enjoyed Carson's companionship and the boy treated his mother better in Carson's presence. Then one day Carson walked in while Brad was in the middle of a meltdown. Carson ordered Brad to calm down and go to his room. Brad stormed off, locked himself in the bathroom, and phoned his father.

Rather than soothe his son, Frank Beecher egged him on. "You don't have to put up with that crap. You've got rights. Tell Carson to go to hell. If you can't take any more, just walk out of the house and I'll pick you up." That is just what Brad did. He ran away from his mother's home, and he was picked up by his father.

CHARACTERISTICS OF SEVERELY ALIENATED CHILDREN

Children who irrationally reject a parent, and do so to a severe degree, present some of the toughest challenges in family law cases. Severe cases of a child's alienation from a parent are distinguished from mild and moderate cases by the extent of the child's rejection of a parent and the degree of negativity in the attitudes and behavior toward the rejected parent. Severely alienated children express extremely polarized views of their parents; they have little if anything positive to say about the rejected parent and often rewrite the history of their relationship to obscure positive elements. They seem content to avoid all contact with the parent, may reject an entire branch of their extended family, and often threaten to defy court-ordered parenting plans that schedule them to be under the care of the rejected parent.

Severe alienation includes behavioral, emotional, and cognitive dimensions (Gardner, 1998; Kelly, 2010). Some custody evaluators and attorneys supplement interviews with litigants with a questionnaire that addresses the child's differential treatment of the parents and sheds light on the three dimensions of alienation: behavioral, emotional and cognitive (Warshak, 2006). The questionnaire report (available at www.wpqonline.com) can alert attorneys to concerns that their clients' children may be exhibiting warning signs of alienation.

Behavioral Impairments

Severely alienated children treat the rejected parent with extreme hostility, disobedience, defiance, and withdrawal. They may resist or refuse contact, vandalize and steal property, threaten violence, and sometimes act on such threats. A boy told the custody evaluator that he would like to give his father a hard kick between the legs, kill him in his sleep, and have him die a horrible death. Unfortunately, children at the severe end of the continuum of parental alienation (PA) typically display such venom. Often these children behave well with all other adults except the rejected parent and people associated with that parent.

Emotional Impairments

When not being openly contemptuous, severely alienated children remain aloof from the rejected parent and express no genuine love, affection, or appreciation. Mother's and Father's Day cards are things of the past. Rather than express contrition for acting in ways that far exceed the bounds of decency and normal behavior toward parents, alienated children show no apparent shame or guilt for their mistreatment of a parent. Severe alienation is not a situation, as one misguided attorney argued, where children merely love one parent a lot more than the other parent. These children harbor strong and irrational aversion toward a parent with whom they formerly enjoyed a close relationship. The aversion may take the form of fear, hatred, or both. On the way to a reunification workshop one night, a child, accompanied by two older siblings, was in a panic, scared to death of his father. He kept repeating, "He'll kill us," and it was clear that he really believed this. By late next morning, half a day into the workshop, the child was playing with the man he had thought would murder him in his sleep. This boy's mother did not predict that the court would judge her as unspeakably cruel for unnecessarily scaring her child. In most cases of severe alienation, however, children are less filled with fear than with hatred.

Cognitive Impairments

The thoughts and statements about the rejected parent, in most cases, are trivial complaints, often in words that echo the favored parent despite the child's claim that the words are his or her own. Two children justified their rejection of their mother with the complaint that while driving them to school each morning she lectured them on how much she loves them. Brad complained that his mother "sprung a cruise" on him. The custody evaluator labeled Brad's attempts to justify his denigration of his mother as shallow and inauthentic. In some cases, when trivial complaints are unsuccessful in severing contact with a parent, favored parents and children lodge accusations of abuse. A week before the court was scheduled to hear Vicki's motion for enforcement of the parenting plan, Brad "remembered" that when he was younger, his mother touched his penis when she was tucking him in bed.

Alienated children's thoughts about their parents become highly skewed and polarized. They seem unable to summon up any positive memories or perceptions about the rejected parent and have difficulty reporting any negative aspects or experiences with the favored parent. They rewrite the history of their relationship with the rejected parent to erase pleasant moments. When confronted with evidence of an affectionate relationship, such as greeting cards, photographs, and family videos, they dismiss the evidence with the claim that they were only pretending. Distorted memories and perceptions sometimes reach bizarre proportions, as in the case of children who came to believe their mother was not their mother and that their stepmother and her family were their only maternal relatives. Uncritical acceptance of the favored parent's representations about the other parent resembles the behavior of cult victims and their dependence on the cult leader (Baker, 2007; Clawar & Rivlin, 1991; Warshak, 2010b).

With children who are severely and irrationally alienated, critical thinking about parents is nowhere in evidence. Instead the children demonstrate knee-jerk support of the favored parent's position in any situation in which the parents disagree. Some children ask to testify against a parent in court, or to speak with the judge to lobby for their favored parent's position in the litigation. One of the most pernicious signs of unreasonable alienation is what has been labeled *hatred by association*–the spread of hatred to people and even objects associated with the rejected parent, such as members of the extended family, therapists, and pets (Warshak, 2010b). Sometimes, in the absence of any intervening contact, children's thoughts about formerly beloved relatives transform from highly positive to complete devaluing.

When Vicki was finally able to get the court to appoint a therapist to work with the family, Brad spit on her during sessions and cussed at her like a sailor. Instead of delivering apologies for his disrespect he said, "She deserves it. She's not a real mother."

Brad witnessed his father cutting Vicki's picture out of old family photos. One day, Brad's father Frank found a photo of Brad and his mother on Brad's dresser. Frank confronted Brad: "What's this doing in my apartment?" and then threw the photo in the trash can. With no more being said, Brad understood that reminders of his mom were unwelcome under his dad's roof. Over time Brad learned that showing any sign of connection with his mom would provoke his father's disfavor and withdrawal and that he could court his father's favor by echoing the father's complaints about Vicki's personality, her behavior, her cooking, and her family.

Like many alienated children, Brad stopped calling his mother "Mom." (Warshak, 2010b). Instead, he referred to her either by her first name or as "the scarecrow," his father's favorite term of derision. Nevertheless, Brad insisted to the custody evaluator and the guardian ad litem (GAL) that his father had nothing to do with his alienation and that his complaints about Vicki were his own. Hostile imperious letters ostensibly written by Brad to his mother were poorly concealed conduits for the father's attacks. Although endowed with high intelligence, the language, punctuation, grammar, and syntax Brad used in these letters revealed his father's handiwork beyond a doubt.

Frank's sister maintained her close and cordial relationship with Vicki. Because of this, Frank regarded his sister as an enemy and was enraged at her "disloyalty." Seemingly overnight, Brad went from loving his aunt to refusing to have anything to do with her. Here again, although the boy's attitudes clearly developed in the shadow of his father's rage, Brad disavowed his father's influence. Instead he blamed his aunt for making him hate her, although he could not say how she did so.

Irrationality of Alienated Children

We must determine where a child's alienation rests on a continuum from rational to irrational and what the relative contributions of each parent's behavior are to the problem. We must distinguish a child who feels more resonance and rapport with one parent than with the other from the child who actively, harshly, and consistently rejects the other parent (Kelly & Johnston, 2001; Warshak, 2002, 2010b, 2010d). It is beyond the scope of this chapter to present the procedures and methods for an unbiased evaluation of the nature and roots of a child's treatment of the parents (Warshak, 2002). It is clear, however, that we cannot infer from children's words, attitudes, and behavior alone what caused them and whether they are reasonable. Alienated children, for instance, commonly disown a parent as a parent. "He is not a real father," they may say. This may be a sign of irrational alienation. Caution is needed before reaching this conclusion because children who come to appreciate that a parent has been abusive will also speak in such terms, particularly if another adult, such as a grandparent, makes up for the parent's deficiencies. (For further discussion of this issue, *see* the section later on "The Role of Mental Health Evidence in the Disposition of Severe Alienation Cases.")

This chapter concerns the subcategory of children whose alienation is not reasonably justified by the rejected parent's behavior and is not proportional to their past experience of the rejected parent. The chapter appears in a book entirely devoted to this phenomenon and not to children whose alienation or estrangement from a parent is warranted by the rejected parent's personality and behavior. Therefore, rather than include a modifying adjective each time this chapter uses the words alienation, estrangement, and PA, it should be understood that the irrational, unreasonable variant is implied if modifying adjectives do not appear before the words. This choice is intended for economy and ease of reading and does not in any way imply the absence of recognition of a category of children whose alienation and estrangement from a parent is reasonably justified by the rejected parent's behavior.

CONSEQUENCES OF SEVERE ALIENATION

Despite differences in conceptualizing and labeling PA, leading authorities regard favored parents' alienating behavior as emotional abuse of the children (Clawar & Rivlin, 1991; Gardner, 1998; Kelly & Johnston, 2001). Society's priority in dealing with abuse is to protect children from further damage and then to help them heal from the consequences of their mistreatment. In opposing interventions for alienated children, however, some advocates deny the possibility that a child's rejection of a parent could have predominantly irrational roots. The prevalence of such denial has prompted surveys addressing the issues of whether children can reject a parent whose behavior does not warrant such rejection and whether the rejection can be due in part to the influence of the favored parent. A survey taken at the Association of Family and Conciliation Courts' annual International Conference reports 98 percent agreement "in support of the basic tenet of PA: children can be manipulated by one parent to reject the other parent who does not deserve to be rejected" (Baker, Jaffe, Bernet & Johnston, 2011). Such findings make it difficult for professionals to maintain credibility while denying the existence of the phenomenon.

Accepting the reality of irrational PA, however, is not equivalent to believing that children with this condition need help to overcome it. Some commentators do not regard it as self-evident that a child who unreasonably rejects a parent is suffering a problem that is a significant departure from the norm and worthy of remediation. Walker and Shapiro (2010), for instance, believe that available data are insufficient to conclude that rejecting a parent is harmful to a child or that alienation will continue over time: "What is being termed as alienation may well be a normal variant of family structure based on many variables in that particular family system and that forcing reunification may itself be more detrimental to the parent-child relationship over a period of time." Sullivan and Kelly (2001) state, "There is no empirical data that indicates whether entrenched alienation and total permanent rejection of a biological parent has long-term deleterious effects on children's psychological development." A custody evaluator who regards Brad's behavior toward his mother as within normal limits, of short duration, and without negative developmental consequences will see little reason to recommend an intervention to overcome Brad's alienation.

The author's previous work presents considerable evidence that PA, even among adolescents, is abnormal, can persist for many years, and is associated with extensive psychological damage (Warshak, 2001, 2003a, 2010c; Hands & Warshak, 2011). In intact and in divorced families, PA is a departure from the norm with only a very small percentage of teenagers being estranged from a parent (Bezilla, 1988; Bibby, 2009; Offer, Ostrov, Howard & Atkinson, 1988). After divorce, most children want more contact, not less, with their parents (Fabricius & Hall, 2000; Parkinson, Cashmore & Single, 2005; Schwartz & Finley, 2009; Wallerstein & Kelly, 1980; Warshak & Santrock, 1983).

Persistence of Parental Alienation

The literature fails to support the idea that PA is a transient blip in a child's developmental trajectory. Warshak (2010c) reports an intervention study in which the average length of time of alienation was 2.5 years, with some children having been alienated for as long as five years, where none gave any indication that the alienation would abate. In a sample of adults who reported being alienated as children, the disrupted parent-child relationship lasted for at least six years in all cases and continued for more than twenty-two years for half the sample (Baker, 2007). Gardner (2001) reports thirty-three cases in which alienation persisted for more than two years. In a sample of college students, 29 percent from divorced homes were alienated from a parent (Hands & Warshak, 2011). Clearly, PA can, but does not necessarily, persist beyond high school. A fifteen to twenty-year follow-up study of thirty-seven young adults who received counseling concluded that "virtually all" subsequently reconciled with the rejected parent during their late teens or early twenties (Johnston & Goldman, 2010). Even the researcher whose work has been cited to support the proposition that PA resolves by the age of eighteen and usually within one or two years refers to the lasting damage caused by parents who manipulate children to turn against their other parent (Wallerstein & Blakeslee, 1989). Missing out on even two formative years of parent-child contact means an accumulation of lost experiences that can never be recovered.

RATIONALE FOR INTERVENTIONS

Some custody evaluators, parents, and attorneys oppose interventions for alienated children if the parent-child relationship problem is seen as an exception to a child's good adjustment in other spheres, such as in school and with peers. Particularly with adolescents, some professionals believe that if the child is doing well in other aspects of life, the child should be empowered to make decisions regarding contact with a parent. Some professionals argue against court-ordered counseling for resistant youth because it is unsuccessful and leaves them feeling angry toward the court or the rejected parent (Johnston & Goldman, 2010). Other professionals counsel a hands-off policy toward these children because of the relative dearth of studies that document long-term damage of growing up irrationally alienated from a parent.

Alleviating Current Impairments

Those who work directly with families in which a child's affections have been poisoned against a parent and other relatives do not believe that good adjustment in other areas trumps the need to relieve children and their parents from unreasonable alienation. Children such as Brad, who suffer irrational anxiety or hatred of a parent and declare a wish to completely erase a good parent from their lives, cannot be said to be functioning reasonably well (Warshak, 2010a). At the very least, unreasonably rejecting a parent is no less serious a problem than are other irrational aversions and anxieties, such as avoidance of school, peers, or open spaces. Severely alienated children suffer significant impairments in their cognitive, emotional, and behavioral development (Johnston, Walters & Olesen, 2005; Kelly, 2010). They maintain a highly distorted view of a parent. They are unable to give and receive love from a good parent. They behave in an extremely negative, defiant, disobedient, and hostile manner. If these children were living in an intact family, we would not doubt the wisdom of addressing rather than ignoring the problem. A family therapist, facing a parent-child conflict in a two-parent home, might advise a parent to temporarily withdraw to her room and regroup when conflict escalates. The therapist, however, would never advise the rejected parent to move out of the home and grant the child's stated wish to have no contact with the parent.

We do not need to cite the long-term consequences of PA in order to justify the importance of addressing the problem. The family's dysfunction in the present is sufficient justification for intervention (Buchanan, Maccoby, & Dornbusch, 1991; Johnston et al., 2005; Lampel, 1996). In addition to alleviating the child's obvious impairments, interventions are needed to improve the functioning of both parents. Some MHPs and lawyers too readily counsel rejected parents to accept the situation and wait passively for the child's return. Those who make recommendations and decisions for these families should understand that the family is suffering and should be aware of the immense tragedy for a child to lose a parent and for a parent to lose a child.

We can better appreciate what is at stake when PA is seen through the eyes of a parent who is the victim. One mother put it this way:

> It is like your child has died, but you can't go through the normal grieving process. Instead you are stuck in this Twilight Zone-like nightmare with no end in sight. You know your child is being abused, and this *is* child abuse pure and simple, but no one will help you save their hijacked souls and you are forced to stand and watch, with your hands tied behind your back. (personal communication)

She described what the literature labels *ambiguous loss* or *complicated loss,* more difficult to resolve than grief over death of a child because it defies closure (Boss, 2006). She also identified the pain of standing by helplessly while the child's character is corrupted.

Vicki witnessed Brad's identity as a person capable of giving and receiving love from two parents slip away, leaving in its wake a hardened, hateful, emotionally handicapped, at times violent, brat. She understood that her son's behavior was symptomatic of great suffering and risks to his character development and future adjustment. She could not understand why the professionals who studied her situation were so reluctant to recommend effective remedies and instead counseled her to accept the situation.

In addition to the emotional impact on families, PA is implicated in violence, suicides, and homicides. An example is a father who alienated his children and then conspired with them to kill their mother. According to the Associated Press article about the case, the district attorney, explicitly recognizing the power of the father's influence, charged the man with having "coerced, persuaded and enticed his children to commit this atrocious crime upon their mother" (Fray, 2010).

Longer-Term Sequelae and Risks

Research on the long-term outcome for families with alienated children is still in its early stages (Baker, 2007; Gordon, 1998; Hands & Warshak, 2011; Rand & Rand, 2006; Wallerstein & Blakeslee, 1989). Nonrandom samples of convenience and the limitations of qualitative research and clinical observations limit how much we can generalize from available results. We can extrapolate long-term outcomes, however, from several well-developed lines of investigation. These include the impact of exposure to poorly managed parental conflict, the consequences of intrusive parenting, and the risks to future development associated with parental absence and unresolved conflicts with parents.

One of the most robust findings in the child development literature on divorce is the negative link between child adjustment and exposure to poorly managed interparental conflict (Kelly, 2005). Children whose parents ask them to carry hostile messages to the other parent or whose parents denigrate each other show more negative sequelae (Buchanan et al., 1991).

The literature on parenting most relevant to understanding the consequences of parental alienating behavior are studies on parental psychological control, also called intrusive parenting. This is defined as parenting behavior that "constrains, invalidates, and manipulates children's psychological and emotional experience and expression" (Barber, 1996; Barber, Stolz & Olsen, 2005). Examples of psychological control include "If I have hurt her feelings, she stops talking to me until I please her again." "Is less friendly to me if I don't see things his way." The concept of intrusive parenting was not created with alienated children in mind, but "manipulating children's psychological and emotional experience and expression" is precisely how authorities on the psychology of alienated children describe the negative influence of the favored parent (Clawar & Rivlin, 1991; Warshak, 2010c). This type of manipulative parenting is linked to subsequent higher levels of depression and antisocial behavior (Barber et al., 2005).

Higher risk for depression is also one of the known long-term hazards of parental absence during childhood (e.g., Amato, 1991). The risk is found regardless of the reason for parental absence. Some of the dynamics of this elevated risk may not apply to situations where parental absence is caused by the child's rejection, but most of the identified reasons for the negative impact of parental absence are relevant to the risks faced by an estranged child growing up apart from a parent and without that parent's psychological contributions to development. In addition, a child who holds a parent in contempt risks feeling contempt for the aspects of his own personality that reflect identifications with the rejected parent. The resulting diminished self-esteem may contribute to depression. A child cannot escape the knowledge that each parent is part of him. It is difficult to harbor great contempt for a parent without, at some level, feeling terribly impaired.

This discussion of the long-term damage associated with PA is concluded by calling attention to the vast literature on theories, research, and experience in the fields of child development and psychotherapy that demonstrates the handicapping effects of damaged and conflicted parent-child relationships on future psychological adjustment. The principle that family-of-origin relationships influence the trajectory of future relationships and life adjustment not only is the foundation of many different schools of psychotherapy and developmental psychology, it has reached the status of a truism in contemporary culture (e.g., Bowen, 1978; Framo, 1992; Sabatelli & Bartle-Haring, 2003). The loss is multiplied when the child is unable to receive and share love with an entire extended family (Levitt, 2005).

PREVENTION OF SEVERE PARENTAL ALIENATION

Overcoming severe alienation usually involves extensive litigation, multiple failed attempts to modify the behaviors of the favored parent and child, and sometimes an intensive intervention, all of which take a lot of money and time. The longer the process takes, the more the losses accumulate. The longer the absence of contact between parent and child, the more lost opportunities for the creation of family memories. School performances, music and dance recitals, scouting trips, science fair projects, sports events, proms, graduation ceremonies–all memories marred by the parent missing from the photographs.

Parent and Child Education Programs

The emotional and financial costs of severe alienation, and the obstacles to its alleviation, highlight the importance of directing resources and efforts to the goal of prevention and early identification of children at risk (Warshak, 2010a, 2011c). Parent education programs are one promising avenue toward this goal. We have strong evidence that many parents going through a divorce can be taught to improve the quality of their parenting and coparenting and that this leads to better outcomes for children (Sigal, Sandler, Wolchik & Braver, 2011).

The effectiveness of court-connected education programs for divorcing parents has yet to be rigorously evaluated. With one significant exception, however, parents report being very satisfied with the program they attended. The exception is the complaint from parents throughout the country that the program failed to prevent a child from aligning with one parent against the other.

Reviews of face-to-face and online divorce education programs provide descriptions of their content and goals (Bowers, Mitchell, Hardesty & Hughes, 2011; Kierstead, 2011; Sigal et al., 2011). An analysis of this content reveals a key omission that accounts for the dissatisfaction expressed by alienated parents. The programs teach about the impact of parental conflict on children and the importance of avoiding alienating behavior. They offer no guidance, however, on how to respond when the other parent engages in alienating behavior that places the children at risk for joining in a campaign of denigration and rejection. The programs exhort parents to refrain from behaviors that encourage alienation, but they make no suggestions to proactively protect children from succumbing to a parent's alienating behavior or to stem the tide of alienation before it becomes severe. In short, parents receive no advice on how to respond effectively to the challenges posed by their children's rejection and provocative, contemptuous behavior. As a result, alienated parents typically make mistakes that compound the problem (Warshak, 2010b). These mistakes make it more difficult for the custody evaluator and court to understand the roots of the problem. Vicki learned from her court-assigned parenting program to avoid bad-mouthing Frank. She learned nothing about what she could do to nip the alienation in the bud.

It is perhaps for this reason that when the focus of litigation is PA, some courts require parents to read and deliver a book report on *Divorce Poison: How to Protect Your Family from Bad-mouthing and Brainwashing* (Warshak, 2010b). Readers of this book sound a common and disturbing theme. They believe that the book's guidance and understanding would have prevented years of suffering. They wish they knew at the onset of their divorce what they know now. Divorce education programs should include modules that fulfill this need.

Parent education programs are only one part of a comprehensive prevention formula. Programs for children who are at risk of becoming alienated may help them develop the skills and mindset to resist efforts by one parent to turn them against the other. Child education programs can include materials such as the video *Welcome Back, Pluto: Understanding, Preventing, and Overcoming Parental Alienation*™, available through plutodvd.com (Warshak & Otis, 2010b). Although the effectiveness of the video has not yet been systematically evaluated, anecdotal reports, comments posted on the Internet; and reviews by children, parents, attorneys, MHPs, and judges are encouraging (Levy & Sauber, 2010). These sources attest to the program's immediate positive impact on children, adolescents, and young adults who are or were subjected to a parent's alienating behavior.

Psychotherapy

Courts will often appoint a psychotherapist or counselor to work with families in which a child is exposed to alienating influences or is beginning to resist contact with a parent. In the early stages of alienation such treatment may help a child avoid aligning with one parent against the other. The literature presents several models and strategies but lacks rigorous outcome data (Carter, 2011; Eddy, 2009; Freeman, Abel, Cowper-Smith & Stein, 2004; Johnston & Goldman, 2010; Sullivan, Ward & Deutsch, 2010). One study reports the successful use of a family-focused intervention to prevent severe alienation in "a considerable number of cases" of children identified as at risk for alienation, with "only a few cases" having negative outcomes (Friedlander & Walters, 2010). The authors base their preliminary conclusions on unspecified "feedback and clinical judgment" that await support by more systematic and reliable outcome data.

In a comprehensive overview of the literature, Fidler and Bala (2010) conclude that "counseling or psychotherapy tend to be suitable for mild and some moderate cases." Psychotherapy is unlikely to prevent the entrenchment of alienation in cases that involve an favored parent who is determined to erase the other parent from the child's life and who suffers a personality disorder or otherwise has little chance of gaining insight about the children's need to maintain a good relationship with the rejected parent. Favored parents will commonly either demean the entire enterprise of mental health treatment or undermine the treatment at the first sign that the therapist believes the alienation is unreasonable and that the child should be required to spend time with the rejected parent.

When the court accepted Vicki's motion for court-appointed counseling, Frank told Brad, "Your mother thinks you're crazy and that's why she is making you see a counselor. You don't need any counseling. She's the crazy one."

Detailed and Unambiguous Court Orders

Parenting coordinators and therapists who work with high-conflict cases agree on the importance of the court's issuing detailed and clear orders. A parent who is intent on obstructing the child's contact with the rejected parent will exploit every loophole and ambiguity in the orders to accomplish this goal. For instance, the parent may claim that the child is coming down with a cold and cannot make the shift between homes will sabotage court-ordered treatment because the orders failed to specify which parent is responsible for getting the child to the therapist. Attorneys who represent rejected parents should anticipate every conceivable excuse to keep children from their clients and then ensure that the orders protect against these contingencies. If this is done at the stage of the initial temporary orders, it could help prevent alienation from taking root and becoming more severe.

Attempts to corrupt a child's view of a parent most effectively crowd out the child's positive feelings and memories when the child has no reminders of the parent's love and no time to enjoy that parent (Gardner, 1998). The child becomes more dependent on the favored parent and more likely to see the rejected parent through the distorting lens of the parent doing the badmouthing.

When their parents separate, children have no norms about what to expect. If they have regular contact with both parents from the outset, this becomes the status quo and the norm. If they lose contact with a parent, this comes to represent what they regard as normal. The longer children are apart from a parent, the stronger the negative attitudes, the more resistance to change, and the more difficulty reuniting children with their rejected parent. The longer the children's wills dominate the behavior of adults, the more difficult it will be for the children to appreciate and accept that decisions about contact are not theirs to make.

Rapid and Effective Enforcement of Court Orders

Even the most unambiguous and detailed orders will not help if they are not enforced. A parent who obstructs the children's contact with the other parent may benefit from the status quo.

In the *Matter of Miller and Todd* (Miller & Todd, 161 N.H.), a New Hampshire court awarded custody to a mother who successfully interfered with the father-child relationship. The court found that the mother alienated the children from their father but reasoned that the children had spent the majority of their lives with her and that was where they felt most comfortable. This is typical for such cases. The absence of contact establishes a status quo that the court honors in order to spare the children drastic changes.

The New Hampshire Supreme Court vacated the award (In the *Matter of James J. Miller and Janet S. Todd*). It recognized that the father was denied contact with his children for more than two years and that awarding custody to the mother because of the lack of father-child contact rewards the mother for violating court orders. The decision quoted the Vermont Supreme Court: "Although obviously well intended, the court's decision effectively condoned a parent's willful alienation of a child from the other parent. Its ruling sends the unacceptable message that others might, with impunity, engage in similar misconduct. Left undisturbed, the court's decision would nullify the principle that the best interests of the child are furthered through a healthy and loving relationship with both parents." (*Begins v. Begins,* 721 A.2d 469, 470-71 [VT. 1998]).

This reasoning gives voice to the most frequent complaint parents make regarding their custody litigation: Repeated violations of orders go unpunished, with some parents making a mockery of the court's authority. Experts agree. According to the well-known divorce authority Joan Kelly

> A significant number of these parents have come to believe that noncompliance with court orders, whether for facilitating contact between the child and rejected parent or attending divorce education classes or therapy, brings no negative consequences. (Kelly, 2010)

Brad remained apart from his mother for four years as the litigation slogged through a quicksand of legal maneuvering and failed psychotherapeutic attempts to remedy the problem. Eventually, Vicki prevailed. The court awarded her sole custody. Brad participated in a Family Bridges intervention developed by Randy Rand and described later, and mother and son recovered a normal relationship.

When asked about the years apart, Brad said that when he ran away he never expected to remain with his father. He knew that "the rules" called for him living part-time with each parent. In the past, when he got mad at a parent, he would go to his room until he calmed down. He assumed that he would return later the same day to his mother. He did not know that things would work differently after divorce. Like many children in his situation, he said that he never really stopped loving his mom and was surprised that the adults, and the court for a long time, allowed him to stay apart from her and essentially take family law into his own hands.

Years of suffering could have been prevented if, on the day Brad ran away, the police retrieved him, gave him a stern lecture, and returned him to his mother. The police were more likely to have done so if Vicki could have shown them court orders that clearly anticipated such an event and directed law enforcement personnel to enforce the parenting plan. Instead, the police told Vicki, "This is a family matter and we cannot intervene. You need to go through the courts." Frank would have been less likely to harbor Brad if Frank expected that the court would act swiftly to sanction him for violating the orders.

The lessons for attorneys who represent clients whose children are at risk for becoming alienated are to: (1) ensure your client's regular contact with the children, (2) secure orders that have teeth in them for noncompliance, and (3) move quickly for sanctions when orders are violated.

DISPOSITION OF SEVERE ALIENATION CASES

When prevention efforts fail or are unavailable and severe alienation cases reach the courtroom, their disposition falls into four general categories (Warshak, 2010c). These four options include variations on two dimensions: (1) the custody and access schedule and (2) the degree to which the court relies on interventions to build healthier family relationships. The first dimension clearly is within the traditional scope of the court's authority. The second raises questions about the proper reach of the court in these matters (Bruch, 2001).

The four options for primary custodial placement of alienated children are with (1) the favored parent accompanied by court-ordered efforts to remedy the problems, (2) the rejected parent, (3) neither parent, and (4) the favored parent with no scheduled contacts with the rejected parent.

Custody with the Favored Parent Plus Efforts To Remedy Alienation

The first option places the child with the favored parent and relies on parent education, counseling, and parenting coordination to promote healing in the family. Variations of this option either accept the child's refusal of contact pending the outcome of counseling; increase the child's scheduled time with the rejected parent, sometimes by as much as half the time; or gradually increase the amount of time the child spends under the care of the rejected parent. In some cases, initial contacts take place with oversight by the counselor or another party.

Many children who participate in court-ordered therapy do so with overt resistance and reluctance. Parents who support or accept their children's rejection of the other parent often lack motivation to participate in therapy aimed at healing the damaged parent-child relationship. Thus, an element of coercion accompanies court-mandated therapy with sanctions for noncompliance. Children who want no contact with a parent are essentially forced against their will to have such contact in, and sometimes out of, therapy sessions. One new program, Overcoming Barriers Family Camp, initially hoped to elicit voluntary attendance from favored parents and alienated children (who live with the favored parent) but soon learned that such cooperation was absent without a court order (Sullivan et al., 2010). This finding comes as no surprise to professionals who have experience working with families with severely alienated children. The organizers of the family camp believed that perhaps they could attract families with less severely alienated children to attend voluntarily; if so, this would situate the program outside the options available for severely alienated children and perhaps more in line with preventive interventions implemented at an earlier stage.

Restricting communication between the children and the favored parent when they are with the other parent can enhance the effectiveness of plans that leave children primarily in their favored parent's care. It is common for favored parents to use communications to suggest to the children that they are not having a good time, to convey the hope that the children are unhappy, to encourage them to ask to come home early, and to encourage them to withdraw from the rejected parent. Rejected parents commonly complain that as soon as the children arrive they receive text messages asking them if they are ready to return home.

The favored parent and child may be more motivated to comply with court orders if the court makes it clear that failure to comply, or unsuccessful repair of the damaged relationship, will most likely lead to an increase in the parenting time awarded to the rejected parent and perhaps supervised, monitored, or suspended contact between the child and the favored parent.

Attempts to remedy alienation while the child lives with the favored parent are most likely to succeed when alienation is in its earlier stages, when counseling has not yet been attempted, when the favored parent is apt to comply with court orders, and when the favored parent is able and willing to get the children to comply with treatment and with a schedule of contact with the rejected parent. The latter condition can be difficult to assess accurately in cases that return to court after a failed course of psychotherapy.

When the favored parent worries that an evaluator, GAL, or the court is likely to hold the favored parent in large measure responsible for the children's alienation and might place the children primarily with the rejected parent, often the favored parent encourages the children to pretend that they have overcome their alienation. Cooperative and polite behavior replaces the former avoidance and disrespect. The children begin to comply willingly with orders for contact. Through such means as texts and greeting cards signed with love, they help create a record that the favored parent subsequently uses to argue in favor of maintaining the status quo.

Evaluators and the court may be taken in by this ploy. As soon as the current round of litigation ends, the children revert to their former disrespectful, resentful, and avoidant behavior. By the time this becomes evident and the rejected parent can get the case back before the judge, it may be too late. The child may reach her or his eighteenth birthday and no longer be subject to family court decisions, or she or he may reach midadolescence, at which time some courts reduce expectations for compliance with a court-ordered residential schedule.

In other instances, the rapid shift in behavior on the eve of litigation accomplishes the opposite result. It exposes the power that the favored parent has wielded all along to remedy the problem and underscores that parent's role in fomenting, strengthening, and supporting the children's suffering. At the same time, it reveals a previously unseen malleability in the behavior of the favored parent and children when sufficiently motivated by the court's authority.

The sham, intended to convince the court to take a hands-off approach, instead helps the evaluator and the court appreciate that the successful resolution of alienation requires the court's unambivalent expectations, oversight, and enforcement. When the children believe that, as far as the court is concerned, failure is not an option, they are more likely to engage meaningfully in efforts to repair the damaged relationship. The fear of getting the favored parent in trouble with the court provides children with a face-saving excuse to "follow the rules" and return to a normal relationship with the other parent. The children then feel relieved to shed the burden of having to disrespect one parent for fear of disappointing the other.

Leaving the children with their favored parent may be less stressful for some children in the short run and may be a default option if the court determines that the rejected parent lacks the capacity to assume full-time care of the children. In terms of alleviating alienation, however, option one has significant drawbacks. According to the consensus of studies, treatment of severely alienated children while they remain apart from the rejected parent and with a parent who has not helped overcome the alienation is more likely to fail than to succeed and may make matters worse by further entrenching the child's distorted perceptions of the rejected parent (Fidler & Bala, 2010; Warshak, 2003a). This is true for all models of treatment of severely alienated children proposed in the literature. Extending unsuccessful treatment while the child remains with the favored parent carries the hazards of delaying, and in some cases preventing, the eventual delivery of effective help.

Custody evaluators and GALs often prefer this option because they believe it is less intrusive and requires less of an adjustment on the children's part than removing the children from the primary care of the favored parent. Typically, court orders for treatment under this option are open ended with vague and nonspecific treatment goals (e.g., to reunify the parent and child or to improve the parent-child relationship). If treatment fails (which is more likely than not with severely alienated children who have no contact with the rejected parent outside of therapy sessions), the rejected parent wants to return to court as soon as possible (assuming finances allow), whereas the favored parent delays the process as long as possible. When the case is back before the court, the judge is likely to order an updated evaluation by the original evaluator. The timing of the reevaluation is subject to the evaluator's schedule and is usually prolonged by the favored parent's obstructive and delay tactics. The longer the delay, the older the children, and the more accustomed they are to living apart from a parent, the less likely the court is to overturn the status quo. For these reasons, recommendations and court orders for option one should include specification of a time frame, criteria for evaluating the success of treatment, and contingency plans in the event that the treatment is ineffective.

In evaluating the impact of interventions accompanying any of the four options, it is essential to determine whether results go beyond superficial or short-lived responses (Freeman et al., 2004; Kelly, 2010; Warshak, 2010c). Intervention outcome studies should distinguish between children's cooperation and enjoyment of a program in its early stages; their understanding of concepts that may facilitate reconciliation; their successful modification of thoughts, emotions, and behaviors associated with the repair of damaged relationships upon completion of a program; and their maintenance of the gains over the long term. For instance, some therapists believe they are making progress when they succeed in arranging for a resistant child to have some contact with a rejected parent. In some cases, the children have contact only during therapy sessions or during the intervention program, and the children regress to an alienated stance upon returning home. In other cases the intervention concludes before bringing the children closer to a positive relationship with the rejected parent. Such programs may not hold much hope for these injured families unless the contacts during the intervention facilitate subsequent successful therapeutic efforts.

Overcoming Barriers, a promising intervention that aims to help children feel freer to show connection with both parents, reports, "In many ways it has been an extraordinarily successful program." A key element for this conclusion apparently stems from participants' ratings of satisfaction given during exit interviews with ten families (Sullivan et al., 2010). Such ratings are encouraging, but we cannot rule out the influence of social desirability and impression management in interpreting the expressed satisfaction. This concern is especially relevant given that the parents, and perhaps some of the children, were aware that the therapists were writing specific recommendations for aftercare treatment and such input might be introduced during subsequent litigation. Follow-up from the five families that participated in the pilot camp is not encouraging when it comes to the behavioral, emotional, and cognitive dimensions of the children's alienation. A relatively large proportion of the rejected parents who participated in the camp subsequently contacted this author to report either no change or intensification of the alienation. The Overcoming Barriers camp has launched alternative programs, apparently tailored to families with less severe alienation. Given the investment of time, the commitment of its organizers, and the considerable personnel cost, with three doctoral-level psychologists and a one-to-one staff-to-camper ratio, the program's disappointing results in families with severely alienated children are a testament to the enormous difficulty of overcoming the problem while children remain with the favored parent..

Custody with the Rejected Parent

The second option places the child with the rejected parent with either temporary or permanent orders. This option may keep contact between the child and the favored parent or may temporarily suspend contact until certain conditions are met. In some cases, children spend the entire summer with the rejected parent. This gives uninterrupted time to repair the relationship but is less of an adjustment for the children, some of whom are used to spending summers on a teen tour or in sleep-away camp apart from both parents. The court may or may not order interventions for the family when children are placed with the rejected parent.

In *In the Matter of James J. Miller and Janet S. Todd* (2011), the New Hampshire Supreme Court cited favorably an opinion from a Vermont case: "Across the country, the great weight of authority holds that conduct by one parent that tends to alienate the child's affections from the other is so inimical to the child's welfare as to be grounds for a denial of custody to, or a change of custody from, the parent guilty of such conduct" (*Renaud v. Renaud*). An analysis of 175 Canadian cases found this option to be the most common response when the court determined that alienation had occurred (Bala, Hunt & McCarney, 2010). Canadian appellate decisions have generally affirmed transfer of custody to the rejected parent (Bala et al., 2010).

Research on this option shows this to be effective in overcoming severe alienation (Warshak, 2003a). A study of 700 cases published by the American Bar Association reports

> Of the approximately four hundred cases we have seen where the courts have increased the contact with the rejected parent (and in half of these, over the objection of the children), there has been positive change in 90% of the relationships between the child and the rejected parent. (Clawar & Rivlin, 1991, p. 150)

A meta-analysis of 515 studies confirms the core proposition of intergroup contact theory that, under the right conditions, contact between opposing groups lessens hostility and prejudice (Brown & Hewstone, 2005; Pettigrew & Tropp, 2006). These findings help to explain the benefits of option two for children who harbor unwarranted hostility fueled by negative stereotypes of the rejected parent.

Courts may temporarily suspend the children's contact with the favored parent in order to: (1) protect the children from what the court determines is an emotionally abusive or unhealthy parenting environment; (2) remove the children from exposure to efforts to undermine their relationship with the rejected parent; (3) make it easier for the children to focus on rebuilding a stable, positive relationship; (4) motivate the children to heal the damaged relationship with the rejected parent; and (5) give the favored parent time and motivation to move from a focus on the presumed flaws of the rejected parent to a focus on his or her own conduct and on how best to meet the children's needs.

A drawback of this approach is that the children may, but do not inevitably, experience more stress in the short run, particularly if the family receives no help to adjust during the transition period. The author and his colleagues offer an intensive educational workshop, Family Bridges, designed to assist families with this transition (Warshak, 2010a, 2010c, Warshak & Otis, 2010a). At the time this text is published, this workshop is the only intervention that has documented a high rate of success in overcoming severe alienation.

Another potential drawback of placement with the rejected parent is that in cases in which the parents live a considerable distance apart from each other, this option may require a change of schools and communities. The court may determine that the risks to the child of losing part of his family far outweigh the risks of adjusting to a change of schools or a geographical change.

In many litigated cases, severely alienated children have long felt empowered and entitled to make their own decisions about whether and under what circumstances they will have contact with the rejected parent. When the court issues an order for placement with the rejected parent, some children threaten to defy court orders, run away, or do violence to themselves or others. Threats to act in dangerous and destructive ways must receive serious attention. Some alienated children are at risk for acting out against the parent they profess to hate. The potential risks must be weighed against the potential benefits and should be taken into account in structuring family transitions. They must also be evaluated in the context of reports that children often make empty threats that evaporate when they realize that the court will not acquiesce to their demands (Clawar & Rivlin, 1991; Warshak, 2010c, 2011b).

No study has ever documented that reversing custody harms severely alienated children. No study has reported that adults, who as children complied with expectations to repair a damaged relationship with a parent, later regret having been obliged to do so. On the other hand, studies of adults who were allowed to disown a parent find that they regret that decision and report long-term problems with guilt and depression that they attribute to having been allowed to reject one of their parents (Baker, 2007).

Placement Apart from Both Parents

The third option places the child apart from both parents. This could be with a relative, boarding school, therapeutic residential school, college preparatory school, military academy, or foster home (Ellis, 2005, Sullivan & Kelly, 2001). It is important to avoid placement with a person whose behavior contributes to or supports the child's irrational alienation. This option may be desirable in cases in which the court wants to reduce the children's contact with the favored parent but the rejected parent is unable to assume the full-time care of the children. It is also an option when the children need to be removed from the favored parent's care but cannot safely live with the rejected parent. In some cases, the placement is temporary or designed to facilitate a subsequent and perhaps gradual transition to the custody of the rejected parent (Gardner, 2001). In some cases children feel freer to reconnect with the rejected parent when they are outside the immediate orbit of their favored parent, as in the case of college students who live away from home (Johnston & Goldman, 2010; Warshak, 2011b).

A benefit of this approach is that it removes children from direct exposure to family tensions and allows them to concentrate on their own development. Psychotherapy conducted with children when they are away from their parents and associated pressures may have greater success assisting them to develop more balanced perceptions of each parent. Sullivan and Kelly (2001) see this as possibly the least detrimental alternative for adolescents who are functioning poorly, are subject to parental pressures to align with one against the other, are exposed to chronic conflict between the parents, and have been unable to find relief from prior interventions.

A drawback of this option is that the child forgoes regular face-to-face contact with both parents, yet may not be spared alienating influences through other means of communication. Also, the expense of residential schools is outside the reach of most families.

No studies have been located that report conclusions about the efficacy of third-party placements in overcoming a child's severe alienation. This author's experience with families who have exercised this option is that it can bring the anticipated benefits. One mother said,

> I have had more contact with my son in the past month that he has been away at school than in the past three years that my children have been alienated from me. The environment at the school has allowed him to be a "normal" 16-year-old boy and not have to live in the day-to-day adult conflict. While I do not see him as often, we have more frequent and better communication. (personal communication)

An additional benefit is that the school keeps the rejected parent informed about the child's schedule; activities; and academic, emotional, and social adjustment. In severe alienation cases, the favored parent usually strives to conceal from the rejected parent any information about the children and their activities.

Custody with the Favored Parent, No Scheduled Contacts with the Rejected Parent, and No Court-Ordered Intervention

The fourth option places the child with the favored parent and suspends contact with the rejected parent unless and until the child elects to make contact. In essence this option surrenders attempts to remedy severe alienation. Instead, the court acquiesces to the child's demands to remove all expectations for contact with the rejected parent and empowers the child to make these decisions. This option is usually seen as a last resort exercised for such reasons as the following:

- The court concludes that time itself will heal the problem and relieve the child's suffering,
- The court concludes that no resolution is possible or feasible without doing greater damage,
- The court determines that it is beyond its power or authority to force a child to have contact with a rejected parent,
- The court concludes that it is helpless to prevent the favored parent and child from sabotaging scheduled contacts with the rejected parent,
- The court determines that the child has sufficient maturity, long-term perspective, and independence of judgment to be competent to make a decision,
- The child will need effective professional assistance to adjust to living with the rejected parent and such help either is unavailable or unaffordable,

- The rejected parent is unable or unwilling to invest the time and money in litigation or unwilling to expect resistant children to participate in an intervention designed to alleviate the problems.

The main benefits of this option are that it may provide short-term relief for the child, avoids potential adjustment problems in overturning the status quo, and may allow the child to function well in the short term in areas not directly related to the parent-child relationship such as school and relationships with peers and other adults.

The drawbacks of this approach, particularly when the child has refused to cooperate with the court-ordered residential schedule, are considerable. They include:

- The child and the favored parent may interpret this as parental abandonment, despite the history of the rejected parent's attempting to re-establish contact.
- The child is encouraged to avoid rather than to manage conflict.
- The child's irrational beliefs about the rejected parent could be reinforced.
- If the favored parent's behavior is considered to be a form of emotional abuse, the court facilitates the child's continued exposure to toxic parenting rather than protecting the child from further mistreatment.
- The child receives no help to better understand her or his relationship with each parent and therefore has no ability to reduce the likelihood of future problems related to a loss of such magnitude.
- A child who has repeatedly flouted court orders for contact, threatens to misbehave if the court does not endorse his or her preferences, and in the end successfully trumps the court's authority will continue to believe that the child is entitled to dictate the terms of his or her relationship with his or her parents. The child will experience his or her disrespect and demands as effective means to gain compliance from adults and may generalize the experience to conclude that the law can be ignored with impunity.
- The child loses the benefits of the rejected parent's contributions, involvement, and expressions of love. Research identifies the importance of the child's healthy relationship with two parents (Kelly & Emery, 2003). In many cases of severe alienation, the child is losing the healthier of the two parents.
- The child runs the risk of suffering a lifelong estrangement from the rejected parent, with all the psychological consequences of such a loss, including the intergenerational loss that the child's future children (the

grandchildren of the rejected parent) may suffer by being deprived of a relationship with their grandparent.

- Even if the child and rejected parent eventually reconcile, they have lost years of involvement, a loss that often includes the extended family.
- In the future, the child may suffer regret, shame, and guilt for having rejected the parent (Warshak, 2003b). This is compounded when the child realizes the grief suffered by a parent who loses a child.

THE ROLE OF MENTAL HEALTH EVIDENCE

Cases with severely alienated children present unique challenges in family law. Their disposition requires a multifactored best-interests analysis rather than a uniform solution (Warshak, 2011a). Testimony by mental health experts in severe alienation cases is most helpful to the court and more likely to be judged as reliable when the witness has the training, credentials, and experience to understand and communicate the nuances of a competent evaluation of alienation allegations.

Some experts proffer opinions on issues related to custody evaluations, such as how to evaluate the relative contributions of each parent to a child's alienation, despite their lack of knowledge, training, or experience in conducting clinical and forensic evaluations. This leaves their testimony open to reliability challenges and impeachment on the grounds of the witness' inadequate qualifications.

Zealous advocates with extreme positions about certain issues (e.g., PA, child abuse, or domestic violence) may see all cases through a single lens. They quickly reach conclusions about the nature and roots of children's alienation with inadequate attention to alternative interpretations of the data. They may selectively and heavily rely on a few studies, often their own, without citing studies that reach different conclusions and without assisting the court in understanding the limitations of their own research. The result is biased testimony that lacks trustworthiness (Campbell & Lorandos, 2001; *Daubert v. Merrell Dow Pharmaceuticals,* 1993; Zervopoulos, 2008).

In some cases, the court relies heavily on mental health expert evidence and testimony in reaching the decision to place a severely alienated child with the favored parent and suspend contact with the rejected parent either with or without ongoing treatment (options one and four discussed earlier). Effective cross-examination of mental health experts often uncovers the absence or paucity of their experience in overcoming severe alienation. With very few exceptions, the expert's experience is limited to working on cases with children who remain primarily in the care of the favored parent or those whom the court places with the rejected parent but they receive no effective help to adjust to the court orders. The expert has no long-term experience with children who present as severely alienated and who, in a reasonable length of time, recover affectionate feelings, correct cognitive distortions, and resume normal behavior with the parent who had been rejected.

Older and smarter children can be very convincing in their accounts of poor treatment at the hands of the rejected parent and in their accounts of a past history that lacks warmth, affection, and good experiences with that parent. They make trenchant criticisms of a parent that appear mature, reasonable, and based on their own experience of the parent. They may convince evaluators and therapists that they are unwilling or incapable of modifying their negative behavior and attitudes about the rejected parent. An expert may believe that because a child apparently feels so strongly about avoiding a parent, the court has no viable option other than to give children what they demand. Such an expert may offer an opinion that is shaped primarily by the degree of the child's expressed resistance to reunification and the expert's unsubstantiated belief that attempted reunification necessarily entails considerable risk to the child's well-being with little expectation of accomplishing the goal of normalizing the relationship. Such an opinion cannot be defended as reliable in the legal sense of being trustworthy (*Daubert,* 1993).

MHPs who have worked with abused children in child protection settings understand that children may protest being removing from a harmful environment yet demonstrate rapid relief once this occurs (Block, Oran, Oran, Baumrind & Goodman, 2010; Goldsmith, Oppenheim & Wanlass, 2004). Experts with sufficient experience in helping children adjust to court orders that place them with the rejected parent and suspend contact with the favored parent for an extended period of time have the opportunity to witness the speed with which children and adolescents recover their submerged desire and ability to relate affectionately to the parent (Warshak, 2010d). Within this context, experts are less apt to be persuaded by children's strong protests and more likely to have confidence in the prospects of a better future for the parent-child relationship.

In cases with alienated adolescents, expert testimony can educate the court about the suggestibility of adolescents, their vulnerability to external influence, and their susceptibility to immature judgment and behavior (Loftus, 2003; Steinberg, Cauffman, Woolard, Graham, & Banich, 2009; Steinberg & Scott, 2003). These limitations are well-known in the fields of adolescent development and neuropsychology and account in part for the consensus view of psychologists that juveniles merit different treatment in the legal system than what adults receive (American Psychological Association, 2004).

Lack of relevant experience leads professionals to: (1) underestimate the difficulty children have in overcoming negative attitudes while remaining exposed to the favored parent; (2) underestimate the likelihood that the child's stated preferences fail to reflect the full range of the child's genuine feelings; (3) overestimate the difficulty of gaining compliance with court orders that place children with the rejected parent; and (4) overestimate the risks of separating the child from the favored parent compared to the risks and tragedy of the child remaining alienated from the rejected parent, missing out on that parent's input, and being unable to give to and receive love from that parent.

Following Brad's participation in a Family Bridges workshop, and the rapid and successful resolution of Brad's alienation, the custody evaluator admitted that the primary reason that he recommended suspending Brad's contact with Vicki was that he could not envision Brad's overcoming his animosity and safely adjusting to living with his mother. Despite being a seasoned custody evaluator, he had no experience with an effective intervention like Family Bridges and little confidence that Brad would come to see his mother in a more realistic and benign light. He simply concluded that Brad and his mother were beyond help.

INTERVENTION RISKS VERSUS STATUS QUO RISKS

Despite the propensity of inexperienced professionals to overestimate the risk of placing children with the tarejectedrget parent, as described earlier each option for dealing with severely alienated children carries potential benefits and risks. The potential risks should be weighed against the potential benefits and taken into account in structuring family transitions.

The main concerns about overriding children's stated wishes are that the children may defy the court's expectations, may commit destructive acts against themselves (e.g., running away or physical harm) or toward the rejected parent, and may lodge false allegations about mistreatment by the rejected parent in order to be removed from that home. No systematic large-scale research compares the risks versus benefits of the four options discussed previously. Warshak (2010c, 2011c) describes the power of the court's firm authority to elicit a recalcitrant child's compliance and reduce the risks of acting out by making it clear to the child that such behavior will not result in the court's appeasing demands to return to the favored parent and may in fact delay the reunification with that parent.

It is impossible to predict with certainty how any child will react to firm attempts to repair a damaged relationship with a parent. Based on their large-scale study, Clawar and Rivlin (1991) conclude:

> There are risks incumbent in any process; however, *a decision has to be made as to what is the greater risk.* It is usually more damaging socially, psychologically, educationally, and/or physically for children to maintain beliefs, values, thoughts, and behaviors that disconnect them from one of their parents (or from telling the truth, as in a criminal case) compared to getting rid of the distortions or false statements. (p. 141 *emphasis in original*)

The potential damage in maintaining the status quo for a severely alienated child is described in detail in the earlier discussion of the drawbacks of suspending required contact between the child and rejected parent and delegating the authority to the child to determine whether and when contact resumes.

When the court determines that a child's interests are best served by reuniting with a rejected parent and that the child's alienation arises in the shadow of, or reflects an identification with, the favored parent's negative attitudes, research and experience suggest the importance of several conditions that favor a successful reunification. These include giving children sufficient time with the rejected parent and reduced contact with people whose negative attitudes have influence over the children (including relatives and friends of the favored parent). Renewed contact with the favored parent should be contingent upon improvement in the children's behavior with the rejected parent, which can be facilitated through skilled intervention for the family and a strong message from the court about the consequences for disobeying court orders. Based on their analysis of the relevant literature, Fidler and Bala (2010) conclude, "All severe and some moderate cases of alienation . . . are likely to require a different and more intrusive approach if the relationship with the rejected parent is not to be abandoned and the alienation is to be successfully corrected."

The social science literature emphasizes the importance of contact between the child and the rejected parent, but in some instances contact alone is insufficient to promote adequate healing. Especially when a child expected the status quo to continue, court orders that place children with the rejected parent and suspend their contact with the favored parent can be quite a shock. In such cases, appropriate interventions with the family can help children adjust to the court orders, recover a positive relationship with the rejected parent, and prepare for the resumption of contact with the favored parent.

FAMILY BRIDGES

Family Bridges: A Workshop for Troubled and Alienated Parent-Child Relationships™ is a structured, four-day, educational and experiential program that assists families in making a safe transition and adjusting to court orders that bring children and their rejected parent together and suspend contact with the favored parent for an extended period (Warshak, 2010a, 2010c; Warshak & Otis, 2010a). Norton (2011) draws on developmental psychology and neurobiology to emphasize the importance of providing children and adolescents with experiences that facilitate empathy, connection, and wellness: "These experiences can help them to create a new narrative about their lives, one that is more cohesive, more hopeful, and allows them to begin to see themselves in a new place and begin to 'let the future in'" (p. 2). Along these lines, Family Bridges helps children re-create their identity as people who can give and receive love from two parents, gives them the experience of relating benevolently to the formerly rejected parent, gives them a face-saving way to correct cognitive distortions, and shows them how to move beyond the past to more rewarding relationships with both parents.

At the time this chapter was written, Family Bridges was (and may still be) the only program for severely alienated children whose success has been documented in a refereed article with follow-up data. A brief description of the program follows. Warshak (2010a, 2010c) provides a comprehensive account of the program's goals, principles, structure, procedures, syllabus, limitations, and preliminary outcomes. A briefer overview and answers to frequently asked questions can be found at www.warshak.com.

Family Bridges works with an individual family rather than a group of families. The four-day workshop usually takes place in a resort setting. The children's reintegration with the rejected parent is accomplished both through the process and the content of the workshop. In line with intergroup contact theory, bringing parent and child together, with the support of the court, to work cooperatively on common goals helps lessen hostility and prejudice (Brown & Hewstone, 2005). The syllabus covers the underlying processes that contribute to PA. Carefully chosen, engaging, entertaining, evocative, and educational audiovisual materials and exercises teach how distortions in memory, perception, and thinking occur. The materials also teach how negative stereotypes form under the influence of suggestion and authority figures, how parental conflict harms children, how to think critically, how children can stay out of the middle of their parents' conflicts, and how the children and parent can better communicate and manage conflict. Children learn how to maintain balanced, realistic, and compassionate views of both parents. The program also offers a workshop for favored parents who attend voluntarily but does not accept referrals of favored parents whose attendance is mandated by the court.

Joan Kelly (2010), a leading authority on divorce, notes the scientific basis for Family Bridges:

> In the overall development of Family Bridges, its goals and principles, and particularly the varied and relevant materials selected for use with parents and children, the incorporation of relevant social science research was evident. Further, the daily structure and manner of presentation of the Family Bridges Workshop were guided by well-established evidence-based instruction principles and incorporated multi-media learning, a positive learning environment, focused lessons addressing relevant concepts, and learning materials providing assistance with integration of materials. The most striking feature of the Family Bridges Workshop was the empirical research foundation underlying the specific content of the four-day educational program. The lessons and materials were drawn from universally accepted research in social, cognitive, and child developmental psychology, sociology, and social neuroscience.

Most of the children who attend Family Bridges have led custody evaluators, parents, and the court to expect no cooperation when it comes to accepting placement with the rejected parent. All the children have had failed experiences with counseling prior to enrollment. Some have threatened to act out, insist that they will not comply with court orders, and act as though they are above the law. Nevertheless, in line with Clawar and Rivlin's (1991) observations, when the court issues its orders, most of the threats give way to muted disappointment in the court and anxiety about the future. By the time they begin the workshop, the children are engaged in making the best of their situation. Early in the process, usually during the first day, the children begin relating positively to the rejected parent and appear relieved to be offered a face-saving way to reconnect. In a study of twenty-three children, twenty-two restored a positive relationship with the rejected parent by the workshop's conclusion. The one holdout was a girl just shy of her eighteenth birthday who made it clear at the outset that she would remain at the workshop to support her younger siblings but had no intention of actively participating (Warshak, 2010c). At follow-up, eighteen of the twenty-two children maintained their gains; those who relapsed had premature contact with the favored parent.

Often a parent, attorney, or judge hopes that the workshop can resolve a custody dispute by repairing a damaged parent-child relationship in a context that fails to meet the enrollment prerequisites or when the favored parent maintains custody and significant residential time with the child or will resume custody upon completion of the workshop. Unfortunately, this program is not designed for such circumstances and thus usually does not accept such referrals. One judge opined that the workshop, coupled with a change in custody, was the only potential remedy for a seventeen-year-old boy who, the court found, was the victim of his father's deliberate behavior to alienate the child from his mother (*S. G. B. v. S. J. L.*, 2010). In her decision, Justice Mesbur ruled, "The Workshop is a last resort. Obviously it would have been better had these problems been identified and corrected early on. . . . Unfortunately, they were not. This leaves the Workshop as [the child's] best last hope" (paragraph 71, p. 14). The boy and his mother did accomplish a successful reunification with the help of Family Bridges.

Anonymous preworkshop and postworkshop program evaluations and follow-up studies are eliciting data that help understand how participants view the overall experience, the specific aspects and components of the workshop, and its impact on their attitudes and behavior. Preliminary review of ratings by parents and children give the program high marks. The children acknowledge that when they first learned of the workshop they felt very negative about having to attend, but that upon its completion their attitudes about the experience are positive and they believe that other families in similar situations would benefit from the program. Their ratings indicate that the workshop successfully accomplished each of its goals and that they experienced it as an educational program in contrast with their previous experiences in counseling. The children report that the workshop leaders treated them with respect and kindness and that the experience in no way harmed them.

In creating the Family Bridges workshop, Randy Rand created an entirely new approach to helping participants modify thoughts, feelings, and behavior. He had the vision to replace the structure of traditional weekly forty-five-minute office sessions with an intensive intervention conducted in a retreat setting. In addition to structural changes, Rand created and selected content and procedures that are fundamentally different from psychotherapists' usual materials and approaches. The experience of Overcoming Barriers, with a summer camp structure reminiscent of Rand's retreat model but lacking the content and procedures of Family Bridges, demonstrates that structural changes alone are insufficient to bring about radical transformations from severe alienation to the recovery of normal relationships. The lesson for aspiring innovators working with families with severely alienated children is that strategies that fail in an office setting are as likely to fail when transplanted to a retreat, camp, or hotel weekend workshop setting.

SEVERE ALIENATION AMONG YOUNG ADULTS

Time, unfortunately, does not always heal the wounds of alienated children (Hands & Warshak, 2011). The passage of time, however, combined with moving outside the orbit of the favored parent and gaining more life experience does help some young adults become more receptive to information that might modify their harsh judgment of the rejected parent (Warshak, 2011b). Professor Linda Nielsen shows the DVD, *Welcome Back, Pluto* (Warshak & Otis, 2010b), to her college classes. She reports that about 70 percent of the college students from divorced families report either in private to the professor or in class discussion that they had an "awakening" from the video and recognized for the first time their favored parent's contributions to their rejection of their other parent. Some subsequently apologize to the rejected parent and reconnect. That an eighty-minute DVD could produce such positive responses is encouraging and suggests that alienated college students may be ripe for reconciliation given the right circumstances.

CONCLUSION

"All the therapists told me to sign over custody to Dad and just let it go," said an alienated mother who works for a family law attorney. "They said there is nothing I can do to reverse the alienation." Fortunately, the therapists are wrong–every successful case in Family Bridges began with the same pessimism.

Severe cases of PA present unique challenges and have long frustrated professionals who try to assist families with this difficult and tragic problem. Fortunately, the availability of books and articles on alienation, educational videos for children, and interventions like Family Bridges is helping to provide an antidote to the discouragement and pessimism that permeates discussions about repairing severely damaged parent-child relationships.

The development of preventive programs that teach parents and children about PA will reduce the number of cases needing more intensive and expensive help. Early identification of children at risk for alienation, and appreciation that divorce poison works swiftly to transform expressions of love into claims of fear and hatred, will help the legal system respond rapidly to protect children from the intensification of alienation (Warshak, 2011c).

Severely alienated children plead with custody evaluators, therapists, attorneys, and judges to allow them to excise from their lives one of the two people on the face of the planet responsible for their care. Despite weathering cruel treatment and untempered hatred that would drive any other person away, most rejected parents maintain a steadfast commitment to their child's welfare and invest considerable resources trying to restore positive relationships. Very often the tragedy extends to an entire half of the child's family who remain astounded and deeply hurt at the formerly loving child's complete estrangement.

Vignette

Bradley Beecher is now an upper classman at a prestigious college. Like many alienated children who reconcile with the rejected parent, Brad admits that all the while he was insisting to the custody evaluator and the GAL that he hated his mother and never wanted to see her again, he never expected the court to take him seriously. He wants people to know that his statements during the litigation did not reflect his genuine feelings about his mother and were an inaccurate account of the history of his relationship with her and her behavior toward him. He thinks that it would have been a huge and tragic mistake for the court to appease his demands and allow him to lose his mother and her family. Despite his insistence at the time that his attitudes were his own, Brad is grateful that the authorities recognized that his attitudes reflected his father's negative influence and were not an expression of mature and independent judgment. Not coincidentally, Brad selected his college specifically for the opportunity to work with one of the world's leading scholars on critical thinking and scientific investigation. Brad first learned of this scientist from a book Dr. Rand left in open view during the Family Bridges workshop.

The outcome of most divorce cases affects each parent's financial situation and the amount and schedule of time they spend with their children. The outcome of cases with severely alienated children spells the difference between an elated parent who recaptures her identity as a parent, versus a bereft parent who mourns the loss of her children and whose children grow up with someone who may be a perpetrator of psychological abuse, who forces them to make a child's version of Sophie's Choice, and who fails to honor their right to love and be loved by two parents. If they do not find their way back to the rejected parent, when these children grow up and have their own children, the next generation is deprived of a legacy. Helping these families is challenging and a heavy responsibility. It is not often that MHPs and legal professionals get the chance to alter the course of generations.

Editors' Notes

- Dr. Warshak describes children with severe and irrational alienation as expressing extremely polarized opinions of their parents, having little if anything positive to say about the rejected parent.
- Dr. Warshak explains the three dimensions of PA: behavioral impairments (e.g., extreme hostility and defiance), emotional impairments (e.g., lack of genuine caring, love, and affection), and cognitive impairments (e.g., rewriting the history and meaning of their relationship with the rejected parent).

- Dr. Warshak illustrates the importance of early intervention because of the serious short- and long-term consequences of this condition, such as depression, disturbed relationships, and poor conflict management.
- Dr. Warshak emphasizes in cases of severe PA that decision-makers usually consider the following four options for primary custodial placement of alienated children: (1) the favored parent accompanied by court-ordered efforts to remedy the problems, (2) the rejected parent, (3) neither parent, and (4) the favored parent with no scheduled contacts with the rejected parent.
- Dr. Warshak described Family Bridges, a research-based, time-limited, and intensive program, empirically designed to address the relationship of severely alienated children with their rejected parents.

REFERENCES

Amato, P. R. (1991). Parental absence during childhood and depression in later life. *The Sociological Quarterly, 32*(5), 543–556.

American Psychological Association. (2004, July 19). Brief for the American Psychological Association and the Missouri Psychological Association as Amici Curiae Supporting Respondent, In *re Roper v. Simmons,* 543 U.S. 551 (2005).

Baker, A. J. L. (2007). *Adult children of parental alienation syndrome: Breaking the ties that bind.* New York: W. W. Norton.

Baker, A., Jaffe, P. G., Bernet, W., & Johnston, J. R. (2011, May). Brief report on parental alienation survey. *Association of Family and Consiliation Courts eNEWS, 30*(2).

Bala, N., Hunt, S., & McCarney, C. (2010). Parental alienation: Canadian court cases 1989–2008. *Family Court Review, 48*(1), 164–179.

Barber, B. K. (1996). Parental psychological control: Revisiting a neglected construct. *Child Development, 67*(6), 3296–3319.

Barber, B. K., Stolz, H. E., & Olsen, J. A. (2005). Parental support, psychological control, and behavioral control: Assessing relevance across time, method, and culture. *Monographs of the Society for Research in Child Development 70*(4), i–147.

Bezilla, R. (1988). *The Gallup study on America's youth: 1977–1988.* Princeton, NJ: The Gallup Organization, Inc.

Bibby, R. W. (2009, May 12). Teens' Enjoyment of Moms . . . and Dads. Project Teen Canada Press Release #1, University of Lethbridge.

Block, S. D., Oran, H., Oran, D., Baumrind, N., & Goodman, G. S. (2010). Abused and neglected children in court: Knowledge and attitudes. *Child Abuse & Neglect, 34*(9), 659–670.

Boss, P. (2006). *Loss, trauma, and resilience: Therapeutic work with ambiguous loss.* New York: W. W. Norton.

Bowen, M. (1978). *Family therapy in clinical practice.* New York: Jason Aronson.

Bowers, J. R., Mitchell, E. T., Hardesty, J. L., & Hughes, R., Jr. (2011). A review of online divorce education programs. *Family Court Review, 49*(4), 776–787.

Brown, R., & Hewstone, H. (2005). An integrative theory of intergroup contact. In M. P. Zanna (Ed.), *Advances in experimental social psychology* (Vol. 37, pp. 255–343). San Diego, CA: Academic Press.

Bruch, C. S. (2001). Parental alienation syndrome and parental alienation: Getting it wrong in child custody cases. *Family Law Quarterly, 35*(3), 527–552.

Buchanan, C., Maccoby, E., & Dornbusch, S. (1991). Caught between parents: Adolescents' experience in divorced homes. *Child Development, 62*(5), 1008–1029.

Campbell, T. W., & Lorandos, D. (2001). *Cross examining experts in the behavioral sciences.* Egan, MN: West group.

Carter, S. (2011). *Family restructuring therapy: Interventions for high conflict divorce.* Scottsdale, AZ: HCI Press.

Clawar, S. S., & Rivlin, B. V. (1991). *Children held hostage: Dealing with programmed and brainwashed children.* Chicago: American Bar Association.

Eddy, B. (2009). *New ways for families: Professional guidebook for judicial officers, lawyers and therapists.* Scottsdale, AZ: High Conflict Institute, LLC.

Ellis, E. M. (2005). Help for the alienated parent. *The American Journal of Family Therapy, 33*(5), 415–426.

Fabricius, W. V., & Hall, J. A. (2000). Young adults' perspective on divorce: Living arrangements. *Family and Conciliation Courts Review, 38*(4), 446–461.

Fidler, B. J., & Bala, N. (2010). Children resisting postseparation contact with a parent: Concepts, controversies, and conundrums. *Family Court Review, 48*(1), 10–47.

Framo, J. L. (1992). *Family-of-origin therapy: An intergenerational approach.* New York: Brunner-Routledge.

Fray, J. (2010, January 25). Arthur Davis III gets 25 years for baseball bat attack on exwife. *LJWorld.com.* Retrieved October 14, 2011, from http://www2.ljworld.com/news/2010/jan/25/arthur-davis-iii-gets-25-years-baseball-attack-ex-/

Freeman, R., Abel, D., Cowper-Smith, M., & Stein, L. (2004). Reconnecting children with absent parents: A model for intervention. *Family Court Review, 42*(3), 439–459.

Friedlander, S., & Walters, M. G. (2010). When a child rejects a parent: Tailoring the intervention to fit the problem. *Family Court Review, 48*(1), 98–111.

Gardner, R. A. (1998). *The parental alienation syndrome: A guide for mental health and legal professionals* (2nd ed.). Cresskill, NJ: Creative Therapeutics.

Gardner, R. A. (2001). *Therapeutic interventions for children with parental alienation syndrome.* Cresskill: NJ: Creative Therapeutics.

Goldsmith, D. F., Oppenheim, D., & Wanlass, J. (2004). Separation and reunification: Using attachment theory and research to inform decisions affecting the placements of children in foster care. *Juvenile and Family Court Journal, 55*(2), 1–13.

Gordon, R. M. (1998). The Medea complex and the parental alienation syndrome: When mothers damage their daughters' ability to love a man. In G. Fenchel (Ed.), *The mother-daughter relationship: Echoes through time* (pp. 207–225). Northvale, NJ: Jason Aronson, Inc.

Hands, A. J., & Warshak, R. A. (2011). Parental alienation among college students. *The American Journal of Family Therapy, 39*(5), 431–433.

Johnston, J. R., & Goldman, J. R. (2010). Outcomes of family counseling interventions with children who resist visitation: An addendum to Friedlander and Walters (2010). *Family Court Review, 48*(1), 112–115.

Johnston, J. R., Walters, M. G., & Olesen, N. W. (2005). The psychological functioning of alienated children in custody disputing families: An exploratory study. *American Journal of Forensic Psychology, 23*(3), 39–64.

Kelly, J. B. (2005). Developing beneficial parenting plan models for children following separation and divorce. *Journal of the American Academy of Matrimonial Lawyers, 19,* 237–254.

Kelly, J. B. (2010). Commentary on "family bridges: using insights from social science to reconnect parents and alienated children" (Warshak, 2010). *Family Court Review, 48*(1), 81–90.

Kelly, J. B., & Emery, R. E. (2003). Children's adjustment following divorce: Risk and resilience perspectives. *Family Relations, 52*(4), 352–362.

Kelly, J. B., & Johnston, J. R. (2001). The alienated child: A reformulation of parental alienation syndrome. *Family Court Review, 39*(3), 249–266.

Kierstead, S. (2011). Parent education programs in family courts: Balancing autonomy and state intervention. *Family Court Review, 49*(1), 140–154.

Lampel, A. (1996). Child's alignment with parents in highly conflicted custody cases. *Family and Conciliation Courts Review, 34*(2), 229–239.

Levitt, M. J. (2005). Social relations in childhood and adolescence. *Human Development, 48*(1-2), 28–47.

Levy, D. L., & Sauber, S. R. (2010). Review of the DVD *Welcome back, Pluto: Understanding, preventing, and overcoming parental alienation. American Journal of Family Therapy, 39*(1), 77–85.

Loftus, E. F. (2003). Make-believe memories. *American Psychologist, 58*(11), 867–873.

Norton, C. L. (2011). Reinventing the wheel: From talk therapy to innovative interventions. In C. L. Norton (Ed.), *Innovative interventions in child and adolescent mental health.* New York: Routledge.

Offer, D., Ostrov, E., Howard, K. I., & Atkinson, R. (1988). *The teenage world: Adolescents' self-image in ten countries.* New York: Springer-Verlag.

Parkinson, P., Cashmore, J., & Single, J. (2005). Adolescents' views on the fairness of parenting and financial arrangements after separation. *Family Court Review, 43*(3), 429–444.

Pettigrew, T. F., & Tropp, L. R. (2006). A meta-analytic test of intergroup contact theory. *Journal of Personality and Social Psychology, 90*(5), 751–783.

Rand, D. C., & Rand, R. (2006). Factors affecting reconciliation between the child and the target parent. In R. Gardner, S. Sauber, & D. Lorandos (Eds.), *The inter-*

national handbook of parental alienation syndrome (pp. 163–176). Springfield, IL: Charles C Thomas.

Sabatelli, R. M., & Bartle-Haring, S. (2003). Family-of-origin experiences and adjustment in married couples. *Journal of Marriage and Family, 65*(1), 159–169.

Schwartz, S. J., & Finley, G. E. (2009). Mothering, fathering, and divorce: The influence of divorce on reports of and desires for maternal and paternal involvement. *Family Court Review, 47*(3), 506–522.

Sigal, A., Sandler, I., Wolchik, S., & Braver, S. (2011). Do parent education programs promote healthy postdivorce parenting? Critical distinctions and a review of the evidence. *Family Court Review, 49*(1), 120–139.

Steinberg, L., Cauffman, E., Woolard, J., Graham, S., & Banich, M. (2009). Are adolescents less mature than adults? Minor's access to abortion, the juvenile death penalty, and the alleged APA "flip-flop." *American Psychologist, 64*(7), 583–594.

Steinberg, L., & Scott, E. (2003). Less guilty by reason of adolescence: Developmental immaturity, diminished responsibility, and the juvenile death penalty. *American Psychologist, 58*(12), 1009–1018.

Sullivan, M. J., & Kelly, J. B. (2001). Legal and psychological management of cases with an alienated child. *Family Court Review, 39*(3), 299–315.

Sullivan, M. J., Ward, P. A., & Deutsch, R. M. (2010). Overcoming Barriers Family Camp: A program for high-conflict divorced families where a child is resisting contact with a parent. *Family Court Review, 48*(1), 116–135.

Walker, L. E., & Shapiro, D. L. (2010). Parental alienation disorder: Why label children with a mental diagnosis? *Journal of Child Custody, 7*(4), 266–286.

Wallerstein, J. S., & Blakeslee, S. (1989). *Second chances: Men, women, and children a decade after divorce.* New York: Ticknor and Fields.

Wallerstein, J. S., & Kelly, J. B. (1980). *Surviving the breakup: How children and parents cope with divorce.* New York: Basic Books.

Warshak, R. A. (2001). Current controversies regarding parental alienation syndrome. *American Journal of Forensic Psychology, 19*(3), 29–59.

Warshak, R. A. (2002). Misdiagnosis of parental alienation syndrome. *American Journal of Forensic Psychology, 20*(2), 31–52

Warshak, R. A. (2003a). Bringing sense to parental alienation: A look at the disputes and the evidence. *Family Law Quarterly, 37*(2), 273–301.

Warshak, R. A. (2003b). Payoffs and Pitfalls of Listening to Children. *Family Relations, 52*(4), 373–384.

Warshak, R. A. (2006). *Warshak parent questionnaire–online version.* Dallas, TX: Clinical Psychology Associates.

Warshak, R. A. (2010a). Alienating audiences from innovation: The perils of polemics, ideology, and innuendo. *Family Court Review, 48*(1), 153–163.

Warshak, R. A. (2010b). *Divorce poison: How to protect your family from bad-mouthing and brainwashing.* New York: HarperCollins.

Warshak, R. A. (2010c). Family Bridges: Using insights from social science to reconnect parents and alienated children. *Family Court Review, 48*(1), 48–80.

Warshak, R. A. (2010d, June). Helping Families with Children Who Reject Parents: Consensus, Controversies and Future Directions. Plenary panel. 47th Annual Conference, Association of Family and Conciliation Courts, Denver, CO.

Warshak, R. A. (2011a). Parenting by the clock: The best interests of the child standard, judicial discretion, and the American Law Institute's "Approximation Rule." *University of Baltimore Law Review, 41,* 83–163.

Warshak, R. A. (2011b, April). *Welcome Back, Pluto: Parental Alienation Evaluation, Prevention, and Intervention.* Keynote speaker, *Parental Alienation: Not Just Another Custody Case.* Annual conference of the Association of Family and Conciliation Courts, Massachusetts chapter, Weston, MA.

Warshak, R. A. (2011c, June). *Plutoed Parents: Preventing and Overcoming Parental Alienation.* 11th Annual Family Law on the Front Lines Conference, University of Texas School of Law, Austin, TX.

Warshak, R. A., & Otis, M. R. (2010a). Helping alienated children with Family Bridges: Practice, research, and the pursuit of "humbition." *Family Court Review, 48*(1), 91–97.

Warshak, R. A., & Otis, M. R. (2010b). *Welcome back, Pluto: Understanding, preventing, and overcoming parental alienation* [DVD]. Dallas, TX: WBP Media.

Warshak, R. A., & Santrock, J. W. (1983). The impact of divorce in father-custody and mother-custody homes: The child's perspective. In L. A. Kurdek (Ed.), *Children and divorce* (pp. 29–46). New York: Jossey-Bass.

Zervopoulos, J. A. (2008). *Confronting mental health evidence.* Chicago, IL: American Bar Association.

Cases

Begins v. Begins, 721 A.2d 469, 470-71 (VT, 1998) as cited in Miller 161 N.H. 630, 20 A.3d 854 (N.H. 2011).

Daubert v. Merrell Dow Pharmaceuticals. 509 U.S. 579 (1993).

In the Matter of James J. Miller and Janet S. Todd. The Supreme Court of New Hampshire. Portsmouth Family Division No. 2009-806. Argued November 17, 2010; opinion issued March 31, 2011.

Miller & Todd [Matter of], 161 N.H. 630, 640, 20 A.3d 854 (2011).

Renaud v. Renaud, 721 A.2d 463, 465-66 (VT, 1988) as cited in Miller 161 N.H. 630, 20 A.3d 854 (N.H. 2011).

S. B. B. v. S.J. L. [Indexed as: B. (S. G.) v. L. (S. J.)]. 2010 ONSC 3717 Superior Court of Justice, Justice Mesbur (June 30, 2010).

Chapter 6

SEXUAL ABUSE ALLEGATIONS IN THE CONTEXT OF CUSTODY AND VISITATION DISPUTES

Terence W. Campbell

In the context of custody and visitation disputes, allegations of sexual abuse can assume all the twists and turns of an Agatha Christie mystery. The following case is an example of how these allegations often unfold.

Vignette

Donna, three and a half years old, was taken by her mother to the outpatient clinic of a local hospital because she was convinced that her daughter had been sexually abused. Donna's parents had been divorced for two years and the mother suspected that her ex-husband had abused their daughter. For almost a year, the mother had worried about the possibility of Donna's abuse. When asked what prompted her worries, she cited Donna's "weird bowel movements." She elaborated how she had observed her daughter's bowel movements to be "at least a foot long." When pressed as to what about Donna's bowel movements necessarily indicated sexual abuse, mother was unable to answer. She also added, however, that Donna seemed to be experiencing nightmares recently and explained that her daughter often seemed upset after visiting her father. The mother offered instances of Donna's episodic oppositionalism and defiance as evidence of her distress.

DEFINING TERMS

Cases such as these prompt asking, "Is this allegation founded in fact, or is it illusory and therefore false?" Responding to such questions necessitates carefully defining terms. "Confirmed allegations" exist when a perpetrator confesses or a chain of reliable evidence identifies a perpetrator beyond a reasonable doubt. "Fabricated allegations" of child sexual abuse (CSA) correspond to those circumstances in which one or more people set out with premeditated malice to direct allegations at an entirely innocent person or persons (Campbell, 1998). "False allegations" of CSA typically originate as rumors and can spiral out of control as the ensuing processes of rumor dissemination gather greater and greater momentum (Campbell, 1992a). False allegations do not involve the malicious premeditation found in fabricated allegations.

Although intentionality is the defining distinction between false and fabricated allegations, intentionality is not a simple dichotomy identified in black and white terms in these cases. In instances of custody and visitation disputes, the parents can substantially lower their thresholds of disbelief when considering rumors directed at an ex-spouse. Situational circumstances providing the opportunity to judge an ex-spouse negatively are a temptation few people can entirely resist. Rumors about each other that would provoke immediate rejection from cooperative ex-spouses can assume more legitimacy than they deserve for disputing ex-spouses struggling with frequent parental conflicts (e.g., "Of course, she is less than honest about what she does with the kids. She lies about everything else. Why should this be any different?").

Considerations of intentionality necessitate asking whether false allegations of sexual abuse–genuinely and sincerely believed by a custodial parent–amount to alienating behaviors that could lead to parental alienation (PA). If PA involves a deliberate, premeditated, knowing campaign to alienate children from a parent, then false allegations of sexual abuse do not by themselves support PA.

Accurately identifying confirmed allegations, fabricated allegations, or false allegations necessitates tracing the background and history of the allegations (Campbell, 1992b). Assessing CSA allegations involves asking how these allegations originated, how they gathered momentum, and how the allegations eventually developed to where they are currently?

THE SEXUAL ALLEGATIONS IN DIVORCE SYNDROME

One of the earliest reviews of CSA related to custody and visitation disputes was reported by Blush and Ross (1987). Working in a clinic operating as an arm of a family court afforded those authors an advantageous perspective. They found that tracking all complaints and motions brought to the court by disputing parents was often informative. In reviewing the court file for any particular case, they could identify what issues provoked parental disputes between these parties and when those disputes originated. Blush and Ross' "syndrome" (Sexual Allegations in Divorce [SAID] or "she said, he said" exchanges) directed evaluators to carefully assess the background and history of a divorce before any allegations of sexual abuse developed. Ross and Blush (1990) referred to factors they identified as "sequence-escalation-timing" (or SET factors) when reviewing the background and history of any particular case.

For Blush and Ross, considering SET factors directed evaluators to look at the context in which the allegations occurred. Did the allegations develop after a sequence of acrimonious exchanges between the parents? Such exchanges can involve disputes related to child support and costs of activities such as sports, music lessons, special camps, and so on. Those acrimonious exchanges can also involve requests to modify visitation or petitions to relocate to another residence far removed from the noncustodial parent.

Carefully reviewing the legal history predating any CSA allegations allows evaluators to identify whether escalating exchanges between the disputing parents triggered the allegations. For example, did a custodial parent seeking increased child support provoke the noncustodial parent to express allegations of visitation denial? In turn, did the animosity between the parents escalate despite their attorneys' attempts at resolving the dispute?

Given an escalating exchange of demands and counter-demands between disputing parents, Blush and Ross also emphasized the necessity of considering the timing of the allegations. Were the allegations timed in such a manner that they gave the accusing parent significantly greater power and influence? In response to CSA, for example, a child protection agency can pursue a custodian's agenda by blocking the noncustodian's visitation.

Assessing CSA in the context of divorce also necessitates identifying whether the divorcing family has broken down into two hostile coalitions that distrust each other. In other words, is it possible to identify a "mother's coalition" or "father's coalition"? If these coalitions exist, it becomes necessary to ascertain whether the child's initial allegations were expressed within a coalition or outside of any coalition. A child telling the mother or someone closely aligned with the mother about the alleged CSA amounts to an "in-coalition" allegation. A child telling a teacher about the alleged abuse in response to a "good touch, bad touch" class discussion is an "out-of-coalition" allegation.

CASE OF DONNA AND SEQUENCE-ESCALATION-TIMING FACTORS

Returning to Donna's case underscores how the background and history predating CSA allegations are important. Until she remarried just two months prior to taking her daughter to the hospital, mother and Donna had lived with mother's parents since her divorce from her first husband. Because of religious differences, the maternal grandparents had never accepted Donna's father even while their daughter was married to him. Since the divorce, they resented his periodic appearances at their home to pick up Donna for visits. Previous disputes between the mother and father about custody and visitation had brought considerable turmoil into the grandparents' home, and they felt less than forgiving toward the father as a result.

Mother's Suspicions and Grandparents' Anxieties

The grandparents adored Donna, and they observed closely to see how she reacted to her father. Because their home acquired an uncharacteristically quiet, sober atmosphere just prior to father's visits, Donna felt awkward and tense. Mother and the grandparents confidently concluded that Donna's awkward, tense behavior indicated apprehensiveness about seeing her father, and they wondered what the father had done to provoke those reactions from her.

Because the grandparents were planning to retire and move to their retirement home in a few months, their worries increased. After their move, they would be separated by almost a thousand miles from their daughter and Donna. They could only imagine what traumas Donna's father might subject her to when they were unable to protect her. Grandmother wondered whether Mike (mother's present husband) could adopt her, but Donna's father emphatically refused to permit adoption. Although mother and grandmother found it difficult to believe him, he insisted that he and his family also loved Donna. The father's alleged sexual abuse profoundly changed this entire situation. As a result of those allegations, the grandparents and mother felt justifiably convinced that such a despicable man would not be allowed to see his daughter again.

Persuading the Therapist

At the hospital, mother and grandmother outlined their evidence of sexual abuse for the therapist assigned to this case. They explained how earlier in the day, Donna had fallen into the toilet while urinating. After her mother retrieved her, she complained that her "pee-pee" hurt. When mother offered to put Vaseline on her genital area, Donna reportedly protested, "No, don't. You'll hurt me like Jimmy does." (While Donna reportedly called Mike, "Dad," her mother clarified that she referred to her father as "Jimmy." That pleased mother and the grandparents endlessly.) Prior to the toilet mishap, mother had previously asked Donna if her father had touched her in her "private places" and Donna had consistently answered, "No." In response to her daughter's statement this time, mother asked again if "Jimmy" had touched her "pee-pee." Donna's affirmative answer spared mother the frustrated disbelief she used to experience in response to her daughter's negative answers. Donna also noticed that Mom seemed to like this answer–it did not make her upset like before.

When Donna saw the therapist by herself, she spontaneously lifted her skirt, pointed to her vaginal area, and announced with a conviction that would have made her mother and grandmother proud, "Jimmy hurt me there." While the therapist's limited experience indicated that sexually abused children rarely react with such spontaneity, she nonetheless regarded this evidence as compelling. The therapist also reviewed the notes of a first-year resident's physical examination that described Donna's recently developed vaginal redness. Impressed by this physical evidence, the therapist overlooked the fact that Donna had not seen her father for more than forty-five days as a result of his military reserve obligations. Instead the therapist assumed that Donna's father had sexually abused her, and she also suggested to mother that she encourage Donna to ventilate her feelings. Additionally, the therapist contacted the court and requested immediate suspension of the father's visitation rights.

Applying Sequence, Escalation, and Timing Factors

Reviewing how the various events in this case unfolded demonstrates the interplay among SET factors. Mother remarries and wishfully fantasizes that Mike was Donna's father (sequence factor). The grandparents contend with their elevated anxiety as they anticipate moving to their retirement home (another sequence factor). Father emphatically and angrily refuses to allow Mike to adopt Donna (escalating factor). Father also reminds mother that as a result of missing visits due to his reserve obligation, he would be demanding make-up visits with Donna (timing factor).

A Wise Detective

As required by law, this matter was also referred to a police agency for criminal investigation. The detective assigned to the case had accumulated many years of experience with his department's sex crime unit. He surprised the therapist by expressing doubts about the credibility of the accusations directed at father. He explained how Donna's recall of her alleged abuse was changing and inconsistent when he interviewed her. He questioned whether the history of custody and visitation disputes between Donna's parents accounted for the mother's allegations. The detective further outlined for the therapist how the mother had long wanted to sever any contact between Donna and her father. He also pointed out that grandmother appeared to be encouraging the mother in her pursuit of this agenda. The information obtained by the detective in his investigation startled the therapist, she had never considered the necessity of evaluating this kind of evidence in similar cases. Nevertheless, she persisted in her conviction that Donna's father had sexually abused her.

Presently, the father has not seen Donna for more than six months. He takes some solace in knowing that the police department will not pursue his prosecution; they cannot find enough evidence to warrant an indictment. However, the father does not know when he will see his daughter again. Meanwhile, the court awaits the outcome of the father's polygraph exam, and Donna's mother continues to take her to the therapist for treatment to alleviate the trauma of her alleged sexual abuse.

United by Donna's apparent crisis, mother and grandmother no longer disagree as they previously did about expectations and limits for Donna's behavior. Subsequently, Donna seems more relaxed and comfortable; she reports no more nightmares, and her former episodes of oppositionality and defiance have disappeared. Moreover, Donna finally appears to be accepting the move from her grandparents' home into the house with her mother and stepfather. Removed from the grandmother's tendency to frequently criticize her maternal skills, the mother feels increased confidence in herself and more comfortable with her daughter. Mother and grandmother credit the therapist's work with Donna for these positive outcomes, and the therapist has graciously accepted their praise.

False Allegations in the Service of Alienation?

In Donna's case, it is quite clear that no one set out with a premeditated agenda, complete with malice aforethought, to alienate Donna and her father. The elevated anxiety levels of the mother and grandparents served as the original impetus provoking these allegations. Mother and grandparents found themselves contending with an exceedingly ambiguous situation. Donna exclaiming, "No! Don't hurt me like Jimmy does," could have been interpreted in many different ways. Rather than carefully think through Donna's statement, mother and grandmother leapt to a premature conclusion. In a similar case, a worried, anxious mother, undergoing a psychological evaluation, was asked, "What would you do if you were the first person in a theater to smell smoke?" This mother replied, "Yell fire so we could all get out of there." That was a rather compelling example of reacting first and thinking later.

The relevant data demonstrate that anxious people interpret ambiguous circumstances in a "worst case scenario" manner (Eysenck, Mogg, May, Richards & Mathews, 1991). In response to the sentence "The doctor examined little Emma's growth," anxious people interpreted "growth" to mean tumor rather than height or stature. Related data also demonstrate that anxious people interpret homophones (mourning/morning), which can be neutral or sad, in a sad manner (Halberstadt, Niedenthal & Kushner, 1995). In other words, when hearing the homophone, they conclude it means "mourning."

The levels of animosity provoked by the SET factors in the case of Donna led to profoundly lowered thresholds of disbelief for the mother, the grandparents, and the therapist. Given their markedly relaxed thresholds of disbelief, they neglected to critically examine the consequences of (1) Donna's shifting and inconsistent descriptions of the alleged abuse, (2) mother's remarriage motivating her attempts at pushing Donna's father entirely out of their lives, and (3) The alliance between mother and grandmother vigorously pursuing the termination of father's parental rights. While viewing these factors as inconsequential coincidences, mother and grandparents welcomed the allegations enthusiastically with open arms. Therefore, did these allegations serve an alienating agenda? Quite clearly, the answer is yes. Nonetheless, these allegations did not amount to premeditated fabrications.

PERSONALITY CHARACTERISTICS OF ALIENATING PARENTS

Donna's case illustrates how SET factors create situations that are misinterpreted, via relaxed thresholds of disbelief, which in turn develop into CSA allegations driven by rumor formation and dissemination (Campbell, 1992b). There are cases of PA in which the personalities of the alienating parent serve as the source driving the alienation. Blush and Ross (1987), for example, described a pattern they termed the "justified vindicator":

> In this instance, a hostile, emotionally expansive and dominant female has directly appealed to "experts" in both the mental health and legal communities. She frequently becomes insistent that formal, punitive legal measures be taken via prosecution before reasonable proofs have been demonstrated. One of the accompanying phenomena with this type of female parent is that she frequently has concurrent criminal action pending with her domestic legal action.

More recently, Gordon, Stoffey, and Bottinelli (2008) reported data demonstrating how alienating parents resort to primitive defenses. Gordon and associates explained that those primitive defenses allow alienating parents to split reality in terms of an "all good parent" and an "all bad parent." In other cases, the primitive defenses motivate vicious attacks directed at the parent targeted by the allegations. Gordon and colleagues reported MMPI-2 data suggesting that either of two MMPI-2 indexes could identify alienating parents. The first index, L + K – F, identifies persistent defensiveness. Elevations on this index would be expected in those cases of parents viewing themselves as "all good parent" and condemning the former spouse as "all bad parent." Gordon and associates also found that the Goldberg Index (Goldberg, 1972) identified those parents whose primitive defenses directed vicious attacks at a target parent.

Gordon and colleagues sought MMPI-2 data from forensic psychologists in Pennsylvania doing custody work. Relying on Gardner's (1987) or Kelly and Johnston's (2001) definitions of parental alienation syndrome, Gordon and coworkers asked the participating psychologists to identify the MMPI-2s of alienating parents, target parents, and controls. The data they obtained are reported in Table 6.1.

Reviewing the interpretive correlates of an elevated MMPI-2 L scale, reported by Butcher and Williams (2000), is informative:

> Unwilling to admit to even minor flaws, Unrealistic proclamation of virtue, Claims adherence to excessively high moral standards, Naive self views, Outright effort to deceive others about motives or adjustment, and Personality adjustment problems in which high repression of conflict is noted. (p. 51)

Butcher and Williams described elevated K scores as corresponding to "an uncooperative attitude and reluctance to disclose personal information" (p. 51). It is not surprising, therefore, that L + K elevations are associated with describing oneself as an "all good parent."

Elevations on Pa (scale 6 of MMPI-2) and Sc (scale 8 of MMPI-2) are associated with the 86/68 profile described by Graham (2000). The correlates of this profile involve the following:

Table 6.1.
T-SCORE MEANS AND STANDARD DEVIATIONS FOR MMPI-2 INDEXES FOR ALIENATING AND CONTROL MOTHERS AND ALIENATING AND CONTROL FATHERS.

	Number of Subjects	**T-Score Means**	**T-Score Standard Deviations**
Mother Alienators: L + K – F			
Alienating Mothers	31	78.32	22.60
Control Mothers	41	55.56	20.18
Mother Alienators: (L + Pa + Sc) – (Hy +Pt)			
Alienating Mothers	31	67.65	15.43
Control Mothers	41	53.15	16.55
Father Alienators: L + K – F			
Alienating Fathers	7	84.57	25.72
Control Fathers	41	60.00	18.11
Father Alienators: (L + Pa + Sc) – (Hy +Pt)			
Alienating Fathers	7	65.14	9.15
Control Fathers	41	52.56	19.13

> Thinking is described as autistic, fragmented, tangential, and circumstantial, and thought content is likely to be bizarre. Difficulties in concentration and attending, deficits in memory, and poor judgment are common. Delusions of persecution and/or grandeur and hallucinations may be present, and feeling of unreality may be reported. Persons with the 68/86 code type often are preoccupied with abstract or theoretical matters to the exclusion of specific, concrete aspects of their life situations. Affect may be blunted, and speech may be rapid and at times incoherent. Effective defenses seem to be lacking, and these persons respond to stress and pressure by withdrawing into fantasy and daydreaming. Often it is difficult for 68/86 persons to differentiate between fantasy and reality. (p. 103)

Autistic, fragmented, and tangential thinking obviously supports false allegations of CSA. In their demands for retribution and vindication, these parents become preoccupied with issues that are abstract and tangential. Consider, for example, the following case of Rachel.

RACHEL AT TRIAL

Although dwarfed by the dimensions of the witness stand surrounding her, nine-year-old Rachel commands hushed silence from the entire courtroom in which she testifies. A jury, three attorneys, and a judge all listen attentively as she graphically details the repeated episodes of sexual abuse she supposedly suffered at the hands of her mother and stepfather. Reactions of shock and sympathy flash across the face of every juror as Rachel recalls the experiences of fellatio and vaginal penetration she reportedly endured.

Dramatic and compelling as Rachel's narration of her alleged nightmare was, her testimony also evoked images of an iceberg–remembering that only one-seventh of an iceberg is visible while the rest remains submerged beneath the surface of the water. The jury in this criminal case also understood that many issues underlying Rachel's sordid revelations demanded closer scrutiny because, after a trial of eleven days, they returned verdicts of not guilty in response to all the charges against her mother and stepfather.

Background and Chronology

Subsequent to her parents' separation, Rachel's father became increasingly suspicious that she had been sexually abused by Mark, the man with whom Rachel and his estranged wife were living. As a result of his suspicions, Daniel (Rachel's father) sought a physical examination for suspected abuse of his then five-year-old daughter. Despite the fact that the initial examination was negative, Daniel obtained another examination for Rachel three months later; it also resulted in a negative finding. Approximately two months later, Daniel obtained Rachel's custody. Rachel's mother (Cindy) did not have the economic resources for legal counsel to contend with her husband's many complaints and petitions before the family court. Daniel then solicited the counseling services of a master's level psychologist (Ms. England) for Rachel.

Over the course of thirteen treatment sessions, Rachel never disclosed any report of sexual abuse to Ms. England. Nevertheless, she reported feeling overwhelmed by the simultaneous demands for her loyalty from each of her parents. Rachel described her ensuing conflicts in somatic terms explaining, "My stomach hurts when I feel a pull from both sides." She moreover clarified, "The hurt starts when I see Mommy and Daddy fight," and she wistfully exclaimed, "I just wish they would stop." As so many other children of divorce, Rachel lamented that she could not choose which parent she most wanted to live with because she still preferred to remain with both of them.

After Cindy and Mark married, David filed a formal complaint with Children's Protective Services (CPS) alleging that Mark had struck Rachel so hard that he left a handprint on her back. CPS undertook a comprehensive investigation and found no cause for substantiation after interviewing both Cindy and Mark. The primary investigator closed this matter, observing that her agency would likely encounter this family again because of their ongoing custody dispute.

Subsequent events verified the investigator's prediction. Three months later, CPS conducted another investigation related to allegations of Rachel's sexual abuse. Like the previous investigation, this inquiry also discovered no basis for substantiation. The second investigator also issued an ominous warning that the frequency with which Rachel was undergoing interviews regarding alleged abuse threatened the reliability of anything she might disclose in the future because of rehearsal effects.

Effects of Play Therapy

Approximately six months after Cindy and Mark married, Daniel met Kathy–a divorced psychiatric nurse–who struck him as particularly sensitive to his assessment of Rachel's problems because she had been sexually abused herself as a child. Kathy recommended play therapy for Rachel with a Ph.D. psychologist, Dr. McKay, at the facility where she worked. Approximately one month after initiating this course of treatment, Dr. McKay's notes indicated Rachel's reporting that Mark had sexually abused her. Rachel's recall of that apparent abuse included her description of how "Mark squirted sticky stuff on my face from his thing." In response to the report and recommendations of Dr. McKay, the court terminated Cindy's visitation except for supervised visits confined to her former husband's residence. Gratified that some official agency finally saw evidence of his former wife's parental cruelty, Daniel took his case to the local prosecutor. When the county prosecutor indicated that this was a case that should be pursued, Daniel felt even more vindicated.

When Dr. McKay resigned her position at the facility treating Rachel, Dr. Will–a child psychiatrist employed at the same facility–assumed responsibility for Rachel's treatment. Dr. Will also advocated expressive play therapy for Rachel, confident that such procedures facilitated necessary "disclosure work." Over the next two years of treatment with Dr. Will, Rachel's disclosures grew at a dramatic rate; in fact, she eventually implicated her mother as participating with Mark in sexually abusing her.

In response to encouragement from Kathy and Daniel, Rachel kept diaries of her thoughts and feelings. With Kathy's support, Daniel explained to Rachel that her diary would help her remember all the things Mark and her mother had done to her. Over a twenty-one-month period, she made 246 separate entries in her diaries. Rachel described her mother negatively on 121 occasions, and Mark was described negatively in 120 entries. Her portrayals of her mother and Mark involved increasing anger and fantasized retribution; in turn, Kathy and Daniel praised Rachel for ventilating her feelings. The frequency of Rachel's cathartic experiences finally led her to the conclusion that referring to her mother as "Cindy"–not as "Mom"–would afford her enormous relief and comfort. Rachel decided to reserve the designation "Mom" for Kathy, a decision that Daniel enthusiastically applauded. Dr. Will also endorsed Rachel's decision, even though the psychiatrist had met Cindy only briefly on one occasion.

The sequence of events outlined in this case stagger the imagination. At five years of age–shortly after Rachel's father assumed her custody–Rachel reported the kinds of loyalty conflicts that often inundate children of divorce. Three years later, after residing continuously in her father's custody, Rachel insists that she endured frequent sexual abuse at the age of five, which was so cruel that it bordered on the sadistic. Rachel's profound revision of her own history underscores how exceedingly vindictive parents can rationalize the revenge they pursue as altogether justified. In addition to encouraging Rachel to write the many entries in her "diary," Daniel also obtained books about CSA, written for children, and sought "book reports" from Rachel. As Rachel's descriptions of her supposed abuse became more graphic and detailed, Daniel expressed greater and greater approval.

The Defense Responds

At trial, a well-informed defense expert carefully traced the many twists and turns in this case. Citing how suggestibility influences can undermine children's memory, the expert explained that children can come to believe events that in fact never occurred. Reviewing Dr. McKay's and Dr. Will's treatment notes made it increasingly evident how the therapists, Daniel, and Kathy influenced what Rachel thought she recalled. The defense expert cited one instance after another of Daniel's shopping for opinions that would support his suspicions of sexual abuse. Although most parents would be relieved if told, "You need not worry. We find no evidence of your daughter's being sexually abused," such feedback left Daniel increasingly frustrated.

In the case of Rachel, the jury became convinced that the CSA allegations were motivated by Daniel's seeking retribution from Cindy. He was overwhelmed with rage at her for leaving him for Mark, and it became clear that he pursued his agenda with single-minded determination. His pursuit of this agenda while ignoring how it might influence Rachel's welfare was particularly sobering.

ASSESSING CHILD SEXUAL ABUSE ALLEGATIONS

Jennifer and Rachel's cases provide us with criteria we can use to assess CSA allegations in the context of custody and visitation disputes. Responding to the following sequence of questions can clarify events that otherwise seem muddled and confusing.

1. **How did these allegations originate?** Was the alleged abuse disclosed within an alleging parent's coalition or outside that coalition? A child's disclosures to the alleging parent, as opposed to someone outside the parent's coalition such as a teacher, are more consistent with false allegations.
2. **Did the allegations develop after a sequence of acrimonious exchanges between the parents?** CSA allegations in the absence of any prior acrimonious exchanges are more likely to be founded in fact. Allegations in the midst of many acrimonious parental exchanges are more likely false or fabricated.
3. **Did the CSA allegations escalate in response to the other parent's denials or counter allegations?** Escalating allegations are also consistent with both false and fabricated allegations.
4. **Were the allegations timed to provide the alleging parent with some kind of strategic advantage?** Affirmative answers to this question are consistent with both false and fabricated allegations.
5. **Did the alleging parent involve various third parties, such as CPS personnel, law-enforcement professionals, and/or mental health professionals, as allies supporting the allegations?** Vigorously seeking allies is consistent with both false and fabricated allegations.
6. **Did the CSA allegations gain momentum via the effects of rumor formation and rumor dissemination?** Both false and fabricated allegations are typically driven by the effects of rumor formation and rumor dissemination.
7. **Does the MMPI-2 of the alleging parent correspond to the L + K – F profile?** Using a T-score profile of 78 and above to rule in alienating behaviors for mothers appears to accurately identify 50 percent of maternal alienators, while also missing the remaining 50 percent (Gordon et al., 2008). Gordon's research demonstrated that a cutoff of 78 and above also appears to mistakenly identify 16 percent of nonalienating mothers as alienating.

For fathers, a L + K - F profile of 84 and above appears to identify 50 percent of father alienators, while missing the remaining 50 percent. A cutoff of 84 and above also appears to mistakenly identify 16 percent of nonalienating fathers.

8. **Does the MMPI-2 profile of the alleging parent correspond to the (L + Pa + Sc) – (Hy + Pt) profile?** Using a T-score profile of 67 and above to rule in alienating behaviors for mothers appears to identify 50 percent of maternal alienators, while also missing the remaining 50 percent (Gordon et al., 2008). A cutoff of 67 and above also appears to mistakenly identify 16 percent of nonalienating mothers.

For fathers, a (L + Pa + Sc) – (Hy + Pt) profile of 65 and above appears to identify 50 pecent of father alienators, while missing the remaining 50 percent. A cut off of 65 and above also appears to mistakenly identify 16 percent of nonalienating fathers.

Cases in which the MMPI-2 profile of the alienating parent satisfies either the L + K – F index or the (L + Pa + Sc) – (Hy + Pt) index warrant tentative classification as fabricated allegations. Recall that either one of those indexes will identify approximately 50 percent of alienators. Moreover, the cutoff scores recommended here are provisional, awaiting data from samples much larger than that available to Gordon and colleagues.

The decision-making criteria discussed previously support developing hypotheses in cases like Donna's and Rachel's. In turn, these hypotheses necessitate additional testing. The differences between false allegations and fabricated allegations are not mutually exclusive, existing at some polar extremes. False allegations, fabricated allegations, and even substantiated allegations fall along a continuum. Substantiated allegations can also respond to exaggerated distortions. What amounts to a single episode of touching can mistakenly become numerous instances of penetration.

SEXUAL ALLEGATION IN DIVORCE CASES AND RELATED MYTHS

Legal and mental health professionals must be aware of the extent of misinformation inundating SAID cases. As a result, those cases often become treacherous minefields posing enormous risks for all who deal with them. The minefields become especially dangerous when armed with the following myths.

Myth 1

Diligent interviewers who go about their work carefully can accurately recall important details from their interviews with children, even when those interviews have not been recorded.

Fortunately, the vast majority of investigative interviews in cases of alleged CSA are electronically recorded. Some states mandate videotaping or audiotaping all investigative interviews with children in abuse or neglect investigations (e.g., California, Florida, Texas). Other states, however, allow local jurisdictions to establish policies for recording interviews (e.g., Michigan). The applicable research clearly demonstrates that, although advocating for the accuracy of their hearsay, interviewer testimony is typically quite mistaken in such circumstances.

A 1999 study examined how accurately twenty-seven experienced interviewers recalled details from their interviews with children between the ages of three and five (Warren & Woodall, 1999). The ages of these interviewers ranged from twenty-eight to fifty-three, average age of 40.59. Their experience in forensic and child protective work ranged from four to twenty-one years, averaging approximately 10.9 years. More than half of these interviewers (57%) had earned master's degrees, 30 percent held bachelor's degrees, and one had a doctoral degree. These interviewers reported a range of 3 to 400 training hours, or a range of 4 to 6 training days.

Those interviewers conducted videotaped interviews of children who, one month earlier, had witnessed two events: (1) a magic show and (2) a silly doctor visit. The interviewers were given one of two cue questions for beginning their interviews: (1) "I understand that a magician came to visit your school. Tell me what the magician did," or (2) "Tell me about the time you went with Tracy to play silly doctor." Except for those cue questions, the interviewers knew nothing else about these two events.

Immediately after their videotaped interviews with the children ended, the researchers audiotaped their interviews with the interviewers. In comparison to the amount of information children related during their videotaped interviews, the interviewers' hearsay accounts involved information loss. Asked what kinds of questions they used to elicit information from the children, most interviewers reported relying primarily on open-ended questions. In fact, however, reviewing the videotapes of the child interviews revealed that more than 80 percent of the questions were specific or close ended, and 16 percent were leading. Interviewers were asked if they could recall any child statements in their "own exact words." Very few interviewers could remember even a two-word or three-word phrase used by the children they interviewed.

In the course of their jobs, interviewers routinely interview many children about similar topics, and substantial amounts of time can elapse between an interview and testifying in a legal proceeding. Such circumstances impose a heavy burden on the memories of interviewers working under those conditions. The details of one interview can easily become confused and contaminated with the details of other interviews.

Warren and Woodall (1999) summarized their findings, emphasizing the following:

> Our results suggest that the hearsay testimony of children's interviewers is degraded. Even immediately after an interview, important content was omitted by hearsay accounts, and the majority of the verbatim (specific wording and content of questions and answers) was lost. Our results also suggest that interviewers are unlikely to be able to accurately reconstruct verbatim information later.

In view of the profound limitations on interviewer recall, attempts at bringing hearsay testimony into legal proceedings should be vigorously challenged.

Myth 2

Well-trained interviewers can record verbatim notes of their interviews that make electronic recordings unneccesary.

A 2000 study investigated the accuracy with which trained, experienced investigators recorded verbatim notes of their interviews (Lamb, Orbach, Sternberg, Hershkowitz & Horowitz, 2000). Specifically, this study compared the audiotaped recordings of twenty forensic interviews of alleged sexual abuse victims (five male and fifteen female four- to fourteen-year-olds) with the investigators' verbatim accounts (notes) of the same interviews. Twenty-five percent of the substantive (i.e., forensically relevant) details provided by the children were not represented in the investigators' notes. The investigators' notes reflected a total of 806 substantive utterances, whereas the audio recordings of the same interviews included 1889 utterances, leaving 1083 utterances (57.3%) unaccounted for by the investigators' supposed verbatim notes.

The investigators' notes misrepresented the utterances used to elicit information from the children. Only 44 percent of the interviewer utterances were accurately identified in the notes. In particular, there was a systematic tendency to mistakenly characterize interviewer questions as open ended when, in fact, the questions were close ended. These interviewers specifically failed to record 53 percent of their suggestive statements. Lamb and his colleagues also found that the interviewers understated their influence in eliciting information, and they also ignored some details of central importance. Lamb and his colleagues emphasized that their study raises "serious questions about the ability of interviewers to recall the content and structure of their interviews with the degree of precision needed for forensic purposes."

When interviewers offer hearsay testimony, we can conclude (1) the accuracy with which they recall what children say is less than reliable, (2) the accuracy with which they recall their own questioning style is less than reliable, (3) their attempts at relying on "contemporaneous/verbatim" notes are less than reliable, and (4) their claims that they complied with an interview protocol are less than reliable.

Myth 3

Sexually abused children exhibit behaviors and symptoms that allow expets to identify them as abused.

Various organizations and agencies have developed lists of behaviors and symptoms for identifying sexually abused children. The Safe Horizon organization, for example, lists "10 Signs of Child Abuse." These signs include returning to earlier behaviors (regression to earlier stages of development), fear of going home, changes in eating (resulting in weight gain or weight loss), sleep disturbances (nightmares or difficulty falling asleep), changes in school performance and attendance, lack of personal care or hygiene, risk-taking behaviors, and inappropriate sexual behaviors (overly sexualized behavior or explicit sexual language).

Relying on behavioral indicators to identify children who have been sexually abused neglects to consider what is known as base rates (Friedrich, 2005). Children who have been sexually abused often exhibit a broad range of non-specific symptoms from depressive withdrawal to aggressive acting out. In fact, the vast majority of children who exhibit this range of nonspecific behavioral symptoms have not been sexually abused. Nonspecific behavioral symptoms ranging from depressive withdrawal to aggressive acting out are high base-rate behaviors. Most children exhibit some symptoms within this range at some point in their development. Fortunately, sexual abuse is a comparatively low base-rate event. Depending on the definition of sexual abuse, only 10 to 20 percent of children are ever sexually abused. Therefore, relying on high base-rate behaviors (behavioral symptoms) to identify a low base-rate event inevitably leads to a substantial frequency of false-positive classifications, mistakenly concluding that a child has been sexually abused when she or he has not.

Consider the following example of mistakenly relying on high base-rate behaviors to identify a low base-rate event.

1. Sexually abused children regularly walk, talk, and drink water.
2. This child regularly walks, talks, and drinks water.
3. Therefore this child has been sexually abused.

To belabor the obvious, these assumptions result in an inordinate number of false-positive classifications.

The following computations also demonstrate the wholesale inadvisability of relying on behavioral indicators or symptoms to identify sexually abused children. Assume we have a sample of 1000 children between the ages of four and sixteen. Further assume that 20 pecent of this sample have been sexually abused. Also assume that 75 pecent of the abused children exhibit sexually inappropriate behavior, as defined earlier. Only 25 pecent of the nonabused children exhibit this kind of sexually inappropriate behavior. At this point, it might seem tempting to use sexually inappropriate behavior to rule in sexual abuse. Doing so, however, involves an unacceptable margin of error. Of our total sample, 200 (20%) of the children have been sexually abused. If 75 pecent of sexually abused children exhibit sexually inappropriate behavior, this equals 150 children. There are also 800 nonabused children remaining in our sample. If only 25 pecent of these 800 children exhibit sexually inappropriate behavior, this equals 200 children. In other words, there are more nonabused children who exhibit sexually inappropriate behavior than abused children exhibiting this behavior.

Myth 4

Body diagrams effectively assist children in identifying and describing where and how they have been touched on their bodies.

Body diagrams depict the outlines of adult males and females and of juvenile males and females. Previously, many child advocacy centers (CACs) used anatomically detailed dolls to assist the interviews of the children they assessed. Laboratory studies have asked two questions related to the dolls: (1) Are children's reports of touching, in response to doll-assisted interviews, sufficiently accurate for forensic purposes? (2) Do the dolls assist children in providing more information compared to verbal questions alone? The answers to both questions have been an emphatic "no" (Poole, Bruck & Pipe, 2011).

As the popularity of anatomical dolls diminished, interviewers increased the frequency with which they relied on body diagrams. Poole and her colleagues (2011) expressed devastating criticisms of body diagrams:

> Controlled laboratory studies that provide accuracy assessments do not support the use of body diagrams to elicit disclosures . . . body diagrams make it easy for children to point to body parts that were not touched during target experiences. Consequently, body diagrams elevate false reports of touching–even among children who actually experienced some touching (i.e., prompting them to report additional touches that had not occurred), and even among school-aged children.

Quite clearly, then, interviewers who continue to rely on body diagrams when interviewing children are insufficiently familiar with the relevant research.

Myth 5

For sexually abused children, disclosure is a process, not a one-time event.

CACs often interview children on multiple occasions in cases of suspected sexual abuse. The rationale for such practices insists that abused children will not disclose their abuse "until they are ready." Because of presumably anticipating retaliation or disbelief, children must "work through and resolve" their reluctance to disclose.

Bruck and Ceci (2004) have reported data demonstrating that more often than not, sexually abused children do not spontaneously disclose their abuse. Reporting the results from various studies, Bruck and Ceci found that only about one third of adults, sexually abused as children, recalled disclosing their abuse in a timely fashion. In a more extensive report of these same data, London, Bruck, Ceci, and Shuman (2005) emphasized that if sexually abused children are directly asked about their abuse, they do not deny but instead they tell. In other words, most sexually abused children do not disclose on their own accord, but if directly asked about any abuse, they promptly report what occurred. Consequently, insisting that disclosure is a process too often amounts to a feeble rationalization for interviewing children repeatedly. In response to repeated interviews, children learn what the interviewers want to hear, and under those circumstances, the children rarely disappoint their interviewers.

Myth 6

Subsequent to disclosing their abuse, sexually abused chidlren often recant their allegations.

Bruck, Ceci, and Hembrooke (1998) reported interviewing twenty-six highly trained child protection workers. These workers insisted that recantation was part of the typical process of disclosure. Recantation refers to children's disavowing their previously expressed allegations of sexual abuse. Those same workers also insisted that the relevant research strongly supported their position. In fact, however, Jones and McGraw (1987) found an an 8 percent recantation rate of only 309 validated sexual abuse cases. Bradley and Wood (1996) found that among 234 validated cases of sexual abuse, 5 percent of the children denied the abuse and only 3 percent recanted their earlier reports. Therefore, although a small percentage of children appear to disclose their abuse reluctantly when directly asked, with a smaller percentage subsequently recanting their disclosures, the overwhelming majority of children appear to maintain their claims and never deny them once they are questioned.

Myth 7

Interviewers undergo effective training and continue to maintain their skills after completing their training.

Many professionals who interview children in cases of alleged sexual abuse make claims about their specialized training. They insist that their training allows them to avoid interviewing children inappropriately. Despite these claims, no one knows how effective specialized training is in the areas of child abuse and child maltreatment. For example, one study in particular assessed the effectiveness of a comprehensive, ten-day, training seminar (Stevenson, Leung & Cheung, 1992). This was a seven-module curriculum–"Child Sexual Abuse Curriculum for Social Workers"–developed by the American Association for Protecting Children (AAPC), a division of the American Humane Association.

The study obtained "before" measurements of assessment skills from the professionals prior to their participating in the training seminar. Upon completing the training, the study also obtained "after" measurements of assessment skills from the participating professionals. The results of this study failed to support the hypothesis that overall assessment skills would improve subsequent to training. For a sample of twelve experienced Kentucky social workers, the average posttest score was slightly, but not significantly, higher than the pretest score. Therefore, training did not result in any reliable improvement for the Kentucky sample completing it.

In a sample of twenty-four experienced California social workers, however, the opposite occurred. Pretest scores were higher than posttest scores were. In other words, the assessment skills of the California sample declined slightly, though not significantly, as a result of the training. The results of that study are especially important because most training programs related to CSA are not so intensive. The usual training program in this area lasts two to three days at the most.

Typical training practices for interviewers too often fail because they rely on a lecture format, thereby reducing participants to passivity. Commenting on its RATAC interview protocol (which refers to Rapport, Anatomy identification, Touch inquiry, Abuse scenario, and Closure) the American Prosecutor's Research Institute advises, "RATAC cannot be learned by simply reading an article or attending a workshop. The protocol must be taught in a course that includes intense hands-on training" (p. 2) (Walters, Holmes, Bauer & Vieth, 2003). Poole and Lamb (1998) have also emphasized, "Whatever training techniques are used, all interviewers, no matter how experienced, benefit from refresher training and opportunities to review and discuss their interviews" (p. 242). Absent these opportunities, interviewers regress back into inappropriate practices (Mart, 2010).

Myth 8

Well-trained interviewers put forth persistent efforts to confirm the allegations of sexual abuse presented to them.

Rather than engage in efforts at confirming allegations, well-trained interviewers consider alternative hypotheses. Wakefield (2006) identified the following as alternative hypotheses when assessing allegations of CSA.

- The allegations are basically valid, but the child substituted a different person for the perpetrator.
- Some of the allegations are valid, but the child has invented or been influenced to make additional allegations that are false.
- The child misperceived innocuous or inappropriate but nonabusive behaviors as sexual abuse.
- The child has been influenced or pressured to make a completely false allegation to serve the needs of someone else.
- The child has fantasized the allegations, possibly because of psychological problems.

- The child initially made up the allegations but has talked to several people about them, and now they have become real to the child.
- The child saw pornographic magazines and pictures, saw a pornographic movie, or observed adults engaged in sexual activities, and that contributed to the allegations she later made.
- The child engaged in sex play with peers or siblings and then accused an adult.
- The child has been questioned repeatedly by adults who believe the child has been abused, and the child began making statements to please the adult, who then reinforced the child with attention or praise.

Testing alternative hypotheses necessitates that inteviewers abandon any single-minded pursuit of ruling in the allegations (Poole & Lamb, 1998).

Myth 9

Sexually abused children more readily disclose their abuse to interviewers whose gender matches their own.

A 2012 study reviewed the cases of 933 children interviewed as a result of alleged CSA at the CAC in Springfield, Missouri, between January 2009 and December 2009 (Fondren-Happel, Fanetti & Visio, 2012). That CAC used the "Cornerhouse Forensic Interview Process," also referred to as RATAC. Female interviewers conducted 65 percent of the interviews (n = 607), and male interviewers conducted 35 percent of the interviews (n = 326). If interviewer gender influenced the disclosures of male or female children, a three-way association between interviewer gender, child gender, and disclosure status would have been evident. No such association was found. Consequently, the relevant data do not support conventional assumptions that advise matching child and interviewer gender.

Myth 10

Play therapy is effective with children exhibiting a broad spectrum of clinical conditions.

Any evidence supporting the effectiveness of play therapy is characterized by its conspicuous absence. For example, play therapy does not appear to enhance academic or intellectual achievement (Clement & Milne, 1967; Clement, Fazzone & Goldstein, 1970). Treatment effects for play therapy are persistently absent when dealing with specific behavioral disorders (Kelly, 1976; Milos & Reiss, 1982). Moreover, play therapy does not improve the interpersonal adjustment of children who participate in it (McBrien & Nelson, 1972; Yates, 1976).

Even more sobering are the data demonstrating that play therapy does not effectively aid children known to have been abused. The study supporting this conclusion reported: "No consistent support was found for the hypothesis that time-limited play therapy would improve the adjustment of maltreated preschoolers who already were attending a therapeutic preschool. This lack of support was evident at both post-test and follow-up" (Reams & Friedrich, 1994).

As long ago as 1975, a review of treatment approaches for children emphasized that the era of blind faith in the activities of play therapy had ended (Davids, 1975). In other words, play therapy amounts to what–at best–is an experimental treatment not known to be effective. The parents of children participating in traditional approaches to child therapy–such as play therapy–view their children as responding positively to treatment. These parental impressions, however, are not supported by objective data. In other words, the outcomes these parents attributed to their children's therapy were influenced more by their excessively optimistic expectations than anything else (Weiss, Catron, Harris & Phung 1999).

Unfortunately, play therapy can distort and confuse the recall of children by undermining the accuracy of what they think they remember. In these cases of distorted memory, the therapist becomes the source of what the child remembers rather than the event in question. For example, one study investigated memories for performed actions compared to imagined actions (e.g., "Did you really touch your nose or did you just imagine yourself touching your nose?") Compared with adults, six-year-old children were far more likely to confuse memories of imagining doing and memories of actually doing (Foley & Johnson, 1985). Similarly, eight-year-old children also had difficulty discriminating actions they imagined another person doing from actions that they saw that person do (Lindsay, Johnson & Kwon, 1991).

Therefore, the "pretending" activities of play therapy can significantly contaminate a child's memory as a result of confusion between actual events and imagined events. Consequently, a play therapist can profoundly distort the memory of a child by suggesting interpretations of what the child supposedly encountered or experienced. In response to the therapist's influence, children accept these interpretations as legitimate. They then resort to their imaginations–though convinced they are searching their memories–inventing anecdotes of past events that appear to validate the therapist's interpretations (Campbell, 1992c).

In their widely recognized and accepted text that has received numerous awards, Ceci and Bruck (1995) advised against children's therapists' becoming involved in the forensic issues of an alleged sexual abuse case:

> Therapists should not attempt to "crack" the case or to discover other aspects of abuse that may be helpful to the courts. In general, they should stay out of the legal arena when the case concerns someone with whom they have a pre-existing therapeutic relationship; in such cases, they should leave forensic activities to another. (p. 290)

Ceci and Bruck moreover explain the danger of therapists eliciting false allegations of sexual abuse from the children they treat:

> [Therapy] involves the danger that the use of some therapeutic techniques that are intended to help a child interpret a victimization experience (e.g., fantasy play, symbolic interpretation, visualizations), and later regain control over it (e.g., self-empowerment training), may lead to co-construction of events and feelings that are not entirely reality based. This becomes a problem when the therapist herself testifies as to the reality of such constructions. (p. 291)

To conclude, mental health professionals and child welfare specialists who endorse any of these myths warrant massive skepticism. This kind of thinking elevates theory over fact, while often confusing one with the other. Ill-informed impressions, relying on what amounts to urban myths, threaten the welfare of children and families alike.

Editors' Notes

- Dr. Campbell points out that false allegations of CSA sometime occur in a case of PA. However, false allegations of CSA can occur without PA; and PA frequently occurs without false allegations of CSA.
- Dr. Campbell uses research on the SAID syndrome to explain how allegations evolve in high-conflict custody disputes. For instance, he explains how the SET factors aid clinicians in understanding the development of a false allegation.
- Dr. Campbell explains how research regarding MMPI-2 scales aids evaluators in differentiating PA-based false allegations from other allegations of CSA.
- Dr. Campbell summarizes a methodology for distinguishing true and false allegations of CSA.
- Dr. Campbell uses peer-reviewed research to describe ten myths regarding CSA allegations.

REFERENCES

Blush, G. J., & Ross, K. L. (1987). Sexual allegations in divorce: The SAID syndrome. *Conciliation Courts Review, 25*(1), 1–11.

Bradley, A. R., & Wood, J. M. (1996). How do children tell? The disclosure process in child sexual abuse. *Child Abuse & Neglect, 20*(9), 881–891.

Bruck, M., & Ceci, S. (2004). Forensic developmental psychology: Unveiling four common misconceptions. *Current Directions in Psychological Science, 13*(6), 229–232.

Bruck, M., Ceci, S. J., & Hembrooke, H. (1998). Reliability and credibility of young chidlren's reports: From research to policy and practice. *American Psychologist, 53*(2), 136–151.

Butcher, J. N., & Williams, C. L. (2000). *Essentials of MMPI-2 and MMPI-A interpretation* (2nd ed.). Minneapolis, MN: University of Minnesota Press.

Campbell, T. W. (1992a). False allegations of sexual abuse and their apparent credibility. *American Journal of Forensic Psychology, 10*(4), 21–35.

Campbell, T. W. (1992b). Psychotherapy with children of divorce: The pitfalls of triangulated relationships. *Psychotherapy, 29*(4), 646–652.

Campbell, T. W. (1992c). False allegations of sexual abuse and the persuasiveness of play therapy. *Issues in Child Abuse Accusations, 4*(3), 118–124.

Campbell, T. W. (1998). *Smoke and mirrors: The devastating effect of false sexual abuse claims.* New York: Plenum Press.

Ceci, S. J., & Bruck, M. (1995). *Jeopardy in the courtroom.* Washington, DC: American Psychological Association.

Clement, P. W., & Milne, D. C. (1967). Group play therapy and tangible reinforcers used to modify the behavior of eight-year-old boys. *Behavior Research and Therapy, 5*(4), 301–312.

Clement, P. W., Fazzone, R. A., & Goldstein, B. (1970). Tangible reinforcers and child group therapy. *Journal of the American Academy of Child and Adolescent Psychiatry, 9*(3), 409–427.

Davids, A. (1975). Therapeutic approaches to children in residential treatment: Changes from the mid-1950s to the mid-1970s. *American Psychologist, 30*(8), 809–814.

Eysenck, M. W., Mogg, K., May, J., Richards, A., & Mathews, A. (1991). Bias in interpretation of ambiguous sentences related to threat in anxiety. *Journal of Abnormal Psychology, 100*(2), 144–150.

Foley, M. A., & Johnson, M. K. (1985). Confusion between memories for performed and imagined actions. *Child Development, 56*(5), 1145–1155.

Fondren-Happel, R. N., Fanetti, M. N., & Visio, M. E. (2012). Effects of gender on rate of disclosure in the forensic interviews of children. *American Journal of Forensic Psychology, 30*(1), 45–57.

Friedrich, B. (2005). Correlates of sexual behavior in your children. *Journal of Child Custody, 2*(3), 41–55.

Gardner, R. A. (1987). *The parental alienation syndrome and the differentiation between fabricated and genuine sex abuse.* Cresskll, NJ: Creative Therapeutics.
Goldberg, L. R. (1972). Man versus mean: The exploitation of group profiles for the construction of diagnostic classification systems. *Journal of Abnormal Psychology, 79*(2), 121–131.
Gordon, R. M., Stoffey, R., & Bottinelli, J. (2008). MMPI-2 findings of primitive defenses in alienating parents. *The American Journal of Family Therapy, 36*(3), 211–228.
Graham, J. R. (2000). *MMPI-2: Assessing personality and psychopathology.* New York: Oxford University Press.
Halberstadt, J. D., Niedenthal, P. M., & Kushner, J. (1995). Resolution of lexical ambiguity by emotional state. *Psychological Science, 6*(5), 278–282.
Jones, D., & McGraw, J. M. (1987). Reliable and fictitous accounts of sexual abuse in children. *Journal of Interpersonal Violence, 2*(1), 27–45.
Kelly, C. (1976). Play desensitization of fear of darkness in preschool children. *Behavior Research and Therapy, 14*(1), 79–81.
Kelly, J. B., & Johnston, J. R. (2001). The alienated child: A reformulation of parental alienation syndrome. *Family Court Review, 39*(3), 249–266.
Lamb, M. E., Orbach, Y., Sternberg, K. J., Hershowitz, I., & Horowitz, D. (2000). Accuracy of investigators' verbatim notes of their forensic interviews with alleged child abuse victims. *Law and Human Behavior, 24*(6), 699–708.
Lindsay, D. S., Johnson, M. K., & Kwon, P. (1991). Developmental changes in memory source monitoring. *Journal of Experimental Child Psychology, 52*(3), 297–318.
London, K., Bruck, M., Ceci, S. J., & Schuman, D. W. (2005). Disclosure of child sexual abuse: What does the research tell us about the ways that children tell? *Psychology, Public Policy, and Law, 11*(1), 194–226.
Mart, E. G. (2010). Common errors in the assessment of allegations of child sexual abuse. *The Journal of Psychiatry & Law, 38,* 325–343.
McBrien, R. J., & Nelson, R. J. (1972). Experimental group strategies with primary grade children. *Elementary School Guidance and Counseling, 6*(3), 170– 174.
Milos, M. E., & Reiss, S. (1982). Effects of three play conditions on separation anxiety in young children. *Journal of Consulting and Clinical Psychology, 50*(3), 389–395.
Poole, D. A., & Lamb, M. E. (1998). *Investigative interviews of children.* Washington, DC: American Psychological Association.
Poole, D. A., Bruck, M., & Pipe, M. E. (2011). Forensic interviewing aids: Do props help children answer questions about touching? *Current Directions in Psychological Science, 20*(1), 11–15.
Reams, R., & Friedrich, W. (1994). The efficacy of time-limited play therapy with maltreated preschoolers. *Journal of Clinical Psychology, 50*(6), 889– 899.
Ross, K. L., & Blush, G. J. (1990). Sexual Abuse Validity Discriminators in the Divorced or Divorcing Family. *Child Abuse Accusations, 2*(1), 1–6.
Stevenson K. M., Leung P., & Cheung K. M. (1992). Competency-based evaluation of interviewing skills in child sexual abuse cases. *Social Work Research and Abstracts, 28*(3), 11–16.

Wakefield, H. (2006). Guidelines on investigatory interviewing of children: What is the consensus of the scientific community? *American Journal of Forensic Psychology, 24*(3), 57–74.

Walters, S., Holmes, L., Bauer, G., & Vieth, V. (2003). *Finding words: Half a nation by 2010–Interviewing and preparing children for court.* Alexandria, VA: American Prosecutors Research Institute.

Warren, A. R., & Woodall, C. E. (1999). The reliability of hearsay testimony: How well do interviewers recall their interviews with children? *Psychology, Public Policy and Law, 5*(2), 355–371.

Weiss, B., Catron, T., Harris, V., & Phung, T. M. (1999). The effectiveness of traditional child psychotherapy. *Journal of Consulting and Clinical Psychology, 67*(1), 82–94.

Yates, L. E. (1976). The use of sociometry as an identifier of a research sample for psychological treatment and quantifier of change among second grade students. *Group Psychotherapy, Psychodrama, and Sociometry, 29,* 102– 110.

Chapter 7

REUNIFICATION PLANNING AND THERAPY

S. Richard Sauber

Vignette

Following the terms of the parents' marital settlement agreement for cooperative shared parental responsibility of their ten-year-old son Sam, this parenting plan was operating effectively for three years. The parents had a 50/50 time-sharing arrangement. Suddenly, an unexplained event occurred and the ten-year-old son protested that he no longer wished to see his father, speak with him, or maintain any contact with him or any of the members of his father's family. The child asserted that his father upset him when he raised his voice because he did not do his chores at his father's home. The mother brought the child to a psychologist to calm her son's distress. The therapist recommended that the ten year old cease having contact with his father while he was attending psychotherapy during the next few months. The father objected both to his exclusion by the doctor, who refused to conduct joint father-son sessions in treating his son and to the fact that he never consented to his son's seeing this doctor, chosen by his former wife. The therapist should not make custodial recommendations, such as stating that he should not have contact with his son for a month or so while the therapist is providing counseling, nor see the child without both parents' consent. Subsequently, the father, with the mother's consent, found another therapist willing to provide family therapy, and this therapist did not address custodial recommendations.

Initially, the second mental health professional (MHP) felt that the child was indoctrinated by the mother against the father, but shortly thereafter, she became convinced by the mother's persuasiveness and charm that the ten year old was justified in being angry with his father. Then, the father withdrew his consent for further counseling, and he brought an ethics complaint against each of these two mental health providers. Usually, it is the alienating parent who files complaints with the state board of regulation, but in this case, it was the father, the target parent.

One year later, the father obtained a court-ordered visitation schedule for bi-weekly contact and a court-ordered appointment for a reunification therapist (RT). This third MHP chose to withdraw from his role of "reunifying" after several office visits, however. The reason given was that the case was too complicated and his inexperience in serving in this capacity as a court-involved therapist caused him discomfort in how to achieve the objective of reunification. The now twelve-year-old immature child receives traditional individual psychotherapy with the same psychologist who originally was asked to provide the reunification therapy. The son claims he has no problems to justify the need for any kind of counseling other than being forced to "waste his time with his father." The puzzled and frustrated father contrasts his prior close and loving relationship with his son to his current detachment, his now acting emotionally aloof, and his continually expressing a nasty, rejecting attitude toward him. The father acts patiently and extends himself with kindness, but his son does not respond accordingly. The mother supports her son in insisting that he should have a choice of whether or not he sees his father or even engages in sports with him. The mother thinks that the father should not have contact with the minor child until he gets professional help for his alleged problems of ineffective parenting and anger management.

Three MHPs, a court-appointed guardian ad litem (GAL), and a court-ordered visitation schedule did not alter Sam's resistance and lack of interest in having access to his father and his father's family. A forensic psychologist conducted a mental status examination of the father and found no impairment in his mental stability, in other words, no anger disorder or deficits in his parental competency. For example, he maintains a positive, healthy relationship with his other children from his former marriage and demonstrates effective parenting in all areas. The mother and her attorney have petitioned the court against the father's repeated requests to have a reunification plan developed by a forensic examiner who would conduct a study of the family. The father has never reconnected with his son, and Sam has never changed his beliefs about him or his resistant attitude about his forced compliance by the court in having to visit with his father. The mother's opinion has not been altered despite the testimony by the forensic examiner that the father has no anger problem or parenting shortcomings. The mother remains firmly entrenched with the assertion and storyline to the court that Sam should not have contact with the father until he gets professional help for his alleged anger management difficulties and parent training for his inappropriate approaches to child discipline. The judge is bewildered as to why the minor child has not resumed normal time-sharing with his father by enjoying his company and feeling the love for him and attachment with him as he did in the past. The only complaint alleged against the father was his insistence that he do his nominal chores in his household to learn responsible behavior instead of being defiant and spoiled in the manner in which he was being raised by his mother.

The presiding judge finally agreed to order a study of the family including interviewing collateral contacts and developing a reunification plan that would be effective because the traditional judicial methods he had available did not work in this case. The reunification plan called for the son to reside with the father for one year, proving an opportunity for them to rebond as their prior positive relationship had been. The collateral contacts attested to the fact that the father previously had a very close relationship with Sam. Evidence was provided that the minor child was moderately alienated, with a prognosis of a "parentectomy" in time had there not been a court intervention for reunification. The mother was permitted standard visitation but no phone calls during the time in which their son was residing with his father. This aspect of the order eliminated the likelihood of the mother-son conspiracy and alignment against the father to continue and prevented interference, which the reunification planner/evaluator determined was likely to occur.

A six-month follow-up indicated the absence of the initial resistance and temper tantrums of the son, as had been expected, and that a successful reintegration and close loving relationship between the father and his son had begun to occur. Brief reunification therapy was helpful to manage the child's initial anger in refusing to speak and interact with his father. The father was a nurturing and empathetic parent by nature who also was able to set limits despite his desire to indulge his son. He was tempted to please him with his whims and win over his affection once again. He was able to demonstrate consistency in managing his alienated child so that no further therapy was necessary. The ongoing option of continuing therapy was described in the reunification plan, and it could commence anytime upon request by either the son or his father. Had the court not ordered sanctions based upon the proposed plan of the reunification evaluation, in other words, temporary reversal of custody and restricted phone or text messaging by the alienating mother, this outcome probably never would have been achieved. The father would have lost contact with his son, as is often the outcome of cases such as this vignette presents.

HISTORY OF REUNIFICATION THERAPY

The term reunification therapy was introduced into the mental health and legal literature much like the new construct of "parenting coordination." However, protective services within the dependency courts have used the term "reunification" because it applies to offending parents enrolled in mandatory substance abuse, domestic violence, parenting, and therapeutic programs. When a parent exhibited child abuse or neglect, the children were placed in protective custody. Efforts were made to reunify the parent with his or her child or children by child welfare workers employed in a variety of social service agencies (*see* the Adoption Assistance and Child Welfare Act of 1980, which was extended in the Adoption and Safe Family Act of 1997 [Child Welfare League of America, 2002]). In mental health practice, as opposed to the social welfare system, the term reconciliation therapy was described. This construct was used in marital therapy from colloquial usage describing couples reconciling their differences. "Reunifying," however, brings to light the fact that there was a break or disruption of a prior-existing relationship within the intact family system or subsystem. The term suggests that fragmentation of the family unit was in need of repair or rehabilitation, hence, reunifying. In contrast to a fragmentation or separation in the core of the family system, reconciliation refers to an issue or issues in conflict causing friction or dissonance, and often is considered a "surface" conflict to resolve. Thus, the dependency courts rather than the family court appropriately used this term to protect a child from abuse or neglect based upon an established codified process of reunification. Parents had to fulfill certain necessary requirements within a specified period of time or face the threat of losing their parental rights.

During the year 2000, reunification became accepted as a construct to describe the progression of reconnecting or reunifying family members through various therapeutic procedures, techniques, and conditions. This approach is still in its experimental phase or infancy stage of development. This new process now becomes part of the types of therapies covered by the classification of court-involved therapy. There are no process and outcome research studies, however, and only theoretical guidance by experienced family forensic and clinical mental health practitioners to offer practice standards. Child welfare workers offer case studies of assessment and program completion as a prerequisite to reunifying. Ethical guidelines need to be established for the RT to follow rather than guessing what to do next and no longer relying on attendance in court-based programs without meeting evaluation criteria for release.

The role of an RT is unique, distinct, and different from that of the traditional role of the mental health counselor or family therapist as depicted in the approach comparison chart in Table 7.1. This new role requires an interdisciplinary way of operating in which the mental health approach interfaces with the legal system much like forensic psychologists must understand how the court operates and how the statutes apply when they become invited guests in this foreign territory. Forensic examiners must understand the laws and the legal implications because these variables affect their professional role and function in following the rules of the court and the ethical guidelines of their profession. Thus, we have the roles of a forensic evaluator and a forensic therapist, currently referred to as court-involved therapist. The latter refers to any court-ordered treatment or court-appointed specialist in which reunification therapy is one particular subspecialty of this type of forensic practice.

Table 7.1.
COMPARISON OF TRADITIONAL PSYCHOTHERAPY WITH REUNIFICATION THERAPY

The chart below explains the essential differences between each of these forms of therapy. There is consideration confusion within the mental health field between individual, couple, and family therapy versus court-ordered therapy. The latter refers to a forensic context in which the order and way in which the therapy is conducted is accountable to legal guidelines and roles and must be followed. This form of therapy does not offer the same freedom of theoretical orientation, therapeutic options and discretion by the therapist to alter procedures, make referrals, and change the goals according to what the MHP determines is most helpful to the patient at the immediate time that this service is provided. The following twenty categories assist the practitioner in identifying the uniqueness and distinction among each approach, the purpose, and the objectives to be achieved.

CATEGORIES/ ISSUES	PSYCHO-THERAPY	REUNIFICATION	CONFLICT TYPE
1. Whose client is patient/litigant?	Mental health practitioner	Attorney, jurisdiction of the court	Professional role
2. Relational privilege that governs disclosure in each relationship	Therapist–patient privilege	Informed consent and/or court order for full disclosure and nonconfidentiality	Professional role

Table 7.1–*Continued*

CATEGORIES/ ISSUES	PSYCHO-THERAPY	REUNIFICATION	CONFLICT TYPE
3. Finances	Self-pay or family member, managed care or insurance reimbursement	Predetermined by attorneys and/or court, percentage or full financial responsibility clearly determined in advance. Unlikely insurance coverage which requires *DSM* diagnosis and other noncovered, nontherapeutic services	Who pays does not determine the process nor the outcome
4. Roles	Latitude may start with one presenting problem and therapist switches roles, e.g., individual sex therapy changed to couples therapy	Limited, restricted, and well-defined role	RT must refer out to another therapist or back to court for therapist appointment to provide psychotherapy, e.g., depression or substance abuse
5. Goals	Therapeutic objectives are mutually determined between the therapist and the patient. Patient defines problem; therapist reframes difficulty according to diagnosis and assessment and a therapeutic plan or contract is established	Client, attorney, and court define narrow objectives and focus on reunification without deviation into other areas that may require a referral for professional attention	Different preferences and goals for the child and each of the parents

continued

Table 7.1–*Continued*

CATEGORIES/ ISSUES	PSYCHO-THERAPY	REUNIFICATION	CONFLICT TYPE
6. Process variables	Alleviation of symptoms and specific behavior changes, such as overcoming depression or relapse prevention	Overcoming visitation refusal, fears, or phobias of reconciliation with target parent and clarification and reframing of foundation for the rejection and unfavorable attitude on the part of either parent or both parents and the child	Maintaining boundaries both in content and in role
7. Selection of MHP	Self-referral recommendation, or managed care list	In mild or moderate cases, parents may agree or the attorney may recommend or submit names to the court or the court will make the court or the court will make the choice. In moderate to severe cases of alienation, target parents select the RT according to their comfort level and the expertise of the RT within this specialized area	Choice by target parent vs. by parental agreement. RT must have no prior relationship with the family to avoid dual roles

Table 7.1–*Continued*

CATEGORIES/ ISSUES	PSYCHO-THERAPY	REUNIFICATION	CONFLICT TYPE
8. Theoretical foundation	Therapist choice according to presenting problem	Family systems model in which the identified patient is the family. Flexibility and documentation are encouraged because RT is in its infancy as a new therapeutic modality. It is a structured and focused intervention. Cognitive-behavioral and in vivo desensitization have been described as helpful techniques	Blame and assignment of fault. No outcome efficacy studies to date support RT theoretical foundation
9. Participants	Patient and collateral individuals	For mild and mild to moderate alienation cases, both parents and children participate; for moderate to severe and severe alienation cases, only the target parent and one or more of the alienated or high-risk children may be designated to participate individuality, conjointly or sucessively	Attempts by the alienating parent to interfere or participate obstructively in the process by undermining the child's attitude and authority of the target parent, attendance and participation in the reunification

continued

Table 7.1–*Continued*

CATEGORIES/ ISSUES	PSYCHO-THERAPY	REUNIFICATION	CONFLICT TYPE
10. Rules or process guidelines	Determined by therapist and patient	Guidelines for practice standards and ethical considerations and specific judicial orders, e.g., reporting requirements for success such as increased frequency of visitation and obstacles encountered from either parent or child requiring court intervention	Parties and attorneys resistant to change
11. Frequency of visits	Weekly or as defined by the patient and therapist	1–3 times per week as defined by the reunification plan, order of the court, or the therapeutic experience or progress of the RT who makes the decision	Resistance to participation by the child and/or alienating/ "favored" parent
12. Cognitive set and evaluative attitude of each MHP	Supportive, empathetic; may be directive or nondirective	Direct, neutral, objective, detached, goal-driven without distraction/ deviation	Structured vs. unstructured approach

Table 7.1–*Continued*

CATEGORIES/ ISSUES	PSYCHO-THERAPY	REUNIFICATION	CONFLICT TYPE
13. The nature and degree of alliance in each relationship	A helping relationahip; allies or advocacy, rarely adversarial	A helping relationship based upon detailed documentation, external pressure for compliance, court sanctions or punitive measures for noncompliance with anticipated resistance by the child supported by the likely adversarial alienating other parent	Sensitivity to feelings and likeability vs. adherence to role and respect for following predetermined procedures and goals
14. The different areas of competency for each expert	Therapy techniques for the treatment of the impairment	Training and experience in the areas of custody evaluations, forensic psychology, divorce mediation and/or parent coordination and family therapy	Adequacy of foundation/ professional qualifications
15. The nature of the hypotheses tested by the mental health professional	Diagnostic criteria for the purpose of therapy	Psycholegal criteria for the purpose of legal adjudication and family reconciliation	Adequacy of foundation/ parent-child contact: frequency and relationship
16. Amount and control of structure in each relationship	Patient-therapist flexibility in establishing the process and techniques	RT structured and relatively inflexible compared to psychotherapy with the control being defined by the specific objectives	Adequacy of foundation/ therapeutic techniques to achieve goals

continued

Table 7.1–*Continued*

CATEGORIES/ ISSUES	PSYCHO-THERAPY	REUNIFICATION	CONFLICT TYPE
17. The scrutiny applied to the information used in the process and the role of historical truth	Patient report with minimum external scrutiny as the truth or accuracy disclosed to the therapist; therapist opinion	Litigant information supplemented with and verified by collateral sources and scrutinized by the RT and the court. Prior to the initiation of RT, RT must review documents and obtain objective history of the case in order to achieve objectives as defined by the court	Adequacy of foundation/ subjective vs. objective information and reporting
18. The goal of the professional in each relationship	Therapist defines treatment goals with patient's participation in an attempt to benefit the patient by working within the therapeutic relationship	RT addresses the goals as defined by the court and later refined by the RT according to progress in achieving stated objectives of alienated child (children) and target parent. Progress affects cooperation vs. resistance of the alienating parent and how this parent will accommodate to the changes taking place, etc., supportive vs. sabotaging. The accom-	Professional role/ patient preferences vs. court order. Real vs. false allegations require clarification. Fabricated complaints such as child endangement from increased visitation with the target parent must be addressed in court, either delaying or suspending RT until complaint resolved

Table 7.1–*Continued*

CATEGORIES/ ISSUES	PSYCHO-THERAPY	REUNIFICATION	CONFLICT TYPE
		modation and/or readjustment of the alienating parent's attitudes and behavior is or will be addressed by his or her individual therapist, the parent coordinator, the GAL, and/or ultimately the presiding judge	
19. The impact of the critical judgment by the mental health professional on the therapeutic relationship, process variables, and outcome	The basis of the relationship is the therapeutic alliance; gains or errors in the critical judgment of the therapist may impair or enchance that alliance, e.g., depression and suicide or drinking and driving. Therapist serves as patient's advocate	The basis of the relationship is successive approximations and objectivity toward the defined goal within an evaluative framework; critical judgment is less likely to cause serious serious emotional harm in contrast to exacerbation of conflict, child temper tantrums, and false allegations generated by the alienating parent. Child safety and the child's well-being always are the priority	Professional role/ relationship determined by therapist-patient vs. court mandate and parental and child compliance to the reunification plan

continued

Table 7.1–*Continued*

CATEGORIES/ ISSUES	PSYCHO-THERAPY	REUNIFICATION	CONFLICT TYPE
20. Criteria for success	Patient satisfaction	Effectiveness based upon evidence and documentation in achieving temporary, and forecasting long-term, reconciliation and stabilization. Success may be defined as ability for alienated child and target parent to be able to interact and maintain a limited visitation schedule, or reestablish a relationship to maintain a visitation schedule and shared parenting, or ideally establish or reestablish a strong emotional bond and attachment with one another and enjoy the frequency to time-sharing and the alienating parent would cease alienation tactics	Adequacy of foundation/party preferences vs. adhering to state statutes for shared parenting responsibility

The process of reunification also is different from parenting coordination, a concept introduced in 2001 and developed by the task forces of the Association of Family Conciliation Courts (AFCC) in 2002 and 2003, resulting in model standards of parenting coordination and finally the published guidelines in 2005. Essentially, it is an alternative dispute resolution process to help parents in conflict make parenting decisions and comply with parental agreements and orders.

The overall objective of the parenting coordinator is to assist high-conflict parents to implement their parenting plan, to monitor compliance with the details of the plan, to resolve conflicts regarding their children and the parenting plan in a timely manner, and to protect and sustain safe, healthy, and meaningful parent-child relationships (Association of Family and Consiliation Courts [AFCC], 2005).

CURRENT DEVELOPMENTS

There are definitions and distinctions among the terms of reunification, reunification plan or reunification evaluation, and reunification therapy. From a historical perspective, reunification was illustrated by the experience of reunification in Germany and the events that took place in 1990. Specifically, in 1989, there was the opening of the Berlin Wall, which had divided the city into two German states since 1945. Some authorities avoid the term reunification and prefer to use the term unification of the two German states. This event is referred to as the "turning point."

The task in the mental health field was to create a suitable framework to describe the process of the reconnection or reunification versus the disconnection or continued separation. That is, it is one thing to classify the etiology resulting from a marital separation and another thing to identify the factors that may cause such an entity as a family to become unified or reunified once a diagnosis has taken place. The family disruption is not necessarily a temporary state but rather a separation that has withstood the test of time against internal and external pressures. Time, in a child's mind, must be a human calculation, not a determination by the calendar.

The process of unifying or the unification of the entity, such as the family, that was previously divided is "the act of coming together again." Specifically, "again" means the family previously was integrated and cohesive. The family may or may not have been stable. Stability refers to a homeostatic condition of high functioning whereas integrated and cohesive have different connotations related to interconnectivity. An alcoholic may well be integrated into the family and his or her presence may be part of the cohesive unit, but nevertheless, instability is exhibited in the episodic behavior of intoxication and alcohol abuse. The mental health field has used the term of reconciliation rather than reunification, most popularly as in the term of "marital reconciliation." The meaning is translated as "to restore again, to settle or resolve a dispute, to bring oneself to accept, to bring into harmony or agreement as to reconcile different points of views between spouses." The child welfare workers within the confines of the dependency court advanced this concept as it is often applied today. As noted in the vignette, nothing helped this family until the judge ordered an evaluative plan, and reunification therapy proceeded according to this plan of working through the initial resistance of the son who was ordered to temporarily reside with his father.

Integrating or reunifying a family in which alienation has taken place can be seen as having multiple levels of experience and meaning. Often a brief review results in a preliminary assumption, but further inspection of the reverberating impact must be examined and understood. For example, the one level could be a father and a child who have previously spent quality time together but who now rejoin in the absence of any emotional feeling, expression, attachment, or bond. This may be considered family time together only because of an obligation or as a result of a court order. In the vignette, this was exemplified by the son's "forced" compliance to visitation prior to the court order for a plan and the commencement of reunification therapy.

The second level of achieved reunification would be that of sharing an activity and spending time with the family members who were disengaged or disjointed. Now, however, the father and son might describe that they are having fun together while swimming and throwing a ball, laughing and experiencing spontaneous expressions of thoughts and feelings. This sharing of a mutually enjoyable activity together certainly goes beyond the first level at terms of obligation. At this second level, the relationship encountered does not reach the level in which there is a meaningful attachment, a close emotional connection, and a feeling of being bonded and truly integrated once again as was experienced in the past as a family subset or subunit of the family. Nonetheless, it gives recognition to the possibility of a mutually pleasant time together.

The third level is based upon evidence of a genuine and natural expression of a desire for those members of the family who previously experienced the strain, divided loyalty, or the split or disconnect to once again rejoice in the love and intimacy they previously shared prior to the martial separation or family disruption. There are no longer any psychological boundaries, family fences of dissention, or even rules that become obstacles to the expression of spontaneity or the expression of joy and the desire for access. The son in the vignette at this level now would be saying to his mother, "I can't wait to see Dad." Sam might call his father, telling him that he misses him and soon again wants to see him. Once the father reciprocates his interest and availability, the child tells his mother that he is going to see his dad either that same day or that weekend. Spontaneous phone calls are an expression of immediacy and good feelings, resembling the natural state of an integrated family that experiences unification even though the family members happened to be physically separated. Examples might include a child calling her paternal grandparent to say hello or e-mailing her paternal cousin to see how she did on her school project or asking her father to accompany her at her feared dental appointment. The child and target parent no longer feel fragmented or distraught in their father-son relationship at this third level.

The process of reunification often is stepwise in the sense that reunification starts with an obligatory visit; then progresses to a fun, shared activity; and eventually results in reliving the time-sharing as if it were in the "good old days" of a genuine, mutually expressed, loving, and caring relationship. Prior to the reunification therapy, the alienated child is likely to refuse any contact or rebel against the visit or the time-sharing that took place under protest, for example, the child sitting alone in her or his room or refusing to look at or speak with the target parent during their scheduled time together.

There are exceptional situations of "spontaneous reunification" in which abrupt, unexpected, or forced events or a crisis create a new circumstance, a new opportunity, a new excuse to allow the reunification to take place. For example, the death, illness, or accident in which the residential parent dies or becomes ill with a life-threatening disease or injury; the target parent is challenged by illness or injury and the child suddenly reacts with an interest in reconnecting; or a circumstance in which the court order requires a reversal of residential custody and the alienating parent no longer has ongoing contact with the child. There also have been situations in which the child attends a college in a distant location from his or her prior residence, which provides an opportunity for spontaneous reunification once the child no longer lives in a home replete with imposed constraints and restraints in communicating with the target parent. This circumstance offers the adolescent a new situation in which he or she is freed from the verbal inculcation and divided loyalty conflicts. Now the teenager can openly speak, without the residential alienating parent listening to his or her conversation; conveying and imposing expectations; programming indoctrinations; and forcing the child to follow the imposed party line.

The AFCC recently published a document that defines and outlines court-ordered therapy as different and distinct from psychotherapy entitled *Guidelines for Court-Involved Therapy* (2010). The suggested standard practices and ethical guidelines developed by the AFCC apply and have direct relevance to reunification therapy as a type of specific court-ordered therapy.

The current practice of reunification therapy most often occurs as a result of a court order that has the advantage of authority and power for the process of reunifying. Unfortunately, the prevailing and common practice of court orders rarely specifies either the nature or rules of the therapy or the conduct requirements of the family members participating. These orders likewise do not offer sanctions to ensure that the therapeutic process is attending to the already identified obstacles that are likely to sabotage any hope or benefit of reunification.

The guidelines formulated by the AFCC are intended to serve as a reference for those who depend on mental health services or on the opinions of MHPs in

> promoting effective treatment and assessing the quality of treatment services. The guidelines also are intended to assist the courts to develop clear and effective court orders and parenting plans that may be necessary for treatment to be effective. The purpose of these guidelines is to educate, highlight common concerns, and to apply relevant, ethical and professional guidelines, standards, and research in handling court-involved families. Family and juvenile court cases involving therapeutic services introduce unique factors and dynamics that require consideration in the treatment process. Both the treatment process and information provided to the therapist are likely to be influenced by the family's involvement in a legal process. While appropriate treatment can offer considerable benefit to the children and families, inappropriate treatment may escalate family conflict and cause significant damage. (AFCC, 2010, p. 1)

The same differentiation that the AFCC made between a court-involved therapist, a court-appointed therapist, and a court-ordered therapist also applies to the RT. The RT may be any MHP providing psychological treatment to a parent, child, or family who at any time during the treatment is involved with the legal system. This role and the goal of reunification therapy are easily confused with family counseling, however, which is not reunification therapy in the formal sense. In reunification work, a court-appointed RT is a MHP providing psychological treatment because the particular therapist was ordered by a judge to specifically provide reunification therapy based upon the client's, attorney's, or judge's belief that this individual is qualified to offer this specialized service. The court order identifies by name the RT and, hopefully, describes the parameters of expected treatment. The greater the detail in the order, the clearer the expectation and accountability of what is planned. A detailed reunification therapy order should provide a blueprint for the RT to follow and for the clients to comply with. In contrast to a therapist providing what they or their clients may call reunification therapy, the preference would be for court-ordered reunification therapy. In cases in which the court order does not designate a specific RT, it should describe a plan of treatment that clarifies the variables that follow.

- Degree of and nature of court involvement
- Degree of and nature of involvement with the parents, children, and collateral contacts
- The difference between the treating RT and the forensic evaluator or MHP forensic expert
- An explanation of the absence of confidentiality, as an ethical duty, and the absence of privilege, a legal right, in reunification therapy.

If a custody evaluation has taken place and the evaluator has figured out the alienation mystery, providing evidence to the court as to the etiology and prognosis, then it is expected that the recommendations will include an effective remedy to the alienation (Sauber & Worenklein, 2012). The detailed suggestions will include the needed blueprint of what is to follow in the reunification process of therapy. Thus, there is no need for a reunification planner or an RT to assess what to do in their therapeutic approach. If the custody evaluator (CE) is inept or misled by the convincing alienator and the emotional presentation of the child or children, however, then it is necessary to have a plan to mitigate the misguided direction set forth by the custody evaluator. Additionally, in cases in which there has been an absence of a custody evaluation, whether by identified need or by the legal proceedings that have taken place, then again the benefit is obvious for a plan. The new role of the planner is to offer the court the required direction and rules for effective intervention or the appointed RT must assess the circumstances and the vast array of professionals and lay persons involved to determine the course to follow, including requests for court sanctions where necessary either before commencing or in the early stages of the reunification.

Mandated informed consent should occur at the start of reunification therapy or preferably already explained to the parties so that it is clear that all information will be not be considered as private but rather available to the clients, attorneys, and the court in much the same manner as in parenting coordination. In contrast, psychotherapy and divorce mediation procedures do not utilize the information beyond the individual or parties involved in the process. HIPAA obligations will not apply because the court will specify that any electronic transmission of treatment information will become accessible to the court as part of the reunification therapy order. This openness and flow of information to certain designated individuals such as the GAL and judge would be explained in an age-appropriate manner to the children.

Inherent in this explanation is the requirement for detailed documentation in order for the court to fully understand the unique reunification approach and procedure. Also included should be the progress and obstacles that have been encountered, the identification of any high-risk variables, the status of the financial arrangements, and any other information discovered or identified that may be pertinent for the court to review. The records of the reunification therapy need continual updating with progress notes included of each session and out-of-session communication that takes place. The court will determine which parties receive what communication at what time. Testimony may occur at any time, as is characteristic of any type of court-involved therapy. RTs must understand the potential impact of the scope and nature of their testimony while recognizing the limits of their knowledge, role, and opinions expressed according to the code of ethics of the MHP discipline that they represent in their education, training, and practice.

The court order also should explain that the natural working alliance applied in general therapy is different in contrast to a legal dispute in which the task and objectives of reunification therapy are defined by the court. In cases of mild, and to some extent moderate, forms of alienation, the court order should require both parents to participate, whereas in some cases of moderate and most cases involving severe alienation, only the target parent generally participates with the child. In the former situation, the alienating parent is willing or receptive or at least says he or she is compliant to changing alienating behavior based upon the instruction and guidance of the RT. In contrast, the latter circumstance shows that the agenda of alienation is quite clear and there is no intention or motivation to alter the behavior that has caused the child's alienation and rejection of the target parent.

The benefit of court-appointment or court-ordered reunification therapy is certainly that the boundaries of the RT are appropriate and that there is no misunderstanding in the defined role or mistaken belief concerning multiple roles. For example, in family therapy, the marital and family therapist (MFT) may occasionally see the episodic alcoholic individually as an adjunct to participation in AA as part of ongoing family treatment goals with the children, or with the spouse. In reunification therapy, there is no boundary crossing in therapeutic roles, and any of the participants in the reunification therapy who need psychotherapy would seek these services as separate and distinct from reunification. The court, not the RT, should arrange for any referrals for the parents or children independent of the RT. Sometimes these referrals may be based upon the suggestion or recommendation of the RT, but this should not be a routine practice. There have been cases reported of the RT sharing office space or in a group practice or even married to another therapist who is simultaneously providing treatment to the alienating parent. This is a clear violation of the mental health ethics of all disciplines and a violation of boundaries that must be avoided in hopes of an outcome of real reunification in alienation cases. A couple team approach is different in traditional family therapy as opposed to an alienated child being reunited to the target parent in court-ordered therapy. The RT is warned to know what they are doing or to seek consultation to escape a malpractice action because of their naïveté or ignorance.

A court order for reunification also should provide that the RT seek additional information about the family and case history during the process while always maintaining professional objectivity. In cases of alienation, the belief exists that "children do not lie" as in other forms of therapy. Alienated children are "brainwashed," however, and the compelling arguments of the alienating parent frequently persuade therapists to change their opinions and may alter the course of therapy. When bias and subjectivity creep into the therapeutic process, an RT should voluntarily and formally withdraw from this role. Otherwise, the therapy is contaminated when the MHP believes the child's absurd complaints about the other parent are justified contrary to the evidence.

Children can be very convincing in that they say what they want and believe that they know what is in their best interests, citing borrowed scenarios from the alienating parent as if it was their original thinking. For example, alienating parents often push the child, their attorney, and the judge to listen to the words of the child as a witness in court. Alienated children are known to be robbed of their own emotions and thoughts through the campaign of programming and denigration by the alienating parent. Their words and actions are contaminated in the true sense of the meaning of the term "contamination" and the child should not be subjected to court testimony which only will further damage the relationship with the target parent. Once adopting a prescribed role while the alienating parent rehearses the child's script will cause the child to be extremely resistant to therapeutic change and reconsideration of her or his fixed point of view that has been presented to the judge as an authority figure in the authoritarian setting of the courtroom of the intimidating courthouse.

As illustrated in the vignette, the child testified against his father and explained to the court how busy he was in his extracurricular activities, team sports, maintaining his honors in his school work, and finding time for his busy social life in going bowling with his friends. He told the court that he did not have the time or the interest in seeing his "worthless" father. In circumstances such as this example, the judge as well as the RT must assign appropriate weight to the child's testimony in court as well as remarks made in the office of the RT. The experience of forensic evaluators shows that the more absurd and unjustified the exclamations of an alienated child, the clearer the severity of the alienation becomes. The proper course of action for what is needed to alter the child's misconceptions and reunify the target parent with the alienated child becomes obvious.

Additionally, a court order for reunification therapy should note that there will occur shifts and changes in the procedural role or techniques of the RT as reunification proceeds. For example, the alienator may realize that his accidental, incidental, or occasional manipulations of his children and their denigrations expressed against the other parent are more detrimental to the children than what he considered would be the result of having the target parent involved in the daily life of their children. In this circumstance, the RT may communicate this finding or change in attitude to the clients, attorneys, GAL, and the court and alter their approach to mild or moderate alienation accordingly.

Further, role shifts may occur if the alienating parent becomes enraged with the progress toward reunifying the "horrible and terrible" target parent with the child who previously refused contact and spoke of the target parent only in terms of hatred. The RT's approach now may become one providing evidence to the court and recommending consideration of a change of residency or custody or the implementation of a supervised visitation of the narcissistic, antisocial, unrelenting compulsive disruptive alienator. Often, this is necessary to manage the interference and efforts to sabotage the reunification process.

The vignette illustrates that the third MHP to undertake an attempt at reunification, this psychologist being court-appointed for this specific purpose, withdrew from the RT role and assumed the role of an individual therapist providing individual child psychotherapy accompanying primarily parent sessions with the mother. This MHP clearly admitted to the parents, attorneys, GAL, and the court that he was neither qualified nor comfortable to continue with such a mission. A forensic evaluator was recommended to be appointed by the court to develop a reunification plan for another MHP to be appointed as the new RT. The next step was the implementation of the developed plan because of the complexity of the reunification process in working with this fragmented alienated family. This kind of role shift from therapist to RT or RT to therapist must be avoided.

Because the ethics and standards are new and being developed by the mental health and legal community, consultation is recommended for the RT. Any consultant to the RT and the RT themselves must, of course, be qualified in the areas of alienation, forensic psychology, family dynamics, child development, mediation, and high-conflict management as well as be skillful in matters of abuse, domestic violence, and sensitivity to ethnic, cultural, and gender differences. Seniority or the number of years of experience in mental health work is insufficient, and a careful inclusion of trained forensic experiences in this area is necessary. Table 7.1 explains the details that must be understood in this transition from psychotherapy to RT. These differences were developed simultaneously and presented at various conferences by this author such as referenced in 2010 and 2011, independently of the AFCC *Guidelines for Court-Involved Therapy.*

There are cases in which either the family members or the attorneys representing the parents have agreed to attempt reunification. However, these attempts do not provide a power of enforcement for the therapist; there must be direct guidance and court sanctions in which there are consequences for non-compliance. Therapeutic ineffectiveness occurs because of the lack of skills or training in this unique subspecialty of the therapist and more often because of the lack of sanctions outlined by the court.

A reunification plan must be developed with general parameters as well as specific rules for the family whose identification of needs may require an assessment by a forensic examiner or forensic planner. For example, a malicious alienating parent who falsely alleges the father has sexually molested their daughter will not be persuaded by tender-minded approaches or the judge's reprimand or a therapist not wanting to garner the mother's disapproval by encouraging the child's overnight visitation. Severe measures must be used to combat severe fabrications and intentional false allegations of the worst kind. Tough-minded approaches are required to stop these kinds of destructive maneuvers to the child and to the innocent target parent. Lip service and scolding are never effective with a vicious parent using deadly emotional weapons.

The RT has a separate and distinct role in which they cannot have any prior experience with the family nor engage in any kind of dual relationship, for example, therapist for the child or parent. The chart presented in Table 7.1 emphasizes twenty different and salient considerations or categorizations between the role of a traditional therapist and that of an RT.

ASSESSMENT OF ALIENATION AND ESTRANGEMENT AND THE DEVELOPMENT OF A PLAN

Whether RTs have the benefit of a reunification plan or must rely upon themselves using documentation to produce their own reunification plan, this role requires an understanding and ability to determine the etiology, diagnosis, prognosis, and treatment variables to differentiate which category–alienation, estrangement, or abuse–may be operating in the family.

There are circumstances in which a child has a realistic, reasonable, or rational reason to reject a parent because of abuse, neglect, abandonment, and/or domestic violence. A plan must draw upon a broader consideration of the previous terms for the distinction between problematic parent behavior, the actions of a child, and alienation factors that should be conceived as the possible reason for the child's rejection of a parent, encompassing all issues that can cause a parent-child conflict including or excluding alienation. The response by an estranged child is justified and proportionate to the behavior of the parent and the past or premarital separation relationship and may be the same as or similar to the divorced relationship between the parents and the child or children.

The RT must remember that there are situations in which a child's rejection of a parent is based upon a combination of one or more of the factors of realistic estrangement and the contributing alienating behavior of the other parent. For example, consider the case of remarriage in which the child becomes upset with the new stepparent and the other parent negatively influences the child because he or she feels threatened by parental replacement. Many of these kinds of variables are discussed in the earlier chapters of the book and an exhaustive list of thirty-nine differentiating factors in the criteria of making a determination between alienation, estrangement, and abuse according to the child and the parent is described elsewhere in more detail (Sauber, 2011).

There also are several questionnaires that have been developed or are in the process of standardization for the purpose of differentiating among alienation, realistic estrangement, and/or abuse. The scale being developed by Sauber and Worenklein is undergoing the standardization process in the samples of cases in West Palm Beach, Florida, and Montreal, Canada. This fifty-item scale will have established norms with reliability and validity indices. The scales by Braver, Coatsworth, and Peralta (2007) and Baker, Burkhard, and Kelly (2012) offer more abbreviated instruments, including fewer items that have not as yet been standardized, that nevertheless are useful for this same determination.

Once the diagnosis is made or the hypotheses are clear and ready for testing, then it is necessary to develop a plan of action for the reunification therapy. Spontaneous treatment interventions by the RT often backfire in alienation cases because of the inherent complexity of visible and disguised matters operating, the presence of false allegations, and the issues of credibility being questioned. A document review and collateral contact interviewing, including contacting prior and current therapists, must take place for the RT to develop a plan based upon evidence rather than intuition. The popular fallback justification of MHPs is asserting "clinical judgment" and "clinical knowledge and experience," but this will not hold up under forensic examination or in the court of law. The RT must be prepared to defend compliance to the plan outline or justify deviation from the blueprint offered by the court. The request of the target parent or reunification planner requires consideration and begs adherence with the court order of conducting reunification therapy. In alienation cases, there generally is one opportunity for the family members to request or comply to the court-ordered reunification. The court is less likely to insist on future motions to continue to try reunification therapy if the first attempt fails. This is why the extra step of having a reunification planner conduct the blueprint of what should be expected, the guidelines to follow, and the court sanctions of what ingredients there are may be necessary to achieve reunification. The planner is an independent court-appointed evaluator who neither conducts the actual reunification therapy nor plays any other role in the case. Both attorneys have the choice of deposing the planner, and the judge certainly has the option of accepting the full proposal or a modification of the espoused plan. In this approach, the plan is discussed or argued prior to the appointment of the RT or the commencement of reunification therapy. The alternative approach more often practiced is for the RT to develop a plan that should be examined by the parties, their attorneys, and the judge but rarely is presented, scrutinized, or questioned by anyone until the reunification fails or even if it succeeds. Success brings objections by the attorney representing the alienating parent to minimize the benefit of the improved relationship between the alienated child and target parent, reminding the court of the history of the target parent and likelihood of the child's regression and once again preference for no or limited contact. The RT must have forensic expertise to require the maintenance of the improvement and a plan for how to keep the progress from being sabotaged by the alienator. The RT must expect and be prepared for testimony and cross-examination during the reunification process and toward the later therapeutic stages.

THE DISTINCT FEATURES OF REUNIFICATION THERAPY

Once a determination has been made as to the cause of the family disturbance, in other words, the disruption of the parent-child relationship, it is necessary to classify the degree of disturbance according to the categories of mild, moderate, and severe alienation. Additionally, the factors incorporating this differentiation must address the child's temperament, such as susceptibility to influence and the external prevailing conditions that affect the child's state of vulnerability. The particular orientation of the RT will be implemented differently depending on the degree of alienation and attention to factors of susceptibility and vulnerability. Attention to the child and alienator variables must measure how successful the alienating parent has been in alienating the child from the target parent. The condition of the child must be examined to understand how or by what methods this alienation was accomplished.

Scenario 1

A malicious mother uses every instance to indoctrinate the child and accuse the father of abuse in terms of child endangerment and sexual molestation. The alienating parent may withhold information about school, medical needs, social activities, or scheduling information as well as engage in unilateral decision-making. Nonetheless, frequent and uninterrupted access takes place with the target parent, but the child in this example experiences minimal impact of the alienation. The child exhibits resistance and nonsusceptibility to the alienating parent's persuasions and attempts to influence. The target parent is very empathetic and sensitive to the child's needs, especially if he already has established a close and strong attachment during the many preceding years to the divorce. This child represents a somewhat immune response pattern to the mother's campaign of denigration.

The RT should aid the target parent in helping his child withstand the continual tactics of alienation. The RT may help in providing therapeutic techniques to counter the alienating parent's presentation to the child by suggesting alternative ways to reframe the allegation in a kind and gentle manner of direct confrontation. This means that the RT must challenge the contrasting reality between the propaganda espoused by the alienating parent through the frequently employed methods of indoctrination and programming versus reminding the child of direct experience she or he has had with the target parent, thus showing the accusations to be false and the acknowledged positive experiences to be true. This provides a possibility, certainly not a guarantee, of the child's thereby cognitively and experientially refuting what the child has been conditioned to believe. This method may stop the creation of the child's delusion and the ultimate confusion with the reality of what really is versus their internalization of the false beliefs being promulgated. When the RT works in this way, the child begins to acknowledge that she or he is no longer scared of the father because he does not raise his voice, he does not lose control of his anger, he does not hit the child, nor does he act as if he were drunk. The father simply does not behave in a frightening or intimidating manner.

The RT will help the target parent to control his frustration and temptation to act out and retaliate against the other parent's false allegations. The target parent must maintain his composure and rise above the fury of the unjustified complaints and accusations. In this way, the target parent learns to remain loving, caring, and consistent in his encouragement and acceptance of the child, which is no easy task for any "helpless" parent placed in this toxic situation.

Scenario 2

The target parent is unable to control his natural impulses to react to and exhibit his anger about the ongoing fabrications and allegations of the alienating parent. In this instance, the target parent may contribute to the realistic estrangement of the child. Consider the impact of repeated embellished storytelling by the alienating parent and the target parent's observing his or her son or daughter becoming increasingly detached and rejecting his or her care and affection. This would exemplify the "hybrid model" of alienation with estrangement contributing to the outcome of the child's behavior. The target parent may begin to participate in the process of blame and castigation of the alienating parent in much the same way as the alienating parent has done with a child. However, the child already is aligned with the favored, alienating parent and becomes defensive with the target parent's attack, withdrawing emotionally and physically from any contact options. The RT would have the target parent cease any reactions that may cause a disruption from the child's reattachment to him or her or collude in the alienating parent's denigration.

Scenario 3

The alienating parent is engaged in mild to moderate programming, but the child is susceptible to this influence, especially feeling vulnerable from the loss of her home and friends in having to relocate. Her parents could no longer afford the marital home, and she has to move to another neighborhood and enroll in a new school system. She feels very insecure about what was going to happen to her on a day-to-day basis. In this instance requiring reality testing, the target parent may say to the child, "I understand that your mother says that I waste money on my dating, buying expensive clothes and leasing a costly car without paying child support and paying for the things that you need and want to avoid moving. However, this is not true as you see I am with you, not dating other women. My clothes are the same outfits that I have worn for years, nothing new. You know that the company I work for has always provided a car for the type of sales work I have to do. The car does not cost me anything, and it is owned by the company for my work. I pay child support regularly and give your mother the money for all of your extracurricular activities and toys you want to buy. What do you think?" The target parent should stay with each theme until the false allegation is completely refuted and the child begins to question the reality of the situation. Now the child begins to believe that the target parent has done nothing wrong in their eyes and thinks about what she has been told as a lie. The RT helps model what the target parent must do because the target parent is not expected to figure out what to do in this Rubik's cube or box that they find themselves.

Scenario 4

In a situation in which the effects of alienation have been internalized and the child begins to internalize these beliefs as if they were true, susceptibility and vulnerability factors may play a less significant role. The RT should teach alternative explanations to present to the child in such a nonthreatening way that the truth may become clearer to the child, as may be illustrated by the father's saying "Your mother may say bad things about me because she is still angry about our getting a divorce. You know for years that we never could get along together and we always were arguing and screaming." Believing the target parent is the first step toward the child's becoming convinced of the truth. The RT should not accept that the child's merely saying that she is convinced of the truth is sufficient. It is necessary to combat the brainwashing by repetition of the accuracy of the theme, details, and the message with repeated inquiry. The target parent should ask the child to explain in her or his own words the subjective understanding of the now objective appreciation of the facts. The intention is to remove the well-implanted internalization of their previously entrenched beliefs by deprogramming. Many target parents have lost their sense of objectivity and express uncertainty about what to say and how to say it to a child who openly expresses hostility against them. The RT should help the target parent to slowly and carefully provide different frames of reference to alienated child. Observational learning is a powerful way to teach the target parent to effectively interact with a hateful and resistant child.

Scenario 5

The alienating parent may be a severe alienator, but the child experiences only mild effects of the alienation programming. The child may feel confusion in being a victim caught in the web of loyalty conflicts between her parents and exhibit signs of depression or repressed anger in being unable to extrude herself from the perceived war zone of her parents' hostilities. The RT may find that parent-child educational approaches can be useful in these circumstances. As shown in the chapter on mild alienation, the educational approach may be sufficient. With mildly alienated children and an obsessed alienator on the rampage, however, the RT should consider the use of the court's sanctioning various options.

A child experiencing severe alienation in a case in which the alienator is only using mild forms of alienation tactics is classified as highly susceptible to influence or persuasion or highly impressionable and exhibits high vulnerability. In contrast, another child might not react or internalize the same tactics used because this child is highly resistant to influence, manipulation, and persuasion and is classified as low in susceptibility. Thus, the alienating parent may use mild, moderate, or severe alienation strategies or behaviors yet the child is affected by internal factors such as their personality features or temperament traits of *susceptibility* or the prevailing external conditions creating *vulnerability*.

The child may be in general resistant to susceptibility but because of the divorce war and causalities, the child may feel vulnerable to the conditions in which she resides and feels exposed and at risk. This means vulnerability applies to the circumstances and the child feels as if she is subjected to the probability of being harmed or injured or even inconvenienced by the existing situation. In this instance, the child would be in a state of easily being affected or open to danger or attack as might be in the example of helpless and vulnerable baby birds.

THE PROCESS OF REUNIFICATION THERAPY

There are basically two approaches to effective reunification therapy, in contrast to ineffective reunification therapy. One of the approaches of the RT is to provide documentation to the courts to facilitate the natural rehabilitation of the damaged parent-child relationship. This necessitates the opening of pathways to healing, challenging false beliefs and irrational assumptions, and questioning the indoctrinated fairy tales about a villain in order to allow the child to become deprogrammed. The child must be able to compare the present reality with the target parent in contrast to what the child had thought, imagined, or been told. Then, the storytelling assumed to be true becomes challenged and the child has the opportunity of questioning its validity and dismissing it as a repeated lie always being asserted by the alienating parent. What limits the progression in this reattachment phenomenon is the "well-meaning" interference of the alienating parent, who may sabotage the therapeutic gains by terminating the therapy or by telling the child that the target parent paid off the therapist. The alienating parent can pretend to take the side of the target parent, seemingly to present a sincere interest in reunification. This forces loyalty conflicts on the child, who can no longer tolerate the pressure. In this circumstance, bonding or rebonding with the target parent becomes too painful for the child, who is caught in the middle of the conflict and must find an escape hatch, usually resulting in alignment with the all-powerful alienating parent. One of the hallmarks of this scenario is that the alienating parent will change therapists with fictitious excuses, like the child did not feel comfortable with or does not like the RT. Thus, documentation and feedback to the attorneys and court are necessary and essential either to prevent the obstruction or to stop the interference before the therapeutic process is beyond repair.

The more effective approach is based on a plan. It includes establishing a foundation and a clear pathway for success by minimizing any resistance and interference for ordering this process. This sort of reunification therapy provides an opportunity for reexperiencing the past good times and fun activities in light of the present context. This includes sharing positive feelings and knowing that the reattachment process is occurring based upon the mutual desire of the child and target parent. This process must begin by following the blueprint of the family analysis after a study has been conducted by a forensic evaluator or planner and then abiding by the created plan for reunification in advance of any attempts to begin or further efforts to restart reunification therapy. The foundation of this approach is that the forensic expert examines and observes the members of the family, speaks with collateral contacts, administers questionnaires as is appropriate, and determines the diagnoses as the cause of the estrangement or alienation. This methodology specifies the necessary and sufficient conditions for successful change. This process is focused on the development of a specific methodology for the reunification process. Once there has been a clear differentiation among alienation, realistic estrangement, and abuse, the forensic examiner will know how to prescribe an effective plan, with a script for each family member to play while defining with clarity the role and focus of the RT. This plan obviously will include and request that certain court-ordered sanctions take place.

In this approach, the RT who is appointed or agreed upon simply follows the plan. In contrast to the former approach, that is, without a reunification plan, the RT has to plot his or her way through the maze, utilizing documentation to justify what will be needed. At the same time, the RT must avoid the expected forces of manipulation, resistance, and interference in the process, especially if progress is expected or being made. This latter approach was developed by this writer because of the repeated failures of reunification reported in the majority of alienation cases. Often recognized is the poorly trained RT who lacks the necessary training and skills needed to deal with the ongoing, unrelenting interference of the alienating parent. Also reported is the insufficient documentation provided by the RT to show her or his inability to control the undermining efforts of the progress that was beginning or has been occurring. The inexperienced RT is extremely defensive as one might expect when his or her ego and professional reputation are being questioned.

Ineffective approaches are highlighted in the vignette at the start of this chapter. Each therapist acted in a traditional capacity without knowing how to proceed or to gain use of the potency of court sanctions. Instead, they had to rely on their customary need for approval by the identified child and the alienating parent who possess the power and the ability to influence the child and the outcome. Why listen to the desperate target parent when the popular parent and her or his well-rehearsed chorus have the ear and the alignment with the child? Reference to Table 7.1 will help to understand the differences in approach, especially as they apply to the diagnosis of children suffering from moderate to severe parental alienation.

What is recommended, once a therapist has been appointed or the case has been referred to a therapist for reunification, consists of assessing what has happened and to identify the factors contributing to the failure to maintain the preexisting parent-child relationship to the divorce or separation or circumstance of disruption. The inability naturally to reunify family members experiencing a transition must be examined.

THE SELECTION OF THE REUNIFICATION THERAPIST

The selection of the RT illuminates the complexity of commencing a process of reunification by bringing to the fore the many competing, complicating, and hidden agendas in the adversary forces that operate in alienation scenarios. The process begins with each attorney submitting to the judge as many as three names for consideration in making an appointment for the RT. Thus, this step of the selection process potentially could consist of six proposed individuals and may include several professionals whom the judge favors.

First, unless the location of the parties is in a large, sophisticated, metropolitan area with many universities, it is unlikely that there would even be six or so qualified RTs in practice from which to choose or who could even be found to have some related expertise in this area. Second, unfortunately, when a client or attorney makes inquiries in their community or contacts MHPs to find an RT, the most frequent response is affirmative because every therapist says they do everything and advertise their services in most every area of mental health practice. Thus, it is very difficult to differentiate between an individual who has heard of or who has a surface knowledge of what reunification therapy is all about and to a seasoned professional who has real expertise and competence in this unique subspecialty. It is more difficult than the motivated target parent may think to differentiate real qualifications during a telephone interview. Often, professionals do not advertise their competence in this area but rather assert family therapy services as their specialty. For example, in a recent case in which a school social worker had an evening practice one night per week consisting of a few clients, she put on her professional cards "MFT" as her specialty. When her experience was reviewed, she had seen two siblings in individual therapy who should have been referred to a specialist in family therapy. She could not even explain the children's problems in concepts of family dynamics nor had she had any training in marriage and family therapy. Her employment as a school social worker did not qualify her to be a competent child therapist. Finding individuals to present to the court for selection is not as easy a task as one may expect. This is exemplified in the vignette of two therapists disciplined for ethical violations and the third court appointed RT's withdrawing from his court-appointed role.

Third, generally one party, the target parent, is the initiating force behind the appointment of a RT to reestablish his or her corrupted relationship with his or her child, whereas the alienating parent is reluctant or resistant or simply refuses to participate in any aspect of the reunification process. As each attorney presents a name, the other side finds an objection or fabricates a reason, such as "I heard that this doctor . . ." in an attempt to exclude each qualified professional presented from the list.

A questionnaire for the RT has been developed by the chapter author and has been prepared to present questions in a relatively nonthreatening manner. This questionnaire, or others like it, can be constructed according to the particular issues of the case in question and presented to either the prospective RT in the selection process or the active RT in the process. The information collected by administering this questionnaire and conducting the collateral contact interview is essential to agreeing to the appointment of an RT or to assess the basic qualifications of the RT struggling to assist the family in need. This process aids in both avoiding the traps that have been encountered with the appointment of a less-qualified RT and identifying a practicing RT who may find himself or herself experiencing difficulty in conducting the reunification. A possible explanation might be that the active RT was unaware of crucial information that otherwise would have been incorporated into a prior plan as a reference guide for him or her to follow. Now, the RT is faced with the dilemma of being unable to adequately present evidence to the court to request appropriate sanctions as a necessary safeguard to continue. Thus, the questionnaire would be helpful to determine as well the progress or the limitations of the current RT appointed to the case. A questionnaire of this type inquires about the RT's view and approach toward reunification in general, the particular role and experience in conducting this kind of unique therapeutic intervention, and how to handle the specific variables inherent to the case in question. Selection of the RT involves the general inquiry among the community of therapists that often engenders such responses as that they are experienced in this type of therapy and every other kind of therapy, that they are qualified to perform any therapy requested, that they are knowledgeable about every form of therapy, and that they have learned about this approach during their prior training placements which is difficult to verify. The long list of services that used to be advertised in the yellow page ads of the telephone directory and is now more often found on the websites of individual therapists and illustrates the point. Thus, this design in a questionnaire will assist the "selection committee" to determine the actual capability, and experience level of court-ordered therapy and the willingness of the therapist to adhere to a well-developed reunification plan or at least participate in the formulation of an effective approach to reunification as the process unfolds. This will include communicating with each of the parties, their attorneys, and, if necessary, the judge. Often, reunification therapy is claimed as an area of specialization of the therapist in working with children and families when in fact most of these MHPs have had no formal education or training in this therapeutic process nor have they never even heard of the American Association of Marriage and Family Therapy (AAMFT) or the AFCC. MHPs with a background and training in divorce mediation, parent coordination, and family therapy would be a good starting point from which to select the RT because they either have had experience in doing reunification or have a sufficient background to learn by doing this kind of unique court-involved therapeutic practice.

Eventually, an agreement is reached, often by selecting a therapist that has a reputation of seeking the approval of others, trying to please everyone, and offering a "middle-of-the-road" approach. This MHP will be amenable to the influence of, or at least not minimize, the position of the alienator's attorney, who vehemently argues to have this timid and impotent therapist appointed by the court. This RT is unlikely to take a strong position supporting the target parent while trying to escape encountering the anger of the alienating parent and dodge committing himself or herself to recommending a methodology that is likely to meet with resistance and hostility from the alienator. Thus, the MHP who is selected as agreeable to the parties is chosen because he or she is malleable, the kind of person who will "go with the flow" in order to keep the therapeutic endeavor continuing. Unfortunately, with all of the positive gains for the target parent that may have resulted from the prior litigation or the disadvantage of unfavorable litigation, the RT assumes a role of critical importance, offering the likelihood of an absence of fruitful changes to take place because of their compromised therapy to reunification at the present time and anticipated in the near future. This error in the selection process can and must be avoided.

Ineffective reunification therapy thus occurs with the focus and goal of balancing the comfort level of each of the parties. This includes not firmly or directly confronting, insisting, or frequently *not* even trying to encourage the child to change negative attitudes. The ineffective RT adopts defensive behavior at the expense of the target parent and protecting the status quo in order to avoid any backlash from the child or the alienating parent. The court is satisfied that an effort has been made, an agreeable solution has been reached, and help is perceived to be forthcoming. The target parent anxiously feels that at least there is some hope and a method with which they can finally reunify with their child or children while the alienating parent is content with the lack of progress. In this way, the alienating parent can maintain the emotional distance, dislike, and reluctance or refusal for their child's visitation with the target parent.

If, on the other hand, an RT known to be highly competent was recommended by one of the attorneys or even the judge, one can expect that the opposing counsel will find multiple reasons why this candidate is unacceptable. An example comes to mind of an actual case in which the opposing counsel and the court-appointed GAL were so vehemently against the expert's appointment that a separate hearing was scheduled to examine the basis, or more properly described as bias, for this opposition. During this hearing, the attorney for the children became the witness, admitting that she had never met the forensic psychologist, never had a case or heard about a case in which he was involved, nor could she identify anyone who even knew him who would offer any positive or negative comments. Nevertheless, extreme opposition was voiced based upon the resume of the expert until the GAL was challenged because the opposing attorney and the GAL wanted "to protect their client" from exposure or examination to a senior forensic evaluator.

A mental health consultant can be very helpful and actually save time and money in selecting a capable MHP by interviewing and examining the credentials of the RT being considered in a different way than an attorney or target parent might go about this seemingly simple but actually complex task (Bone & Sauber, 2012).

THE REUNIFICATION PLAN DEFINES THE THERAPY

The vignette offered at the beginning of the chapter presented no other solution other than a court-ordered investigation for the development of a reunification plan. The judge delayed ruling on the original motion for an assessment of the family for more than a year, until it was evident that the three prior attempts of the RT failed. The evaluative approach advocated here suggests to the court the safeguards and sanctions necessary to impose an order to effectively reunify the family or at least initiate access between the child and the target parent. A skillful navigator RT understands the value of documentation and the assumption and utilization of power from their experience of conducting family therapy and forensic practices. Without a reunification plan, the skillful RT can only proceed cautiously with the intension of developing a plan as they progress. Potential difficulties, such as allegations of domestic violence, sexual molestation, child abuse, and neglect; plus the alienating parent's efforts to undermine the process, such as reporting that the child complains that the RT smells, the RT has been bribed, or the child does not feel comfortable with the RT's questions; and the biased attitude of supporting the target parent must be anticipated and documented. The skillful RT will expect that the alienating parent may use charm to win the sympathy of the RT and provide many compelling horror stories of the "demonized," "despicable" target parent to strengthen an alliance with the therapist.

Documentation must be used because reunification is intended to halt the alienating parent from temporarily or permanently damaging the relationship of the children with the other parent. The skillful RT always will be mindful that reunification is the cure for the alienation dilemma, and it is the antithesis of what the alienating parent wishes to accomplish. Doing this kind of work must include the realistic awareness of the difficulties inherent in the process and the challenges to be faced in rescuing the child from the abuse of the alienating parent perceived by the child as their "champion" and "savior." It is the author's hope that the skillful RT will use these guidelines to be effective in helping the alienated child and his or her family reunite.

DIFFERENT SCENARIOS, DIFFERENT APPROACHES

Taking into consideration these variables, there is a difference in the approach to reunification therapy according to whether the mental condition of the child represents mild or moderate versus severe alienation and whether the behavioral tactics of the alienator are classified as mild, moderate, or severe. In cases of milder degrees of alienation, there would be an invitation for both parents to participate in the selection of the RT and the process of reunification. The reunification therapy process would include an educational and therapeutic component. In the situation in which the alienating behavior is of the more severe variety, however, only the target parent would select the therapist and only she or he and the victimized, alienated child would participate in reunification effort. The alienating parent would be too committed to obstructing the process and acting in a malicious way to avoid cooperation and facilitation of the reconnecting of the target parent with the disconnected child. The alienating parent would be resistant to any form of parent education or therapeutic effort to coparent and understand and appreciate the best interests of the child. Moderate alienation cases could go either way in this approach depending on the alienating parent's capacity for insight and a genuine willingness to change.

If there were a case in which the child was mildly alienated either due to just beginning the brainwashing process or because the campaign of denigration has been mitigated by the target parent's ongoing presence and persistent sensitivity, then the parent attempting severe tactics has to be excluded from the reunification process before further damage can be caused to the potentially susceptible, suggestible, vulnerable child. If, on the other hand, the alienating parent only occasionally or somewhat randomly or as a trigger reaction would bad-mouth the other parent, even with a child who is highly susceptible, then the alienating parent still would be included in the reunification therapy. The RT would be alert to the child's temperament of susceptibility and the prevailing conditions related to the variables in the child's potential vulnerability in working with this family.

The hope in mild cases is that the alienator can be persuaded through education or brief therapy that speaking with the child by using derogatory comments about the other parent only hurts the child. The cost of retaliation to the target parent is not worth the emotional problems caused to the child. In these cases, the child may express reluctance to have contact with the target parent because the child reflects or mirrors the alienating parent's behaviors, feelings, and attitudes against the other parent. In moderate cases in which the child feels alienated, the child is likely to resent forced compliance to the time-sharing or visitation and may show oppositional defiance to having any contact with the target parent. The RT is expected to point out to the alienating parent her or his destructive ways whether it is based upon their naïve, unconscious attitudes or the impulsive expression of their anger. Acting out is counterproductive and damaging to their loved ones. Obviously, there are benefits to the child's having a relationship with both parents, for example, positive role development and modeling of each parent plus having the other parent actively involved in the raising of the child. The alienating parent will be allotted time off and relief from the daily responsibilities of childcare as the state statutes intend. The advantage of shared parental responsibility, of course, results in a better adjustment for the children of divorce, supported by research and common sense. High coparental conflict is the number one cause of injuries to children of divorce, and the evidence shows a number of deleterious consequences to the child's sense of well-being and confidence, school performance, adaptation to social morals and rules such as juvenile delinquency and substance abuse. The consequences are so intense that adults often exhibit or repeat similar unwanted behaviors in harming themselves and their children.

In cases of mild alienation, visitation often takes place out of obligation and mandatory adherence to the rules, much like going to school when the child does not feel like attending. Once the child is with the target parent, the child may be able to enjoy, in part, the activities of the day. The RT should be mindful, however, that the child may adopt the negative outlook after being bombarded with the alienating parent's attitudes constantly being conveyed. Usually, this occurs by using a cell phoneor texting during the visit with the target parent. This defiance may be initiated by the child or the alienating parent as an unwarranted conditioned response to the target parent. Upon return to the child's residential placement, however, the child begins to feel the alienation, distance, and distaste for the association or presence of the target parent. The child has to prepare for the transition by changing his or her mind-set to coincide with the alienating parent's expectations to reduce anticipated dissonance. The child is expected to report how unpleasant it was for her or him to have forced access against the child's will and wishes with the other parent.

In cases of moderate or severe alienation, in other words, the child refuses contact and the alienating parent is unrelenting in his or her attacks on the target parent, it is best for the court to impose sanctions against the interfering parent in order to allow the repair and healing of the fractured relationship.

Responsibility to assist and correct the behavior of the alienating parent would be assigned to the attorney representing that parent and/or the therapist treating this parent. The RT should encourage the attorney, as an officer of the court, to try to control his or her client's obstreperous attempts to sabotage the reunification and to inform the client of the potential sanctions by the court. The RT must realize that the alienating parent's destructive behavior is under the scrutiny of the court, although alienators are unlikely to alter their behavior because they feel their actions are above the law. Alienating parents feel they can do whatever they wish to do, as in the past, and no consequences will result. These parents have felt powerful and justified in their actions for so long that they feel the court will be unable to regulate their influence and choices. Unfortunately, alienating parents are often correct because the court by nature is not oriented toward attending to these kinds of unlawful behaviors exhibited under the radar. This is why the development of a reunification plan as a blueprint in advance of any efforts at reunification therapy makes sense.

The RT must work with the therapist of the alienator to help the therapy process and stop the therapist from being a good friend and cheerleader to the client by supporting and approving of his or her tactics. The therapist must not get caught up with the alienating parent's compelling and convincing arguments to justify her or his actions against the other "terrible, horrible parent." Instead, the therapist's role is to explore the patient's underlying motivation and dynamics for this conduct, and identify the personality disorder causing the behavior, whether it be narcissistic, borderline, or antisocial. The RT should help the therapist to accept his or her responsibility, not being co-opted by the manipulating alienator. Providing legitimate treatment and directly advising the patient to cease in her or his harmful, inappropriate conduct is necessary.

In moderate cases, the objections or temper tantrums to resist time-sharing may be short-lived, and the child will accept that he or she must participate in the scheduled visitation. The child is expected to not experience any pleasure in being with the rejected parent or have fun engaging in any of the activities planned but instead will complete the "time sentence." This obligation is not a matter of choice for the child as the alienating parent will advocate and reinforce. The RT must emphasize that repetition in compliance with the agreed-upon parenting plan or court-ordered visitation schedule is necessary and offers partial hope for resolution in time. Ideally, children will learn to cope and understand that they must make the best of a bad situation. Once the child accepts this notion, the RT should help the child play the role of relating in a more positive way to the target parent.

In extreme or severe alienation cases, often the only way to cause a therapeutic and emotional breakthrough for the rebonding between the target parent and the alienated child may be that of reversing custody. The child would be required to reside with the target parent without the continuous prompting and programming of the alienator. The child would not have the chore of reporting to one parent while spying on the other parent's activities. Now the target parent has the refreshing opportunity to know about the child's school performance and extracurricular activities and be able to demonstrate a genuine interest and participate in a meaningful way. The RT can help the child make peace with the target parent, to coexist and to have a reprieve from her or his own cognitive dissonance. The RT should advocate for a specified period of suspended contact to ensure that the malicious parent would not readily have access to obstruct the process of reunification. The intended purpose for the alienating parent is to understand and appreciate the power of the judicial sanctions such as a no-contact order and then supervised visitation in hopes of minimizing his or her abuse of power and violation of court orders. Enforcement may be the only solution for these emotionally disturbed, highly manipulative parents.

The RT should recommend that as the child's relationship with the target parent becomes stronger, the alienating parent may have supervised visitation. This procedure is recommended to guarantee that the alienator is compliant with appropriate standards of parenting until the target parent's relationship with the child is restored and the alienating parent ceases undermining the authority and relationship of the target parent with the child. The RT should be unencumbered in offering attachment and bonding therapy and successfully deprogram the indoctrinated erroneous beliefs that the child had been conditioned to believe as true. At times, the therapy may resemble the techniques used with cult members when they are returned to their home environment to begin a new life and reestablish their relationship with their taught "enemy" parents while maintaining absolutely no contact with the cult leaders and the cult members.

The RT should be aware of other programs and methods of helping the alienated child. Warshak (2010) and Warshak and Otis (2010a) offer an alternative approach in which the target parent and the alienated child travel to a program site that may be either a family home or a vacation resort for four consecutive days. This model is educational and experiential. Other programs have been treatment oriented and hospital based. The family members reside in an inpatient setting while participating in various group-centered methodologies. Gardner (1998, 2001) originally used psychiatric hospitalizations to contain the acting-out, rejecting child who professed hatred, refusing to ever speak with or have any further contact with their target parent. The child was court ordered to attend these hospital-based treatment settings, but the judges expressed considerable reluctance to sign an order for this forced or involuntary admission approach to child reunification with the target parent who had become victimized.

Other approaches for the RT that are less intensive and costly and have been shown to be helpful with alienated children include *Welcome Back, Pluto: Understanding, Preventing, and Overcoming Parental Alienation* (DVD) by Warshak and Otis (2010b). This video describes the complex psychological situation of alienation in which the problem is defined, and is manifestation, and intervention techniques are included for its control and abatement with children and adolescents. The video assists in explaining how a vulnerable child might be parroting what the favored parent wants the child to say against the target parent. It is the first program of its type designed for parents and the child to watch together. *Toxic Divorce: A Workbook for Alienated Parents by Reay* (2011) has exercises and strategies for the alienated child and parent to complete and follows the written therapeutic homework assignment model for clinical practice as advocated and described by Luciano L'Abate in his many books on this subject. Gardner's textbook, *Therapeutic Interventions for Children with Parental Alienation Syndrome* (2001) contains 445 pages of rich suggestions that incorporate his theory and symptoms for identification while explaining various interventions with the alienator and the target parent. The last chapter on recantation and reconciliation is particularly revealing.

RT is not for everyone. In fact, alienation cases are the most challenging forms of therapeutic endeavors. This applies to attorneys, GALs, parenting coordinators, and custody evaluators and includes individual and family therapists providing services to the alienated child, alienating parent, or target parent. What appears to be real is often an illusion carefully and skillfully constructed by the alienating parent. How can a trained psychologist compete with an antisocial personality disorder in which the alienating parent has years of experience at presenting narcissistic and histrionic stories to captivate the audience while knowing how to enact a borderline level of functioning in subtly programming the innocent mind of the child? How can an RT alter one child's indoctrination when an older sibling already convinced of the alienator's propaganda undermines the therapeutic techniques toward reunification by reaching the younger sibling? The RT new to these kinds of cases has to decide whether or not to be a part of this brand of treatment. Often, the RT thinks that court-ordered therapy will expand her or his practice and ventures into uncharted waters. Many RTs have experienced a tough cross-examination, and they will disclose their future intention to decline an invitation to work with alienation cases regardless of roles available. It takes courage and the ability to withstand the social disapproval and applause of the majority of the parties and players in these cases. The RT must possess the confidence and skills to cope with unwarranted criticism and attacks in moving forward to accomplish a reunion when the forces against them are all encompassing and powerful. Once the RT masters this challenge, however, the work offers the most rewarding of professional satisfaction in accomplishing a mission often described as "impossible."

Editors' Notes

- Dr. Sauber explains the difference between court-ordered reunification therapy and traditional psychotherapy according to twenty different categories for consideration. For example, he illustrates cases in which either or both of the parents and/or the child needs psychotherapy. The next step is for the RT to notify the parents' attorneys of her or his recommendation. Then, a motion is filed in court to have one or more therapists appointed to provide these service(s). RTs should never compromise their own role of having a dual relationship and find themselves providing dual roles of reunification therapy and traditional therapy either simultaneously or successively.
- Dr. Sauber defines the importance and significance of reunification and how the development of a plan is essential, especially if the custody evaluation is flawed or if there was no custody evaluation to offer specific recommendations and specific guidelines to the RT. The RT must follow the court-ordered instructions as to how to conduct the reunification therapy, including judicial sanctions to prevent any obstacles, landmines, or interference that may be displayed or occur by either of the parents or the child. For example, the child says she is uncomfortable with and dislikes the RT and the alienating father wants her to see another RT. The court order addresses this expectation and ensures the continual role of the RT in alienation cases.
- Dr. Sauber points out the necessity of differentiating between parental alienation, realistic estrangement, and abuse and how each of these classifications must logically determine the plan for reunification therapy. In cases in which alienation is diagnosed, the next consideration is whether the child has experienced mild, moderate, or severe alienation. Each of these demarcations as well determines the specific approach to be used by the RT. These factors must be incorporated in the development of the reunification plan in bringing about a closer, nonobstructive relationship between the target parent and the alienated child. The foundation for the plan and approach must be based upon valid, objective information as opposed to distorted and fictitious storytelling or malicious programming as evidenced in the child.
- Dr. Sauber offers a vignette and numerous case scenarios to exemplify different situations requiring different plans and different approaches. This presentation emphasizes the importance of an effective, *a priori* blueprint of action before reunification therapy actually takes place, offering an outline or decision tree to follow as one implements the initial, middle, and later stages of reunification therapy.

- Throughout the chapter, Dr. Sauber offers suggestions for the RT to enhance the effectiveness of this role by performing a unique type of court-ordered therapy. For example, he points out how the RT should assist the target parent in responding to her rejecting son making false allegations against her that are both absurd and clearly represent a borrowed scenario from the alienator.

REFERENCES

Association of Family and Conciliation Courts (AFCC). (2005). *Guidelines for parenting coordination.* May, 2005. Available from AFCC, 329 W. Wilson St., Madison, WI 53703.

Association of Family and Conciliation Courts (AFCC). (2010). *Guidelines for court-ordered therapy.* October, 2010. Available from AFCC, 329 W. Wilson St., Madison, WI 53703.

Baker, A. J. L., Burkhard, B., & Kelly, J. (2012). Differentiating alienated from not alienated children: A pilot study. *Journal of Divorce and Remarriage, 53*(3), 178–193.

Bone, J. M., & Sauber, S. R.(2012). The essential role of the mental health consultant in parental alienation cases. In A. J. L. Baker & S. R. Sauber (Eds.), *Working with alienated children and families: a clinical guidebook* (pp. 71–89). New York: Routledge.

Braver, S. L., Coatsworth, D., & Peralta, K. (2007 July). *Alienating behavior within divorced and intact families: matched parents' and now-young-adult children's reports.* Presented at the Association of Family and Conciliation Courts, Washington, DC.

Child Welfare League of America. (2002). *Summary of Adoption and Safe Families Act of 1997.* Retrieved from: http:/www.cwla.org/advocacy/asfap1105-89summary .htm (Accessed May 28, 2004).

Gardner, R. A. (1998). *The parental alienation syndrome: A guide for mental health and legal professionals* (2nd ed). Cresskill, NJ: Creative Therapeutics.

Gardner, R. A. (2001). *Therapeutic interventions for children with parental alienation syndrome.* Cresskill, NJ: Creative Therapeutics.

Reay, K. M. (2011). *Toxic divorce: A workbook for alienated parents.* Penticton, British Columbia, Vancouver: Self-published.

Sauber, S. R. (2011 May). *Differentiation between alienation, estrangement and bona fide abuse for the development of the reunification plan.* Presented at the Canadian Symposium for Parental Alienation Syndrome, Dawson College: Montreal, Canada.

Sauber, S. R., & Worenklein, A. (2013). Custody evaluations in alienation cases. In A. J. L. Baker & S. R. Sauber (Eds.), *Working with alienated children and families: a clinical guidebook* (pp. 47–70). New York: Rutledge.

Warshak, R. (2010). Family bridges: Using insights from social sciences to reconnect parents and alienated children. *Family Court Review, 48*(1), 48–80.

Warshak, R., & Otis, M. R. (2010a). Helping alienated children with family bridges: Practice, research and the pursuit of "humbition." *Family Court Review, 48*(1), 91–97.

Warshak, R., & Otis, M. R. (2010b). *Welcome back Pluto: Understanding, preventing and overcoming parental alienation* [DVD]. Dallas, TX: WBP Media.

Chapter 8

LEGAL INTERVENTIONS IN CASES OF PARENTAL ALIENATION

DEMOSTHENES LORANDOS

This chapter will use a vignette throughout to illustrate the planning, preparation, and presentation of a case based upon parental alienation syndrome (PAS) behaviors. The vignette will encompass a criminal, custody, and licensure case. Where significant marital assets and/or clients with professional backgrounds are involved, counsel must anticipate a "three-ring circus."

Vignette

David Connelly and his ex-wife Susan arrive for their appointment with counsel. David is a sixty-year-old CEO in manufacturing. Susan moved to Massachusetts after they split amicably, and she now works as a pharmaceutical representative. David and Susan have come to the appointment together because their son Richard has been arrested for physical abuse and criminal neglect of a minor. Richard has recently graduated with a master's degree in social work from an expensive university and opened a private clinic. His soon-to-be ex-wife Jane is a high school teacher who has gone to divorce court and, based on the arrest, secured a restraining order to keep Richard out of their home and away from Adrian, their three-year-old daughter. The child has a vivid welt on the right side of her face and a black eye. Jane has pictures and she has posted them on her Facebook page. The Connellys inform counsel that, because of the arrest, the Board of Social Work and Richard's malpractice insurance carrier have advised him that he may not see clients until the criminal charges are resolved. This is particularly galling for David and Susan, because when Richard graduated they helped him buy a building so that Richard could establish a clinic with two partners. One false allegation and Richard has lost his home, his daughter, his marriage, his clinic, and because Jane's attorney claims that the building in which the clinic is located is a marital asset, Jane wants that too. Not only is there a criminal case to fight, but Richard must also fight in divorce court, with Children's Protective Services (CPS), with the Social Work Licensure Board, and with his malpractice carrier. With tears in his eyes, David exclaims that Richard would never hurt Adrian, takes out his checkbook, and begs counsel to save his son and only grandchild.

FACT ANALYSIS AND PRE-TRIAL PLANNING

In order to organize and prepare many years' worth of convoluted facts for the witnesses who will be called, the Clancy Method should be employed. This is a trial planning and presentation methodology developed by Patrick Clancy of the Innocence Team in California and this author. After law school and a stint in the California Public Defender's Office, Mr. Clancy became a certified criminal law specialist. In these convoluted cases, Mr. Clancy developed a method for electronically scanning, organizing, and categorizing trial materials. Several years ago, in association with this author's company PsychLaw.net, a five-part video seminar series was developed to teach certified family law and certified criminal law specialists how to successfully defend against well-organized false allegations of child abuse. Part five of this series concerns trial preparation and the use of technology. The five-part series is available free on the web from PsychLaw.net.

While Richard's parents are still in town, counsel should have her researcher and/or investigator meet with David and Susan. The researcher must get her hands on every video, photo, card, letter, document, or *tchotchke* that relates to the married life of Richard and Jane and to their daughter Adrian. Armed with the case file and what she has procured, the researcher will begin the preparation process.

First, this method requires the creation of a master document file. This means electronically scanning into Adobe Acrobat (.pdf) every document, picture, witness statement, or transcript. The filing system for these documents is very important. Each document should be named by date, in the following format: 2012.01.05 Plaintiff Motion for Visitation. If the files are named in this manner, they will organize themselves in the electronic files in chronological order. Next, files should be created for each type of document. For example, there could be separate files named motions, notices, orders, subpoenas, and so on.

Second, the method requires creating a master chronology of three columns in a program such as Excel. Column one, the date of each event of any significance to the case; column two, the who, what, how, and why do we care information about each significant event; and column three, the "how do we prove" information about the event. Notably, column three holds the exact file folder, file name, and Adobe page, paragraph, and line of the proof needed for trial. That is why everything must be scanned.

The third step in the process involves creating a master witness list for friendly and opposing witnesses with contact information and citations to relevant places in the master document and chronology files. This means that counsel will order witness development according to the case proof and presentation plan. When the master chronology is completed, individual subchronologies for each witness are created from the master document and master chronology files. Because all of the relevant facts and the witnesses involved in those facts are catalogued and interrelated, counsel and support staff must produce a "what do we need from this witness?" chart for each expected witness, for direct examination and cross-examination. Counsel should present these charts to the other team members in routine meetings. In this way, support staff can comment and then add additional facts and legal argument citations.

While the staff is working on the Clancy Method, counsel must select an expert for the defense team. Counsel's expert must know and be able to explain essential peer-reviewed, scientific treatises in each selected content area. One must pick experts who not only know their stuff, but who "fit" the dynamics *and dramatics* of the case. This defense team expert must be thoroughly familiar with parental alienation (PA) and false allegations of abuse. This defense team expert must also be able to participate in planning, in intervention with the client, and in team meetings. Further, counsel must quickly contact the prosecutor working on Richard's criminal case. An arraignment and bail hearing, as well as bond, must be scheduled by staff. Next, counsel should contact the investigators in law enforcement in order to get the police records and contact CPS for their records in order to begin the process by which their file is obtained. Counsel should also line up a private polygrapher familiar with PA and false allegations of abuse. There are two separate strategies to use here, and these are important: with the police, CPS, and the prosecutor, counsel should ask how to get to the bottom of this situation to find the truth, because counsel is particularly concerned with the child and her psychological and physical well-being. This is why counsel is in this field. With the private polygrapher and chosen defense team expert, counsel should promise the police, CPS, and the assigned prosecutor to bring them the truth about the case. Counsel should emphasize that the promise to tell them the truth will be backed up by the documents the researcher is gathering. Counsel's public focus must be on the child and saving her from the sequelae of PA. Of course the police, CPS, and the assigned prosecutor are adversaries, but they will find out what counsel will bring to the triers of fact. Every effort should be made to stop and dismiss the criminal case at every step. It never hurts to try.

The second strategy is to build awareness in counsel's office among members of the defense team of the process of PA. The defense team must organize all data to explicate PA. The diagnostic criteria include a campaign of denigration against the target parent by the child; frivolous rationalizations by the child for her criticism of the target parent; a lack of ambivalence in the child over her description and treatment of the target parent; a manifestation referred to as "the independent-thinker phenomenon" by the child whereby she says her denigration is all her own idea; reflexive support by the child of the preferred parent against the target parent; an absence of guilt in the child over their exploitation and mistreatment of the target parent; a demonstration of borrowed scenarios from the alienating parent by the child; a notable spread of animosity toward the target parent's extended family by the child. These are all described in greater detail in Chapter 1 of this text.

Fidler and Bala (2010a) reported that clinical observations, case reviews and qualitative as well as empirical studies indicated that alienated children may exhibit

- poor reality testing
- illogical cognitive operations
- simplistic and rigid information processing
- inaccurate or distorted interpersonal perceptions
- disturbed and compromised interpersonal functioning
- self-hatred
- low self-esteem or inflated self-esteem or omnipotence
- pseudo-maturity
- gender-identity problems
- poor differentiation of self (enmeshment)
- aggression and conduct disorders
- disregard for social norms and authority
- poor impulse control
- emotional constriction, passivity, or dependency
- lack of remorse or guilt

All of these characteristics should be kept in mind, and wherever possible, there should be proofs and witness charts oriented to demonstrating their occurrence in Adrian.

Next, counsel must visit Richard in jail and get his signature on the retainer agreement. From past experience, counsel is aware that many clients cannot handle the pressures of cases like these (much less on all fronts, as Richard is facing). Counsel must make sure that Richard does not cave to the pressure and begin "explaining" himself to willing listeners. Clearly, Richard is desperate to explain the narrowly averted auto accident, the panicked stop, and the origin of Adrian's black eye. He is abject in his self-recrimination because Adrian's seat belt was not properly fastened. Counsel must take the time to listen to Richard and to be compassionate because his entire life is falling apart, and this is not conducive to sane behavior. Counsel must listen carefully to Richard's recitation of Adrian's colliding with the rear passenger doorpost but remind him that jail is not the place for conversation. He must keep his mouth shut. He may not talk to anyone other than counsel because there may be prosecution "plants" in jail. Remind him that conversations are often recorded and of course there may be defendants in jail who will relate conversations in hopes of a deal in their own case. Counsel must explain to Richard that the discovery available in the family law case in the form of interrogatories and requests for production of documents, examinations, and depositions will save his life. The family case discovery must be utilized in this fashion and the criminal case won. The criminal case must be counsel's most important priority.

Counsel should begin legal research with the excellent treatise, *Right to Present a Defense.* This is an ongoing web document continually updated by National Association of Criminal Defense Lawyers (NACDL) contributor Mark J. Mahoney (2009). Although it is aimed at criminal defense, the relevancy arguments concerning the right to tell one's own story is of great value in custody or dependency cases as well. Counsel should be mindful that the court might not be aware of state and sister-state precedent on salient issues. Counsel must think through relevant legal issues, prepare *points* and *authorities* to use if need be at trial, and set her or his sights on diligently making a record for review. To aid in this endeavor, counsel should download and then conform to his or her state-specific precedent motions available from Thomson-Reuters West's two-volume *Cross Examining Experts in the Behavioral Sciences* (Campbell & Lorandos, 2001, updated annually). Special attention should be spent on *Daubert* or *Frye* challenges, taint motions asserting that a child's memory is compromised (therefore she cannot testify from "personal knowledge"), and motions to defeat "outcry" (the always questionable hearsay testimony from adults who have allegedly heard a child's complaints). Again, these are available to counsel from *PsychLaw.net,* the NACDL and The Innocence Team in California. After bond, counsel should demand a preliminary examination and file detailed motions for discovery in both the family and the criminal cases. All of the immediate discovery battles, subpoenas, and depositions must be diligently fought in the family case, because most jurisdictions do not allow depositions in criminal cases.

Counsel must immediately contact the Board of Social Work to let them know that Richard has representation. Counsel must research and push "prior restraint" with the Social Work Board. Because Richard is innocent until proven guilty, the Social Work Board should not have the mandate to restrain Richard from working until after adjudication. If they are reluctant to negotiate, counsel should file against the Social Work Board in Federal Court, because Richard's license and ability to work is a property right. If possible, counsel should negotiate that Richard at least be allowed to see adult patients in a supervised setting. Counsel should use the defense team expert and her connections to help Richard find a clinic in which he can get back to work immediately.

While pushing the discovery process, counsel should work with David and Susan to find and quickly furnish an alternate living environment for Richard. Counsel should also use the chosen defense team expert and her connections to find Richard a therapist to help him deal with the pressures of the multiple cases facing him. If confidentiality law is not inviolate in counsel's jurisdiction, counsel should arrange to employ the therapist as part of the defense team. Richard must be functional so that he can get right to work helping David and Susan and the researcher get all the materials for the master document and master chronology files. As soon as practical, counsel must have a conversation with CPS.

Upon speaking to Adrian's caseworker Jessica Stein, counsel discovers that she has a B.A. in human services and no training or experience in criminal child abuse cases beyond a twenty-hour workshop at the local children's advocacy center (CAC). Counsel must be mindful of the kind of training folks like Jessica actually get at CACs. In this vein, counsel should refer to peer-reviewed, published research on this topic (Herman, 2005, 2009; Lorandos & Campbell, 1995, 2005). Jessica relates that Adrian said, "Daddy hurt me," and on the advice of her attorney, Jane brought Adrian to the CAC to be interviewed. Counsel learns from Jessica that the interviewer who talked to Adrian has been an interviewer for one year and was trained solely by attending a workshop in Huntsville, Alabama, on interviewing children. Counsel should be mindful of the training people like the CAC interviewer actually get at the Huntsville center (Horner, Guyer & Kalter 1992a , 1992b; Stevenson, Leung & Cheung 1992; Horner & Guyer 1991). Jessica states that the interviewer reported that Adrian made it clear, "Daddy hurt me." During the CAC "forensic interview" Adrian was repeatedly questioned about

Daddy hurting her and how many times Daddy hurt her, and when pushed she began to cry. While crying, Adrian told the interviewer she was "scared." Jessica informs counsel that based upon what Adrian said, CPS is going to move to terminate Richard's parental rights and will participate with the prosecutor in the criminal case. Jessica from CPS informs that Richard is not to see his child under any circumstances.

Reading up on the process the CPS went through and, more specifically, the methodology employed by the CAC, counsel and the defense team expert should remember Richard Gardner's description of the difference between "evaluators" and "validators." Gardner described how validators use behavioral lists and "consistent-with-abuse" reasoning. He reminded readers of the draconian condemnation of normal childhood behaviors in the late nineteenth century and concluded that validators lack common sense and are a product of an eroded educational system. He suggested that they often get through college without taking any rigorous courses, such as mathematics, physics, and chemistry, which would teach them critical reasoning skills. He wrote that these validators demonstrate a

> Holier-Than-Thou Phenomenon: Validators often manifest this patronizing attitude. They, unlike the rest of us, are there to protect children. They unlike the rest of us 'believe the children.' . . . It provides these examiners with a feeling of special importance, which likely serves to compensate for basic feelings of inadequacy. (Gardner, 1991, p. 49)

Gardner (1991) described the outcome of the work of these less than well-trained "experts"

> The Golden Rule has essentially become a quaint anachronism. . . . There is an element of psychopathology apparent in a person who would see a three-year-old child for a few minutes and then write a note stating that a particular individual (the father, the stepfather, a nursery school teacher) sexually abused that child. It takes a defect in the mechanisms of conscience to do such an abominable thing. (pp. 50–51)

Blending this sense of validators with the research on training for interviewers will prove invaluable when counsel attempts to understand and explain suggestibility research.

After counsel's researcher interviews Richard for many hours, Richard mentions as an aside that he is concerned about Jane because she was coping during the last months of the marriage by drinking more. The researcher points out in the next defense team meeting that counsel must look into Jane's drinking. Counsel should ask the defense team expert to communicate with Richard's therapist and explore Richard's denial and whether Richard and Jane have been in a "negotiated maladjustment contract." This is a concept that grew out of marital therapy research. It predates the notion of "co-dependence" and holds that in return for behaviors that meet the compelling needs of both partners, one or both of them perform behaviors that are self-injurious, deviant, or maladaptive (Carson, 1969; Gehrke & Moxom, 1969). Additionally, Richard's therapist should be asked to deal with Richard's lack of efficient thinking, inability to focus, anxiety, and multiplicity of storylines. The goal of pushing Richard's therapy is to confront his denial, prepare him for two–maybe three–trials, and help him be more effective in developing a plan for Adrian. As part of his recovery from this temporary disaster, Richard should be encouraged to go into "research mode." Counsel should encourage him to begin by studying the famous abuse cases of the 1980s and 1990s–McMartin, Kern County, Kelly Michaels, and Wenatchee. Richard should watch Sean Penn's documentary *Witch Hunt* and learn how the manipulation of the children in the Kern County, California, case was done (Penn, 2008).

In the family case, Jane and her attorney are insisting on exclusive use of the marital home. Jane and Steven, one of the therapists at Richard's clinic, have entered into an agreement to keep the clinic operating without Richard. Counsel's investigator and researcher should be charged with looking into whether Jane and Steven might have a deeper relationship. As the researcher works on the chronology with Richard and the defense team expert, they realize that because Richard was in school for the last four years and working part time, Richard was the one around Adrian the most. Jane left for work at 7:30 AM, and was not home until at least 4:30 PM–sometimes not until 7:30 or 8:00 PM. This information should also go to Richard's therapist, to aid in pushing on Richard's denial.

Having been ordered to mandatory mediation, Jane and Richard file their narratives for the custody mediator. Jane's narrative describes Jane as the primary caregiver for Adrian. Jane claims that she is the best candidate for the role of single parent for the child and that she is more responsible. Jane accuses Richard of being a mama's boy, dependent upon his parents to prop him up and extricate him from any messes. To counter this expected gambit, counsel has been vigorously conducting discovery in the family case, and the private investigator has uncovered several disciplinary actions against Jane at the high school where she teaches. These disciplinary actions were for tardiness, for absenteeism, and suspicion of intoxication. Richard is shocked–he had no inkling of the depths of Jane's problem. Counsel's private investigator finds that Jane's relationship with Steven, the clinic therapist, has developed. Jane has begun attending support groups for "mistreated women" with Steven's sister Janice, a militant advocate for abused women. Jane complains to Janice about the "inconclusive" finding from Adrian's pediatrician who says that in three years of caring for Adrian, she's never seen indications of abuse. Steven's sister Janice refers Jane to a physician who is more oriented to their point of view. This physician has developed a reputation in the state for finding indications of abuse in little girls and boys. In the physical exam, Jane tells the physician that Adrian has often complained of being hurt by Daddy. The physician examines Jane's photographs of Adrian's facial injuries and repeatedly asks the child how many times Daddy has hurt her. One should remember what the philosopher Goethe taught: "We look for what we know. We find what we look for."

While the case is winding through discovery in the family court, psychological evaluations to determine the "best interests" of Adrian are ordered. Counsel should work to get this process started with an evaluator who has some sense of PA. Counsel should negotiate with opposing counsel to pick a skilled evaluator, and with the family court judge to obtain a protective order stating that Richard does not have to begin the evaluation until the criminal case is concluded. In the likely event that counsel is stuck with someone's favorite evaluator, it will be important to work with the defense team expert to slowly spoon feed the evaluator with recent research on the psychological evaluation of alienating and target parents. The defense team expert should provide a brief on research into alienating parents that has found alienators perceive themselves to be flawless and virtuous, and they externalize responsibility onto others. They lack insight into their own behavior and the impact their behavior has on others (Bagby, Nicholson, Buis, Radovanovic & Fidler, 1999; Bathurst, Gottfried & Gottfried, 1997; Siegel, 1996). To this brief for the evaluator, the defense team expert should add the literature that describes psychological disturbance (including histrionic, paranoid, and narcissistic personality disorders or characteristics) as well as psychosis, suicidal behavior, and substance abuse as being common among alienator parents (Baker, 2006; Clawar & Rivlin, 1991; Gardner, 1992; Hoppe & Kenney, 1994; Johnston & Campbell, 1988; Johnston, Walters & Olesen, 2005; Kopetski, 1998a, 1998b; Lampel, 1996; Rand, 1997a, 1997b; Racusin, Copans & Mills, 1994; Siegel & Langford, 1998; Turkat, 1994, 1999; Warshak, 2010a). Counsel's brief, designed to educate the chosen evaluator, must include a discussion of two important MMPI-2 studies comparing alienator parents with target parents and controls (Gordon, Stoffey & Bottinelli, 2008; Siegel & Langford, 1998).

As the weeks go by, Jane associates with a number of like-minded people in her support meetings. They begin to attend court sessions with Jane. In the hallways of the courthouse, counsel must step around a developing cadre of people infused with righteous anger, staring Richard down. What is happening here? Counsel, in the criminal and family court pleadings, has described PA. This has aroused the ire of persons who argue that men misogynistically use the concept of PA in court to defeat women who are trying to stand up for themselves and their children. Counsel must be aware of the arguments these detractors rely upon (Lorandos, 2006).

While advocacy is playing out in the family court, the CAC has been giving Adrian "therapy." Through discovery in the criminal case, counsel learns that the child is receiving play therapy, a particularly controversial modality that encourages the child to use her imagination and narrative skills to express herself (Campbell, 1992a–d; Lindsay, Johnson & Kwon 1991). Records delivered in discovery document that Adrian's stories are getting more and more detailed as Adrian goes to therapy once a week and sometimes twice if she's particularly "anxious." The master document file and chronology hold data demonstrating that the double visits are occurring on the weeks in which there is a court date.

Adrian's increasingly detailed stories make their way into the court record through Jane's filings. Jane, Janice (Steven's sister), and her supporters seize on this, and counsel is met with a barrage of blog posts, news articles, website articles about PA, and articles accusing Richard Gardner of being a protector of abusers. Jane and her supporters appear on a local talk show, specifically stating, "Richard Connelly abused his three-year-old daughter." The townspeople are sharpening their pitchforks, and a whiff of bonfire is in the air. A normal reaction would be to speak out. Counsel must remember *Gentile v. State Bar of Nevada* (1991) and circle the wagons. In *Gentile,* an attorney gave a press conference hours after his client was indicted on criminal charges. The Nevada State Bar filed a complaint alleging that the attorney violated a rule prohibiting an attorney from making an extrajudicial statement that could have "a substantial likelihood of materially prejudicing an adjudicative proceeding." It was a mess. Counsel, "don't fire until you see the white of their eyes."

In the criminal case, counsel must do every bit of discovery possible in Richard's preliminary examination. Put Jane on the stand, and Adrian too. Counsel should ask as many specific questions as possible, because the devil is in the details. Once counsel gets Jane and Adrian's stories at the preliminary examination, support staff must compare them to every statement from every other place the "Daddy hurt me" allegation has been repeated. Staff must compare police reports, CAC records, therapy records, and Jane's appearances in the media. With these data, support staff must compile charts of the inconsistencies between each actor's stories. Counsel's researcher and the defense team expert must analyze all of the interviews and the credentials of the professionals involved in the case from within this scientific perspective.

Before counsel attempts Jane's deposition in the family case, counsel should depose other actors, such as therapist Steven and sister Janice. Counsel must depose the CAC therapist, making sure to focus on finding out what Adrian has stated in therapy. Counsel must politely question the CAC therapist about what she does in play therapy, getting as many details as possible. In Jane's deposition, counsel must confront Jane with the things the private investigator has uncovered, as well as what counsel has found while deposing other individuals. Counsel should not work for a Perry Mason moment here; just get Jane to lie, again and again and again. Counsel's goal must be to link Adrian's statements (from interviews, therapy, and Adrian's teachers) to statements by Jane. They will all be cross-referenced by staff in the "inconsistencies" charts. Later they will be used to show Jane's parental influence on Adrian. Counsel must push the criminal trial and base the defense on science.

THE SCIENCE

Psychologist researcher Hollida Wakefield and Lutheran minister turned clinical psychologist Ralph Underwager taught that the "natural history" (origin, timing, and nature) of a child abuse allegation must be examined (Wakefield & Underwager, 1990, 1991). Although they focused primarily on sexual abuse accusations, their strategy is applicable to other forms of alleged abuse as well. They provided preliminary guidelines for the determination of true versus false accusations. They defined factors behind false allegations of sexual abuse, including the character of the accuser; the persons who aid, and in many cases abet, the accuser; and the use of leading or manipulative questioning. Counsel and the defense team should be mindful of the list Wakefield and Underwager (1990, 1991) provided to differentiate between real and false allegations. They suggested the fact finder examine the

- origin of the disclosure
- timing of the allegations
- age of the child
- behavior of the accusing parent
- nature of the allegations
- characteristics of the child's statement
- personality characteristics of the parties involved
- behavior of the professionals involved

For this reason, counsel, the staff researcher, and the defense team expert must carefully analyze every statement made by Adrian, every statement attributed to Adrian by another, and specifically how the CPS and the CAC personnel arrived at their conclusions. The CAC videorecorded "forensic" interviews must be analyzed, second by second, for indications of parental influences; interviewer bias; leading, suggestive, or repetitive questions; interviewer modifications of what was said; questions that suggested new content; questions that denigrated Richard; and so forth. Each utterance must be coded as to *when* it was made, *what* specifically was said and to *whom* the statement was made. Lacking a skilled researcher, this process can be replicated by any attorney near a university. A little searching (try *Craig's List*) will find a social sciences graduate student who is already plugged into numerous medical and behavioral science databases through her or his study. They all need money, and the good ones can break down the science jargon easily. The statements analysis should then be laid out in an Excel spreadsheet. These coded lists should be cross-referenced because they will form the basis for cross-examination of the accuser and other witnesses over their inconsistencies, contradictions, and outright fabrications.

In Richard's case, counsel will prepare specific science content areas to deal with the alleged "Daddy hurt me" statement and its aftermath. Review of the natural history of the allegation shows that some time before little Adrian is said to have made the "Daddy hurt me" statement, Jane was away at a continuing education seminar and Adrian and Richard traveled to a hotel and theme park. On the return trip to the family home, Richard was cut off in traffic by an elderly couple driving through a red light. When he slammed on the brakes, Adrian's improperly fastened seat belt gave way and the child collided with the rear passenger doorpost. Her black eye and bruises took several hours to appear. When they arrived home, Jane grabbed Adrian and left the home. To educate the trier of fact about what Jane has been saying to Adrian and how the "Daddy hurt me" statement came about is counsel's first science content area: *parental influences on children's memory.* When Jane took little Adrian to CPS, the investigator sent Jane and Adrian to the local CAC for a forensic interview. With respect to the interview and the effects of the play therapy on Adrian, counsel's second science content area is *children's suggestibility.*

Over the course of months since the alleged "Daddy hurt me" statement, the play therapist has carefully noted the many additional statements Adrian has made involving "Daddy" and "hurting" and "a long time." Jane's counsel, the prosecutor and the play therapist all say that Adrian's alleged "Daddy hurt me" statement is clearly a *delayed disclosure.* This, then, is the third science content area counsel must develop.

ESSENTIAL TREATISES IN THREE SCIENCE CONTENT AREAS

In the cross-examination of proposed experts, counsel must be mindful that one can find a great deal to illuminate for the court by exploring *what they do not know.* If they *survive voir dire,* what they think they know is for direct examination. Cross-examination is all about contrasting the seriousness of the circumstances with what they *should know* but do not. The Clancy Method and *Cross Examining Experts in the Behavioral Sciences* (Campbell & Lorandos, 2001) explain this important use of cross-examination at length. Once learned, it is easy to do.

In preparing for the criminal trial, the defense team carefully prepares with each fact witness with individual *What do we need from this witness?* (WDWNFTW) charts. All of them are keyed to the Gardner (1992) and Fidler and Bala (2010a) criteria. Simultaneously, counsel, the researcher, and the defense team expert pull the three science content areas together with learned treatises.

Parental Influences on Children's Memory

Counsel must show the trier of fact what anxious parents can do to children's memories. Counsel's expert must explain that the coded statements charts and the numerous interviews and CPS materials that were reviewed demonstrated that Adrian's stories of what she "remembered" changed dramatically under parental questioning. Counsel should not plan to begin this explication by denigrating anxious parents. The PA case does not need to be won in the early stages of the criminal trial. Consequently, counsel should tailor the proofs of the science of parental influences by starting with a description of how worried and anxious parents can make mountains out of molehills. For example, "maternal over reporting of anxious symptoms was related systematically to the level of maternal anxiety" (Frick, Silverthorn & Evans, 1994, p. 376).

Concerning Janice, Jane's supporters, and their impact on what Jane said to Adrian, counsel's expert should be prepared to explain the serious effects of rumor. A good place to start is with the work of forensic psychologist Terence Campbell (1992a):

> Once a parent suspects that his or her child has been sexually abused, the parent struggles with a very difficult situation. As long as the child denies any abuse, a worried parent must contend with a gnawing, unrelenting sense of anxious uncertainty. . . . The intense needs of people to obtain information under these circumstances motivates them to exchange imaginative

> speculations with each other. In turn, these speculative exchanges create fertile ground for a bountiful harvest of rumors. . . . [In these circumstances parents often think that] We agree, therefore we must be right! . . .
>
> When children finally respond to questions regarding alleged sexual abuse by indicating, "Yes he did it . . ." the parent experiences a paradoxical sense of relief . . . the parent no longer contends with the agonizing paralysis of doubting uncertainty.

Counsel should plan to add an explanation that "Young children interpret adult questions such as 'Are you sure?' or 'What about this one?' as a cue that their first answer must have been incorrect and that they should produce a different response" (Ricci, Beal & Dekle, 1996, p. 497). Counsel should also use the defense team expert to introduce research that mothers are not "able to accurately recall whether [statements] were the child's own words or if her statement is a reconstruction of a conversation in which the child provided one-word answers to a series of direct and possibly leading questions from the mother" (Bruck, Ceci & Francoeur, 1999). Working closely with the defense team expert, counsel may conclude this portion of the science explication with Debra Poole and Stephen Lindsay's stunning report of the "Mr. Science" experiments in which parents merely suggested a behavior that Mr. Science may have performed: "Misinformation provided by parents is an extremely powerful contaminant of preschoolers' testimonies" (Poole & Lindsay, 1995, p. 147).

Suggestibility

In this field, counsel must be familiar with concepts such as confirmatory bias, the repeated question effect, and source monitoring error. For these concepts counsel should have on hand standard texts in the field of suggestibility, such as Campbell, 1998; Ceci & Bruck, 1995; Ceci, Ross & Toglia, 1989; Ceci, Toglia & Ross, 1987; Doris, 1991; Kuehnle & Connell, 2009; Poole & Lamb, 1998; Wakefield & Underwager, 1990. Counsel should plan to use this foundation in cross-examination. Next, counsel should use the defense team expert and quotes from *Jeopardy in the Courtroom* to describe the deleterious effects of therapy for children in these circumstances:

> Adults may tilt the odds toward false disclosures for two reasons. First, the presence of extra adults, all of whom share the same beliefs about what may have transpired, may induce a child to join them. Second, extra adults multiply the number of questions that the child is asked about the same theme: "Tell us how you were sexually abused." (Ceci & Bruck, 1995, p. 155)

> And the harmful part of the so-called treatment is that there was no attempt to help the child with their reality testing, so that manifestly implausible things . . . were simply accepted at face value. . . . You do harm to the child because you don't help the child to distinguish between what is possible, what is real, what is not real; what is a fantasy and what is real. . . . So a lot of these children got worse in the course of treatment. (Ceci & Bruck, 1995, p. 226)

> On the basis of what we now know, it would be imprudent to use fantasy inductions, imagery play, and "memory work" during the therapy sessions conducted before the completion of forensic interviews. These practices can be saved for after the legal resolution. Prior to it, therapy should be restricted to working on everyday coping strategies. . . . (Ceci & Bruck, 1995, p. 289)

Concerning the kind of therapy Adrian has been receiving, Campbell (1992a) explained,

> A play therapist can profoundly distort the memory of a child by suggesting interpretations of what the child supposedly encountered or experienced. In response to the therapist's influence, children accept these interpretations as legitimate. They then resort to their imaginations–though convinced they are searching their memories–inventing anecdotes of past events which appear to validate the therapist's interpretations.

Counsel should prepare to cross-examine Adrian's play therapist with these quotes, and then the defense team expert should hit all of them home. The trier of fact should be informed by the defense team expert about the standard reported experiments in child suggestibility, such as

- The Mousetrap study (Ceci, Huffman, Smith & Loftus, 1994)
- The Sam Stone study (Leichtman & Ceci, 1995)
- The Simon Says study (Lepore & Sesco, 1994)

These three experiments are discussed for lay audiences in Ceci and Bruck's *Jeopardy in the Courtroom: A Scientific Analysis of Children's Testimony* (1995).

Counsel should prepare the second-by-second analysis of Adrian's CAC interview with the defense team expert to describe memory interference and explain the effects of modifications by interviewers and therapists. "Modification" is a form of suggestive questioning in which the interviewer contradicts or incorrectly restates what the child just said, and "Children frequently agree with interviewers who either reword their statements in a way that changes their meaning or who claim that the children made statements they did not make" (Warren, Woodall, Hunt & Perry, 1996, p. 241). When reviewing actual forensic interviews, these researchers found 93.9 percent of them overflowing with modifications. In a follow-up study, Warren and Marsil found that this form of suggestive questioning "may be equally or even more detrimental to children's testimonial veracity than leading questions" (Warren & Marsil, 2002). Citing a high rate of modifications by police and forensic interviewers and a low rate of disagreement from children like Adrian in actual interviews, researchers Hunt and Borgida (2001) explained that these "commonly used interviewing techniques can have serious, deleterious effects on children's testimony." Memory researcher Elizabeth Loftus has repeatedly demonstrated that when people do not have an original memory, they can and do accept misinformation and adopt it as their own memory (Loftus & Hoffman, 1989). The defense team expert should also be prepared to point out that researchers Orbach and Lamb (2000) documented that

> Option posing, yes/no, and suggestive questions subvert children's competency, foster acquiescence to misleading information, and increase the retrieval of erroneous information. . . . Option posing utterances . . . focus the child's attention on details or aspects of the alleged incident that the child has not previously mentioned.

This is the point in cross-examination, and then in the direct examination of the defense team expert, at which counsel must be prepared to bring in the issue of CAC staff training, "validators" versus "evaluators," and the analysis of the natural history of the allegation.

Delayed Disclosure

To perfect Jane's claims, the CAC interviewer, play therapist, and Jane's support group referred specialty physician will testify that there is good research to support the idea that Adrian's "Daddy hurt me" statement was a delayed disclosure. The implication is that the "hurting" has been going on for a long time. After all, Adrian has been repeatedly questioned about "how many times" and "when did it start" and that she was "so scared." When pushed, these witnesses will exclaim that the research of Sorensen and Snow (1991) made it clear that children delayed their disclosure of abuse events. As a strategic point for courtroom practice: Counsel should never use the word disclosure. This word has a psycholinguistic charge via subliminal connotation: when something is disclosed, we imagine that it was hidden and now, due to someone's wonderful work, it has been revealed. That is the prosecutor's game. Defense counsel must call it a "story." Defense counsel must say "the child said" or "the child related," never, "the child disclosed."

To deal with the article by Sorensen and Snow (1991), counsel should prepare the following materials for cross-examination of the opposing witnesses and conclude with the defense team expert describing the value of these resources. Reputable research into the Sorenson and Snow idea of delayed disclosure does "not support the view that disclosure is a quasi-developmental process with 'stages' that can be 'resolved'" (Bradley & Wood, 1996). Indeed, when actual cases are closely scrutinized, denial or delayed disclosure occurs "in 6% of cases, and recantation in 4%." Dealing with the idea that it is only through persistent questioning or therapy that a child can come to describe episodes of abuse, one quality study found that "83% of all allegations and disclosures were elicited through free-recall questions . . . and . . . these data dispel the belief that interviewers need to bombard children with suggestive techniques in order to elicit details of trauma" (Bruck & Ceci & 2004; *see also* Lamb, Sternberg, Orbach, Esplin, Stewart & Mitchell, 2003). To really drive home the point with the trier of fact about how the Sorensen and Snow paper is, there are two cases from the Utah Supreme Court (Sorensen and Snow's home state):

> the victims' statements related through Barbara Snow and other experts were simply so unreliable that they should not have been admissible. In sum, the tainting, indeed the inducing of testimony in this case, was not benign–it was the product of a misdirected zealousness and the failure to adhere to any scientific standards for the eliciting of truthful testimony. (*State v. Bullock*)

and even more damaging:

> testimony from law enforcement personnel that false information deliberately "fed" by them to Barbara Snow in their investigatory work promptly appeared in the statements of children she interviewed . . . one police officer who described how the children in Dr. Snow's care were able to reproduce specific information after he had suggested it to Dr. Snow that such information should be present in their statements. (*State v. Hadfield*)

These criticisms of Snow's work were directly based on the way she developed and reported data.

Because this delayed disclosure idea had its origin in the junk science concept the "Child Sexual Abuse Accommodation Syndrome" (CSAAS) (Lorandos & Campbell, 2005) counsel and counsel's expert should use two recent studies to explain how degrading this idea actually is. Here's an example: "The research on denial and recantation shows that when directly questioned in a formal setting, only a small percentage of abused children demonstrate these behaviors" (London, Bruck, Ceci & Shuman, 2005; London, Bruck, Wright & Ceci, 2008).

Prepared with the master document file, the master chronology file, the inconsistencies charts, a thoroughly prepared expert, thoroughly prepared fact witnesses, all of the discovery information obtained in the family case, and the WDWNFTW charts and exhibits, counsel is ready for motion hearings in criminal court. The prosecution will argue that Adrian should not take the stand, and her "Daddy hurt me" and numerous additional play therapy-generated statements should be admitted through adults under a hearsay exception commonly called outcry. Counsel must be prepared to counter with a request for a taint hearing regarding Adrian's memory. A motion and brief for a taint hearing can be obtained in the Thomson-Reuters West two-volume *Cross Examining Experts in the Behavioral Sciences* (Campbell & Lorandos, 2001). Counsel must be prepared to lead with the defense team expert to point out that this child's memory is not her own. The defense team expert must be prepared to educate the court with video segments of the "Mousetrap" experiments (Ceci et al., 1994), as well as footage from *60 Minutes, Dateline, 20/20, Nightline,* and PBS *Frontline* news documentaries on the infamous daycare cases in the 1980s and 1990s. It is likely that the judge will erroneously rule that what the child knows or does not know goes to the weight of her testimony. Therefore, the prosecutor must prove the child is unavailable if she wishes to use adults to relay her alleged statements via hearsay to the jury. In order to do this, the prosecutor will call Adrian to the stand. It is very likely that the child, not having seen her demonized father for many months, will be too scared to answer the prosecutor's questions. The judge will likely suggest that it appears Adrian is truly unavailable. Defense counsel must be prepared to examine the child, and counsel must understand how to cross-examine children. Counsel must know that in order to talk to a three year old, counsel must be a person that a three year old wants to talk to. If counsel cannot do this, perhaps another line of work is called for.

A properly prepared defense attorney should be able to have the child laughing and giggling on the stand with all the silly things the two of them are talking about. The court must rule that Adrian is "available" and, via the taint hearing, that there are insufficient guarantees of trustworthiness surrounding the giving of the alleged statements to let them come in via hearsay (*Idaho v. Wright,* 1990). At the same time as the taint hearing, counsel should hold a *Daubert,* or *Frye,* or *Mohan* hearing (depending on local law) to disqualify the CAC interviewer and therapist. At this hearing, the court must make a detailed finding that the proposed experts really are experts pursuant to current expert evidence law. With respect to the behavioral sciences, these motions can be obtained in the Thomson-Reuters West set *Cross Examining Experts in the Behavioral Sciences* (Campbell & Lorandos, 2001). Because there have been numerous opportunities to convince the assigned assistant prosecutor to dismiss if counsel follows this method along the way, it is likely that the criminal case will be over. *One down, two to go.*

Next, counsel must return to the licensure case. In the beginning of counsel's representation of Richard, counsel negotiated with the Board of Social Work that Richard be allowed to see adult patients in a supervised setting. After the criminal case is dismissed, the operating agreement negotiated with the Board of Social Work should autoextinguish. Negotiating on the use of his building in the family court, Richard should now be able to return to his practice. Counsel should confirm with the Board of Social Work, reminding that Richard has a stellar record with no improprieties. Counsel should make a record that the only stain on his reputation is the one that Jane created. *Two down, one to go.*

Finally, the defense team has the custody trial to win. The defense team has used the master chronology to find witnesses who were present in the home while Richard was parenting Adrian. The chronology reveals that Richard held study groups in his home while in school because he was located close to campus. Counsel has kept the team's investigator busy, and the team has discovered that four months prior to the allegation, Jane was seen with Steven at a coffee house. Jane and Steven were seen again two months prior to the allegation, this time at the local Bed Bath & Beyond®. With this new information, the defense team must reformat every one of the proofs developed for the criminal case with the Gardner (1992) and/or Fidler and Bala (2010a) criteria as a central focus. Counsel and the team must prepare to show that Richard was caring for Adrian at home while Jane was gadding about, doing who knows what. Counsel must also prepare to show the court that the PA coming from Adrian is the product of Jane and her supporters and the poison they have been spewing. Adrian has demonstrated that she knows about the legal cases involving her parents in detail. This information can only have come from Jane.

PREPARING FOR EXPERT TESTIMONY

Because counsel has carefully chosen an expert to explicate the signs and symptoms of PA in this matter, the expert will have in her possession highlighted, dog-eared copies of at least the following:

- *Children Held Hostage: Dealing with Programmed and Brainwashed Children* (Clawar & Rivlin, 1991)
- *The International Handbook of Parental Alienation Syndrome: Conceptual, Clinical and Legal Considerations* (Gardner, Sauber & Lorandos, 2006)
- *Adult Children of Parental Alienation Syndrome: Breaking the Ties That Bind* (Baker, 2007)
- *Special Issue on Alienated Children in Divorce and Separation: Emerging Approaches for Families and Court* (Fidler & Bala, 2010b)
- *Parental Alienation, DSM-5, and ICD-11* (Bernet, 2010)

Depending on the expert's field, the expert must also have and bring the following to planning meetings and to court:

Psychologists

- Ethical Principles of Psychologists and Code of Conduct with 2010 Amendments
- Specialty Guidelines for Forensic Psychology
- Record Keeping Guidelines
- Guidelines for Child Custody Evaluations In Family Law Proceedings
- Guidelines for Psychological Evaluations in Child Protection Matters

Psychiatrists

- Principles of Medical Ethics of the American Medical Association
- American Psychiatric Association's Principles of Medical Ethics with Annotations Especially Applicable to Psychiatry
- American Academy of Child and Adolescent Psychiatry Code of Ethics
- American Academy of Child and Adolescent Psychiatry–Practice Parameters for Child Custody Evaluation
- American Academy of Psychiatry and the Law: Ethics Guidelines for the Practice of Forensic Psychiatry

Social Workers

- Code of Ethics

Furthermore, counsel must be sure the chosen expert has done everything she can to speak to all parties in the case. The cheap shot cross-examination technique of "Well, you didn't talk to my client, did you?" should be addressed in the first planning meetings. The differential diagnosis of estrangement versus alienation requires data developed from many sources. An interview with the child involved may be possible. Perhaps caregivers other than counsel's client can bring the child to the expert. This should never be attempted clandestinely. Experts must be apprised of who may and who may not bring the child in for an interview. When in doubt, ask the court (Baker, 2007b; Bernet, 1983; Eisner, 2010; Stahl, 2003; Woody, 2009).

In addition, counsel and the chosen expert must be steadfast in the syntax used in testimony. Experts should never say, "So and So *is* . . ." or, "Analysis of test responses indicates that So and So *will* . . ." Experts who pontificate that a particular person *is* this or that or that this particular person *will* do this or that should be avoided. The data reviewed can only be compared to a particular person or a situation, and there are limits in the validity and reliability of any comparison. Admittedly, the more and better data an expert has, the better the comparison of a particular person or circumstance to *what the research tells us.* An ethical expert will always describe the limits of the data and the range of error in comparisons and predictions.

In preparing with the chosen expert, counsel must remember that it is in contested custody cases that experts are attacked, grieved, and sued. The chosen expert likely knows this, but counsel must underscore this potential difficulty. Counsel should always seek an order from the presiding judge that any and all "ethical complaints" or standard of care concerns be contained in a separate record and dealt with outside the confines of the issues concerning the child victims of PA. Also in this vein, counsel and the chosen expert should work out a sign or signal from the expert that there is more that must be said but only concerning legal or ethical issues. Too many experts from the behavioral sciences are left hanging by unprepared attorneys and not allowed to address a misconception that may have arisen in cross-examination. Counsel should not allow the expert to signal whenever he or she wishes to make an additional point concerning the research literature. To reiterate, this should only occur to address legal or ethical issues that may otherwise require the expert to hire an outside attorney to correct the record.

Counsel must prepare with the chosen expert concerning the criticisms of PA and PAS research. Gardner's explication of PAS was lauded by some and criticized by others, but it was Gardner's description of false sexual abuse allegations as a tactic that found him pilloried. The *ad hominem* attacks and shoddy scholarship that characterized Gardner's critics in the two decades that followed his 1985 paper are well-illustrated by three examples.

The criticisms of social worker Kathleen Faller (1998, 2000) with respect to Gardner and his formulation of PAS seemed to be based on Faller's lack of methodological awareness and a frank desire to mislead readers. She began her 2000 *Arkansas Little Rock Law Review* article by citing a 1995 article she wrote with student social worker Ellen DeVoe entitled *Allegations of*

Sexual Abuse in Divorce (Faller & DeVoe, 1995). The purpose for citing this work was to refute Gardner's proposition that in the highly charged atmosphere of child custody litigation, many allegations of child sexual abuse appeared to be fabricated. A close look at Faller and DeVoe's 1995 study revealed serious methodological problems. It seemed that in the mid-1990s, Faller and her "Faller Group" developed a reputation for wildly skewed and improper methodology replete with leading questions and forced focus on the genitals of anatomically detailed dolls. A special panel of the Michigan courts was created to review Faller's work (*Bielaska v. Orley*, 1996) and found their work to be "suggestive," "coercive," and "untrustworthy." The analysis she offered in her Gardner criticisms was worthy of the same adjectives (Lorandos, 2006; Warshak, 2003).

Hobbs (2006) described the impact of shoddy scholarship on the treatment of children in the courts of the United Kingdom. To illustrate, Hobbs pointed to the impact of a report by Claire Sturge and Danya Glaser in 2000 that relied solely on Faller's criticism of Gardner. Hobbs, a researcher and teacher at Keele University in England, was an associate fellow of the British Psychological Society and a chartered psychologist. He explained that in their report to the court, Sturge and Glaser (2000) made reference to only Faller's specious work about PA and, with no critical analysis whatsoever, used it to support a denial that PA existed. Hobbs argued that these specially commissioned experts gave the court no indication whatsoever of the existence of a large PA research literature, or of the many judicial decisions in other countries successfully based on it. Unfortunately, argued Hobbs, although Sturge and Glaser failed to mention these crucial facts, the sole article on which they relied had itself already been significantly discredited just a short time later in the very same journal in which it had been published. He argued that the national significance of the Sturge and Glaser report should not be underestimated, because the entire Family Division of the Court of Appeal, the Lord Chancellor's Childrens' Act Subcommittee, and the government itself via the Lord Chancellor were not made aware of the increasing global scientific and judicial recognition and acceptance of PA and PAS. "This was a direct result of their bona fide trusted experts' serious failure to provide the relevant comprehensive and impartial review required." Hobbs went on to explain that

> What is of particularly crucial relevance to the UK's recognition and management of PAS subsequent to Sturge and Glaser's findings on PAS, is that the 1998 Human Rights Act came into force throughout the UK in October 2000. Since that time, all domestic legislation and previous precedent case

> law must be construed in accordance with the enacted portions of the 1950 European Convention on Human Rights, and, of course, in accordance with the judgments of the European Court of Human Rights. (p. 81)

Consequently, because the Chancellor was not made aware of the significant research in PA, the acceptance and recognition of strategies to aid families and children caught in the process were delayed in the United Kingdom.

Describing herself as a "research professor of law," Carol Bruch, in a 2001 work, relied upon newspaper articles and nine citations to Faller's material to support her arguments. In her criticism of Gardner's formulation of PAS, Bruch informed that it is always "deeply troubling" when one confronts an "overwhelming absence of careful analysis and attention to scientific rigor" (Bruch, 2001). Curiously, Bruch ignored 200 years of case precedent concerning parents alienating children from another parent and two decades of careful, peer-reviewed research from the behavioral sciences to rely on Kathleen Faller and newspaper articles. In so doing, she ignored the research described earlier and years of hard scholarship by the likes of Hetherington, Lamb, Emery, Cox or the interdisciplinary work: *Legal and Mental Health Perspectives on Custody Law: A Deskbook for Judges* (Benedek & Levy, 1998). In a work that seemed to use hyperbole as a substitute for clear thinking, Bruch also relied on a "study" by Karen Winner. Some digging uncovered that Ms. Winner is a private investigator and author of an issue book for women. Winner has a bachelor's degree in social work and has submitted a number of women's issue pieces to newspapers around the country. She "investigates" and lectures on such topics as how women are subjected to "dirty tricks" by opposing lawyers and discriminated against by "prejudiced judges." Winner maintained a business and website, *The Justice Seekers, Inc.,* where she advertised:

> Need an expert to debunk the fraudulent diagnosis, "Parental Alienation Syndrome?" Need an expert to evaluate whether your divorce lawyer has engaged in business practices that put his or her financial interests above the client's welfare? This small but growing list is a free public service to help litigants in divorce and custody cases find the experts they need. Check back periodically to see new additions. *Courtesy of the Justice Seekers, Inc.* (Winner, 2002)

This from Carol Bruch, the "research professor of law," who argued that it is "deeply troubling" when one confronts an "overwhelming absence of careful analysis and attention to scientific rigor."

With respect to the significant shortcomings in scholarship by Faller and Bruch, researchers Fidler and Bala (2010a) explained that these "feminist advocates" claim they are acting in a name of helping women. Fidler and Bala reasoned that in this way shoddy scholarship does a great disservice to the many mothers who are unjustifiably alienated from their children, often by abusive men. These Canadian researchers went on to point out that hyperbole instead of scholarship does a great disservice to the children caught in an alienation scenario.

Counsel must prepare with the defense team expert to describe the sequelae of PA. In this vein, an explication of the research into the consequences in the lives of children of this difficult dysfunction must be developed. Counsel should use Clawar and Rivlin's *Children Held Hostage* (1991), Baker's 2005 study for the *American Journal of Family Therapy* and her 2007 book *Adult Children of Parental Alienation Syndrome: Breaking the Ties That Bind,* as well as selected chapters from the materials described earlier. Counsel must prepare with the defense team expert to show that if this alienation is not halted, Adrian will have a terrible time of it–*just like Jane did.* The team must work hard to draw parallels between Jane's upbringing and her resultant inability to relate to men in a healthy way. Perhaps this may be buttressed by having the defense team's private investigator look into the backgrounds of Jane's supporters. It is likely there is much to discover there. Finally, counsel must carefully prepare with the defense team expert to demonstrate Adrian's life *before* the allegation, *during* the trajectory of the allegations and criminal case, and *now.*

While the defense team's preparation is developing, and through vigorous advocacy, counsel has obtained supervised visitation for Richard and Adrian at a visitation center. At the visitation center, Richard is given a long list of rules. He must bring things to play with Adrian, but the restrictions are tight. Adrian's favorite thing to do was play dress up, but Richard cannot bring costumes. Richard had been teaching Adrian about the Bible, but Bibles are forbidden at the center. Richard has been advised by the expert to try to rekindle good memories in Adrian, but Richard is not allowed to bring photos. The game "Candyland" is expressly forbidden. Richard is told that all of the things that he wanted to do with Adrian could be seen as evidence that he was "grooming" Adrian to keep quiet about abuse. The center itself is filthy and bleak, and Richard and Adrian are very uncomfortable there, especially with the supervisor there. Counsel must use the expert and Richard's therapist to instruct that the supervised visitation process and the reports that are generated are nothing more than a beauty contest. Make an analogy, make a joke: "Evening wear . . ." "Talent . . ." "World Peace. . . ."

The consequences of many months of alienation and indoctrination that counsel explicated in the criminal case will have taken a toll on Adrian. Counsel must use the defense team expert's connections in the behavioral sciences community to find a suitable reunification therapist to guide Richard's reintegration process with Adrian. Counsel and the defense team expert should utilize the questionnaire developed by Sauber (2012) to search for and vet potential specialists.

Because Jane and her attorney have hired an expert, counsel must prepare a cross-examination just as was done for the criminal defense. When the cross-examination begins, counsel discovers that Jane's expert is actually a nice old guy who wants to get the parties to hold hands and sing *Kumbaya.* Gently but with force, counsel must expose that this expert's ideas about what to do are not supported in the research (Fidler & Bala, 2010a; Kelly, 2010; Warshak, 2010b). The court, through the defense team's painstaking work of laying out the entire timeline of Adrian's indoctrination, is beginning to see that Jane is a liar. The key themes in the defense team's expert testimony will provide a veritable road map for the family court judge. The tipping point comes when the court is shown a few home videos, showing Adrian as a happy and healthy little girl with Daddy and his social work study group. The contrast with the Adrian the judge sees now is undeniable. Adrian is destabilized and now has behavioral problems that manifest at school and at home. She is now almost five years old, and in the two years that her mother has been campaigning against her father, Adrian has grown more and more destructive.

Counsel and the defense team have taken great pains to document and then present to the court Jane's lies and outright fabrications. Even the child custody evaluator has seen Jane's pathology when the defense team briefed the research for her. Following the submission to the court of counsel's brief describing the many, many cases from developed countries the world over where a custodial change is in the child's best interests, the court sees the light and orders Adrian into an intensive reunification program like *Family Bridges* (Kelly, 2010; Warshak, 2010b). Jane is ordered into therapy if she wishes to interact with Adrian again in supervised visitation. Jane is ordered to pay 75 percent of Richard's legal fees. The entire amount is deducted from her share of the marital estate.

Editors' Notes

- The author explains a methodology for pretrial planning that involves an integration of fact proofs with the scientific data on the manipulation of children's memories, child suggestibility, interviewing, and delayed disclosure of distorted recollections.
- The author's trial planning methodology is described in detail and is grounded in a distribution of fact development responsibilities among

staff and science data integration between attorney and chosen expert. The specific use of scientific research data is illustrated.

- The author's experience with client management and expert selection and collaboration is described. The author cites the reader to criteria for expert selection and direct as well as cross-examination preparation. The common pitfalls for experts testifying about parental alienation are described and recommendations given for handling them.
- The author recommends that any attorney or litigant preparing a PA case use the research cases and sample motions contained in this volume's Supplemental Reference Guide.

REFERENCES

Bagby, R. M., Nicholson, R. A., Buis, T., Radovanovic, H., & Fidler, B. J. (1999). Defensive responding on the MMPI-2 in family custody and access evaluations. *Psychological Assessment, 11*(1), 24–28.

Baker, A. J. L. (2005). The long-term effects of parental alienation on adult children: A qualitative research study. *American Journal of Family Therapy, 33*(4), 289–302.

Baker, A. J. L. (2006). Patterns of parental alienation syndrome: A qualitative study of adults who were alienated from a parent as a child. *American Journal of Family Therapy, 34*(1), 63–78.

Baker, A. J. L. (2007a). *Adult children of parental alienation syndrome: Breaking the ties that bind.* New York: W. W. Norton.

Baker, A. J. L. (2007b). Knowledge and attitudes about the parental alienation syndrome: A survey of custody evaluators. *American Journal of Family Therapy, 35*(1), 1–19.

Bathurst, K., Gottfried, A. W., & Gottfried, A. E. (1997). Normative data for the MMPI-2 in child custody litigation. *Psychological Assessment, 9*(3), 205–211.

Benedek, E., Levy, R., & National Interdisciplinary Colloquium on Child Custody Law. (1998). *Legal and mental health perspectives on custody law: A deskbook for judges.* Egan, MN: West Group.

Bernet W. (1983). The therapist's role in child custody disputes. *Journal of Child Psychiatry, 22*(2), 180–183.

Bernet, W. (2010). *Parental alienation, DSM-5, and ICD-11.* Springfield, IL: Charles C Thomas Publisher.

Bradley, A. R., & Wood, J. M. (1996) How do children tell? The disclosure process in child sexual abuse. *Child Abuse and Neglect, 20*(9), 881–891.

Bruch, C. (2001). Parental alienation syndrome and parental alienation: Getting it wrong in child custody. *Family Law Quarterly, 35*(3), 527–552.

Bruck, M., Ceci, S. J., & Francoeur, E. (1999). The accuracy of mothers' memories of conversations with their preschool children. *Journal of Experimental Psychology: Applied, 5*(1), 89–106.

Bruck, M., & Ceci, S. J. (2004). Forensic developmental psychology: Unveiling four common misconceptions. *Current Directions in Psychological Science, 13*(6), 229–232.

Campbell, T. W. (1992a). False allegations of sexual abuse and their apparent credibility. *American Journal of Forensic Psychology, 10*(4), 21–35.

Campbell, T. W. (1992b). False allegations of sexual abuse and the persuasiveness of play therapy. *Issues in Child Abuse Accusations, 4*(3), 118–124.

Campbell, T. W. (1992c). Promoting Play therapy: Marketing dream or empirical nightmare. *Issues in Child Abuse Accusations, 4*(3), 111–117.

Campbell, T. W. (1992d). Psychotherapy with children of divorce: The pitfalls of triangulated relationships. *Psychotherapy, 29*(4), 646–652.

Campbell, T. W. (1998) *Smoke and mirrors: The devastating effect of false sexual abuse claims.* New York: Insight Books.

Campbell, T. W., & Lorandos, D. (2001) *Cross examining experts in the behavioral sciences* (two volumes, annual updates). Egan, MN; West Group.

Carson, R. (1969). *Interaction concepts of personality.* Chicago: Aldine.

Ceci, S. J., & Bruck, M. (1995). *Jeopardy in the courtroom: A scientific analysis of children's testimony.* Washington, DC: American Psychological Association.

Ceci, S. J., Huffman, M. L. C., Smith, E., & Loftus, E. (1994). Repeatedly thinking about a non-event: Source misattributions among preschoolers. *Consciousness and Cognition: An International Journal, 3*(4), 388–407.

Ceci, S. J., Ross, D. F., & Toglia, M. P. (Eds.). (1989). *Perspectives on children's testimony.* New York: Springer-Verlag.

Ceci, S. J., Toglia, M. P., & Ross, D. F. (Eds.). (1987). *Children's eyewitness memory.* New York: Springer-Verlag.

Clawar, S. S., & Rivlin, B. V. (1991). *Children held hostage: Dealing with programmed and brainwashed children.* Washington, DC: American Bar Association Section of Family Law.

Doris, J. (Ed.). (1991). *The suggestibility of children's recollections: Implications for eyewitness testimony.* Washington, DC: American Psychological Association.

Eisner, D. (2010). Expert witness mental health testimony: Handling deposition and trial traps. *American Journal of Forensic Psychology, 28,* 47–65.

Faller, K. (1998). The parental alienation syndrome: What is it and what data support it? *Child Maltreatment, 3*(2), 100–115.

Faller, K. (2000). Child maltreatment and endangerment in the context of divorce [essay]. *University of Arkansas Little Rock Law Review, 22*(429).

Faller, K., & DeVoe, E. (1995). Allegations of sexual abuse in divorce. *Journal of Child Sexual Abuse, 4*(4), 1–25.

Fidler, B. J., & Bala, N. (2010a). Children resisting post-Sseparation contact with a parent: Concepts, controversies, and conundrums. *Family Court Review, 48*(1), 10–47.

Fidler, B. & Bala, N. (Eds.)(2010b). Special issue: Alienated children in divorce and separation: Emerging approaches for families and courts. *Family Court Review, 48*(1).

Frick, P. J., Silverthorn, P., & Evans, C. E. (1994). Assessment of childhood anxiety using structured interviews: Patterns of agreement among informants and association with maternal anxiety. *Psychological Assessment, 6*(4), 372–379.

Gardner, R. A. (1991). The "validators" and other examiners. *Issues in Child Abuse Accusations, 2,* 38-53.

Gardner, R. A. (1992). *The parental alienation syndrome: A guide for mental health and legal professionals.* Cresskill, NJ: Creative Therapeutics.

Gardner, R. A., Sauber, S. R., & Lorandos, D. (Eds.). (2006). *The international handbook of parental alienation syndrome: Conceptual, clinical and legal considerations.* Springfield, IL: Charles C Thomas Publisher.

Gehrke, S., & Moxom, J. (1969). Diagnostic classifications and treatment techniques in marriage counseling. *Family Process, 1*(2), 253–264.

Gordon, R. M., Stoffey, R., & Bottinelli, J. (2008). MMPI-2 findings of primitive defenses in alienating parents. *American Journal of Family Therapy, 36*(3), 211–228.

Herman, S. (2005). Improving decision making in forensic child sexual abuse evaluations. *Law and Human Behavior, 29*(1), 87–120.

Herman, S. (2009). Forensic child sexual abuse evaluations: Accuracy, ethics, and admissibility. In K. F. Kuehnle & M. Connell (Eds.), *The evaluation of child sexual abuse allegations: A comprehensive guide to assessment and testimony.* Hoboken, NJ: Wiley & Sons, Inc.

Hobbs, T. (2006). PAS in the United Kingdom: Problems in recognition and management. In R. A. Gardner, S. R. Sauber, & D. Lorandos (Eds.), *The international handbook of parental alienation syndrome: Conceptual, clinical and legal considerations* (pp. 71–89). Springfield, IL: Charles C Thomas Publisher.

Hoppe, C., & Kenney, L. (1994). *A Rorschach study of the psychological characteristics of parents engaged in child custody/visitation disputes.* Paper presented at the 102nd Annual Convention of the American Psychological Association, Los Angeles, CA, August 12–16.

Horner, T. M., & Guyer, M. (1991). Prediction, prevention, and clinical expertise in child custody cases in which allegations of child sexual abuse have been made: I. Predictable rates of diagnostic error in relation to various clinical decision making strategies. *Family Law Quarterly, 25*(2), 217–252.

Horner, T. M., Guyer, M. J., & Kalter, N. M. (1992a). Prediction, prevention, and clinical expertise in child custody cases in which allegations of child sexual abuse have been made: II. Studies of expert opinion formation. *Family Law Quarterly, 25*(3), 381–409.

Horner, T. M., Guyer, M. J., & Kalter, N. M. (1992b). Prediction, prevention and clinical expertise in child custody cases in which allegations of child sexual abuse have been made: III. Studies of expert opinion formation. *Family Law Quarterly, 26,* 141–170.

Hunt, J. S., & Borgida, E. (2001). Is that what I said? Witnesses' responses to interviewer modifications. *Law and Human Behavior, 25*(6), 583–603.

Johnston, J. R., & Campbell, L. E. (1988). *Impasses of divorce: The dynamics and resolution of family conflict.* New York: The Free Press.

Johnston, J. R., Walters, M. G., & Olesen, N. W. (2005). Clinical ratings of parenting capacity and Rorschach protocols of custody-disputing parents: An exploratory study. *Journal of Child Custody, 2*(1-2), 159–178.

Kelly, J. B. (2010). Commentary on "Family Bridges: Using insights from social science to reconnect parents and alienated children" (Warshak 2010). *Family Court Review, 48*(1), 81–90.

Kopetski, L. (1998a). Identifying cases of parent alienation syndrome, Part I. *Colorado Lawyer, 27*(2), 65–68.

Kopetski, L. (1998b). Identifying cases of parent alienation syndrome, Part II. *Colorado Lawyer, 27*(3), 61–64.

Kuehnle, K., & Connell, M. (Eds.). (2009). *The evaluation of child sexual abuse allegations: A comprehensive guide to assessment and testimony.* Hoboken, NJ: Wiley & Sons, Inc.

Lamb, M. E., Sternberg, K. J., Orbach, Y., Esplin, P. W., Stewart, H., & Mitchell, S. (2003). Age differences in young children's responses to open-ended invitations on the course of forensic interviews. *Journal of Consulting and Clinical Psychology, 71*(5), 926–934.

Lampel, A. (1996). Children's alignment with parents in highly conflicted custody cases. *Family and Conciliation Courts Review, 34*(2), 229–239.

Leichtman, M., & Ceci, S. (1995). The effects of stereotypes and suggestions on preschoolers' reports. *Developmental Psychology , 31*(4), 568–578.

Lepore, S. J., & Sesco, B. (1994). Distorting children's reports and interpretations of events through suggestion. *Journal of Applied Psychology, 79*(1), 108–120.

Lindsay, D. S., Johnson, M. K., & Kwon, P. (1991). Developmental changes in memory source monitoring. *Journal of Experimental Child Psychology, 52*(3), 297–318.

Loftus, E. F., & Hoffman, H. G. (1989). Misinformation and memory: The creation of new memories. *Journal of Experimental Psychology: General, 118*(1), 100–104.

London, K., Bruck, M. Ceci, S. J., & Shuman, D. W. (2005). Disclosure of child sexual abuse: What does the research tell us about the ways that children tell? *Psychology, Public Policy and Law, 11*(1), 194–226.

London, K., Bruck, M., Wright, D., & Ceci, S. J. (2008). Review of the contemporary literature on how children report sexual abuse to others: Findings, methodological issues, and implications for forensic interviewers. *Memory, 16*(1), 29–47.

Lorandos, D., & Campbell, T. W. (1995). Myths and realities of sexual abuse evaluation and diagnosis: A call for judicial guidelines. *Issues in Child Abuse Accusations, 7*(1), 1–18.

Lorandos, D., & Campbell, T. W. (2005). Benchbook in the behavioral sciences: Psychiatry–Psychology–Social work. Durham, NC: Carolina Academic Press.

Lorandos, D. (2006). Parental alienation syndrome: Detractors and the junk science vacuum. In R. A. Gardner, S. R. Sauber & D. Lorandos (Eds.), *The international handbook of parental alienation syndrome: Conceptual, clinical and legal considerations* (pp. 397–418). Springfield, IL: Charles C Thomas.

Maloney, M. J. (2009). *The right to present a defense.* Retrieved from: http://www.harringtonmahoney.com/documents/Rtpad2009v1.pdf

Orbach, Y., & Lamb, M. E. (2000). The relationship between within–Interview contradictions and eliciting interviewer utterances. *Child Abuse and Neglect, 25*(3), 323–333.

Penn, S. (Producer), & Handy, D., & Nachman, D. (Directors). (2008). *Witch hunt.* [Motion picture]. Berkeley, CA: Hand-Nac Movie, LLC.

Poole, D. A., & Lamb, M. E. (1998). *Investigative interviews of children: A guide for helping professionals.* Washington DC: American Psychological Association.

Poole, D. A., & Lindsay, D. S. (1995). Interviewing preschoolers: Effects of nonsuggestive techniques, parental coaching and leading questions on reports of nonexperienced events. *Journal of Experimental Child Psychology, 60*(1), 129–154.

Racusin, R., Copans, S. A., & Mills, P. (1994). Characteristics of families of children who refuse post-divorce visits. *Journal of Clinical Psychology, 50*(5), 792–801.

Rand, D. (1997a). The spectrum of parental alienation syndrome, Part I. *American Journal of Forensic Psychology, 15*(3), 23–52.

Rand, D. (1997b). The spectrum of parental alienation syndrome, Part II. *American Journal of Forensic Psychology, 15*(4), 39–92.

Ricci, C. M., Beal, C. R., & Dekle, D. J. (1996). The effect of parent versus unfamiliar interviewers on children's eyewitness memory and identification accuracy. *Law and Human Behavior, 20*(5), 483–500.

Sauber, S. R. (2013). Reunification planning and therapy. In D. Lorandos, W. Bernet & S. R. Sauber (Eds.), *Parental alienation: Handbook for mental health and legal professionals* (pp. 190–231). Springfield, IL: Charles C Thomas Publisher.

Siegel, J. (1996). Traditional MMPI-2 validity indicators and initial presentation in custody evaluations. *American Journal of Forensic Psychology, 13*(3), 55–63.

Siegel, J., & Langford, J. (1998). MMPI-2 validity scales and suspected parental alienation syndrome. *American Journal of Forensic Psychology, 16*(4), 5–14.

Sorensen, T., & Snow, B. (1990). How children tell: The process of disclosure in child sexual abuse. *Child Welfare, 70*(1), 3–15.

Stahl, P. M. (2003). Understanding and evaluating alienation in high-conflict custody cases. *Wisconsin Journal of Family Law,* 24(1), 20–26.

Stevenson, K. M., Leung, P., & Cheung, K. M. (1992). Competency-based evaluation of interviewing skills in child sexual abuse cases. *Social Work Research and Abstracts, 28*(3), 11–16.

Sturge, C., & Glaser, D. (2000). Contact and domestic violence: The experts' court report. *Family Law,* 615–629.

Turkat, I. D. (1994). Child visitation interference in divorce. *Clinical Psychology Review, 14*(8), 737–742.

Turkat, I. D. (1999). Divorce-related malicious parent syndrome. *Journal of Family Violence, 14*(1), 95–97.

Wakefield, H., & Underwager, R. (1990). Personality characteristics of parents making false accusations of sexual abuse in custody disputes. *Issues in Child Abuse Accusations, 2*(3), 121–136.

Wakefield, H., & Underwager, R. (1991). Sexual abuse allegations in divorce and custody disputes. *Behavioral Sciences and the Law, 9*(4), 451–468.

Warren, A. R., Woodall, C. E., Hunt, J. S., & Perry, N. W. (1996). "It sounds good in theory but . . .": Do investigative interviewers follow guidelines based on memory research? *Child Maltreatment, 1,* 231–245.
Warren, A. R., & Marsil, D. F. (2002). Why children's suggestibility remains a serious concern. *Law and Contemporary Problems, 65*(1), 127–147.
Warshak, R. A. (2003). Bringing sense to parental alienation: A look at the disputes and the evidence. *Family Law Quarterly, 37*(2), 273–301.
Warshak, R. A. (2010a). Alienating audiences from innovation: The perils of polemics, ideology, and innuendo. *Family Court Review, 48*(1), 153–163.
Warshak, R. A. (2010b). Family bridges: Using insights from social science to reconnect parents and alienated children. *Family Court Review, 48*(1), 48–80.
Winner, K. (2002). The Justice Seekers Inc. Retrieved from http://www.divorcedfromjustice.com/home.html
Woody, R. (2009). Ethical considerations of multiple roles in forensic services. *Ethics and Behavior, 19*(1), 79–87.

Cases

Bielaska v Orley, Michigan Court of Appeals Docket Nos. 173666; 174949; 175287 and 175388 Slip Opinion July 19th, 1996.
Gentile v. State Bar of Nevada, 111 S. Ct. 2720 (1991).
Idaho v Wright, 497 US 805, 110 S Ct 3139 (1990).
State v. Bullock, 791 P.2d 155, 176 (Supreme Court of Utah, 1989).
State v. Hadfield, 788 P.2d 506, 508 (Supreme Court of Utah, 1990).

Chapter 9

PROTECTING THE INTEGRITY OF THE FAMILY LAW SYSTEM: MULTIDISCIPLINARY PROCESSES AND FAMILY LAW REFORM

R. Christopher Barden

The family law system is burdened by the widespread use of antiquated and unreliable practices. Reliance on ineffective traditional litigation practices, unscientific assessment tools, unproven therapy procedures, and unreliable opinions based upon "clinical judgment" too often taint the integrity of family law. The unpredictable, stressful, threatening uncertainty of traditional family law practices too often creates powerful incentives for embattled parents to seek control via extreme litigation strategies, including generating parental alienation (PA) processes. Informed, effective, multidisciplinary reforms, including the use of effective science-intensive litigation practices, will help restore the integrity of the family law system, protect the rights of families, and reduce the incidence of PA.

Science-intensive litigation methods are essential to improve antiquated, traditional practices in family law, civil law, and criminal law across America. Science-intensive litigation emphasizes published research from the relevant scientific (not clinical) community and real-time multidisciplinary analyses in all aspects of the litigation process. Science-intensive litigation is most effective when a national science expert/consultant assists local litigators and the court in real-time to improve the quality and reliability of the information and methodologies available to the legal process. Such assistance includes improving cross-examinations and *Frye* or *Daubert* analyses of the underlying–and all too often improper–methodologies of local therapists, custody evaluators, and "expert" witnesses (Barden, 2006; Grove & Barden,

2000; *Daubert v. Merrell Dow Pharmaceuticals, Inc.*, 1993; *Kumho Tire, Inc. v. Carmichael,* 1999).

Science-intensive litigation practices provide concrete and effective reforms replacing or improving the antiquated litigation methods still widely used in family law cases. Traditional antiquated practices fail to involve science (not clinical) experts or conduct systematic *Frye* or *Daubert* methodological analyses and thus typically permit the introduction of unreliable, junk-science assessment, custody evaluation, and treatment methods that often mislead and confuse courts, attorneys, and families.

The application of effective, science-based, multidisciplinary practices in family law litigation is overdue; a rising tide of PA cases has stained the integrity of the family law system. Although many analysts have focused on the theory that parental alienators are troubled, manipulative individuals, an essential alternative hypothesis is that many previously well-functioning parents have been driven by the unpredictable stresses of systemic defects in the current family law system to the extreme litigation strategy of inducing PA in their children.

Science-intensive litigation practices not only are overwhelmingly successful in individual cases but also provide the foundation for ongoing efforts to systemically reform the family law system. Recent historical examples of rapid, substantive, significant reforms in the emergency medical and mental health systems demonstrate the power and efficacy of science-intensive, multidisciplinary reform efforts, including litigation, public education (such as national media), legislation (state and federal), and regulation (i.e., licensing and funding). Reforming family law via science-intensive multidisciplinary efforts will protect the health and rights of children and families and reduce the epidemic of PA.

The family is the essential unit of civilization. Families and children deserve competent, informed, professional services from the family law and mental health systems. Family law practice and affiliated mental health expert testimony involve enormously important responsibilities. Although civil, business, and criminal legal systems developed over hundreds of years of theory, trial, error, and correction, much of the family law system–including child custody processes–has been cobbled together since the 1960s. Responsible family law reforms based upon reliable, science-based, methodologies are urgently needed. Family law reform is especially important to our nation because fundamental U.S. Constitutional rights of parents and children are often at stake in family litigation. Notably, the U.S. Supreme Court ruled, "We have recognized on numerous occasions that the relationship between parent and child is constitutionally protected" (*Parham v. J.R.*, 1979, p. 602). Also, "In light of extensive precedent, it cannot now be doubted that

U.S. courts will protect the fundamental right of parents to make decisions concerning the care, custody, and control of their children" (*Santosky v. Kramer,* 1982).

It is universally agreed that families and children should be vigorously protected from all forms of mistreatment, including neglect; physical abuse; sexual abuse; and emotional abuse, including PA; as well as damages produced by inadequately trained legal and mental health professionals. Given the systemic problems of unreliable methodologies and counterproductive financial incentives that currently plague the U.S. family law system, effective systemic reforms should be a top priority. Efforts to reform the family law system should be based in fact rather than prejudice, science rather than hysteria, and reason rather than political ideology (Barden, 2006). The national tragedy of PA appears at least partly and perhaps mostly due to systemic defects in family law that generate unnecessarily high levels of contention and uncertainty, thus energizing the proclivity of alienators to seek greater personal control over custody decisions. Informed use of effective science-intensive litigation practices will produce a less contentious, more predictable, increasingly reasonable, and more efficient family law system. A science-reformed family law system would greatly reduce PA processes (Barden, 2001).

- **Parental alienation processes are an extreme example of socialization–a well-researched, universally accepted psychological process.**

It is important that family law and affiliated mental health professionals realize that the basic psychological processes underlying PA–socialization and social influence–have been well-documented in the peer-reviewed scientific literature and published in the highest quality peer-reviewed journals for decades. Parental socialization influences on children, including PA, are some of the most reliable and best documented of all psychological and anthropological processes (Ceci & Bruck, 1996; Cialdini, 1993).

Academic and clinical researchers in the fields of developmental psychology, social psychology, anthropology, clinical psychology, and psychiatry have spent decades documenting the ways in which children's memories, emotions, and attitudes can be influenced by parents and authority figures. It is uncontested in the relevant scientific communities that parental influence processes are well-understood and widely documented in peer-reviewed, reputable science journals. The successful transmission of culture itself depends on the ability of parents to instill beliefs, emotions, and even memories in children (Ceci & Bruck, 1996; Clawar & Rivlin, 1991). Given the universal acceptance of the power of parents to influence children, it is unfortunate that in reviewing PA issues, some courts (and some poorly trained mental health professionals) have stumbled over the meaning of technical terms such as "syndrome," thus missing the ethical and investigational obligation to carefully review the ongoing influence of parents, therapists, or other adults on the attitudes, beliefs, and even memories of children (Bruck & Ceci, 1995; Ceci, Huffman & Smith, 1994).

- **Science-intensive litigation methods review and expose improper economic conflicts of interest, thus reducing incentives for parental alienation.**

Science-intensive legal practices–the informed use of scientific experts, information, and methodologies–should include an economic analysis of financial incentives and hidden conflicts of interest. A common and serious conflict of interest seen in many cases involves local family lawyers and local mental health-affiliated professionals (e.g., custody evaluators, therapists, and parenting coordinators) sharing hidden financial incentives in multiple ongoing family law cases. These powerful, ongoing, unreported financial and social ties and overly cozy professional relationships too often create a system in which proper litigation–truly zealous representation of conflicting parties–does not actually take place. For example, clients should be, but typically are not, informed if the opposing expert will not actually be cross-examined because the attorney needs that expert in the attorney's next five cases. Such unethical arrangements often generate high levels of anger, contention, and alienation processes as some parents increasingly come to perceive the family law system as "rigged" and proceed to take matters into their own hands–via PA.

Typical examples of such misconduct include local attorneys who refuse to expose the unreliable, junk-science practices; hidden records; improperly scored psychological testing; and other misconduct of local therapists. For instance, in one case a local attorney failed to represent her client. An investigation exposed that the local therapist was a close social friend of the lawyer and also deeply involved in several of the attorney's upcoming lucrative cases as a supporting expert. This kind of corruption is tragically common in many family law jurisdictions. Fair and impartial litigation is hardly possible under such circumstances, and families trapped in such a system are often exposed to wildly contentious, overly stressful, and tragically expensive litigation.

In such tainted family law systems, desperate parents may resort to PA processes in an attempt to gain predictable control over what they (often correctly) view as a corrupt, destructive local family law system. It is uncontestable that family law legal professionals and affiliated mental health professionals do, in fact, receive larger overall payments in cases involving more PA, more contention, more testing, more therapy, more evaluations, more motions, and more hearings. Given these powerful financial incentives rewarding greater contention and PA, it is not surprising that the incidence of PA cases seems to have soared (Clawar & Rivlin, 1991; Dunne & Hedrick, 1994; Johnston, 1993; Kopetski, 1998a, 1998b). Actor Alec Baldwin, in his book *A Promise to Ourselves: A Journey through Fatherhood and Divorce,* offered this instructive analogy: "[Judge] Robbins introduced me to the concept of the family law judge as Las Vegas pit boss. In the end, her role was to get out of the way of the litigants gambling at the tables. Her ultimate function was to ensure that the gaming went on uninterrupted. The house always won" (Baldwin, 2008, p. 136).

• Science-intensive litigation methods expose and reduce improper conflicts of interest and junk-science assessments and testimony while reducing parental alienation processes.

Science-intensive litigation methods are stunningly effective in exposing and eliminating antiquated, junk-science methods, procedures, practices, and conclusions. Reviewing litigated cases in more than thirty states, examples of improper conflicts of interest leading to an improper reliance on junk-science methods are easy to recall. In one such case, the attorney–let's call him Mr. Legal–failed to vigorously question or file a *Frye* or *Daubert* challenge against expert witness Dr. Psyche. Unknown to the client, Dr. Psyche was also scheduled to use the same unreliable junk-science methodology (e.g., failure to disclose controversies with projective assessment methods; failure to state alternative hypotheses; failure to accurately quote from records; failure to produce peer-reviewed journal articles to support conclusions; failure to obtain and quote from collateral sources, including school records; failure to accurately inform the court of limitations on expert methodologies, etc.) to testify in several future lucrative cases for none other than Attorney Legal. Although Attorney Legal clearly had an ethical obligation to inform the client of the existing, serious financial conflict of interest and offer to resign from the case, he never did. The hapless, uninformed client paid a fortune to lose custody of her child to Mr. Legal's improper failure to apply the *Daubert* doctrines to exclude Dr. Psyche's junk-science methods and conclusions.

In another case, a child protection social worker–let's call her MSW Sherlock–lacked basic training in science, logic, or methodology. MSW Sherlock did not understand the importance of alternative investigational hypotheses nor the dangers of confirmatory bias. MSW Sherlock always sent alleged abuse cases to her close personal friend and therapist, Dr. Confirmer, whom Sherlock knew would rapidly "validate" any abuse allegation, no matter how suspicious. Biased, improperly trained, child protection workers like Sherlock should retire from investigations or seek retraining, but they virtually never do. Such professionals cannot withstand *Daubert* scrutiny in court, but local attorneys rarely challenge and exclude them.

Consider also the case of a "well-respected," senior psychologist and custody evaluator–let's call her Dr. Projective–who consistently used controversial methodologies without fairly and accurately disclosing the scientific and methodological problems and controversies involved (e.g., failure to accurately discuss controversies regarding "ink blot," "drawing," and "play therapy" assessment methods; failure to state alternative hypotheses; failure to accurately cite to the record; failure to produce peer-reviewed journal articles; failure to accurately inform the court of limitations on expert methodologies, including "clinical judgment," etc.). Dr. Projective often used these controversial methods to determine custody issues, validate abuse allegations, and mislabel citizens with no actual history of mental illness as "requiring years of [expensive] therapy." Dr. Projective failed not only to disclose the controversial nature of her assessment procedures but also to cite to any peer-reviewed science articles, to offer alternative investigational hypotheses, and to cite actual–often contradictory–evidence from collateral sources (e.g., school or medical records). By failing to disclose the controversial nature of her procedures while uniformly confirming abuse and pathology, Dr. Projective was assured of a steady stream of lucrative investigation referrals from local attorneys who never asked about her methodology and never filed essential *Frye* or *Daubert* challenges. Dr. Projective's family law-affiliated therapist friends were also assured a steady stream of paying patients via Dr. Projective's frequent recommendations that previously normal families now "required" years of court-ordered, expensive psychotherapy. In still other cases within this tainted system, Dr. Projective's therapist friends served as evaluators, and they would also opine that the court should order previously normal parents into therapy–with Dr. Projective. This local band of financially linked family law-affiliated legal and mental health professionals profited handsomely over many years from this all-too-typical, undisclosed, unethical, court-ordered circular referral arrangement. Hapless parents were often infuriated by being psychiatrically mislabeled and forced into expensive (often junk-science-based) "therapy" by a process they correctly viewed as corrupt. At no stage in this process were competent *Frye* or *Daubert* evaluations conducted. At no point in this process were vigorous science-intensive cross-examinations conducted of any of the myriad of "expert" witnesses and "therapists." Many families were finally freed from a cycle of court-ordered "therapy," further evaluations, motions, and hearings by bankruptcy. A proper, vigorous, science-intensive, cross-examination can quickly destroy the credibility of experts like Dr. Projective and quite often wins the case (Campbell & Lorandos, 2001).

In another case, Attorney Hideaway failed to disclose financial conflicts of interest with a local therapist and evaluator, Dr. Inkblot. Even worse, Attorney Hideaway acted to protect Dr. Inkblot from basic discovery requests. Attorney Hideaway filed motions to block discovery of even basic records (e.g., raw test data, therapy records, dates of service, or consent forms) and easily obtained highly improper "protective orders" to hide the essential records in the case. These "protective orders," blocking basic discovery of essential evidence, were issued by Judge Fairway, Attorney Hideaway's weekend golf buddy.

In these tragic, real-life cases, the most basic function of the legal system–full, fair, accurate, and complete disclosure of all relevant and essential evidence–failed. Such hidden financial and social conflicts of interest pose grave dangers to the integrity of the family law system and preclude due process for many families. Such practices can quickly lead to the increased stress and unnecessary contention that so often promote PA processes. Producing a more ethical, open, transparent, predictable, science-informed, family law process would reduce the incidence of PA.

• Science-intensive litigation practices, including informed *Frye* and/or *Daubert* analyses, protect the fundamental rights of families and children.

Science-intensive litigation practices, including informed *Frye* or *Daubert* challenges, prevent family law cases from devolving into an all too common morass of unreliable, pseudoscientific ideas and practices. By the 1990s, the U.S. Supreme Court and state courts had instituted *Frye* and/or *Daubert* methodological guidelines that govern the analysis and exclusion of unreliable expert testimony (Campbell & Lorandos, 2001; Fisher, 2002; Grove & Barden, 2000). Although currently family law is by far the most junk-science-contaminated area of American law, few family lawyers are properly trained in using science-informed *Frye* or *Daubert* challenges to protect the integrity of the litigation process. Even fewer family lawyers work with actual scientists in multidisciplinary teams to effectively apply Frye or Daubert challenges in a science-informed manner. Instead, most family lawyers rely upon local, science-illiterate, mental health clinicians (therapists, evaluators, etc.) who are, tragically, often just as confused on essential science issues as J.D.-only attorneys. Multidisciplinary litigation teams typically and quickly demolish antiquated, science-illiterate litigation practices. Multidisciplinary team processes applying reliable methodologies are currently at work improving efficiency and reliability in medicine, business, aviation, the military, and many other areas of human endeavor. Why not family law?

Although unknown to most family lawyers and clinical "experts," it is well-documented in widely available peer-reviewed, published, scientific journal articles that many of the methods currently employed by mental health experts in family law cases are unreliable, controversial, or unethical, thus failing basic *Frye* or *Daubert* analyses (Campbell & Lorandos, 2001; Dawes, 1997; Dawes, Faust & Meehl, 1989; Dineen, 1996; Emery, Otto & O'Donohue, 2005; Fisher, 2002; Garb, 1989, 1998; Grove & Barden, 2000; Grove, Barden, Garb & Lilienfeld, 2002; Hagen, 1997). The widespread use of unreliable assessment and diagnostic processes in family law often generates the enormous uncertainty, stress, and anger that can lead to PA. Coordinated multidisciplinary litigation including vigorous science-based cross-examinations and *Frye* or *Daubert* challenges will rapidly reform family law systems, protect the rights of litigants, protect children from unnecessary stress, and reduce PA.

- **Antiquated, traditional, "horse and buggy" legal practices produce ineffective, confused litigation leading to stress, contention, and parental alienation processes.**

Widespread reliance upon antiquated, single-profession, "horse and buggy" family law practices poses ongoing dangers to the integrity of the legal system. The term "horse and buggy" law brings to mind those hard working, independent health care practitioners of the early 1900s who drove a horse and buggy to serve the sick. On errands of mercy the isolated physicians of yesteryear brought a leather bag and the best of intentions but also dangerous, pseudoscientific methodologies that often resulted in iatrogenic injury, pain, suffering, and premature death (Bloch, 1988). Today, in sharp contrast, the most advanced medical practitioners–think of surgeons in a major medical center–work in integrated, multidisciplinary teams applying empirically validated methodologies (e.g., radiology, bacteriology, virology, hematology, engineering, and pharmaceutical research) to alleviate suffering (Barden, 1990; Barden, Ford, Wilhelm, Rogers-Salyer & Salyer, 1988).

In contrast to the efficient medical team approach of modern hospitals, many legal practitioners continue to practice in the kind of methodological isolation familiar to the horse-and-buggy physicians of long ago. Too many attorneys continue to try cases with little or no consultation with actual science experts (i.e., professionals who have conducted scientific research and publish in peer-reviewed science journals) in the relevant fields. Such science illiterate attorneys are too easily misled by poorly trained, confused, or duplicitous mental health clinicians, most of whom are also science illiterate. State licensing systems simply lack the resources to ensure the quality of family law-affiliated mental health professionals. Many family law-affiliated mental health professionals currently rely on unsound, unscientific practices (e.g., failing to disclose controversies regarding unreliable "clinical judgments"; failing to disclose controversies regarding forms of psychotherapy; failing to disclose controversies regarding "projective tests," "drawing tests," and other errors) because they lack basic knowledge in scientific methodology. J.D.-only family attorneys rarely read–and cannot actually understand in any meaningful way–relevant technical, scientific journal publications on testing, assessment, clinical judgment, coping, resilience, memory contamination, iatrogenic treatments, interviewing errors, developmental psychopathology, social psychology, suicide prediction, influence, interviewing, posttraumatic stress disorder, violence, anxiety, depression, psychopharmacology, behavioral genetics, suggestibility, hypnotic processes, and many other areas of pertinent essential science. In addition, many family law attorneys have not carefully reviewed and do not carefully apply the ethics codes of the professionals who testify before them (e.g., American Psychological Association, 2010). Given these systemic deficits, much of the expert testimony in family law hearings fails minimal standards of ethics and scientific reliability (Campbell & Lorandos, 2001; Grove & Barden, 2000). Even brief consultations with multidisciplinary science experts could produce much more effective and powerful litigation strategies and practices for local attorneys. Improved litigation practices would eliminate many of the most glaring weaknesses in the current system, thus reducing stress, contention, and PA processes.

Effective multidisciplinary teams should involve actual scientists, including "members of the relevant scientific community." Such professionals, crucial in all *Frye* and *Daubert* analyses, are scientists who personally conduct, write, edit, review, obtain grants to fund, and publish scientific research in reputable peer-reviewed science journals. Such experts in scientific methodology can investigate, review, and opine regarding the opinions of the relevant scientific community and draft questions to document the unreliable practices, methods, procedures, and opinions so often seen in family law hearings. Having an actual science expert present in the courtroom to draft real-time cross-examination questions on methodology and science journal information is a stunningly effective and powerful litigation practice that improves and assists the legal process. Having a licensed clinician on the team who is also a real scientist (i.e., obtains research grants; is an editor of journals; and publishes in science, not clinical, journals) is optimal. Alternatively, conference call links to expert scientists who transmit questions to the local attorney in real-time via e-mail is another very successful procedure. Global methodological questions can also be transmitted in advance. In sum, an actual science expert (not just a clinician) is essential for all informed *Frye* or *Daubert* challenges and effective family law litigation. Such technical methodological analysis protects the integrity of the legal system while reducing anger, stress, contention, and thus the risk of PA processes.

- **Science-intensive litigation practices compel disclosure of controversies regarding clinical methodologies.**

For effective, reliable legal processes, science, or clinical work, proper methodology matters. Our overly narrow professional education system ensures that the vast majority of attorneys in family law simply do not receive sufficient, or any, training in the methodologies of science, much less social science. Such attorneys are rarely able to conduct the kind of sophisticated, methodological, cross-examination required to prevent harm from the unfortunately common pseudoscientific practices of family law-affiliated mental health professionals. Many legal professionals remain unaware of the fact that for most of the past century a methodological "civil war" has raged between the relevant scientific community in psychology and psychiatry and many of the practicing clinicians in those troubled fields. The battles continue to this day. For example, an international expert on scientific methodology entitled his illuminating book on clinical practices *House of Cards: Psychol-*

ogy and Psychotherapy Built on Myth (Dawes, 1997). This feud between practicing clinicians and scientists over the unreliability of popular clinical methods is well-known in the relevant professions and should be properly and honestly disclosed in each and every report or trial testimony of a mental health professional. For example, Professor Walter Mischel of Columbia University, a former president of the Association for Psychological Science, recently stated, "The disconnect between much of clinical practice and the advances in psychological science is an unconscionable embarrassment" (Mischel, 2008). Too few family lawyers currently complete the basic due diligence investigation necessary to understand these important issues so they can be properly litigated. In many cases, consulting with multidisciplinary experts, especially relevant scientists, is the most efficient and effective way to prepare for complex science/law/clinical issues, including child custody quandaries. The science-intensive litigation approach is routinely successful and often easily overwhelms traditional horse-and-buggy litigation practices.

Although many clinician mental health experts portray themselves as seasoned veterans with dozens of years of experience seeing hundreds of patients, their testimony can be grossly misleading and unethical without an honest explanation that the relevant scientific community has demonstrated that "clinical experience" and "clinical judgment" are often of little value (Campbell & Lorandos, 2001). Consider the following: "Mental health experts often justify diagnostic and predictive judgments on the basis of 'years of experience' with a particular type of person. . . . However, research shows that *the validity of clinical judgment and amount of clinical experience are unrelated"* [emphasis added] (Dawes, 1989). Also, "[Research studies] generally fail to support the value of on-the-job experience in mental health fields" (Garb, 1989). Similarly, clinicians may "have considerable difficulties distinguishing valid and invalid variables" (Dawes, Faust, & Meehl, 1989). The current epidemic of PA has often been enabled by the unchallenged use of unscientific "clinical judgment" testimony, including therapists who claim powers of discernment or lie detection far beyond the abilities of mere mortals (Ekman & O'Sullivan, 1991; McNally, 2005a; Rosen & Phillips, 2004; Vrij, Granhag & Porter, 2010). Informed multidisciplinary Frye or Daubert challenges could quickly eliminate the testimony of such expert witnesses.

- **The improper use of controversial and unreliable assessment measures produces stress, contention, and increased risks of parental alienation.**

The use of psychological assessment measures in family law, including personality testing for otherwise normal parents in custody cases, remains a controversial subject. Professor Eleanor Maccoby (2005), former chair of the Standord University Psychology Department, has noted,

> Standard measures of parents' and children's intelligence, personality traits, and emotional states are wholly inappropriate for custody evaluations, and that even the measures and constructs that have been designed specifically to assess child custody arrangements for individual children have no proven validity as predictors of a child's well-being in the care of one or the other of two disputing parents.

More specifically, the use of "projective testing" (e.g., ink blots, pictures, sentence completion, etc.) has been quite controversial. International experts have called for the exclusion of such testing from courts of law (Campbell & Lorandos, 2001; Grove & Barden, 2000; Grove et al., 2002). Experts using such methods should–at least–fully, fairly, and honestly disclose the associated controversies. Family lawyers should be properly prepared to cross-examine experts or evaluators who rely upon such unreliable and controversial methods. Litigators and judges should note that controversial methods have *not,* by definition, been accepted by the relevant scientific community. Some attorneys and even a few courts have failed to notice that "controversial" and "generally accepted" are logically incompatible labels. PA, in contrast, is simply a form of socialization, one of the most widely accepted and least controversial of all psychological processes.

National experts have opined that competent *Frye* or *Daubert* hearings would exclude many of the "expert" practices commonly seen in family law courts (Fisher, 2002; Grove & Barden, 2000). These points have been carefully made and updated annually for more than a decade by Campbell and Lorandos in their two-volume work for West Group, *Cross Examining Experts in the Behavioral Sciences* (Campbell & Lorandos, 2001). Incompetent, unreliable assessment methods often hasten, deepen, and expand chaotic, unpredictable PA processes.

It is difficult to see how the current tide of PA cases can be significantly reduced without systemic multidisciplinary reforms and improvements in the legal system, especially consistent, informed implementation of *Frye* or *Daubert* judicial gatekeeping to exclude unreliable methods and practices. The integrity and efficiency of family law cases would be greatly improved and streamlined by informed *Frye* or *Daubert* challenges. Such a reformed system could greatly reduce the incidence of PA cases.

• In science-intensive litigation, expert witnesses properly assist the court with peer-reviewed scientific journal citations and quotations.

Competent experts respect the gatekeeping role of the court and carefully cite peer-reviewed scientific research articles that provide useful scientific information to augment the expert's opinions, hypotheses, use of testing, and other methodologies. Virtually all forensic psychological reports and testimony should contain and be grounded on actual citations to scientific research published in peer-reviewed journals or authoritative texts. Experts have an affirmative civic and professional duty–independent of the competence of local attorneys to expose and correct testimonial errors on cross-examination–to tell the whole truth and avoid misleading the court (Bersoff, 2003). Minimal standards for expert witnesses practices should include the following guidelines. Experts should (1) discuss and disclose limitations on the methodologies used in the report, assessment, and/or testimony; (2) offer citations to actual evidence including verbatim quotes from medical/school/counseling or other records; (3) provide cites to and inclusions of actual scientific information from peer-reviewed published scientific research in science journals; and (4) offer helpful and informative investigational hypotheses and investigational recommendations to the court.

Finally, given the long and tragic history of unreliable and iatrogenic treatments in the mental health system, courts should avoid ordering citizens into "psychotherapy" without properly investigating and making a clear record of the peer-reviewed scientific research documenting the expected risks and benefits of each proposed "treatment" (Chambless & Hollon, 1998; Singer & Lalich, 1996; Watters & Ofshe, 1999; Winslade, 1995). The use of empirically supported treatments (e.g., cognitive behavioral therapy for depression and anxiety) could be an initial investigational hypothesis for many families and individuals (Angell, 2011; Carlat, 2010; Fournier et al., 2010; Kirsch, 2011; Whitaker, 2010). It should be considered improper for attorneys or courts to recommend or order a citizen into treatment without supplying peer-reviewed journal citations documenting that such treatments have been demonstrated reliably safe and effective.

• Multidisciplinary analysis is a stunningly powerful litigation, public policy, and legislative method and has previously produced systemic reforms in the emergency medicine and mental health systems.

Recent history provides illustrative examples of multidisciplinary methods that have produced rapid and significant reforms in the medical and mental health systems. Such methods will be essential to effective and efficient reform of family law and affiliated mental health systems. A key, highly successful methodology for effective rapid societal reform includes the use of multidisciplinary analysis and interactive practices in law, public policy, psychology, and economics. Such up-to-date science-intensive practices are stunningly successful in the courtroom and typically overwhelm traditional legal practitioners who lack awareness of key scientific methods and knowledge. More globally, over the past 20 and more years, carefully coordinated multidisciplinary teams have applied the combined power of law and science to generate and maintain important reforms in the medical, mental health, and legal systems. Significant reductions in PA via family law and mental health reforms should be the next step in multidisciplinary reform efforts.

Effective multidisciplinary reform teams have employed an integrated approach including education ("from CLEs to the BBC"), legislation (state and federal), litigation (civil malpractice, criminal prosecution, and family law), regulation (including licensing actions), experimentation (scientific research to clarify key issues), and prosecution (joint efforts with state attorneys general, county prosecutors, the U.S. Justice Department, and the Federal Bureau of Investigation [FBI]). These methods rapidly produced important systemic reforms in the medical and mental health fields and can similarly reform the family law system.

• Multidisciplinary efforts produced important reforms in the U.S. emergency system for children. These reforms provide a clear road map to reducing parental alienation.

A series of internationally reported, successful multidisciplinary reform projects began with legislative and regulatory reforms to the U.S. Emergency Medical System for Children (EMSC) in the late 1980s and early 1990s. Injury was then, and remains, the single most important public health problem for American children, however it is measured: number of deaths, dollar costs for treatment, or relative rankings with other health problems (Centers for Disease Control, 1990). Tragically, as of the late 1980s, emergency medical treatment for children in many hospital and ambulance systems failed to incorporate even basic equipment for children (e.g., a lack of infant or child-sized oxygen masks or spinal stability boards) or appropriate medical training (e.g., the differential pediatric assessment of shock). Such systemic errors led to the unnecessary deaths of thousands of children annually (Williams & Kotch, 1990). To assess and address this complex problem, a team of national experts in economics, pediatrics, surgery, public policy, emergency medicine, hospital administration, law, psychology, and other fields was gathered to provide a multidisciplinary analysis, draft corrective legislation, obtain national media attention, work to enact reform legislation, and thus prevent the unnecessary deaths of thousands of children annually (Barden et al., 1993).

Coordinated national legislative, regulatory, educative, and litigation methods successfully led to the passage of EMSC reform legislation and improved standards of care (Barden et al., 1993). Several former U.S. surgeons general have noted that these EMSC legislative and regulatory reforms–energized by far-reaching media exposés–improved care for seriously injured children and saved thousands of lives across the United States (C. E. Koop, personal communication, October 28, 1992). Buoyed by the relatively rapid yet significant legislative, legal, and medical success of this complex project, multidisciplinary reform efforts were next applied to the U.S. mental health system. Such efforts provide an illustrative example for those working to improve the family law and mental health systems.

• Initial legislative efforts to provide informed consent protections for psychotherapy patients failed, leading to successful reforms via litigation, education, and regulation.

Multidisciplinary family law reformers should strive to ensure that troubled families requiring psychotherapy will be offered only safe and effective, scientifically validated treatments. To ensure families and courts make appropriate choices regarding psychotherapy, truly informed consent is essential. The successful battle to obtain informed consent for psychotherapy patients provides an enlightening history and another example of how multidisciplinary efforts can improve and reform entrenched yet maladaptive institutional and professional systems. A similar process could ameliorate the plight of many PA litigants.

Throughout virtually all of the twentieth century, psychotherapy patients were uniformly denied the basic protections of informed consent. Although informed consent protocols were universally in use in the surgical and general medical worlds by the 1970s, the psychotherapy professions had successfully resisted calls to provide psychotherapy patients with accurate information on the scientifically documented risks and benefits of proposed therapies, alternative therapies, and no therapy at all. Following a national 1990s wave of widely publicized and uniformly successful litigation against psychotherapists who failed to obtain informed consent, industry leaders' views rapidly evolved to the reform position that psychotherapists must properly obtain informed consent from patients, just like other health care professionals (Beahrs & Gutheil, 2001).

Institutional progress in obtaining informed consent rights for psychotherapy patients was a positive side effect of the national wave of litigation that ended one of the most damaging of all mental health practices, "recovered memory therapy." During the 1990s, controversies surrounded recovered memory therapy; a chorus of scientists and patient advocates viewed such treatments as "reckless experimentation on human subjects" without proper consent. Energized by the public health debacle of recovered memory therapy, the most dangerous form of mental health quackery since lobotomies, demands that all psychotherapy patients receive the protections of informed consent grew into a national movement, including the formation of the National Association for Consumer Protection in Mental Health Practices.

The debate over informed consent and psychotherapy came to a historic plateau on August 8, 1994, as many leaders in the mental health field and social science fields (including several past presidents of national professional organizations) sent a public letter, "A Proclamation for Mental Health Reforms," to U.S. Congressional leaders urging them to legislatively require informed consent protections for psychotherapy patients (Barden, 2001). As the Proclamation stated:

> Consumer, patient, and professional groups are just now realizing that psychotherapy patients across America are being subjected to experimental and potentially dangerous forms of "psychotherapy," including "memory retrieval/enhancement" therapy, at taxpayer expense. Even more disturbing is the almost universal practice of subjecting patients to controversial and potentially dangerous procedures without any semblance of informed consent. We believe that fraud investigations by the F.B.I. and other agencies would reveal that virtually none of the therapists engaged in "memory retrieval" or "memory enhancement" procedures are informing their patients (or insurance companies) of the experimental, very controversial and potentially dangerous nature of these "treatments." (Barden, 1996)

Further, the 1994 Proclamation sought to link informed consent with tax-funded health care reimbursements and thus ban tax-funded payments for all so-called "treatments" lacking empirical validation. This "Proclamation for

Mental Health Reforms" (a.k.a. the "Barden Letter") created a national firestorm of controversy that in many ways endures to the present (Barden, 1994). It is clear, however, that over the past decades the fundamental ideas expressed in the Proclamation–that informed consent does indeed apply to psychotherapy and that reimbursed "therapies" should be limited to empirically supported treatments–have become widely accepted and enforced in the legal, public policy, insurance, health care management, and mental health systems. To oppose the 1994 Proclamation, national practitioner associations reportedly waged a million-dollar lobbying effort that successfully blocked passage of the Proclamation's associated legislation, the "Truth and Responsibility in Mental Health Practices Act" (Barden, 1996). Halted in the U.S. Congress, coordinated, multidisciplinary efforts to reform the mental health system moved into state courtrooms. In this way, the litigation battle for mental health reform began in earnest.

- **Coordinated litigation and licensing actions ended the "repressed memory therapy" epidemic providing another road map for reducing parental alienation.**

The mental health system of the twentieth century featured a staggering array of controversial, dangerous, and/or injurious pseudoscientific practices. Although endlessly debated in academic, professional association, and clinical circles, several continued to injure the public for many years. These dangerous and controversial methods included lobotomies, orgone energy therapy, primal scream therapy, Rolfing, recovered memory therapy, cathartic therapies, age regression, neurolinguistic programming, rebirthing therapy, reparenting therapy, attachment therapy, holding therapy, facilitated communication, therapeutic touch, neural organization techniques, and many other examples of how therapists can become dangerous peddlers of pernicious influence (Singer & Lalich, 1996).

Tragically, the legal system, which has employed financial incentives (i.e., malpractice suits) for improved quality standards in the general medical world for decades, was unable to generate a wave of financially viable psychotherapy malpractice suits until the groundbreaking *Hamanne v. Humenansky* case (1995) in St. Paul, Minnesota. In this case, the first financially viable, full-trial, psychotherapy lawsuit, a jury awarded over $2.46 million to Vynette Hamanne, who had originally sought treatment for anxiety (Gustafson, 1995). Her psychiatrist, Dr. Diane Humenansky, diagnosed Hamanne as suffering from multiple personality disorder (MPD) and told Hamanne that she "must have experienced childhood sexual and ritual abuse" despite contrary evaluations and the patient's lack of any memories of such abuse. The treatments used by Dr. Humenansky to "recover repressed memories" included hypnosis, guided imagery, suggestive lectures, antidepressants, and lengthy hospitalizations, all without proper informed consent. Vynette Hamanne gradually came to accept her new "memories" of horrific abuse, became much more depressed, and ended contact with her previously beloved parents. Eventually freed of Dr. Humenansky's ongoing hypnotic influence and overmedication, Hamanne realized she had been cruelly damaged by experimental, reckless practices. Patient Hamanne won a multimillion dollar jury verdict following an internationally publicized six-week trial involving national experts on both sides of the issue. This landmark case launched hundreds of similar suits across America. Unfortunately earlier lawsuits, even apparent "winners" like the Ramona case in California, actually cost more to litigate than the jury verdict recovered. Such suits were viewed as financial liabilities and failed to generate a national wave of interest in prosecuting such actions (Gustafson, 1995). Prior to *Hamanne v. Humenansky,* national experts in litigation firmly believed that legal actions for harmful therapy could not be financially viable and were "impossible to win" (e.g., cannot prove damages, no standards of care, patient plaintiffs are too ill for the stress of litigation, etc.). *Hamanne v. Humenansky* was the game changer that launched reform via litigation and began the end of "recovered memory therapy" and "multiple personality disorder therapy."

Following the internationally reported jury verdict–and a second $2.6 million, internationally reported verdict in the related *Carlson v. Humenansky* malpractice case–it quickly became possible for Hamanne's science-litigation expert to coordinate and place many dozens of therapy malpractice cases with local plaintiff attorneys across America (Guthrey & Kaplan, 1996).

A national wave of carefully coordinated lawsuits was thus organized against "recovered memory" therapists with an initial focus on prominent members of the "recovered memory" community. This wave of multidisciplinary, science-intensive litigation culminated in the November 1997 world record $10.6 million settlement in the *Burgus v. Braun* case (Belluck, 1997). Reported on page one, column one of the *New York Times* and throughout the world media, this case starkly demonstrated the overwhelming power of multidisciplinary, science-intensive litigation to successfully prosecute and actually eliminate harmful mental health therapies–and therapists (Acocella, 1998).

Following the international media storm of the multimillion dollar *Burgus v. Braun* settlement, hospitals, clinics, and therapists fled from "recovered memory therapy" practices. The few remaining practitioners went "underground." Faced with the power of the U.S. legal system in the form of angry, vengeful juries, the iatrogenic epidemic of "multiple personality disorder" and "satanic cult abuse" ended much more quickly than it began. The use of coordinated multidisciplinary litigation teams–coupled with coordinated licensing revocation actions in many states–ended the "recovered memory" and MPD epidemics in just a few years (Barden, 2001). The historic victory of these science-intensive litigation teams not only was instrumental in closing down the "recovered memory/MPD" industry but also is a stellar example of how significant national reforms can be achieved rather rapidly using the combined powers of law and science (Belluck, 1997; Freyd, 1992; Gustafson, 1995; Guthrey & Kaplan, 1996; Loftus & Davis, 2006; McNally, 2005b; Ofshe & Watters, 1996; Pope, Oliva & Hudson, 2005).

Unlike the seemingly ineffectual, academic, and clinical debates that permitted some controversial "therapies" to injure the public for decades, science-intensive litigation–by leveraging the power of the U.S. legal system through jury verdicts, legal settlements, licensing revocations, and license restrictions–rapidly ended the dangers posed by "recovered memory therapy/MPD" practitioners and even compelled insurance companies to end or revise malpractice coverage for several hazardous pseudoscientific practices (DiStefano, 2003; Donovan, 1999; Gustafson, 1997; Lerner, 1999; "Psychiatrist loses license," 1999; Wallace, 1996).

Given the rapid, transformative success of this coordinated, multidisciplinary process, the same science-intensive litigation strategies were employed to end the dangerous practice known as "rebirthing therapy" (wherein a patient is tightly confined in blankets and must wriggle free to be "reborn" to waiting parents). Following the death of young Candace Newmaker in Colorado during a holding-rebirthing psychotherapy session, a criminal trial employing multidisciplinary methods resulted in lengthy prison sentences for prominent holding-rebirthing therapists. Combined with coordinated state legislation banning rebirthing practices as well as national television, radio, and newspaper media coverage, these efforts again demonstrated the combined power of multidisciplinary teamwork, informed media, and the legal system to rapidly eliminate dangerous forms of mental health treatments and treaters (Belluck, 1997; "Controversial holding therapy," 2005; Janofsky, 2001; Lowe, 2001a; Lowe, 2001b; Walters & Roberts, 2001).

In the twenty-first century, multidisciplinary litigation, legislative hearings, media attention, and licensing prosecutions were again employed to close down a national "holding therapy" clinic ("Controversial holding therapy," 2005; Santini, 2002). Federal and state legislation to prohibit health care payments for such dangerous "holding" pseudotherapies was also drafted, passed, and implemented. For example, the 109th U.S. Congress 2nd Session, U.S. House of Representatives, Departments of Labor, Health and Human Services, Education, and Related Agencies Appropriations Bill, 2007, states "The Committee expects that none of the funds provided for the Substance Abuse and Mental Health Services Administration will be used to support attachment therapy (AT), a controversial 'treatment' . . . AT is an unvalidated intervention" (*see also,* Texas Admin. Code, Dept. Family and Protective Services, Title 40, Part 19, Chap. 749, Sub.G, Rule §749.1021. Children's Rights [January 1, 2007]). Yet again, coordinated multidisciplinary teams employed the power of litigation, legislation, regulation, and media to circumvent the often ineffectual and seemingly endless debates of the academic and clinical worlds and quickly end real and present dangers to the public.

With regard to winning the "recovered memory wars" and implementing informed consent protections for psychotherapy patients, probably the single most important and powerful reform process involved behind-the-scenes, coordinated, multidisciplinary consultations, sometimes lasting years, with a variety of state attorneys general. Such consultations were an important component of the national process that revoked or restricted the professional licenses of many leading proponents of dangerous pseudotherapies. Coordinated licensing investigations played an essential role in ending the practices known as recovered memory therapy, reintegration therapy, reparenting, rebirthing, coercive holding therapy, and related controversial practices (Gustafson, 1997; Lerner, 1999; "Psychiatrist loses license," 1999; Wallace, 1996).

Successful multidisciplinary reform methods will prove useful in ameliorating current systemic family law troubles including, and especially, the ongoing epidemic of PA. Reforming family law defects and reducing PA appears a far less daunting task than the previously successful significant reforms of the emergency medical and mental health systems of the United States.

• Historically successful science-intensive litigation methods will reduce parental alienation.

It is time to reform the U.S. family law system. The well-documented and well-publicized efforts of highly trained, coordinated, experienced multidisciplinary teams have already generated significant reforms in the emergency medical system for children and the mental health system of the United States. Multidisciplinary, science-based litigation teamwork ended the national tragedies of repressed memory therapy, MPD clinics, rebirthing centers, and other dangers to citizens. Similar reforms will greatly reduce the stress, contention, and unpredictability of the current family law process and reduce the tragedy of PA. Science-based family law reform is a worthy and achievable goal.

Editors' Notes

- In this chapter, Dr. Barden explains that one of the reasons for the increased incidence of PA is the highly contentious, frustrating, and unscientific nature of the family law system in the United States. He says that some parents may deal with their frustration by inducing PA in their children. It follows that reducing the amount of conflict and increasing the level of scientific inquiry in the area of family law should reduce the incidence of PA.
- Dr. Barden states he has seen many cases of family law marked by blatant conflicts of interest, such as unrevealed alliances between judges and attorneys and among attorneys, mental health experts, and mental health clinicians. These cases frequently feature unscientific methods of evaluation and recommendations for unproven methods of treatment.
- Dr. Barden emphasizes that the unethical conflicts of interest and the junk-science methods adopted by both experts and clinicians can be defeated through the proper use of *Daubert* and *Frye* challenges. He says this requires a team approach, including knowledgeable attorneys and experts and consultants from various scholarly areas who are familiar with the underlying science pertaining to the case.
- Dr. Barden speaks from extensive experience, because he and his colleagues applied the concept of "multidisciplinary reform" to several important projects: the reform of the emergency medical system for children in the 1980s; the adoption of informed consent for psychotherapy in the 1990s; and the abolition of dangerous forms of "psychotherapy," such as "recovered memory therapy" and "holding-rebirthing therapy."

REFERENCES

Acocella, J. (1998). The politics of hysteria. *The New Yorker,* April 6, 64–79.

American Psychological Association. (2010). Ethical principles of psychologists and code of conduct. Accessed at http://www.apa.org/ethics/code/index.aspx

Angell, M. (2011, June 23). The epidemic of mental illness: Why? [Review of the books *The emperor's new drugs: Exploding the antidepressant myth,* by I. Kirsch, *Anatomy of an epidemic: Magic bullets, psychiatric drugs, and the astonishing rise of mental illness in America,* by R. Whitaker, and *Unhinged: The trouble with psychiatry–A doctor's revelations about a profession in crisis,* by D. Carlat]. New York Review of Books. Accessed at http://www.nybooks.com/articles/archives/2011/jun/23/epidemic-mental-illness-why/?pagination=false

Baldwin, A. (2008). *A promise to ourselves: A journey through fatherhood and divorce.* New York: St. Martin's Press.

Barden, R. C. (1990). The effects of craniofacial deformity, chronic illness, and physical handicaps on patient and familial adjustment: Research and clinical perspectives. In B. Lahey & A. Kazdin (Eds.), *Advances in clinical child psychology* (Vol. 13) (pp. 343–375). New York: Plenum Press.

Barden, R. C. (1996). Truth and responsibility in Mental Health Practices Act. In T. Dineen (Ed.), *Manufacturing victims* (1st ed.) (pp. 322–326). Montreal: Robert Davies Publishing.

Barden, R. C. (2001). Informed consent in psychotherapy: A multidisciplinary perspective. *The Journal of the American Academy of Psychiatry and the Law, 29*(2), 160–166.

Barden, R. C. (2006). Protecting the fundamental rights of children and families: Parental alienation syndrome and family law reform. In R. Gardner, R. Sauber & D. Lorandos (Eds.), *The international handbook of parental alienation syndrome: Conceptual, clinical and legal considerations* (pp. 419–432). Springfield, IL: Charles C Thomas Publisher.

Barden, R. C., Ford, M. E., Wilhelm, W. M., Rogers-Salyer, M., & Salyer, K. E. (1988). Emotional and behavioral reactions to facially deformed patients before and after craniofacial surgery. *Plastic & Reconstructive Surgery, 82*(3), 409–416.

Barden, R. C., Kinscherff, R., George, W., Flyer, R., Seidel, J., & Henderson, D. (1993). Emergency medical care and injury prevention systems for children: An economic-medical-legal-psychological analysis and legislative proposals. *Harvard Journal on Legislation, 30*(2), 461–497.

Barden, R.C. (1994). Letter regarding Mental Health Reforms to the U.S. Congress (with signatories Paul E. Meehl, Terence W. Campbell, Richard Ofshe, Richard A. Gardner, M.D., Margaret Singer, William Grove, Michael D. Yapko, Robyn Dawes, Richard Flyer, M.D., Robert Kinscherff, J.D., Mel Guyer, J.D., Francis Fincham, Thom Moore, Henry E. Adams, E. Mark Cummings, Lewis P. Lipsitt, Donald M. Kaplan, Robert R. Holt, Richard M. McFall, Hans H. Strupp, Stephen J. Lepore, Lee Sechrest, Paul Ekman, Hans J. Eysenck; Version II Jerome Kagan, George Stricker, Debra Ann Poole, Mark L. Howe, J. Don Read, Howard Shevrin) (1994). Reprinted in T. Dineen, *Manufacturing victims* (pp. 322–326). Montreal, Canada: Robert Davies Publishing, 1996. Accessed at http://www.stopbadtherapy.com/reform/letter.shtml

Beahrs, J. O., & Gutheil, T. G. (2001). Informed consent in psychotherapy. *American Journal of Psychiatry, 158*(1), 4–10.

Belluck, P. (1997, November 6). Memory therapy leads to a lawsuit and big settlement. New York Times, p. 1. Retrieved from: http://www.nytimes.com/1997/11/06/us/memory-therapy-leads-to-a-lawsuit-and-big-settlement.html?pagewanted=print&src=pm

Bersoff, D. N. (Ed.). (2003). *Ethical conflicts in psychology* (3rd ed.). Washington, DC: American Psychological Association.

Bloch, H. (1988). Medicine and science in the 19th and 20th centuries. *Journal of the National Medical Association, 80*(2), 229–232.

Bruck, M., & Ceci, S. J. (1995). Amicus brief for the case of State of New Jersey v. Michaels presented by Committee of Concerned Social Scientists. *Psychology, Public Policy, and Law, 1*(2), 272–322.

Campbell, T. W., & Lorandos, D. (2001 and annual updates). *Cross examining experts in the behavioral sciences* (2 vols.). Eagan, MN: Thomson Reuters Westlaw.

Carlat, D. (2010). *Unhinged: The trouble with psychiatry–A doctor's revelations about a profession in crisis.* New York: Free Press.

Ceci, S., & Bruck, M. (1996). *Jeopardy in the courtroom: A scientific analysis of children's testimony.* Washington, DC: American Psychological Association Press.

Ceci, S., Huffman, M. L. C., & Smith, E. (1994). Repeatedly thinking about a non-event: Source misattributions among preschoolers. *Consciousness and Cognition, 3*(3-4), 388–407.

Centers for Disease Control, U.S. Department of Health and Human Services. (1990). *Childhood injuries in the United States.* Washington, DC: U.S. Government Printing Office.

Chambless, D., & Hollon, S. (1998). Defining empirically supported therapies. *Journal of Consulting and Clinical Psychology, 66*(1), 7–18.

Cialdini, R. B. (1993). *Influence: Science and practice.* New York: Harper Collins Press.

Clawar, S. S., & Rivlin, B. V. (1991). *Children held hostage: Dealing with programmed and brainwashed children.* Chicago, IL: American Bar Association Press.

Controversial holding therapy, used on troubled children, could be finished in Utah. (2005, February 15). *USA Today.*

Dawes, R. M. (1989). Experience and validity of clinical judgment: The illusory correlation. *Behavioral Sciences & the Law, 7*(4), 457–467.

Dawes, R. M. (1997). *House of cards: Psychology and psychotherapy built on myth.* New York: Free Press.

Dawes, R. M., Faust, D., & Meehl, P. E. (1989). Clinical versus actuarial judgment. *Science, 243*(4899), 1668–1674.

Dineen, T. (1996). *Manufacturing victims: What the psychology industry is doing to people.* Montreal, Canada: Robert Davies Multimedia Publishing.

DiStefano, J. N. (2003, June 30). Pennsylvania liquidates the American Psychiatric Association Insurance Trust. *Philadelphia Inquirer,* p. D-1.

Donovan, L. (1999, October 8). Controversial psychiatrist suspended: Recovered memory case spurs state move. Chicago Tribune. Retrieved from: http://articles.chicagotribune.com/1999-10-08/news/9910080262_1_dissociative-identity-disorder-bennett-braun-satanic

Dunne, J. E., & Hedrick, M. (1994). The parental alienation syndrome. *Journal of Divorce and Remarriage, 21*(3), 21–38.
Ekman, P., & O'Sullivan, M. (1991). Who can catch a liar? *American Psychologist, 46,* 913–920.
Emery, R. E., Otto, R. K., & O'Donohue, W. T. (2005). A critical assessment of child custody evaluations: Limited science and a flawed system. *Psychological Science in the Public Interest, 6*(1), 1–29.
Fisher, G. (2002). *Evidence.* New York: Foundation Press - West Group.
Fournier, J. C., DeRubeis, R. J., Hollon, S. D., Dimidjian, S., Amsterdam, J. D., Shelton, R. C., & Fawcett, J. (2010). Antidepressant drug effects and depression severity: A patient-level meta-analysis. *JAMA, 303*(1), 47–53.
Freyd, P. (Ed.) (1992). *False memory syndrome foundation newsletter.* Philadelphia, PA: FMS Foundation.
Garb, H. N. (1989). Clinical judgment, clinical training, and professional experience. *Psychological Bulletin, 105*(3), 387–396.
Garb, H. N. (1998). Studying the clinician: Judgment research and psychological assessment. In H. N. Garb (Ed.), *Psychodiagnosis* (pp. 39–83). Washington, DC: American Psychological Association.
Grove, W. M., & Barden, R. C. (2000). Protecting the integrity of the legal system: The admissibility of testimony from mental health experts under Daubert/Kumho analyses. *Psychology, Public Policy, and Law, 5*(1), 234–242.
Grove, W. M., Barden, R. C., Garb, H. N., & Lilienfeld, S. O. (2002). The failure of Rorschach-Comprehensive-System-based testimony to be admissible under the Daubert-Joiner-Kumho standards. *Psychology, Public Policy, and Law, 8*(2), 216–234.
Gustafson, P. (1995, August 1). Jury awards patient $2.6 million: Verdict finds therapist Humenansky liable in repressed memory trial. *Minneapolis/St. Paul StarTribune,* p. 1B.
Gustafson, P. (1997, February 8). Board suspends license of psychiatrist Diane Humenansky. *Minneapolis/St. Paul StarTribune,* p. 1B.
Guthrey, M., & Kaplan, T. (1996, January 25). 2nd patient wins against psychiatrist: Accusation of planting memories brings multi-million dollar verdict. *St. Paul Pioneer Press,* p. 4B.
Hagen, M. (1997). *Whores of the court: The fraud of psychiatric testimony and the rape of American justice.* New York: Harper Collins Press.
Janofsky, M. (2001, April 18). Girl's death brings ban on kind of 'therapy.' New York Times. Retrieved from: http://www.nytimes.com/2001/04/18/us/girl-s-death-brings-ban-on-a-kind-of-therapy.html?pagewanted=print&src=pm
Johnston, J. R. (1993). Children of divorce who refuse visitation. In C. E. Depner & J. H. Brah (Eds.), *Nonresidential parenting: New vistas in family living* (pp. 109–135). Thousand Oaks, CA: Sage Publications.
Kirsch, I. (2011). *The emperor's new drugs: Exploding the antidepressant myth.* New York: Basic Books.
Kopetski, L. M. (1998a). Identifying cases of parental alienation syndrome, part I. *Colorado Lawyer, 27*(2), 65–68.

Kopetski, L. M. (1998b). Identifying cases of parental alienation syndrome, part II. *Colorado Lawyer, 27*(3), 61–64.

Lerner, M. (1999, June 3). Psychologist barred from treating cases involving false memories. *Minneapolis/St. Paul StarTribune.*

Loftus, E. F., & Davis, D. (2006). Recovered memories. *Annual Review of Clinical Psychology, 2,* 469–498.

Lowe, P. (2001a, April 13). Ethics specialist blasts 'rebirthing.' Rocky Mountain News. Retrieved from: http://m.rockymountainnews.com/news/2001/apr/14/ethics-specialist-blasts-rebirthing/

Lowe, P. (2001, April 21). Rebirthing team convicted: Two therapists face mandatory terms of 16 to 48 years in jail. Rocky Mountain News. Retrieved from: http://m.rockymountainnews.com/news/2001/apr/21/rebirthing-team-convicted/

Maccoby, E. E. (2005). A cogent case for a new child custody standard. *Psychological Science in the Public Interest, 6*(1), i–ii.

McNally, R. J. (2005a). Troubles in traumatology. *Canadian Journal of Psychiatry 50,* 815–816.

McNally, R. J. (2005b). *Remembering trauma.* Cambridge, MA: Belknap Press/ Harvard University Press.

Mischel, W. (2008). Connecting clinical practice to scientific progress. *Psychological Science in the Public Interest, 9*(2), i–ii.

Ofshe, R., & Watters, E. (1996). *Making monsters: False memories, psychotherapy, and sexual hysteria* (2nd ed.). Berkeley, CA: University of California Press.

Pope, H., Oliva, P., & Hudson, J. (2005). Repressed memories. The scientific status of research on repressed memories. In D. Faigman, D. Kaye, M. Saks & J. Sanders (Eds.), *Modern scientific evidence: The law and science of expert testimony* (Social and Behavioral Science, 2005–2006 ed.) (pp. 408–447). Eagan, MN: West Group.

Psychiatrist loses license over satanic allegations. (1999, October 8). *Chicago Tribune.* Retrieved from: http://www.deseretnews.com/article/721716/News-capsules.html?pg=all

Rosen, G. M., & Phillips, W.R. (2004). A cautionary lesson from simulated patients. *Journal of the American Academy of Psychiatry and Law, 32,* 132–133.

Santini, J. (2002, September 20). Legislative panel backs measure that would ban 'holding therapy.' *Salt Lake Tribune,* p. A10.

Singer, M. T., & Lalich, J. (1996). *Crazy therapies.* Hoboken, NJ: Jossey-Bass.

Vrij, A., Granhag, P., & Porter, S. (2010). Pitfalls and opportunities in nonverbal and verbal lie detection. *Psychological Science in the Public Interest, 11*(3), 89–121.

Wallace, C. G. (1996, July 3). State board suspends psychologist's license. *Idaho Falls Post Register,* p. A-8.

Walters, B. (Anchor), & Roberts, D. (Reporter). (2001, June 15). Little girl lost: 10 year old dies from controversial rebirthing therapy, interview of R.C. Barden [Television news program]. *20/20.* New York: ABC News.

Watters, E., & Ofshe, R. (1999). *Therapy's delusions.* New York: Scribner.

Whitaker, R. (2010). *Anatomy of an epidemic: Magic bullets, psychiatric drugs, and the astonishing rise of mental illness in America.* New York: Crown Publishing.

Williams, B. C., & Kotch, J. B. (1990). Excess injury mortality among children in the United States: Comparison of recent international statistics. *Pediatrics, 86,* 1067–1072.

Winslade, W. J. (1995). Ethics in psychiatry. In H. I. Kaplan & B. J. Sadock (Eds.), *Comprehensive textbook of psychiatry* (5th ed., Vol. 2, pp. 2124–2131). Baltimore, MD: Williams & Wilkins.

Cases

Burgus v. Braun, Rush Presbyterian, Circuit Ct., Cook Co., IL, No. 91L08493/93L14050 (1997).

Carlson v. Humenansky, Dist. Ct., 2nd Dist., MN, No. CX-93-7260 (1996).

Daubert v. Merrell Dow Pharmaceuticals, Inc., 509 U.S. 579 (1993).

Hamanne v. Humenansky, U.S. Dist. Ct., 2nd Dist., MN, No. C4-94-203 (1995).

Kumho Tire, Inc. v. Carmichael, 119 S.Ct.1167 (1999).

Parham v. J.R., 442 U.S. 584 (1979).

Santosky v. Kramer, 455 U.S. 745, 753, 71 L. Ed. 2d 599, 102 S. Ct. 1388 (1982).

Section II

Foundations of Parental Alienation: Historical, Scientific, and Legal

Chapter 10

THE HISTORY OF PARENTAL ALIENATION FROM EARLY DAYS TO MODERN TIMES

Deirdre C. Rand

INTRODUCTION

The idea that divorce creates a context in which a distraught parent may seek to turn the child against the other parent is not new. Terms such as "poisoning the child's mind" and "alienating the child's affection" have been used in historic legal cases and understood by the general public for almost 200 years. Precursors to the phenomenon that Richard Gardner called parental alienation syndrome (PAS) began to appear in the psychiatric literature forty years before Gardner introduced the term.

In the 1970s, changes in the divorce laws gave rise to a dramatic increase in the divorce rate and a burgeoning of child custody litigation unparalleled in history. In response to these developments, two major research projects on children of divorce got underway. The American Bar Association (ABA) commissioned a study of 700 divorced families that utilized the social psychology concepts of "brainwashing" and "programming" as the theoretical framework. Also, a group of mental health researchers in Marin County, California, launched the California Children of Divorce Project, which focused on children's normative responses to divorce and included a brief therapy component. Findings of both these projects would provide independent support for many of Gardner's observations regarding PAS.

Gardner's perspective was rooted in his training as a child psychiatrist and psychoanalyst. He had been working with children of divorce for twenty years when he introduced the term parental alienation syndrome to describe a special type of divorce-related psychological disturbance in children, primarily in the context of custody disputes. Gardner's description of PAS struck a chord with legal and mental health practitioners across the country who, like Gardner, had been encountering a growing number of these troubling cases themselves.

A number of practitioners found PAS to be a useful concept and became involved in elaborating and refining the concept. Others suggested different names and alternative formulations for the problem. Some primarily criticized Gardner's work on PAS and argued that the concept should be done away with altogether. By the mid-1990s, debate about PAS and how to remedy it was becoming increasingly heated and politicized. More recently, there are signs of renewed interest and consensus building within the professional community. There appears to be considerable interest in PAS among members of the general public, some of whom have made important contributions to our understanding of the problem by writing about their experiences with PAS. Divorce professionals and members of the lay community have come together to create a groundswell of support for including parental alienation (PA) in the *Diagnostic and Statistical Manual of Mental Disorders* (*DSM-5*) (American Psychiatric Association, 2013).

PRECURSORS OF PARENTAL ALIENATION FOUND IN HISTORIC LEGAL CASES

Terms such as poisoning the child's mind, inoculating the child with hatred, and alienating the child have been used in historic divorce cases since the early 1800s. Both mothers and fathers have been described as engaging in these kinds of behaviors. Similar terminology can be found in legal cases to this day, such as *Schutz v. Schutz,* in which the judge described the mother as "dripping poison" into the minds of the children against their father (Palmer, 1988). The legal cases described in this section were collected by historian Richard Stephens (Stephens & Gunsberg, 2010).

In 1818 in England, the Marchioness of Westmeath sought a divorce on the grounds of domestic violence and adultery. The Marquess agreed that the mother could have custody of their young daughter but reneged on the agreement, alleging that the mother was poisoning the child's mind against him. The judge decided to override the stipulated custody agreement and awarded custody to the father on common law grounds. The Marquess then moved away with the child and instructed members of his household never to allow the mother to see or communicate with her. The mother later quoted her daughter as saying, "Papa and the Duke of Buckingham have pointed out what sort of woman you was [sic]. I never wish to see your face again" (Stone, 1993, pp. 313–314).

In another high profile English case (*Ball v. Ball,* 1827), the mother alleged an "illicit connexion [sic] between her husband and his niece" and was granted a divorce. The parents disputed custody of their daughter, with the mother claiming she had been prevented from seeing the child, and counter allegations by the father that mother had endeavored to "alienate the affections of the child" from him.

Similar terminology was used in historic American cases. In *Guillot v. Guillot* (1887), the mother alleged that her husband was "vilifying her character and poisoning the minds of their children against her." In *Carter v. Carter* (1904), the mother alleged that the father and his family had exercised an "undue influence" over their son and "inoculated him with hatred toward her." In 1923, a mother named Ethel Crum was awarded $25,000 in damages after persuading a jury of her claim that her ex-husband and his relatives had prevented her from seeing her daughter and had alienated the child's affections from her.

The *Oakland Tribune* in California reported regarding *Sparks v. Sparks* (1917), "Child Alienated; Mother is Suicide." The couple's young daughter was quoted as saying, "You are not my Mamma," words allegedly taught her by the father. In the Reventlow case (1944), a nine-year-old boy wrote in code to his mother, "The hell with my father. I would like it if he died." Mother reportedly wrote back that she enjoyed the letter very much and asked her son to send her more such letters.

Testamentary Kidnapping

Lucy Stone was a prominent suffragist and the first woman in Massachusetts to obtain a college degree. In 1902, she spoke out against laws that enabled men, whether or not they were of age, to will custody of their children to someone other than the mother, regardless of the mother's wishes (Stone, 1902). The practice of using a will to keep the child from the other parent posthumously is known as testamentary kidnapping. Mothers have been known to use this tactic as well. For example, an embittered divorcee named Mrs. Needham left a fortune to her ten-year-old son, on the condition that the boy must never associate with his father or his father's parents. The *Washington Post* (Dec. 11, 1904) described this as a "legacy of hate received by the lad," and bemoaned the fact that "the boy receives this unnatural legacy gladly."

Albert Einstein's Understanding of Parental Alienation

Maleva Maric, Einstein's first wife, was brilliant in her own right and the only woman in Einstein's section at the Polytechnic in Zurich, where they met. Maric bore Einstein two sons during their ten years of marriage. During their acrimonious divorce, Einstein wrote several letters expressing his concerns that Maric was "poisoning" the children against him and that, "My fine boy had been alienated from me . . . by my wife, who has a vengeful disposition" (Isaacson, 2007, p. 210).

Ultimately, Einstein and Maric agreed that Maric would have primary physical custody of the children, and Einstein would give her and the children all the money that he anticipated receiving when he won the Nobel Prize. Having reached a settlement, the relationship between Einstein and Maric improved dramatically. For example, Einstein did not hold Maric responsible for the falling out he had with his oldest son over Einstein's disapproval of the young man's decision to become an engineer. Hans Albert went forward with his career plans and eventually reconciled with his father, who helped bring Hans Albert to America before the Nazis took power.

PRECURSORS IN THE PSYCHIATRIC AND PSYCHOANALYTIC LITERATURE

In 1945, forty years before Gardner introduced the term PAS, an Austrian-American psychoanalyst named Wilhelm Reich suggested that parents of certain character types would seek to defend themselves against narcissistic injury in divorce by fighting for the child and defaming the other parent. Reich wrote, "The child is told, in order to alienate him or her from the partner, that this person is an alcoholic or psychotic, which does not correspond to the truth" (1945, p. 349).

In one of the first books on children of divorce, child psychiatrist Louise Despert (1953) described the harm to children when the parent with physical custody gives in to the temptation to break down the child's love for the other parent, who was no longer living in the family home. Gardner subscribed to Despert's view that what is best for the child will ultimately be better for the parents as well. He cited Despert in *Psychotherapy with Children of Divorce* (Gardner, 1976) and *Family Evaluation in Child Custody Litigation* (Gardner, 1982).

In 1970, Westman, Cline, Swift, and Kramer published a peer-reviewed article on the role of child psychiatry in divorce, providing their own description of parents who enlist their children as allies against the other parent. According to Westman and colleagues,

> Another pattern is found in which one parent and the child team up to produce an effect on the other parent. Not infrequently a child sides with one

> parent or the other, though feeling ambivalent underneath. In these cases one parent appears to deliberately undermine the other through the child. (p. 419)

Interestingly, that article was published in the same year as *The Boys and Girls Book about Divorce,* in which Gardner (1970) explained how parents sometimes use their children as weapons. Gardner advised children not to take sides and to resist pressure to say mean things to the other parent. Gardner cited Westman and associates in *Psychotherapy with Children of Divorce.*

E. James Anthony (1970) was among the first to systematically study *folie à deux* between a parent and child. The idea that delusional ideas could be transferred to children was quite new and had received little attention in the literature. The study focused on mother-child dyads primarily in intact families, utilizing a child development framework to explain how the *folie à deux* was formed. Anthony opined that the normal symbiosis between mother and infant could become pathological when the mother prevented the child from progressing to the separation-individuation stage and deliberately fostered extreme dependency on the mother as the child grew older.

Several years later, a sensational case report of parent-child *folie à deux* in divorce appeared in the *American Journal of Psychiatry* (Tucker & Cornwall, 1977). The case involved attempted patricide by a ten-year-old boy, arising from a *folie à deux* relationship with his psychotic mother. The contributions by Anthony and by Tucker and Cornwall were precursors to Gardner's observation that symptoms of severe PAS in the child may be the result of a *folie à deux* relationship with the custodial mother in which mother and child share paranoid delusions about the father (Gardner, 1989).

In 1978, child psychiatrist Alan Levy proposed a case typology for evaluating children's statements regarding parental preference in custody disputes. Levy divided children's preferences into four categories: (1) child who will not take sides; (2) child with an ambivalent preference; (3) child with a realistically unambivalent preference; and (4) *child who is pathologically unambivalent in rejecting a parent or refusing to visit, seemingly brainwashed by the preferred parent* [emphasis added] (Levy, 1978). Gardner found this typology useful and cited Levy in his books on family evaluation in child custody.

Findings of the California Children of Divorce Project were published in *Surviving the Breakup* by Wallerstein and Kelly (1980). Those contributors were studying children's normative responses to divorce, and Gardner cited their work. He was particularly interested in their observation that children age nine to eleven had normal developmental issues that made them particularly vulnerable to getting caught up in divorce disputes between the parents. Children in that age group were prone to taking sides and had a tendency to see one parent as all good and the other as all bad. They readily involved themselves as weapons in the parents' conflicts. Wallerstein and Kelly had Ph.D.s in social work and psychology, respectively. They were not psychiatrists, but many of their early findings were published in psychiatric journals, such as the *American Journal of Orthopsychiatry* and the *Journal of the American Academy of Child Psychiatry.*

In 1985, at least two articles were published that described the PAS phenomenon, but without the name. Writing from a psychiatric perspective, Benedek and Schetky (1985) described how some parents pressure the child to take sides in the divorce, making the child feel guilty about visiting the other parent and, in extreme cases, resorting to brainwashing. Brynne Rivlin, a clinical social worker at the Bryn Mawr Counseling Center in Pennsylvania, reported on her study of 200 divorced families (1985). The article appeared in *Conciliation Courts Review.* Rivlin found that children in custody-conflicted families had a tendency to form strong allegiances with one parent. If the preferred parent encouraged the alliance, the other parent could find himself or herself treated as the enemy. These observations were elaborated on in Clawar and Rivlin's twelve-year study of 700 divorced families, commissioned in the 1970s by the ABA and published in 1991.

GARDNER'S WORK ON PARENTAL ALIENATION SYNDROME

Introducing the Term Parental Alienation Syndrome

As a child psychiatrist, Gardner saw a trend emerging in the early 1980s in which a growing number of children were presenting as obsessed with denigrating a once-loved parent in the context of disputes over child custody. Gardner worked to codify his observations of the phenomenon and opined that it should have a special name, due to its rapidly growing frequency. In 1985, Gardner introduced the term parental alienation syndrome in *Academy Forum,* a publication of the American Academy of Psychoanalysis. The following year, in 1986, he delivered the Ninth Annual Herschfeld Lecture at St. Joseph's Medical Center on the topic of PAS.

Gardner conceptualized PAS as a divorce-specific psychological disturbance of the child for which the primary manifestation was the child's campaign of denigration against a parent, with a litany of complaints that mirrored those of the aligned parent and were not well-founded in reality. The term PAS was not applicable if there had been *bona fide* child abuse by the rejected parent. In Gardner's view, the child's symptoms were caused by a combination of three factors: parental brainwashing (conscious or unconscious); the child's own contributions (e.g., emotional or developmental issues); and situational factors, which could be anything from length and content of the litigation to the advent of a new partner in the life of one of the parents. He used the term brainwashing in talking about alienating parents because it described the tactics a person uses to influence another to accept certain beliefs. There was more to PAS than parental brainwashing, however, which is why Gardner suggested a special name for the phenomenon of children obsessed with denigration of a parent in the divorce context.

Gardner's First Book on Parental Alienation Syndrome and the Controversy over Child Sex Abuse

Gardner's book (1987b) *The Parental Alienation Syndrome and the Differentiation between Fabricated and Genuine Child Sex Abuse* was published in 1987. When Gardner introduced the term PAS, he observed that false allegations of sex abuse seemed to be on the rise and that false allegations of sex abuse were a spin-off of PAS in some cases because they were such a powerful weapon. He recognized that *bona fide* abuse occurred in the context of divorce but believed that there was a higher probability of fabrication in that situation. In Gardner's view, false allegations of sex abuse were such an important problem that he devoted a significant portion of his 1987 book to his criteria for differentiating between fabricated and genuine child sex abuse, which he called the Sex Abuse Legitimacy Scale (SALS). The SALS was intended for use in a broad range of contexts, not just in situations involving divorce and PAS.

As an experienced child psychiatrist, Gardner had worked with child victims of physical and sexual abuse. He noted that the child's preoccupation with denigrating the rejected parent in PAS was different. He was clear on the point that it was a child's *unreasonable* rejection of a parent that warranted a diagnosis of PAS. If there was *bona fide* abuse by the alienated parent, the child's rejection was justified and the term PAS did not apply. Gardner took the position in his 1987 book that allegations of child abuse should be thoroughly investigated and that genuine abuse had to be ruled out before a diagnosis of PAS could be made (1987b).

The idea that false allegations of abuse occurred ran contrary to the child advocacy agenda of the 1980s and the maxim that "children never lie about abuse." Gardner's views concerning false allegations drew strong negative reactions in some circles. The fact that he devoted a significant portion of his first book on PAS to discussing his criteria for differentiating between *bona fide* and fabricated sex abuse allegations prompted critics to reject his ideas about PAS as well. The first critics to speak out against PAS gave the mistaken impression that sex abuse was an essential feature of PAS. They tended to confuse Gardner's SALS criteria with his criteria for PAS and to portray the concept of PAS as a means of determining whether child abuse allegations were true or false (Faller, 1998; Myers, 1997; Wood, 1994). Those misunderstandings took on a life of their own and were repeated by subsequent PAS critics (Bruch, 2001; Williams, 2001; Zirogiannis, 2001).

Gardner was not alone in his views on the higher incidence of sex abuse allegations in divorce. The American Academy of Child and Adolescent Psychiatry (1988) described the explosion of cases involving allegations of child sex abuse and cautioned that the possibility of false allegations should always be considered, especially if the parents were engaged in a custody dispute. Clawar and Rivlin (1991) made similar observations in their study of 700 divorce families. In their book, *Jeopardy in the Courtroom,* Ceci and Bruck (1995) concluded that there probably was a higher rate of false abuse reports in the divorce context, although as many as 50 percent of abuse reports in divorce were probably true.

Gardner's Guide for Legal and Mental Health Professionals

Gardner decided to make minimal reference to "the sex-abuse factor" in his 1992 book, *The Parental Alienation Syndrome: A Guide for Mental Health and Legal Professionals.* In that book, Gardner clarified his view that false allegations of sex abuse were a spin-off of PAS, found in about 10 percent of PAS cases. He presented diagnostic criteria for mild, moderate, and severe PAS in its generic form and offered therapeutic and legal approaches appropriate for each level of severity. He also included a section on "The Programming Father" for the first time.

In the second edition of *The Parental Alienation Syndrome* (1998b), Gardner reported that the gender ratio of alienating parents appeared to have shifted to 60 percent mothers and 40 percent fathers. Gardner described characteristic motivations and behaviors of alienating fathers, which differed in some respects from the presentation of alienating mothers. There was an extensive discussion of criteria for differentiating between PAS and *bona fide* abuse and neglect by a rejected parent. A chart at the end of the book summarized Gardner's *diagnostic* criteria for mild, moderate, and severe PAS, based on manifestations in the child. A second chart summarized the psychotherapeutic and legal approaches he recommended for *treatment* of PAS that take into account the quality of the child's bond with the alienating parent and the severity of the alienating parent's behavior. The idea of custodial transfer only came into play if the child's PAS symptoms were moderate to severe and there was a disturbed alienating parent who had an unhealthy relationship with the child.

Gardner's Articles on Parental Alienation Syndrome

Gardner was a prolific writer and published numerous articles on PAS in professional journals. *Academy Forum,* which featured Gardner's 1985 article introducing the term PAS, published a follow-up article on Gardner's perspective on PAS 16 years later (2001a). Gardner discussed PAS extensively in an article that appeared in the *New Jersey Family Lawyer* (1987a) aimed at helping judges with the unfamiliar job of interviewing children in custody litigation. Subsequently, a journal of the American Judge's Association called *Court Review* included an article devoted to legal and psychotherapeutic approaches for the three levels of PAS (Gardner, 1991).

As recognition of PAS grew, peer-reviewed journals published a growing number of articles by Gardner regarding his work. Gardner discussed various aspects of PAS from a practical perspective, addressing topics such as dealing with alienating parents (1998a); differentiating between PAS and *bona fide* abuse (1999a); family therapy of moderate PAS (1999b); follow-up data on ninety-nine PAS children to answer the question "Should courts order PAS children to visit/reside with the alienated parent?" (2001b); empowerment of children as a contributing factor to PAS (2002c); how denial of PAS harms women (2002b); whether evaluators should use the term PAS versus PA (2002a); the role of the judiciary in entrenching PAS (2003a); and diagnosis and management of the three levels of PAS (2004b).

Gardner's Work Reaches an International Audience

As the PAS phenomenon was increasingly observed in other countries, interest in Gardner's work expanded to reach an international audience. (*See* Chapter 13, "Parental Alienation Initiatives around the World.") In October 2002, Gardner was invited to give the keynote address at an international conference on PAS in Frankfurt/Main, Germany (Gardner, 2003b). Shortly before he died, Gardner brought together thirty-one contributors from seven countries for *The International Handbook of Parental Alienation Syndrome,* which was published posthumously (Gardner, Sauber & Lorandos, 2006).

RECOGNITION, ELABORATION, AND REFINEMENT OF PARENTAL ALIENATION SYNDROME

Early Recognition of Parental Alienation Syndrome

By the late 1980s, mental health and legal professionals who had been encountering these troubling cases were beginning to make significant use of the concept of PA (Bala, Fidler, Goldberg & Houston, 2007). References to Gardner's 1985 article on PAS began to appear in the literature. Dorothy Huntington, a psychologist and researcher, referenced Gardner in a chapter titled "Fathers: The Forgotten Figures in Divorce" (1986). Huntington brought attention to the simultaneous rise in the divorce rate and the incidence of postdivorce parental kidnapping, which she described as a new form of child abuse. Psychiatrist John Jacobs referenced Gardner's 1985 article in a case study of severe divorce pathology, using the term Medea complex to describe an alienating mother with an overriding need for revenge (1988).

In Florida, attorney Nancy Palmer (1988) argued for legal recognition of PAS. Attorney Anne Goldwater (1991) argued for legal recognition of PAS in Canada. Goldwater described Gardner's 1989 book on *Family Evaluation* as the primary source document regarding PAS, thereby skirting the controversy over PAS and false allegations of sex abuse.

The *Australian Family Lawyer* published an article on PAS by a forensic psychologist named Ken Byrne. Byrne (1989) described Gardner's concept of PAS as complex, due to the interaction between factors in the alienating parent, who propelled the alienation, and factors in the child, who might have psychological reasons of their own for rejecting one parent in the divorce. An article by Byrne and Maloney (1993) described a successful intervention in a PAS case in which the children were refusing visitation with their father.

Leona Kopetski was a custody evaluator in Colorado when she learned of Gardner's work on PAS in 1987. She recalled the astonishment she felt to find that his independently derived observations of the characteristics of PAS families were remarkably similar to her own (Rand, Rand & Kopetski, 2005). In his 1992 book on PAS, Gardner reported having a personal communication with Kopetski in 1988. In 1991, Kopetski presented her data on eighty-four PAS families at the fifteenth Annual Child Custody Conference in Keystone, Colorado (Kopetski, 2006). Kopetski's career was cut short when health problems forced her to retire. Colleagues encouraged her to write up her observations regarding PAS, which were published in *The Colorado Lawyer* (1998a, 1998b).

The Children's Rights Council (CRC) was founded in 1985 with the overarching goal of helping children maintain relationships with both parents following divorce. Psychologist Richard Sauber, founding editor of The *American Journal of Family Therapy,* recalls meeting Dr. Gardner at CRC's annual conference in 1988, when both men did presentations on their new books, Gardner's on PAS, Sauber's on divorce mediation (Marlow & Sauber, 1990).

In 1990, PAS was the theme of the keynote address at the Fifth Annual Conference of the National Council for Children's Rights, delivered by Frank Williams, M.D., Director of Family and Child Psychiatry at Cedars-Sinai in Los Angeles. The text of the speech suggests that, at the time, issues surrounding determinations of joint versus sole custody were more controversial than the concept of PAS per se. According to Williams, Gardner's criteria for making custody recommendations were sometimes misunderstood and misused by mental health professionals advocating for sole custody to one parent.

Elaboration and Refinement of Parental Alienation Syndrome in the 1990s

Citations to Gardner's 1987 book on PAS began to appear in the literature on divorce and related issues, including two of this author's articles on a contemporary variant of Münchausen syndrome by proxy (MSP), in which an adult caretaker fabricates sex abuse of the child, presenting the child for repeated interviews and exams to validate abuse by someone else (Rand, 1990, 1993). As the title of the second article suggests, MSP is a complex type of emotional abuse responsible for some false allegations of abuse in divorce. Campbell referenced Gardner's 1987 book in an article on the pitfalls of triangulated relationships in psychotherapy with children of divorce (1992b) and another on false allegations of sex abuse (1992a).

Clawar and Rivlin (1991) referenced Gardner's work on PAS in *Children Held Hostage,* but chose to use different terminology. They used the social psychology concepts of programming and brainwashing for their research, concepts that were utilized in studies of thought reform methods in Communist China. Clawar and Rivlin opined that most professionals involved in child custody disputes agreed that some degree of parental brainwashing was present in virtually all cases.

By 1993, the phenomenon that Gardner termed PAS was widely recognized and understood by legal and mental health professionals in the family law arena, according to attorney Carol Sanders in South Carolina. Sanders (1993) addressed three problematic issues in divorce litigation: bad-faith relocation, fabricated child sexual abuse, and PA. She noted that terminology other than PAS was sometimes used to describe the phenomenon.

At least half a dozen articles on PAS and PA appeared in family law journals in the 1990s, some of them a product of psychologist/attorney collaboration (Bone & Walsh, 1999; Darnall, 1999; Garber, 1996; Waldron & Joanis, 1996; Walsh & Bone, 1997; Ward, Campbell & Harvey, 1993).

Janet Johnston, Director of Research at the Center for Families in Transition in California, referenced Gardner's work on PAS in a chapter on children who refuse visitation (Johnston, 1993). She opined that strong alignments between a child and alienating parent were probably similar to the behavioral phenomenon that Gardner termed PAS. Johnston suggested that children caught in a *folie à deux* relationship with a psychotic alienating parent might need psychiatric hospitalization or residential treatment to safely separate from the disturbed parent.

In Canada, Glenn Cartwright, a professor in the Department of Educational Psychology at McGill University, published an article titled "Expanding the Parameters of PAS" (1993). Cartwright observed that PAS can be motivated by disputes over child support, not just custody, and that alienating parents sometimes used the *hint* of sexual abuse to create an aura of suspicion about the other parent. One of Cartwright's students did an ethnographic study of the lost parent's perspective in PAS (Vassiliou & Cartwright, 2001). Meanwhile, the Canadian Bar Association gave the 1995 Leiff Award to law student Lisa Cooke (1995) for her comprehensive paper on PAS.

Ira Turkat, a psychologist with the University of Florida School of Medicine, discussed PAS in a pair of articles on chronic visitation interference by custodial parents with severe personality disorders (1994, 1997). Turkat opined that Gardner had contributed significantly to our understanding of what children of divorce experience and described Gardner's work on PAS as pioneering. Turkat used the term "malicious parent syndrome" for a subgroup of custodial parents who engaged in vicious behavior toward the other parent that went beyond alienating the children (1999). He went on to write articles specifically about PAS and PA (2002, 2005).

In 1994, Dunne and Hedrick in Seattle published the first qualitative study of severe PAS families. Therapeutic approaches alone were found to be ineffective. The only cases in which alienation was interrupted were those in which the child was placed in the custody of the target parent. Also in 1994, an article on PAS appeared in the *Journal of Psychosocial Nursing* (Price & Pioske, 1994). Custody evaluation guidelines for psychologists, issued by the American Psychological Association (1994), listed three of Gardner's books under Pertinent Literature, including his 1992 book on PAS.

Psychologist Mary Lund in Southern California contributed an article on PAS, written from a therapist's perspective (1995). Lund examined factors in addition to parental programming that could contribute to a child's rejection of a parent. Lund cautioned that therapists, especially individual child therapists, could become unwitting participants in the PAS dynamic.

In the mid-1990s, this author decided to undertake a comprehensive review of the literature on PAS and related topics, which she naïvely thought would take two months to complete. The volume of material was such that "The Spectrum of Parental Alienation Syndrome" took two years to write and had to be divided into two articles (Rand, 1997a, 1997b). In part II (1997b), this author discussed the model of psychological maltreatment of children developed by Garbarino, Guttman, and Seeley (1986) and used their concepts to operationally define just how PAS and parental abduction could constitute child abuse. The Kopetski Follow-up Study, which examined the efficacy of various legal and therapeutic interventions in more severe cases of PAS, became "The Spectrum of Parental Alienation Syndrome, Part III" (Rand, Rand & Kopetski, 2005).

In 1997, the American Academy of Child and Adolescent Psychiatry published "Practice Parameters for Child Custody Evaluation." That document had a section headed, "Parental Alienation," which included the statement, "Sometimes, negative feelings toward one parent are catalyzed and fostered by the other parent; sometimes, they are an outgrowth of serious problems in the relationship with the rejected parent."

A psychologist in Ohio, Douglas Darnall, published a book on PA called *Divorce Casualties* that is now in its second edition (1998, 2008). Darnall described three types of alienating parents: naïve alienators, active alienators, and obsessed alienators. There is a brief discussion of Gardner's work on PAS and a bibliography of works by Gardner and other contributors, including this author's first two "Spectrum" articles, published the year before.

An article on mediation and PAS was selected as the winning entry in the 1998 Student Essay Contest of the ABA Section on Dispute Resolution (Vestal, 1999). In 1999, Family Resolution Services in Canada published a manual introducing the concept of Hostile Aggressive Parenting (HAP), a term used to describe the behaviors of divorcing parents who seek to eliminate the other parent from the child's life (Hostile Aggressive Parenting, 1999). The difference between HAP and Gardner's concept of PAS was that HAP focused on parental behaviors, whereas Gardner focused on manifestations in the child. The manual cautioned that children's behavior could be misleading if looked at in isolation; thus, the child's behavior should be cross referenced with the known behavior patterns of the parents.

California psychologist Philip Stahl began his book on complex issues in custody evaluations with a chapter titled "Alienation and Alignment of Children" (1999b). An article with this title also appeared in the *California*

Psychologist (Stahl, 1999a). Stahl referenced Gardner's books on PAS along with works by contributors of different views. He reported that there was significant dispute among the experts about whether PA was a syndrome, as well as widespread disagreement about solutions. Gardner's suggestion that a change of custody to the target parent should be considered in more severe cases was especially controversial.

A manual on expert testimony, published by the Texas Bar in 1999, included a chapter on PAS by psychologist Richard Warshak (1999), a clinical professor at the University of Texas Southwestern Medical Center and author of *The Custody Revolution* (1992). Warshak would go on to become a major contributor to the literature on PAS.

Elaboration and Refinement of Parental Alienation Syndrome in 2000 and Beyond

In the year 2000, a private benefactor brought together Gardner and a group of PAS experts from across the country for three days of dialogue in Washington, DC. The author and her psychologist husband were among the invitees. Most of us had never met Dr. Gardner in person, nor did we know each other. The exchange of ideas was exhilarating. The professionals assembled were primarily interested in advancing the cause of research on PAS. We developed a wish list of research priorities; research on interventions and long-term follow-up of children's relationship with the target parent was at the top of the list.

The author had been thinking for some time that Leona Kopetski's data on eighty-four PAS families (1998a, 1998b) might make a good foundation for a follow-up study. She called Kopetski from Washington, DC, and the Kopetski Follow-up Study was born (Rand, Rand & Kopetski, 2005). Gardner responded to the call for research by publishing a follow-up study of ninety-nine PAS children from his own practice, using statistics to analyze his data (2001b). The author and her husband met Richard Warshak for the first time, and the three of us would eventually collaborate on developing the Family Bridges Program for Severely Alienated Parent-Child Relationships (Warshak, 2010b; Warshak & Otis, 2010).

Also in 2000, the American Psychological Association published a comprehensive, well-researched book called *Divorce Wars: Interventions with Families in Conflict* by Elizabeth Ellis, a Georgia psychologist and author of *Raising a Responsible Child* (1995). Ellis reported that the term PAS had come into common usage for describing this phenomenon. She noted that Gardner used PAS to refer to the child's behavior but also used it with reference to the alienating parent's behavior, which had contributed to confusion in the field.

Ellis went on to publish several articles on PAS and PA (2005, 2007; Ellis & Boyan, 2010).

Bricklin and Elliot (2000) contributed an article for judges, lawyers, and mental health professionals on dealing with children of high-conflict divorce. Those authors believed it was important to include a section on "the parental alienation concept Richard Gardner has done so much to explicate" (p. 517). They expressed concern about the "negative commentary" in recent articles and "shop-talk" among professionals that were dismissive of Gardner's contributions. Some of that occurred at the thirty-seventh Annual Conference of the Association of Family and Conciliation Courts in 2000. Some of the presentations there involved a "reformulation of PAS" that would be the subject of a special issue of *Family Court Review* the following year (Schepard, Johnston & Kelly, 2001).

Warshak's article on remarriage as a trigger for PAS came out in 2000, followed by an article on current controversies regarding PAS (2001a). In 2003, *Family Court Quarterly* published Warshak's article, "Bringing Sense to Parental Alienation: A Look at the Disputes and the Evidence," which was particularly well-received. The list goes on. Warshak wrote a best-selling book on PAS, *Divorce Poison,* which was published in 2001 and is now in its third edition (2010a). The book was written for a wide audience, including divorced and divorcing parents and professionals in the family law arena. Warshak is a prolific writer whose work has elevated the debate about PAS, as suggested by his 2005 article on the importance of "objectivity versus polemic" in social science. Recently, he was involved in a study of PA among college students (Hands & Warshak, 2011).

Law professor Sandra Berns in Australia conducted a study of PAS cases in an effort to answer concerns raised about allegations of PAS being misused by fathers, with the backing of father's rights groups (2001). She found that courts seemed able to discriminate whether allegations of PAS were valid and that the involvement of father's rights groups was negligible.

Using the alienated child model, Kelly and Johnston (2001) concluded that both parents, as well as vulnerabilities within the child, contribute to the problem of alienation. Two papers by Johnston (2003) and Johnston, Walters, and Olesen (2005) reported on empirical studies of parental alignment and child alienation, utilizing data from earlier studies of children of divorce.

An article examining the validity of PAS amid the controversy appeared in a Florida family law journal (Bone, 2003). A two-part article titled "Father, What Father?" was featured in a journal of the New York Bar Family Law Section (Steinberger, 2006a, 2006b). The articles emphasized the effects of PAS on children.

The topic of reconciliation between the child and target parent was addressed in a systematic way for the first time in two chapters of *The*

International Handbook of Parental Alienation Syndrome. Cartwright (2006) described the process by which alienated children sometimes reconcile with the rejected parent on their own, after a significant period of physical and/or psychological separation. A chapter by Rand and Rand (2006) identified factors associated with spontaneous parent-child reconciliation, based on case reports from a variety of sources. A review of cases in which children remained alienated into adulthood illustrated the potentially lethal consequences of failure to interrupt alienation when the child is still a minor. Two articles in the *American Journal of Family Therapy* elaborated on the theme of spontaneous reunification with the alienated child (Darnall & Steinberg, 2008a, 2008b).

Amy Baker is a developmental psychologist who became known for her qualitative research with adults who were alienated as children (2005a, 2005b, 2005c). She elaborated on that research in her groundbreaking book, *Adult Children of Parental Alienation Syndrome* (2007). Baker recorded interviews of forty individuals who agreed to participate in her study, then analyzed the recordings using an ethnographic method, similar to that of an anthropologist. The book contains a number of quotations from adults alienated as children, providing a poignant view of what these children actually experience and how they perceive their parents during and after divorce.

A Handbook of Divorce and Custody, edited by Gunsberg and Hymowitz, included a chapter on PA by Shopper (2005), written from a psychoanalytic perspective. *Challenging Issues in Child Custody Assessments* was the work of Canadian contributors Fidler, Bala, Birnbaum, and Kavassalis (2008) and included two chapters on PA. The authors did a good job of integrating the contributions of Gardner and other PAS contributors with the ideas of critics who have a different perspective. *The Essentials of Parental Alienation Syndrome* was written by psychologists Robert Evans and Michael Bone (2011). They dedicated their book to Gardner's pioneering contributions: "Without his work as a basis, we would not have made the progress we have to educate–even more fully–both professionals and parents to change what can have a devastating effect on children and their families" (p. v).

PARENTAL ALIENATION CRITICS AND THE POLITICS OF SCIENCE

In 2006, this author developed an online continuing education course on PAS and PA, offered through the Zur Institute. Dr. Ofer Zur asked the author to address the criticisms and controversies surrounding PAS, and the material developed on that topic evolved into a journal article titled "Parental Alienation Critics and the Politics of Science" (Rand, 2011). The article discussed the views of the Johnston/Kelly group, who decided to reformulate PAS, and the views of critics who identify with a feminist/child advocate agenda and take the position that PAS is junk science and does not exist.

In 2001, *Family Court Review* published a special issue devoted to a reformulation of Gardner's PAS by a group of mental health professionals in California, headed by two renowned contributors to the field of high-conflict divorce, Janet Johnston and Joan Kelly, who also acted as guest editors of the special issue. Johnston and Kelly recognized the existence of the PAS phenomenon but believed there were too many problems with PAS as Gardner conceived it. They took issue with what was characterized as "Gardner's overly simplistic focus" on the brainwashing parent as the primary causal agent of child alienation and "Gardner's one-size-fits-all remedy" of changing custody to the alienated parent. The Johnston/Kelly group set out to develop "a more complex and useful understanding" of the range of factors that can contribute to a child's rejection of a parent. They developed their own model, which they called the "alienated child" (Kelly & Johnston, 2001). The authors acknowledged that their ideas and views were based largely based on practical experience and clinical insights.

The definition of "alienated child" is quite similar in many respects to Gardner's diagnostic criteria for PAS. There is a difference in emphasis, however, with the Johnston/Kelly critics pointing to causal factors other than the influence of an alienating parent. Another difference is Gardner's recommendations for treatment of moderate to severe PAS, which rely heavily on the degree of pathology exhibited by the alienating parent and the severity of the alienating behavior. Gardner's response to the Johnston/Kelly critics was published posthumously in a 2004 issue of *Family Court Review,* which included Johnston and Kelly's rejoinder to Gardner's comments (Gardner, 2004a; Johnson & Kelly, 2004). The rejoinder was adversarial in tone and failed to correct factual errors, such as the mistaken assertion that Gardner's work on PAS was not published in peer-reviewed journals.

Feminist and child advocate critics such as law professor Carol Bruch take the position that the phenomenon Gardner called PAS does not exist or, if it does, it is not a problem in need of fixing. Bruch noticed that PAS was being discussed by other names by some highly respected contributors. She responded by expanding her criticisms to include all contributors who recognized the existence of the PAS phenomenon, whether they called it "parental alienation" without the "syndrome" or the "alienated child." The National Organization for Women, which sought to make use of the term PAS a crime in California, has embraced Bruch's views and came out against PA as well as PAS. Critics in that group opine that PAS is a theory Gardner invented to defend child molesters. In their view, courts rely on PAS testimony to give custody to abusive fathers and PAS should not be admissible in court. That perspective has gained widespread support among prosecutors (Ragland & Fields, 2003).

Some practitioners in the family law arena have adopted the alienated child model, while others continue to use the term PAS or decided to use the term PA, rather than get bogged down in the controversy over calling the problem a syndrome.

RENEWED INTEREST AND CONSENSUS-BUILDING IN THE PROFESSIONAL COMMUNITY

Some of the criticisms of Gardner's work on PAS appear to be due to misunderstandings of his writings (Fidler et al., 2008; Rand, 2011). The process of sorting these out appears to have resulted in a broad consensus among experienced professionals in the family law arena that some children do become unreasonably alienated from a parent and few reject Gardner's views outright.

In 2010, *Family Court Review* published an updated special issue on alienated children. Canadian psychologist Barbara Fidler and attorney Nicholas Bala, a professor at Queen's College, were invited to be the guest editors (Fidler & Bala, 2010a). They also contributed an article on children who resist contact with a parent in the context of divorce and separation (Fidler & Bala, 2010b). The impetus for the special issue in 2001 was the reformulation of PAS, and all the articles were by like-minded contributors. The impetus for the special issue in 2010 was an article by Richard Warshak, introducing the Family Bridges Workshop for Alienated Parent-Child Relationships in a peer-reviewed journal for the first time (Warshak, 2010b; Warshak & Otis, 2010). Family Bridges is a postlitigation program designed to help severely alienated and recovered abducted children with the transition to living with a target or left-behind parent who has sole legal and physical custody. As a codeveloper of the Family Bridge's program, the author is pleased to see that Warshak's article on Family Bridges seems to have sparked renewed interest in ameliorating the problem of pathological alienation from a parent.

Most of the contributors to the 2001 issue are represented in the special issue of 2010, which includes a thoughtful commentary by Joan Kelly on Warshak's Family Bridge's article, along with articles by new contributors who express a range of views (Kelly, 2010). Guest editors Fidler and Bala set the tone, noting that the ultimate objective shared by all contributors to the

2010 special issue was to better serve children who are not maintaining healthy relationships with both parents. They engaged in an active editorial process with the contributing authors in an effort to clarify perspectives and concerns. The result was a toning down of the rhetoric and a narrowing of disagreements.

According to Fidler and Bala, there has been renewed public and professional interest in alienation in recent years. The Association of Family and Conciliation Courts selected PA as the theme for its annual international conference in 2010, attended by judges, lawyers, mediators, and mental health professionals from eight countries. Despite sharp differences on topics such as the status of PA as a syndrome and the desirability of its inclusion in *DSM-5,* a consensus emerged from this conference that irrational PA is a genuine problem, universally observed by judges, lawyers, custody evaluators, and therapists (Baker, Jaffee, Bernet & Johnston, 2011).

PARENTAL ALIENATION IN THE POPULAR LITERATURE

Precursors to Parental Alienation Syndrome in the Popular Literature

In 1935, the movie *O'Shaughnessy's Boy* was novelized and published as a book for young readers (Boleslawski, 1935; Mitchell, 1935). The book tells of a father's eventually successful struggle to find his son after the mother and her older sister ran off with the boy when he was five years old. The father was a famous animal tamer for the circus. The mother was a trapeze artist who hated the circus life. When the father found the boy in his teens, the mother had been killed in a circus accident, and the boy blamed the father, under the aunt's nefarious influence. As one might expect, animals were instrumental in helping father and son to reconcile.

Marjory Stoneman Douglas was a journalist and early suffragette who led the crusade to save the Florida Everglades by turning them into a national park. Her autobiography (1987) contains a poignant account of the rupture in her relationship with her father when her parents divorced, and her reunion with him years later in 1915. Her mother was a troubled woman and Douglas was her primary emotional caretaker. The reunion with her father was precipitated when the man Douglas married tried to get money from her father by fraud. Her father reached out to her through his brother and helped Douglas get a divorce, which was frowned on at that time. Douglas went to work for her father, at the paper that became *The Miami Herald,* and lived with him for the rest of her life.

Somewhere Child by Bonnie Black (1981) is a compelling autobiographical account of a mother's fight to maintain a relationship with her daughter, who was abducted as an infant by the father and his parents. When Black discovered that they were living with her daughter in Rhodesia, she quit her job and moved to Africa in order to have standing in a custody trial there. The Rhodesian court eventually awarded her custody. Father and his parents disappeared with the child again, and Black lost her daughter for good. Black poured her love for her daughter into writing this book, drawing on material from diaries, letters, and court documents. Although she had never heard of PAS, her account contains detailed descriptions of the kinds of things that severely alienating parents say and do to destroy the child's love bond with the other parent, and the impact those behaviors have on the child.

Books by Alienated Parents in the Contemporary Popular Literature

Since 1985, when the term PAS was introduced, a growing number of parents have written books about their personal experiences with losing a child to PAS, and the fight to reestablish or maintain a postdivorce relationship with their child when there is a strong pull for alienation. This section discusses a sampling of six such books.

Lost Children (2000) was written by an English woman named Penny Cross, who turned to writing as a means of self-examination and healing after her oldest son committed suicide at twenty-two. According to Cross, her son was severely alienated and left a will that stated his categorical wish that she and her relatives be banned from attending his funeral. Cross recounts her decision to end a troubled marriage, leaving the children with their father while she settled into her new home. She naïvely believed that the children would gradually adjust to the changes and that her relationship with them would continue as before. She describes the shock and pain she felt when she realized that the children had closed ranks with their father and turned on her almost overnight. Cross had completed the first draft of *Lost Children* when she first learned of Gardner's work on PAS. Reflecting back, she thought that knowledge of PAS would have helped her at the time she was making decisions about her children and the divorce. She included material about PAS by Gardner and other contributors in the hopes that the information would help others make more informed decisions about leaving a bad marriage when children are involved.

Icebound (Nielsen & Vollers, 2001) is the story of a physician who decided to leave her children with their father rather than put them through a contentious custody battle. There is no indication that Jerri Nielsen had heard of

PAS or thought that her children might reject her when she decided to end the marriage and left them with their father. After taking a job as the physician at the South Pole Research Station, Nielsen discovered she had breast cancer. The station was snowed in, and the daring rescue mission that saved her life made national headlines. Nielsen recounts that her ex-husband told reporters that she made up the story about breast cancer to get attention. Her oldest daughter reportedly said she did not care what happened to her mother. Nielsen died of cancer at fifty-seven, but continued giving motivational talks until three months before her death in 2009.

A Kidnapped Mind (Richardson & Broweleit, 2006) was written by a Canadian mother whose alienated son Dash committed suicide at sixteen. According to Richardson, Dash had a destructive, enmeshed relationship with his alcoholic father, who was determined to sever Dash's bond with his mother. After an acrimonious custody battle, the court gave custody to the father, and Dash became increasingly alienated from his mother. Richardson recounts that Dash had a row with his father just before committing suicide and that his father died of alcoholism two years later. According to Richardson, "PAS touches tens of thousands of people in this world, and none of them get off lightly. They–we–feel the fallout" (p. 8). Psychologist Reena Sommer wrote in the forward, "I think that *A Kidnapped Mind* will provide important insights into the needs of children of divorcing parents in a way that the theoretical or empirical contributions of academics have not been able to achieve" (p. 10).

They Are My Children, Too (Meyer & Quinn, 1999) recounts the story of Lady Catherine Meyer, who cofounded the international arm of the National Center for Missing Children and is the wife of a now-retired British ambassador. Although Meyer had custody of the children in England, their father refused to return them to London after a summer visit with him in Germany. German authorities declined to enforce the British custody orders and refused to return the boys to their mother. A protracted legal battle in English and German courts ensued. Meyer did not see her sons for almost ten years. According to Meyer, the aim of parents who abduct their children out of the country is to flee from one judicial system in favor of another in order to reverse previously permanent custody decisions and destroy the child's relationship with the left-behind parent. Meyer found PAS to be an important concept, noting that she has had personal experience with it, as have many of parents who contacted her.

A Family's Heartbreak (Jeffries & Davies, 2008) was written from the perspective of an alienated father but was intended for alienated mothers as well. According to Jeffries, his introduction to PA began in 2004, when he filed for divorce and his eleven-year-old son turned on him literally overnight. "I never saw it coming," Jeffries wrote, similar to Penny Cross. Jeffries reports that many of the professionals involved in his case had never heard of PA and that those who did were unsure how to deal with a severe case. Gardner's book on PAS became Jeffries's bible. According to Jeffries, PAS may not be in the *DSM,* but alienating behavior still inflicts pain and heartache on parents, children, and extended family members. "Parents on the receiving end of alienating behavior don't really care if professionals classify the behavior as a syndrome or a bad alignment of the stars" (p. viii).

A Promise to Ourselves (Baldwin & Tabb, 2008) chronicles the seven-year custody battle of actor Alec Baldwin after his wife, actress Kim Basinger, filed for divorce. Baldwin acknowledged making mistakes but said that the cause of the bitter custody litigation was his desire to be a real father and his refusal to give up his relationship with his daughter. "The system punished me for that," he wrote. Public sources have sometimes portrayed Baldwin as promoting Gardner and PAS, but Baldwin simply described his relationship with his daughter as a casualty of PA.

PARENTAL ALIENATION AND THE *DSM-5* CAMPAIGN

At the time Gardner introduced the term PAS in 1985, the *DSM* was in its third edition. In the early 1990s, when *DSM* committees were meeting to consider the inclusion of additional disorders in the *DSM-IV,* there was no proposal to include PAS because there were too few articles on PAS in the literature to warrant such a submission (Gardner, 2002a).

A group of mental health and legal professionals was invited to submit a formal proposal to the *DSM-5* Work Group on Disorders of Childhood and Adolescence. William Bernet, M.D., a professor of psychiatry at Vanderbilt University School of Medicine, spearheaded the writing of the proposal (2010; Bernet, Boch-Galhan, Baker & Morrison, 2010). The debate over inclusion of PA disorder has become highly politicized, and political pressures will likely play a role in determining whether a child's obsession with denigrating a once loved parent in divorce will be included as a disorder in *DSM-5.*

The PAS phenomenon exists whether or not it becomes a formal diagnosis in *DSM-5.* Labels are something we use to communicate with each other about common human experiences. They are communication shortcuts for mental and emotional experiences that are a source of real suffering to real people. Parents who have lost a child to PAS describe the pain as worse than the pain of a physical death. For children, loss of a parent is a profound loss, regardless of the reason. We must hang on to our compassion if we are to help parents and children maintain loving relationships in the wake of conflicted divorce.

Editors' Notes

- Dr. Rand discussed precursors of PA found in historic legal cases and also in the psychiatric and psychoanalytic literature. In that regard, she noted the writings of Wilhelm Reich, Louise Despert, Jack Westman and his colleagues, James Anthony, Alan Levy, and Judith Wallerstein and Joan Kelly.
- Dr. Rand provided an overview of Richard Gardner's publications regarding PAS, including his seminal 1985 article in *Academy Forum,* his 1987 book *The Parental Alienation Syndrome and the Differentiation Between Fabricated and Genuine Child Sex Abuse,* his 1992 book *The Parental Alienation Syndrome: A Guide for Mental Health and Legal Professionals,* and his subsequent writings.
- Dr. Rand explained how other authors recognized, elaborated upon, and refined the concept of PAS in the 1990s and the 2000s. For example, she discussed the work of psychologist Dorothy Huntington, attorney Nancy Palmer, social worker Leona Kopetski, psychiatrist Frank Williams, sociologist Janet Johnston, psychologist Ira Turket, and psychiatrist John Dunne. She highlighted the important book *Children Held Hostage* by Stanley Clawar and Brynne Rivlin. Dr. Rand commented on the important work of psychologists Douglas Darnall, Philip Stahl, and Richard Warshak.
- Dr. Deirdre Rand explained how she and Dr. Randy Rand collaborated with Dr. Richard Warshak in developing Family Bridges, a treatment program for severely alienated children and adolescents.
- With regard to research on PA and PAS, Dr. Rand summarized the work of Leona Kopetski, Elizabeth Ellis, Barry Bricklin, Sandra Berns, Janet Johnston, Amy Baker, Barbara Fidler, and others.
- Finally, Dr. Rand commented on the portrayal of PA in popular literature. She noted several autobiographical books related to PA, including *Somewhere Child, Lost Children, A Kidnapped Mind, They Are My Children Too,* and *A Family's Heartbreak.*

REFERENCES

American Academy of Child and Adolescent Psychiatry. (1988). Guidelines for the clinical evaluation of child and adolescent sexual abuse [Position paper]. *Journal of the American Academy of Child and Adolescent Psychiatry, 27*(5), 655–657.

American Academy of Child and Adolescent Psychiatry. (1997). Practice parameters for child custody evaluation. *Journal of the American Academy of Child and Adolescent Psychiatry, 36*(10 supplement), 57S–68S.

American Psychiatric Association. (2013). *Diagnostic and statistical manual of mental disorders,* Fifth Edition. Arlington, VA: American Psychiatric Association

American Psychological Association. (1994). Guidelines for child custody evaluations in divorce proceedings. *American Psychologist, 49*(4), 677–80.

Anthony, E. J. (1970). The influence of maternal psychosis on children - folie à deux. In E. J. Anthony & T. Benedek (Eds.), *Parenthood: Its psychology and psychopathology* (pp. 571-595). London: Little, Brown and Co.

Baker A. J. L. (2005a). Parent alienation strategies: A qualitative study of adults who experienced parental alienation as a child. *American Journal of Forensic Psychology, 23*(4), 43–62.

Baker, A. J. L. (2005b). The cult of parenthood: A qualitative study of parental alienation. *Cultic Studies Review, 4*(1), np.

Baker, A. J. L. (2005c). The long-term effects of parental alienation on adult children: A qualitative research study. *American Journal of Family Therapy, 33*(4), 289–302.

Baker, A. J. L. (2007). *Adult children of parental alienation syndrome: Breaking the ties that bind.* New York: W. W. Norton.

Baker, A. J. L., Jaffee, P. G., Bernet, W., & Johnston, J. R. (2011). Brief report on parental alienation survey. *The Association of Family and Conciliation Courts eNEWS 30*(2).

Bala, N., Fidler, B. J., Goldberg, D., & Houston, C. (2007). Alienated children and parental separation: Legal responses in Canada's family courts. *Queen's Law Journal, 33,* 79–138.

Baldwin, A., & Tabb, M. (2008). *A promise to ourselves: A journey through fatherhood and divorce.* New York: St. Martin's Press.

Benedek, E. P., & Schetky, D. H. (1985). Custody and visitation: Problems and perspectives. *Psychiatric Clinics of North America, 8*(4), 857–873.

Bernet, W., Boch-Galhau, W. V., Baker, A. J. L., & Morrison, S. L. (2010). Parental alienation, DSM-5, and ICD-11. *American Journal of Family Therapy, 38*(2), 76–187.

Bernet, W. (2010). *Parental alienation, DSM-5, and ICD-11.* Springfield, IL: Charles C Thomas Publisher.

Berns, S. S. (2001). Parental alienation syndrome in the family court: Magic bullet or poisoned chalice? *Australian Journal of Family Law, 15*(3), 191–214.

Black, B. L. (1980). *Somewhere child.* New York: Viking Press.

Boleslawski, R. (Director). (1935). *O'Shaughnessy's boy.* United States: Metro-Goldwyn-Mayer.

Bone, M. J. (2003). The parental alienation syndrome: Examining the validity amid controversy. *Family Law Section Commentator, 20*(1), 24–27.

Bone, M. J., & Walsh, M. R. (1999). Parental alienation syndrome: How to detect it and what to do about it. *Florida Bar Journal, 73*(3), 44–47.

Bricklin, B., & Elliot, G. (2000). Qualifications of and techniques to be used by judges, attorneys, and mental health professionals who deal with children in high conflict divorce cases. *University of Arkansas at Little Rock Law Review, 122*(3), 501–528.

Bruch, C. S. (2001). Parental alienation syndrome and parental alienation: Getting it wrong in child custody cases. *Family Law Quarterly, 14*(4), 381–400.

Byrne, K. (1989). Brainwashing in custody cases: The parental alienation syndrome. *Australian Family Lawyer, 4*(3), 1–5.

Byrne, K., & Maloney, L. (1993). Intractable access: Is there a cure? *Australian Family Lawyer, 8*(4): 22–27.

Campbell, T. W. (1992a). False allegations of sexual abuse and their apparent credibility. *American Journal of Forensic Psychology, 10*(4), 21–35.

Campbell, T. W. (1992b). Psychotherapy with children of divorce: The pitfall of triangulated relationships. *Psychotherapy: Theory, Research, Practice, and Training, 29*(4), 646–52.

Cartwright, G. F. (1993). Expanding the parameters of parental alienation syndrome. *American Journal of Family Therapy, 21*(3), 205–215.

Cartwright, G. F. (2006). Beyond parental alienation syndrome: Reconciling the alienated child and the lost parent. In R. A. Gardner, S. R. Sauber, & D. Lorandos (Eds.), *The international handbook of parental alienation syndrome: Conceptual, clinical and legal considerations* (pp. 286–291). Springfield, IL: Charles C Thomas.

Ceci, S. J., & Bruck, M. (1995). *Jeopardy in the courtroom: A scientific analysis of children's testimony.* Washington, DC: American Psychological Association.

Clawar, S., & Rivlin, B. V. (1991). *Children held hostage: Dealing with programmed and brainwashed children.* Chicago, IL: American Bar Association.

Cooke, L. (1995). *Parental alienation syndrome: A hidden facet of custody disputes.* First Place, Lieff Award, Canadian Bar Association, Ottawa, Ontario.

Cross, P. (2000). *Lost children: A guide for separating parents.* London: Velvet Glove Publishing.

Darnall, D. (1998). *Divorce casualties.* Dallas, TX: Taylor Trade Publishing.

Darnall, D. (1999). *Parental alienation: Not in the best interest of the children.* North Dakota Law Review, 75, 323–364.

Darnall, D. (2008). *Divorce casualties: Understanding parental alienation* (2nd ed.). Lanham, MD: National Book Network.

Darnall, D., & Steinberg, B. F. (2008a). Motivational models for spontaneous reunification with the alienated child: Part I. *American Journal of Family Therapy, 36*(2), 107–115.

Darnall, D., & Steinberg, B. F. (2008b). Motivational models for spontaneous reunification with the alienated child: Part II. *The American Journal of Family Therapy, 36*(3), 253–261.

Despert, J. L. (1953). *Children of divorce.* New York: Doubleday.

Douglas, M. J. (1978). *Voice of the river: An autobiography with John Rothchild.* Sarasota, FL: Pineapple Press, Inc.

Dunne, J., & Hedrick, M. (1994). The parental alienation syndrome: An analysis of sixteen selected cases. *Journal of Divorce & Remarriage, 21*(3/4), 21–38.

Ellis, E. M. (1995). *Raising a responsible child.* New York: Birchlane Press.

Ellis, E. M. (2000). *Divorce wars: Interventions with families in conflict.* Washington, DC: American Psychological Association.

Ellis, E. M. (2005). Help for the alienated parent. *American Journal of Family Therapy, 33*(5), 415–426.

Ellis, E. M. (2007). A stepwise approach to evaluating children for parental alienation syndrome. *Journal of Child Custody, 4*(1/2), 55–78.

Ellis, M., & Boyan, S. (2010). Intervention strategies for parent coordinators in parental alienation cases. *The American Journal of Family Therapy, 38*(3), 218–236.

Evans, R. A., & Bone, J. M. (2011). *The essentials of parental alienation syndrome.* Palm Harbor, FL: The Center for Human Potential, Inc.

Faller, K. C. (1998). The parental alienation syndrome: What is it and what data support it? *Child Maltreatment, 3*(2), 100–115.

Fidler, B. J., & Bala, N. (2010a). Guest editors' introduction to special issue on alienated children in divorce and separation; Emerging approaches for families and courts. *Family Court Review, 48*(1), 6–9.

Fidler, B. J., & Bala, N. (2010b). Children resisting post separation contact with a parent: Concepts, controversies, and conundrums. *Family Court Review, 48*(1), 10–47.

Fidler, B. J., Bala, N., Birnbaum, R., & Kavassalis, K. (2008). *Challenging issues in child custody assessments: A guide for legal and mental health professionals.* Toronto: Thomson Carswell.

Garbarino, J., Guttman, E., & Seeley, J. W. (1986). *The psychologically battered child.* San Francisco, CA: Jossey-Bass Publishers.

Garber, B. D. (1996). Alternatives to parental alienation syndrome: Acknowledging the broader scope of children's emotional difficulties during parental separation and divorce. *New Hampshire Bar Journal, 37*(1), 51–54.

Gardner, R. A. (1970). *The boys and girls book about divorce.* New York: Jason Aronson, Inc.

Gardner, R. A. (1976). *Psychotherapy with children of divorce.* New York: Jason Aronson, Inc.

Gardner, R. A. (1982). *Family evaluation in child custody litigation.* Cresskill, NJ: Creative Therapeutics, Inc.

Gardner, R. A. (1985). Recent trends in divorce and custody litigation. *Academy Forum, 29*(2), 3–7.

Gardner, R. A. (1986, June 11). *The parental alienation syndrome.* Paper presented at the Ninth Annual Herschfeld Lecture, St. Joseph's Hospital and Medical Center, Paterson, NJ.

Gardner, R. A. (1987a). Judges interviewing children in custody/visitation litigation. *New Jersey Family Lawyer, 7*(2), 26-30, 43–47.

Gardner, R. A. (1987b). *The parental alienation syndrome and the differentiation between fabricated and genuine child sex abuse.* Cresskill, NJ: Creative Therapeutics.

Gardner, R. A. (1989). *Family evaluation in child custody mediation, arbitration, and litigation: A guide for parents and mental health professionals.* Cresskill, NJ: Creative Therapeutics.

Gardner, R. A. (1991). Legal and psychotherapeutic approaches to the three types of parental alienation syndrome families: When psychiatry and the law join forces. *Court Review, 28*(1), 14–21.

Gardner, R. A. (1992). *The parental alienation syndrome: A guide for mental health and legal professionals.* Cresskill, NJ: Creative Therapeutics.

Gardner, R. A. (1998a). Recommendations for dealing with parents who induce a parental alienation syndrome in their children. *Journal of Divorce & Remarriage, 28*(3/4), 1–23.

Gardner, R. A. (1998b). *The parental alienation syndrome: A guide for mental health and legal professionals* (2nd ed.). Cresskill, NJ: Creative Therapeutics.

Gardner, R. A. (1999a). Differentiating between the parental alienation syndrome and bona fide abuse/neglect. *American Journal of Family Therapy, 27*(3), 195–212.

Gardner, R. A. (1999b). Family therapy of the moderate type of parental alienation syndrome. *American Journal of Family Therapy, 27*(2), 97–107.

Gardner, R. A. (2001a). Parental alienation syndrome (PAS): Sixteen years later. *Academy Forum, 45*(1), 10–12.

Gardner, R. A. (2001b). Should courts order PAS children to visit/reside with the alienated parent? A follow-up study. *American Journal of Forensic Psychology, 19*(3), 61–106.

Gardner, R. A. (2002a). Parental alienation syndrome vs. parental alienation: Which diagnosis should evaluators use in child-custody litigation? *The American Journal of Family Therapy, 30*(2), 93–115.

Gardner, R. A. (2002b). The denial of parental alienation syndrome (PAS) also harms woman. *The American Journal of Family Therapy, 30*(3), 191–202.

Gardner, R. A. (2002c). The empowerment of children in the development of parental alienation syndrome. *American Journal of Forensic Psychology, 22*(2), 5–29.

Gardner, R. A. (2003a). The judiciary's role in the entrenchment of the parental alienation syndrome (PAS). *American Journal of Forensic Psychology, 21*(1), 39–64.

Gardner, R. A. (2003b). The parental alienation syndrome: Past, present, and future. In W. v. Boch-Galhau, U. Kodjoe, W. Andritzky, & P. Koeppel (Eds.), *Das Parental Alienation Syndrom: Eine interdisziplinäre Herausforderung für scheidungsbegleitende Berufe* [*The parental alienation syndrome (PAS): An interdisciplinary challenge for professionals involved in divorce*] (pp. 89–124). Berlin, Germany:Verlag für Wissenschaft und Bildung.

Gardner, R. A. (2004a). Commentary on Kelly and Johnston's "The alienated child: A reformulation of parental alienation syndrome." *Family Court Review, 42*(4), 611–621.

Gardner, R. A. (2004b). The three levels of parental alienation syndrome: Differential diagnosis and management. *American Journal of Forensic Psychiatry, 25*(3), 41–76.

Gardner, R. A., Sauber, S. R., & Lorandos, D. (Eds.). (2006). *The international handbook of parental alienation syndrome: Conceptual, clinical and legal considerations.* Springfield, IL: Charles C Thomas.

Goldwater, A. F. (1991). Le syndrome d'aliénation parentale [Parental alienation syndrome]. In *Dévelopment récents en droit familial* [*Recent developments in family law*] (pp. 121–145). Cowansville, Quebec: Éditions Yvon Blais.

Hands, A. J., & Warshak, R. A. (2011). Parental alienation among college students. *American Journal of Family Therapy, 39*(5), 431–443.

Hostile Aggressive Parenting. (1999). Ontario, Canada: Family Resolution Services.

Huntington, D. S. (1986). Fathers: The forgotten figures in divorce. In J. W. Jacobs (Ed.), *Divorce and fatherhood: The struggle for parental identity* (pp. 55–81). Washington, DC: American Psychiatric Press, Inc.

Isaacson, W. (2007). Einstein: His life and universe. New York: Simon and Schuster.

Jacobs, J. W. (1988). Euripides' Medea: A psychodynamic model of severe divorce pathology. *American Journal of Psychotherapy, 42*(2), 308–319.

Jeffries, M., & Davies, J. (2008). *A family's heartbreak: A parent's introduction to parental alienation.* Stamford, CT: A Family's Heartbreak, LLC.

Johnston, J. R. (1993). Children of divorce who refuse visitation. In C. Depner, & J. Bray (Eds.), *Nonresidential parenting: New vistas in family living* (pp. 109–135). Newbury Park, CA: Sage Publications.

Johnston, J. R. (2003). Parental alignments and rejection: An empirical study of alienation in children of divorce. *The Journal of the American Academy of Psychiatry and the Law, 31,* 158–70.

Johnston, J. R., & Kelly, J. B. (2004). Rejoinder to Gardner's Commentary on Kelly and Johnston's "The alienated child: A reformulation of parental alienation syndrome." *Family Court Review, 42*(4), 622–628.

Johnston, J. R., Walters, M. G., & Olesen, N. W. (2005). The psychological functioning of alienated children in custody disputes: An exploratory study. *American Journal of Forensic Psychology, 39*(3), 39–64.

Kelly, J. B. (2010). Commentary on "Family Bridges: Using insights from social science to reconnect parents and alienated children." *Family Court Review, 48*(1), 81–90.

Kelly, J. B., & Johnston, J. R. (2001). The alienated child: A reformulation of parental alienation syndrome. *Family Court Review, 39*(3), 249–266.

Kopetski, L. M. (1998a). Identifying cases of parent alienation syndrome, Part I. *The Colorado Lawyer, 27*(2), 65–68.

Kopetski, L. M. (1998b). Identifying cases of parent alienation syndrome, Part II. *The Colorado Lawyer, 27*(3), 61–64.

Kopetski, L. M. (2006). Commentary: Parental alienation syndrome. In R. A. Gardner, R. Sauber, & D. Lorandos (Eds.), *The international handbook of parental alienation syndrome: Conceptual, clinical and legal considerations* (pp. 378–390). Springfield, IL: Charles C Thomas.

Levy, A. M. (1978). Child custody determination: A proposed psychiatric methodology and its resultant case typology. *Journal of Psychiatry and Law, 6*(2), 189–214.

Lund, M. (1995). A therapist's view of parental alienation syndrome. *Family & Conciliation Courts Review, 33*(3), 308–316.

Marlow, L., & Sauber, S. R. (1990). *The handbook of divorce mediation.* New York: Plenum Press.

Meyer, C. L., & Quinn, S. (1999). *They are my children too: A mother's struggle for her sons.* New York: Public Affairs.

Mitchell, L. (1935). *O'Shaughnessy's boy.* New York: Lynn Publishing Company.

Myers, J. E. B. (1997). What is parental alienation syndrome, and why is it so often used against mothers? In *A mother's nightmare–incest: A practical legal guide for parents and professionals* (pp. 135–137). Thousand Oaks, CA: Sage.

Nielsen, J., & Vollers, M. (2001). *Icebound: A doctor's incredible battle for survival at the South Pole.* New York: Hyperion Press.

Palmer, N. R. (1988). Legal recognition of the parental alienation syndrome. *American Journal of Family Therapy, 16*(4), 361–363.

Price, J. L., & Pioske, J. S. (1994). Parental alienation syndrome: A developmental analysis of a vulnerable population. *Journal of Psychosocial Nursing, 32*(11), 9–12.

Ragland, E. R., & Fields, H. (2003). Parental alienation syndrome: What professionals need to know, Part 1 of 2. *National Center for Prosecution of Child Abuse Update Newsletter, 16*(6).

Rand, D. C. (1990). Munchausen syndrome by proxy: Integration of classic and contemporary types. *Issues in Child Abuse Accusations, 2*(2), 83–89.

Rand, D. C. (1993). Munchausen syndrome by proxy: A complex type of emotional abuse responsible for some false allegations of child abuse in divorce. *Issues in Child Abuse Accusations, 5*(3), 135–155.

Rand, D. C. (1997a). The spectrum of parental alienation syndrome (part I). *American Journal of Forensic Psychology, 15*(3), 23–52.

Rand, D. C. (1997b). The spectrum of parental alienation syndrome (part II). *American Journal of Forensic Psychology, 15*(4), 1–33.

Rand, D. C. (2011). Parental alienation critics and the politics of science. *American Journal of Family Therapy, 39*(1), 48–79.

Rand, D. C., Rand, R., & Kopetski, L. M. (2005). The spectrum of parental alienation syndrome (part III). The Kopetski follow-up study. *American Journal of Forensic Psychology, 23*(1), 15–43.

Rand, D. C., & Rand, R. (2006). Factors affecting reconciliation between the child and target parent. In R. A. Gardner, S. R. Sauber, & D. Lorandos (Eds.), *The international handbook of parental alienation syndrome: Conceptual, clinical and legal considerations* (pp. 163–176). Springfield, IL: Charles C Thomas.

Reich, W. (1945). *Character analysis.* New York: WR Farrar, Straus, and Giroux/Noonday Press.

Richardson, P., & Broweleit, J. (2006). *A kidnapped mind: A mother's heartbreaking story of parental alienation syndrome.* Toronto: Dundurn Press.

Rivlin, B. V. (1985). Manipulative techniques of children in the transitional family. *Conciliation Courts Review, 23*(1), 21–26.

Sanders, C. H. (1993, Winter). When you suspect the worst: Bad-faith relocation, fabricated child sexual abuse, and parental alienation. *Family Advocate,* 54–56.

Schepard, A., Johnston, J., & Kelly, J. (Eds.). (2001). Alienated children in divorce [Special Issue]. *Family Court Review, 39*(3).
Schepard, A., Fidler, B. J., & Bala, N. (Eds.). (2010). Alienated children in divorce [Special Issue]. *Family Court Review, 48*(1).
Shopper, M. (2005). Parental alienation: The creation of a false reality. In L. Gunsberg & P. Hymowitz (Eds.), *The handbook of divorce and custody: Forensic, developmental and clinical perspectives* (pp. 109–125). Hillsdale, NJ: Analytic Press.
Stahl, P. M. (1999a). Alienation and alignment of children. *California Psychologist, 32*(3), 23–29.
Stahl, P. M. (1999b). *Complex issues in child custody evaluations.* Thousand Oaks, CA: Sage.
Steinberger, C. (2006a). Father? What father? Parental alienation and its effect on children. Part I. *Family Law Review: A publication of the Family Law Section of the New York State Bar Association, 38*(1), 10–24.
Steinberger, C. (2006b). Father? What father? Parental alienation and its effect on children. Part II. *Family Law Review: A publication of the Family Law Section of the New York State Bar Association, 38*(2), 9–19.
Stephens, R. K., & Gunsberg, L. (2010, October 2). *History speaks for itself: The phenomenon and emotional pain of parental alienation.* Paper presented at the Canadian Symposium for Parental Alienation Syndrome: Parental Alienation Syndrome, Past, Present and Future, Mt. Sinai School of Medicine, New York.
Stone, L. (1902). *Mothers' right to children.* Newport Mercury, Newport, RI. Mar. 29, 1902.
Stone, L. (1993). *Broken lives: Separation and divorce in England, 1660–1857.* Oxford: Oxford University Press.
Tucker, L. S. Jr. & Cornwall, T. P. (1977). Mother-son folie a deux: A case of attempted patricide. *American Journal of Psychiatry, 134,* 1146–1147.
Turkat, I. D. (1994). Child visitation interference in divorce. *Clinical Psychology Review, 14*(8), 737–742.
Turkat, I. D. (1997). Management of visitation interference. *Judge's Journal, 36*(2), 17–47.
Turkat, I. D. (1999). Divorce related malicious parent syndrome. *Journal of Family Violence, 14*(1), 95–97.
Turkat, I. D. (2002). Parental alienation syndrome: A review of critical issues. *Journal of the American Academy of Matrimonial Lawyers, 18*(1):131–176.
Turkat, I. D. (2005). False allegations of parental alienation. *American Journal of Family Law, 19,* 1–15.
Vassiliou, D., & Cartwright, G. F. (2001). The lost parent's perspective on parental alienation syndrome. *American Journal of Family Therapy, 29*(3), 181–191.
Vestal, A. (1999). Mediation and parental alienation syndrome: Considerations for an intervention model. *Family and Conciliation Courts Review, 37*(4), 487–503.
Waldron, K. H., & Joanis, D. E. (1996). Understanding and collaboratively treating parental alienation syndrome. *American Journal of Family Law, 10*(3), 121–33.
Wallerstein, J. S., & Kelly, J. B. (1980). *Surviving the breakup.* New York: Basic Books.

Walsh, M. R., & Bone, J. M. (1997). Parental alienation syndrome: An age-old custody problem. *Florida Bar Journal, 71*(6), 93–96.

Ward, P., Campbell, J., & Harvey, H. (1993). Family wars: The alienation of children. *New Hampshire Bar Journal, 34*(1), 30–40.

Warshak, R. A. (1992). *The custody revolution: Father custody and the motherhood mystique.* New York: Simon and Schuster.

Warshak, R. A. (1999). Psychological syndromes: Parental alienation syndrome. In R. Orsinger (Ed.), *Expert Witness Manual* (pp. 3:32:1–3:32:27). Dallas, TX: State Bar of Texas, Family Law Section.

Warshak, R. A. (2000). Remarriage as a trigger of parental alienation syndrome. *American Journal of Family Therapy, 28*(3), 229–241.

Warshak, R. A. (2001a). Current controversies regarding parental alienation syndrome. *American Journal of Forensic Psychology, 19*(3), 29–59.

Warshak, R. A. (2001b). *Divorce poison: Protecting the parent-child bond from a vindictive ex.* New York: Harper Collins.

Warshak, R. A. (2003). Bringing sense to parental alienation: A look at the disputes and the evidence. Family Law Quarterly, 37(2), 273–301.

Warshak, R. A. (2005). Eltern-kind-entfremdung und sozialwissenschaften–sachlichkeit statt polemik [Parent-child alienation and social science–Objectivity instead of polemics]. *Zentralblatt fur Jugendrecht, 92*(5), 186–200.

Warshak, R. A. (2010a). *Divorce poison new and updated edition: How to protect your family from bad-mouthing and brainwashing.* New York: Harper Collins.

Warshak, R. A. (2010b). Family bridges: Using insights from social science to reconnect parents and alienated children. *Family Court Review, 48*(1), 48–80.

Warshak, R. A., & Otis, M. R. (2010). Helping alienated children with family bridges: Practice, research and the pursuit of humbition. *Family Court Review, 48*(1), 91–97.

Westman, J. C., Cline, D. W., Swift, W. J., & Kramer, D. A. (1970). Role of child psychiatry in divorce. *Archives of General Psychiatry, 23*(5), 416–420.

Williams, F. S. (1990, October 20). *Preventing Parentectomy Following Divorce.* Paper presented at the Fifth Annual Conference of the National Children's Rights Council, Washington, DC.

Williams, R. J. (2001). Should judges close the gate on PAS and PA? *Family Court Review, 39*(3), 267–281.

Wood, C. (1994). The parental alienation syndrome: A dangerous aura of reliability. *Loyola of Los Angeles Law Review, 27,* 1367–1415.

Zirogiannis, L. (2001). Evidentiary issues with parental alienation syndrome. *Family Court Review, 39*(3), 334–343.

Chapter 11

PARENTAL ALIENATION RESEARCH AND THE *DAUBERT* STANDARDS

AMY J. L. BAKER

Case Example

Mr. and Mrs. X divorced when Mrs. X was pregnant with the couple's fifth child. Extensive documents indicate that since the birth of their first child, Mr. X had been an involved and active father, teaching his children academic subjects while they were homeschooled as well as actively encouraging their various extra-curricular activities (piano lessons, skiing, gymnastics, baseball, and so forth). At the onset of the marital dissolution, Mrs. X, according to numerous documents, engaged in a series of behaviors designed to undermine the children's confidence in their father and interfere with his contact with them (i.e., making a missing children's report while the children were with their father during his parenting time). Over a dozen child abuse claims were filed against him, none of which were indicated or founded. Ironically, it was on her watch that the family's youngest child nearly drowned, and it was during her parenting time that she abused drugs, using child support payments to cover her weekend drug habit. Once she remarried, she used her new husband's name on school forms and began to schedule competing activities for the children during the time they were supposed to be with their father. Although Mr. X was interpersonally intense, ascribed to unorthodox political conspiracy theories, and was a congregant at a church of what some might consider a fringe sect of the Catholic faith, he was never found to be abusive or neglectful of his children. After ten years of concerted campaigning on the part of Mrs. X and her new husband, however, the children came to vehemently reject their father, refusing any visitation or contact with him whatsoever. Despite a compelling and PAS-informed custody evaluation, Mr. X has not yet been able to prevail upon the court to impose sanctions on Mrs. X for her interference and noncompliance with the court-ordered parenting plan. Currently, the children are severely alienated and show signs of serious mental health problems. Perhaps not surprisingly, Mrs. X had children from a prior marriage whom she had hidden from their father for over a decade, demonstrating that alienation is often a result of a proclivity on the part of one parent as opposed to a result of the relationship between two parents. Despite all of this evidence, during an extensive hearing to determine the "best interests" of the children, counsel for the mother attempted to neutralize the custody evaluator and the father's experts by discrediting the concepts of parental alienation (PA) and parental alienation syndrome (PAS).

OVERVIEW

The purpose of this chapter is to provide an overview of the standards that courts in the United States use to ascertain the scientific merit of psychological theories such as PA and to demonstrate how PA meets those standards. For sake of clarity, the term parental alienation strategies (PA strategies) is used to describe the behaviors, actions, and attitudes exhibited by a parent that are likely to create an unjustified psychological breach between the child and the other parent. Parental alienation syndrome (PAS) is the term used to describe the behaviors of a child who rejects one parent without rational cause, usually in response to exposure to PA strategies.

Daubert and *Frye*

In the 1923 *Frye v. United States,* decision, the admissibility of polygraph test data was disputed, which resulted in the court's making a ruling about the conditions under which scientific evidence can be admitted. The court held that expert testimony must be based on scientific methods that are sufficiently established and accepted, writing that, "Just when a scientific principle or discovery crosses the line between the experimental and demonstrable stages is difficult to define. Somewhere in this twilight zone the evidential force of the principle must be recognized, and while the courts will go a long way in admitting experimental testimony deduced from a well-recognized scientific principle or discovery, the thing from which the deduction is made must be sufficiently established to have gained general acceptance in the particular field in which it belongs." For this reason, *Frye* is referred to as the general acceptance theory.

More recently, in *Daubert v. Merrell Dow Pharmaceuticals* (1993), the Supreme Court held that the Federal Rules of Evidence superseded Frye as the standard for admissibility of expert evidence in federal courts. In Daubert, the Court agreed on the following guidelines for admitting scientific expert testimony: (1) the judge is the gatekeeper, ensuring that scientific expert testimony truly proceeds from scientific knowledge. (2) The trial judge must ensure that the expert's testimony is "relevant to the task at hand" and that it rests "on a reliable foundation." (3) The judge must find it more likely than not that the expert's methods are reliable and reliably applied to the facts at hand. That is, the knowledge is gained through the scientific method, defined as (a) the process of formulating hypotheses and then conducting empirical experiments to prove or falsify the hypotheses, (b) being subject to peer review and publication, (c) having a known or potential error rate and the existence and maintenance of standards and controls concerning its operation, and (d) having theory and technique that is generally accepted by the relevant scientific community.

In *Daubert,* the courts determined that expert testimony must be derived from the scientific method as well as subject to peer review and generally accepted. To be deemed scientific, a method must be based on gathering empirical and measurable evidence. Although specific procedures vary from one field of science to another, common features differentiate scientific inquiry from other ways of obtaining knowledge (such as from intuition or clinical experience). In brief, the scientific method involves researchers proposing hypotheses and designing studies to test these hypotheses using reliable and valid measures. Findings are subject to peer review and when found worthy are published in peer-reviewed journals.

What follows next in this chapter is a description of each of the relevant terms identified by the Daubert standards for ascertaining whether scientific testimony is based on the knowledge gained from the scientific method. Although internal validity is not mentioned specifically as a *Daubert* standard, it is included because it is a concept integral to the scientific method (Baker & Charvat, 2008).

Formulation of Testable, Falsifiable Hypotheses

The scientific methodology begins with the formulation of a testable hypothesis. If a theory cannot result in the identification of testable hypotheses, the theory is not falsifiable and hence does meet this *Daubert* standard. An example of an unfalsifiable statement is that all Martians are green. This cannot be tested because we do not have access to information about the skin color of Martians (or that there are in fact Martians). The concept of falsifiability is attributed to Karl Popper (1934, 1977), who is widely considered the first person to articulate the scientific method. He was concerned with the problem of invalid inferences in which a single instance was used as the basis of universal conclusions. For example, in the single instance of seeing a white swan, one concludes that all swans are white. In order to prevent science from being comprised of these types of invalid inferences, Popper proposed the use of falsification as a standard. He noticed that although a single instance of seeing a white swan cannot be used to conclude that all swans are white, it can be used to disconfirm the statement that all swans are black. With respect to PA, falsifiability is relevant, for example, when recruiting subjects to a study based on the statement, "one parent turned you against the other parent." While this would not support the conclusion that all adults would report this experience, it does refute the notion that no adult would report this experience.

In scientific studies, hypotheses are developed *a priori,* meaning prior to the collection and analysis of the data. Hypotheses are statements about what the data will show. Hypotheses are falsifiable when the results could either support or refute them. For example, in a study of the long-term effects of PAS it must be possible that none of the subjects experienced negative effects in order to test the hypothesis that PAS is associated with negative outcomes. Thus, recruiting subjects for the study from a pool of people with known mental health disorders (such a psychiatric hospital or outpatient clinic) would not be appropriate.

Reliability of Measurement Instruments

Reliability is the term researchers use to describe how accurate a measurement instrument is. It is understood that in any measurement tool there is some error involved. A person completing a survey might circle the wrong item by mistake or might misunderstand the question being asked. Likewise, a person completing a form on Monday might answer questions one way but on Tuesday might answer them a different way. Two researchers watching the same video of a parent and child interacting might each code the parent's sensitivity differently or one might think that the child was exhibiting one of the eight behavioral manifestations of PAS while the other coder might see two manifestations. The typical visual presentation of reliability is a target with the arrow hitting the bull's-eye each time. That is the ideal, in which there is no error in the score at all. In social science, however, it is understood that there is always some error involved in a person's score on a measurement instrument, although the goal is to have as little error as possible. Each method of establishing the reliability of a measure is aimed at measuring the amount of error in the score. If a measurement tool has too much error, then the score has no meaning. It is basically a random number. In social science, there are four ways to statistically determine measurement reliability: interrater/interobserver reliability, test-retest reliability, parallel-forms reliability, and internal consistency reliability. In most situations, it will be necessary to establish reliability, but there are two exceptions: (1) A researcher using an existing measure that has already been established as reliable may not need to establish the reliability of the measure again. It will depend on the specific study. (2) A clinician using an existing measure that has already been established as reliable for the population for which the clinician wants to use it will not need to establish the reliability of the measure in order to use it in a clinical setting (i.e., for assessment or diagnostic purposes).

The first type of reliability is called in interrater or interobserver reliability and refers to a situation in which two (or more) people make an independent judgment (without knowing the other's judgment and without discussing the case prior to making his or her own judgment) about characteristics being observed. Examples include two custody evaluators independently reviewing a case file and determining whether PA is a factor in the case, two clinicians observing or interviewing parents and children and determining whether alienation is the cause of the child's rejection of the parent, and two researchers coding a child's responses to a questionnaire and determining presence or absence of PAS in the child. Reliability is established as either a percentage of agreement between the coders or as a kappa statistic, which takes into account chance agreement and is, therefore, considered a more stringent test of reliability. Interrater reliability is typically considered adequate if it is .80 or better. So, for example, if two custody evaluators review ten case files and agree on nine of them regarding the presence or absence of PAS in the child then interrater reliability, if expressed as the percentage of agreement, would be 90 percent. As a kappa, the figure would depend on the nature of the scoring and the types of agreement and disagreement. A kappa statistic is usually lower than the percentage of agreement. For example, even with 90 percent agreement, the kappa could be considerably lower depending upon the pattern of responses. It is necessary to establish interrater reliability each time the coding system is used because it is necessary to determine that the coders themselves are using the system appropriately. A clinician using a rating system to code children's behaviors for clinical or diagnostic purposes either employ a second person with whom to establish interrater reliability or could establish that she or he is qualified to accurately code the data (for example, has attended training on how to score the data).

The second type of reliability is called test-retest reliability and refers to the extent to which a person's score on the same test is consistent at two different test-taking sessions. The test is taken and then retaken after an interval and the agreement between the two scores is calculated. This form of reliability is appropriate only under the condition in which it is assumed that there would be no change in the person's score and that taking the test the first time would not affect the person's responses on the test the second time. For example, if a child's attitudes toward a parent are assessed for presence or absence of the eight behavioral manifestations of PAS and then the child is exposed to reunification therapy and tested again, it would not be appropriate to assume that the child's attitudes (and, hence, scores) would remain stable. The purpose of the reunification therapy is to effectuate a change in the child's attitudes. A change in scores would be expected. Thus, test-retest would not be the right choice to establish that the attitude measure was reliable. Likewise, if an alienating parent completed an attitude measure that led him or her to realize that it would be advisable to appear as if he or she supported the child's relationship with the rejected parent, that parent might change his or her responses on the measure at the time of the reassessment with the intention of appearing a certain way to the evaluator. Again, test-retest would not be an appropriate reliability approach in such a situation. Another PAS-related scenario in which it would not be appropriate (but could be instructive for other reasons) to give the same test at points in time is when a custody evaluator administers a test to a child (for example, the Bricklin Perceptual Tests [Bricklin, 1995] in which the child is asked to rate each parent) once when brought by the favored parent and once when brought by the rejected parent. If the child is brought to one session by the alienating/favored parent and to the second session by the rejected/targeted parent, the child's responses might vary widely from one testing session to another. This does not necessarily indicate lack of reliability of the measure. Rather it reflects that alienated children behave differently depending upon which parent is observing them. It would be comparable to having two different children complete the form and expect concordance of their responses. In the case of the X family described at the opening of the chapter, one child completed a report card on the father (the rejected parent) when brought to the session by his mother. At that time he gave the father all "F"s. When brought to the session by the father, the child changed his markings to a much more balanced perspective. In this case, the low test-retest was diagnostic (along with other information) of the child's difficulty demonstrating positive thoughts and feelings about his father when in the presence of his mother.

When the measurement instrument is not likely to change a person's responses nor is the person subject to experiences that are likely to be reflected in a changed set of responses to the measure (such as an alienated child being brought by the alienating parent and then by the rejected parent), however, then test-retest is an acceptable approach. That is, when it is expected that there would be no change in the person's responses, test-retest is a logical choice for establishing reliability of a measure. In that situation, change in responses would reflect lack of reliability of the measure.

Calculation of test-retest reliability is determined by the extent to which there is agreement in the two sets of scores (time 1 and time 2) for a group of people. The sample size needed for this analysis depends upon the number of items on the test (the more items, the larger the sample needed). The specific statistic used will depend on the type of items on the test and the type of scoring. For example, if the measurement instrument results in a single score of alienated = one and not alienated = zero, then the appropriate statistic would be a kappa. If the measurement instrument results in a continuous score in which the higher the number, the more alienated the child is, the appropriate statistic would be a correlation.

Once a measure has been established as having adequate test-rest reliability, it is not necessary for a researcher or clinician to repeat the process for each use of the instrument, unless the measure is being used in a different population than that for which reliability has already been established. For example, if a clinician is using a measure that has already been established as reliable for young children with an older population, it is probably important to determine that it is reliable in that older population as well.

Logistically, test-retest poses a significant challenge in that all of the people who participated in the first testing session must be available for the second testing session within a relatively short period of time (usually one or two weeks), and testing conditions need to be relatively consistent from one testing session to the next. A significant change in the conditions (more noise, more distractions, a more lenient proctor, etc.) could also account for changes in scores and undermine the process of ascertaining whether the scores are stable.

Parallel-forms reliability is comparable to test-retest reliability but avoids some of the logistical problems of having to find a group of people willing to be tested on the same measurement instrument at two points in time. Parallel-forms reliability solves this problem by administering two versions of the test at the same time. This approach assumes that there are in fact two comparable versions of the same instrument that are available, which is obviously not always the case. Another version of parallel forms is to consider two halves of the same measure parallel forms. That is, a person's responses to one half are examined to see if they are comparable to the person's responses to the other half. Because of fatigue that can set in over the course of completing a lengthy instrument, it is not advised to compare the first half with the second half. Comparing odd number items to the even number items is the preferred approach. Parallel-forms reliability is only suitable for situations in which the measurement instrument has many items designed to measure the same construct (say the child's lack of ambivalence about the rejected parent), however. If a measurement instrument is designed to assess several constructs at once, parallel forms would not be advisable because it would not necessarily be expected that a child's scores on one construct would be comparable to another. For example, parallel-forms reliability could be calculated with a fifty-item depression inventory when every item is expected to measure depression. If there is a thirty-item personality test with ten items about depression and ten items about anxiety and ten items about cognitive styles, parallel-forms reliability would not be appropriate.

Once a measure has been established as having adequate parallel-forms reliability, it is not necessary for a researcher or clinician to repeat the process for each use of the instrument, unless the measure is being used in a different population than that for which reliability has already been established.

Internal consistency, as the fourth form of reliability, aims to determine the extent to which items on a measure belong to the same scale. When the reliability is acceptable, then the items can be summed to create a total score that can then be used in analyses. This is helpful because it is often parsimonious to conduct data analyses with a few summary scores rather than dozens of individual items. An example might be an eight-item measure of a child's rejection of one parent. The researcher would want to add the eight items together to create a total summary score representing the child's overall rejection. Before doing so, however, the researcher must establish that the items are internally consistent. Otherwise, it is not advisable to create a scale out of the summed items. To determine internal consistency, a statistic known as a Cronbach's alpha can be calculated to determine whether there is sufficient internal consistency of the items to allow for the creation of a summary score. An alpha of .80 or above is considered adequate internal consistency for the creation of a summary score. An option when conducting a Cronbach's alpha is to examine what the alpha would be if each item were removed. This allows the researcher to determine whether a particular item is actually reducing the internal consistency and should be removed. One bad item can lower the alpha, and it is allowable to create a summary score omitting one item if the analysis suggests that this is warranted.

Every time the measurement instrument is used and a researcher wants to create summary scores, it is advised to calculate internal consistency scores. A clinician using the measurement tool on a single case, however, does not need to do that as long as the instrument manual is followed in terms of appropriate procedures for the creation of summary scores.

Validity of Measurement Instruments

Validity refers to a measurement instrument measuring what it is supposed to measure. A depression scale is supposed to measure depression. An anxiety scale is supposed to measure anxiety. A measure of a child's unwarranted rejection of a parent is supposed to measure a child's unwarranted rejection of a parent. If reliability is visualized as the arrow hitting the bull's-eye each time, validity is visualized as the arrow hitting the correct target. A measure could be reliable but not valid. That is, it could accurately and consistently measure a construct although the construct it is measuring happens to be a different one than what was intended. There are six types of validity.

Face validity refers to the items on a measure appearing to measure the construct of interest according to experts (either the person creating the form or, ideally, independent experts in the field). Establishing face validity can be achieved by comparing the items on a measure to a theoretically derived description of the construct of interest. A researcher creates a measure and then examines the items and makes a determination regarding whether the measure seems to be measuring what it is supposed to be measuring. There is no statistic and no specific threshold of validity to achieve. Face validity is a process that is based on the qualifications of the experts making the judgment.

Content validity involves a systematic review of the items on an instrument to determine whether all content areas are covered. Here the focus is on thoroughness of the content being covered. If a researcher constructed a measure of the child's alienation, a review of Gardner's (1998) eight behavioral manifestations would be a good starting place to determine whether the items on the measure cover all eight. Like face validity, this is a nonstatistical form of validity that is considered a good starting place in developing a new measure but not sufficient for validating it.

The next four types of validity each involve comparing the scores of the measurement instrument in question to scores on other measurement instruments and hence represent a statistical form of validity.

Predictive validity involves examining concordance between the scores on the measure in question to scores on a related construct measured at some point in the future. Thus, the question being addressed is whether scores on the measure predict scores on a different measure in the future. An example might be measuring a parent's use of PA strategies at one point in time and then determining whether that predicted the child's alienation in the future. The theory suggests that exposure to PA is associated with the child's adoption of false ideas and feelings about the targeted parent. Thus, exposure to the strategies should be related to subsequent alienation of the child. This form of validity is helpful when the researcher has access to the same sample at two points in time and when intervention is unlikely and not ethically dictated. For example, although severe depression might lead to suicide, it would not be ethically appropriate for researchers to measure depression and then withhold treatment in order to determine whether that is the case. In cases in which there is no known treatment or for other reasons treatment is not advised, predictive validity can be a powerful research tool.

Concurrent validity refers to the degree to which the measure in question is associated with other measures of the same construct that are measured at the same point in time. Researchers might have created a new measure of parental sociopathy that they want to validate because it would be easier for clinicians to use in custody evaluations than existing measures of the same construct. In order to ascertain the new measure's validity, researchers can administer the new measure and an existing measure that has already been established as reliable and valid and determine the extent to which scores on the two measures are concordant. Concordance of .80 or higher is considered an indication of concurrent validity. Of course, there are not always existing reliable and valid measures of the construct of interest, which would rule out this form of validity.

Convergent and discriminant validity refer to the extent to which the measure in question is concordant with measures of other constructs it should be associated with (convergent validity) and not concordant with measures of other constructs it should not be associated with (discriminant validity). These constructs are based on theory. For example, a measure of PA strategies should be associated with some type of Axis II personality disorder but not necessarily an Axis I disorder. Thus, a measure of PA strategies could be convergently and discriminately validated with measures of Axis I and Axis II diagnoses.

Error Rate

Error rate has two related meanings with respect to measures: the first is as a form of reliability and the second is as a form of validity. With respect to reliability, error rate refers to the extent to which a measurement instrument is calibrated to reduce measurement error. An example would be a scale that needs to be set to zero in order to properly measure a person's weight. When the *Daubert* ruling mentions, "the existence and maintenance of standards and controls concerning its operation" it suggests that this is the type of error rate to which they are referring. In social science, this is less of a concern than it is in hard science, in which measurement tools can break down or change in their calibration in a way that would affect the data being collected. However, there is another way to think about error rate which relates to validity. In this way of thinking, error rate pertains to the extent to which a measure is able to accurately classify cases according to a known measurement of the cases. Thus, it is a form of concurrent validity in which the new measure aims to classify cases as true or false cases of a phenomenon (say, alienated or not alienated), which can be compared to a concurrent measure that has known validity. The error rate can be ascertained when the new measure's classifications are tested against the existing (i.e., concurrent) classification. In this type of analysis, there are two types of errors: a true case can be classified as a not true case (called a false-negative, also called a Type 2 error) and a not true case can be classified as a true case (called a false-positive, also known as a Type I error). Sensitivity is the term used to connote the extent to which the measure accurately classifies the true cases (i.e., has a low false-negative rate) and specificity is the term used to connote the extent to which the measure accurately classifies the not true cases (i.e., has a low false-positive rate). It is advisable to have both high sensitivity and high specificity, although exactly what is considered high depends upon many factors. For example, in medicine if the risk of death is high for missing a true case and there are few side effects of the medicine used for treating a case that was falsely (incorrectly) diagnosed, it would be more important to not miss any true cases than it would be to avoid a false-positive. Thus, high sensitivity would be very important, whereas high specificity would not. With respect to PAS, ideally a measure should be able to identify most of the true PAS cases as well as most of the non-PAS cases. It would not be helpful to classify all of the cases as PAS because, although it would accurately catch all of the true cases, it would also catch all of the non-PAS cases. Likewise it would not be helpful for a measure to consider all cases as non-PAS, which would accurately classify all of the non-PAS cases but would misclassify all of the PAS cases. A good measure of PAS must be good at classifying the true cases as well as classifying the not true cases.

A third meaning of error rate pertains to a study (as opposed to a particular measurement instrument). In this meaning, the error pertains to the likelihood that the statistical findings are due to chance or error as opposed to representing an actual association between variables. The standard in the field for considering a finding real and not due to error is .05, meaning that only 5 times in 100 would those findings be due to chance, or error.

Internal Validity of Design

Although not specifically mentioned in the Daubert ruling, the validity of the design is an important consideration in scientific methodology. Internal validity refers to the extent to which the design reduces flaws that would interfere with the researcher having confidence in the data collected. Campbell and Stanley (1963) identified seven threats to internal validity of experiments, each of which represents a plausible alternative explanation as to why participants might improve over time other than the intended cause of the improvement. These primarily apply to experimental designs in which some intervention or manipulation is administered in order to ascertain its presumed effect. Examples include psycho-educational interventions for alienated children, reunification therapy for alienated children and rejected parents, and coparenting classes to reduce parental conflict. In each case, there is an interest in establishing whether the intervention led to a change in the participants. In order to do so, the seven threats to internal validity need to be ruled out or controlled in some manner. The threats are (1) history, any event that occurred that could lead to a change in the participants other than the intervention; (2) maturation, changes in the participants due to the passage of time or their development; (3) testing, the effects of taking a pre-test; (4) instrumentation, changes in the measures; (5) regression to the mean, a statistical artifact when subjects with extreme scores are selected to participate in an intervention; (6) mortality, the loss of subjects over time that changes the composition of the samples; and (7) selection, bias introduced into the study based on how the sample was selected.

Most of the research on the topics of PA strategies and PAS, however, are not experimental designs in which interventions are tested for their effectiveness. Thus, these seven threats are not relevant to many studies conducted in the field to date.

Peer Review

The *Daubert* standard also asserts that articles cited to support proffered testimony must be submitted to and accepted by a blind peer review process in order to ensure that the study and its description meet scholarly academic standards. Blind refers to the process by which the submitted manuscript is absent any identifiers of the authors. This allows the reviewers to assess the quality of the work free from any preconceived biases based on familiarity with the person or the work of the authors. Peer-review refers to the fact that the people conducting the review process are respected scholars in the field (i.e., peers), known for their fair and accurate reviews of other's work. Most if not all academic journals are peer reviewed. One way to know for certain whether a journal is peer reviewed is to examine its website and to determine whether it is indexed by the American Psychological Association's (APA) own database, known as PsycINFO®. According to the APA website, Psyc-

INFO is an abstracting and indexing database devoted to peer-reviewed literature in the behavioral sciences and mental health. Thus, journals that are indexed in the PsycINFO database are presumed to be peer reviewed. Gardner has been criticized for being self-published (meaning, he did not submit his work to the scrutiny of blind peer reviewers). Thus, whether other PAS-related work has been peer reviewed becomes more important than usual. Much of Gardner's work on PAS was published in peer-reviewed journals (e.g., Gardner, 2001, 2002, 2004), however.

Summary of Daubert Standards

According to the *Daubert* standards, scientific theory must be testable and falsifiable, must use reliable and valid measures, must have a known error rate when applicable, and must be subject to peer review. In Table 11.1, the key studies in the field of PA are presented with respect to these features. It is important to note that four types of studies were not included. The first type is comprised of clinical descriptions of PA strategies or PAS that do not include testable hypotheses. For example, Dunne and Hedrick (1994) conducted a qualitative analysis of sixteen PAS cases in order to identify common themes. The second category is empirical studies in related fields, such as children of divorce, that happen to confirm parts of PA theory but also relate to divorce more generally. An example is provided by Buchanan, Maccoby, and Dornbusch (1991), who studied adolescents whose parents divorced and found that adolescents' experience of feeling caught between parents was related to poor adjustment outcomes. The third set of studies excluded are those in which some portion of PAS theory is presented as if it were being tested but due to design flaws it actually was not. Johnston (2003) exemplifies this category. In that study she found that children in 20 percent of her cases exhibited extreme rejection of one parent yet she concluded that "most children were not aligned" with the implication that PAS theory is refuted by these numbers. Further, because she combined in her analyses parents who might have been abusive or neglectful and hence responsible for the warranted rejection by their children in addition to parents who were not abusive or neglectful and hence not responsible for the unwarranted rejection by their children, results regarding predictors of children's rejection are not valid. In addition to the previously mentioned categories of excluded empirical studies, all nonempirical writings on PA strategies and PAS were excluded from the chart, although this represents an extensive body of knowledge about these constructs (Bernet, Boch-Galhau, Baker & Morrison, 2010).

Table 11.1
OVERVIEW OF EMPIRICAL STUDIES IN THE FIELD OF PA STRATEGIES OR PAS

	Study 1	**Study 2**
Reference	Baker, A. J. L. (2010)	Baker, A. J. L. (2007a)
Overview	252 adults completed measures of psychological maltreatment as well as responded to a single item regarding one parent trying to turn them against the other parent	40 adults were interviewed about their experiences growing up. Selection of sample was based on response to flyer asking for adults who–when they were children–had been turned against one parent by the other parent.
Construct	PA strategies	PA strategies
Hypotheses	Respondents who endorsed the item would have statistically significantly higher scores on measures of psychological maltreatment.	Research questions: (1) Did anyone self-identify as having been turned against one parent by the other? (2) What effects did they perceive this to have? (3) What parental strategies did they identify as affecting them?
Falsifiable	If none of the respondents had endorsed the item or if no statistical associations between PA strategies and psychological maltreatment.	If no one had responded to flyers or if all who had responded reported that the experience of alienation had not negatively affected them.
Measure Validity	Concurrent validity of the item in that scores on all measures of psychological maltreatment were statistically significantly higher for those who endorsed the "tried to turn" item than for those who did not.	Validity of construct in that the findings were consistent with theory regarding presence of PA strategies and impact of alienation on functioning.
Measure Reliability	N/A, PA strategies measured with a single item.	N/A, qualitative data
Error Rate	N/A for the measure but all effects were significant at $p < .05$ or better.	N/A
Design Validity	No threats although all data are self-report and retrospective.	No obvious flaws, although all data are self-report and retrospective and qualitative data coded by author.
Peer Review	*Journal of Divorce & Remarriage*	Book published by W. W. Norton. Articles published by *American Journal of Family Therapy, Cultic Studies Review,* and *American Journal of Forensic Psychology.*

continued

Table 11.1–*Continued*

	Study 3	Study 4
Reference	Baker, A. J. L. (2007b)	Baker, A. J. L. & Ben Ami, N. (2011)
Overview	106 custody evaluators rated how possible they thought it was for one parent to turn a child against the other parent.	118 adult children of divorce completed the Baker Strategies Questionnaire (BSQ) along with standardized measures of self-esteem, substance abuse, self-sufficiency, psychological maltreatment, and attachment style.
Construct	PAS	PA strategies
Hypotheses	Research questions: (1) What proportion of custody evaluators endorsed the concept of PAS? (1) What predicted their endorsement?	Scores on the BSQ would be statistically significantly associated with identified outcomes.
Falsifiable	If none of the evaluators had endorsed the concept of PAS?	If none of the respondents had endorsed the items on the BSQ.
Measure	Item had face validity. Data demonstrated validity of the construct in that 100% of sample endosed the statement that it was somewhat or very much possible for a parent to turn a child against the other parent.	Content validity of the BSQ in that it matched the content identified in other studies of PA strategies. Concurrent validity of the BSQ measure and the construct of PA strategies established in that scores on the BSQ measure and the construct of PA strategies established in that scores on the BSQ were statistically significantly correlated with psychological maltreatment, self-sufficiency, and self-esteem that was associated with depression and attachment.
Measure Reliability	N/A, a single item	Internal reliability established via Cronbach's alpha of BSQ of .96.
Error Rate	N/A for the measure but all effects were significant at $p < .05$ or better.	N/A for the measure, but all effects were significant at $p < .05$ or better.
Design Validity	No threats to internal validity	No threats although all data are self-report and retrospective.
Peer Review	*American Journal of Family Therapy*	*Journal of Divorce & Remarriage*

Table 11.1–*Continued*

	Study 5	**Study 6**
Reference	Baker, A. J. L., & Brassard, M. R. (in press)	Baker, A. J. L., Burkhard, B., & Kelly, J. (2012)
Overview	188 high school students completed a short form of the Baker Strategies Questionnaire (BSQ) along with measures of psychological maltreatment, depression, and acting out.	40 children completed the Baker Alienation Questionnaire (BAQ). 19 of the children were sent for reunification therapy, and 21 were sent for treatment due to problems related to high-conflict divorce. Independent teams of clinicans rated cooperation of the youth and history of abuse.
Construct	PA strategies	PAS
Hypotheses	(1) Scores on the BSQ would be higher in youth from nonintact families? (2) Scores on the BSQ would be higher for those who endorsed the item, "one parent tried to turn me against the other parent." (3) Scores on the BSQ would be associated with concurrent measures of well-being and with reports of child maltreatment.	(1) Youth sent for reunification therapy would be above the cutoff on the BAQ where youth sent for other treatment would not be above the cutoff. (2) Youth above the cutoff on the BAQ would be less cooperative than youth below the cutoff. (3) Youth above the cutoff on the BAQ would be less likely to have been abused than youth below the cutoff.
Falsifiable	If none of the youth had endorsed the items on the BSQ.	If none of the children had responded to the questionnaire items in a manner consistent with alienation or if there were no associations between the BAQ and other measures.
Measure Validity	BSQ has content validity. Concurrent validity of the BSQ established in that total scores are higher in the sample from nonintact families and correlated with all three types of child maltreatment as well as with concurrent depressive symptoms.	The BAQ has face validity as well as concurrent validity in that 18 of the 19 19 cases sent for reunification therapy (RT) were classified as alienated based on BAQ scores. None of the abused children were rated as alienated. Half of the alienated cases were deemed uncooperative with treatment.
Measure Reliability	Internal consistency of the BSQ established with a Cronbach's alpha of .86.	Interrater reliability established with 97% agreement between independent coders.
Error Rate	N/A for the measure but all effects were significant at $p < .05$ or better.	87.5% cases correctly reclassified and all effects significant at $p < .05$ or better.
Design Validity	No threats, although all data are self-report.	No threats but data are dependent on validity of the judicial decision regarding reunification therapy or not.
Peer Review	*Journal of Divorce & Remarriage*	*Journal of Divorce & Remarriage*

continued

Table 11.1–*Continued*

	Study 7	**Study 8**
Reference	Baker, A. J. L., & Chambers, J. (2007)	Baker, A. J. L., & Darnall, D. (2011)
Overview	106 adults were surveyed about their experiences growing up. They rated the frequency of the 17 PA strategies using the Baker Strategies Questionnaire (BSQ).	68 targeted parents compled a survey about their child's behavior.
Construct	PA strategies	PAS
Hypotheses	(1) Scores on the BSQ would be higher in the sample from nonintact families. (2) Scores on the BSQ would be higher for those who endorsed the item that one parent tried to turn them against the other parent.	Parents of alienated children would endorse the 8 behavioral manifestations of PAS as being descriptive of their children.
Falsifiable	If none of the respondents had endorsed the 17 PA strategies.	If none of the parents had endorsed the items as descriptive of their children.
Measure Validity	Items on the BSQ have face and content validity. Concurrent validity of the BSQ is established in that each item was rated statistically significantly more frequently by those with divorced parents and by those who said that one parent tried to turn them against the other parent.	The survey had face validity and content validity. The study established validity of the PAS construct in that the behaviors described matched with theory regarding how alienated children should behave.
Measure Reliability	Internal validity of the BSQ was established with a Cronbach's alpha of .93.	N/A
Error Rate	N/A for the measure but all effects were significant at $p < .05$ or better.	N/A
Design Validity	No threats although all data are self-report and retrospective.	Survey respondents could have responded based on their knowledge of PAS theory rather than their actual experience with their children although this was mitigated by asking for stories to explain their responses as a validity check. Sample bias might also be relevant in that subjects were recruited from a convenience sample.
Peer Review	*Journal of Divorce & Remarriage*	*Journal of Divorce & Remarriage*

Table 11.1–*Continued*

	Study 9	Study 10
Reference	Baker, A. J. L., & Darnall, D. (2006)	Ben Ami, N., & Baker, A. J. L. (2012)
Overview	97 targeted parents were surveyed about the behaviors of the other parents	118 adult children of divorce responded to a single item regarding one parent trying to turn them against the other parent along with standardized measures of self-esteem, substance abuse, self-sufficiency, psychological maltreatment and attachment style.
Construct	PA strategies	PA strategies
Hypotheses	Research question: (1) What strategies do targeted parents report the other parents as using?	Respondents who endorsed the item "one parent tried to turn me against the other parent" would have statistically significantly lower scores on measures of well-being.
Falsifiable	If none of the parents had generated a list of PA strategies.	If none of the respondents had endorsed the item, "One parent tried to turn me against the other parent."
Measure Validity	Measure validity is not applicable because it was an open-ended item. Validity of the construct was established in that the behaviors described matched the theory regarding how alienating parents should behave.	The item has face validity. The study established concurrent Validity in that those who endorsed the item were more likely to report psychological maltreatment, difficulties with self-sufficiency, low self-esteem, depression, and insecure attachment style.
Measure Reliability	1,300 behaviors were produced that were independently coded by the two authors. Interrater reliability was achieved with a kappa of .88.	N/A, a single item
Error Rate	N/A	N/A for the measure but all effects were significant at $p < .05$ or better.
Design Validity	Sample bias might be relevant in that subjects were recruited from a convenience sample.	No threats although all data are self-report and retrospective.
Peer Review	*Journal of Divorce & Remarriage*	*American Journal of Family Therapy*

continued

Table 11.1–*Continued*

	Study 11	**Study 12**
Reference	Bow, J. N., Gould, J. W., & Flens, J. R. (2008)	Bricklin, B., & Halbert, M. C. (2004)
Overview	448 professionals involved in child custody cases completed a survey about PA and PAS. They all reported having some knowledge of the concept and the average percentage of cases with PAS present was reported to be 26%.	93 children were given the Bricklin Perceptual Scales (BPS) measure at two different times with a six-month lapse. 127 children were given the Perception-of-Relationships Test (PORT).
Construct	PAS	PAS
Hypotheses	Research question: (1) How do professionals view the concepts of PA and PAS?	Children's scores on the BPS and the PORT would be stable over a six-month period.
Falsifiable	If none of the survey respondents had endorsed the concept.	If the scores had not been stable.
Measure Validity	Face validity of survey items	Criterion validity of the BPS established with correlations with mental health professionals 8 months later. Validity is reported at 91%. Criterion validity of PORT established with correlations with mental health professionals 8 months later. Validity is reported at 91%.
Measure Reliability	N/A	Test-retest reliability of the BPS established at 92.5%. Test-retest reliability of the PORT established at 92.9% agreement.
Error Rate	N/A	PORT error rate was 89%.
Design Validity	No threats to internal validity	No threats to internal validity
Peer Review	*American Journal of Family Therapy*	*American Journal of Family Therapy* and Brunner/Mazel

Table 11.1–*Continued*

	Study 13	Study 14
Reference	Clawar, S., & Rivlin, B. (1991)	Cookston, J. T., & Fung, W. W. (2011)
Overview	Divorce cases for 700 children were reviewed for presence of programming/ brainwashing.	61 parents participated in the KidsTurn intervention and completed measures including one about PA strategies on the part of the other parent.
Construct	PA strategies	PA strategies
Hypotheses	Would programming/brainwashing be prevalent in custody cases?	Parental reports of PA strategies would decrease from time 1 to time 2.
Falsifiable	If brainwashing had not been found in the cases.	If no parent had endorsed the items about PA.
Measure Validity	Insufficient information in book to determine validity of measurement.	Items on the PA scale had face validity.
Measure Reliability	Insufficient information in book to determine reliability of measure.	PA scale established internal consistency with a Cronbach's alpha of .80.
Error Rate	Insufficient information in study to determine error rate.	N/A for the measure, but all efforts were significant at $p < .05$ or better.
Design Validity	Insufficient information in study to determine internal validity of study design.	History and matruation ruled out due to how short the program is. Regression is not relevant as sample not selected based on scores on a measure. Instrumentation ruled out as not relevant for paper and pencil measures. Sample selection might be an issue, but many sample characteristics controlled statistically. Mortality might be an issue, but design allows for examination of effectiveness for completers, which is valid. Testing might be an issue but ruled out in that multiple informants are used.
Peer Review	American Bar Association	*Family Court Review*

continued

Table 11.1–*Continued*

	Study 15	Study 16
Reference	Gordon, R. M., Stoffey, R., & Bottinelli, J. (2008)	Kruk, E. (2011)
Overview	158 parents involved in custody disputes were given the MMPI-2. Cases were classified by evaluators as cases of alienation (n = 76) or not (n = 82). Primitive defenses were compared and found to differ by group. Hypotheses 1 and 2 supported but not hypothesis 3.	Qualitative study of 14 mothers who lost custody of their children. PA was a theme identified by the mothers as reasons for losing custody.
Construct	PA strategies	PA strategies
Hypotheses	(1) Alienating parents would have higher primitive defenses than non-alienating parents. (2) Targeted parents would not differ from comparison group on extent of primitive defenses. (3) Targeted parents would be higher than comparison group parents on primitive defenses, following Kelly and Johnston reformulation of Gardner's theory.	Research question: What issues are discussed by mothers who lose custody?
Falsifiable	If hypotheses 1 and 2 were not supported and hypothesis 3 was supported.	If no mother had rasied the issue of PA strategies on the part of the favored parent.
Measure Validity	MMPI-2 has demonstrated validity.	Narrative data subject to content analysis.
Measure Reliability	MMPI-2 has demonstrated reliability.	N/A, qualitiative data
Error Rate	Hit rate of the validity scales on the MMPI are above 80% (Bagby et al., 1994), and all effects significant at $p < .05$ or better.	N/A
Design Validity	Insufficient information about how cases were classified as PAS or no PAS.	No threats to internal validity.
Peer Review	*American Journal of Family Therapy*	*Journal of Divorce & Remarriage*

Table 11.1–*Continued*

	Study 17	Study 18
Reference	Rueda, C. (2004)	Siegal, J. C., & Langford, J. S. (1998)
Overview	14 independent raters coded 5 vignettes for presence of PAS using Gardner's 8 criteria.	Mothers deemed to be alienating will have higher scores on the K and F scale than nonalienating mothers will.
Construct	PAS	PA strategies
Falsifiable	If there had been no agreement among raters or if none of the raters had agreed to participate in the study.	If no associations had been found between alienation and MMPI scores.
Measure Validity	Insufficient information to determine whether vignettes actually described PAS according to the theory.	MMPI has demonstrated validity. Study established concurrent validity of the presence/absence of PA strategies in that mean scores on the K scale and F scale were statistically significantly higher for the PA group than the non-PA group.
Measure Reliability	In 4 of the 5 cases agreement was .70 or higher.	MMPI has demonstrated reliability. Reliability of PA coding not provided.
Error Rate	N/A	Hit rate of the validity scales of the MMPI are above 80% (Bagby et al., 1994) and all effects significant at $p < .05$ or better.
Design Validity	No internal threats other than as noted above in measure validity.	No internal threats.
Peer Review	*American Journal of Family Therapy*	*American Journal of Forensic Psychology*

continued

Parental Alienation and *Daubert*

As of this writing, PA and/or PAS have been subjected to two *Daubert* hearings and one *Mohan* hearing with this author as the proposed expert. The first case, Hendren v. Lee, in July 2011 was in Massachusetts. As a result of the hearing, the special master concluded, "I find that parental alienation is a subject generally accepted by the relevant mental health community." In September 2012 in Connecticut, the court held a *Porter/Daubert* hearing in the case of *Mastrangelo v. Formica.* Following the hearing the judge made an oral decision allowing PA and PAS testimony, which he later reversed. The ultimate decision was that testimony regarding PA was admissible while PAS was not. In March 2013 a *Mohan* hearing was held in Ontario, Canada, in the *Fielding v. Fielding* case. The judge concluded that the 17 parental alienation behaviors and the 8 child manifestations of alienation "are supported by Dr. Baker's own research and appear to be well accepted in the literature and science community." These cases have not been addressed by appellate courts, so they have not been published.

PA and PAS has been addressed in hundreds of family law cases in the United States and Canada. (*See* examples in Chapter 12, Parental Alienation and North American Law, and the second section of the *Supplemental Reference Guide* of this book.) In some of those cases, there presumably had been *Daubert, Frye,* or *Mohan* hearings at the trial level, but that was not noted by the appellate court. However, the trial courts and appellate courts in the cases in Chapter 12 and the *Supplemental Reference Guide* considered PA and/or PAS to be valid and reliable scientific concepts because the courts based their decisions on testimony regarding PA and/or PAS.

NEXT STEPS FOR THE FIELD

Continued research is clearly needed to build on the knowledge base on several different important fronts. With respect to reliability of the PAS construct, more work is needed in large prospective samples regarding the presence of the eight behavioral manifestations of the syndrome. This is the single most important piece of work that needs to be done. Interrater reliability of coding of children's behavior as well as interrater reliability of children's responses to survey questions would be very helpful for advancing the field. Bricklin and Halbert's (2004) validation study of the Perception-of-Relationships Test (PORT) and the Baker Strategies Questionnaire (BPS) are helpful but incomplete because they do not map onto the eight behavioral manifestations. Rather, they assess the child's campaign of denigration and lack of ambivalence and perhaps some of the other behavioral manifestations but not the full and complete set of eight as described by Gardner (1998).

Reliability of the seventeen PA strategies could also be improved through independent ratings of case files. This could be conducted by both researchers as well as clinicians who represent key stakeholders in the measure development field and the primary potential consumers of any measures to be developed.

Once measures have been deemed reliable, large-scale studies could be conducted to ascertain various forms of validity (concurrent, convergent, discriminant, and predictive). It would also be helpful to establish valid cutoff scores based on age- and gender-specific norms so that clinicians could determine for any single case whether a parent is exhibiting PA strategies (yes or no) and whether the child is exhibiting the PAS (at the mild, moderate, or severe levels).

Another very important direction for future research will be to conduct studies in which alienated children are compared to children who refuse or resist visitation for other reasons as well as to children who have been physically abused or neglected in order to ascertain whether they exhibit different behaviors and experience different concurrent correlates and longitudinal outcomes. Although some argue that it is not possible to differentiate alienated from estranged children or that all cases of visitation refusal reflect a hybrid of causal factors that make clean distinctions between alienated and not alienated impossible, others contend that alienated children present a unique clinical portrait and that once one knows what to look for it is actually quite easy to detect the different types of cases. The data collected to date in the field support the contention that alienated children behave differently, but clearly more work needs to be done in order to solidify these findings and utilize them to help children and families affected by PA.

REFERENCES

Bagby, R. M., Rogers, R., Buis, T., & Katemba, V. (1994). Malingered and defensive styleson the MMPI-2: An examination of validity scales. *Assessment, 1*(1), 31–38.

Baker, R. M., Rogers, R., Buis, T., & Katemba, V. (1994). Malingered and defensive styles on the MMPI-2: An examination of validity scales. *Assessment, 1*(1), 31–38.

Baker, A. J. L. (2007a). *Adult children of parental alienation syndrome: Breaking the ties that bind.* New York: W. W. Norton.

Baker, A. J. L. (2007b). Knowledge and attitudes about the parental alienation syndrome: A survey of custody evaluators. *American Journal of Family Therapy, 35*(1), 1–20.

Baker, A. J. L. (2010). Adult recall of parental alienation in a community sample: Prevalence and associations with psychological maltreatment. *Journal of Divorce and Remarriage, 51,* 1–20.

Baker, A. J. L., & Ben Ami, N. (2011). To turn a child against a parent is to turn a child against himself. *Journal of Divorce and Remarriage, 54*(2), 203–219.

Baker, A. J. L., & Brassard, M. R. (in press). Schoolchildren Caught in Parental Loyalty Conflicts: Correlates with Well-Being and Implications for School Psychologists. *Journal of Divorce and Remarriage.*

Baker, A. J. L., Burkhard, B., & Kelley, J. (2012). Differentiating alienated from not alienated children: A pilot study. *Journal of Divorce and Remarriage, 53*(3), 178–193.

Baker, A. J. L., & Chambers, J. (2011). Adult recall of childhood exposure to parental conflict: Unpacking the black box of parental alienation. *Journal of Divorce and Remarriage, 52*(1), 55–76.

Baker, A. J. L., & Charvat, B. C. (2008). *Child welfare research methods.* New York: Columbia University Press.

Baker, A. J. L., & Darnall, D. (2007). A construct study of the eight symptoms of severe parental alienation syndrome: A survey of parental experiences. *Journal of Divorce and Remarriage, 47*(1), 55–75.

Baker, A. J. L., & Darnall, D. (2006). Behaviors and strategies of parental alienation: A survey of parental experiences. *Journal of Divorce and Remarriage, 45*(1/2), 97–124.

Ben Ami, N., & Baker, A. J. L. (2012). The long-term correlates of childhood exposure to parental alienation on adult self-sufficiency and well-being. *American Journal of Family Therapy, 40*(2), 169–183.

Bernet, W., Boch-Galhau, W. v., Baker, A. J. L., & Morrison, S. (2010). Parental Alienation, DSM-V, and ICD-11. *American Journal of Family Therapy, 38,* 76–187.

Bow, J. N., Gould, J. W., & Flens, J. R. (2008). Examining parental alienation in child custody cases: A survey of mental health and legal professionals. *American Journal of Family Therapy, 37*(2), 127–145.

Bricklin, B. (1995). *The custody evaluation handbook.* New York: Bruner/Mazel.

Bricklin, B., & Halbert, M. C. (2004). Can child custody data be generated scientifically? *American Journal of Family Therapy, 32,* 119–138.

Buchanan, C. M., Maccoby, E. E., & Dornbusch, S. M. (1991). Caught between parents: Adolescents' experience in divorced homes. *Child Development, 62,* 1008–1029.

Campbell, D., & Stanley, J. (1963). *Experimental and quasi-experimental designs for research.* Chicago: Rand-McNally.

Clawar, S., & Rivlin, B. V. (1991). *Children held hostage.* Chicago: American Bar Association.

Cookston, J. T., & Fung, W. W. (2011). The Kids' Turn program evaluation: Probing change within a community-based intervention for separating families. *Family Court Review, 49*(2), 348–363.

Dunne, J., & Hedrick, M. (1994). The parental alienation syndrome: An analysis of sixteen selected cases. *Journal of Divorce & Remarriage, 21*(3–4), 21–38.

Gardner, R. A. (1998). *The parental alienation syndrome: A guide for mental health and legal professionals.* Cresskill, NJ: Creative Therapeutics.

Gardner, R. A. (2001). Should courts order PAS children to visit/reside with the alienated parent? A follow-up study. *American Journal of Forensic Psychology, 19*(3), 3–7.

Gardner, R. A. (2002). Parental alienation syndrome vs. parental alienation: Which diagnosis should evaluators use in child custody litigation? *American Journal of Family Therapy, 30*(2), 93–115.

Gardner, R. A. (2004). Commentary on Kelly and Johnston's The Alienated Child: A Reformulation of Parental Alienation Syndrome. *Family Court Review, 42*(4), 611–621.

Gordon, R. M., Stoffey, R., & Bottinelli, J. (2008). MMPI-2 findings of primitive defenses in alienating parents. *American Journal of Family Therapy, 36*(3), 211–228.

Johnston, J. (2003). Parental alignments and rejection: An empirical study of alienation in children of divorce. *Journal of the American Academy of Psychiatry and the Law, 31*(2), 158–170.

Kruk, E. (2001). Collateral damage: The lived experiences of divorced mothers without custody. *Journal of Divorce & Remarriage, 51*(8), 526–543.

Popper, K. (1934; 1977). *The logic of scientific discovery.* New York: Routledge.

Rueda, C. A. (2004). An inter-rater reliability study of parental alienation syndrome. *American Journal of Family Therapy, 32*, 391–403.

Siegel, J. C., & Langford, J. S. (1998). MMPI-2 validity scales and suspected parental alienation syndrome. *American Journal of Forensic Psychology, 16*(4), 5–14.

Cases

Daubert v. Merrell Dow Pharmaceuticals, 509 U.S. 579 (1993)

Frye v. United States, 293 F. 1013 (D.C. Cir. 1923)

Chapter 12

PARENTAL ALIENATION AND NORTH AMERICAN LAW

DEMOSTHENES LORANDOS

PURPOSE

The purpose for building this chapter was two fold: *First,* to give the reader representative examples of parental alienation (PA) cases from the United States and Canada. One goal in developing this material has been to provide professional and lay readers with a source with which they can easily see the similarities in alienator, child victim, and target parent behaviors as it was seen and described by legal authorities. An additional goal has been to offer the reader a source with which they can become familiar with the contours of the courts' response to alienators, and their child and target parent victims. Another goal has been to assemble material from which readers can find brief descriptions of PA patterns that may be similar to cases in which they are enmeshed. Hopefully, the material can be added to a brief, a lecture, a shared story, and it will help to curtail the pain and suffering alienators inflict on so many people.

Second, to provide brief but accurate descriptions of many alienation cases across a twenty-five-year period to illustrate that PA deniers do not seem to know the data. Bruch, Faller, Hoult, and other nonscientifically based critics maintain that PA does not exist but is a plan or plot by pedophiles to take defenseless children from protective women. Curiously, there is no evidence that a court took children away from a protective woman because of proofs concerning PA and gave them to a man in any of the thousands of cases reviewed. Like global warming deniers and creationists, the PA deniers thrive in a post-fact/Fox News world. A tutorial on critical thinking and how the PA deniers do not value evidence-based empiricism would be beyond the scope of this chapter, so the approach taken here was to provide the reader with the evidence distilled from 3,000 PA cases in the United States and Canada.

METHOD

The method used to distill these examples was as follows:

First, court reports, opinions, and citations to PA cases were obtained from the files of persons who had been involved in them as experts or litigators. This proved unsatisfactory because many of the 280 cases that were reviewed from these sources were incomplete, lacked signatures, had incorrect citations, or could not be found in the public domain.

Second, a query was developed and the ALLSTATES and CAN-ALL-CASES Westlaw databases were searched. The query was (alienat! /3 (mother father son daughter parent!)) & da (aft(1984) & bef(2012)). This search delivered only cases that met three criteria: (1) The case contained the sequence of letters "alienat"; (2) The "alienat" sequence appeared three or fewer words removed from any one of the words "mother," "father," "son," or "daughter," or the sequence of letters "parent"; and (3) The case was published after 1984 and before 2012. The query obtained 1104 cases in the initial United States query pool and 1642 cases in the initial Canadian query pool.

Third, these 2,746 cases were individually reviewed and cases were removed that did not contain at least one of the following two criteria: (1) An independent evaluating expert testified on the subject of PA, whether or not the expert found PA; (2) the court found on any basis that there was PA whether or not there was expert testimony. None of the following were considered "experts" on PA, for the purposes of inclusion: the parties, their children, their therapists, their children's therapists, their attorneys, guardians ad litem, child advocates, mediators, parenting coordinators, custody conciliators, law enforcement officers or Child Protective Services (CPS) personnel. No testimony on PA by any of these persons qualified a case for inclusion. Further, if the court did no more than speculate concerning PA, or if the court's action was to appoint an expert to examine the extent to which there may be PA, the case was not included for further review. Cases with opinions only in French (all from the province of Quebec) were also manually excluded. This refining analysis yielded 482 cases of severe PA.

Fourth, the 482 cases were reviewed again in depth. Each case was scrutinized for description of background facts, clarity of the findings of fact, reliance on statutory and case precedent, and availability of the case in the public domain.

Fifth, the annotated cases were divided into target parent mother and target parent father groupings. From this sort, thirty cases from the United States and thirty cases from Canada, equally divided among target parent mother and target parent father, were selected by this author for description.

Sixth, the cases were organized chronologically and each case was read and annotated again. Phrases, sentences, and paragraphs, which accurately described the case process and record were extracted and sorted for chronological clarity. The verbatim extracted material was chronologically organized and the summaries prepared. In developing the summaries, the author endeavored to turn what was in some cases tortured legalese into prose. Every effort was made to be accurate. Difficult syntax, long and convoluted sentences, temporal inconsistencies, punctuation anomalies, and language differences made the process an arduous one. For example, in the United States there are very few published and available opinions by trial court judges, but this is *de rigueur* in Canada. In the United States, psychologists and psychiatrists aiding the court are typically referred to as evaluators, but the same folks are assessors in Canada. Spelling differences such as counseling/counselling; behavior/behaviour; and judgment/judgement, were changed to American English spellings by the Microsoft spell checker. Tenses in the opinions, which were contemporaneous for the most part, were changed to the past tense for readability. With apologies to the reader, this author left extremely long sentences (judges love long sentences) intact but set them out with semicolons. The names of the various courts: Provincial, Magistrate, District, Circuit, Supreme, Superior, were reduced to "trial court" or "appellate court" for readability. The titles of the various judges were also reduced to "judge." Quotation marks were dispensed with and the citations customary in legal and scholarly writing were jettisoned. The reader will find exact wording in the case reports themselves and citations to find them are given at the end of this chapter. Finally, every effort was made to conceal the identities of the parties and particularly the child and target parent victims. Many cases in Canadian jurisprudence are identified by initials only. In the PA context, this is laudable. The author made every attempt to conceal those names the courts printed in their written opinions. This book is aimed at ameliorating PA, not restigmatizing its victims.

PART ONE
SELECTED CASES FROM THE UNITED STATES

Target Parent Mother

In re M.K.T., 1993–Pennsylvania

This was a 1993 PA by foster mother case. It began in the 1980s when Pennsylvania's office of Children and Youth Services (CYS) and foster mother Myrna Hagan became involved with the family. It seems that the father held an M.B.A. and worked as a computer consultant. The mother was employed as a secretary. In 1989, K., then age sixteen, ran away from home and refused to return when apprehended by the police. The girl alleged that she feared her father because he routinely used excessive physical discipline on her and her siblings. CYS personnel interviewed the children in their home. All three children expressed fear of their father and requested that they be removed from their home. There seemed to be no serious complaints about the mother. The children were placed in shelter care pending a hearing. The father admitted to a CYS caseworker that he had used physical discipline in the form of paddling and slapping across the face. Explaining quite clearly that the complaint of CYS and their "expert" were "shallow and picayune," the appellate court chastised their lower court judge, saying that a review of the record in this case compelled only one conclusion. The appellate panel insisted that the conclusion was so clear that they were puzzled how either the trial court or CYS could maintain a contrary position. Concerning the mother's right to parent her children, the appellate panel apologized: "Unfortunately, the trial court lost sight of the goal."

In this difficult case, at least six behavioral scientists were involved over the "shallow and picayune" CYS process. There was one handpicked psychologist for CYS, Dr. Neil Rosenblum, and five neutral experts: Dr. Susan Nathan, Dr. Donald Hazlett, Dr. Kenneth Stanko, Dr. Robert Saul, and Dr. Anna Marie Breaux. To perfect their shallow process, CYS had Rosenblum meet each of the children alone once and each child in an interactional session with foster mother Myrna Hagan. Rosenblum never met the parents but testified on behalf of CYS. Dr. Robert Saul also testified after meeting with the children and foster mother. Saul expressed that he had concerns about the foster mother's strong views concerning the return of the children to their parents and feared what the foster mother might communicate to the children. Dr. Saul also stated that the foster mother's views about the parents very possibly would have a detrimental effect on the goal of reunifying the family, and, given that the children had become attached to Hagan, they would be influenced by her even more. Clearly, between Hagan and the mother, Hagan was winning their hearts.

Although Dr. Kenneth Stanko admitted that the father's methods of discipline were detrimental to the children's upbringing, he was consistent and emphatic in his belief that the parents had worked very hard at changing their behavior and ridding themselves of inappropriate ways of parenting. He stated that they read many books, both those given by him and those they obtained themselves. They underlined relevant portions and sought him out with questions. Dr. Stanko testified that the parents put this information to use in their parenting of a child who had moved back home without incident. Dr. Stanko emphasized that Hagan's attitude was a serious problem to the stated goal of reunification. He testified that to a reasonable degree of medical certainty, placement of the children with Hagan was not conducive to reunification of the family.

Dr. Anna Marie Breaux spent twenty-one and one-quarter hours in direct evaluation with the family. Dr. Breaux testified that the parents exhibited a great degree of motivation to get the family reunited. The crux of the problem, according to Breaux, was the children's belief that they had to choose between their foster mother and their mother. Dr. Breaux stated that Hagan was competitive with the parents rather than being neutral to the relationship with their children. Dr. Breaux testified that the children were being done a disservice by continued placement with foster mother Hagan. Dr. Breaux opined that this foster mother had explicitly and implicitly taken actions leading to the children's alienation from their parents.

The only evidence that supported the conclusion that visitation with the parents posed a threat to the children still held by CYS was the testimony of Dr. Rosenblum for CYS at the hearing, and it was not *competent* evidence according to the appellate panel reviewing the matter. The appellate court determined that the other expert testimony in the case was significant, both in quantity and in quality. The record demonstrates that for over three years, every psychologist or psychiatrist who treated this family said the same thing: the parents acknowledged their wrongdoing, worked very hard to rectify it, and proved themselves in their care of the child who returned, but they were prevented from reunification with the other children due solely to the efforts of the foster mother and her influence over them. The appellate court chastised their trial judge and ruled that the order terminating visitation with the parents was reversed. They demanded their trial court hold an expedited hearing to determine whether the children may be returned forthwith to their parents' home.

In re Marriage of R., 1994–Iowa

In this case two doctors of osteopathy and "Trudi" were at war. In this difficult matter, the trial court spent eighteen days listening to the mother's twenty-one witnesses, including seven by deposition, and the father's thirty-five witnesses, including five by deposition. The trial court extracted from the voluminous evidence several specific examples of what it considered conduct on the part of the father's new wife (Trudi) and the father to alienate the children from their mother. The first involved a Fourth of July weekend. The mother asked to trade holidays because she had to work a sixty-hour weekend. The father refused to change the holiday schedule and, although he knew the mother was working, he got the son up to get ready for his mother's visitation and let the child sit for two hours with his bag by the window watching for his mother, who did not come. When she did not come on Monday, the same scene was reenacted.

The second was an attempt to charge the mother or someone who cared for the son with or for the mother with sexually molesting the child. Trudi took the boy to doctors four times on two separate occasions with her complaints. All medical opinions refuted Trudi's claims, but Trudi told others about them, including their rabbi, and she then made her complaints in front of the child. In another example of alienation seen as telling by the court of appeals, the mother volunteered with the school to accompany one of the child's classes on a field trip. When the father learned about it, he called the school and complained. He also insisted that the mother take the hours she had chaperoned the field trip as her visitation time. The trial judge found this was a case of parental alienation syndrome (PAS) and it was severe. The appellate court, as did the trial court, found that Trudi contributed substantially to the discord. The trial court in its findings noted the fact that Trudi had alienated her three children from a prior marriage from their father after she divorced him. She seemed to view the children as items to be secreted and was manipulative, forbidding the son to talk to his mother at school and religious functions. The trial court's award of custody of the children to the target parent mother was affirmed.

G. v. G., 1995–Texas

In this Texas case, a modification was sought within one year of the original decree. As it was in Texas, the custody dispute was tried before a jury in 1992. The record indicated that the father had a history of severe emotional outbursts and had engaged in threatening behavior toward the mother and the children. There was testimony that the father was destructive as well.

Mother testified about her belief that the child was afraid of his dad, and that the father had no real love for their son and was only using him. The child had problems controlling his bowels, which the mother believed were stress related. The record reflects that the father wanted the four-year-old daughter to fly unescorted from San Antonio to Houston and back, and the father admitted he refused to let the boy talk to the guardian ad litem alone.

Dr. Kit Harrison, the court-appointed psychologist, described the father as very bombastic, loud, combative, verbally argumentative, and very power oriented and that he referred to the four-year-old as "the girl." Dr. Harrison testified that the son acted as his father's messenger or robot and that he was "brainwashed." It was Dr. Harrison's opinion that the father exploited both children. He testified that the father's behavior was extremely detrimental to the children because it completely stifled growth and development. Dr. Harrison's expert opinion was that the son was subject to his domineering and extremely controlling father and that the father was alienating the child from his mother. Dr. Harrison further testified he suspected that the father had a personality disorder. After hearing all the evidence, custody was changed to the target parent mother. Father's appeal was dismissed.

A. v. A., 1999–Delaware

In this case, the mother made a 911 call when the father pulled her out of the room, dragged her downstairs, said he was going to shoot her, started to strangle her, and threatened to "do" her whole family. The father was found guilty of assault and, after an appeal, was again found guilty by the reviewing court.

The record reveals that the court-appointed evaluator Dr. Marsha Orlov testified that she saw the parties together with one of the children. She found that the father constantly shifted the focus to negative comments regarding mother's behavior. He continually alleged that the mother was not capable of parenting and that she had a variety of sexual affairs, including one with her sister's husband. The sister denied that any affair occurred. The record also reflects the opinion that the reported complaints by one child were exaggerated and that instead of encouraging the children to evaluate their relationship with their mother, the father encouraged negativism towards her.

Evaluator Orlov assessed that the older child had been severely damaged by the process. The Court met with the son twice on the record. The Court observed that he exaggerated his complaints against his mother and lied, in part, on less significant items from the past. Dr. Orlov's testimony concerning the son's truthfulness was consistent with the Court's observation. Dr. Orlov testified that, unlike the daughter, who was adept at lying, the son was not yet. The mother presented the testimony of Donna D. in support of her claim that the father was alienating the son from her. Ms. D. was the mother of another of this father's children. Ms. D. believed that her daughter was alienated from her due to the father's and the older child's influence.

The Court listened carefully to a microcassette tape submitted into evidence by the father. Despite testimony by the older child that the tape had been recorded by him and submitted to father who, in turn submitted it to the court without alteration, Mr. James B. Reames, President of JBR Technology and an expert in forensic science, testified otherwise. Mr. Reames determined that the cassette tape had been altered in the section containing the pertinent information. Mr. Reames noted that certain erasure marks on the tape were inconsistent with normal playback and recording. He stated that information had been added to the tape. Mr. Reames determined that a different recorder made these marks on the tape. The result was that custody of the younger child was awarded to the target parent mother.

B. v. B., 1998–Vermont

The parties were married in 1974; the mother was eighteen and the father was nineteen. They had two sons, who were fifteen and thirteen years old at the time of trial. The parties' interests grew apart over the course of their twenty-year marriage.

The court found that prior to the separation, the mother had been the primary care provider for the children, but after the parties separated, the boys began to spend more time with their father, and their relationship with their mother deteriorated. The court found that the father had encouraged the sons' animosity by unfairly blaming her for the parties' marital problems and by making disparaging remarks about her lifestyle. Concerning a letter the court received from the younger boy expressing a preference to live with father, the court observed that it was not the product of an eighth grader. The boy's recriminations against his mother, the court concluded, clearly reflected discussions with the father and further persuaded the court of the father's role in corroding both boys' relationship with their mother.

The court expressly found that father had encouraged the boys' hostility toward the mother and that although several factors had contributed to the estrangement between mother and sons, the single most significant factor was the constant poisoning of the relationship by the father. The appellate court opined that the findings raised serious doubts about the father's fitness to serve as the custodial parent. The father's conduct and attitude demonstrated virtually no capacity to place the interests of the children above his own in fostering a positive relationship with the mother. The trial judge explained: "The father may not deserve to win custody of the boys, but he has effectively done so" as a result of his own misconduct. So the trial judge awarded the father sole physical and legal rights for the children and granted the mother limited visitation.

The three-judge appellate panel categorically rejected this reasoning. They instructed that a parent who willfully alienates a child from the other parent may not be awarded custody. They recognized the practical considerations that impelled the family court to its conclusion. They did not contend that an award to the mother would magically negate the father's baleful influence or effect an immediate reconciliation with the children. Nevertheless, they reversed the trial court's custody order and sent the case back for a more appropriate custody award for the target parent mother.

Matter of P., 1995–Tennessee

In this case, a child was born out of wedlock during a time when the parties were living together. The father originally denied paternity, but the child was ultimately legitimated, at the age of two, after results of blood tests. The conflicts and discord in the case were long standing and, despite the efforts of many participants, showed very few, if any, signs of improvement.

In 1991, the mother was undergoing physical, emotional, and financial difficulties. In light of these problems, she agreed that the father could have custody of their son and a consent order was entered. The father's refusal to enter counseling; his continued frustration of the mother's visitation; and intimidation of the mother, the Court Appointed Special Advocate (CASA), and school personnel brought about a reevaluation. The father then based his claim of better comparative fitness on the fact that mother was a lesbian and lived with her lesbian partner. The trial judge believed that underlying the father's behavior was his hostility at the mother's admission that she was a lesbian. The issue was not formally raised until just before the trial, and there was never any allegation of inappropriate conduct or behavior by the mother or her partner. On the contrary, the Center for Children in Crisis found the mother's partner to be the more mature of the adults in the boy's life. The father of the mother's two other children testified that the mother was a good mother, his children were well-adjusted, and his relationship with his children was quite good.

The record revealed that the alienating father here was unable to see how his behavior affected his son. He refused to address the child's difficulties in school and lack of peer friendships; he demonstrated an unwillingness to follow court orders regarding visitations and counseling; and continued to make negative commentary regarding the mother in a manner that caused the child to choose sides. The reports of CASA and the guardian ad litem contained factual details of the father's personality and behavioral disorder as diagnosed by the Center for Children in Crisis. The father's only affirmative response to these issues was an attempt to leave the jurisdiction of the court. The record demonstrated that the mother made considerable progress in improving her physical and mental condition and regained the ability to care for her son. The court ruled that there were changed circumstances that warranted a revision in custody arrangements and the appellate court affirmed a change to target parent mother.

M. v. M., 2001–Vermont

In this case, the Supreme Court of Vermont dealt with a cultural clash over PA and religion. In this case, the father and mother had two daughters together. At the time of their divorce in 1995, the father and mother stipulated to joint parental rights and responsibilities for the girls. There was extensive cooperation on issues regarding the girls immediately following the divorce, including shared access to one another's homes, the exchange and transport of the children's belongings between the two homes, frequent and open communication between mother and father without limitation, joint parent-teacher meetings, and flexibility about time and contact with each parent. There was a significant change for the worse starting in the latter half of 1996. By June 1999, the mother moved to modify the parties' original divorce decree, seeking both sole legal and sole physical rights and responsibilities for the children. The mother told the court that the changes included the father's prohibiting the girls from contacting her while they were in his care, prohibiting her from entering his home, and refusing to communicate with her except in writing. The mother testified to symptoms of anxiety in both girls, including nightmares, stomachaches, and a constricted throat; the younger girl was very clingy and sucking her thumb. The mother explained the changes as coincidental to the father's deepening involvement with the Jehovah's Witness religion.

The father argued that the portion of the court's order providing that he not bring the girls to any Jehovah's Witness religious gatherings or attempt to raise the girls as Jehovah's Witnesses was unconstitutional. The record and legal argument on this point was extensive. The Vermont Supreme Court reasoned that their trial courts may take into account a parent's religious practices when making a custodial determination if there is evidence that the practices have a direct and negative impact on a child's physical or mental health. In this case noted the court, the mother presented extensive evidence that the conflicting practices and rules in each household that stemmed from her and the father's disparate religious beliefs were causing the children to experience extreme confusion and anxiety.

The trial court made specific findings regarding the negative effects on the children of mother's and father's differing sets of beliefs, including the children's feelings of disloyalty, guilt, confusion, and anxiety. Thus, not only was evidence of harm presented, but also the trial court made specific findings that the conflicting beliefs and practices in each household were having a palpable negative impact on the children and would continue to do so. The Vermont Supreme Court upheld the trial court's prohibition. Additionally, there was extensive evidence in the record of the father's attempting to alienate the girls from their mother that independently supported the court's disposition in the case. The father refused to communicate with her in person on repeated occasions in front of the children. There was testimony about the father's refusing to answer the door for her, refusing to roll down the car window while she attempted to talk to him at an exchange of the children, communicating to her through the stepmother while he stood by silently during exchanges, and hanging up the phone on her. For the reasons cited, custody was awarded to the target parent mother.

S. v. P., 2003–Washington

The marriage in this case was dissolved by decree of the court in 1996. At that time the parties agreed on a parenting order. The plan provided for joint decision making. In late 1999, the boys were spending every overnight with their father. The record indicated that this had resulted from his intimidation that caused subtle but persistent alienation of the boys' natural affections for their mother. The disintegration of the mother-son relationships was helped by the reluctant acquiescence by the mother, who felt helpless to deal with the alienation and who hoped to alleviate pressure on the boys by going along with the father's demands. The mother asked the father to try mediation in accord with the terms of the parenting plan in order to resolve the ongoing dispute as to the residential schedule, but the father insisted upon reading his response to the mother's request for mediation out loud, in front of the boys. The record documents that the father blocked the mother's car from leaving the driveway when the father persisted in this effort to read his manifesto and the mother attempted to leave.

At the next court date, the court denied the father's petition to end overnights for the mother, finding that it was not with the mother's consent but was based instead on the father's threats and intimidation of the mother. The court noted that the father's persistent and subtle alienation of the boys from their mother was so serious that they had been robbed of a relationship with her. The court also found the father to be in contempt of court for his willful disregard of the original parenting plan, including the residential schedule, the transportation provisions, the respect-for-the-other parent clause, and the requirement for joint decision making. The court found that the boys were so thoroughly alienated from their mother that they would require ongoing therapy. The court found that the father had engaged in abusive use of conflict to the detriment of the boys and that the opportunity for further PA should be minimized. For these reasons, the court set out a detailed residential schedule. Eight weeks later, based on a posttrial motion by the mother, the trial court found the father to be in contempt of court for, among other things, continued PA, failure to abide by parenting plan provisions, and failure to obtain PA counseling as directed. The ruling regarding continued PA was based in part on the mother's revelation that she had taped and transcribed a telephone conversation between the boys and their father during which the father encouraged the boys to let their grades slip at school and to defy their mother. The court found that the father had had the ability to comply with the court's previous orders but had failed in bad faith to do so. The order contained a warning that unless the father complied with the order to obtain PA counseling within three weeks, his residential time would be suspended until he did comply. The court awarded the mother attorney fees and costs incurred for the contempt proceeding.

Six months later, the trial court held the father in contempt once again, ordering jail time for his failure to obtain PA therapy as previously ordered. The court ruled that the father could purge himself of contempt by paying the overdue guardian ad litem fees and by beginning alienation counseling. The father finally obeyed the two court orders one day before he was due to report to the county jail. According to a court-appointed evaluator, the father was out to prove that the mother was a bad parent. The record documents that the father made various reports to police and school authorities that the mother beat the boys. Although investigations showed these allegations to be false, the mother was repeatedly confronted by police at her front door, who were there to investigate the welfare of the children because of these reports. The father told the wife's sister's husband that he would do anything to get the children away from their mother and that he would do whatever it took to get his way. Affirming the court's order, the appellate panel noted that their experienced trial judge in this case viewed the father's systematic alienation of the children from their mother to be very serious. The appellate panel upheld the change of custody to the target parent mother.

J.H. v. P.F., 2004–New York

In this case, the father met the mother when he began working as a "bouncer" and she was a sales associate. Testimony indicated that the mother was terrified when father became more antagonistic toward her, threatening to kill her, "mulch" her, stating, "You never know what could happen in the middle of the night." The mother alleged that the father would wake her up in the middle of the night screaming at her and calling her a loser and "a filthy disgusting animal who can't keep her legs shut."

The court-appointed evaluator noted that the mother presented as a frightened recipient of the father's rage. She had serious difficulty negotiating with him because of her fear. The trial court found that the mother was a sincere and credible witness. She was timid but a kind and loving mother, committed to the well-being of her child. All witnesses, other than the father and his mother, confirmed her substantial involvement in the child's life, from birth to present.

At one point in the case, the father went home and had a "powwow" with his wife and the child that he characterized as an open family discussion. The father presented notes of the powwow to court evaluator Dr. Reubins. The psychologist testified that during the course of his evaluation he met with the parties and the child cumulatively forty-two times and prepared an extensive report. Dr. Reubins characterized the powwow notes presented to him by the father as "the most compelling example of parental alienation I've ever seen." When Dr. Reubins expressed his surprise that the father would say these things to the child, the father replied that he had talked openly with the child for years. Dr. Reubins stated that the father's powwow was tantamount to brainwashing, by attempting to teach the child what she should believe. The powwow was further described by the evaluator in his report as a candid example of negative influencing of a child against the mother and positive brainwashing toward that goal.

The trial court reasoned that not only did the father show a complete disregard for the child's relationship with her mother by the powwow he held, he also sought to frustrate the mother's temporary order of visitation by denying her the very overnight visitation that the parties previously stipulated to in open court. Based on the many examples of alienation and the pattern of the father's disparagement of the mother, the court changed custody to the target parent mother.

S. v. S., 2007–Ohio

At the beginning of this case, the mother was a linguist in the United States Navy, stationed in Spain. The parents lived in Spain until 1998, when the father moved to his parents' home in Cardington, Ohio, with the children. At the time, the mother was at sea on a tour of duty. The father did not advise the mother of his decision to move, and the mother had another year of service to fulfill. While she was at sea, the father filed a complaint for divorce. The trial court issued orders designating father the children's temporary residential parent and granting the mother visitation pursuant to a long-distance schedule.

In 2002, the case was tried, but the magistrate judge did not render a decision until twenty-four months later. The mother filed objections to the Magistrate's decision. Three and a half years after the trial by the Magistrate, the trial court wrote that the father had been alienating the children against the mother for the past five years. Thus, in 2007, the Ohio trial court finally realized that the children had been severely alienated against their mother by the father. The 2007 court offered that the father had shown that he would never change or recognize that he ever did anything wrong. Not only did the father alienate the children but also, as the court wrote, he had not helped his situation when he resigned his job and showed no desire to obtain employment. Further, the father never established his own home for himself and the girls but instead lived with his mother. This was all magnified by the fact that it appeared the paternal grandmother had not been a positive influence for the girls and their relationship with the mother while they had lived with her. Curiously, the record shows that through all the PA exhibited by the father, the mother appeared to bear no animosity toward him.

The court in 2007 summarized that the father exhibited a total lack of understanding of the importance of both parents' involvement in the children's lives. After the separation, observed the court in 2007, she was a mother that wanted to see her children and the father did all he could to prevent that from happening. The court went on to report that it gave him control and he abused it. The Ohio appellate court offered that their trial courts generally do not make a change of custody under these circumstances, but PA trumps that generalization. The harm that can be done to children is inconceivable wrote the appellate panel while affirming a change in custody to the target parent mother.

M. v. M., 2007–Texas

In this Texas case the mother filed a petition for divorce and a suit for damages against father based on assault and intentional infliction of emotional distress. The father answered with a general denial and a counter petition for divorce. The case was tried before a jury. The mother alleged that the father assaulted her in 1995 by throwing a microwave at her, shaking her by her arms, and sexually assaulting her. The mother and others testified that on a daily basis the father told her that she was completely crazy and that everything bad that happened was her fault. The record reflects that the father told her in the presence of the children that G. was the smart child and must have inherited her intelligence from him, whereas P. was the dumb one, like her. The mother testified that before the children's bedtime, he would tickle them, getting them excited, and then expect them to go straight to sleep. When the children would leave their bedroom, the father would get upset and spank them.

Another assault incident occurred during the summer of 2001, when the father asked the mother for sex and she refused. He insisted she did not have a choice and demanded she take off her clothes. The mother testified that when she took off her clothes, the father covered their bed with a shower curtain, "lathered himself" up with baby oil, and forced her to have anal intercourse. The mother's medical records were admitted by the court and documented the mother's complaints of forced sex. The father testified that the sexual incidents the mother described were consensual. However, Dr. Maria Arango testified that the mother presented with anal fissures on an August 2001 visit, which, according to Dr. Arango's testimony, made her allegation of forced anal intercourse more believable.

When the father appealed, the appellate court assigned to the case noted that the testimony of the mother and Dr. Arango, coupled with the mother's medical records, constituted legally sufficient evidence to support the assault claim. The jury appointed mother sole managing conservator and found that the father assaulted her and intentionally inflicted severe emotional distress on her. The jury awarded her $165,000 in past compensatory damags, and $250,000 in exemplary damages. The appellate court noted that considering all of the evidence, the record was both legally and factually sufficient to support the jury's finding. The result: $415,000 and sole custody to the target parent mother.

S. v. S., 2007–Connecticut

In this matter, the Connecticut appellate court noted that after eight years of university study, earning two master's degrees, acceptance into a Ph.D. program, and being offered a teaching position for at least the first year while writing her dissertation, the mother deferred a potential career as a university teacher to have a family with the father in the United States. When the relationship soured, the father made a false allegation to federal immigration authorities that she had forged his signature on papers she filed to obtain permanent residency in the United States.

While fighting the false charges, she was stuck in Russia for ten months. In addition, she denied his allegations, made numerous times, that she intended to spirit the children away to Russia and testified instead that she wanted to stay permanently in the United States with her children. She testified that the numerous arrests for family violence orchestrated by the father occurred after incidents in which the father physically or emotionally abused her. He would then falsely accuse her of domestic violence. The trial judge explained that after considering all of the evidence presented, it found the mother's testimony about her marriage and her relationship with the father to be credible and true. The implication of that finding, wrote the court, was that her separation from the children for ten months while she was in Russia, the damage to her parental bond with the children during that time, the need thereafter to reintroduce herself to the children as their mother through supervised therapeutic visitations, and the restrictions on her access to the children because of her husband's claims that she had untreated mental problems and would flee with them to Russia all resulted from efforts by the father to alienate the children from their mother. The court also found as true her testimony that the family violence incidents were all initiated by the father. The court found that the father constantly criticized her for working too much and accused her during the marriage of marrying him just to get a green card and his financial support and that her loss of her college and public school teaching positions was caused in large part by the arrests and his accusations of impure motives for marrying him. The court found that the mother's decision to live in a battered woman's shelter and transitional living program for the two years before the trial was a reasonable effort on her part to protect herself and get on her feet financially.

The court went on to note that nothing in the evidence credibly suggested any serious concerns about the mother's parenting or her ability to care for the children. Her ten-month separation from the children when they were young so seriously damaged her relationship that upon her return she was a stranger to them. The court also expressed concern about the father's mental health. The court noted that the evidence was replete with examples of paranoid and obsessive behavior and the conclusions of the professionals who worked with him were that he needed a psychiatric or psychological evaluation. The court agreed with the conclusion of the family relations counselor that his concerted effort to affect the children's relationship with their mother and his intense feelings of paranoia in which everyone was out to get him evidenced ongoing mental health issues. Dr. Thomas, a Yale Child Study Center psychiatry fellow, testified that the father perseverated on a number of suspicious or persecutory themes and appeared quite preoccupied with discussing negative portrayals of the mother as an abusive, exploiting wife and neglectful mother. This occurred again and again despite several prompts by the doctor to redirect him to speak to the question at hand.

Working to reintegrate the mother, now a stranger to her children into their lives, the court issued strict orders and concluded that an order of joint legal custody, with final decision-making assigned to the target parent mother, was in the children's best interest.

P. v. M., 2009–Louisiana

This case was a child custody and visitation dispute between two mothers–a biological mother M. and an adoptive mother P.–of an eleven-year-old girl.

For twenty-four years, M. and P. were lesbian partners. During that time, they jointly decided to have a child by artificial insemination. The child was born in 1997. For more than six years, the trio lived together as a family, first in California and then in Louisiana. When the relationship between M. and P. ended, a dispute arose between them over custody and visitation. Following a lengthy trial, judgment was rendered awarding M. sole custody and terminating P.'s visitation rights. P. appealed and the Lousiana appellate court reversed the trial court's visitation ruling and remanded for a hearing to immediately set the parameters of visitation.

The record documents that in the spring of 1979, M. and P. began a lesbian relationship. In the summer of 1979, they began sharing an apartment. Both M. and P. graduated from college while living in New Orleans. M. obtained a bachelor's degree in elementary education and a master's degree in biological science. P. obtained two bachelor's degrees: mechanical engineering and business management. Thereafter, they moved to California and bought a house together. While living in California, M. attended university in Berkeley and received a Ph.D. in zoology. After living together for about seventeen years, they decided to have a child by artificial insemination. They mutually agreed on the selection of the sperm donor. M. then became pregnant in 1996.

During 2004, the parties separated. According to P., the cause of the breakup of their relationship was M.'s having a lesbian relationship with a married woman, C.P. M., on the other hand, characterized her relationship with Mrs. P. as a platonic friendship and attributed the breakup to other causes. In the fall of 2004, M. moved into an apartment located not far from the family home. For approximately one year after they separated, the parties coparented their daughter and equally shared physical custody. In 2005, M. moved herself and the daughter out of the family home. She, along with the child, moved to a new house that she had just purchased but did not inform P. of the move until after the fact by leaving a phone message for her. Soon

M. caused sexual assault allegations to be made against P. Dr. Brian Jordan was appointed by the court as the custody evaluator to make recommendations regarding custody and visitation.

In a December, 2005, letter to the court, Dr. Jordan advised the court that he found no grounds to support allegations that P. had engaged in sex abuse of her adopted daughter. Dr. Jordan opined the child's current alienation towards P. stemmed from alienation tactics employed by M. An example appearing in the record was that in December, 2005, when M. dropped the girl off at P.'s home, M., in the presence of the child, verbally denigrated P. regarding her living conditions; forced the child's dog into P.'s car, causing severe anxiety and distress for the child; and screamed at P. that she was "separating a child from her mother" and was a "monster" for doing so. M. then instructed the child to call 911 in the event that P. touched or hurt her. Two months later, M. filed a demand seeking to set aside P.'s adoption of their child and to obtain a declaration that M. was the child's sole parent. M. argued that the California adoption was invalid because an adoption by unmarried lesbian partners would not be allowed under Louisiana law.

In 2006, P. filed a motion to appoint Dr. Alicia Pellegrin as a second court-appointed evaluator. The court granted the motion and continued M.'s motion to terminate visitation. Dr. Pellegrin conducted her evaluation over a three-month period. Dr. Pellegrin described the preseparation relationship between the parties as a committed, monogamous relationship. Witnesses indicated that M. and P. saw themselves as a model lesbian couple and described the child as extremely attached to both of her moms. Witnesses indicated that before the separation there was no difference between P.'s and M.'s interaction with the child. As to the sudden vitriol, Dr. Pellegrin explained that in order for M. to refute the lifestyle and sexual orientation that she voluntarily chose and into which she voluntarily chose to bring the child, M. had to reject P. Dr. Pellegrin opined that although it was M.'s right to make a different decision for herself regarding her sexual interests, she had no right to demonize homosexuality because she and P. made a choice to bring a child into their then homosexual lifestyle. Dr. Pellegrin went on to testify that to now characterize P.'s sexual orientation as wrong and/or sinful could serve no purpose but to alienate the child from P., which was exactly what happened. Dr. Pellegrin also noted that M. told her that the child changed her last name from P. to M. on her schoolbooks and papers and distanced herself from P. in every way. Dr. Pellegrin described the child's responses regarding her negative feelings towards P. as rehearsed and characterized the girl's communication with P. as rude and disrespectful. For example, she pointed out that the child's contact name on her cell phone for P. was "stupid" and that the child spat on the target parent mother.

A silly but confounding variable occurred when Dr. Jordan testified about his view of maternal bonding. He testified that at some point a child will psychologically bond to one person as his or her mother, but a child will not bond to two mothers. Dr. Jeffery Lockman, was qualified as an expert in the area of development psychology and child development. Dr. Lockman was critical of Dr. Jordan's finding of no maternal bonding and Dr. Jordan's apparent lack of knowledge of current attachment theory. Because P. was consistently available in providing care for the child during the sensitive period, Dr. Lockman opined that parental bonding between P. and the girl was almost certain. More witnesses described the relationship prior to the separation between P. and her daughter as an endearing, warm, loving mother-daughter relationship and testified that the girl was excited to see P. when she came to pick her up in the afternoons. Even M.'s younger sister testified that the daughter referred to both P. and her sister by their first names. M.'s sister acknowledged that up until the separation P. took an active role in caring for the child: fed her, bathed her, dressed her, took her to school, and took her to the doctor.

Reviewing the entire record and especially the termination of P.'s relationship with her child, the appellate panel wrote that they recognized the apparent frustration of the trial judge in his attempt to resolve an obviously bitter custody dispute. However, given that neither Dr. Pellegrin nor Dr. Jordan voiced any concern that would warrant denying visitation rights to P. and that there was no other evidence of abuse warranting denying such rights, the appellate court concluded their trial court erred in terminating P.'s visitation rights. On remand, the target parent mother's rights were restored and the appellate court recommended appointing a parenting coordinator to facilitate contact.

In re Marriage of Y. and A., 2010–California

In this matter, the California court record documents five years of stressful history after the trial court awarded sole legal and primary physical custody to the mother, with two hours of monitored visitation for father. The court ordered the father to pay the mother child support of $898 per month, found that the father was capable of earning in excess of the amount the mother earned, and found that the father had engaged in PA. As a sanction, the court ordered that the father pay $5,000 to cover the mother's attorney's fees and expenses. During the case an evaluator reported that the father had threatened the mother's stepsister, who lived with the mother and their mother, with physical harm if she testified in court on behalf of the mother. After hearing this testimony, the trial court reduced father's visitation. His visitation was reduced again after a hearing in April, 2006. The father appealed.

The case records document that the father claimed that the mother's attorney "and her gang made huge plots, lies, fraud, swindle and deception to take our children from my Father, and me, and gave them to the mother and her Mother, to live with them in their brothel, teach my sisters lying, and the ingratitude to their father." The father's efforts at PA during his time with the children found his daughter telling Sheriff's department personnel that she did not want to go back to her mother because her mother would beat her. Again the court responded and in August 2007 provided that the target parent mother had sole legal and physical custody and ordered that the child be returned to her mother "forthwith." The father then informed the mother he would not be returning the child to her and that he would be seeking a different judge and a different court to hear his complaints. An attorney for the child confirmed that. The trial court asked children's counsel for a report on the status of the involvement of the Department of Children and Family Services (DCFS). Counsel indicted that DCFS had met the parties and determined that the father's allegations against mother for neglect and abuse had no basis.

More evidence in the record indicated that the father acted as executor of the estate of his uncle. The documents also reflected that father disbursed estate assets of $411,479 to unidentified persons who had allegedly submitted "informal claims." At trial the father claimed that he could not recall who the funds were paid to. The court also found that during the course of the action, the father had been improperly diverting income due to him to his relatives, who were supporting him, in order to artificially reduce his income for purposes of support calculations. The court ultimately found that the father engaged in a clear pattern of PA and willfully violated the court's orders in an effort to interfere with and thwart the mother's relationship with and custody of the children. The appellate panel affirmed custody and decision-making authority being solely vested in this target parent mother.

In re Marriage of B., 2011–Iowa

This case documents that the father and mother married in 2000 and divorced in 2010. Under the dissolution decree, the mother received physical custody. For two years, the couple operated under a temporary order that provided for joint physical care. The court found that the father encouraged the children to become involved in the paternal communication difficulties, permitted disrespectful behavior from the girls to their mother, and effectively pressured them to take sides. The father and several of his witnesses admitted that he called the mother demeaning names in front of the children. Indeed, the mother testified that the children came to view these names as normal and also began using them. Father also admitted to making over 300 calls to the mother in a one-month period and hiding tape recorders in the home to monitor her conversations. He followed the mother, tracked the people who came and went from the home as well as her after-work activities, and made unfounded accusations about her personal life. Based on this evidence as well as evidence of physical abuse during the marriage, mother's therapist testified that the mother was a victim of domestic violence and that the father had issues of power and control.

This testimony was corroborated by the testimony of the children's therapist, who stated: "In 20 years that I have been in this–this is probably the most significant case of parent alienation I've ever witnessed." Custody was awarded to the target parent mother and affirmed on appeal.

Target Parent Father

G. v. S., 1988–Missouri

In this matter, the father filed a motion to modify the custody provision of a dissolution decree. The trial court denied the motion, entered a judgment of civil contempt against the father, and awarded the mother a judgment against the father for $2500 in attorney fees and a fee of $1000 to the guardian ad litem. The father appealed and the appellate panel reversed the judgment. The panel noted that the case had a voluminous history. Some sixty motions had been filed since the divorce decree was entered, the majority of which were filed by the mother raising complaints about custody and visitation with the children The evidence, including the mother and stepfather's own testimony, indicated that they held the father in low regard, degraded him in the child's presence, depicted him as an evil person with whom the child should have no contact, and engaged in persistent efforts to destroy the child's natural affection for her father. The mother expressed it as her preference that the child have nothing to do with her father.

The appellate court ruled that this state of facts showing an attempt by one parent to alienate a child from the other parent was a changed condition and could form the basis for a modification of custody. After considering all of the evidence in the record, the appellate court wrote of their firm belief that the trial court erred in not ordering a change of the child's custody from the alienating mother to the target parent father and a similar belief that such a custody change would be in the child's best interest. The court instructed that when a parent who has custody makes disrespectful and abusive statements against the other parent and attempts to wean the children away, the decree can properly be modified and the custody changed. The overwhelming evidence of the daughter's relationship with her mother and stepfather and the hostility by the mother to the father supported a change of custody to the target parent father. The appellate court ruled that costs on appeal were assessed against the alienating mother.

K.B. v. C.M., 1991–New York

This case involved spurious allegations of child sexual abuse and the trial judge's extensive efforts to find the facts. The record reveals that in 1990, four-year-old child M. allegedly told her mother that she had been sexually abused by her father. Mom told a friend, and this friend interviewed M. at home. When the friend called the Department of Social Services (DSS), social worker Sally Conkling investigated. In her third interview with a concerned adult, M. recounted a story about daddy and sexual abuse. Following M.'s story, the DSS social worker referred M. to Bette Malachowski, a master's level psychologist, under contract with them.

Ms. Malachowski testified that the alienating mother seemed to be repeating the story of abuse by rote. When asked what the witness meant by the expression rote, Malachowski testified that the mother had to start from the beginning and repeat the whole story each time. She could not respond to questions without starting from the beginning and completing the entire story. In her interviews with the child, Malachowski noted there was no sex play, and the child repeatedly told her she was making believe. Malachowski went on to testify that, in her judgment, the mother had a vested interest in the outcome of the case. The trial judge took the testimony of the child's pediatrician, who had examined and interviewed the child. The pediatrician testified that the mother brought M. to him for an examination and his physical examination of the child revealed nothing. He testified that the child denied that anything had happened. After collating all of these data, the DSS concluded that the mother's allegation was unfounded.

The alienating mother waited five months and started the whole process up again. This time another worker was assigned who also interviewed M. By the time M. was interviewed by the sixth concerned adult, she had developed a story about an "electric dinkie." Mom found a polygrapher to interact with M. Despite the fact that the polygrapher admitted he had never attempted a validation process with a young child, the "electric dinkie" story seemed to have an impact on him. On cross-examination, the polygrapher stated that he was familiar with the SAID syndrome which describes increased numbers of false allegations, when the factors he admitted to are present. [*See* Chapter 6, "Sexual Abuse Allegations in the Context of Custody and Visitation Disputes."]

The trial judge took the testimony of M.'s pre-school teacher, a probation officer, and a certified social worker in the mental health clinic, none of whom observed any fear of the father by the child. Following a review of a lengthy law guardian report, the trial judge noted that Malachowski conducted numerous interviews with the child and concluded no abuse had taken place. When reading the polygrapher's report, Malachowski testified that the statements the child reportedly made to the polygrapher were "an almost exact verbatim statement to her . . ." from the mother.

The trial judge noted that when asked to provide details, the youngster was either unable to do so or created a scenario for the purposes of the interview. In subsequent interviews a different scenario was presented. Therefore, he found the child's descriptions of sexual activity between herself and her father varied considerably depending upon whether she was talking to this adult interviewer or that adult interviewer. Cutting through it all, the trial judge found that there was no credible testimony to suggest that the child was afraid of her father and in fact the testimony suggested a relaxed and warm relationship. The judge went on to conclude that there was no testimony to suggest that M. had any awareness of her sexuality nor had become involved in any sexual activity. The judge summarized that he had the unique opportunity of observing the demeanor of all the witnesses who appeared before him and concluded that the testimony of the father was more credible than that of the mother. The court agreed that the mother programmed her daughter to accuse the father of sexually abusing the child so that she could obtain sole custody and control or even preclude any contact that the father might have with his daughter. Rather eloquently, the judge concluded: "In the opinion of this Court, any parent that would denigrate the other by casting the false aspersion of child sex abuse and involving the child as an instrument to achieve his or her selfish purpose is not fit to continue in the role of a parent. . . . Like Medea, she is ready to sacrifice her child to accomplish her selfish goal." Custody was changed to the target parent father.

B. v. B., 1993–Louisiana

The parents were married in 1984 and divorced in early 1989. Joint custody was ordered and the mother was named the domiciliary parent. The record documented that the two little boys knew a lot about sexual conduct. Dr. Deborah Myers, a pediatrician, saw the boys when they were four and three years old and talked to them. She said that these children knew a whole lot more about sex than they ought to. Psychologist evaluator, Dr. Lonowski, concluded that the children had been exposed to inappropriate sexual behavior. It appeared to him that the children believed that their father had sexually abused them. Additional evaluator Dr. Simoneaux believed that the children had almost certainly been exposed to sophisticated sexual behavior in some fashion, explaining that children so young could not conceive of the things they knew unless they had been taught about the concept or the act was demonstrated. Dr. Simoneaux concluded that the mother and her current husband were doing whatever they could do to discourage the children's relationship with their father and his family and using the children as pawns in their continuing battle with father. The record reflects that Dr. Simoneaux found that the mother had had almost exclusive control of the children and he felt that her exclusive control, combined with her efforts at removing the father's family from any sphere of influence, posed a risk to the children that was not in their best interests.

The trial judge was faced with a hard decision in this case. He gave a detailed and well-reasoned explanation for his decision said the appellate court. In it, he made several credibility calls. In his written reasons he explained that the problem he was faced with was the damage caused by sexual abuse weighed against the damage caused by emotional abuse and false allegations based on exposure to sexual knowledge. He found that the children had received a great degree of improper sexual knowledge. He did not believe that the allegations of sexual abuse were well-founded. Therefore, he found that the father was not guilty of sexual abuse of the children and that the mother made it all up and planted the notion in the children's heads in order to alienate their father forever.

The reviewing court explained that a parent who will deliberately use such means to further selfish interests is acting in his or her own interests and not in the child's interest. When one parent embarks on a planned course of action to destroy the parent-child relationship between the child and the other parent, it cannot be in the best interest of the child, wrote the appellate panel. This reviewing court went on to write that civilized people abhor and condemn child sexual abuse, but bringing false charges of parental sexual abuse of children, and the deliberate use of the children as pawns to validate the charges, is equally despicable and condemnable. The appellate court went on to note that when that course of action involves planting in a child's mind knowledge of sexual practices that cannot be reasonably associated with sex education, and the inculcation of that knowledge is falsely attributed to child abuse by the other spouse, it takes no expert to realize that the resulting damage to the child is incalculable. The trial court ruled and the appellate court affirmed custody to the target parent father.

W. v. W., 1995–Indiana

In this case, witnesses testified that the mother displayed anger and hostility. They testified that they saw the mother kick the child. The mother then requested that the parties utilize the services of Dr. Lawlor, a clinical psychologist who conducted a custody evaluation. Dr. Lawlor testified at trial that it would be in the best interests of the children for the trial court to award sole custody to the father because the mother was engaging in PAS, which he defined as a series of actions and maneuvers by which she would attempt to exclude the father and to denigrate him in the eyes of the children. Furthermore, a significant portion of the father's evidence revealed that the mother had a volatile temper and that she displayed socially inappropriate behavior. Testimony also revealed concern over the fact that the five-year-old daughter had yet to be fully potty trained while under the mother's primary supervision.

The father testified that the mother was uncooperative and inflexible with respect to his access to the children. He also said that the mother consistently acted in an angry and acrimonious manner toward him in the presence of the children. The father believed that his relationship with the children was becoming increasingly strained and remote as a result of these activities. The mother argued to the appellate court that the trial court committed reversible error in not allowing her ten-year-old alienated son to rebut Dr. Lawlor's allegations that she restricted the children's access to their father, as well as the allegations that the mother kicked him. The trial court and the appellate court took up the issue of having a ten year old to rebut the custody evaluator. Although it may be good policy to exclude some otherwise competent persons, including children, from the adversarial and confrontational setting, reasoned the appellate court, articulation of such a policy should be left to the legislature. The appellate panel reasoned that their rules of evidence clearly indicated that a party in civil litigation is free to call and to obtain the testimony of competent witnesses, and their trial court lacks discretion to accept or reject those witnesses. However, the appellate court reasoned that the error the trial judge committed in precluding the ten-year-old alienated boy from rebutting allegations that the mother kicked him did not mandate reversal. The appellate panel affirmed the trial court's vesting of custody of the children in the target parent father.

B. v. O., 1996–Michigan

Rarely do courts have the benefit of an objective analysis of the work of a proposed expert, but three objective analyses of what Kathleen Faller and her Faller Group actually did (as opposed to what Faller says they do), was accomplished in Michigan. In *B. v. O.,* a specialty panel of the Michigan Court of Appeals was assembled to review Faller and her group's work in a case involving PA-derived allegations of child sexual abuse. The panel was composed of the former Chief Justice of the Michigan Supreme Court, a member of the Court of Appeals nominated by the White House for a Federal judgeship, and a well-respected member of the Michigan trial court. The special panel began a forty-nine-page opinion by explaining that they had undertaken a "painstaking review of the entire record." It is important to note that this objective panel also watched six hours of Faller and her group on videotape.

The Court noted numerous inaccuracies and deficiencies in the Faller Group's work. The court noted with approval the deposition of the then president of the American Psychiatric Association, Ellissa Benedek, which severely criticized Faller's techniques in assessing child sexual abuse. Dr. Benedek testified, after having reviewed a videotaped interview of a child done by Kathleen Faller, that she did not believe the interview met the standards for unbiased interviewing regarding the question whether sexual abuse occurred. Dr. Benedek opined Faller's interview was replete with leading questions, and that Faller engaged in repeated questioning while giving the child rare opportunity to tell her story.

The special panel adopted the findings of two forensic psychologists, Drs. Patricia Wallace and Terence Campbell. They wrote, "We have viewed the taped interviews in their entirety and agree with Campbell's and Wallace's assessment of them." According to their review, this special panel noted that after Dr. Wallace reviewed all of the Faller Group's notes, records and videotapes, she opined: "The younger child was being coached, rehearsed and prepared to tell what the interviewer and defendant . . . want her to say; the adults clapped for the younger child when she said what they wanted her to say; the children were set up verbally several times about what they were going to have to testify to, or what they were going to have to talk to me about; if they wanted the child to say, 'yes', you are right. They would end up with a high voice." Dr. Wallace testified that in her estimation the interviewers both had information or ideas that sex abuse had occurred and that it was the dad who had committed it and that the child should be frightened of or uncomfortable with the father. Dr. Wallace went on to testify that the interviewer undressed the anatomically detailed male doll and fumbled with the penis while the older child was asked leading penis-related questions. The forensic psychologist continued by explaining that the danger in that type of questioning is that it presumes the existence of a fact and the child is unable to separate what is real or true from what is expected at the time. The special panel noted that Dr. Wallace concluded by explaining that in the videotape the Faller Group interviewer brought up the term "finger." Finger had not been used anywhere in the dialogue. The interviewer spontaneously brought up, "Was his finger inside or outside?," so the interviewer showed the child both visually and auditorially what she should say.

The opinion of the special panel went on to cite with approval forensic psychologist Terence Campbell, indicating that after he reviewed all of the Faller Group's notes, records, and videotapes, Dr. Campbell opined that the interviewers asked slanted one-sided questions that were designed to obtain only information that was consistent with the hypothesis that the children had been sexually abused. The interviewers simply went in and began asking questions; they did not ask questions that could obtain information that disconfirmed their expectations. Dr. Campbell opined that under those circumstances the probability of a biased interview soars. Dr. Campbell went on to note that the interviewers' series of repeated questions seemed to suggest that the children did not get it right before and they better change their answers to what this big person expected. The special panel of the court of appeals noted that Campbell explained that the interviewers' questions created imagery in the children's mind. Over time, said Dr. Campbell, what the child imagines and what the child remembers may become confused.

The specially constituted appellate panel independently concluded the work of Kathleen Faller and "the Faller Group" was suggestive, coercive, and untrustworthy. They found that the statements made by the children during the tapes and reported by the therapists were not trustworthy. The panel went on to write that the statements made by the children during the videotaped interviews followed leading and repeated questioning. The panel noted the record and that there was expert testimony by Drs. Campbell and Wallace that the Faller Group's questioning was coercive and suggestive and wrote that their independent review of the tapes led them to the same conclusion. They wrote in their opinion that Drs. Wallace and Campbell testified the alienating mother encouraged certain answers and that her presence would affect the interview, and their independent review was in accord. The panel summarized that when the tapes were viewed in their entirety, it was clear that the interviewers assumed the veracity of the alienating mother and assumed that the abuse had occurred; the children were subjected to repeated questioning until the desired response was obtained. The panel also made clear that their independent review found the alienating mother and a Faller Group interviewer had coached the children about what to tell the judge.

The award of custody to the alienating mother was summarily reversed and the children placed with the target parent father.

K. v. K., 1996–Connecticut

In this case, the record revealed that the mother had a trouble-filled history. Her parents separated. Her father had what she described as a nervous breakdown and later returned to the family. He was an alcoholic who was verbally, physically, and sexually abusive. She described both of her parents as dysfunctional. Her first marriage, when she was 19, was to a man she described as an alcoholic who was sexually and physically abusive. When the marriage in this case began breaking down, the mother's behavior became increasingly bizarre. She began accusing the father of having affairs with other women and of being a homosexual. She described him as a "faggot" and other foul nouns, often in front of the children. In August, 1993, while in a restaurant with the children, the mother told them a man in the restaurant was going to kidnap them.

The record revealed that the next day, the mother asked the father if he was having the police follow her because she saw them everywhere she stopped. The mother also told the children that someone who was making phone calls to her had been killed, because she "could smell the gun smoke in the air." The next morning, the mother told the children that she knew what the father was doing to them. The children cried and denied the mother's claims, but the mother's behavior got worse, and her pressure on the children increased. In spite of the the children's protests, she demanded the father leave the home. Next, the mother brought the children to a deserted theater, where she and the children huddled for the night. The mother's behavior so frightened faculty at her daughter's elementary school that the school called the police and had a restraining order entered. Four days after "gun smoke in the air," an investigative worker for DCFS made an unannounced home visit to the mother. The worker testified that the mother's physical condition worried him, as did the condition of the home. The police arrived, spoke to the family, agreed with the DCFS investigator that the children were in danger from their mother, called an ambulance, and had the mother removed to the psychiatric hospital. She was discharged two weeks later with a diagnosis of psychotic disorder. After she left the hospital, the mother increased her effort to systematically alienate the children from their father.

Reviewing the entire record, the trial court determined that in a calculated series of inappropriate behaviors, the mother manipulated the children and achieved her goal of alienating them from their father. She also gained sympathy as someone who was the victim of a conspiracy. She bothered and annoyed the father, calling him at all hours, and accusing him of having her put away and of taking the children. Nevertheless, the father behaved with dignity and caring throughout the mother's most outrageous period. Custody was changed to the target parent father.

H. v. S., 1997–Indiana

This matter began in 1995 when the mother and father's marriage was dissolved. Two months later, the mother started taking their daughter to Michelle Crane, a child psychologist. The mother made repeated allegations of sexual abuse against the father. During the sessions with Crane, the mother repeatedly indicated that she desired a modification in the child custody arrangement, stating that she suspected the father of sexually abusing their daughter and that he had a long history of "psych" treatment. The child also heard mother repeatedly call the father "Satan" and accuse him of being homosexual. The mother in the presence of the child accused the father of disrupting the child's class and making her cry, told him to go to hell, indicated that he was going to get AIDS, and informed the child that she would need to be decontaminated after the father placed his stocking cap on her head.

Visitation exchanges became troublesome, so the father hired Norman Borders, a private investigator, to accompany him as a witness when he exchanged the child at the mother's residence. The father testified that this was because he believed the mother would attempt to fabricate allegations against him. On one occasion, the mother, father, and private investigator Borders met at a truck stop to exchange the child. Shortly after the exchange, the mother returned to the truck stop, saw P.I. Borders, and began to follow his vehicle. In response, Borders began backing his vehicle towards the mother's car. After blocking the mother's car, Borders drove away. Shortly thereafter, the mother reported the incident to the police, stating that Borders looked like the "Unabomber" and that he could have been a hit man. As a result of this misconduct, the father was forced to obtain a restraining order, seek a change of judge, and prepare to defend against the mother's sexual abuse allegations at trial. The father argued that the mother had engaged in a pattern of PA with the child that was affecting her long-term emotional and psychological needs. In support of these arguments, the father presented the testimony of a child psychologist, who, after reviewing records and reports from CPS, Michelle Crane, and several other counselors, indicated that the mother's comments and allegations against the father were directed at alienating the child from the father and that the mother's behavior endangered the child's emotional and psychological development.

The trial court awarded the father approximately $65,200 in attorney's fees, based on his attorney's efforts in obtaining child support and defending against the mother's baseless claims. The appellate court reasoned that the evidence presented at the modification hearing revealed that immediately after the father and the mother were awarded joint custody of the child, numerous disputes arose. Specifically, the appellate court noted that the mother made repeated allegations of sexual abuse against the father, none of which were substantiated. The appellate panel noted that despite the fact that the trial court attempted to minimize the hostility by restricting the parties' interaction and communication to visitation issues, the animosity escalated to the point that a private investigator and the police were involved in simple exchanges. Additionally, the evidence, as set forth in the trial court's findings of fact indicated that the mother made numerous disparaging comments about, and allegations against, the father in front of the child and others, including comments that the child would have to be decontaminated.

The appellate court affirmed their trial court's determination that mother had engaged in a concerted effort to destroy the child's relationship with the father and awarded sole physical and legal custody of the child to this target parent father. Additionally, the panel affirmed the denial of the mother's visitation for a period of sixty days, followed by two hours of supervised visitation with the child every two weeks for three months. Simply put, the Indiana appellate court upheld the custody change to the target parent father as well as the fines and the finding that the mother was in contempt of court.

Matter of J.F. v. L.F., 1999–New York

The parents in this custody proceeding had a long, difficult history in the courts regarding custody and visitation issues. The difficulties were heard before numerous judges over the course of a decade. The animosity that the mother, the physical custodial parent, harbored for the father did not lessen with time. As predicted by the mental health professionals at the inception of the case, the mother succeeded in causing PA of the children from their father.

The record in this matter reveals that Dr. Herbert Lessow, a board-certified psychiatrist, conducted psychiatric evaluations of the parents and children. He found the father to be normal and testified that the father had insight. He further reported that the mother continued to have a psychiatric diagnosis of moderate-to-severe personality disorder, with borderline, obsessive, and passive-aggressive features. He stated, that the mother had clearly won the war over the children's minds and hearts and the father was generally helpless to offset that. He opined that the children were deeply attached in a symbiotic fashion with their mother. According to this evaluator, the father was painted in a highly derogatory and negative fashion, way out of proportion to any possible deficiencies that he may have had. The doctor opined that this was clearly a borderline mental device within the mother's psychology that was duplicated in the children. Even with expert psychiatric assistance, the overall prognosis for any major change in their attitude would appear to be quite limited at this time, said Lessow.

Dr. Feinberg, a diplomate in psychiatry and neurology, a member of the American Academy of Psychiatry and the Law, and a diplomate of the American College of Forensic Examiners, testified that as he predicted in testimony in 1994, the alienation from the father had become more severe, probably the most severe case of alienation he had personally witnessed in his thirty-three years in child psychiatry. Dr. Feinberg testified that all of the classic signs of alienation were present and had been in place since at least 1991. If the children were allowed to remain with their mother, reasoned the psychiatrist, their paranoia would harden into pathological personality traits as so clearly seen in their mother and her extended family. If the children were placed in their father's custody, reasoned Feinberg, emotional upset and some possible turmoil in the short term may occur. The court next appointed psychologist, Melvin Sinowitz, Ph.D., who concluded in his reports that the PAS was clear and definite with both children. Dr. Sinowitz found that the mother had poisoned the children's childhood. He found that both children used identical language in dismissing the happy times they spent with their father as evidenced in the videotape and picture album as "Kodak moments." The children denied anything positive in their relationship with their father to an unnatural extreme. The court was convinced that the children had been alienated from their father by their mother. Their negative view of their father was out of all proportion to reality. Custody was changed to the target parent father.

P. v. P., 2000–South Dakota

When the parties were initially divorced, a custody evaluation was conducted. After testing the children, interviewing several individuals, and observing the parties with the children, the evaluator recommended that the father have sole custody of the two oldest boys and that father and mother share joint custody of the younger children, with primary physical custody held by the father. The evaluator further recommended that the mother undergo a complete psychological evaluation.

The trial court interviewed one of the children in chambers for twenty-five minutes, with both attorneys present. During this interview, the child expressed a strong preference to live with his mother due to his close relationship with her and his feeling that the mother's boyfriend, whom mother lived with, would provide a safe environment for him. The trial court found that mother was able to provide special attention to this child by spending more time with him and working with him on his learning disability. The trial court determined there was no evidence of the mother exerting influence over the child.

Shortly after the trial court decision that physical custody be changed to the alienating mother, the child met with a certified professional counselor in Sioux Falls. The reviewing appellate panel noted that the report of the counselor reflected that the child was prompted for years by the mother to say he wanted to live with her. The appellate court noted that by 1999, the mother had not completed any of the evaluator's recommendations. The mother referred to the father as "your dumb father"; accused the father of an affair, which destroyed the marriage; and commented that the father might get AIDS from sleeping with his fiancée, which was OK with mother. The reviewing appellate panel noted that given the history of the mother's belittling the father to the children and attempting to influence them, there was little reason to believe that anything had changed since 1994, the date of the last custody evaluation.

Based on the record evidence, the appellate panel determined that their trial court abused its discretion in awarding physical custody to the alienating mother. The panel reminded their trial judge that the predominant concern is the child's best interest and considering the mother's history of attempting to alienate the child from the father and her expression of anger for father to the child, the panel was convinced that the father was the parent best equipped to handle the child's temporal, mental, and moral welfare. The appellate panel held that the trial court was clearly wrong, abused its discretion, and reversed the custody decision; custody to target parent father.

In re Disciplinary Proceedings Against Nichols, 2002–Wisconsin

Wisconsin attorney David Nichols represented the alienating mother of a child that was the focus of a custody and placement dispute. A psychologist testified on behalf of the child's father that he saw evidence of "emotional incest" and PAS attributable to attorney Nichols' client. Attorney Nichols subsequently filed an action on behalf of the mother against the psychologist and his medical malpractice insurer, claiming that the psychologist's opinions were negligent and defamatory.

The record reveals that attorney Nichols was admitted to practice law in Wisconsin in 1981. In 1993 he consented to a public reprimand imposed by the Board of Attorneys Professional Responsibility for misconduct. In 1995 his license was suspended for sixty days as discipline for professional misconduct. His license was again suspended in 2000. The complaint litigated in this matter involved two cases filed by the board alleging misconduct. In the psychologist lawsuit, summary judgment in the defendant's favor was granted. The circuit court concluded that the suit was frivolous. When dismissing the lawsuit the circuit court stated that a motivation was to send a chilling message to the psychologist to pull out of his patient-doctor relationship with the father and thus be unavailable to provide opinions in court. The judge in charge of the psychologist lawsuit reasoned that that was a misuse of the court system. The judge opined that there was no basis in fact or a reasonable extension of any law that could provide for the kind of harassing and frivolous suit that attorney Nichols filed on behalf of the mother. In 1999 the Court of Appeals issued an order upholding the circuit court's finding of frivolousness. The case report simply closes with the statement that "...the license of David L. Nichols to practice law in Wisconsin shall remain suspended until further order of the court. . . ."

S. v. S., 2004–Vermont

In this case the father and mother divorced in 1998. At the time of their divorce, they agreed that the mother would have sole parental rights and responsibilities over the parties' two children. They also agreed that the father would have contact with the children every other weekend, two weeks in the summer, and shared holidays.

The record documents that a year later the father filed a motion to modify the parties' parental rights and responsibilities. Although the court denied the motion, it found that the mother had been engaging in a pattern of behavior that had frustrated the father's ability to have parent-child contact. The court found that the mother's negative behavior had begun to have an adverse impact on the children. The trial court concluded that the mother had substantially interfered with the father's relationship with the children. The trial court concluded that it was not in the children's best interests to transfer custody to father but warned the mother, however, that it viewed the situation as extremely serious and that if the mother persisted in her negative behavior, the court would have no choice but to change custody.

Problems between the mother and father continued, and both parties filed numerous motions with the court. In 2001, the father again moved to modify the parties parental rights and responsibilities, complaining that the mother continued to interfere with his relationship with the children. Again, the court denied the father's motion. A hearing on the pending motions was held in April 2003, and both parties appeared without attorneys. Based on the evidence presented, the court found it crystal clear that the mother had intentionally and repeatedly sabotaged the father's ability to have contact with the children. She had also intentionally attempted to interfere with the father's ability to obtain school information and to participate in their religious upbringing. The court found the mother's demeanor in court to be snide and disrespectful to both father and the court and stated that mother clearly had a deep level of hostility that had not receded over the five years since the parties' divorce. The court found that mother was unable to place the children's needs ahead of her own anger and vindictiveness. In contrast to mother, the court found that father had maintained a calm and reasonable demeanor in court and with the children, in spite of the mother's mistreatment of him and his frustration with being unable to contact the children. The court concluded that the father showed an understanding of the damage that this situation was inflicting on the children and an appropriate concern for their well-being.

The court explained that the mother had been warned that her ongoing negative behavior was likely to lead to a loss of custody, and the court found that, despite these warnings, her improper behavior continued and in fact had escalated. The court concluded that the best interests of the children required that they be removed from her environment. When the alienated mother appealed the change of custody order, the appellate panel wrote that they recognized that obstruction of visitation and attempts at PA were not in a child's best interests, and they may form the basis for a change in custody. They rejected the alienating mother's assertion that the family court's findings as to the mother's interference with the father's contact were not supported by the evidence or were erroneous. The record provides support for each, reasoned the appellate court as the change of custody to the target parent father was upheld.

H. v. H., 2010–Arkansas

This appellate case arose from a long and contentious series of domestic battles conducted in and out of the courtroom after the parties ended their twenty-year marriage. According to the appellate review panel in 2010, the parties' two children were trapped in the no-man's-land of the parties' internecine struggles. The appellate panel reviewed the record in which psychiatrist Bradley Dine testified. Dr. Dine opined that the mother was attempting to align the children against the father and trying to alienate the children from him. He expressed concern about the mother's not getting counseling to help her deal with her history of childhood sexual abuse. He opined that her experience seemed to have made her hypersensitive about the possibility of molestation involving their daughter.

When questioned at the hearing, the mother declared that she thought the father was abusive and was looting the children's trust. The record indicates that she thought that the father was engaging in sexually perverse conduct with their daughter despite some half-hearted statements to the contrary, such as she "hoped" it was not so. She also confirmed that her personal assistant Jeanne Nutter had told the daughter about Jeanne's being molested as a child and asked the daughter if she had been inappropriately touched by the father. Jeanne Nutter testified about the events surrounding her disclosure to the daughter that she had been sexually molested as a fourteen-year-old. Nutter claimed she shared that story because the child did not want to visit her father that day. Nutter admitted that she previously made defamatory remarks about the father, which resulted in the father receiving a $31,000 settlement when he threatened to sue.

The attorney for the children opined that, based almost exclusively on the testimony of mother, the children would be better served by being placed in their father's custody. Conversely, he found the father to be mature and thoughtful as it related to the custody of the children. The trial judge supported her decision with more than thirty-five pages of oral findings. Based on the child's testimony that she would do anything to live with her mother, including making false accusations that her father had inappropriately touched her, the trial judge found that the mother had caused irreparable damage to the relationship between the child and her father. The reviewing appellate court held that contrary to the mother's assertion, when a trial court finds a custodial parent is causig PA, it is not necessary that he or she complete the process before the trial court is justified in changing custody. The result: custody of both children summarily changed to target parent father.

L.R. v. T.R., 2010–New York

State Supreme Court Justice Robert A. Ross led a movement to change New York's matrimonial system. In *L. R. v. T. R.,* Justice Ross held hearings over the course of twenty-three days into a celebrated custody battle. In this case, Justice Ross faced a mother described as "a vengeful roadblock, the barbed wire standing in the way of her two daughters and their desperate dad" according to the New York press. On the other side of the trauma was the father, an alienated fifty-two-year-old marketing executive. In months of hearings consuming over $200,000 in fees and costs, the story of mother's behavior unfolded. The court records documented that the mother intentionally scheduled one of their children's birthday party on a Sunday afternoon during the father's weekend visitation and then refused to permit the father to attend. This alienating mother threatened to cancel the child's party and warned her that her sister too, would be punished "big time" for wanting to spend time with her father. When the mother completed the children's registration cards for their schools she wrote that the father was not authorized to take them: "I have custody. Please call me." She wrote to school personnel demanding that they restrict their conversations with the children's father as she was "solely responsible" for academic progress and emotional wellbeing. The alienating mother identified her new husband as the children's parent/guardian.

Justice Ross carefully analyzed the extensive testimony and noted that the record documented that there were countless times when the mother deliberately scheduled theater tickets, family events, and social activities for the girls during their father's visitation, and he was compelled to consent or risk disappointing the girls. The judge found that these occurrences continued even during the time span of proceedings before the court. He continued that the mother testified that it was the two girls who refused to see their father because they were angry with the "choices" he had made on their behalf. The "choices," noted Justice Ross, were those that the mother had forced the father into after the fact. The judge took special note that the two girls parroted their mother's demands and on several occasions they actually read from a script during dinners at their father's they were allowed to attend. The judge reasoned that the fact that the children were as angry as they were with the father demonstrated that the mother's efforts to alienate the children and their father were effective. The mother's contention before the court was that she had no involvement in the children's issues, but this was belied by the fact that the children had intimate knowledge of their mother's position on all of the issues.

This New York trial judge was quite taken by the way the mother sabotaged the family holidays, saying that he observed the mother smirk in the courtroom as the father emotionally related how he was deprived of spending Hanukkah with his children and was relegated to lighting a menorah and watching his daughters open their grandparents' presents in the back of his truck at the base of mother's driveway on a December evening. The court found the proofs so compelling, he found that they went past the usual clear and convincing standard and rose to proofs beyond a reasonable doubt. He was especially troubled that this alienating mother frequently disparaged the father in the presence of the children, calling him a deadbeat, loser, scumbag, and f––––g asshole. On one particular occasion, while holding the girls in her arms, the mother said to the father "We all hope you die from cancer." The record revealed that the mother's conduct involved accusations of sexual abuse as well. She falsely accused the father of sexual misconduct shortly after the father moved to his new home, and the children's friends were enjoying play dates there. The record documents that the mother pursued a campaign to report the father to CPS. To facilitate this, she spoke with a psychologist at the school a child attended, advised the children's pediatrician that the father inappropriately touched one of the girls, and also told her story to numerous other professionals and family friends. The record documents that after a thorough investigation, CPS found the entire allegation to be baseless. The court explained that by making such allegations, the mother needlessly subjected the child to an investigation, placing her own interests above those of the child.

Described as an "an extraordinary supervising judge," Justice Ross won numerous awards including a Memorial Tribute from the Nassau County Bar Association Matrimonial Law Committee. His findings of law were a veritable template for judges in the United States. In brief, this is what he did:

1. He explicitly and in great detail explained the court's jurisdiction in custody cases and the various mechanisms available for enforcement of the court's orders in these matters.
2. He explained in detail the court's powers to maintain jurisdiction in postjudgment custody cases in contradiction to arguments of *res judicata.*
3. He outlined statutes and cases that state, "Visitation is a joint right of the noncustodial parent and of the child."
4. He outlined how a court must determine what is "in the best interests of the child" in custody cases and laid out the standards in these cases.
5. He cited with specificity cases that have found that parental alienation is *not* in the best interests of the child and how it amounts to custodial interference, how it is a pernicious violation of courtorders in these cases and a direct violation of the target parent's rights.
6. He explained the resultant court procedures in his jurisdiction and specifically pointed out how it is in the best interests of the child that there be a prompt evidentiary hearing to determine appropriate custody/visitation time and any remedial issues that may be necessary to insure that the court's orders be followed and the target parent's rights are restored.
7. He explained the appropriate procedure for determining if criminal contempt charges are appropriate, where that court power derives from, what the burden of proof is, and how it is met.
8. He explained how and why the target parent father reached his burden of proof.

9. He delivered the factual findings with very specific details and specifically included his impressions and observations of the alienator mother both during her own testimony and the testimony of the target parent father. He included with painstaking detail, many instances of the alienator's egregious behavior and the effects on both the target parent and the children.
10. He explained exactly what remedies in civil contempt, criminal contempt, criminal sanction via the state's law prohibiting custodial/visitation interference, and remedies in tort for money damages there were.
11. He summarized from precedent and the record before him, reiterating the court's role in custody hearings, specifically in cases of parental alienation, and again explained why and how the court maintains jurisdiction in in the children's best interests.
12. Justice Ross concluded by setting up a hearing to determine the alienating mother's responsibility for the hundreds of thousands of dollars in costs and attorney fees then sentenced mother to twelve days in jail.

E. v. E., 2011–Connecticut

When the court temporarily gave sole custody to the father on December 1, 2010, the court found that the mother had made baseless complaints to DCFS, was making efforts to cause the child to hate her father, and was manipulating the child for the express purpose of creating evidence that would result in limiting the father's access to his daughter. The court concluded that mother was causing emotional harm to her daughter. The record substantiates the mother's lengthy pattern of contemptuous conduct, the expenses and financial waste caused by the mother, the substantial financial drain on the resources of the father and the guardian ad litem caused by the mother, and the pattern of PA with prior false reports of abuse and/or neglect to governmental entities.

Because of the mother's pattern and practice of interfering with the father's relationship with the child, her refusal to communicate appropriately with the child or the father, and her refusal to foster or support a relationship between the child and the father, the court ordered that sole physical and legal custody of the child was vested in the target parent father. The court went on to order that the mother could only move for modification of the physical and legal custody arrangements once she had completed all additional coparenting classes and/or training recommended by her therapist. The focus of the therapy had to be on the acceptance of responsibility for the PA she committed; how to support a positive, nurturing relationship between the father and the child; and any treatment necessary to address the mother's mental health issues.

W. v. W., 2011–Connecticut

In this case, even though parenting plans called for joint custody, it became clear that there were serious problems regarding custody issues. The plan named David Israel, a psychologist, as the therapist for the family, expanding his prior role of coparenting counselor. The record also reflects that the mother was to begin treatment with a psychiatrist. The treatment was expected to include medication as well as therapy.

The testimony of the majority of professionals involved with this family was that the child had been alienated from his father and that alienation was in the moderate to severe range. The professionals offered that the boy perceived his father through his mother's eyes, which created a negative reaction in the boy that he could not articulate. The guardian ad litem characterized the child as the "foot soldier" in the parental dispute during her testimony. The court found the testimony of the child's therapist Dr. Israel, Dr. Horowitz, and the guardian ad litem to be persuasive and convincing. Dr. Israel testified that after forty sessions working with the father and son toward reunification, he could not find one reason to substantiate the child's fear of his father, which was expressed in a very charged and emotional manner. Dr. Mayer, the boy's therapist for a good part of 2007, testified that he could not find a cause for the problems between the father and son. The professionals in this case credited the father with an eagerness to learn and to improve as a parent. Dr. Israel testified that he was amazed by the patience and restraint the father showed in their three-way sessions.

After carefully reviewing all of the evidence entered during the trial, including the testimony of the many witnesses presented by both sides, the court found that the mother had an unhealthy and negative influence on the child's perception of his father. The court found that this had endangered the father-son relationship and placed the mental health of the child at risk. For these reasons, sole legal custody of the minor child was changed to the target parent father.

PART TWO
SELECTED CASES FROM CANADA

Target Parent Mother

R. v. K., 1991–Ontario

This matter involved a severe case of PA. The mother was to have custody of all three children and the court provided specific access for the father. The father then moved next door to the mother, and his conduct made it impossible for the mother and children to continue to reside in that area. Shortly thereafter, the father was charged by the police with threatening harm to the mother and was required to undergo mandatory psychiatric counseling. The court record indicated that the father was a fanatic and obsessed with his hatred of the mother to the point of being oblivious of its detrimental effects on his children. The court determined that the father was not consciously aware of his brainwashing and had no insight into its consequences. The court record described the father as consumed with rage and vengeance against the mother, possibly for having been abandoned by her. The court determined that the father continued to use one child as his surrogate to undermine the minds of the two other children and the affection that they otherwise would have had for their mother. An evaluator recommended that there be no contact, and the court vested custody in the target parent mother.

O. (S.) v. O. (S.C.), 1999–New Brunswick

The parties in this case were married in Ontario in 1988. They separated in 1998. The mother left the children in the care of the father, went to Toronto for work, and lived there with her sister. The record indicates that the mother borrowed $10,000 from her mother and sent it home to pay family bills. This was, in effect, her mother's life savings and only a little bit was paid back at the time of the court hearing. The money that the mother earned was also sent back to the father to meet their living expenses. At that time, the father was working on his General Education Development test. In 1997, when he was visiting in Toronto, the mother said she had a week's vacation and wanted to return to New Brunswick because she missed the children. The father made a terrible scene when he found her back at the family home. The record also indicates that the mother had been involved in a car accident in 1997 and had suffered personal injuries. The father compelled her to settle her claim for $10,000 against the advice of her lawyer, and in court proceedings, he admitted taking the money. The father then told the mother "I'm prepared to divorce you and you've got 48 hours to change my mind."

Soon thereafter the mother discovered a tape recorder in the home. The father admitted he had been taping her. By that time, the father was involving the children in his struggle against the mother and the court determined this resulted in confusion, distress, and a general malaise in the children, which greatly increased their stress. The court relied on the affidavit of the psychologist assessor, which stated in part that the children were suffering from PA. The assessor psychologist defined PA as an emotional disturbance whereby the children were preoccupied by the depreciation and criticism by their father of their mother.

PA, said the psychologist in 1998, was a form of mental abuse that would affect not only the children's relationship with their mother but also all spheres of their lives: personal, social, and educational. The psychologist also told the court that the mother had been psychologically abused by the father for several years. The psychologist told the court that psychological abuse was a means of controlling women by threatening them and the people who are dear to them. It can take various forms, said the psychologist, such as harassment, threats of suicide, verbal attacks that humiliate them or make them feel insecure, constant criticism, unfair accusations, isolation from friends, and forcible participation in degrading acts. The psychologist also told the court that the children were in a constant state of confusion. He said the children were receiving mixed messages and a barrage of negative comments about their mother. The psychologist assessor went on to say that the children exhibited aggressive behavior and would often refuse to take instructions from their mother. They challenged her authority and it was extremely difficult for her to parent them. The record documented that the father, on the other hand, did nothing to assist the mother and kept up his efforts to make things as difficult as possible for her. The court ordered custody to the target parent mother and suspended father's access.

S. v. S., 2002–Manitoba

In this case, the father told the court he should be the primary caregiver because as a farmer he could spend more time with the children than could the mother and could offer them a farm life, which both children enjoyed. The record documents that the father was never able to admit that the situation he offered the children was anything short of perfection. After a lengthy court hearing the court opined that the father cooperated only if he got his way. The record also documents that the father had problems dealing with anger and conflict.

The court opined that credibility plays an important role in the determination of any custody issue and, at that point, the court had considerable trouble accepting anything the father said as true when it conflicted with the evidence of the mother or her witnesses. The court determined that it was clear on the evidence that the custodial/access arrangement that existed at the time resulted in almost unbearable stress and conflict for the children and those around them and would ultimately lead to the children's alienation from their mother. The court opined that the sad state of affairs was due solely to the father, who had gone to considerable lengths to undermine the smooth working of the parenting arrangement and whose hatred of the mother poisoned any chance of stress-free time sharing of the children's lives. The court concluded that the best interests of the children called for the target parent mother to have sole custody of the children and to be the sole decision-maker for them. The father's access to the children was dramatically reduced.

R. (F.D.) v. P. (M.D.), 2004–Alberta

In this matter, the parents moved in together in 1993 and had baby boy together in 1996. The mother became the primary caregiver for the child but under the stress of the relationship suffered a mental breakdown in 2001. She was tentatively diagnosed as having a bipolar disorder, and the couple separated shortly thereafter. The father sought sole custody of the son and interim sole custody was awarded to him. The record reveals that the father was surprised and not happy that the mother was released from the hospital. A review of the hospital record indicated that the mother had suffered a brief psychotic episode of uncertain origin that had substantially subsided by the time she left the hospital. Within weeks she was asymptomatic. The court noted that the shadow of this illness dogged the mother for the next three and one-half years and was the primary reason that her son had only supervised access with her. The father was able to move with their son to Saskatchewan without court order and to keep the boy away from the mother. The court record documents that bipolar disorder was ruled out but that the father's position with respect to the mother's illness was ignorance or at worst, wrote the judge, cruelty.

The court record documented that the mother had two adult daughters from a previous marriage, both of whom were well-educated, one as a nurse and one as a teacher. Both had been very supportive of their mother through the ordeal that culminated in these court proceedings. The record also documented that as soon as father was granted interim sole custody he alleged sexual interference by the mother with their son. The son told a psychologist that his mother came into his bedroom and touched his crotch for several seconds until he asked her to stop. This caused the court to suspend all access for mother.

As can be seen from the court record, the son was effectively deprived of his mother except for supervised visits every two weeks for three years after these events and then entirely for eight months without reason. The court opined that this was a nightmare of Orwellian proportions for the mother and closely examined the questions involved in the father's allegations of sexual improprieties. The court simply found that it did not believe that the mother did what was alleged. Rather, hearing all of the evidence, the court found that the father could not understand the mother's illness and reacted with a fear that became malice to the point that what was an innocent childhood moment became a tool to further distance the child from his mother. The court went on to find that there was other objective evidence to support the conclusion that the father's attitude towards the mother and his sense of ownership of the child was a negative with respect to future access. The court found that the evidence at trial painted a graphic picture of the three and one half years in the lives of the son and his parents. The court saw a pattern of actions by the father to cast off his former spouse in the middle of a mental health crisis and take the opportunity to remove their son from her by creating emotional distance through imposing his pejorative views of the illness on the son. The court concluded that it was in the child's best interests that he reside with the target parent mother in Calgary.

T. v. T., 2006–Ontario

This was a "toxic grandmother" case. Things got out of hand when the mother and father argued over a picture that the father had taken. The mother claimed that the father assaulted her. The daughter witnessed at least part of the altercation, but fortunately the other children did not. The mother called the police and after interviewing both parents and the daughter, the police took the father and charged him with assault. One of the conditions of his bail was that he not have any contact with the mother. Upon release, the father went to the home of his sister and did not return to the matrimonial home. When the son and daughter returned to their mother after an overnight with their father, the son yelled and swore at his mother saying, "You're a terrible parent. You lied. Drop the charges. Dad said you lied." The daughter cried and said, "You ruined my life. Dad told me he can't come to my Bat Mitzvah and it's your fault." Mother described both children as "out of control."

The court materials reveal that the mother was quickly cut out of her older children's lives. The father's mother replaced the children's mother as the primary caregiver. During court proceedings, the mother expressed concerns about the impact of the father's mother on her children and on their relationship. The record made clear that although there was a court order that the children could not be with either of their grandmothers when they were together, there was no evidence of concern with respect to them being with their maternal grandmother. During court proceedings, the father presented his mother as a warm and loving mother and grandmother. However, the record reveals that their rabbi reported that the father had spoken to him many times in the past about how difficult his mother was. The rabbi described the relationship between the father and his mother as one that was fraught with anxieties and testified that the father had described his mother to him as "toxic."

The record reveals that the court's assessor, Dr. Goldstein, had been a psychiatrist for forty years. He had conducted an estimated 500 custody and access assessments since 1968. The record indicated that Dr. Goldstein described the environment in the father's household as toxic and felt that the situation needed to be changed urgently. He likened the situation of the children to prisoners of war in that their identities had been taken away from them and their minds worked on. He called it the ultimate in child abuse. Dr. Goldstein acknowledged in his testimony that his terminology was extreme but explained that this was because he felt that the situation was extreme. In Dr. Goldstein's opinion, this was not so much a struggle between father and mother but between father/grandmother and mother. The result: custody to target parent mother.

L. (R.A.) v. R. (R.D.), 2007–Alberta

This matter documents a sad case of manipulation and prostitution. In this case, the parties married in 1987 and separated in 1997. They had one child, a daughter age thirteen at the time of the trial. In the same year, father had another child, a son, with a girlfriend, and this extramarital relationship was the reason for the marriage breakdown. The record reveals that the father's girlfriend moved into the matrimonial home after the mother left but had since moved out with her child. The mother brought an action seeking sole custody of her daughter with no access for the father because she claimed the father was trying to alienate the child from her.

The court record documents that the father had an alternative sexual lifestyle and attended swingers clubs and participated in group sex. The record also reveals that the father had convinced his girlfriend to engage in prostitution in order to make money and set up a web site to promote it. The father's testimony demonstrated that he considered prostitution a legitimate career for a loved one, and the mother worried that this thinking could affect their teenage daughter. At the trial on the target mother's petition, the testimony of the father's girlfriend during and after the parties' separation was taken. Ms. V.H. testified that she lived with the father and the children for four years. She testified that she witnessed firsthand the relationship between the mother's child and the father. She also had extensive knowledge of what the father intended, planned, and did over the years they were together. The court determined that she was uniquely placed to give evidence concerning the father's strategic objectives. The record also reveals that much of V.H.'s testimony directly corroborated the mother's testimony. Her evidence provided part of the factual foundation for the mother's fear that the father had been alienating the child against her.

In part, the evidence of V.H. was that the father was manipulative and controlling, gave priority to his own wants, and would say or do whatever he believed was required to obtain his desired end. Once he decided upon a course of action, she testified, he would work on her to enlist her participation and support to accomplish it. The trial judge expressed great concern that V.H. was engaged in prostitution when she lived with the father. V.H. testified and the court accepted, that it was the father who convinced V.H. that she should engage in Internet-based prostitution. He told her that they needed the money and that having other men find her sexually attractive would increase her self-esteem. Her evidence was that he worked to attempt to secure her agreement over a period of time, and she described the manner in which he set up the web site to solicit sex for her. He would then make comments on her web site about the nature and quality of her services. He would post comments using various pseudonyms as part of a strategy to create interest in her and build her business. Some of these posted comments were in evidence. The father claimed this was entirely her idea and she set up the web site herself. However, the court found that it was the father who was the computer expert. The court noted that this was the same computer that was available to the child. Consequently the court found that the father established the web site, posted messages under a graphic pseudonym, and induced V.H. to prostitution and benefitted from it.

The court-appointed assessor, Dr. Edwards, was deeply concerned with the father's behavior. The doctor reported that he was concerned about the degree and extent of the father's disturbed behavior, hostility, negativity, criticality, self-righteousness, lack of insight and manipulativeness. The assessor went on to opine that, in addition, the father was oblivious to his impact on others, was over-involved with the child, and had endless hostility toward the mother. Dr. Edwards thought that in all likelihood the father was personality disordered, and he was surprised by the level of chronic anger demonstrated by him. Dr. Edwards found that the father saw himself as the savior and advocate for the child and that that was dangerous and self-deluding.

The court found that the circumstances were very troubling indeed. The father's persuasiveness and persistence, opined the court, convinced a bright and articulate adult woman to engage in sex with strangers for money. The court found the father's actions demonstrated he was prepared to use his longtime girlfriend as a means to his end and that type of thinking could affect his teenage daughter. The result: custody to target parent mother, father's access suspended.

S. (C.) v. S. (M.), 2007–Ontario

This case involved the Canadian group Court Watch and Justice Craig Perkins of the Ontario Superior Court. By January 2004, the situation in the mother's home had deteriorated seriously. The second child had become increasingly hostile to the mother and called the Children's Aid Society (CAS) to lodge a complaint about the mother, saying that mother was constantly badmouthing the father and driving while intoxicated. The CAS investigated but did not intervene.

The court noted that the father involved Canada Court Watch Project in his cause. The record documented that Court Watch is a lobby group whose stated aims include bringing "an end to the needless injustices being perpetrated against many innocent children and families by institutions such as our family court system and branches of the Children's Aid Society." Much information about the family and various professionals associated with it was posted on the Court Watch web site. Two representatives of Court Watch testified at the trial.

The record documents that the national chairman of the Canada Court Watch Project (and of the National Association for Public and Private Accountability and of the Family Justice Review Committee) was Dorian Baxter, often referred to in testimony and on the Court Watch web site as "The Archbishop Dorian Baxter." Court records document that Baxter was an Elvis Presley impersonator and ordained clergyman. He was responsible for the content of the Court Watch web site, approving or at least aware of what goes on the site, although he was not personally the author of the content. Court Watch operated a "Family Justice Review Committee" that it said was basically like a jury system: a group of people called together to review documents or circumstances of a case to see if a complaint is justified or if action should be taken. The court record documented that Court Watch held itself out as a resource to help parents and families who were not satisfied with the performance of the justice system or the CAS.

In this case, the judge opined that Court Watch was a haven, if not a magnet, for disgruntled parties, whether or not their dissatisfaction was justified and whether or not there were any grounds for complaint against the system or the institutions involved. The judge noted that in this case, Court Watch took the children's very personal stories and published them for the entire world to see and hear. Court Watch helped the third child run away from the lawful care of CAS. Here, opined the court, Court Watch and its representatives set themselves up as investigator, prosecutor, judge, jury and executioner concerning the family justice and child protection system involving this specific family. As the court explained, however, they had no training, no legal mandate, and no standing on behalf of the public to do so.

The court noted that the principal actor in the Court Watch organization involved in this case appeared to be Vernon Beck. Mr. Black was a semiretired heating and air conditioning consultant by training and occupation. Court testimony verified that Mr. Black volunteered his time to Court Watch as an investigative reporter, mediator, advocate for children and families, interviewer, recorder and adviser of children, letter writer, affidavit drafter, and web site text writer. He had no formal training or instruction in any of these fields and was self-taught. He was the Court Watch point of contact for the father and then the children.

The court went on to write that Vernon Beck interviewed the youngest child in this case and made a videotape of what the child had to say. Court Watch helped the children in this case with some of the many letters they wrote to therapists, politicians, and other persons in authority. Court materials documented that another service offered by Court Watch was preparing affidavits for children. The judge noted that the "template affidavit" on the Court Watch web site was a sample or model for other children to use. The court noted that this template included an accusation that the mother called the police in order to have the child apprehended and forced to go with them, so as to "force me out of my dad's house and into foster care as part of her campaign to make my life and my dad's life as difficult as possible." It further accused CAS workers of threatening and coercing the child in an attempt to force the child to return to live with the abusive mother. The judge noted that the template affidavit carried on for some twelve pages with a litany of complaints and accusations against the mother, the CAS and its workers, the police, the foster home, the lawyer appointed for the child, and the presiding judge at a hearing the child attended. Justice Perkins wrote that the template complains about unlicensed social workers being employed by the CAS and went on to note that this was the kind of help in family and child protection cases that Court Watch had to offer.

The court opinion informs that a month after the court's decision in this case was released, the Justice himself was added to the site in an article dated December 20, 2006. The court found that the story quoted members of the family, including the children, and "many of their friends and neighbors in the community, including professionals," all of whom went unnamed. Justice Perkins went on to note that the language in the story was extreme and monumentally one sided. The various people who had been involved in this family's troubles and in the case were painted as evildoers.

Records in the case document that the father arranged for a psychologist, Dr. Marty McKay of Toronto, to perform a psychological assessment of the youngest child while the child was in hiding from the CAS in 2004. Dr. McKay was identified by a witness as being on an advisory body to Court Watch. The father said he found Dr. McKay through Court Watch and, one afternoon in his testimony at trial, said he took the child to her. The next morning, he said he did not take the child, he merely arranged for the assessment and the child arranged for a ride to get there. Dr. McKay did not testify at the trial. Curiously, her report was offered by the mother, not the father, and not because she adopted it. Rather, the point was to show that the father, Court Watch, and Dr. McKay were involved together in frustrating the court order that placed the child in the care of the CAS. Dr. McKay's assessment took place without the knowledge or permission of the CAS or for that matter the mother who held joint custodial rights with the father, before CAS intervention.

Court records document that there were many incidents reported by the mother and other witnesses of explosive, disproportionate anger by the father that far exceeded any evidence of irrational behavior by the mother from the father and his witnesses. The father's anger went beyond mere flashes. The woman the father lived with testified about hearing the father tell two of his children to go and pour acid on a neighbor's prized flower garden, which they proceeded to do. This act was done in retaliation for some slight to the father. Court testimony documented that father supplied the acid. The father denied, minimized, deflected, and explained away all incidents of violence. As to the involvement of the siblings, the court opined that PAS children were recruited by the alienating parent and alienated siblings to the alienating parent's cause. In this case, the then twelve-year-old child was recruited by the second child, who actually gave instructions in writing on what to do in order to cause trouble for the mother. This same child later engaged in a letter writing campaign with the help of Court Watch. According to court materials, this was done at the father's instigation, and the second child became a hero to the father's and Court Watch's cause.

Justice Perkins went on to write that he found the mother to be a good historian. Her version of events was usually borne out by documentation or other witnesses' testimony. When confronted with unfavorable or unpleasant aspects of her own behavior, by her own lawyer or the father's, she conceded her errors and several times apologized for her bad judgment. In vesting custody in this target parent mother, Justice Perkins wrote that given the history and actions by the father in this case and given his proclivity to disobey the various court orders and to acquiesce in the three oldest children's disobedience of court orders, there was a need to bolster the order for no access with some fairly detailed restraints on the father. As to Court Watch, Justice Perkins offered that his comments about them and their members were made because they were active participants in events that helped shape the outcome of the case. They helped the father drive the wedge in further between the two camps–the father and the three oldest children versus the mother–wrote the judge. They made the prospect of any relationship between the camps more remote than ever. Their intervention helped solidify the three oldest children's alienation from their mother and increased the risk of harm to their sibling if contact were to be restored.

L. (J.K.) v. S. (N.C.), 2008–Ontario

This case involved a trumped-up arrest. The parties married in 1982, their son was born in 1994, and they separated in March 2005 when a physical altercation broke out between them in the presence of the child.

During the assault, the child was urged to call 911, and the police came to the scene. The mother was charged with assault and ultimately found not guilty after a trial at which her son was called to testify against her. From the time of her arrest, the mother was required to live outside the matrimonial home. After the incident, the father removed all pictures of the mother from the family's home.

The court appointed assessor Dr. George Awad to complete an assessment of the family for the court. In its opinion, the court noted that it carefully considered Dr. Awad's report and opined that the report was thorough, frank, and exceptionally well-written. Dr. Awad found that the child was alienated from his mother, and the doctor noted that the father himself had no relationship with his own mother or his brother. The assessor noted that the father's closest relationship was to his father and his sister. In the evaluation process, the father was described as an enraged man. Dr. Awad found that the father had a hateful attitude towards the target parent mother and towards his own mother. In short, the father had a hatred for women. The assessor determined that from the history given by the father, the mother was the only adult heterosexual relationship the father had experienced. Dr. Awad concluded that the father actively worked at alienating the boy from his mother and recommended the removal of the child from the father's custody.

Court records document that Dr. Richard Warshak testified that he worked with a team in remedying situations in which a child was in conflict with a parent. He testified that the associates with whom he worked were Dr. Randy Rand and Dr. Deirdre Rand, who were both qualified psychologists. The "Family Workshop for Alienated Children," as described by Dr. Warshak, was a structured, standardized, and highly specialized program developed by Dr. Randy Rand to assist families in which children have become so alienated from one parent and other relatives that they either refuse contact with the alienated parent or show extreme reluctance to spend time with that parent.

After hearing the proofs and the extent of the alienation, the court vested custody in the target parent mother and ordered that she at her discretion, utilize the services of Dr. Richard Warshak to enable a transition of least conflict for the child. The court went on to order that if the mother chose to engage Dr. Warshak's services, the mother, the father, and the child must participate in Dr. Warshak's follow-up counseling

P. v. P., 2008–Saskatchewan

This case involved what the experts called an obsessed alienator. The father and mother were married in 1990 and separated in 2005. They had two children who were fifteen and thirteen years old at the time of trial. The court records document that the mother was somewhat timid and withdrawn, especially when faced with an aggressive individual like the father in this case. Following their separation the possessive and domineering father moved onto the same block on the same street as the mother and, as the court noted, increased his hold on the children. The court opined that the father used the children as pawns to deliver notes, demanding that the mother reconcile with him or that she was an unfit mother and a prostitute.

According to testimony that was not refuted, the father only worked for three years in the previous twenty. He spent much of his time during this period enjoying life on a small patch of land outside of town. His only source of income appeared to have been Workers' Compensation and social benefits.

The court found that in spite of court orders and the Children's Voices Report to the contrary, the father continued to facilitate the development of PA of the mother by her children. The court had no doubt that the children were well-aware of the wrath of their father if they were to suggest any desire for visitation time with their mother. The report of the assessor noted that this was a classic sign of PA. Authorities quoted in the assessor's report described an obsessed alienator as enmeshing the children's personalities and beliefs into his or her own. The report filed with the court indicated strong evidence of this obsessed alienation behavior in interviews completed with the father and the children in the home.

Reviewing all of the testimony and documentary evidence, the court ruled that the primary residence of the children would immediately be with the target parent mother. Further, the court ruled that there would be no contact directly or indirectly between the father and either of the children by any means, including telephone, text messages, facsimile, e-mail, regular mail, other web-based text, audio or video.

B. v. B., 2009–British Columbia

This case involved a very angry man. The court records indicated that the father was an abusive husband to the mother during their marriage. He was charged with assault in 1999 and agreed to a peace bond that mandated anger management counseling.

The court noted that the father had engaged in physical as well as emotional abuse on an ongoing basis. The father denied that he verbally abused the mother during their marriage; however, he admitted using derogatory words when referring to her or to her actions. Although he also denied calling the mother "stupid," he volunteered that many people said he had used names like this when referring to her. The court found that the father's testimony concerning his behavior during the parties' marriage was quite disingenuous. He minimized his behavior and emphasized the mother's overreaction to his conduct at every opportunity. With respect to the children, the court opined that it was clear the father damaged their emotional and psychological well-being in a variety of ways. The court opined that the father's behavior alienated the children from their mother; that he made the children, and particularly a daughter, his own emotional caretaker; and that he convinced them that any affection they had for their mother was an act of disloyalty and a betrayal of their father.

Psychologist Dr. Korpach concluded that the father had been engaging in consistent behaviors that alienated the children from their mother and that a joint parenting relationship would irreparably damage the children's relationship with her. As a result of her conclusions, Dr. Korpach made several recommendations. First, she recommended that the mother have sole custody of the children based on her conclusion that the father's difficulties containing his anger and his alienating behavior would destroy the children's relationship with their mother in any form of joint parenting. Second, due to her finding that the father was forceful, manipulative, and disregarding of the children's needs in favor of his own, Dr. Korpach recommended that the mother retain sole guardianship rights with an obligation to consider input from the father only in writing. Third, to ensure the children were able to develop a relationship with both parents and extended families, Dr. Korpach recommended that the father have no unsupervised access to the children, including contact via the Internet or by telephone. Visits were to be professionally supervised and occur on a weekly basis. The visitation guidelines were to be developed with the assistance of the children's counselor and were to include no negative discussion of the mother.

Considering the proofs in the record, the court agreed with Dr. Korpach's recommendation that the target parent mother be awarded sole custody of the children. Considering the father's difficulties controlling his anger and what the court determined to be his persistent behaviors and statements that alienated the children from their mother, the father posed a risk to the children's emotional health and well-being. The court went on to determine that this was because he was simply not willing to take the steps necessary to address his difficulties. Therefore, the court ruled that the mother, as the custodial parent, should have the sole right to make decisions about the children's moral and social upbringing, as well as their day-to-day care, discipline, and behavior.

J. v. J., 2010–Ontario

In this case, the parties were married in 1991. It was a first marriage for both. They had two boys C. age fifteen and M. age nine at the time of trial. Both parents agreed that C. suffered from attention-deficit/hyperactivity disorder (ADHD) and obsessive compulsive disorder (OCD) and that M. had a learning disability. Both parents remained in home where court testimony indicated, the father sabotaged the mother's disciplining of the children, broke into the mother's room, called the mother names, swore at and threatened the mother, turned off power and cable, walked around in a towel and exposed himself. Records also documented that the father spoke to his own mother about blowing up the house. There was evidence of self-mutilation in the oldest child C. (carving his initials into his skin).

Court records indicated that the father had a personality disorder and was modeling unhealthy behaviors that had influenced the children. Extended exposure to these behaviors in the father was seen as having long-term negative impact. Court records document that the experts thought that tasking father with day-to-day parenting would stress him and could trigger an explosive reaction.

The court found that the father demonstrated many alienating behaviors. He called the mother names in front of the boys and they then mimicked him, and he undermined mother's efforts to impose bedtimes and discipline. Further, the court found that the father tried to paint himself as the victim in his voice mail messages and in his own diary entries. The court determined that the father undermined the mother's attempts to discipline C. when he assaulted her, and the father sabotaged the mother's summer access as well. He allowed C. to evade schoolwork by permitting him to come to his house. He did not follow up with the schools to verify the mother's claims that C. was simply avoiding work. The result: custody to target parent mother.

S. (I.M.M.) v. S. (D.J.), 2010–British Columbia

This case involved a serious and ongoing lack of cooperation and active PA. This lack of cooperation by the father was demonstrated by difficulties in planning for the scheduling of vacations and extracurricular activities for the children during the school year and many other alienating and undercutting behaviors as well.

Court assessor Brown had thirty years of experience according to the court and was a highly experienced, professional registered clinical counselor. Ms. Brown reported to the court that this couple could not work cooperatively together to parent the children and that the father would continue to behave so as to alienate his sons from their mother. Ms. Brown strongly recommended that the father participate in counseling to help him deal with his anger in relation to the mother. The court noted that assessor Brown saw aspects of the father's behavior as both an active and an obsessive alienator. She determined that he was strongly influencing his sons to his way of thinking by portraying himself as a "victim of their mother's greed."

The court determined it was clear on the evidence that the father manifested entrenched behaviors that were likely to seriously damage or even destroy the children's relationship with the mother. The court determined that despite the various difficulties the mother encountered in trying to parent with the father, she persisted in a calm and committed way, because she firmly believed it was in the children's best interests for them to have a relationship with their father. In contrast, the father told the children that upon reaching the age of twelve years, they may choose which parent they wish to reside with and continued to undercut the mother. Further, the father refused to pay an outstanding order concerning his share of special expenses and did not move with any dispatch to comply with the orders of the court regarding property division. The trial judge cited to significant case precedent and vested custody in the target parent mother.

S. v. S., 2010–Ontario

This case found experts describing the consequences of PA in stark terms. Court records document that Jacqueline Vanbetlehem, MSW, and Ted Horowitz (Ph.D. in social work) agreed that the children had been heavily influenced by the father to have unrealistic and unjustified negative feelings toward the mother. Despite the father's repeated attempts to get the experts to agree that the children were justified or at least reasonable in rejecting the mother, both experts regarded the father's active alienation as by far the more pressing problem. Both witnesses described the long-term serious effects of unresolved alienation in children when they become adults. According to the two experts in this case, alienated children have significantly higher rates of mental and emotional problems, substance abuse or addiction, and marriage or relationship breakdown than do children who have a relationship with both their parents.

The trial judge offered that it was interesting to hear the father's submissions, which bore out what the mother and the two expert witnesses had said. Barely a minute into his testimony wrote the trial judge, the father veered sharply from addressing what arrangements would be in the best interests of the boys to talk extensively about how the mother had betrayed him and the family by acting independently as soon as she began earning a significant income. The father insisted that the mother began neglecting him and the children, abandoning them and forming a new relationship, all in the interest of money. His bitterness was palpable wrote the court. He accused her of stealing the wealth of the family away from him, in terms similar to those the children repeated to the mother and the two expert witnesses. He also questioned the mother's willingness and even her intellectual capacity to recognize the needs of the children and make any changes necessary to meet them. After hearing all of the testimony and reviewing the reports of the experts, the court ruled that both children would reside with the target parent mother. The father's access to each of the children was suspended.

D. (S.) v. C. (A.S.), 2011–Manitoba

This was an appeal of a case the trial court let drag on and on. Ever since their separation in 2004, the parents in this case had a history of disputes regarding the custody of their three children. In 2006, Dr. Golfman, a psychologist, and a social worker, Ms. Frankel, completed an extensive assessment of the situation. Their report and testimony at trial formed a basis for the judge's conclusion at the 2008 trial that the father was deliberately alienating the children from their mother. Curiously, the judge ordered primary care and control to the father. She did so on condition that the father hire a reunification expert and encourage access between the children and their mother. That access did not take place.

At a second trial in 2010, the reunification expert, Ms. Mercedes, testified that the father was not cooperating. In their updated report, Ms. Frankel and Dr. Golfman stated that the children remained pathologically alienated from their mother as a result of the actions of the father initially and, subsequently the environment with the older siblings and extended family. This time, the judge changed the custody of the youngest child from the father to the mother. At the 2010 trial, the mother decided that, because of the lack of effective help from the Manitoba courts for six years and given the older children's ages (seventeen and fifteen), she would not pursue a change of custody for them, only for the youngest daughter. The trial judge awarded sole custody of the youngest child to this target parent mother, with supervised-only access to the father.

A. v. A., 2011–Alberta

In this case, the alienating father tried to manipulate the assessor evaluation before it began. An assessor was engaged to acquire input from the children on the parenting arrangements. However, the father took the children to his lawyer's office prior to their attendance at the assessor's office and the admittedly untrained lawyer interviewed them. The mother discovered that the children had been interviewed by the father's attorney and also coached into secrecy about it when the assessor referenced it in his report. In this report, the assessor suggested that the expression of the children's wishes could not be relied upon given the tainting that had occurred. Considering this and other evidence of alienation, the court opined that this glaring incident occurred in the face of a court order carefully prescribing a protocol for interviewing the children. When cross-examined about the clandestine interview with the children, the father brushed it off as his lawyer's decision. Although this may have been the case wrote the judge, the father complied all too eagerly without thought to possible harm to the children. In cross-examination, the father demonstrated little or no insight into the fact that this was the very thing the protocol sought to avoid. The court determined that this was a clear example of PA assisted by the father's counsel. The result was that the alienating father's time with the children was drastically reduced in favor of the target parent mother.

Target Parent Father

S. v. K., 1999–British Columbia

The parents in this case separated after a four-year relationship during which they had two children. The mother was awarded permanent custody of the children and the father was awarded access. Soon after the divorce the mother's drinking problem resulted in several alcohol-related incidents in front of the children. Conflicts between the parents continued, and when the father applied for a change in custody the court noted two significant and material changes since the mother was awarded custody. These were that the mother had put the children at risk with her drinking and that the emotional health of the children was damaged by the mother's attempts to alienate the children from their father.

In its written opinion, the court noted that in 1994 the court awarded custody of the parties' two daughters to the mother, but in 1997 the mother, while she was with the two children, collapsed on a public street as a result of her alcohol intake. The court's opinion also noted that between 1994 and 1997, there were numerous applications regarding access and guardianship. An assessor was agreed upon as an independent expert by counsel for the parents, and the assessor's views on the mother's alcoholism were added to the record. The assessor opined that the mother was not convincing as a person who was committed to an alcohol-free lifestyle, and she certainly had not taken responsibility for her drinking. The assessor noted that the mother had been given many chances over the years by treators and the courts. The assessor noted that there was a clearer picture of the mother's alcohol-related incidents because of updated information, in-depth psychological testing results, and changing symptoms in the two children as they had evolved over the last years.

With respect to the impact of the mother's actions on the couple's daughter, the assessor wrote that the child was described by the individuals who had treated her in the last months as "fused" with her mother in an unhealthy attachment. The daughter had clearly integrated the stance of her mother as a disempowered victim of her father's "cunning manipulations" opined the assessor. She believed, as her mother had often told her, that her father did not love her but that he sought custody and access changes only to annoy and persecute the mother. The assessor added that this young girl was deeply and tragically alienated from her father and was made to choose loyalties from a young age in order to retain her mother's love and attention. The assessor made twelve detailed recommendations, including that the father should have sole custody of the children for a minimum of two years and that access by the mother should be supervised for a period of eighteen months and the supervisors had to be independent. After hearing all of the evidence, the court agreed with the assessor and vested custody of the children in the target parent father, no access for alienating mother.

L. (D.) v. Listuguj Police Service, 1999–Québec

This case deals with parental abduction of twin girls, born in California in 1988. They were abducted in October 1995 and brought to Canada despite a specific restraining order handed down by a California Court. They were held on the Mi'kmaq community reserve of Listuguj from that time on, rarely being allowed to venture off the reserve in order to avoid a 1996 Canadian court order from being executed and returning them to their father in the United States.

The court documents reveal that the mother, age forty, lived the first twenty years of her life on the reserve. During this time, at eight years old she left her parents to live with her grandmother for three years. From a broken home on the reserve, she moved to the United States at age twenty, but admittedly never really fit in with her work environment and neighbors once outside the reserve. Court materials indicated that from time to time, she sought psychological help and counseling for her problems. Court records document that the mother could neither manage the workplace nor cope with the separation judgment, much less the preparation for a final divorce hearing. She was unable to cope with the stress of it all and, overcome with her admitted emotional and financial insecurity, her solution was to abduct the six and one-half-year old twins and go to her psychological hideout in Canada, the Listuguj (Mi'kmaq) reserve. To complicate matters, the Council on the reserve passed a resolution supporting the abducting parent and affording those charged with peacekeeping–the Listuguj Police Service on the reserve of some 2,000 inhabitants–with an excuse to ignore, refuse to execute or comply with the Canadian Superior Court judgment ordering the return of the children to their father.

The assigned judge wrote that these blonde freckled twins were held on the reserve, out of the reach of the law and their father, from October 1995 until March 1999. These two young children were literally indoctrinated into First Nation culture, to the exclusion of what they had previously known. The court found that they grew up to believe judges were bad and that their father was a bad guy with a beard. The court went on to point out that the mother taught the children to live as outlaws. Finally, the court determined that as it had heard all the proof, it was convinced that the best interest of the children was that they should be in the custody of their father and rediscover the world outside the reserve. Custody was vested in the target parent father.

C. v. C., 2004–Ontario

This was a very litigious case before the court for approximately seven years. There were multiple motions and approximately fifteen interim orders. The record reveals that the parents were married in 1973 and separated in 1998, at which time the father left the matrimonial home at the request of the mother. Since that time, the father was unable to have access or visits with his daughters.

In the trial the mother argued that she followed along every step of the way doing what her lawyer and counselor instructed. She claimed that she was faultless, but the court found that her position and her testimony were completely contradictory to all other evidence before the court. After years of inaction, the court found that mother's sabotaging actions were knowing, willful, and deliberate. Consequently, the court ruled that the mother's actions and lack thereof constituted contempt and were obviously contrary to the best interests of all three children. Reviewing the record, the court offered that there was no evidence before the court that would indicate that the target parent was anything but a good father, a loving father, and a father who was steadfast.

The 2004 opinion notes that the behavior of the mother in the case created a "travesty." As a result of the mother's behavior, the children had little or no relationship with the father who loved them, who tried to be a good father, and who had been a good provider throughout their lives. If it were not for the age of the youngest child and the fact that at the time of the trial she was a young woman attached to her mother and who would shortly be leaving home, the assigned judge offered that the court would be looking to the father as the appropriate custodial parent. Instead, the court ruled that the alienating mother must pay a fine of $10,000 forthwith. The court also ordered that the mother had to immediately arrange and be supportive of counseling for the children. The court further ruled that the mother would be responsible to ensure that the youngest got to and from these appointments twice per month without exception. Finally, the court ruled that if the mother breached the order for any reason directly or indirectly, she would be considered in contempt of court and required to pay a fine in the amount of $15,000.

W. v. W., 2005–Nova Scotia

This family had extensive involvement with child protection agencies and the police. Since the marital separation, the family was in a constant state of crisis. The court noted that the parents continually relied on external agents and the courts to address their never-ending issues. Further, the court determined that there was no evidence to suggest that these parents' relationship would improve in the foreseeable future.

The record reveals that the court had the benefit of a custody and access assessment prepared by Rilda van Feggelen, a senior member of her profession. She was a registered psychologist with expertise in the area of children and the family. Ms. van Feggelen testified that the status quo could not continue. She felt the children were at risk and as such needed to be "rescued" from their circumstances. Based on the testimony and the record, the court found that the mother in this case was prepared to ignore court orders if they were at variance with her views of the world. She perceived herself as a victim and felt she was always at war with anyone she felt was a threat to her control of her family unit. The assessor and the court found that the mother was unable to control her emotions in front of her children or her community. The court noted that the mother continually defended her choices by stating that the father was, and continued to be, physically abusive to her. The court found that her professed position was nothing more than a tool to defend otherwise indefensible positions. The court also noted that the children developed an unhealthy relationship with their mother such that their future relationships would be significantly affected. The court ruled that the present access situation and the boys' mental state amounted to a change in the conditions and circumstances of the children and their parents' ability to meet their needs. The record reflects that the court also found that these changes materially affected the boys and that they were not foreseen at the time of the original order.

On the other hand, the court found that the father had shown that he knew what was best for the boys. He made a concerted effort to shield the boys from parental issues and conflict. The father had moved on since the separation and was forward looking in his perspectives, wrote the judge. The court finally determined that this was one of those exceptional cases where drastic action was required to meet the best interests of the children. It is one of those few cases, ruled the court, where the parental rights of one parent had to be severely curtailed in the interests of creating a healthy family environment for the children. The result: sole custody to target parent father.

M. v. M., 2005–Ontario

In this case, the parents were married in 2000, had one child, and separated in 2003. The record documents that from the separation, the mother worked to sabotage the relationship between the father and the child. The child was residing with her parents in Mississauga, Ontario, until early in 2003, when the mother took the child to visit with her parents in Aylmer, Quebec. While there, the mother informed the father, through a text message that she was separating from him and that she and the child would remain in Quebec.

In an attempt to avoid the Ontario court, the mother petitioned the court in Quebec to suspend the father's access just prior to trial. Despite the distance imposed by the mother's unilateral move to Quebec, the father pursued a relationship with the child in every way he could. The record documents that the mother brought a spurious sexual abuse allegation despite the fact that she knew it was false. The mother accompanied the child to an examination by a pediatrician, and the report documenting that there were no indications of sexual abuse was known to her when she purposefully misled the trial court.

The record in the trial court documents that the father made numerous court appearances prior to trial, and the mother disobeyed the court orders resulting from these appearances. The father brought motions for contempt against the mother, but his motions were adjourned again and again. Finally, the trial court determined that the mother's conduct in creating a false sexual abuse allegation and frustrating access was contrary to best interests of the child and created substantial and compelling reasons to review custody. Reviewing the entire record, the court determined that the mother's behavior was a form of child abuse and her fitness as a parent was questionable at best. Based on the record and mother's conduct a finding of contempt by reason of disobedience of three court orders was entered by the trial court. Father's costs for the contempt motions was fixed at $9,426.36 and awarded to him by the court. The court also ordered the mother to pay a fine of $5,000 and changed custody of the child to the target parent father.

F. v. V., 2006–Ontario

In this case the father was sixty years of age and retired from Canada Customs and Revenue. The mother was fifty-five years of age; she was born in Yugoslavia and immigrated to Canada in 1990. Reviewing all of the records, the court noted that the father and child endured a life of harassment by the mother for the previous eleven years. The mother made a career of making false allegations that were trivial and heinous concerning the father's care of the daughter and against him personally since their separation in 1994. The mother falsely alleged physical, emotional, and sexual abuse over and over and over again, wrote the court. In all, the mother made approximately thirty-one calls with allegations to the police and approximately thirty-six calls with allegations to the CAS. All the allegations were determined to be unfounded. Court records revealed that this alienating mother could not be trusted to refrain from pressuring the child to take sides, telling lies, or speaking derogatorily about the father either to or in presence of the child.

The case languished in the courts from 2002 through 2006, when the court finally held that the mother had no concept of the truth. Her false allegations, outright lies, distortions, half-truths, and complete fabrications left her with no credibility before the court. The heinous and ridiculous false allegations made against the father by the mother, wrote the court in 2006, included an allegation of masturbating in front of the child and denying the father access because the court order was allegedly fraudulent. As a result of the mother's false allegations, the father had numerous criminal charges laid against him and numerous investigations undertaken by the police. The record documented that all the investigations and the charges were initiated by the mother. The result: sole custody to target parent father and mother held in contempt with a $5,000 fine.

F. (C.J.) v. G. (R.C.), 2007–British Columbia

In 1997, the mother made the first of many serious allegations of abuse against the father and his family. This dispute involved the ministry of the provincial government responsible for child protection, variously named at different times so referred to here as "the Ministry." The mother was unmarried and moved frequently, having four changes of address between 2005 and 2007. She was forty-one years old and was estranged from her extended family. She alleged that the father had sexually abused the couple's boys, causing the Ministry to undertake an investigation that resulted in negative findings after both boys had been examined.

The record reveals that following the allegations of sexual abuse, the mother refused the father access to the children for six months, and then in January 2000, the mother reported to the Ministry that the paternal grandfather had abused the children. The mother then alleged that the father's fiancée planned to remove the children to Mexico. In January 2001, the mother alleged more physical abuse by the father. Matters continued much the same until August 2004 when the mother alleged that the paternal grandmother had sexually assaulted the boys and the grandfather had physically abused them. The children were again interviewed by social workers, and it became clear that the grandparents provided a stable, secure and loving environment for the boys.

In May 2006, the mother sought a referral from a pediatrician for a psychiatric assessment of one of the children. The court found that the psychologist's report was replete with misinformation from the mother. She attempted to color the psychologist's report with expressed concerns that the father had alienated one of the children from her, that the father would curtail the child's school and activities, that the paternal grandmother had sexually abused one of the children, and that the stepmother emotionally and physically abused the children with the concurrence of the father. The court record documented that the mother told the psychologist that the father and stepmother constantly argued and were alcoholics and that the stepdaughters were barely clothed in the house. She did not tell the psychologist that the Ministry had found that the child the psychologist was seeing was in need of protection from her.

In 2007, the assigned judge wrote that there were credibility gaps with the mother's testimony. The mother told the court that the stepmother's daycare had been shut down by the licensing authority after her accusations of abuse, which was inaccurate except for her unfounded allegations. She engaged in misinformation to responsible experts with the obvious goal of coloring opinions against the father. According to the record, the mother provided inappropriate information and attitude in front of the children as reported by the general practitioner and as demonstrable in reports of psychologists and the supervisor of access. She blatantly failed to provide access, contrary to orders, including the most recent order, wrote the assigned judge in 2007. The mother actively alienated the children from their father and any others who had not adjusted to her wishes. The mother's conduct aimed at destruction of the father's familial relationship with the boys was so serious, wrote the court, as to warrant a change of custody on its own. The result: sole custody to the target parent father.

W. (S.L.) v. W. (W.N.), 2007–Alberta

Because of severe PA, custody of the children was vested with the target parent father. The mother appealed and requested a stay of the enforcement of the order. The children, ages eight, seven, and five years old, had been residing with their mother when the emergency order was made on the Court's own motion after receiving a copy of the psychologist's report. Prior to making the emergency order, the court viewed evidence, some of which came from the mother's own computer transmissions, confirming her ongoing alienation of the children from their father and stepmother. The court determined the materials demonstrated that the children were being seriously and significantly alienated from their father by their mother's behavior. The judge eloquently wrote that such a situation cried out for a change to salvage some possibility for the children to form a positive and loving relationship with their father and stepmother and hopefully retain some of the loving relationship that they had with their mother.

The mother swore in two affidavits in support of her request to stay the change of custody order that the children were at risk of harm in their father's home. The court took notice of the assessor's work where it was reported that in light of mother's openly contemptuous attitude with respect to complying with court orders, her history of noncompliance, and her open statements that she would rather go to jail, it appeared that the issue of sanctions for noncompliance had to be addressed. The assessor went on to report that it was virtually impossible to work on supporting the children's relationship with their father when their mother continued to remain openly hostile towards their stepmother and continued to allow the children to determine when and if they would go to spend time with them.

The assessor told the court that the longer the children were exposed to the mother's defiance, the greater the likelihood she would succeed in undermining their relationship with their father. The alienating mother's request to stay the transfer of custody of the children to the target parent father was dismissed.

L. (R.) v. L. (N.), 2007–New Brunswick

In this case, the assessor explained that the evaluation was incomplete because it was impossible to engage the mother in the process, nor was it possible to establish a connection with the child. The father, on the other hand, was compliant and cooperative throughout. The assessor listed all the times she tried to reach the mother and the times she talked to her in court. A risk assessment was done and the assessor testified that, in his opinion, the child presented as a little girl groomed systematically and methodically to cease having a relationship with her father. The risk assessor went on to say that there was considerable evidence that the father had a very good relationship with the child before the separation and for a year postseparation.

Cheryl Brown, a person the court referred to as an expert in children's counseling therapy, saw the father and helped with relationship building and reconciliation. Ms. Brown testified that she discovered two signs under a protocol that indicated PA to her. She identified the two indicators as emotional maltreatment and isolation. From the first interview, she felt obligated to report this to Child Protection as she considered the mother's behavior of isolating the child and requiring the child to only turn to one parent for support to be abuse. Considering all of the evidence, the court determined that custody should be vested in the target parent father, and the mother was to have no contact directly or indirectly until a qualified child therapist informed the court that it was in the child's best interest to see her. The court also noted that the case dragged on due to the actions of the mother and awarded costs to the target parent father.

L. v. L., 2009–British Columbia

The record in this case documented that after the return from access time in 2004, there were allegations that the father had physically neglected and sexually abused the child. The father denied these allegations and voluntarily suspended his access while the police and representatives of the provincial government responsible for the welfare of children conducted an investigation. In addition to his voluntary suspension of access, the father, on his own initiative, submitted to two polygraph examinations and to a psychological assessment to determine whether there were indicators of a potential for abusive behaviors. The investigation included interviews by the police and social workers and established no basis for any reasonable belief that the father neglected or in any way abused the child. Test results indicated that the father presented no risk to the child whatsoever. Trial on the issue of permanent custody was finally set for a hearing in 2008. The mother did not attend. Nevertheless, the trial went ahead and the trial judge ordered counsel for the father to present all the material in his possession.

The circumstances were that the father applied for an order for permanent custody of the child. The court reviewed voluminous records and determined that the mother's avoidance of the courts of British Columbia was not due to a lack of energy or resources. She fought the case out in Nebraska, where she had relocated, and through her attorney, participated in hearings before the Judicial Committee of the Nebraska Legislature. She was so tireless in her advocacy, the Canadian court expressed shock that the Nebraska Legislature saw fit to amend their child custody legislation following her participation and stories.

Ostensibly on the child's behalf, this alienating mother began a court action in the Nebraska District Court in which she purported to raise the very allegations that were raised in proceedings before the same court in her application for a temporary emergency jurisdiction order to stop the father's visitation. The British Columbia court expressed that it was of considerable interest that the mother succeeded in obtaining findings of fact in Nebraska when trying to get the Nebraska court's temporary emergency jurisdiction. The Canadian judge noted that the Nebraska courts expected a full hearing on the exact same allegations but in the British Columbia Supreme Court. This strategic move on the mother's part laid the groundwork for the circumvention of the findings of both the District and the Supreme Courts of Nebraska that confirmed the jurisdiction of the British Columbia Supreme Court.

Because of the alienating mother's shenanigans, the Canadian court, noting mother's abuse, ruled that the mother was determined to obstruct a full hearing of the allegations she herself made and the custodial arrangements that would best serve the child's interests. In compliance with the expectation of the Nebraska courts, the court with jurisdiction over the child ruled for an immediate return of the child to Canada, custody to target parent father, and costs to be paid by the mother.

M.A. v. M.A., 2009–Ontario

In this case the parties had three children. The 2002 divorce judgment provided that the father was to have custody of the children with specified access to the mother. Shortly before the judgment was delivered, the mother moved herself and the children to Geraldton, Ontario, in violation of an interim court order that required that neither party remove the children from the jurisdiction of Thunder Bay. The children were returned to the father, with the assistance of the Ontario Provincial Police. Almost immediately after the children were returned, the mother began contacting the CAS alleging that the father was abusing them. There was a prior allegation made to the CAS by the mother against the father in 2001 during the course of the parties' initial litigation that was found to be baseless. The mother began calling the CAS again in May 2002.

When the mother's plans to obtain the children through CAS action did not work out, she seemed to disappear. Court records document that between June 2003 and June 2007 the mother did not contact the father or the children. She failed to tell them her whereabouts, she did not send the children birthday cards or other gifts, she essentially disappeared from their lives. In 2007, the mother was residing in Winnipeg when she received a call from the parties' daughter. The mother immediately travelled to Thunder Bay and brought a motion to change custody on an emergency *ex parte* basis. At this same time, the mother again began to contact CAS and again alleged the father was abusing their daughters.

The children left with the mother for a visit to Portage La Prairie, Manitoba, and the mother began to refuse the father access. She denied the father's access by changing her telephone number and then making additional unfounded allegations of sexual abuse against the father in Manitoba. This prevented the father from enforcing the Ontario court order during the course of the investigation. Next, the mother moved the children's residence and schools outside of Portage la Prairie in violation of the court order. She did not inform the father where she was living, and at the time this case was called her whereabouts were unknown.

The court record revealed that the father had not seen the children since they left with the mother in 2008. This seems to have occurred because between June 2008 and December 2008 the police in both Manitoba and Thunder Bay investigated the allegations of sexual assault. All of the police agencies closed their files because the allegations were not substantiated. With respect to an investigation of the mother, the court noted that she was described by the assessor as a person having difficulties managing her own life. The assessor's report documented that psychological testing indicated that the mother demonstrated difficulty with paranoia. The court's assessor was of the opinion that the mother was unable to exercise good judgment. The judge at the time outlined ten separate concerns he had with the mother's ability to parent the children. Some of these concerns were her history of failing to supervise them at a time when they were still infants, that she often exhibited rage and violence toward the children and the father, that she had an inability to recognize the children's legitimate medical and other needs, that she had an inability to tell the truth, and her lifestyle of moving from city to city and thus moving the children from school to school. Considering the record, the assessor's work, and testimony, the court ordered an immediate change to sole custody for target parent father.

Catholic Children's Aid Society of Toronto v. H. (L.D.), 2008–Ontario

This was Ontario's infamous Hu Ha case. Here the father separated from the mother in January 2005. CAS filed an amended protection application seeking an order that the two children were in need of protection and an order that the children be removed from the care and custody of their mother and placed in the care and custody of their father. In the tortured history of the case, one expert testified that she was manipulated by the mother to remove two sentences in her report. Further, the expert testified that she felt pressured by the mother to include things in her report with which she was not comfortable. The records document that the mother would go to any ends to accomplish her purpose. Unfortunately, CAS told the court that it was not until the most recent assessment was completed by Dr. Amin that the extent of the damage to the children and the mother's dysfunctional parenting became clear. Only then did CAS become convinced that it was in the best interests of the children that the society ask the court to remove the children from her care and place them with their father.

The court heard the trial of this application over eighteen days. The mother alleged that her former husband had physically abused her during the marriage and sexually abused their young children during access visits. The children, who were five and ten years old at the time of the trial, made vague statements to investigators that appeared to support some of the mother's allegations, but the court record documents that ultimately several independent mental health professionals and a child protection investigation concluded that the incidents did not occur. The experts, including an access supervisor, concluded that the allegations were unfounded and that the mother's anger and point of view were transmitted to her children, including their stated reluctance to visit their father. Partway through the case the court, in hearing the CAS case, concluded that there was a need to reverse the process of alienation while keeping the children in the care of the mother who was, at the time, the primary caregiver. The court ordered structured access, as well as counseling for the parents and children. The father was awarded legal custody to ensure his right to access to information about the children.

In the 2008 Ontario case (it went before Judge Brownstone in 2010 with similar results) the court made many findings and determined that the mother simply did not want the father to have access. The court considered the allegations of domestic violence from the parties' past and accepted that Dr. Amin gave these issues consideration. The court accepted his conclusion that the father did not pose an emotional or physical threat to the children and that he could provide a safe and nurturing environment. The judge went on to find that there was irrefutable evidence that the primary aspects of PAS were present in the mother's relationship with the father. The mother engaged in a campaign of denigration wrote the court, also finding that the mother's hostility towards the father was unabated. The court found that the mother's influence over the children was virtually overwhelming by reviewing their verbal and written communications to the father, to the society, to the court, and to the previous judge. Despite court orders not to do so, the court found that the mother provided her children with unending amounts of personal information concerning the father as well as constant information as to the conflicts and struggles between herself and the professionals. The court wrote that the mother continually advised the society and the court of her belief that the children were old enough to make up their own minds whether they wished to visit with their father, and she simply was not able to force them to visit. The court determined that the mother constantly attempted to control and manipulate the minds of her children in spite of clear warnings not to do so. She subtly but blatantly ignored the court orders of physical and telephone access by the father, and her expressed views as to the propriety of her conduct indicated little or no prospect that she would conduct herself differently in the future. The court noted that there are few, if any, expressions of regret by the mother and found the children to be in need of protection from her. The court determined that father was able and willing to provide for his children's guidance, education, and necessities of life. Therefore, the court ruled that the children would be placed immediately in the primary care of their father for a period of twelve months with the supervision of the society.

Children's Aid Society of Waterloo v. L. (K.A.), 2010–Ontario

In this case the parents married in 1996, had a daughter in 1997 and a son in 1999, and separated in 2000 and again in 2002. The divorce proceedings involved high conflict but after a 2005 trial, the parents were awarded joint custody with week-about sharing of the children. There were problems with the father's access. Their son died in 2008 and the CAS brought an application for orders that the children were in need of protection from an alienating mother and to place the children with the father subject to their supervision.

The court found that in its view, all the indicia of PA were present in this case. Access was rarely without problems and the mother demonstrated unwillingness to follow any court order unless it favored her position, showed no respect for the father and his family, and was blind to the daughter's psychological needs. The court found that the girl was aligned with her mother and that they saw themselves as a team against everyone else. The assigned judge wrote that the mother demonstrated contempt for the father's caregiving abilities, questioning his decisions, and demonstrated contempt for the father's involvement. Further, the court wrote that after hearing the evidence, it was impossible to come to any conclusion other than that the mother had embarked on a campaign to alienate the children for years. The court found that it was evident that she was unable to accept the concept of equal time and continued to try to erode whatever relationship the daughter and father had in order to accomplish what she did not accomplish at the first trial. The time has come, wrote the court, to do something far more drastic to end the conflict and the need for these parents to associate with each other in any way. The court and the CAS reasoned that moving the girl to her father's home and imposing terms of supervision that the society would enforce would take the girl out of the middle and give her time to adjust and reconnect with her father. The result: custody to target parent father with the help of CAS. Mother's contact severely limited and supervised.

L. (T.L.L.) v. L. (J.J.), 2011–Manitoba

This was an appellate case. In the record of the court, the materials document that in April 2007, just as the trial court was about to deliver its decision, the mother launched yet another sexual assault allegation against the father and appeared in court with a motion to hear new evidence based on her new allegation. By the time of the trial before the judge, the mother was already frequently in contempt of the interim orders by denying the father his time with the children. Of equal concern to the court, the mother had made numerous allegations of sexual assault not just against the father but also against other individuals before the trial. None of her allegations had sufficient merit to result in the laying of a criminal charge by the police or any further action by any investigating agency. Every one of her allegations was found to be unsubstantiated.

With her campaign of serial false allegations, the mother succeeded in stopping the father from seeing his sons for months at a time. On each occasion that she made a complaint, the child caring agency and the Winnipeg Police Service had to complete their required protocol of interviewing the children and the father, preparing their reports, and ultimately clearing the father of any wrongdoing. Because of the backlog that the agencies and police had, each of these unsubstantiated complaints took several months to wind its way through the system.

The court in 2009 noted that of great import was a 100 page comprehensive family assessment prepared by Dr. Linda Rhodes. This assessor was described by the court as quite experienced, and it was clear that she believed the father to be the better parent. Dr. Rhodes found that the mother was engaging in classic alienator behavior that had almost completely alienated the oldest boy and would soon succeed in alienating the two younger boys, if it was not stopped. Based on her assessment of the mother, Dr. Rhodes had little confidence that the mother was capable of change or of developing insight into her destructive behavior.

The trial took approximately two weeks. Eleven witnesses were called. The mother alleged that the father was abusive and that he had sexually assaulted all three boys for years. She did not accept the opinions of the social workers, police, Dr. Rhodes, and other professionals on any of these issues. She firmly believed that she was the children's only real advocate. In contrast to the mother's delight in her serial allegations, it was clear to the court that the father was nearing his breaking point in his battle for his sons. While working as a chaplain within the justice system, he was investigated by the police and child caring agencies for allegations of sexual assault and physical abuse, all of which were eventually shown to be unsubstantiated.

His job security and emotional well-being were continually threatened by the mother's repeated sexual assault allegations.

The court determined that the recurrent theme during the entire case was the pattern of sexual abuse allegations by the mother. The judge pointed out that there were three more allegations by the mother since the last trial. The first one was made as the court was about to pronounce his order on in 2007. The next allegation was made shortly after the two younger boys started unsupervised visits with their father. The last investigation involved just the youngest boy and was made after his visits recommenced with his father following the second interruption. The court opined that the investigations resulted in a loss of precious and irreplaceable time for the father with his sons. While the mother's complaints to the agency became increasingly graphic and disturbing, the witnesses confirmed that the children never reported anything remotely close to the sexual or unusual abuse described by the mother. Dr. Rhodes was so concerned about the mother's pattern of unsubstantiated reporting that she declined to describe the symptoms that she would have expected to see in an actual child who had been sexually abused because she did not want to provide the mother with a "how to" manual for her next inevitable set of false claims.

Reviewing the history of the case, reports, and witness testimony, the assigned judge found as fact that there was no evidence that supported any of the mother's sexual abuse allegations over the years. The court explained that it was unable to conclude whether the pattern of sexual assault allegations was born out of the mother's malice, psychopathology, or other indiscernible motivation. The court went on to find that the mother had shown no insight, no remorse, and no motivation to change. The court found that she had no understanding that it was in her children's best interests to be free to love their father and have a relationship with him. Even with contempt proceedings hanging over her head the mother would not assure the court that she would follow the court orders if she disagreed with them. Her conduct over the past few years had been emotionally destructive to her sons' well-being, wrote the court in its opinion. The long-term implications of her dysfunctional behavior were clearly contrary to her son's best interests. The court reasoned that this was one of those exceptional cases in which drastic action was required and that a complete reversal of custody would best meet the needs of the children. The court ruled that the children needed a period of time to heal and bond again with their father in a safe, nurturing environment. The ruling was simply that the target parent father would have sole custody of all three children.

In this appeal, the appellate court began its analysis by offering a summary of the numerous court proceedings between the parties, which began for their purposes in 2006. They reviewed the record wherein there was a two-week trial, in which the trial judge, despite his finding that the mother had deliberately withheld access from the father, confirmed the joint custody order. The appellate panel noted that after another two-week trial at which both parties represented themselves, a different trial judge concluded that the mother had engaged in a ceaseless and deliberate campaign to alienate the children from the father, including making numerous baseless allegations of sexual abuse. The appellate court explained that at the conclusion of the subsequent trial the court granted sole custody of the children to the target parent father and made a finding of contempt. The appellate court affirmed the order that the alienating mother was to pay costs in the amount of $10,000 and while dismissing her appeal, ordered her to pay costs again.

L. v. S., 2011–British Columbia

This case documents eight years of PA before decisive court action. The high-conflict custody dispute that was originally started in Provincial Court included approximately twenty-seven Provincial Court orders, two appeals to the Supreme Court, one application to the Court of Appeal for leave to appeal, and four Supreme Court orders. The trial itself in the Supreme Court took twenty-nine days. The voluminous court record documents that the father was an accountant, thirty-nine years of age. The mother was forty-three years of age and a legal secretary. The parties began dating while the mother was addicted to cocaine. Shortly before a 2003 family case conference, the mother delivered a report authored by a psychologist, Dr. Steane. Records document that this report was undertaken without the consent or knowledge of the father or the court. The failure of the mother to obtain the father's consent to retain Dr. Steane was considered by the trial judge as a prime example of the disrespect that the mother had for court orders.

A review of the record documents that according to the mother, beginning in June 2005, the child made complaints about having a "sore bottom." These complaints continued and escalated and it was only when mother says she understood that the child's reference to her bottom actually meant her vagina, that the mother realized the gravity of the situation. This brought on the involvement of the Ministry of Children and Family Development and the Royal Canadian Mounted Police (RCMP). The child was taken to a drop-in clinic and was examined by a physician, who found no physical evidence of sexual abuse. Undeterred, the mother made an allegation twice on the child's birthday in 2005 that the father burned his daughter's bottom with a stick. Contrary to the alienating mother's claims, the father's evidence documented that he did not see his daughter on her birthday. The child was also examined by the sexual assault unit at the Children's & Women's Health Centre at the British Columbia Children's Hospital, and there was no physical evidence of any assault.

When the report of Dr. Carr, the court's assessor, was released, the mother had been seeing Dr. Hay, a psychiatrist, for approximately three years. Dr. Hay expressed concerned about Dr. Carr's report and more particularly about Dr. Carr's finding that the mother had a borderline personality disorder. After listening to both experts the court refused to accept the evidence of Dr. Hay. The court reasoned that he was an advocate and appeared to be prepared to do or say whatever was necessary to assist his client, even if it meant attempting to destroy the reputation of Dr. Carr. Further, the judge wrote that Dr. Hay was also prepared to allow his client's mother to edit his letter of support for the mother. During the court proceedings the mother was nonresponsive and often evasive in her answers. She also denied ever using drugs while pregnant to Dr. Carr, the Ministry, the RCMP, in her thirteen-page police report, and to Dr. Hay. Indeed, she reported to the Ministry that she had not used drugs since January 2001. Nevertheless, during the trial she admitted to using cocaine when pregnant. Dr. Hay's intake forms revealed that she attempted suicide by ingesting sleeping pills. For these and other reasons the court gave the evidence of the mother very little weight and preferred the evidence of the father and his wife when their evidence was inconsistent with the mother's. Simply put, the court found that the father was a truthful witness and gave his evidence in a responsible and thoughtful fashion.

The trial court also noted that the mother and her parents held negative and distorted beliefs about the father and his family and communicated those views directly to the child. It was clear, wrote the court, that this unhealthy atmosphere of disrespect, which was created by the mother, had adversely affected the child. The court went on to explain that the atmosphere of disrespect was not just in the defendant's home but in the grandparents' home, in the school that the child attended, and in the afterschool care that the mother used. The findings of the assessor, Dr. Elterman, noted that the mother had difficulty separating her own emotions from that of the child's. Dr. Elterman wrote that the mother demonstrated her thinking when she said that it would be different if the child felt loved and secure and had a bond with her father. When asked why she believed that no bond existed, the mother told the assessor that one only has to talk to the child to find out that there was no bond.

Despite the mother's allegations, the court determined that the father did not sexually abuse his daughter. The court found that the mother refused to accept the evidence of the two doctors who examined the child, the conclusions of the RCMP that there was no sexual assault, and the Ministry of Children and Family Development's concluding that there was no sexual assault. The trial judge found it disturbing that even after the publication of Dr. Elterman's report and finding of alienation, there was no evidence that the mother accepted these findings and no evidence that she took any steps whatsoever to change her behavior. The long-term psychological effect that mother's campaign of alienation would have on the child when she reaches adolescence, wrote the judge, was clearly pointed out by numerous experts in the case. The result: sole custody to target parent father.

CONCLUSIONS

Two themes emerge from these cases. One is alienator behavior. It seems the behavior of alienators is strikingly similar whether they are alienating fathers or alienating mothers. Perhaps it can be said that alienating mothers with serial fraudulent claims of abuse are harder for court personnel to stop, but the tactics are the same. The alienators in this sample manifest a sense of entitlement and ownership of their children, and the use of children as pawns demonstrates not only the lack of insight but a general heartlessness to their infliction of consternation and pain on their children and the target parents. Alienating parents in this sample engaged in harassment: repeated false allegations, hiding tape recorders, stalking, and the publishing of private facts to the public. The alienators in this sample seemed to work to build coalitions of support for their terrible behavior and gravitated to special interest groups who engage in no fact checking whatsoever. The alienators in this sample manifested a sense of being untouchable. They felt they could say anything and do anything on the telephone, in letters and e-mails, and in front of witnesses and there would be no consequences. These alienators were adept at using the inertia endemic to social welfare agencies, law enforcement, and the courts.

The other theme that emerged from these cases is that for the most part, it took so long and was so very difficult to extricate the child victims from the clutches of the alienators. Why did the mother in *In re M.K.T.* have to wait years for the appellate court in Pennsylvania to set things right? Why did the Vermont mother in *B. v. B.* have to sit by and watch a misguided trial judge give custody of her child to the alienator? Why did the Ohio mother in *S. v. S.* have to wait ten years while the courts took little or no action to help her? How come the Missouri father in *G. v. S.* had to lose precious parent-child time while he waited for the appellate court to reverse the judgment of custody to the alienator? In the *Matter of J.F. v. L.F.*, why did the target parent father in New York have to wait through ten years of ridiculous allegations and court inaction when all of the tragedy he and his children had to endure was predicted on the record at the very beginning? Why did the South Dakota court in *P. v. P.* vest custody in the alienator when it was clear to the appellate court that she had been working on the child for years? Why did the Vermont father in *S. v. S.* have to file over and over and over again and have to wait till the state's supreme court set things right? Why was the child in *R. (F.D.) v. P. (M.D.)* deprived of his mother for so long by a dull and inactive Alberta court? Why did the mother in *C. (S.) v. C. (A.S.)*, have to give up on the two older and completely alienated children in Manitoba? Why did the Ontario court sit idly by as the alienating mother from Yugoslavia made a career out of serial false sexual abuse allegations for eleven years? When the alienating mother made crazy allegation after crazy allegation in *G. (C.J.) v. G. (R.C.)*, why did the courts of British Columbia let her get away with it for ten years? Why did the target parent fathers each have to wait eight years in *L. (T.L.L.) v. L. (J.J.)* and *L. v. S.* while the Manitoba and British Columbia courts did nothing? When custody of the child victims was finally changed to the target parents in these tragic cases was it too late? Were the fines the alienating parents had to pay worth the heartache?

What was it about the judges in New York's *K.B. v. C.M.* and *L.R. v. T.R.* that they got it right immediately? How did the Ontario judge in *M. v. M.*, get it right? The answer that emerged from these sixty cases is that it was the lawyers. The successful lawyers knew that their judges placed a great emphasis on logic, thinking, rationality, fairness, rights, and rules (Daicoff, 1997). The successful and dogged Canadian and U.S. lawyers knew that their judges tended to be dependable and practical with a respect for facts who would emphasize analysis, logic, and decisiveness (Miller, 1967) if only the lawyers could present the material so that it was palatable. The successful lawyers knew that their judges tended in the main to have a low interest in emotions or others' feelings (Shneidman, 1984). These dogged lawyers understood that, for the most part, their judges tended to emphasize logic and linear thinking rather than express concern for emotional suffering or for the feelings of others (Nachmann, 1960; Watson, 1968). In brief, their judges had to be presented with the data and facts of PA in a way they could process and understand. It is hoped that this book provides the material to do just that.

REFERENCES

United States Reference Cases

A. v. A., 1999 WL 33100154 (Del.Fam.Ct.)
B. v. B., 168 Vt. 298, 721 A.2d 469 (Vt.,1998.)
B. v. B., 613 So.2d 275 (La. App. 3 Cir., 1993.)
B. v. O., 1996 WL 33324080 (Mich.App.)
E. v. E., 2011 WL 1566201 (Conn. Super.)
G. v. G., 1995 WL 222085 (Tex.App.-Hous. (14 Dist.))
G. v. S., 754 S.W.2d 579 (Mo. App. W.D., 1988.)
H. v. H., 2010 Ark. App. 58 (Ark. App., 2010.)
H. v. S., 685 N.E.2d 71 (Ind. App., 1997.)
In re Disciplinary Proceedings Against Nichols, 253 Wis.2d 149, 645 N.W.2d 270, 2002 WI 60 (Wis., 2002.)
In re Marriage of B., 804 N.W.2d 314, 2011 WL 3128058 (Iowa App.)
In re Marriage of R., 524 N.W.2d 212 (Iowa App.,1994.)
In re Marriage of Y. and A., 2010 WL 4970285 (Cal.App. 2 Dist.,2010.)
In re M.K.T., 427 Pa.Super. 515, 629 A.2d 988 (Pa.Super.,1993.)
J. H. v. P. F., 6 Misc.3d 1013(A), 800 N.Y.S.2d 348 (N.Y.Fam.Ct. 2004.)
K. v. K., 1996 WL 898369 (Conn. Super.)
K. B. v. C. M., 151 Misc.2d 794,574 N.Y.S.2d 267 (N.Y. Fam . Ct., 1991.)
L. R. v. T. R., 27 Misc.3d 1227(A), 911 N.Y.S.2d 693 (N.Y.Sup. 2010).
M. of J.F. v. L.F., 181 Misc.2d 722, 694 N.Y.S.2d 592 (N.Y.Fam .Ct., 1999.)
Matter of P., 914 S.W.2d 889 (Tenn.App.,1995.)
M. v. M., 173 Vt. 195, 789 A.2d 921 (Vt.,2001.)
M. v. M., 2007 WL 2128882 (Tex.App.-Corpus Christi)
P. v. M., 10 So.3d 748, 2008-0075 (La.App. 4 Cir. 1/7/09)
P. v. P., 611 N.W.2d 425, 2000 SD 64 (S.D., 2000.)
S. v. P., 117 Wash.App. 1017, 2003 WL 21321829 (Wash.App. Div. 1)
S. v. S., 177 Vt. 577, 865 A.2d 358, 2004 VT 106 (Vt., 2004.)
S. v. S., 2007 WL 80039 (Ohio App. 5 Dist.)
S. v. S., 2007 WL 2570428 (Conn.Super.)
W. v. W., 655 N.E.2d 523 (Ind. App., 1995.)
W. v. W., 2011 WL 8199263 (Conn. Super.)

Canadian Reference Cases

A. v. A., 2011 CarswellAlta 948, 2011 ABQB 306, [2011] A.W.L.D. 3470, [2011] A.W.L.D. 3467, [2011] A.W.L.D. 3465, [2011] A.W.L.D. 3462, [2011] W.D.F.L. 4569, [2011] W.D.F.L. 4539, [2011] W.D.F.L. 4519, [2011] W.D.F.L. 4583, 5 R.F.L. (7th) 258, 53 Alta. L.R. (5th) 20
B. v. B., 2009 CarswellBC 3282, 2009 BCSC 1666, [2010] B.C.W.L.D. 1866, [2010] B.C.W.L.D. 1849, [2010] W.D.F.L. 985, [2010] W.D.F.L. 1044

C. v. C., 2004 CarswellOnt 5255, [2005] W.D.F.L. 711, [2005] W.D.F.L. 695, [2005] W.D.F.L. 642, [2004] O.T.C. 1106, 135 A.C.W.S. (3d) 880

C. (S.) v. C. (A.S.), 2011 CarswellMan 443, 2011 MBCA 70, 2 R.F.L. (7th) 30, 268 Man. R. (2d) 282, 206 A.C.W.S. (3d) 461

Catholic Children's Aid Society of Toronto v. H. (L.D.), 2008 CarswellOnt 9401, 2008 ONCJ 783, [2010] W.D.F.L. 3226, [2010] W.D.F.L. 3229

Children's Aid Society of Waterloo (Regional Municipality) v. L. (K.A.), 2010 CarswellOnt 7373, 2010 ONCJ 80, [2011] W.D.F.L. 1105, [2011] W.D.F.L. 1123, 92 R.F.L. (6th) 363

F. v. V., 2006 CarswellOnt 159, [2006] W.D.F.L. 1160, [2006] W.D.F.L. 1155, [2006] W.D.F.L. 1221, [2006] W.D.F.L. 1217, [2006] W.D.F.L. 1265, 145 A.C.W.S. (3d) 101, 69 W.C.B. (2d) 107

G. (C.J.) v. G. (R.C.), 2007 CarswellBC 215, 2007 BCSC 161, [2007] B.C.W.L.D. 4401, [2007] B.C.W.L.D. 4399, [2007] W.D.F.L. 3272, [2007] W.D.F.L. 3262

J. v. J., 2010 CarswellOnt 2922, 2010 ONSC 6, [2010] W.D.F.L. 4643, [2010] W.D.F.L. 4583, [2010] W.D.F.L. 4572

L. v. L., 2009 CarswellBC 670, 2009 BCSC 359, [2009] B.C.W.L.D. 2510, [2009] B.C.W.L.D. 2553, [2009] W.D.F.L. 1683, [2009] W.D.F.L. 1727

L. v. S., 2010 CarswellBC 2035, 2010 BCSC 1081, [2011] B.C.W.L.D. 492, [2011] B.C.W.L.D. 491, [2011] B.C.W.L.D. 489, [2011] W.D.F.L. 369, [2011] W.D.F.L. 358, [2011] W.D.F.L. 345

L. (D.) v. Listuguj Police Service, 1999 CarswellQue 3725, [2000] R.D.F. 35, REJB 1999-15479, J.E. 2000-58

L. (J.K.) v. S. (N.C.), 2008 CarswellOnt 2903, [2008] W.D.F.L. 3437, [2008] W.D.F.L. 3430, [2008] W.D.F.L. 3431, 54 R.F.L. (6th) 74.

L. (R.) v. L. (N.), 2007 CarswellNB 684, [2009] W.D.F.L. 1100, [2009] W.D.F.L. 1156, 65 R.F.L. (6th) 117

L. (R.A.) v. R. (R.D.), 2007 CarswellAlta 183, 2007 ABQB 79, [2007] W.D.F.L. 3055, [2007] W.D.F.L. 3050, [2007] W.D.F.L. 3088, [2007] W.D.F.L. 3091, [2007] A.W.L.D. 2707, [2007] A.W.L.D. 2705, [2007] A.W.L.D. 2715, [2007] A.W.L.D. 2716.

L. (T.L.L.) v. L. (J.J.), 2011 CarswellMan 18, 2011 MBCA 10, [2011] W.D.F.L. 1372, [2011] W.D.F.L. 1445, 262 Man. R. (2d) 124, 507 W.A.C. 124

M. v. M., 2005 CarswellOnt 2630, 140 A.C.W.S. (3d) 505

M.A. v. M.A., 2009 CarswellOnt 2231, [2009] W.D.F.L. 4074, 176 A.C.W.S. (3d) 758

O. (S.) v. O. (S.C.), 1999 CarswellNB 289, 215 N.B.R. (2d) 129, 551 A.P.R. 129.

P. v. P., 2008 CarswellSask 160, 2008 SKQB 63, [2008] W.D.F.L. 2408.

R. v. K., 1991 CarswellOnt 1326, [1992] W.D.F.L. 049.

R. (F.D.) v. P. (M.D.), 2004 CarswellAlta 1743, 2004 ABQB 956.

S. v. K., 1999 CarswellBC 993

S. v. S., 2002 CarswellMan 108, 2002 MBQB 73, 162 Man. R. (2d) 199

S. v. S., 2010 CarswellOnt 10860, [2011] W.D.F.L. 4633, 7 R.F.L. (7th) 167

S. (C.) v. S. (M.), 2007 CarswellOnt 1267, 37 R.F.L. (6th) 373, 155 A.C.W.S. (3d) 605, [2007] W.D.F.L. 2939, [2007] W.D.F.L. 2944.

S. (I.M.M.) v. S. (D.J.), 2010 CarswellBC 538, 2010 BCSC 306, [2010] B.C.W.L.D. 4666, [2010] W.D.F.L. 2722, 83 R.F.L. (6th) 333

T. v. T., 2006 CarswellOnt 8553, [2007] W.D.F.L. 2581, [2007] W.D.F.L. 2597, [2007] W.D.F.L. 2647, [2007] W.D.F.L. 2671, [2007] W.D.F.L. 2583, [2007] W.D.F.L. 2612, [2007] W.D.F.L. 2632, [2007] W.D.F.L. 2590, [2007] W.D.F.L. 2589, [2007] W.D.F.L. 2620, [2007] W.D.F.L. 2626, [2007] W.D.F.L. 2640, [2007] W.D.F.L. 2656, [2007] W.D.F.L. 2637, 154 A.C.W.S. (3d) 1125.

W. (S.L.) v. W. (W.N.), 2007 CarswellAlta 875, 2007 ABQB 420, [2007] A.W.L.D. 3851, [2007] W.D.F.L. 4526

W. v. W., 2005 CarswellNS 7, 2005 NSSF 2, [2005] W.D.F.L. 1133, 229 N.S.R. (2d) 168, 725 A.P.R. 168

Science

Daicoff, S. (1997). Lawyer, know thyself: A review of empirical research on Attorney attributes bearing on professionalism. *American University Law Review, 46,* 1337–1427.

Miller, P. V. R. (1967). Personality differences and student survival in law school. *Journal of Legal Education, 19,* 460–467.

Nachman, B. (1960). Childhood experience and vocational choice in law, dentistry, and social work. *Journal of Counseling Psychology* 7(4), 243–250.

Shneidman, E. N. (1984). Personality and "success" among a selected group of lawyers. *Journal of Personality Assessment 48*(6), 609–616.

Watson, A. S. (1968). The quest for professional competence: Psychological aspects of legal education. *University of Cincinnati Law Review 37,* 91.

Chapter 13

PARENTAL ALIENATION INITIATIVES AROUND THE WORLD

CHRISTIAN T. DUM

Since parental alienation (PA) is an expression of human behavior, it is not surprising that it occurs worldwide and with much the same behavioral patterns. There are some aspects of PA that do vary from country to country, however. The frequency with which the problem occurs, the attention the problem gets, and the environment for dealing with it differ considerably from place to place, depending on the country's history, social traditions, and–because PA is most frequently seen in the context of separation or divorce–its legal system. In this chapter we will compare how various aspects of PA have developed around the world, with the aim of encouraging both mental health and legal professionals to consider adopting successful approaches from other countries to the cultural, social, and legal framework of their own country.

PARENTAL ALIENATION AWARENESS ACROSS CULTURES

Because developments regarding PA in English-speaking countries are covered in other chapters of this book and are more easily accessible to readers, this chapter will focus on other areas of the world. This chapter disproves absurd claims that PA is an "American invention" or simply "Gardner's theory." Also, this chapter complements the demonstration of the worldwide existence of PA studies in the proceedings of an international conference in Germany (Boch-Galhau, Kodjoe, Andritzky & Koeppel, 2003), *The International Handbook of Parental Alienation Syndrome* (Gardner, Sauber & Lorandos, 2006); and *Parental Alienation, DSM-5, and ICD-11* (Bernet, 2010). In fact, with the term parental alienation, due to Gardner, as key words, perhaps in translation or transliteration, one can find evidence of PA awareness nearly everywhere one cares to look, aided also by the fact that his book (Gardner, 1992) was most often its starting point. Awareness means relief to many affected parents and children, as they learn that their experience is not unique but rather common, and it has a name.

PA is not confined to Western culture or countries with no-fault divorce, although religion and cultural traditions may influence frequency and handling. For example, PA was recognized as a problem in Malta (Vassalo, 2009) well before legal divorce was made possible in 2011. Also, PA awareness exists in the Philippines, where to date no legal divorce is possible, only legal separation under rather stringent conditions. The Civil Code (Article 363) as amended by the Family Code of 1998 (Article 213), states in that case, "No child under seven years of age shall be separated from the mother, unless the court finds compelling reasons to order otherwise." These statutes, understood to imply sole maternal custody, were at issue in a case before the Supreme Court of the Philippines (*Dacasin v. Dacasin,* 2010).

In a Separate Opinion, Justice Roberto Abad detailed why he feels uncomfortable with the proposition that an agreement between the mother and the father on joint custody over a child below seven years of age is void for being contrary to law and public policy. He states,

> To declare that a joint custody agreement over minors of tender age contravenes Philippine laws will only discourage separating couples from sharing parental duties and responsibilities. It will render shared parenthood illegal and unduly promote *paternal alienation* [emphasis added]. It also presumes that separated parents cannot cooperate and compromise for the welfare of their children. It constitutes undue interference in the parents' intrinsic right to direct their relations with their child. (Dacasin v. Dacasin, 2010)

PA awareness is also evident in states in which ancient religious traditions play a significant role. In India this influence is reflected in the Hindu Marriage Act of 1955, which applies to Hindus, Sikhs, and Buddhists but not to Christians or Jews. In 2008 the Children's Rights Initiative for Shared Parenting (CRISP) was created in India by people who recognized the serious effects of PA on children due to single parent families on account of divorce or separation. CRISP is focusing on furthering the rights of children to remain connected with both parents. Its web site (www.crisp-india.org) has extensive information on PA.

Israel has two somewhat parallel court systems, Civil Family Courts and Rabbinical Courts. The latter addressed PA at an annual conference, Rabbinical Courts and Parental Alienation (2007).

In Malaysia, which is a multiethnic society but with Islam as the dominant and state religion, one finds a very informative web site on PA (www .pemalik.org), as well as reports in newspapers and on the official web site of the Malaysian Bar. Shared custody, which also impacts PA, is an issue, as the Marriage and Divorce Act of 1976 (http://www.commonlii.org/my/legis /consol_act/lrada1976272/) states in Part VIII, §88(3): "There shall be a rebuttable presumption that it is for the good of a child below the age of seven years to be with his or her mother, but in deciding whether that presumption applies to the facts of any particular case, the court shall have regard to the undesirability of disturbing the life of a child by changes of custody."

A preference for maternal custody in early childhood also exists in the Islamic Maghreb states of North Africa. Some evidence of PA awareness can be found in all of them (e.g., in Morocco, Divorce des parents, 2009). A thesis from Algeria (Benghalem, 2010) not only contains very interesting information on Islamic custody law but also theoretical and empirical sections directly relevant to PA.

EDUCATING THE GENERAL PUBLIC AND PROFESSIONALS

Even a small survey of countries, such as just given, shows that in our era of global Internet, self-help groups and advocacy organizations are often at the forefront of PA awareness. If their information is as objective and accurate as possible, they can play a significant role in educating the general public and in gaining the broad support of professionals and politicians, which is necessary for solving the problem. The proponents of the Brazilian law on PA (Oliveira, 2008), in force since 2010 and to be discussed later, acknowledge that it was inspired by an article written by law professor Rosana Barbosa Cypriano Simão (Cypriano Simão, 2007) in a book from "Associação de Pais e Mães Separados" (Association of Separated Fathers and Mothers) (www.apase.org.br), the web site of "SOS Papai e Mamãe"(www.sos-papai .org), and by suggestions from individual members of these and other associations.

Italy has taken an interesting approach by forming a head organization, Adiantum (www.adiantum.it), of various parent-child organizations to represent their agenda more effectively. In a hearing by the Italian Senate on July 26, 2011, Adiantum advocated the inclusion of PA in the current shared custody reform project. There is a very informative web site on PA developments in Italy: www.alienazione.genitoriale.com.

In France, the Association contre l'alienation parentale pour le maintien du lien familial (ACALPA) (Association against Parental Alienation and for the Maintenance of Family Ties), founded by Olga Odinetz in 2004, informs about PA, interacts with the media, participates in related conferences, and has even trained police about PA in order to aid in their duty to enforce parenting time orders. The web site of ACALPA is www.acalpa.org.

The experience of the German organization Väter für Kinder (Fathers for Children), founded in 1988 by family lawyer Peter Koeppel, which informs on psychological and legal aspects of custody, is also very positive. The web site (www.beideeltern.de) is frequently consulted by parents, professionals, students, and the media. The Federal Ministry of Justice regularly asks for comments on any new law drafts related to family law, and sometimes the German Supreme Court does as well, before custody-related decisions. Their web pages on PA are some of the most frequently consulted. They were started by this author soon after discovering a brief reference to Gardner's book in a seminal article on "rituals of obstructing parenting time" (Klenner, 1995). An important conclusion to draw from this experience, which applies also to other web sites that report on developments from other countries and also to translations in print, is that only if these reports closely relate to the situation in their own country will there be a significant resonance.

The breakthrough in Germany came when Kodjoe and Koeppel (1998) related PA to existing German family law and to what they called "Leuchtturmurteile" (lighthouse judgments) that independently had described the same behavioral patterns Gardner summarized. Although this fact was also used by some for discarding PA as "old wine in new skins" (Stadler & Salzgeber, 1999), there were soon more papers, seminars, media reports, and also new judgments explicitly referring to PA.

Then a climate change occurred, however, and it is important to analyze why. Apparently a chief reason is that this enthusiastic discussion of PA was not followed up by original, empirically based research. Most of the papers were merely an exchange of opinions, repeating also the all too well-known controversies, just shifted in time. This situation was encouraged by the fact that peer review as a fair and effective tool for quality assurance is largely unknown, although it is standard practice in Germany in natural sciences such as biology or physics (Dum, 2003). This also makes acceptance of papers for publication a rather nontransparent process. A sad consequence is that so far only a single paper on PA from Germany (Napp-Peters, 2005) made it as peer reviewed into the largest psychological database, PsycINFO®, of the American Psychological Association. This database generally lists only peer-reviewed papers, currently some 210 with the key words "parental alienation."

Almost needless to say, the polemical article by Bruch (2001) was published in translation in the most widely circulated German family law journal, but it was extremely difficult to also get even a very brief rebuttal by Gardner printed. Bruch's article then served as the key reference to PA in a yearly appearing prestigious handbook on case law, the "Palandt," which is on practically every lawyer's and judge's desk. Bruch's article thus entered some judgments for rejecting PA. It is perhaps a minor miracle that in Palandt, Bassenge, and Brudermüller (2006) and also in 2007 to 2008 it was replaced as key PA reference by an extended version of earlier work by Warshak (2005b), translated by this author and commented jointly with Boch-Galhau.

Although the followers of the "alienated child" concept de-emphasize the role of alienating parents, compared to Gardner's original formulations especially, but do not deny, of course, that there are alienated children, an article by Johnston (2007) appeared in a German family law journal with an arbitrarily altered title, "Entfremdete Scheidungskinder?" ("Alienated Children of Divorce?"). In a flawed, but also slanted translation, Johnston's characterization of Bruch as a "women's advocate" became the equivalent of "attorney for women." Also, more on the funny side, the colloquial "goodies" for enticements was translated as the equivalent of "sweets." More seriously, "role-reversal" became the equivalent of "overidentification," although German mental health professionals can also be expected to be familiar with the phenomenon of parentification and the German term: Parentifizierung. There are other serious flaws in that paper. In 2008, the article was added as a PA reference in the "Palandt."

Starting with the 2010 edition of Palandt, only a court decision of 2005, which rejects PA with reference to Bruch (2001), is listed. This likely can be blamed on the fact that there have been no German publications on PA since 2007, not even in translation.

In the Czech Republic, Gardner's book *The Parental Alienation Syndrome* (1992) was translated in 1994 and Warshak's book *Divorce Poison* (2001) was translated in 2003. *Divorce Poison,* which is primarily directed toward PA-affected parents, was also published in Korea (2005a), Croatia (2008), Finland (2012a), and Japan (2012b). Attempts to convince German publishers to publish these books or others on PA have failed so far, although publications in German would have a much larger audience. There is to date not a single comprehensive book on PA for professionals in German, although one is most needed.

The tradition of training about PA that we see in other countries, organized by professional organizations and in part also sponsored by government agencies, is unfortunately also still absent in Germany. In Italy, it continues to this day in an impressive manner. For example, a course, "Bambini privati dei loro genitori. Approfondimento di due tematiche emergenti:

alienazione genitoriale e allontanamenti istituzionali" ("Children Deprived of Their Parents. Thorough Examination of Two Emerging Issues: Parental Alienation and Institutional Placements") (2011) was organized by Prospettive Associazione per la valorizzazione delle risorse umane (Association for the Promotion of Human Resources) from October 2011 to April 2012. It stood under the patronage of the provincial government of Trento and offered credits for continued education.

In Italy, PA studies were from the very beginning connected to academic teaching and research, with the first publication (Buzzi, 1997) and then Gulotta (1998) already included an empirical study. Accordingly, there are a number of comprehensive Italian books for professionals on PA, for example, Gulotta, Cavedon, and Liberatore (2008); Parrini (2008), and Cavedon and Magro (2010). They are complemented by peer-reviewed articles that have appeared mostly in the journal *Maltrattamento e Abuso all'Infanzia,* with a special edition on PA in 2005 (Malagoli Togliatti & Franci, 2005) and another special edition on "Threats to the parent-child relationship" in 2009 (Malagoli Togliatti & Lubrano Lavadera, 2009).

In Spain, the first National Symposium on Parental Alienation took place in 2006, organized by the Ilustre Colegio Oficial de Medicos de Madrid (Official College of Physicians of Madrid). It was followed in 2007 and 2008 by other such symposia for professionals. The Asociación Pro Derechos del Niño SOS Papá (Association for the Rights of the Child) has already organized its Fourth International Congress on PA and Shared Parenting with broad participation by experts on PA from Spain and abroad (www.congresointernacionalsap.org). Although these conferences meet the same scientific standards as earlier national symposia, the organization by what is primarily a father's association especially infuriates anti-PA lobbies.

Most professionals in Germany now prefer to just describe the PA phenomenon without explicitly referring to the term "parental alienation" or "parental alienation syndrome." A former judge at an appeals court, open to PA as shown by a number of "PA decisions" in which he had participated, gives this advice:

> The attorney, however, should consider, if it is advisable to immediately (in the preliminaries or in court) operate with the term "PAS." It could raise certain aversions at the bench, as once by trying to win points with allegations of sexual abuse. The main object should be to avoid escalation on part of everyone involved! (Weychardt, 2007)

Although there is certainly no point in just dropping the "PA words" without specifying what actually happened in the case, omitting any reference to PA unfortunately makes it difficult to retrieve such cases or the vast amount of corresponding literature from databases, the Internet, and so on.

It is remarkable that despite the now-prevailing climate, self-help groups, in particular a group of mostly alienated mothers, PAS Eltern e. V. (PAS Parents Association), managed to get the attention of the Children's Commission of the Bavarian State Diet to organize in the parliament in March 2011 an expert meeting on PA, attended also by senior state government officials (Eltern-Kind-Entfremdung, 2011). The commission seems determined to keep PA on the parliamentary agenda. In March 2012 the State Family Ministry in cooperation with medical organizations and universities issued guidelines for physicians (*Gewalt gegen Kinder und Jugendliche,* 2012) which in Section 3.4.2.4 describes involving children in the parental conflict as a special form of psychological abuse that may result in a parental alienation syndrome and illustrates it with an example. Actually using the PAS term in these guidelines, although very controversial in Germany still, should open up a vast amount of literature. See, for example, Andritzky (2006).

REACTION AGAINST PARENTAL ALIENATION

Critical discussion is essential for the progress of science, but reaction against PA is most often based upon nonscientific arguments, even on just the fact that most affected parents, and thus also self-help group members, are alienated fathers. That alienation is not a question of gender but is largely connected with being the residential parent or not should have been emphasized by the early PA pioneers. This fact is becoming ever more evident with increasing numbers of fathers as primary residential parents. At the same time an increasing number of alienated mothers, who even suffer additionally, because it is still believed, also in Western societies, that especially smaller children "normally belong" to the mother after separation or divorce (Kruk, 2010). It is helpful that more and more mothers and grandparents–who are usually not subject to allegations of using PA to cover up abuse and domestic violence–become active in PA self-help or PA advocacy groups.

Nevertheless, it is doubtful that this reality will sufficiently impress certain groups of PA detractors, especially when their claims and activities are at least indirectly supported by some professionals and even through government agencies and public funding. This may occur by articles such as "Parental Alienation oder [or] Parental Accusation Syndrome?" (Fegert, 2001) and in other ways. It is bizarre that, in view of the large number of peer-reviewed publications outside Germany, the detractor groups claim that PA is just Gardner's or an American "invention" with no scientific significance, but also that PA is just being discussed in Germany still, while already reduced to insignificance in the country it came from. Sadly, such claims were even echoed by spokespeople of a supposed expert body on custody and of a federal ministry.

In Spain, anti-PA lobbies have succeeded in what is hopefully only a temporary climate change. The Dean of the College of Psychologists of Madrid, Fernando Chacon (2008), wrote

> [The controversy about parental alienation is] completely sterile. It is fed by interest groups, carried out by disqualifications, and is devoid of scientific arguments: The key for psychologists is to ask, if there are fathers or mothers who manipulate their child to predispose him or her against the other parent and finally to refuse contact, and if this has negative effects for the welfare of the child. If the answer to these questions is yes, you might consider the necessity of referring to cases that exhibit the characteristics common in a certain (universal) way; we could call it 'X'. Now, deciding on a specific name or not does not deny the ontological reality of individual cases, which are our primary concern.

Recently, militant groups, it seems, could channel their protests to make Spain apparently the only country in which government agencies had urged judges, prosecutors, and legal experts against acceptance of the PA concept. In 2011 the Center for Domestic Violence and Gender, part of the Ministry of Health, Social Policy, and Equality, issued a report that warned that PAS represented "dangerous consequences for mothers and children." In an article in the newspaper *El País,* Miguel Lorente, coordinator of the institutes of forensic medicine in Andalusia and author on the "battered wife syndrome," is quoted saying, "Certainly there are mothers, but also fathers who foment aversion against the other parent, but if the relation to the child is healthy and intense, it will not get interrupted," adding, "If a child rejects a parent, it is due to this parent being violent and aggressive. With this many experts agree" (Prades, 2011). The government report was coordinated by Ana María Pérez del Campo (2010), president of the Association of Separated Mothers. One of the authors of the report is also the first author of an anti-PA book (Vaccaro & Barea Payueta, 2009).

Family judges, such as Ángel Luis Campo (Oviedo, 2011), however, felt that the government should not tell judges, who are independent, what position to take on PA. Judges do not have to decide on the appropriateness of the term PA but on what is behind the term. There can hardly be a doubt that there are parents who try to manipulate a child to refuse contact with the other parent and judges must act accordingly. Francisco Serrano Castro (2011), another family judge, pointed out that the authors of this report were chosen to represent gender ideology and subsidized lobbies. These self-styled experts have refused any cooperation with other groups. Also, denying the reality of PA, because it is not listed as a disease in the *DSM,* is equal to denying that there are battered women, because the "battered wife syndrome" is not in the *DSM.* Serrano Castro declared himself more inclined to be guided by the judgments of the European Court of Human Rights, relating to the recognition of PA, rather than by the government's representative for gender violence saying that the report is directed against sexist judges.

The governing body of the professional Asociación Española Multidisciplinar de Investigation Sobre Interferencias Parentales (ASEMIP) (Multidisciplinary Spanish Association for the Investigation of Parental Interference) also replied to this "False Debate on PAS" (Fariña Rivera & Tovar Escudero, 2011). ASEMIP (2010) endorsed the inclusion of PA in *DSM-5* and *ICD-11* and has issued a very comprehensive report on parental interference in separation and divorce (Fariña, Arce, Novo & Seijo, 2010).

EMPIRICAL RESEARCH ON PARENTAL ALIENATION

Clinical observations by mental health practitioners stood at the beginning of PA studies and still play an important role in providing input for more extensive empirical studies. There are specific limitations to empirical research on PA, in that outside a forensic setting it proves mostly impossible to interview or test alienating parents or, for legal and ethical reasons, the affected children. The most important subjects of such studies, the children, can usually only be interviewed as adults, such as in the cross-sectional studies of Baker (2007). They provide a retrospective view and information about long-term effects, but knowing more about their immediate experience as a child and the needs they felt then would also be most important for improving the way PA cases are handled. Boch-Galhau and Kodjoe (2006) were able to carry out such studies in Germany with some children, by interviewing them at the earliest possible moment after custody was transferred to the previously alienated target parent. They also interviewed children who on their own decided to live with the target parent, and in one case when the child was returned to the parents from institutional alienation after specific PA therapy. Boch-Galhau (2012) conducted very interesting follow-up interviews with these children or then young adults.

Extensive studies have been carried out in Sweden by Hellblom Sjögren (2006, 2012) on institutional PA by social agencies placing children with foster parents or in shelters without adequate measures for supporting their earliest possible return to their parents. They dramatically highlight the need for

PA training of social workers and of judges who ultimately decide on such cases.

Various authors (e.g., Lund, 1995) have emphasized that PA is a relational problem in which it is important to consider the entire family system, rather than just the kind of cause and effect model of alienating parent-child, as may be suggested by Gardner's presentations. The child's resistance to contact with a parent can also arise from efforts to cope with being in the middle of intense parental conflict or could be connected with the target parent's inability to develop a positive relationship with the child or even with abusive behavior (which, it is agreed, precludes the applicability of PA). With prolonged conflict, resistance to contact may also be due to fully developed PA, with psychodynamics in the child or young adult as now an autonomous cause for this rejection. Some authors designate this stage of the child as "parental alienation syndrome (PAS)," as distinct from "parental alienation (PA)," the influence (programming) by a caretaker (Darnall, 1998).

Assessing these factors is important for deciding how to proceed with legal measures or therapy. The recent book for professionals by Cavedon and Magro (2010) specifically deals with this differential diagnosis. They discuss interview techniques and a number of diagnostic tests that might be helpful in evaluating the relation between family members and the family dynamics. These techniques are illustrated by PA and non-PA cases. Such cases, including cases with allegations of sexual abuse and a case of genuine preference for one of the parents, were also discussed in the comprehensive monograph by Gulotta and colleagues (2008). They show how a psycholinguistic examination and what they call microanalysis of the communication between parents, psychological expert, and child can be used for a refined differential diagnosis of PA. Tracing the nuances of language, following Watzlawick, Beavin Bavelas, and Jackson (1967), can reveal alienating behavior of a parent or dissonances in the child's story, which demonstrate indoctrination. Symptoms of alienation, such as mimicking adult speech, can also be revealed by using software for the analysis of readability and complexity of texts by the use of uncommon words and other indexes.

A very recent study (Lubrano Lavadera, Ferracuti & Malagoli Togliatti, 2012) analyzed twelve Italian court-ordered psychological expert evaluations in which PA had been diagnosed. Twelve evaluations that did not receive a PA diagnosis served as a control group. The study highlights the family characteristics in these two groups.

A team (Cartié et al., 2005) attached to the courts of Barcelona was able to study the characteristics of sixty-nine "PA families" (eighty-nine children), selected on the basis of a template that included a variety of family characteristics in addition to eleven PA symptoms identified by Gardner. Those cases amounted to about 10 percent of the cases with conflicts over custody referred to the team. It was found that PA symptoms occurred with different frequencies, which also depended significantly on the age of the child. Correlation was found within two clusters: independent-thinker phenomenon, campaign of rejection or denigration, animosity towards the alienated parent's extended family, and absence of guilt formed the first cluster. Adult speech and frivolous, absurd rationalizations formed the second. Borrowed scenarios, lack of ambivalence, and reflexive support of one parent against the other were not correlated with other symptoms. There was no correlation between the number of symptoms present and the severity of PA. Cartié and colleagues (2008) extended that work to focus more on characteristics of the "rejected" parent and to improve diagnostics by designing a structured interview, which in suspected PA cases was carried out independently by two experts. Their sample consisted of thirteen families, with five interviewed by two experts.

Both studies built on a thesis by Bolaños Cartujo (2000), with a detailed description of the legal, demographic, socioeconomic, and cultural characteristics of fifty (later 100) families litigating over custody, in which there was rejection of a parent, and a same size control group without rejection. Rejection appeared unrelated to the causes for separation and to economic issues but depended significantly on the age of the children and the existence of new partners. High socioeconomic level, especially of the mothers, was significantly more frequent in the rejection group, and the same applied to high cultural level. This is interesting, because it indicates that alienating behavior is not simply a matter of lacking the educational background for understanding the dire consequences for the child but rather of personality characteristics. The study distinguishes between primary rejection concurrent with separation and secondary rejection, later after separation or divorce is legally in force, with mothers significantly more frequently affected by primary rejection. In a pilot study, it was found that mediation with the family system is effective in mild to moderate PA cases, if carried out in conjunction with the court. In 74 percent of rejection cases, some agreement could be reached, with total restoration of contact in 38 percent of cases. Mediation techniques are discussed in Bolaños Cartujo (2008) and illustrated by case stories.

Vilalta Suárez (2011) evaluated from thirty-nine family court records the frequency of fourteen characteristics indicative of PA for the child, twenty-eight for the residential parent, five for the nonresidential parent, and nine contextual variables of the conflict. The classic PA symptoms were significantly more frequent in cases with interruption of parent-child contacts, and their intercorrelation corresponded to the results of Cartié and associates

(2005). There was a significant correlation between PA-related characteristics of the child and such characteristics of the residential parent, but none with variables related to psychological problems of the nonresidential parent. As in other studies (Cartié et al., 2008; Gordon, Stoffey & Bottinelli, 2008), the characteristics of target parents did not differ from those of a control group.

French psychiatrist and psychoanalyst Marie-France Hirigoyen was a best-selling author with her book on psychological harassment (1998). In her newest book, *Abus de faiblesse et autres manipulations* (*Abuse of Weakness and Other Manipulations*) (2012), Hirigoyen illustrates PA from case stories. This text leaves no doubt as to the reality of emotional abuse by PA and its serious consequences. Hirigoyen analyzes the psychological characteristics of the participants in the PA relational problem: an alienating parent, often with narcissistic personality disorder and related to problems in his or her own childhood (transgenerational effect); the extremely difficult situation of a child caught in the middle of parental conflict and his or her coping attempts; and a target parent with an overwhelming feeling of being powerless. She strongly advises alienated parents to somehow stay present in the life of the child but without exerting pressure and strictly avoiding attempts to impress "the truth" on the child while clearly responding to unjust allegations.

It is difficult to extend empirical studies from small convenience samples to statistically more relevant large cohorts. Templates for data collection, semistructured interviews and various psychological tests may be helpful, but there is currently no specific test for PA and much still depends on the experience of the expert examining an individual case. Interruption of parent-child contacts is a relatively simple criterion to apply. It will, however, exclude what are generally considered mild to moderate PA cases in which contacts still take place, but include cases in which interruption has causes other than PA. In any case, an operational definition for selecting samples must not be circular, that is, hypotheses to be tested must remain falsifiable in principle (Popper, 1959).

Although a number of longitudinal studies exist on children of divorce that indicate increased likelihood of more serious and longer lasting effects on children when parental conflict continues, longitudinal studies specifically on "PA children" would be desirable. The outcome may depend on resilience factors, such as identified in the famous long-term Kauai Study (Werner & Smith, 1992, pp. 197–198) and in the divorce study of Benghalem (2010).

Only universities and research institutions, rather than practitioners, are likely able to carry out large-scale empirical studies with statistically significant large cohorts and control groups. The same applies to longitudinal studies over extended periods. The connection of PA to academic teaching and research that exists in some countries more than in others is therefore a significant factor for progress.

LEGAL ASPECTS OF PARENTAL ALIENATION

> The laws of every people governed by statutes and customs are partly peculiar to itself, partly common to all mankind. The rules established by a given state for its own members are peculiar to itself, and are called *jus civile;* the rules constituted by natural reason for all are observed by all nations alike, and are called *jus gentium.* So the laws of the people of Rome are partly peculiar to itself, partly common to all nations; and this distinction shall be explained in detail in each place as it occurs. (Gaius, 160 AD/1904)

The diversity between nations in their legal systems, in their social support systems, as well as the administrative systems that go with them still exists today. It largely also explains the diversity with which the problem of PA is handled. As common to all nations in the sense Gaius described, we can consider various international treaties with an impact on national legislation. Although national custody laws usually will contain provisions for the contact of the child with both parents, some states have in addition introduced special legislation on PA that foresees specific measures for dealing with the problem and raises the awareness of the justice system regarding PA.

UNITED NATIONS CONVENTION ON THE RIGHTS OF THE CHILD

The convictions that "The family, as the fundamental group of society and the natural environment for the growth and well-being of all its members and particularly children, should be afforded the necessary protection and assistance so that it can fully assume its responsibilities within the community," and that "The child, for the full and harmonious development of his or her personality, should grow up in a family environment, in an atmosphere of happiness, love and understanding" can be said to be shared by all nations, even if they are not signatories of the United Nations Convention on the Rights of the Child (CRC) (United Nations, 1989). (The U.S. is a signatory to the CRC, but has not ratified it.)

The quotations are from the CRC's preamble. The articles that apply most directly to children of separated parents are as follows:

Article 3

1. In all actions concerning children, whether undertaken by public or private social welfare institutions, courts of law, administrative authorities or legislative bodies, the best interests of the child shall be a primary consideration.

Article 8

1. States Parties undertake to respect the right of the child to preserve his or her identity, including nationality, name and family relations as recognized by law without unlawful interference.

2. Where a child is illegally deprived of some or all of the elements of his or her identity, States Parties shall provide appropriate assistance and protection, with a view to re-establishing speedily his or her identity.

Article 9

1. State Parties shall ensure that a child shall not be separated from his or her parents against their will, except when competent authorities subject to judicial review determine, in accordance with applicable law and procedures, that such separation is necessary for the best interests of the child. Such determination may be necessary in a particular case such as one involving abuse or neglect of the child by the parents, or one where the parents are living separately and a decision must be made as to the child's place of residence.

2. In any proceedings pursuant to paragraph 1 of the present article, all interested parties shall be given an opportunity to participate in the proceedings and make their views known.

3. States Parties shall respect the right of the child who is separated from one or both parents to maintain personal relations and direct contact with both parents on a regular basis, except if it is contrary to the child's best interests.

Article 12

1. States Parties shall assure to the child who is capable of forming his or her own views the right to express those views freely in all matters affecting the child, the views of the child being given due weight in accordance with the age and maturity of the child.

2. For this purpose, the child shall in particular be provided the opportunity to be heard in any judicial and administrative proceedings affecting the child, either directly, or through a representative or an appropriate body, in a manner consistent with the procedural rules of national law.

Article 18
1. States Parties shall use their best efforts to ensure recognition of the principle that both parents have common responsibilities for the upbringing and development of the child. The best interests the child will be their basic concern. (United Nations, 1989)

It is clear how these rights are violated if a state fails to protect children against alienating influences or if a child of sufficient maturity is not heard in family court proceedings. The professional Unión Latinoamericana de Entidades de Psicología (Latin American Union of Organizations of Psychology) issued a strong statement on PA, based on the UN's CRC and with reference to the entry on relational problems in *DSM-IV,* considering "parentectomy" a very serious problem (Declaración de la Unión Latinoamericana, 2011).

The committee overseeing the CRC does not accept complaints by individuals, although they may be directed to other UN committees, such as the Human Rights Committee, located in Geneva. Some states are considering the incorporation of the convention in their constitution, as Austria did in February 2011, in order to make it directly applicable domestic law. Since February 28, 2012, a new Optional Protocol of the UN's CRC is open for signature. It will provide a complaints procedure for children, enabling them to seek redress for violations of their rights, after national mechanisms have been exhausted.

EUROPEAN CONVENTION ON HUMAN RIGHTS

The European Convention on Human Rights has been ratified by the forty-seven member states of the Council of Europe, not just the member states of the European Union. With the European Court of Human Rights, it provides a very powerful instrument for enforcement. The Court's judgments and its case law make the Convention an effective instrument for advancing and harmonizing the rule of law in Europe.

The proceedings are conducted in either English or French, and judgments are freely available on the Internet. Thus, they are open to a much larger audience than any national proceedings and also provide an excellent view of the legal and administrative system of the state concerned. Judgments originate from complaints (called "applications") mostly by private individuals or legal entities over legal or administrative practices of a state (or states), once litigants have exhausted the national remedies. A judge from that state is also one of the seven members of the Chamber addressing the complaint. Exceptional cases may be referred to a Grand Chamber of seventeen judges. If the Court finds a violation of the Convention, the "applicant" is entitled to "just satisfaction" (Article 41) (Council of Europe, 1950/2010). It usually includes, in addition to moral satisfaction by a judgment from this highly prestigious court, compensation for expenses and nonpecuniary damages. The judgment is binding for the member state but does not directly overrule national decisions or annul national laws. National laws, however, had to be modified after the Court found them to be in conflict with the Convention. In Austria, the Convention is immediately applicable domestic law of constitutional rank, rather than just an international treaty the state has submitted to.

Regarding custody and parenting time, the proceedings are mostly based upon the following articles:

> Article 6–Right to a fair trial
> 1. In the determination of his civil rights and obligations or of any criminal charge against him, everyone is entitled to a fair and public hearing within a reasonable time by an independent and impartial tribunal established by law. Judgment shall be pronounced publicly but the press and public may be excluded from all or part of the trial in the interests of morals, public order or national security in a democratic society, where the interests of juveniles or the protection of the private life of the parties so require, or to the extent strictly necessary in the opinion of the court in special circumstances where publicity would prejudice the interests of justice.
>
> Article 8–Right to respect for private and family life
> 1. Everyone has the right to respect for his private and family life, his home and his correspondence.
>
> 2. There shall be no interference by a public authority with the exercise of this right except such as is in accordance with the law and is necessary in a democratic society in the interests of national security, public safety or the economic well-being of the country, for the prevention of disorder or crime, for the protection of health or morals, or for the protection of the rights and freedoms of others.
>
> Article 13–Right to an effective remedy
> Everyone whose rights and freedoms as set forth in this Convention are violated shall have an effective remedy before a national authority notwithstanding that the violation has been committed by persons acting in an official capacity.

Article 6 is the article most frequently cited, especially regarding the length of proceedings. It is crucial in family matters because, as the Court reiterates time and again, the excessive length of proceedings can predetermine their outcome, with "alienation" progressing in time, even to a point of no return, and in any case no way to recover the lost years of childhood.

Different from family court, of concern to the European Court of Human Rights are only possible violations of the rights of the applicant by the state's authorities in handling the case. The Court thus does not hear the other parent or the child, nor are new psychological evaluations ordered. The Court bases its judgment solely on the evidence available from the national proceedings, brought forward by the applicant or as counterarguments by the representative of the concerned state. These are very important points to keep in mind when asking whether this highly prestigious supranational court recognizes PA. It can be said to be true, if the Court specifically refers to PA as a relevant factor for its decision. That is most likely to happen when PA arguments already played a significant role in the national proceedings.

As of April 2012, PA was such a factor in 8 decisions among twenty-three judgments in which the terms parental alienation (parental alienation syndrome) or aliénation parentale (syndrome d'aliénation parentale) appeared. In the remaining cases PA was mentioned just by the applicant, although sometimes also by national courts.

The eight decisions specifically using PA arguments were

- *Sommerfeld v. Germany* (Application no. 31871/96), July 8, 2003
- *Koudelka c. République Tchèque* (Requête no. 1633/05), July 20, 2006
- *Zavřel c. République Tchèque* (Requête no. 14044/05), January 18, 2007
- *Patera c. République Tchèque* (Requête no. 25326/03), April 27, 2007
- *Mincheva c. Bulgarie* (Requête no. 21558/03), September 2, 2010
- *Piazzi c. Italie* (Requête no. 36168/09), November 2, 2010
- *Bordeianu c. Moldavia* (Requête no. 49868/08), January 11, 2011
- *Diamante and Pelliccioni v. San Marino* (Application no. 32250/08), September 27, 2011.

The case of *Elsholz v. Germany* (2000) was the first with a reference to PA (by the applicant) and received a lot of attention but did not yet represent a recognition of PA by the Court. The same applies to the case *Kutzner v. Germany* (2002), in which young children were taken to a shelter by social services. The Court merely used "alienation" in a more general sense, for drifting apart, becoming strangers due to lack of contact, without necessarily implying that someone was trying to turn the children against the applicants or that the children were rejecting a parent.

In *Sommerfeld v. Germany* (2003), PA is not mentioned in the majority decision, but PA and fundamental questions regarding the child's true wishes and best interests were discussed in the dissenting opinion of Judge Rees

(Germany), joined by Judges Pastor Ridruejo (Spain) and R. Türmen (Turkey), thus paving the way for PA recognition by the Court. They said,

> The procedural requirement to have up-to-date psychological expert evidence in order to obtain correct and complete information on the child's relationship with the applicant as the parent seeking access to the child would seem an indispensable prerequisite for establishing a child's true wishes and thereby striking a fair balance between the interests at stake. This procedural requirement is endorsed even more by recent research on the so-called parental alienation syndrome ("PAS"), which has been described by Richard A. Gardner in the *American Journal of Forensic Psychology* (2001, pp. 61–106) under the title "Should courts order PAS children to visit/reside with the alienated parent? A follow-up study," and which has received an increasing amount of attention. Courts should therefore address the question whether parental alienation syndrome is present and what specific consequences such a syndrome could have on the child's development and–as the Chamber put it–on the establishment of "a child's true wishes." . . . It is true that the District Court judge, in the second set of proceedings, heard the thirteen-year-old M., who stated that she did not wish to talk to or see the applicant. However, since the last and only psychological expert opinion (a one-page submission) was submitted in April 1992, there was no other opinion about the truthfulness of the wishes expressed by the child and the question how far and how strongly she was influenced by her mother and her stepfather. . . . The statements of a ten- or thirteen-year-old girl, whether she is heard in court or not, cannot always be decisive or even indicative of her true wishes. In such a complex situation, where the alienation of the child from her natural father by the strong influence of her mother and her stepfather can be perceived, a more thorough approach has to be taken and an effective and genuine chance of participation has to be given to the natural father. (*Sommerfeld v. Germany,* 2003)

The case *Mincheva c. Bulgarie* (2010) is remarkable in that there is no direct mention in the application (as summarized by the Court) of the child (abducted by the father) showing signs of PA, but the Court on its own stated

> The Court also considers that in failing to act diligently, national authorities, through their behavior, fostered a process of parental alienation to the detriment of the applicant, thus ignoring her right to respect for family life guaranteed by Art. 8. (*Mincheva c. Bulgarie,* 2010)

In the other cases PA had played a significant role already in the national proceedings. In all of the previous cases, as in many others in which PA is not mentioned, the key question for the Court to decide was if the national authorities had undertaken all necessary measures in their power according to national law to facilitate the contact between the applicant and his or her child when this contact was in the best interest of the child; that is, when it was established that this parent was fit to raise the child and had given no reasons for the lack of contact. The Court does not shy away from calling influencing a child toward contact refusal "programming" that must be stopped, if necessary also by coercive measures such as fines or prison terms. Here is an illustration from *Zavřel c. République Tchèque* (2007):

> In view of the above facts, the Court admits that non-fulfillment of visitation rights of the applicant was due primarily to the manifest refusal by the mother, then to that of the child, programmed by the latter. However, a lack of cooperation between separated parents cannot dispense the competent authorities from implementing all possible means for allowing the maintenance of family ties (. . .); it was the duty of the authorities to take adequate measures to sanction the behavior of the mother. Indeed, although coercive actions toward children are not desirable in this delicate area, the use of sanctions should not be ruled out in the case of clearly illegal behavior of the parent with whom the child lives (. . .). . . .In this regard the Court notes that according to the expert report of 25 March 2004 the parental alienation syndrome was not yet at that time very developed in the child and his meeting with the applicant in the office of the expert went smoothly. ... If appropriate measures had been implemented quickly, it would therefore not have been difficult for the minor to get used to visits by his father, as had also been found by the Regional Court eighteen months ago. (*Zavřel c. République Tchèque,* 2007) (internal citations omitted)

See also *Koudelka c. République Tchèque* for another case in which the court endorsed coercive measures to stop parental "programming."

The European Court of Human Rights has supported the transfer of custody in case of severe PA, as in *Bordeianu c. Moldavia* (2011):

> The Court notes that the meeting between the parties dated August 10, 2007, was a failure, because of the refusal of the girl to join the applicant. It follows that at the time of the execution procedure the authorities could no longer ignore the fact that parental alienation of the girl had reached a level that threatened the implementation of the judgment and the solution of the problem required a complex approach with the participation of experts. It's at that time at the latest that the authorities should have become aware of the seriousness of the problem and implement a system of measures to prepare the transfer of the child from one parent to the other. The Court observes that no such action has been taken in this case. The bailiff decided to return the writ of execution November 27, 2007. (*Bordeianu c. Moldavia,* 2011)

The Court sees a violation, if measures were carried out only halfheartedly or were not followed up, or if they were not carried out with the necessary urgency, because PA progresses with time, even to the point of no return. For example, in *Koudelka c. République Tchèque* (2006), the Court wrote

> In the opinion of the Court, national courts have allowed in this case that the dispute is settled by the mere passage of time, so that the restoration of ties between the applicant and his daughter no longer seems possible today. (*Koudelka c. République Tchèque,* 2006)

Thus, as of now there are eight significant family law cases in which this high supranational court used arguments related to PA in its own assessment of the case. This can be seen as a clear recognition of the phenomenon. In addition, the Court has in other cases pointed out behavioral patterns that signal PA to most of us, but without actually using this term. That twelve of the twenty-three admitted cases mentioning PA are from the relatively small Czech Republic certainly should not lead to the conclusion that PA is more prevalent there than elsewhere, but rather that awareness of the phenomenon is better there than elsewhere. In fact, as Bakalář (1998) reported, a translation of Gardner's 1992 book *The Parental Alienation Syndrome* was requested by the Ministry of Labor and Social Affairs in 1994 and entered in manuals for social workers, whose job, among other things, is the representation of minors in custody proceedings. It apparently made the Czech Republic the first non-English-speaking country to be widely aware of Gardner's work and of the developments in PA in North America. Studies in the Czech Republic mostly go by the name "Syndrom zavrženého rodiče" (syndrome of rejected parents).

HAGUE CONVENTION AND INTERNATIONAL CHILD ABDUCTION

Child abduction may result in some of the worst cases of PA, because the abductor will necessarily have to "explain" to the child why there is no contact with the other parent. The international treaty that addresses child abduction is the Hague Convention of 25 October 1980 on the Civil Aspects of International Child Abduction. That treaty has only an indirect impact on PA, because its essence is the prompt return of the child to the country of habitual residence, with any custody proceedings or mental health intervention only to be conducted there. Impressive testimonies of PA brought about by international abduction may be found in Finkelstein (2003), the DVD

Victims of Another War: The Aftermath of Parental Alienation (Gebhard, 2005), and the web site Take Root (www.takeroot.org).

LEGISLATION REGARDING PARENTAL ALIENATION

Mexico

In 2004, the Federal District of Mexico was the first jurisdiction to adopt a reference to PA in its civil code:

> Article 411: Whoever exercises parental authority must ensure respect and consistent contact of the children with the other parent who also exercises custody. Accordingly, each parent must avoid any act of manipulation, parental alienation aimed at producing in the child resentment or rejection of the other parent.

In 2006, however, a countermovement, using the familiar identification of PA by some lobbies with sexual abuse and *ad hominem* attacks on Richard Gardner, eliminated that reference (Diario de los Debates, 2006, pp. 8–26). Yet, the same article was later adopted into the civil code of the state of Morelos, Mexico, as Article 224 (Ikeda, 2008, p. 81).

In the state of Aguascalientes, Mexico, the Civil Code was modified on November 19, 2007, by adding

> Article 439. . . . With both parents at all times is the obligation to avoid any conduct of parental alienation toward their children.
>
> Article 440. . . . Those who exercise parental authority, even if they have no custody, have the right to contact with the children, unless there is danger for them. . . . Any time that parental alienation is lodged on the part of either parent, the court shall ex officio order the therapeutic measures necessary for minor children, in order to restore healthy contact with both parents. To this effect, both parents have the obligation to cooperate in the implementation of measures that are determined. The judge may make use of enforcement measures established by civil law, with the power, if necessary, to order the suspension of the previously established custody or contact. (Periodico Oficial, 2007, p. 8)

On June 23, 2011, the state of Querétaro, Mexico, approved the inclusion of PA in its Codigo Civil, Articles 443 to 449. The proposal included an extensive justification, partially reproduced here:

1. Parental alienation occurs mainly in the context of custody disputes between parents. Its primary manifestation is a campaign of denigration of a child against one of the parents, a campaign that has no justification.

2. That such behavior is characterized by a set of symptoms resulting from the process by which one parent transforms the conscience of their children through various strategies in order to prevent, hinder, or destroy their links with the other parent.

3. It is necessary to integrate this behavior in domestic legislation, as there are severe cases in which the rejected parent, who was once loved and had a good relationship with the child, sees his or her link of affection permanently destroyed.

5. That the devastating effects of alienation on children are manifested in all aspects of their life, not only in their affections. The consequences go far beyond their own understanding of what is happening to them and immaturity with respect to relationships. The alienated children are betrayed by a parent, especially one who should care for them and protect them; one who provides welfare and they are physically and emotionally dependent on.

7. That some behaviors and obstructive strategies alienating parents use can be to refuse passing telephone calls to the children; organizing various activities for children during the period that the other parent must normally exercise visitation; introduce the new spouse to the children as their new mother or new father; intercept mail and packages sent to the children; denigrate and insult the other parent in front of children; refuse to inform the other parent of activities in which the children are involved, such as sporting events, school activities, among others; discuss in a discourteous manner the new spouse of the other parent; prevent the other parent to exercise their visitation rights; . . . among many other behaviors.

8. That PA occurs when there is no justified case for rejection, can be detected by the destruction of good memories of the parent, the use of language inappropriate for the age of the child, as if he or she were an adult, extension to the family of the alienated parent, claims of absurd and weak reasons that this animosity is exclusively his/her work, including behaviors that should be determined by experts and of which one must consider the type of relationship the child and the alienated parent had maintained before the separation.

11. That PA is a form of abuse of minors and the state must protect children from all forms of abuse perpetrated by parents or any other responsible person.

> 12. That judges should consider the arguments that professionals in the field provide, based on scientific literature and not on mere repetition of simplistic recipes of one case extrapolated to another, as well on statements made to that effect by the children involved. (Dictamen de la Iniciativa, 2011, pp. 9–12)

After revision, the Civil Code of the state of Querétaro adds in Article 443 that parental authority is suspended for "engaging in behaviors of parental alienation" and adds

> Title Nine, Article 447. Every child of minor age has the right to live with his or her parents, but when they do not cohabit or are divorced, they establish the basis for custody, so he/she will have the right to maintain regular contact and visit with them. . . . When someone who has temporary or permanent custody of minors carries out behaviors of parental alienation or any other aimed at the avoidance of contacts of them with the person or persons entitled thereto, in more than one occasion and without due cause justified in the opinion of the judge, he shall apply the measures provided for in the Code of Civil Procedure of the State of Querétaro, and may even declare a change of custody of minors.
>
> Article 449 c. Parental alienation is the manipulation that a parent or relative subjects a minor to by disapproval or criticism, in order to denigrate the other parent or their families and in order to produce in the child, rejection, rancor, hatred or contempt for him/her. The manipulation must be severe enough to induce in the child rejection of contact with the parent or relative. A person who commits any of the behaviors in the first paragraph is considered alienating. Every parent or family member has the duty to prevent and bring to the attention of the court any conduct of parental alienation.
>
> Article 449 d. At the time that the court is aware that a parent or family member commits acts of parental alienation, it must use the measures established by law, to safeguard the integrity and the right of the child. (Dictamen de la Iniciativa, 2011, pp. 9–12)

Similar parliamentary proposals for including definitions of PA in the Civil Code and measures against it have also been made in the Mexican states of Michoacán de Ocampo (Dictamen con Proyecto, 2010), Chihuahua (Propone PAN, 2011), and Morelos (Iniciativa que Reforma, 2011, pp. 21–23).

Brazil

In Brazil, Lei No. 12.318 (2010) went into effect on August 26, 2010. It defines PA and institutes specific measures for the courts to deal with the problem. The proposal, as presented on October 7, 2008, to the Chamber of Deputies (Oliveira, 2008), explained the reasoning for introducing a special law when the civil or penal codes of Brazil, like those of other countries, already contained provisions that require compliance with custody regulations and prohibit in particular the impediment of contacts between child and nonresident parent. As the proposal states,

> PA deserves state reprimand, because it is a form of abuse in the exercise of family power and disrespects rights of the child's personality formation. It clearly involves matters of public interest, given the need to demand a responsible paternity and motherhood, committed to the constitutional dictates as well as the duty to safeguard the mental health of our children.

The proposal concluded by citing for its importance and wealth from the article on PA by former Judge Maria Berenice Dias (2009). The article by Judge Dias appeared in *Revista do Cao Civel,* an official publication of the Brazilian government, which also included in the same issue other articles on PA.

The law is designed to facilitate the legal recognition of the conduct of PA and proposes specific tools that allow a clear and responsive judicial intervention. Because it is a very compact prescription, and it has already served as a model case for other, similar initiatives, Chapter 14 is devoted to a detailed presentation of that important legislation.

Italy

Gulotta and colleagues (2008) cite from a case as early as June 19, 1998, in which the Juvenile Court of Milan explicitly refers to PA:

> . . . between the two a relationship had been established which seriously damages the psychological integrity of the child: the child was gradually assuming the paranoid personality traits of his father and seemed to suffer from what some experts call "parental alienation syndrome." . . . (*Tribunale per i Minorenni di Milano,* ord. 19.6.1998, proc. n. 1652/E/97)

Cases in which a child was removed from the care of a parent on account of PA received considerable attention also in the media (Casi di allontanamento per PAS in Italia, 2011). An early such case, *Alessandria* (1999), which was upheld by the appeals court of Torino, is mentioned in a proposal (Disegno di Legge N. 957, 2008) in the Italian Senate for the reform of the shared parenting law of 2006.

The proposal speaks of the need to end attempts at manipulation by a parent, usually the primary residential parent, to completely eliminate the other parent from the life of the children, inducing in them the rejection of any contact. The project describes this as "a malaise which goes by the name Sindrome di alienazione genitoriale (PAS, Parental Alienation Syndrome)." The proposal points out that there is a large body of literature on PA, including Italian publications. The law project would modify Article 709 of the code of civil procedures by replacing a mere warning against the one-sided measures of a parent and adding a statement on PA: "The proven conditioning of the will of the child, especially if aimed at the rejection of the other parent by activating the parental alienation syndrome constitutes a serious misconduct, which can result in exclusion from parenting."

Article 709 in its present form had already been used in a number of cases related to PA, but the additional reference to PA predictably is causing opposition from the familiar lobbies. There is an alternate law proposal in the Senate, DDL 2454, which in essence adds the same sentence about programming the child and its consequences to Article 709 but without explicit reference to PA.

A proposal for the modification of the shared custody law of 2006 was also submitted in the Italian Chamber of Deputies on February 16, 2009 (Proposta di legge, 2009). It also refers to the need to act against PA and proposes in Article 2:

> For the decision on custody of children to one parent or a third party, the judge must evaluate, making use of experts appointed for the purpose, any environmental influences that may cause in the child a parental alienation syndrome of a severe or intermediate stage, and any material impediment to prevent the offspring to maintain a joint relationship, balanced and continuous contact with both parents.

According to Article 5 of this proposal, the judge hearing the child has to ascertain the presence of PA.

It should be mentioned that in 2004 the province of Liguria approved guidelines for its social services that include PA as a form of child abuse (Indirizzi in materia, 2004, p. 3799):

> 2 (f). Parental alienation syndrome: psychological state experienced by children in the middle of a parental conflict as inhibition to frequent one of the parents; is especially evident in cases of conflictual separation or divorce.

The Società Italiana di Neuropsichiatria dell'Infanzia e dell'Adolescenza (SINPIA) (Italian Society of Neuropsychiatry of Childhood and Adolescence) also described PA as psychological abuse in its official guidelines (SINPIA, 2007), as did an official report to the provincial government of Trento on violence and abuse within families (Savona & Caneppele, 2006).

Belgium

On November 23, 2010, Christine Defraigne (2010) introduced a proposal in the Belgian Senate to reduce the risk of a rupture of the relation between the child and one of the parents. This proposal describes in some detail various formulations of PA, starting with Richard Gardner and then in particular the work of Van Dieren, de Hemptinne, and Renchon (2011) on parental collaboration for reducing this risk of rupture. Articles 2 to 5 of the proposal set the legal framework for parental guidance by a psychological expert in cases of loss of relation between the child and a parent or the risk of it. The proposal foresees regular progress reports by the expert to the judge and, if necessary, measures of enforcement, such as fines and change of residence of the child. Article 6 of the proposal adds a paragraph to the penal code titled "Of Parental Alienation." It mandates eight days to one year in prison and fines between 26 and 1000 Euros for any parent who deliberately impedes the exercise of parental authority by repeated acts or manipulations aimed at the degradation or breakdown of the emotional connection to the other parent.

Austria

On December 7, 2011, an initiative in the Austrian National Assembly requested the government to develop a law proposal that defines PA and deals with it as a form of child abuse. The document presents the Brazilian law regarding PA as a model and refers to the extensive PA literature as summarized in *Parental Alienation, DSM-5, and ICD-11* (Bernet, 2010). The initiative points out international and Austrian studies on child abuse (Fichtenbauer, 2011).

OTHER LEGAL MEASURES FOR DEALING WITH PARENTAL ALIENATION

The Belgian law proposal is the only one the author is aware of that would explicitly add PA to the penal code, but other states have entries in their penal codes that punish behavior relevant to PA. Argentina, in 1993, adopted Ley 24.270, which provides penalties for a parent or third person who impedes or obstructs contact of a minor with his or her nonresident parent. The penalty is one month to one year in prison, increased to six months to three years in the case of children under 10 or handicapped persons. The same penalties apply to an unauthorized change of address designed to impede the contact between child and nonresident parent. If the child is moved abroad, the penalty is increased. Manonellas (2005) discussed that law in detail, also in connection with PA cases.

France has similar entries in its Code Pénal, Articles 227-5 to 227-11, for undermining the exercise of parental authority by impeding parenting time, and so on. Those acts are punishable with a fine of up to 15,000 Euros and one year in prison, and if carried out by persons without custody rights or if the child is illegally moved abroad, fines are increased. If the residential parent moves the child to another location without notifying the parent with visitation rights within one month, the fine is up to 7,500 Euros and six months in prison.

Although such entries in the penal code may be a deterrent to alienating parents, the problem is in avoiding harm to the child. The primary purpose should be to protect the child and his or her relationship with both parents, rather than to punish a parent. In fact, statistics for France show that only 10 to 15 percent of the cases of parenting time obstruction were pursued, leading to a sentence, with less than 1 percent in prison terms. Other cases were resolved alternatively, with mediation even at the initiative of the state prosecutor. (*See* the report of the French Senate in L'exercice du droit de visite, 2006.)

Even civil enforcement measures are often difficult to carry out and present a similar dilemma. Fines, whether based on a criminal or civil code, may not be applicable simply for lack of money, and transferring a child to the other parent with the help of a bailiff and police may not be a desirable option.

These practical difficulties, however, must not lead to total inaction, such that court orders on parenting time can be ignored with impunity over extended periods, which inevitably leads to alienation, or even PA (or PAS), often to the point of no return. The cases highlighted from the database of the European Court of Human Rights already give ample evidence for these practical difficulties and also of the consequences of inaction by the authorities.

If at all possible, an effective and more desirable alternative to an imposed court decision and its enforcement is to seek the collaboration of both parents in the interest of their child by counseling and mediation, and to do this at the earliest possible moment. The authority of the court is needed as the coordinator and for the power it has for enforcing decisions by possible sanctions or a change of custody. It will in any case, even if just in the background, help to increase the motivation for reaching a solution.

In Germany it seems impossible, perhaps for experiences from more recent history, to order any kind of counseling, mediation, or therapy in family court cases–not even the kind of mandatory courses on consequences of divorce for minor children or a mediation attempt at working out a parenting plan as they exist in various U.S. states–as preconditions for granting divorce. Such orders are seen as unacceptable coercion, with orders for therapy, even if issued for very good reasons, regularly quashed by the appeals court or even the constitutional court.

What has shown considerable success in Germany, however, is voluntary cooperation and close networking of all professionals involved, including the lawyers on both sides, with the common aim to settle the parental conflict by a unanimous solution. In this circumstance, the parents face a closed phalanx of professionals, led by the judge, with thus little choice but to cooperate. Early timing and leaves for counseling or mediation are important elements of this practice, first developed in the court district of Cochem, starting about 1992, but now spreading to more and more court districts in Germany (Rudolph, 2007).

Elements of this practice were incorporated into the reform of civil procedures in 2009. Custody cases must be treated preferentially, with the first hearing within a month. The chief aim is to reach a unanimous settlement. For this purpose, the court may *suggest* counseling and mediation (although not *order* it), with possible effects on the distribution of court fees in case of noncooperation. An important step is that now a psychological expert can be asked to try by "solution oriented diagnosis" to find a unanimous solution between the parents, rather than just do a diagnosis of the current status with recommendations regarding custody and parenting time to the court. Although early field tests with court-associated mediation by specialized professionals were seen positively, even by parents who were at first skeptical of such an approach, in Germany it has remained by mere recommendations even as the European Union wants to give mediation more priority.

A system, such as has already existed for a number of years in Austria, of comediation by a psychologist and a family lawyer, preferably also female and male, and with high qualifications set by statute certainly seems preferable as far more effective. It is accessible to anyone, because fees are based on income, with the rest assumed by the state. The Austrian custody reform of 2012 also foresees that (an attempt at) mediation can be mandated by the court. In Algeria, Croatia, and other countries it is already a precondition for divorce.

CONCLUSION

This chapter sufficiently demonstrates that PA is part of the spectrum of human behavior and as such is not restricted to a particular culture, nor to the Western world, nor to no-fault divorce. In fact, with "parental alienation" as the search term, perhaps in translation or transliteration, one can find evidence of PA awareness nearly everywhere one cares to look. Awareness already means some relief to many affected parents and children, learning that their experience is not unique but rather common and has a name. For professionals, awareness of advanced developments in other countries should also be helpful, but for methods of handling the problem to be successful, they have to be adapted to the cultural, social, legal, and administrative system of their country. Scientifically rigorous, empirically based research is not only a necessary foundation for progress on the subject but likely can also largely prevent the many controversies that have beset the PA topic from the very beginning. Of course, it cannot be overlooked that PA is most frequently connected to separation and divorce, which is often a highly controversial process in itself.

Editors' Notes

- Dr. Dum points out that PA is a worldwide phenomenon that is not restricted to a particular culture, country, or continent. Through the Internet, a person can find information about PA almost everywhere one looks.
- Dr. Dum says that knowledge of advanced developments in other countries should be helpful to mental health and legal professionals in devising methods for addressing PA in their own countries.
- He emphasizes that scientifically rigorous, empirically based research is a necessary foundation for progress on the subject of PA. That applies to research in psychology, sociology, and the law. Such research will likely resolve many of the controversies that have marked the history of PA.
- Dr. Dum explains how the United Nations Convention on the Rights of the Child, the European Convention on Human Rights, and the Hague Convention regarding child abduction are important international agreements that have implications for PA. He describes legal initiatives regarding PA in Mexico, Brazil, Italy, Austria, Belgium, and other countries.

REFERENCES

Andritzky, W. (2006). The role of medical reports in the development of parental alienation syndrome. In R. A. Gardner, S. R. Sauber, & D. Lorandos (Eds.), *The international handbook of parental alienation syndrome: Conceptual, clinical and legal considerations* (pp. 195–208). Springfield, IL: Charles C Thomas.

ASEMIP apoya la inclusión del trastorno de alienación parental en la quinta edición del DSM (2010). [The position of the Spanish Association for Multidisciplinary Research on Parental Interference (ASEMIP) concerning the inclusion of parental alienation disorder in the fifth edition of *Diagnostic and Statistical Manual of Mental Disorders (DSM-5)*]. Retrieved from http://www.asemip.org/?page=4

Bakalář, E. (1998). Das "Parental Alienation Syndrome" (PAS) in der Tschechischen Republik [The "Parental Alienation Syndrome" in the Czech Republic]. *Zentralblatt für Jugendrecht, 85*(6), 268.

Baker, A. J. L. (2007). *Adult children of parental alienation syndrome: Breaking the ties that bind.* New York: W. W. Norton & Co.

Bambini privati dei loro genitori. Approfondimento di due tematiche emergenti: alienazione genitoriale e allontanamenti istituzionali. (2011). [Children deprived of their parents. Thorough examination of two emerging issues: Parental alienation and institutional placements]. Retrieved from http://www.associazione prospettive.it/index.php/ricerca-e-formazione/documenti/finish/3-prospettive /2-percorso-di-formazione-bambini-privati-dei-loro-genitori/0

Benghalem, I. (2010). Études des facteurs de résilience (facteurs de protection) chez les enfants victimes de divorce [Study of the factors of resilience (factors of protection) in child victims of divorce]. (Master thesis). Retrieved from http://bu .umc.edu.dz/theses/psychologie/BEN1243.pdf.

Bernet, W. (Ed.). (2010). *Parental alienation, DSM-5, and ICD-11.* Springfield, IL: Charles C Thomas.

Boch-Galhau, W. v. (2012). *Parental Alienation und Parental Alienation Syndrome/ Disorder: Eine ernst zu nehmende Form von psychischer Kindesmisshandlung–mit Fallbeispielen.* English edition: (2013) *Parental alienation and parental alienation syndrome/disorder: A serious form of psychological child abuse–with case examples.* Berlin: Verlag für Wissenschaft und Bildung.

Boch-Galhau, W. v., & Kodjoe, U. (2006). Psychological consequences of PAS indoctrination for adult children of divorce and the effects of alienation on parents. In R. A. Gardner, S. R. Sauber, & D. Lorandos (Eds.), *The international handbook of parental alienation syndrome: Conceptual, clinical and legal considerations* (pp. 310–322). Springfield, IL: Charles C Thomas.

Boch-Galhau, W. v., Kodjoe, U., Andritzky, W., & Koeppel, P. (Eds.). (2003). *Das Parental Alienation Syndrom: Eine interdisziplinäre Herausforderung für scheidungsbegleitende Berufe* [*The parental alienation syndrome: An interdisciplinary challenge for professionals involved with divorce*]. Berlin: Verlag für Wissenschaft und Bildung.

Bolaños Cartujo, I. (2000). Estudio descriptivo del síndrome de alienación parental en procesos de separación y divorcio. Diseño y aplicación de un programa piloto de mediación familiar [Descriptive study of the parental alienation syndrome in the course of separation and divorce. Design and application of a pilot program in family mediation]. (Doctoral thesis). Retrieved from http://www.tdx.cat/handle/10803/4733;jsessionid=4D57A0B433F9DE68C5C302D15C5E9DE9.tdx2

Bolaños Cartujo, I. (2008). *Hijos alineados y padres alienados. Mediación familiar en rupturas conflictivas [Aligned children and alienated parents: Family mediation in conflictual separations]*. Madrid: Reus.

Bruch, C. S. (2001). Parental alienation syndrome and parental alienation: Getting it wrong in child custody cases. *Family Law Quarterly, 35,* 527–552.

Buzzi, I. (1997). La sindrome di alienazione genitoriale [Parental alienation syndrome]. In V. Cigoli, G. Gulotta, & G. Santi (Eds.), *Separazione, divorzio e affidamento dei figli [Separation, divorce and custody of children]* (pp. 177–187). Milano, Italy: Giuffré.

Cartié, M., Casany, R., Domínguez, R., Gamero, C., Garcia, C., & González, M. (2008). *Síndrome d'alienació parental (SAP). Aproximació al perfil de competències parentals del progenitor alienat, elaboració d'una guia d'exploració tècnica [Parental alienation syndrome (PAS): Approach to a profile of parental skills of alienated parent, development of a guide for diagnostic interviews.]*. Centre d'Estudis Jurídics i Formació Especialitzada. Barcelona: Generalitat de Catalunya. Departament de Justicia. Retrieved from http://www20.gencat.cat/docs/Justicia/Documents/ARXIUS/AJ-3240-08.pdf

Cartié, M., Casany, R., Domínguez, R., Gamero, C., Garcia, C., González, M., & Pastor, C. (2005). Análisis descriptivo de las características asociadas al síndrome de alienación parental. [Descriptive analysis of the characteristics associated with the parental alienation syndrome]. *Psicopatología Clínica, Legal y Forense, 5,* 5–29.

Cavedon, A., & Magro, T. (2010). *Dalla separazione all'alienazione parentale. Come giungere a una valutazione peritale [From separation to parental alienation: How to arrive at an expert evaluation]*. Milano, Italy: FrancoAngelli.

Chacon, F. (2008). El conceptualismo de Guillermo de Ockham y el debate sobre la existencia del síndrome de alienación parental (SAP) [Conceptualism of William Ockham and the debate about the existence of parental alienation syndrome (PAS)]. *Guía del Psicólogo, 284,* 3.

Council of Europe. (1950/2010). European convention on human rights. Retrieved from http://www.echr.coe.int/Documents/Convention_ENG.pdf

Cypriano Simão, R. B. (2007). Soluções judiciais concretas contra a perniciosa prática da alienação parental [Concrete judicial solutions against the pernicious practice of parental alienation]. In Associação de Pais e Mães Separados (APASE) (Eds.), *Síndrome da alienação parental e a tirania do duardião. Aspectos psicológicos, sociais e jurídicos [Parental alienation syndrome and the tyranny of the guardian: Psychological, social and legal aspects]*. São Paulo, Brazil: Editora Equilibrio.

Darnall, D. (1998). *Divorce casualties: Protecting your children from parental alienation.*

Dallas: Taylor Publishing Company.
Declaración de la Unión Latinoamericana de Entidades de Psicología sobre la alienación parental. (2011). [Declaration of the Latin American Union of Organizations of Psychology on parental alienation]. Retrieved from http://www.ofcostarica.com/anasap/index.php?view=article&catid=%2037%3Aap&id=65%3Adeclaracion-ulapsi&format=pdf&option=%20com_content&Itemid=61
Defraigne, C. (2010). Proposition de loi instaurant la guidance parentale sous mandat judiciaire [Proposition of a law installing parental guidance under a legal mandate]. Retrieved from http://www.senate.be/www/?MIval=/publications/viewPub.html&COLL=S&LEG=5&NR=520&VOLGNR=1&LANG=fr
Diario de los debates de la Asamblea Legislative del Distrito Federal, Num. 40, 28 de diciembre de 2006. (2006). [Journal of debates of the Legislative Assembly of the Federal District, No. 40, December 28, 2006]. Retrieved from http://www.aldf.gob.mx/archivo-f766b2adde3e1c817008b399a14834e5.pdf
Dias, M. B. (2009). Síndrome da alienação parental, o que é isso? [Parental alienation syndrome, what is it?]. *Revista do Cao Cível, 11*(15), 45–48. Retrieved from https://www2.mp.pa.gov.br/sistemas/gcsubsites/upload/25/REVISTA%20DO%20CAO%20CIVEL%2015(3).pdf
Dictamen de la Iniciativa de Ley que reforma el artículo 443, el párrafo tercero del artículo 447 y adiciona el Capítulo Sexto del Título Noveno, del Libro Primero y los artículos 449 ter, 449 quater y 449 quintus del Código Civil del Estado de Querétaro. Presentado por la Comisión de Administración y Procuración de Justicia. (2011). [Law proposal]. Gaceta Legislativa, Number 058 of June 23, 2011. Legislatura del Estado de Querétaro. Retrieved from http://www.legislaturaqro.gob.mx/files/asuntos_leg/gacetas2/GACETA%20058,%2023%20JUNIO%202011%20PLENO.pdf
Dictamen con Proyecto de Decreto que Reforma Diversas Disposiciones del Codigo Familiar PARA el Estado de Michoacán de Occampo, Elaborado por las Comisiones de Justicia; de Gobernacion; Y de Grupos Vulnerables, Equidad y Genero. (2010) [Law proposal]. Gaceta Parlamentaria, Volume IX Number 206 H of December 21, 2010. Retrieved from http://www.congresomich.gob.mx/Modulos/mod_Gaceta/archivos/1567_bib.pdf
Disegno di Legge N. 957 (2008). Modifiche al codice civile e al codice di procedura civile in materia di affidamento condiviso. Senato della Repubblica XVI Legislatura. [Law proposal]. Retrieved from http://www.senato.it/leg/16/BGT/Schede/Ddliter/testi/32138_testi.htm
Divorce des parents. (2009, October 1). [Parental divorce]. *Le Matin,* Morocco.
Dum, C. T. (2003). Begutachtete Aufsätze in Fachzeitschriften und das Parental Alienation Syndrom [Peer-reviewed articles in professional journals and the parental alienation syndrome]. In W. von Boch-Galhau, U. Kodjoe, W. Andritzky, & P. Koeppel (Eds.), *Das parental aalienation syndrom: Eine interdisziplinäre Herausforderung für scheidungsbegleitende Berufe* [*The parental alienation syndrome: An interdisciplinary challenge for professionals involved with divorce*] (pp. 384–389). Berlin: Verlag für Wissenschaft und Bildung.
Eltern-Kind-Entfremdung: Fachgespräch und Fotoausstellung im Landtag. (2011).

[Parent-child-alienation: Expert meeting and photo exhibit in the State Diet]. Retrieved from http://www.bayern.landtag.de/cps/rde/xchg/landtag/x/-/www1/2261_7448.htm

Fariña, F., Arce, R., Novo, M., & Seijo, D. (2010). Separación y divorcio: Interferencias parentales [Separation and divorce: Parental interference]. Asociación Española Multidisciplinar de Investigación sobre Interferencias Parentales (ASEMIP). Retrieved from http://www.asemip.org/system/files/1217/original/Ponencias-I-Congreso-Interferencias-Parentales-ASEMIP-V2-2010.pdf?1341991727

Fariña Rivera, F., & Tovar Escudero, C. (2011). El falso debate sobre el SAP [The false debate on PAS]. Revista Digital de Derecho de Familia. Retrieved from http://www.lexfamily.es/revista.php?codigo=899

Fegert, J. M. (2001). Parental Alienation oder Parental Accusation Syndrome? Die Frage der Suggestibilität, Beeinflussung und Induktion in Umgangsrechtsgutachten [Parental alienation or parental accusation syndrome? The question of suggestibility, influencing and induction in parenting time expert reports]. *Kindschaftsrechtliche Praxis, 4,* 3–7, 39–42.

Fichtenbauer, P. (2011). Schaffung eines Gesetzes zum Elternentfremdungssyndrom = Parental Alienation Syndrom (PAS) [Creating a law on Parental Alienation Syndrome]. Retrieved from http://www.parlament.gv.at/PAKT/VHG/XXIV/A/A_01805/index.shtml

Finkelstein, C. S. (2003). The heart of an abducted and alienated child (pp. 175–177); Sarah or Cecilie: The identity issue (pp. 183–185); PAS perspectives: An adult, parentally abducted and alienated as a child, reflects on current PAS treatment modules (pp. 367-371). In W. v. Boch-Galhau, U. Kodjoe, W. Andritzky, & P. Koeppel (Eds.), *Das Parental Alienation Syndrom: Eine interdisziplinäre Herausforderung für scheidungsbegleitende Berufe* [*The Parental Alienation Syndrome: An Interdisciplinary Challenge for Professionals Involved with Divorce*]. Berlin: Verlag für Wissenschaft und Bildung.

Gaius (160 A.D./1904). On civil law and natural law. In *Institutes of Roman law* (4th ed.). (Edward Poste, Trans.). Oxford: Clarendon Press.

Gardner, R. A. (1992). *The parental alienation syndrome: A guide for mental health and legal professionals.* Cresskill, NJ: Creative Therapeutics.

Gardner, R. A., Sauber, S. R., & Lorandos, D. (Eds.) (2006). *The international handbook of parental alienation syndrome: Conceptual, clinical and legal considerations.* Springfield, IL: Charles C Thomas.

Gebhard, G. (Director). (2005). *Victims of another war: The aftermath of parental alienation* [DVD]. United States: Pacific View Productions.

Gewalt gegen Kinder und Jugendliche. Erkennen und Handeln. (2012). [*Violence against children and adolescents: Recognizing it and acting*]. Bayerisches Staatsministerium für Arbeit und Sozialordnung, Familie und Frauen [Bavarian State Ministry of Labor and Social Affairs, Family, and Women]. Retrieved from http://www.stmas.bayern.de/imperia/md/content/stmas/stmas_internet/jugend/aerzteleitfaden_interaktiv.pdf

Gordon, R., Stoffey, R., & Bottinelli, J. (2008). MMPI-2 findings of primitive defenses in alienating parents. *American Journal of Family Therapy, 36,* 211–228.

Gulotta, G. (1998). La sindrome di alienazione genitoriale: Definizione e descrizione [The parental alienation syndrome: Definition and description]. *Pianeta Infanzia, 4,* 27–36.

Gulotta, G., Cavedon, A., & Liberatore, M. (2008). *La Sindrome di alienazione parentale (PAS): Lavaggio del cervello e programmazione dei figli in danno dell'altro genitore [The parental alienation syndrome (PAS): Brainwashing and programming of children to the detriment of the other parent*]. Milan: Giuffrè.

Hellblom Sjögren, L. (2006). PAS in compulsory public custody conflicts. In R. A. Gardner, S. R. Sauber, & D. Lorandos (Eds.), *The international handbook of parental alienation syndrome: Conceptual, clinical and legal considerations* (pp. 131–152). Springfield, IL: Charles C Thomas.

Hellblom Sjögren, L. (2012). *Barnets rätt till familjeliv. 25 svenska fall av föräldra alienation [The child s right to family life: 25 Swedish cases of parental alienation*]. Lund, Sweden: Studentlitteratur.

Hirigoyen, M. (1998). *Le harcèlement moral, la violence perverse au quotidian [Psychological harassment: Perverse everyday violence*]. Paris: Éditions La Découverte. English edition: (2000). *Stalking the soul: Emotional abuse and the erosion of identity.* New York: Helen Marx Books.

Hirigoyen, M. (2012). *Abus de faiblesse et autres manipulations [Abuse of weakness and other manipulations*]. Paris: Éditions JC Lattès.

Ikeda, J. K. (2008). *Propuesta legislativa para el Estado de Morelos sobre la custodia compartida y la alienación parental [Legislative proposal for the state of Morelos on shared custody and parental alienation*]. (Thesis). Available from Lulu.com.

Indirizzi in materia di maltrattamento, abuso e sfruttamento sessuale a danno dei minori. (2004). [Guidelines on abuse, sexual abuse, and exploitation against children]. Bollettino Ufficiale Della Regione Liguria, Parte II. Retrieved from http://www.alienazione.genitoriale.com/wp-content/uploads/2011/01/delibera_liguria.pdf

Iniciativa que Reforma Diversas Disposiciones del Codigo Familiar del Estado de Morelos. (2011). [Law proposal. Gaceta Legislativa Congreso del Estado de Morelos, Number 081. Retrieved from http://www.transparenciacongresomorelos.gob.mx/acceso/Gaceta/09/Gaceta_81.pdf

Johnston, J. R. (2007). Entfremdete Scheidungskinder? [Alienated children of divorce?]. Kindschaftsrecht und Jugendhilfe, (6), 218-224. Based on Children of divorce who reject a parent and refuse visitation: Recent research and social policy implications for the alienated child. (2005). *Family Law Quarterly, 38,* 757–775.

Klenner, W. (1995). Rituale der Umgangsvereitelung bei getrennt lebenden oder geschiedenen Eltern [Rituals of contact obstruction by parents in separation or divorce]. *Zeitschrift für das gesamte Familienrecht, 42,* 529–535.

Kodjoe, U., & Koeppel, P. (1998). The Parental Alienation Syndrome (PAS) I. *Der Amtsvormund, 72,* 9–26.

Kruk, E. (2010). Collateral damage: The lived experiences of divorced mothers without custody. *Journal of Divorce & Remarriage, 51,* 526–543.

L'exercice du droit de visite et d'hébergement: l'insuffisante efficacité des sanctions à l'égard des parents n'assumant pas leurs obligations à l'égard de leurs enfants et d'hébergement. (2006). [The exercise of the rights of visitation and accommodation: Insufficient efficiency of sanctions regarding parents who are not assuming their responsibilities with regard to their children and accommodation]. Retrieved from http://www.senat.fr/rap/r05-388/r05-38850.html#toc387

Lei No 12.318, de 26 de Agosto de 2010. Retrieved from http://www.planalto.gov.br/ccivil_03/_Ato2007-2010/2010/Lei/L12318.htm

Lubrano Lavadera, A., Ferracuti, S., & Malagoli Togliatti, M. (2012). Parental alienation syndrome in Italian legal judgments: An exploratory study. International *Journal of Law and Psychiatry 35*(4), 334–342.

Lund, M. (1995). A therapist's view of parental alienation syndrome. *Family and Conciliation Courts Review, 33,* 308–316.

Malagoli Togliatti, M., & Franci, M. (2005). La syndrome di alienazione genitoriale (PAS): Studi e ricerche [The parental alienation syndrome (PAS): Studies and research.]. *Maltrattamento e Abuso all'Infanzia, 7*(3), 39–63. Special issue on PAS.

Malagoli Togliati, M., & Lubrano Lavadera, A. (2009). Il rifiuto e il disagio dei figli nei casi di separazione conflittuale: Possibili percorsi evolutivi [Denial and maladjustment of children in cases of conflictual divorce: Possible developmental pathways] [Italian]. *Maltrattamento e Abuso all'Infanzia, 11*(3), 27-38. Special issue on Minacce al legame genitori-figli [Threats to the parent-child relationship].

Manonellas, G. N. (2005). *Responsibilidad penal del padre obstculazador, La Ley 24270. Sindrome de alienacion parental (SAP)* [*Criminal responsibility of the obstructing parent, the Law 24270: Parental alienation syndrome (PAS)*]. Buenos Aires: Ad-Hoc.

Napp-Peters, A. (2005). Mehrelternfamilien als "Normal"-Familien - Ausgrenzung und Eltern-Kind-Entfremdung nach Trennung und Scheidung [Multi-parent families as "normal" families: Segregation and parent-child alienation after separation and divorce]. Praxis der *Kinderpsychologie und Kinderpsychiatrie, 54,* 792–801.

Oliveira, R. de (2008). Projeto de Lei Nr. 4053, de 2008, Dispõe sobre a alienação parental. [Law Project 4053, of 2008, Provides for parental Alienation]. Retrieved from http://www.camara.gov.br/proposicoesWeb/prop_mostrarintegra?codteor=601514&filename=Tramitacao-PL+4053/2008

Oviedo, M. S. M. (2011, January 11). El Gobierno insta a los jueces a descartar el síndrome de manipulación de los progenitores [The government urged judges to discard the syndrome of parental manipulation]. La Nueva España. Retrieved from http://www.lne.es/sociedad-cultura/2011/01/11/gobierno-insta-jueces-descartar-sindrome-manipulacion-progenitores/1017998.html

Palandt, O., Bassenge, P., & Brudermüller, G. (2006). Bürgerliches Gesetzbuch [German Civil Code] [German] (65th ed.) Munich: Beck Juristischer Verlag.

Parrini, A. (2008). *Separazioni distruttive tra conflittualità e alienazione. Aspetti psicologici e giuridici* [*Destructive separations between conflict and alienation: Psychological and legal aspects*]. Francavilla al Mare, Italy: Edizioni Psionline.

Pérez del Campo, A. M. (Ed.). (2010). Informe del grupo de trabajo de investigación

sobre el llamado síndrome de alienación parental [Report of the working group on the so-called parental alienation syndrome]. Madrid: Ministerio de Sanidad, Política Social e Igualdad.
Periodico Oficial del Estado de Aguascalientes, Tomo LXX, Núm. 47 Primera Sección, p. 8 (2007). [Law proposal]. Retrieved from www.ordenjuridico.gob.mx/Estatal/AGUASCALIENTES/Decretos/AGSDEC11.pdf
Popper, K. (1959). *The logic of scientific discovery.* London: Routledge Classics.
Prades, J. (2011, January 10). El Gobierno insta a los jueces a no esgrimir una patología inexistente [The government urged judges not to wield a non-existent pathology]. *El Pais.* Retrieved from http://elpais.com/diario/2011/01/10/sociedad/1294614003_850215.html
Propone PAN incorporar al código civil la figura de alienación parental. (2011). [PAN (National Action Party) proposes to incorporate parental alienation into the civil code]. Retrieved from http://tl.diputadospanchihuahua.org/?p=816
Proposta di legge: Nuove norme in materia di affidamento condiviso dei figli (Proposed law: New rules on shared custody of children]. (2009). Retrieved from http://www.camera.it/_dati/leg16/lavori/stampati/pdf/16PDL0023760.pdf
Rabbinical courts and parental alienation (2007). Retrieved from www.kipa.co.il/family/show.asp?id=22178
Rudolph, J. (2007). *Du bist mein Kind* [*You are my child*]. Berlin: Schwarzkopf & Schwarzkopf.
Savona, E. U., & Caneppele, S. (Eds.). (2006). *Violenze e maltrattamenti in famiglia* [*Violence and maltreatment in families*]. Trento: Giunta Provincia Autonoma di Trento. Retrieved from http://transcrime.cs.unitn.it/tc/fso/pubblicazioni/RS/08_Ottavo_rapporto_sulla_sicurezza_nel_Trentino-App_1.pdf
Serrano Castro, F. (2011, January 26). Síndrome de alienación parental [Parental alienation syndrome]. *El Mundo.* Retrieved from http://apfsaragon.com/es/index.php?mod=content_detail&id=1113
SINPIA (Società Italiana di Neuropsichiatria dell'Infanzia e dell'Adolescenza). (2007). Linee guida in tema di abuso sui minori. [*Guidelines on the subject of child abuse*]. Trento, Italy: Edizioni Centro Studi Erickson. Retrieved from: http://www.sinpia.eu/atom/allegato/154.pdf
Stadler, M., & Salzgeber, J. (1999). Parental Alienation Syndrom (PAS)–alter Wein in neuen Schläuchen? [Parental alienation syndrome (PAS)–old wine in new skins?]. *Familie, Partnerschaft und Recht, 4,* 231–235.
United Nations (1989). Convention on the rights of the child. Retrieved from http://www.ohchr.org/EN/ProfessionalInterest/Pages/CRC.aspx
Vaccaro, S., & Barea Payueta, C. (2009). *El pretendo síndrome de alienación parental. Un instrumento que perpetúa el maltrato y la violencia* [*The so-called parental alienation syndrome: An instrument perpetuating abuse and violence*]. Madrid: Ed. Desclée de Brower.
Van Dieren, B., de Hemptinne, M., & Renchon, J.-L. (2011). Le risque de rupture du lien parent-enfant et l'expertise axée sur la collaboration parentale [The risk of a rupture of parent-child relationship and the expertise oriented on the parental

collaboration]. *Revue Trimestrielle de Droit Familial* (2), 261–298.
Vassalo, I. (2009, August 19). Tug of war–The alienated child during marital separation. *The Malta Independent.* Retrieved from http://www.independent.com.mt/news2.asp?artid=92764
Vilalta Suárez, R. J. (2011). Descripción del síndrome de alienación parental en una muestra forense [Description of parental alienation syndrome in a forensic sample]. *Psicothema, 23,* 636–641.
Warshak, R. A. (2001). *Divorce poison: Protecting the parent-child bond from a vindictive ex.* New York: Harper Collins.
Translations of *Divorce Poison.*
Warshak, R. A. (2003). *Rozvodové jedy* [Czech]. Prague: Triton.
Warshak, R. A. (2005a). _______ [Korean]. Seoul: ____ [Morning Dew].
Warshak, R. A. (2008). Otrov razvoda: Zaštita veze izmedu roditelja i djeteta od osvetoljubivog bivšeg partnera [Croatian]. Zagreb: Algoritam.
Warshak, R. A. (2012a). Eromyrkky–kuinka suojella lasta avioerotilanteessa [Finnish]. Helsinki: Gummerus Kustannus.
Warshak, R. (2012b). _______________ [Japanese, trans. by Satoshi Aoki]. Tokyo: Seishin Shobo K.K.
Warshak, R. A. (2005b). Eltern-Kind-Entfremdung und Sozialwissenschaften–Sachlichheit statt Polemik [Parent-child-alienation and social sciences–objectivity instead of polemics]. *Zentralblatt für Jugendrecht, 92*(5), 186–200.
Watzlawick, P., Beavin Bavelas, J., & Jackson, D. (1967). *Pragmatics of human communication: A study of interactional patterns, pathologies and paradoxes.* New York: W. W. Norton & Company.
Werner, E. E., & Smith, R. S. (1992). *Overcoming the odds: High risk children from birth to adulthood.* Ithaca, NY: Cornell University Press.
Weychardt, D. W. (2007). Vortragsmanuskript zur elterlichen Verantwortung [Lecture manuscript on parental responsibility]. Retrieved from http://www.hefam.de/koll/wey20070528.doc

Cases

Alessandria, No. 318/99 (Alessandria, June 24, 1999. Confirmed by Court of Appeal of Turin, Italy).
Bordeianu c. Moldavia, Requête no. 49868/08 (European Court of Human Rights, January 11, 2011).
Casi di allontanamento per PAS in Italia. (2011). Retrieved from http://www.alienazione.genitoriale.com/casi-di-allontanamento-per-pas-in-italia
Dacasin v. Dacasin, G.R. No. 168785 (Supreme Court of the Philippines, February 5, 2010). Retrieved from http://www.lawphil.net/judjuris/juri2010/feb2010/gr_168785_2010.html
Diamante and Pelliccioni v. San Marino, Application no. 32250/08 (European Court of Human Rights, September 27, 2011).
Elsholz v. Germany, Application no. 25735/94 (European Court of Human Rights,

July 13, 2000).

Koudelka c. République Tchèque, Requête no. 1633/05 (European Court of Human Rights, July 20, 2006).

Kutzner v. Germany, Application no. 46544/99 (European Court of Human Rights, February 26, 2002).

Mincheva c. Bulgarie, Requête no. 21558/03 (European Court of Human Rights, September 2, 2010).

Patera c. République Tchèque, Requête no. 25326/03 (European Court of Human Rights, April 27, 2007).

Piazzi c. Italie, Requête no. 36168/09 (European Court of Human Rights, November 2, 2010).

Sommerfeld v. Germany, Application no. 31871/96 (European Court of Human Rights, July 8, 2003).

Tribunale per i Minorenni di Milano, ord. 19.6.1998, proc. n. 1652/E/97.

Zavřel c. République Tchèque, Requête no. 14044/05 (European Court of Human Rights, January 18, 2007).

Chapter 14

PARENTAL ALIENATION AND THE NEW BRAZILIAN LAW

TAMARA BROCKHAUSEN

In August 2010, Brazil became the first country to adopt national legislation regarding parental alienation (PA).The Brazilian law (which is called Lei No. 12.318) defines PA and provides for specific civil remedies that courts can use to address the problem. This chapter explains how Lei 12.318 came about and relates some early examples of how the law was implemented. The heading of the official government version of Lei 12.318–in Portuguese–is in Figure 14.1. The complete text of Lei 12.318–in English–is in Box 14.2. (Lei 12.318 may be accessed at http://www.planalto.gov.br/ccivil_03/_Ato2007-2010/2010/Lei/L12318.htm)

BRIEF HISTORY OF CUSTODY LEGISLATION IN BRAZIL

In Brazil, there is a long history of mothers receiving exclusive legal and physical custody of children after separation or divorce. The text of the civil law prior to 2002 stated that in the absence of blame in the separation, custody was to be given to women in priority. Many years before, however, decisions in court regarding custody ceased to base themselves on this law. Legislative changes in the Estatuto da Criança e do Adolescente (ECA) (Civil Code for Children and Adolescents) and the Federal Constitution, such as equality between men and women and priority to children's welfare, rendered the laws in question obsolete.

It was only in 2002 that a change was made in Brazilian legislation regarding the preference given to women in obtaining legal custody. At that time, civil law began to grant custody to the parent with the better chances to exercise it, leaving aside the granting of custody linked to the gender issue. Nevertheless, in spite of removing the sexist character from the law's text, due to how recent the change is, even today the bias of granting the woman custodial priority remains. Sometimes the magistrate's preference to grant custody to the mother is explicit. The 2003 census conducted by the Instituto Brasileiro de Estatística e Geografia (Brazilian Institute of Statistics and Geography) showed that mothers have custody of the children 92 percent of the time. As such one can see the unfortunate matriarchal rule in Brazilian legal practice.

In 2009, Brazilian law adopted a preference for shared custody, thus becoming yet another theme to be considered. Only a small number of the legal decisions have made use of this law, however. Currently, one can note that shared custody is granted when there is consensus between the couple regarding it. The magistrates defend this by claiming they avoid giving shared custody in cases of litigation because it becomes impractical if there is no agreement between the parents regarding decisions about their children's lives.

That said, legal practice in Brazil is still very conservative regarding custody, and it is granted unilaterally in the vast majority of the cases. This logic, which continues to reign in legal circles, can be explained in the origins of Brazilian law. Today in Brazil, there continues to be a debate regarding custody and visiting rights after parents separate, whereas in Europe and the United States, that debate after separation has become obsolete. In those countries, the only discussion following separation concerns how the children will live with each of their parents.

The model in Brazil–where one parent has legal and physical custody and the second parent has visitation–tends to create issues regarding the institution of custody and parental authority. That is because granting unilateral custody can foster a sense of ownership of the offspring, giving rise to abusive interpretations. Granting unilateral custody fails to regulate parental abuse of power, the principal issue in situations involving PA.

According to Brito (2004),

> The claim that in our country parental authority belongs to both father and mother, who are responsible for their offspring, ends up confirming the hypothesis that we do not need to divide them into two categories after marital separation: that of guardians and visitors. As exemplified in other countries, we can abolish the term custody, leaving only the expression parental authority. In the case of needing to use the term *custody,* it should be accompanied by the adjective *shared,* facilitating the interpretation of fairness between father and mother, as well as an indication of a child's broad contact with both parents.

Given this scenario, one can understand the Brazilian context in which Lei 12.318 came to be, which addresses PA. There was a social context that pressed for effective tools in regulating a more balanced coexistence of children with both parents after separation, and also for a more efficient legislative and legal model to administer abuse of parental authority.

Around the year 2000, the term parental alienation syndrome (PAS) appeared for the first time on web sites, from entities that fought for the rights of divorced parents, mostly men. The knowledge of PAS, until the years 2008 to 2009, was confined to laymen, parents who were members of online discussion groups, until little by little it spread through the proposed law to professionals from different fields (legal, psychological, educational, and social).

Therefore, the movement for the new law met little resistance until its implementation began. Adopted on August 26, 2010, Lei 12.318 was widely distributed by the mass media, attracting a large number of criticisms. The law's adoption meant that the country experienced a rapid profusion of information on the topic of PA, along with a need for professional studies and

Box 14.1.
THE POLITICAL STRUCTURE OF BRAZIL

The Federative Republic of Brazil is the world's fifth largest country, both in geographic size and in population. A former colony of Portugal, Brazil became an independent country in 1822. Brazil consists of the federation of 26 states, more than 5,000 municipalities, and the Federal District, Brasília.

Brazil is a democracy in which voting is compulsory. The president's term in office is four years, and he or she can be reelected. The legislature consists of the bicameral Congresso Nacional do Brasil (National Congress of Brazil), which includes the Federal Senate (with 81 senators) and the Chamber of Deputies (with 513 deputies).

There are many political parties in Brazil, and about twenty parties are represented in the National Congress. Senators and deputies are identified by their political party and the state that they represent. For instance, in this chapter, the following political parties are designated by their respective abbreviations: Brazilian Democratic Movement Party (PMDB), Communist Party of Brazil (PCdoB), Democrats (DEM); Social Progressive Party (PSP), and Workers Party (PT). Also, the following states are designated by their abbreviations: Pará (PA), Rio Grande do Sul (RS), Santa Catarina (SC), and São Paulo (SP).

research. Currently, there are only a few publications in the professional literature of Brazil, and they lack depth and diversified discussions. The judicial system also lacks the structure to accommodate the new demand created by cases involving PA. Therefore, the new law comes amid challenges in the professional setting.

HISTORY OF LEI 12.318

The first initiative to create the proposed bill to curb PA in Brazil appeared in May 2008. The judge drafting it, Elizio Luiz Perez, a father who participated in the online discussion groups, decided to expose his innovative idea. At that time the issue of PA was already circulating in the Internet in associations of divorced parents, such as Associação de Mães e Pais Separados do Brasil (AMASEP) (Association of Separated Mothers and Fathers of Brazil); Associação de Pais e Mães Separados (APASE) (Association of Separated Fathers and Mothers); Parents for Justice; Taking Part; and SOS Father Mother.

The text of the bill, after it was written by Judge Elizio Luiz Perez, was exposed through social networks and discussion forums to a large number of professionals and lay people as a way to gather comments and suggestions. Thus, there emerged a social organization, constituted mainly from the discussion forums of these organizations for the movement toward making the proposal a law. The group sought, through its members, to inform members of parliament about PA. They sought to disseminate technical issues and reports from people on the drama of their lives through visits to the Federal District (Brasília) and through e-mails.

In June 2008, a month after the public display of the proposed law to the Internet groups, another father, Celso Dias, a member of the network of associations on the Internet, sought out Congressman Regis Oliveira (PSP-SP) to find political patrons willing to represent the drafted bill. In subsequent months, the group made several mobilizations seeking parliamentary representation in their state to present the bill. Karla Mendes, journalist; Igor Shasha, lawyer; and Elizio Luiz Perez, judge and author of the bill met and went to the National Congress (Brasília) to mobilize congressmen.

In October 2008, Congressman Regis Oliveira presented the bill, which received the number 4053/08. The group once again paid a visit to Congress, aiming to deliver the informative material on PA to the offices of the congressmen. At this time, the drafted bill was granted urgent status, so that it required consideration by a smaller number of commissions (just by the Chamber of Deputies and the Senate), so as to be approved more quickly.

In December 2008, the group returned to Congress for a meeting with Comissão de Seguridade Social e Família (CSSF) (Commission on Social Security and Family) of the House of Representatives; Congressman Jofran Frejat (DEM-SP); and the rapporteur appointed to the bill, Congressman Jose Aristodemo Pinotti (DEM-SP). The members of parents' associations sent separate e-mails to lawmakers urging support for the project. In February 2009, Congressman Pinotti resigned from office for health reasons. For this reason, the vote for approval of the bill had to be postponed until the appointment of a new rapporteur.

In April 2009, the first documentary about PA was released in Brazil–*A Morte Inventada (Death Invented)*–by the filmmaker and father, Alan Mines, thus helping to publicize the issue. In the same month, the group went once more to Congress to visit the new rapporteur of the bill, Congressman Acélio Casa Grande (PMDB-SC). The group asked Congressman Elcione Barbalho (PMDB-PA), chairman of the CSSF in the Chamber of Deputies, for expediency in handling the project. In subsequent months, the group conducted a series of visits to Congress and members who could offer support to the bill.

In June 2009 came the first resistance to the project. At the time of voting the bill in the CSSF, Congresswoman Jô Moraes (PCdoB) asked that the project be removed from the voting agenda. The groups of parents' associations sent her e-mails asking for explanations. In July 2009, Congressman Acélio Casagrande, the rapporteur of the bill, asked the group to a meeting in his office along with Congresswoman Jô Moraes. The congresswoman explained she had been approached by two entities, Rodrigo Dias, founder of one of the associations of divorced parents (Parents Forever), and the Centro Feminista de Estudos e Assessoria (CFEMEA) (Center for Feminist Studies and Advisory Services), a nongovernment organization linked to the feminist movement. They justified their disagreement with certain points of the bill. The group clarified the points of divergence to the congresswoman, who then agreed to schedule a meeting with congressmen and the CFEMEA group, so that this might be clarified.

Among the justifications for opposing the bill, Rodrigo Dias stated that the project would increase the power of the judge in cases of PA without going through technical studies in health (psychology and social work).The group, during their meeting with the CFEMEA, explained that the bill was focused on child protection and not on the father or mother. That explanation helped establish an atmosphere of understanding among the parties and dispel any misunderstanding that the law might stigmatize women.

In July 2009, the substitute bill by Congressman Acélio Casagrande was unanimously approved by the CSSF, passing through the sieve of the

Comissão de Constituição, Justiça e Cidadania (CCJ) (Commission on Justice and Citizenship). In August 2009, Congresswoman Maria do Rosario (PT-RS) was named the new rapporteur of the bill in the CCJ. In the same month, the group went to Congress to distribute informational materials about PA. The congresswoman received numerous anonymous e-mails disagreeing with the bill, as a result of which a public hearing was requested to discuss the project with interested parties.

In October 2009, a public hearing was held, one of the most tense moments of the progress of the bill. Composing the table were Judge Elizio Luiz Perez; Dr. Sandra Baccara, a psychologist; Dr. Cynthia Ciarallo, representative of the Conselho Federal de Psicologia (CFP) (Federal Council of Psychology); the former federal judge, Maria Berenice Dias; Karla Mendes, a journalist; and Congresswoman Maria do Rosario. Among the criticisms levied against the bill, a representative of the CFP explained that it could result in excessive state intervention in a family's private life. He further justified that the discussion about PA would engender greater rivalry between parents and overshadow the institution of shared custody. In the bill's defense, Dr. Sandra Baccara argued that the position of the psychologist of the CFP did not reflect the position of all professional psychology. At this point, Judge Maria Berenice, also in favor of the bill, asked the CFP representative if she was representing an isolated position or whether the CFP was officially opposing the bill. The representative said it had not been formally discussed by the body and was thus not an official position. At the end, the representative of the CFP requested a new public hearing with the attendance of Conselho Nacionaldos Direitos da Criança e do Adolescente (CONANDA) (National Council for the Rights of Children and Adolescents) an agency of the government that organizes legislation involving the rights of children and adolescents.

On November 19, 2009, the law project was approved in the CCJ of the House of Representatives and it was referred to the second step, its approval in the Senate.

In April 2010, the group resumed the work of mobilizing congressmen through visits in the Federal District. Senator Paulo Paim (PT-RS), appointed rapporteur of the bill in the Human Rights Commission, said it would hold a new public hearing to debate it. Being an election year, the public hearing would delay its processing. For this reason, members of the movement of the bill asked the congressman to cancel the public hearing. In May 2010, the office of Senator Paulo Paim said it would hold a public hearing at the request of the CFP. In the same month, Senator Paulo Paim said the public hearing was no longer planned as the CFP had not made a formal request nor appointed representatives.

In June 2010, the Human Rights Commission of the Senate unanimously approved the bill without amendments to the text approved by the Chamber of Deputies. In the same month, the new rapporteur of the bill was named, this time from the CCJ of the Senate, Senator Pedro Simon (PMDB-RS). In July 2010, the project was again approved unanimously by the Commission and was sent for the President's approval. The members of the movement returned to disseminate information about PA for the President's Secretariat for Legal Affairs.

On August 26, 2010, President Luiz Inácio Lula da Silva signed the bill. On August 27, 2010, Lei 12.318 became law providing for Acts of Parental Alienation.

Two articles of Lei 12.318 were vetoed at the request of the Ministry of Justice. It was explained that the articles were vetoed because they were contrary to the public interest. The first vetoed article, Article 9, provided for the possibility of mediation as a form of alternative dispute resolution in cases of PA. The Public Prosecutor explained that since enforcing the rights of chil-

Presidência da República
Casa Civil
Subchefia para Assuntos Juridicos

LEI No 12.318, DE 26 AGOSTO DE 2010.

Mensagem de veto	Disõe sobre a alienação parental o art. 236 da Leino8.060, de 13 de julho de 1990.

O PRESIDENTE DA REP´UBLICA Faço saber que o Congresso Nacional decreta e eu sanciono a seguinte Lei:

Art. 10 Esta Lei dispõe sobre a alienação parental.

Art. 20 Considera-se ato de alienção parental a interferência na formação psicológica da criança ou do adolescente promovida ou induzida por um dos genitores, pelos avós ou pelos que tenham a crinça ou adolescente sob a sua autoridade, guarda ou vigilância para que repudie genitor ou que cause prejuizo ao estabelecimento ou á manutenção de vículos com este.

Figure 14.1.

dren and adolescents to family life is not available outside of the legal setting, it is not appropriate to use extrajudicial mechanisms for resolving disputes. The protective measures for minors should be exercised exclusively by the authorities.

The second veto, Article 10, concerned the possibility of criminal sanctions, in other words, restriction of children and adolescents' living with the parent who submits false reports to police authorities. One of the reasons given for the veto of Article 10 was that the ECA already included mechanisms to inhibit the effects of PA, such as reversal of custody, fines, and even suspension of parental authority. Furthermore the effects of criminal punishment of the parents could be harmful to children and adolescents, whose rights the law supposedly sought to protect.

JURISPRUDENCE BEFORE AND AFTER LEI 12.318

There have already been legal cases in which the court's decision relied on Lie 12.318, and several cases are summarized in this chapter. In the following decision in the state of São Paulo, the court found both parents as possibly guilty of alienating and gave both a warning.

> The right to visits is not only a right of the parent, but also a right of the child. According to reports by the Council, as well as the technical report, the Magistrate noted the intense animosity between the parties. Nonetheless, the animosity between the parties may not reflect in children and their development. *Moreover, it is extremely likely that the parties have committed acts of parental alienation. On the other hand, the intense emotional imbalance of both parties can not harm the child's visits* [emphasis added]. I rule that the author and defendant be forwarded to psychological treatment in this city, to be referred to the county's Secretary of Health. I stress that the initiation of treatment should be reported in this case, adding the name of the professional treating them. (R.C.D.C. and D.B.S., 2011)

In the following case, one can find warnings given to a variety of family members who acted in conjunction with the alienating parents, as published in the Official Gazette of São Paulo on February 18, 2011:

> As rightly pointed out by the distinguished representative of the prosecution, it does not seem appropriate to transfer custody of the child for two months for a social study without the influence of the paternal family, but I do not consider an abrupt change of custody reasonable, even if the goal is further evaluation. The measure is extreme and does not seem proportion-

> al to the objective pursued. *Nevertheless, the father and the paternal grandmother of the minor should be aware of the gravity of their conduct of deliberately alienating the child from his mother. Currently, according to the Law 12318/2010, it is considered an act of parental alienation in influencing the child's psychological development, promoted or induced by parents or grandparents* [emphasis added]. If the existence of typical acts of parental alienation is shown, or any conduct that hampers the coexistence of the child with the parent, the magistrate may, without prejudice, resulting from civil or criminal liability, take one of the measures spelled out in Article 6 of the aforementioned law, which include a change in the custody and a suspension of parental authority. We are not yet concluding the existence of typical acts of parental alienation, but according to the opinion of the technical sector, there is evidence to that effect. *Therefore, the defendant and his mother (grandmother of the minor) must be aware of the importance of not interfering with the coexistence between mother and daughter* [emphasis added]. (A.C.F. and C.R.D.M., 2011, p. 176)

Both before and after the adoption of Lei 12.318, one can find legal decisions regarding compliance with visitations under penalty of criminal contempt and condemnation. We cite two decisions like this in the state of São Paulo. In June 2011, after the advent of the new law,

> All these [previous] measures were frustrated in the face of the daughter's resistance to leave in the company of her father the condominium where she resides with her mother. *There is evidence that resistance may result from the daughter suffering parental alienation by the mother, or at least the utter failure of the latter to encourage her daughter to accompany her father (which likewise can be characterized parental alienation by willful default)* [emphasis added]. In any case, these mere traces were not considered sufficient to immediately discard the possibility that the minor's resistance results from her own insecurity. Precisely in the face of these doubts . . . , it was always determined that the will of the minor not be disrespected. Such a restriction aimed to: a) first, to prevent the minor from suffering psychological trauma should she be required to accompany her father, b) secondly, to enable the parents and the minor to adapt to the new routine, c) third, allow enough time for the minor to be convinced by her mother to accompany her father, d) and fourth and lastly, to give time to the parents (especially the mother) to propose revisions regarding the visitation structure in the event the current regime proves inconvenient or incompatible with the will and the possibilities of the minor daughter. Having exhausted all previous attempts, we now urge a new approach be adopted, because: a) there was enough time for the parents and minor to adjust to the visitation regime in place, b) the mother had enough time to convince her daughter to accompany the parent, or in the presence of any relevant reason, to take action in order to revise the current system of visits, c) there is no news that the visitation regime was proposed for revi-

> sions, even less than the mother obtained anticipated custody so that the daughter might not be taken by the father. In the face of such circumstances, the mother must strictly comply with the visitation regime in force and convince her daughter to accompany her father. *That said, I grant the request for the mother to be ordered to take effective and immediate action to comply with the visitation regime in force, in order to convince her daughter to accompany the defendant* [emphasis added] under penalty of a) a crime of disobedience, for which the timely measures will be adopted according to Art.40 of the CPP, b) a fine of R$545.00, payable cumulatively for every noncompliance (every failed attempt to carry out the visits outside the mother's residence), pursuant to Art. 461, § 5, of the CPC. (W.R. and S.B., 2011, p. 2065)

In a second decision in the State of São Paulo on December 12, 2009, prior to the ratification of the law in question,

> Outright grant of judicial protection under Article 461, § 3, of the CPC, determining the defendant is to fully satisfy the visitation regime approved by sentence . . . , immediately resuming the visits of the claimant, in accordance with the stipulations of the festivities for the year-end holidays and January vacation . . . , with a fixed penalty fine of R$ 2,000.00 (two thousand Reals) for each failure to comply. In case of disobedience, beyond the fine, search and seizure warrant may be issued for the execution of visits, notwithstanding the delivery of parts to the criminal court for appropriate action (Art. 461, §§ 4 and 5, CPC). Consigning to the writ of summons and subpoena of the defendant, and the diligence be performed by the bailiff, with urgency. (Case number 100.09.345500-2, 2009, p. 413)

Prior to the adoption of Lei 12.318, there already had been decisions based on PA. Maria Berenice Dias, who subsequently advocated for Lei 12.318, was a judge of the Court of Rio Grande do Sul, a state appellate court. In June 2006, Judge Berenice Dias made the following decision:

> In viewing the presence of parental alienation syndrome in the mother's attitude, which can compromise the daughter's psychological well-being, in the best interest of the infant, she will be placed under the temporary custody of the paternal grandmother. (Rio Grande do Sol Tribunal of Justice, 2006)

As for the type of court orders related to the topic of PA, many are first-instance decisions in the courts of various states of the country. Basically, these decisions have warned parents to back off any practice of PA. For example, in the most common decisions before the prevention of visits, the magistrates have restrained under penalty the conduct of (1) declaration of potential PA, (2) the initiation of a procedure to verify the hypothesis of PA, (3) reversal of custody, (4) loss or suspension of parental authority, (5) suspension of visits, (6) reversal of the obligation to take their children on visits, and (7) fine every frustrated visit. The fines have been fixed between the minimum wage (about 600 Reals) and 2000 Reals for each frustrated visit. It has also been usual for first-instance judgments to request urgent psychological analysis due to evidence of PA. Other decisions have denied requests for suspension of visiting rights due to evidence of PA.

Two court decisions from the state of São Paulo indicate stronger stances on the part of judges. The first occurred in May 2011:

> In preparation to exonerating, I determine: (1) clarification by the father regarding obstruction of visits determined by the judgment (pages 136/138), and the observance of which had been subpoenaed personally; (2) indication of close relatives of the parties (ascending and/or collateral, to the third degree) residing in the city, in case of any need for compulsory change of custody, should the hypothesis of parental alienation be confirmed, thus avoiding protective institutionalization [emphasis added]. Deadline: 10 (ten) days. (M.K.D.C. and J.C.P.D.C., 2011)

The second decision occurred in June 2011:

> Given what is on the record and the agreement of the prosecution, I grant the request for . . . Search and seizure of minor E.R.S. and her delivery to the defendant, who will remain the weekend in his company, removing the minor on Saturday at 10 a.m. and returning her on Sunday at 7 p.m. *Notwithstanding, I order prosecution for parental alienation, noting that the defendant may lose custody of the child and the application of a fine. From this moment on, I authorize the use of police force and forceful entry at the discretion of the bailiff, as necessary* [emphasis added]. Providing and executing as necessary. This is to be done, with urgency. (R.C.D.S.T. and E.L.D.S., 2011)

There have already been a number of decisions from a variety of state appellate courts, which upheld the lower court's reversing custody on the ground of PA. For example, the state court of Rio de Janeiro said:

> Judgment on the merits to determine the reversal of custody, withdrawing and handing her from the mother to the father, because of the profound process of parental alienation practiced by mother, who has not managed with care the child's activities. Agreement with the sentence handed down in line with the positioning Ministerial collected [sic] in both first and second levels of jurisdiction. (Rio de Janeiro Tribunal of Justice, 2010)

Also, the state court of São Paulo turned down the request for suspension of visiting rights in face of the PA practiced by the appellant:

> Obstruction presented by the parent is harmful to the child. Individualism of the mother should be removed from the plan. Procedure of appellant characterizes parental alienation. Appellant had already proposed action to destitute parental rights from the defendant, but without success. Belligerency between the parties can not affect the relationship with the child. (São Paulo Tribunal of Justice, 2010)

COMMENTS ON TEXT OF LEI 12.318

Brazilian Law, which provides for acts of PA inaugurated a specific concept, but because it was grounded in the model of Richard Gardner, it can be analyzed and compared to the interventional proposal of that author. According to Lei 12.318, the "act of parental alienation" is defined as "the interference in a child's or adolescent's psychological education promoted or induced by either parent, by grandparents, or by those who hold the child or adolescent under their authority, guardianship, or surveillance to reject one of the parents, or that hampers building or maintaining bonds with them."

Also found in the text of the law is an illustrative list of alienating behaviors: carrying out campaigns for disqualifying a parent's behavior upon exercising his or her parenthood; obstructing the exercise of parental authority; obstructing the contact between a child or adolescent with one of her or his parents; obstructing the legal right to exercise family life; deliberately withholding from a parent relevant personal information on the child or adolescent, including school-related, medical, and address changes; filing false charges against a parent, or their family members or against grandparents to obstruct or prevent their presence in the child or adolescent's life; and changing residence to a distant place, without justification, in order to make it difficult for the child or adolescent to live with the other parent, his or her family member, or grandparents.

Two terms are mentioned, "act of parental alienation" and "parental alienation." The legal definition does not directly involve notions of family dynamics, pathology, or even use the term "parental alienation syndrome." The law also refers to terms such as "carrying out campaigns for disqualifying a parent's behavior upon exercising his or her parenthood" and "interference in a child's or adolescent's psychological education promoted or induced by either parent . . . to reject one of the parents." Thus, the alienation under Lei 12.318 is approached a certain way, in that the notions of "parent programmer" and "brainwashing" are present in the concept of

Gardner. It can be inferred therefore that a notion of parental alienation is established as a form of psychological child abuse. In this respect, the third article of the law states, "The practice of PA infringes a fundamental right the child or adolescent has in having a healthy family life . . . and constitutes moral abuse on the child or adolescent."

Contrary to the interventional model proposed by Gardner, however, the model proposed by Lei 12.318 does not require for the child to show signs of PAS for which measures are applied. That is, the child does not need to reject the parent for legal action to be undertaken. In this sense, one can say that the Brazilian definition involves primarily a preventive character against PA. The penalty is about the attitudes and behavior of those who practice such acts, whether or not they are a typical programmer and whether or not PAS is present in the child.

The author of the draft bill, Elizio Luiz Perez (2010), commented on this point:

> Regardless of the presence of Parental Alienation Syndrome (PAS) or other consequences, it appears that the psychological process of parental alienation is itself a form of emotional abuse against the child or adolescent. Here's the first point that the law turned: avoid, in origin, the practice of this form of abuse, giving visibility to the context in which they practice it, and the risks inherent to it, though it need not already infer disorder for the child or teenager. (p. 68)

Later he adds,

> Such was the motivation for the original project, of a preventive character, to remove the absurd practical situation of having to wait for the implementation of imminent harm to the child to allow intervention. It is not the State's option to pronounce such lesions and act on complaints of abuse (or threat), albeit of a psychic nature. (p. 69)

Also found in Lei 12.318 is a definition of PA¸ "acts of parental alienation," which specifically do not have a psychologizing notion of this phenomenon in the Gardnerian definition of "brainwashing," "campaign of denigration," and "programming." For example, according to Article 2 of Lei 12.318, PA in isolation is conceptualized as attitudes to hamper the coexistence of the child with the alienated parent, omit information about the child or adolescent, create false accusations, or change the child's address to a distant location. It appears therefore that the legal definition includes different scopes of what is meant by PA, such as the "acts of parental alienation." Thus, there is no need for the requirement of a campaign of denigration by the programmer in order for the judge to intervene protectively for the child. Any acts of PA, even isolated, can be restrained by the magistrate, so there is no need to characterize any pathology in the child or the parent to take action.

In this sense, the concept in Lei 12.318 departs from a psychologizing and pathologizing notion found in Gardner's model. As Brockhausen (2011) said, "While the definition of 'acts' amplifies what is meant by parental alienation, the model of Gardner pathologizes these situations because it includes the most severe cases of obstruction linked to issues important to the alienating parent and psychological violence" (p. 63). From this comparison, one can weave consequences to the model of the Brazilian Law. For Gardner, both parents can incite PAS in children, but only one can install it. The reason is because PAS represents alignment of the child with one side. Therefore, in the approach of Gardner, only one parent should be blamed for the PAS. In the format of the Brazilian Law, however, by basing its focus on the attitudes of the alienator, this opens the possibility for both parents to commit acts of PA, and there may be sanctions for two or more responsible individuals.

The notion proposed by Gardner pathologizes and restricts such situations, the Brazilian legal concept extends the concept of the term. If the model of Gardner gathers the most problematic family situations, the Brazilian model includes milder dynamics and family conflicts. The Brazilian definition carries out a prevention of the installation of PAS, and one can thus trivialize use of the term. In this case, the implicit risk is to decrease the effectiveness of the operation of the judiciary in the most severe cases of PA, just those who need faster and more forceful measures.

Another consequence of the Brazilian model can be seen in the increase in the power of the magistrate to make decisions because there is no need for help from health professionals for the judge to determine the presence of PA. So if on the one hand Lei 12.318 carries out prevention, it encompasses other milder conflicting dynamics that could have good results with alternative interventions, such as therapy and mediation.

Returning to the scope of the concept of PA provided in Article 2 of Lei 12.318, it is expected to find other possible types of PA besides those explicit under the law. To clarify, Lei 12.318 allows for any other possible form of PA found by the judge or diagnosed by the expert that does not fit the assumptions listed in the text. Thus, the legal text seeks to cover situations not specified.

Another point that should be emphasized is that PA in the text of Lei 12.318 is not restricted to family situations involving separation and divorce, because there is no mention in the law of whether the parents are separated or divorced. Also, the definition of PA is not restricted to the behavior of the alienating parent but can involve other persons. That can be seen from this excerpt, that PA is "the interference in a child's or adolescent's psychological education *promoted or induced by either parent, by grandparents, or by those who hold the child or adolescent under their authority* [emphasis added], guardianship, or surveillance to reject one of the parents, or that hampers building or maintaining bonds with them." In continuation in the same article, it can be seen that Lei 12.318 provides for the secondary alienating figure defined by Gardner although he does not specifically use the term. The text says that forms of PA may be "either directly committed or with the aid of third parties."

Brazilian law, prior to the enactment of Lei 12.318, already had suitable legal instruments to curb cases of PA. One should observe that the coercive measures envisioned in Article 6 (imposing a fine, reversal of custody, suspension of parental authority, requiring psychological care) are provided for in specific laws such as the Civil Code for Children and Adolescents and the Constitution. In this sense, legal authors have criticized the redundant nature of the law. According to Duarte (2010),

> In these cases, using the tools included in the legal proceedings, the magistrate already had the appropriate means to stop the abuse of the guardian in the impediment of the other's right to visit, or of the non-guardian committing parental abandonment, or who also abuses their right in not returning the child after finishing the visiting period.

In a presentation to a professional organization, Judge Antônio Carlos Mathias Coltro (2010) also criticized the new law, stating that the judge already had instruments to implement the planned measures, highlighting the judicializing character of family issues.

One cannot help noticing that the definition of the law on PA, being as broad as it is, might encourage the widespread use by lawyers in the judicial system as a tool of empowerment, bargaining, or threat. It is up to judges and prosecutors through their work to control the unmeasured use. Lei 12.318, however, establishes specificity and arranges instruments generating greater comfort to magistrates to intervene. The power to enforce decisions is ensured only by coercive measures that are often avoided by the magistrate of the area of the family. The law also avoids following up on clarifying allegations and determines punishments, thus removing the greatest sense of justice.

According to Bedaque,

> What we can no longer be accepted is the presumed link between the civil judge to the so-called formal truth, with the real truth prevailing only in criminal matters. Such expressions are among those that should be banished from procedural science. Formal truth is synonymous with formal lies, since

> they are two faces of the same phenomenon: the judgment made in the light of insufficient evidence to verify the judicial-material reality. When one does not see that one's rights recognized, pursuant to an unfair ruling, then one cease to believe in the judicial function. (2009, p. 17)

However, one cannot fail to mention the social effects when coining the concept of PA, now recognized as legitimate under the law. Nor can one fail to recognize the effect of Lei 12.318 to reaffirm the power of the magistrate, making it more comfortable to act more firmly in these cases. If on the one hand the judge is given more power, on the other hard he should demonstrate greater sensitivity and understanding when intervening more forcefully so as not to induce greater harm to the child or adolescent.

The necessity of the law in Brazil can be understood, in part, in terms of the narrow interpretation of the legal operators as to the meaning of the child's family life rights. The practice reveals a determination of restricted visits and inaction of law operators in situations of contact obstruction, false allegations, and requests to change cities, which are granted without further examination regarding the possibility of PA. Rarely, when an allegation of abuse is proven false, is custody reversed. Applications for suspension of visits are trivially granted when accusations are made, often without establishing an assisted visit, suddenly breaking an important emotional bond.

For Souza, the Civil Code makes rules pertaining to custody confusing for not reserving isolated treatment of the subject. In this sense, Souza argues that several new laws in question like Lei 12.318 have emerged to clarify the meaning of the institution of custody. He said,

> Unfortunately what we see in practice is that the spouse who has custody actually exercises sole parental authority, when this situation should only exist in pathological cases of suspension or dismissal of parental authority. This vicious custom is an affront to law and harms the children of ample family life. (2008, p. 9)

The need of the law arose aiming to regulate situations that went unseen in the eyes of the judges. When facing parental conflicts, legal operators tend to act via generalizations, glossing over the different levels of responsibilities and difficulties of each parent and providing rationalizations such as "the two fight." Thus they retreat from cases of PA.

The author of this chapter said,

> It is about giving the correct accent to certain issues in the psycho-legal field. Minor difficulties in the parenting of the alienated parent have been equated to the systematic psychological violence practiced by the alienating par-

> ent in relation to the offspring, as two elements that equally influence the hostility of the children against the rejected parent. (Brockhausen, 2012)

The judicial practice, being complicit with this kind of situation, is detrimental to a culture complicit with alienation. Later, the author stated,

> As a legal psychologist, I found that, with the delay or silence of the judiciary, some parents gave up trying to maintain contact with their children, while others committed transgressional acts, ironically to keep their right to visit their children. In denying the application of the law to curb the whims of a parent who uses the child as a means of retaliation, the judiciary is complicit with the transgression, participating in the cycle of violence. It was possible to observe the perverse effect if a lack of enforcement of sanctions. How to transmit the law to the child, an essential element for parental love, when parents are denied the law that provides them with the right to a parent-child relationship? Love needs the law and its limits. Among the new symptoms of modernity, Parental Alienation seems to coincide with the pathology of family relationships in modern life. (Brockhausen, 2012)

Moreover, in many states of the United States, some domestic laws can be identified as regulating devices of PAS or PA. In the states of Arizona and California, for example, the presumption for custody takes into account the parent who ensures greater coexistence with the child's other parent. In these states, they also take into account, when determining custody, whether either of the parents is guilty of any false accusations. In the state of New Jersey, the competent court for family matters is the one where the child resided for the previous six months. Leaving the state is forbidden without the express permission of both parents (*see* http://www.womenslaw.org for statutes regarding family law in every state).

The attribution of custody is also conditional on the parent who has the greater ability to agree, communicate, and cooperate regarding the child's matters. When the parents cannot reach an agreement regarding custody, the court can demand that each parent present a proposal. An ample offer of contact will be taken into consideration by the magistrate in awarding custody. To take or prevent a minor child, aiming to hide him from the other parent or deprive them of contact with the child, is a crime in that same state.

Also provided for in New Jersey law is an obligatory educational program for divorced parents, twice a month, to help them redeem their conflicts resulting from the separation and its affect on their children. These types of devices create a differentiated and self-regulating cultural situation against the abuse of parental authority, whereas in Brazil, lacking a more coherent judicial regulation, divorce disputes can reach enormous proportions of psychological violence in children. Brazilian legislation is mild in such cases and prevention of visiting right is not considered a crime, contrary to the practice in other countries.

Analyzing it, Brazil shows itself to have few social and legal regulatory devices on PA or abuse of parental authority. Comparative law shows that the private life of Brazilian families suffers little state intervention and as a result does not efficiently regulate a variety of abusive situations. It is perhaps for this reason that Brazil is the only country in the world with a law dedicated to PA.

Editors' Notes

- In this chapter, Ms. Brockhausen summarized the history of custody legislation and litigation in Brazil and also the legislative history of Lei 12.318, the proposal regarding PA that became law in August 2010.
- Lei 12.318 provides a definition of PA: "the interference in a child's or adolescent's psychological education promoted or induced by either parent . . . to reject one of the parents, or that happens building or maintaining bonds with them." The law cites several examples of alienating behavior, such as "obstructing contact between a child and a parent" and "filing false charges by a parent."
- Ms. Brockhausen points out that Lei 12.318 may be applied broadly to inappropriate parenting activities. For example, the law simply describes alienating behaviors and does not require that the child has actually become alienated from a parent. Also, the law includes the alienating behaviors of grandparents and other third parties.
- Lei 12.318 provides several options for judges who identify PA, such as increasing parenting time for the alienated parent, fining the alienating parent, and even changing the child's custody. Ms. Brockhausen summarized several recent legal cases in which the court took action based on Lei 12.318.

REFERENCES

Bedaque, J. R. d. S. (2009). *Investigative powers of the judge* (4th ed.). São Paulo: RT Publisher.

Brito, L. M. T. (2004). Guarda conjunta: conceitos, preconceitos e prática no consenso e no litígio [Shared custody: Concepts, prejudices, and consensus and litigation practice]. In R. C. Pereira (Ed.), *Afeto, ética, família e o novo código civil* [Affection, ethics, family and the new civil code] (pp. 355–367). Belo Horizonte, Brazil: Del Rey.

Brockhausen, T. (2011). *SAP e psicanálise no campo psicojurídico: de um amorexaltadoaodom do amor* [*PAS and psychoanalysis in the psycho-legal field: From an exalted love to the gift of love*]. (Unpublished master's thesis). Institute of Psychology, University of São Paulo, São Paulo.

Brockhausen, T. (2012). Alienação parental: Caminhosnecessários [Parental alienation: Required paths]. *PsicologiaCiência e Profissão: Diálogos, 9*(8), 15–17.

Duarte, M. (2010). Alienação parental: Comentários iniciais à Lei 12.318/2010 [Parental alienation: Initial comments on Law 12.318/2010]. Instituto Brasileiro de Direito de Família (IBDFAM). Retrieved from http://www.ibdfam.org.br/?artigos&artigo=697

Mathias Coltro, A. C. (2010, November 22). Lecture presented to the Lawyers Association of São Paulo (SP-AASP).

Perez, E. L. (2010). Breves comentários acerca da lei de alienação parental [Brief comments on the law on parental alienation]. In M. B. Dias (Ed.), *Incesto e alienação parental: Realidades que a justiça insiste em nãover* [*Incest and parental alienation: Realities that the justice refuses to see*] (2nd ed., pp. 61–94). São Paulo: Editora Revista dos Tribunais.

Souza, R. P. R. (2008). A tirania do guardião [The tyranny of the guardian]. In APASE, *Síndrome da alienação parental e a tirania do guardião: Aspectos psicológicos, sociais e jurídicos* [*Parental alienation syndrome and the tyranny of the guardian: Psychological, social, and legal aspects*] (pp. 14–26). Porto Alegre, Brazil: Equilíbrio.

Cases

A.C.F. and C.R.D.M. (2011, February 2). *Publicação Oficial do Tribunal de Justiça do Estado de São Paulo.*

Case number 100.09.345500-2 (2009, December 12). *Publicação Oficial do Tribunal de Justiça do Estado de São Paulo.*

M.K.D.C. and J.C.P.D.C. (2011, May 27). *Publicação Oficial do Tribunal de Justiça do Estado de São Paulo.*

R.C.D.C. and D.B.S. (2011, May 17). *Publicação Oficial do Tribunal de Justiça do Estado de São Paulo.*

R.C.D.S.T. and E.L.D.S. (2011, June 15). Diário da Justiça Eletrônico de São Paolo.

Rio de Janeiro Tribunal of Justice (2010, October 27). Case number 0142612-80.2005.8.19.0001. Judge Marco Aurelio Froes.

Rio Grande do Sol Tribunal of Justice (2006, June 7). Case number 70014814479. Judge Maria Berenice Dias.

São Paulo Tribunal of Justice (2010, November 11). Case number 990.10.217441-7. Judge Natan Arruda Zelinschi

W.R. and S.B. (2011, June 20). *Publicação Oficial do Tribunal de Justiça do Estado de São Paulo.*

Box 14.2
LAW # 12.318 OF AUGUST 26th, 2010

The PRESIDENT OF THE REPUBLIC

makes it known that the National Congress has passed, and that he enacts the following Law:

Art. 1st This law rules on parental alienation.

Art. 2nd An act of parental alienation is deemed the interference in a child's or adolescent's psychological education promoted or induced by either parent, by grandparents, or by those who hold the child or adolescent under their authority, guardianship, or surveillance to reject one of the parents, or that hampers building or maintaining bonds with them.

Sole paragraph. Illustrative forms of parental alienation, in addition to those so determined by a judge or ascertained by experts, either directly committed or with the aid of third parties are:

I—to carry out campaigns for disqualifying a parent's behaviour upon exercising his/her parenthood;

II—to obstruct the exercise of parental authority;

III—to obstruct the contact between a child or adolescent with one of their parents;

IV—to obstruct the legal right to exercise family life;

V—to deliberately withhold from a parent relevant personal information on the child or adolescent, including school-related, medical, and address changes;

VI—to file false charges against a parent, their family members, or against grandparents, to obstruct or prevent their presence in the child or adolescent's life;

VII—to change residence to a distant place, without justification, in order to make it difficult for the child or adolescent to live with the other parent, their family member, or grandparents.

Box 14.2—*Continued*

Art. 3rd The practice of parental alienation infringes a fundamental right the child or adolescent has in having a healthy family life, impairs affection in their relationship with the parent and other family members, and constitutes moral abuse on the child or adolescent, in breach of the duties inherent to parental authority, or to guardianship or custody.

Art. 4th Once an act of parental alienation has been so stipulated, either on a motion or by default, at any stage of the proceedings, either on a lawsuit or after an incident, proceedings shall have priority, and the judge shall determine expeditiously, after the Public Prosecutor has been heard, the provisionary action required to preserve the child or adolescent's psychological integrity, including to assure their life with the parent, or to facilitate the actual reapproximation between both, if applicable.

Sole paragraph. Both the child or adolescent shall have ensured minimum assisted visits, except in cases where there is imminent risk to the child or adolescent's physical or psychological integrity, so attested by a professional eventually appointed by the judge to assist such visits.

Art. 5th Whenever there is evidence of parental alienation practice, brought by a lawsuit or after an incident, the judge, if necessary, shall determine a psychological or bio psychosocial expert assessment.

§ 1st The expert report shall be based on a wide psychological or biopsychosocial assessment, as applicable, also including interviews with the parties, review of court records, history of the couple's relationship and separation, chronology of incidents, assessment of the involved parties' personalities, and an examination of the child or adolescent's response to a possible charge against one of their parents.

§ 2nd The expert assessment shall be carried out by a qualified professional or multifunctional team, requiring, in any case, proven qualification from either professional or academic records in diagnosing parental alienation acts.

§ 3rd The expert or multifunctional team assigned to determine the occurrence of parental alienation will have up to 90 (ninety) days to submit their expert report, such time being extended solely on court order based on properly grounded justification.

continued

Box 14.2—*Continued*

Art. 6th After having ascertained typical acts of parental alienation or any behaviour obstructing the life of a child or adolescent with either parent, either brought by a lawsuit or after an incident, the judge may, either cumulatively or not, with no prejudice to any civil or criminal liability, widely using the procedural instruments capable of inhibiting or mitigating their effects, according the severity of the case:

I—declare the occurrence of parental alienation and notify the alienator;

II—extend the family life schedule in favour of the alienated parent;

III—apply a fine to the alienator;

IV—determine psychological or bio psychosocial counseling;

V—determine change of custody to joint custody, or its reversal;

VI—determine, by restraining order, the place of residence of the child or adolescent;

VII—declare the suspension of parental authority.

Sole paragraph. Once an abusive address change, obstruction or prevention of family life, has been ascertained, the judge may also reverse the duty of taking the child or adolescent to or from the parent's home upon their changing the place of family life.

Art. 7th Guardianship attribution or modification shall be made in favour of the parent who makes the life of the child or adolescent feasible with the other parent, in cases where shared custody is not viable.

Art. 8th Changes in the child or adolescent's domicile is irrelevant for determining competence over lawsuits grounded on the right to family life, except as arising from mutual agreement between parents, or a court ruling.

Art. 9th (ANNULLED)

Art. 10th (ANNULLED)

Art. 11th This Law becomes effective as of the day of its publication.

Chapter 15

PARENTAL ALIENATION, *DSM-5,* AND *ICD-11*

WILLIAM BERNET

Some clinicians say it does not matter whether parental alienation (PA) is a formal diagnosis in the *Diagnostic and Statistical Manual of Mental Disorders* (*DSM,* published by the American Psychiatric Association) or the *International Classification of Diseases* (*ICD,* published by the World Health Organization [WHO], the public health arm of the United Nations). They say that any knowledgeable and motivated mental health professional can treat family members who are affected by PA, regardless of whether the condition is an official diagnosis. They say that in conducting evaluations and developing treatment plans, they use appropriate, acceptable, Axis I diagnoses, such as separation anxiety disorder, oppositional defiant disorder, and parent-child relational problem. In very severe cases of PA, they may use the diagnosis of shared psychotic disorder. Also, experienced forensic evaluators say there is no need for PA to be a *DSM* diagnosis when they testify in a legal proceeding. As an expert witness, they can simply describe what they observed in the family they evaluated (for example, one parent purposefully undermined the child's relationship with the other parent) with no need to label the end result (that is, the child's alienation from the previously loved, now rejected parent) with a formal diagnosis.

On the other hand, many writers say it matters a great deal, that the concept of PA and the actual words parental alienation, should certainly be included–one way or another–in both *DSM-5* and *ICD-11.* The advocates of PA as a recognized diagnosis typically present the following arguments: (1) It simply reflects reality; that is, the construct of PA is just as valid and just as real as mental conditions such as reactive attachment disorder, attention-deficit/hyperactivity disorder, and conduct disorder. (2) It is important for trainees to learn about PA and for practitioners to be familiar with PA, so the condition will be recognized earlier when it is more treatable. Professional and general public awareness of PA will be heightened when the condition becomes an accepted diagnostic term. (3) When it is necessary to testify about PA in court, the testimony will be given more serious consideration if the concept of PA has been accepted by the American Psychiatric Association and WHO. (4) With less controversy and more awareness about PA, the concept and term PA will appear more regularly in psychological and medical literature, which thus would facilitate retrieving literature on the phenomenon and promote scientific investigation regarding PA.

PARENTAL ALIENATION AND DSM-IV

When *DSM-IV* was published in 1994, the concept of PA was fairly well known. Although they used varying terminology and somewhat different definitions, PA had been observed and identified by several independent researchers during the 1980s, including Janet Johnston, Linda Campbell, and Sharon Mayes (1985), who identified a "strong alliance" in children of divorce, "defined as a strong, consistent overt (publically stated) verbal and behavioral preference for one parent together with rejection and denigration of the other"; Richard Gardner (1985), who defined "parental alienation syndrome" (PAS); Judith Wallerstein and Sandra Blakeslee (1989), who discussed "the Medea syndrome" extensively in *Second Chances: Men, Women, and Children a Decade after Divorce,* saying, "A child may be used as an agent of revenge against the other parent"; and Stanley Clawar and Brynne Rivlin (1991) in *Children Held Hostage.* Although there was a growing literature regarding PA, no one submitted a formal proposal to the American Psychiatric Association that PA be included in *DSM-IV* (Allen Frances, personal communication, July 2012).

PARENTAL ALIENATION AND DSM-5

Almost twenty years passed between the publication of *DSM-IV* in 1994 and *DSM-5* in 2013. During that time, many mental health practitioners validated in their own clinical work the findings of Johnston, Gardner, Wallerstein, and Clawar and Rivlin and the other seminal writers. The discussion spread from the United States and Canada to other countries in Europe, South America, and Asia. Hundreds of writers from six continents described cases of PA (*see* the bibliography in Bernet, 2010). Many custody evaluators and other mental health experts introduced the terms, "parental alienation" and "parental alienation syndrome" in courts in the United States, Canada, South America, and Europe. A number of books were published, some of them by and for mental health professionals, some of them for the general public, and some of them the personal stories of alienated parents. In addition to a multitude of case reports, systematic research regarding PA and PAS began to appear. PA and PAS were defined and discussed in *Wikipedia* as well as scholarly works such as the *Encyclopedia of Forensic Science* and the *Encyclopedia of Clinical Psychology.* Parental alienation became household words that the average person recognized and understood. It was time for PA to become a diagnosis formally recognized by mental health professionals.

2008: CONTACTING THE DSM-5 TASK FORCE

The leadership of the American Psychiatric Association started planning for *DSM-V* as far back as 2000. The *DSM-V* Task Force was appointed in 2006, under the leadership of Chairman David Kupfer, M.D., and Vice Chairman Darrel Regier, M.D. William Narrow, M.D., was appointed research director of *DSM-V.* (The abbreviation for the next version of *DSM* was later changed from *DSM-V* to *DSM-5.*) The active task of revising *DSM-IV-TR* started seriously in May 2008, when the members of the various work groups were named. For example, the Childhood and Adolescent Disorders Work Group (CADWG), under Chairman Daniel Pine, M.D., included prominent child and adolescent psychiatrists James Leckman, M.D.; Ellen Leibenluft, M.D.; Judith Rapoport, M.D.; and Charles Zeanah, M.D. David Schaffer, M.D., initially a member of the CADWG, became chairman of ADHD and Disruptive Behavior Disorders Work Group.

After the work groups and their members were announced in May 2008, this author wanted to know whether PA or PAS was already on their list of diagnoses to consider for inclusion in *DSM-5.* The author contacted Dr. Daniel Pine, the chairman of the CADWG, who replied that the Task Force had not received a formal proposal regarding PA or PAS. Dr. Pine said that interested parties could submit such a proposal, which he thought should be about twenty pages long. He requested that the formal proposal be sent to him by August 2008, about six weeks off. Before starting to work on the proposal, this author conferred with Demosthenes Lorandos, Ph.D., J.D., and S. Richard Sauber, Ph.D., who had been the editors, along with Richard Gardner, M.D. (2006), of the recently published *International Handbook of Parental Alienation Syndrome.* In a conference call, we discussed the advantages and disadvantages of submitting a formal proposal that PA, or some variation of it, be included in *DSM-5.* We agreed to proceed and submitted an initial proposal to Dr. Pine and the *DSM-5* Task Force by the due date. We created the term parental alienation disorder, in order to conform to the vocabulary in *DSM.* Dr. Sauber, the editor of *The American Journal of Family Therapy,* arranged for that initial proposal, "Parental Alienation Disorder and *DSM-V,*" to be published a few months later (Bernet, 2008). The initial proposal was also supported by Wilfrid von Boch-Galhau, M.D. (from Germany), Lena Hellblom Sjögren, Ph.D. (from Sweden), James S. Walker, Ph.D. (my colleague at Vanderbilt University Department of Psychiatry), and others.

2009: NEXT STEPS

When Dr. Pine responded to our initial proposal in September 2008, he reported that he had discussed it with the CADWG, and he had some feedback for us. Of primary concern, according to Dr. Pine, was that the fifty-six-page proposal that had been submitted did not cite enough research regarding the validity of parental alienation disorder as a concept or the reliability of the proposed criteria for the diagnosis of parental alienation disorder for this novel condition to be included in *DSM-5* as a mental disorder. About the same time, we started to receive comments from clinical psychologists and psychiatrists who had heard about our proposal. They expressed discomfort with PA's becoming a mental disorder in the front part of *DSM-5.* Their arguments against its inclusion were not that it did not exist, as none doubted the reality of PA as an actual phenomenon and a serious mental condition that needed to be identified and treated. Rather, they had concerns about "labeling the victim," in other words, the child, with a mental disorder. Further, they pointed out that the American Psychiatric Association was emphasizing the biological basis for most mental disorders, which PA lacked. Several clinicians said they thought that PA seemed to fit the general definition of a relational problem, and that it seemed similar to parent-child relational problem, which was already a diagnosis in *DSM-IV-TR.* After considering available options for several months, it was decided to continue advocating for the inclusion of PA in *DSM-5* in the following manner: (1) We would expand the section of the proposal that presented the peer-reviewed research foundation for the concept of PA. (2) We would invite additional professionals as contributing authors of the proposal, with an emphasis on international authors who had studied PA or PAS. (3) We would modify the proposal to include a recommendation that PA be included in *DSM-5* as *either* a mental disorder in the front part of the book *or* as a relational problem in the chapter of *DSM-5,* "Other Conditions That May Be of Clinical Interest," *or* as a proposed diagnosis in the appendix of DSM-5, "Criteria Sets for Further Study."

THE COMMITTEE OF FLORENCE

In April 2009, the annual meeting of the World Psychiatric Association took place in Florence, Italy. In one of the plenary presentations, the senior officials who were developing *ICD-11* and *DSM-5* reported on the progress of their work, including how they intended to coordinate the diagnoses and the diagnostic criteria between those two nosological systems. One of the presenters from WHO was Geoffrey Reed, Ph.D., a staff member of the American Psychological Association who had been assigned to WHO to develop the sections of *ICD-11* that pertained to behavioral disorders. The author met Dr. Reed and agreed to send him a copy of the original proposal regarding PA that had already been submitted to the *DSM-5* Task Force.

At the same time in Florence, Dr. Boch-Galhau brought together a group of European colleagues who were interested in discussing PA and PAS, including the possibility of the concept's being included in the next editions of *DSM* and *ICD.* In addition to Dr. Boch-Galhau and the author of this chapter, the informal meeting was attended by Eduard Bakalář, C.Sc. (from the Czech Republic); Paul Bensussan, M.D. (France); Christian Dum, Ph.D. (Germany); Anja Hannuniemi, LL.Lic. (Finland); Lena Hellblom Sjögren, Ph.D. (Sweden); Ursula Kodjoe, M.A. (Germany); Olga Odinetz, Ph.D. (France); and Benoit Van Dieren, Ph.D. (Belgium). The group became known as the "Committee of Florence," although subsequent meetings were held in Fagersta, Sweden; St. Moritz, Switzerland; and Würzburg, Germany. In some meetings, the participants also included Nils-Göran Areskoug, M.D., Ph.D. (Sweden); Asunción Tejedor Huerta, Ph.D. (Spain); and Terje Torgersen, M.D. (Norway). Our European colleagues–experts in PA–agreed to help develop the new, enlarged proposal that Dr. Pine said was required if we wanted to be taken seriously by the *DSM-5* Task Force. The Committee of Florence also agreed that it would be important to develop a comprehensive proposal that would be submitted to both the *DSM-5* Task Force and the *ICD-10* Revision Commission of WHO.

2010: PUBLICATION OF THE FORMAL PROPOSAL

The second version of the formal proposal was submitted to *DSM-5* and *ICD-11* personnel in November 2009. At 179 pages, including a bibliography of about 600 references, the second proposal was much more comprehensive than the initial, 56-page document. In March 2010, the second formal proposal was published in the *American Journal of Family Therapy* (Bernet, Boch-Galhau, Baker, & Morrison, 2010). We also arranged to publish the second proposal–along with additional chapters, a more extensive bibliography, and fifteen case vignettes–in the form of a monograph, *Parental Alienation, DSM-5, and ICD-11* (Bernet, 2010). The publisher Charles C Thomas had previously published *The International Handbook of Parental Alienation Syndrome* (Gardner et al., 2006) and is the publisher of this book. All three books regarding PA were included in the American Series in Behavioral Science and Law, which has been edited by Ralph Slovenko, Ph.D.

Parental Alienation, DSM-5, and ICD-11 received both positive and negative reviews. Positive reviews were published in the *Journal of the American Academy of Child and Adolescent Psychiatry* (Shapiro, 2011), the *Journal of Forensic Sciences* (Gray and Billick, 2011), the *American Journal of Family Therapy* (Kaslow, 2011), and Deutsches Ärzteblatt, a medical journal in Germany (Andritzky, 2012). Three articles about the proposal and the book were critical:Walker and Shapiro (2010) in the *Journal of Child Custody;* Houchin, Ranseen, Hash, and Bartnicki (2012) in the *Journal of the American Academy of Psychiatry and the Law;* and Pepiton, Alvis, Allen, and Logid (2012), a review essay in the *Journal of Child Sexual Abuse.* The articles by Walker and Shapiro, Houchin and coworkers, and Pepiton and associates were critiqued in turn by Bernet and Baker (2013).

2011: PARENTAL ALIENATION STUDY GROUP

The writing of *Parental Alienation, DSM-5, and ICD-11,* with its extensive bibliography, was accomplished by an editor and seventy contributing authors, mostly mental health and legal professionals, from twelve countries. After the publication of the book, many additional individuals expressed an interest in advocating that PA be included in *DSM-5* and *ICD-11.* In order to coordinate our efforts, we organized ourselves as the Parental Alienation Study Group (PASG), which quickly grew to about 130 individuals from thirty countries. Although the initial purpose of PASG was to focus on the inclusion of PA in *DSM-5* and *ICD-11,* we also intended to encourage research in the causes, prevention, and treatment of PA; education of mental health and legal practitioners; and education of the general public.

EDUCATING PROFESSIONALS

In recent years, there has been a proliferation of presentations regarding PA at regional, national, and international conferences for mental health and legal professionals. For example, there were presentations regarding PA at meetings of the following organizations, listed in chronological order:

- American Academy of Forensic Sciences (February 2010 and February 2012)
- Association of Family and Conciliation Courts (June 2010)
- International Cultic Studies Association (July 2010)
- International Council of Psychologists (August 2010)
- European Association for Forensic Child and Adolescent Psychiatry, Basel, Switzerland (September 2010)
- American Academy of Psychiatry and the Law (October 2010)
- Forensic Mental Health Association of California (March 2011)
- VI Congreso Nacional de Psicologia Juridica y Forense, Spain (April 2011)
- School Social Work Association of America (April 2011)
- American Psychiatric Association (May 2011 and May 2013)
- American Psychological Association (August 2011)
- International Cultic Studies Association, Montreal (July 2012)
- American Academy of Child and Adolescent Psychiatry (October 2012)
- International Society for Interpersonal Acceptance and Rejection, Chandigarh, India (January 2013)
- International Academy of Law and Mental Health, Amsterdam (July 2013

There have been several professional meetings devoted exclusively to PA or PAS. For example, the international conference regarding PAS in Frankfurt, Germany (October 2002)¸ the proceedings of which were published by Boch-Galhau, Kodjoe, Andritzky, and Koeppel (2003). There have been two national symposiums on PAS in Spain (Madrid, March 2006; Santiago de Compostela, Galicia, December 2008). There have been four international conferences called "Síndrome de Alienación Parental y Custodia Compartida," in Spain (Léon, September 2009; Madrid, May 2010; Zaragoza, March 2011; and Valencia, March 2012). They were elaborate events with about twenty speakers over three days. In Italy, a conference regarding PA was organized by the Fondazione Guglielmo Gulotta and Unitå Psicoforense (Milan, March 2012). In most of those meetings, the presenters and attendees discussed the pros and cons of whether PA should become an official diagnosis for use by mental health professionals.

In the United States and Canada, four meetings organized by the Canadian Symposium for Parental Alienation Syndrome (CS-PAS) (Toronto, March 2009; Toronto, October 2009; New York City, October 2010; and Montreal, May 2011) were attended by hundreds of mental health practitioners, legal professionals, and members of the general public interested in that topic. The founder of CS-PAS, Joseph Goldberg, organized those meetings and brought together leading authors and scholars to make presentations, including Amy J. L. Baker, Ph.D.; William Bernet, M.D.; Glenn R. Caddy, Ph.D.; Terence W. Campbell, Ph.D.; Demosthenes Lorandos, J.D., Ph.D.; Brian Ludmer, L.L.B.; Jayne Major, Ph.D.; Kathleen Reay, Ph.D.; S. Richard Sauber, Ph.D.; and Abraham Worenklein, Ph.D. Goldberg also arranged for a discussion of PA to be included in the curriculum of the didactic programs that are required in many states for divorcing parents. In addition to the CS-PAS, the Parental Alienation Awareness Organization (PAAO) and the International Support Network for Alienated Families (ISNAF) have organized regional meetings for mental health and legal professionals as well as family members affected by PA.

The flourishing interest in PA has been manifested by many recently published books. Since the publication of *Parental Alienation, DSM-5, and ICD-11* in 2010, with its lengthy bibliography, the following books and other materials have been published regarding PA or PAS:

- *Adult Children of Parental Alienation Syndrome: Breaking the Ties that Bind,* by Amy J. L. Baker, was published in Italian (Baker, 2011)
- *Working with Alienated Children and Families: A Clinical Guidebook,* by Amy J. L. Baker and S. Richard Sauber, 2013
- *Parental Alienation und Parental Alienation Syndrome/Disorder: Eine ernst zunehmende Form von psychischer Kindesmisshandlung–mit Fallbeispielen* [*Parental Alienation and Parental Alienation Syndrome/Disorder: A Serious Form of Psychological Child Abuse–With Examples*] (German), by Wilfrid von Boch-Galhau, 2012. The English edition appeared in 2013.
- *Dalla Separazione All'Alienazione Parentale: Come Giungere a Una Valutazione Peritale* [*Separation from Parental Alienation: How to Arrive at an Expert Evaluation*] (Italian), by Adele Cavedon and Tiziana Magro, 2010
- *The Essentials of Parental Alienation Syndrome (PAS): It's Real, It's Here, and It Hurts,* by Robert Evans and Michael Bone, 2011
- *Parental Alienation 911 Workbook,* by Jill Egizii and Michele Lowrance, 2012
- *Padres Separados: Cómo Criar Juntos a Sus Hijos* [*Separated Parents: How to Raise Your Kids Together*] (Spanish), by Jorge Ferrari and Nelson Zicavo, 2012
- *Children Who Resist Postseparation Parental Contact: A Differential Approach for Legal and Mental Health Professionals,* by Barbara Jo Fidler, Nicholas Bala, and Michael A. Saini, 2012

- *Parental Alienation Syndrome: A Family Therapy and Collaborative Systems Approach to Amelioration,* by Linda Gottlieb, 2012
- *Barnetsrätt till familjeliv: 25 svenska fallstudier av föräldraalienation* [*The Child's Right to Family Life: 25 Swedish Case Studies of Parental Alienation*] (Swedish), by Lena Hellblom Sjögren, 2012
- *Abus de Faiblesse et Autres Manipulations* [*Abuse of Weakness and Other Manipulations*] (French)¸ by Marie-France Hirigoyen, 2012
- *Where Did I Go Wrong? How Did I Miss the Signs? Dealing with Hostile Parenting and Parental Alienation,* by Joan Kloth-Zanard, 2012
- *The Good Karma Divorce: Avoid Litigation, Turn Negative Emotions into Positive Actions, and Get On with the Rest of Your Life,* by Michele Lowrance, 2010
- *Child Less Parent: "Snapshots" of Parental Alienation,* by Jennifer McBride, 2012
- *Divorce, Séparation: Les Enfants Sont-ils Protégés* [*Divorce and Separation: Are the Children Protected?*] (French), by Jacqueline Phélep and Maurice Berger, 2012
- *Toxic Divorce: A Workbook for Alienated Parents,* by Kathleen Reay, 2011
- *Brainwashing Children,* by John Steinbeck, 2011.
- *Welcome Back Pluto: Understanding, Preventing, and Overcoming Parental Alienation,* a DVD written by Richard A. Warshak and Mark R. Otis, 2010
- *Divorce Poison,* by Richard A. Warshak, was published in Finnish (2012a) and in Japanese (2012b)
- *Crianza Compartida* [*Shared Parenting*] (Spanish), by Nelson Zicavo Martinez¸ 2010
- Special edition of *Papa-Ya: Das Magazin für Kind-gerechte Familienpolitik* [*The Magazine for Child-Oriented Family Policy*] (German) with twelve articles regarding PA, 2012

DSM-5 TASK FORCE RECEIVES MANY COMMENTS

Between 2009 and 2012, the members of PASG and many other individuals provided the *DSM-5* Task Force with articles from the mental health and legal professional literature, book chapters, books, and DVDs regarding PA. Task Force members were repeatedly reminded that PA could be included in *DSM-5* in several different ways: as a mental disorder that is "located" in the child, as a relational problem between the child and the rejected parent, as a relational problem subtype or specifier, as an example of shared psychotic disorder, and in the *DSM-5* chapter for diagnoses that need further study. Also, hundreds of parents and other family members of affected children wrote letters to Task Force members, at times relating in detail their personal nightmares involving PA. An advocacy organization, Fathers and Families, encouraged its members to write the Task Force in support of our proposal. Task Force members reported that most of the correspondence they received on this topic supported the inclusion of PA in *DSM-5.*

The Task Force also received statements from individuals and organizations opposing the inclusion of PA as a diagnosis in *DSM-5.* For example, Janet R. Johnston, Ph.D., and Joan B. Kelly, Ph.D., wrote a letter to Dr. Daniel Pine, saying "We have serious concerns regarding the inclusion of parental alienation in any capacity, particularly as a mental disorder but also as a V code, i.e., a parent-child relationship problem. We consider that it is premature to include parental alienation in the DSM because of the lack of an adequate research foundation" (Johnston and Kelly, personal communication, 2009). The president of the National Organization for Women Foundation wrote a letter to Dr. Daniel Pine and the CADWG in which she expressed the concern, "We believe that if the proposed subject disorder is added to the *DSM-V* it will be given an undeserved credibility as it is used unfairly against protective parents–usually mothers–in the courts" (O'Neill, 2010). Paul Fink, M.D., a former president of the American Psychiatric Association and current president of the Leadership Council on Child Abuse and Interpersonal Violence–whose "mission is to promote the ethical application of psychological science to human welfare"–repeatedly spoke out against PAS. For example, Dr. Fink made the preposterous allegation that advocates of our proposals include "'father's rights' groups who don't like to be interfered with when they are sexually abusing their children. The group has petitioned the DSM task force to include PAS in the publication" (Fink, 2010a). Dr. Fink subsequently withdrew his statements, saying, "I apologize for suggesting that all fathers who accuse mothers of PAS are sexually abusing their children. That was clearly an overstatement that I retract. . . . I do not deny that parental alienation occurs and that a lot of people are hurt when there is an alienator" (Fink, 2010b). The concerns raised by the PA opposition were addressed in an excellent article, "Parental Alienation Critics and the Politics of Science" (Rand 2011).

2012: RESPONSE FROM DSM-5 TASK FORCE

Task Force members responded to our proposals, letters, and e-mails and minimally addressed our three primary recommendations, that is, that PA should be included in *DSM-5* as a mental disorder *or* PA should be discussed in the section of *DSM-5* pertaining to relational problems *or* PA should be included as a proposed diagnosis in the appendix of *DSM-5,* "Criteria Sets for Further Study."

Parental Alienation as a Mental Disorder

Senior members of the *DSM-5* Task Force said several times they did not think PA should be considered a mental disorder because it is not "located" in the child. For example, Dr. Darrel Regier wrote, "The requirement that a disorder exists as an internal condition residing within an individual and not merely as a relational problem would be inconsistent with the current conceptualization of PAS" (Regier, personal communication, January 24, 2012). With regard to that statement, many advocates of PA thought that the opinion of the *DSM-5* Task Force was both arbitrary and incorrect.

There are recognized *DSM* diagnoses in which the association between interpersonal relationships and the child's mental disorder is precisely analogous to what occurs in PA. That is, in PA, Parent A interacts with the child in a way that causes the child to internalize false beliefs and feelings regarding Parent B, and the child acts on those beliefs and feelings by rejecting Parent B. That dynamic is comparable to what happens in reactive attachment disorder (RAD), a diagnosis currently in *DSM-IV-TR.* In RAD, the child's early caregivers interact with the child in ways that cause the child to internalize maladaptive patterns of attachment, and the child acts on those maladaptive patterns by forming pathological relationships with future caregivers. PA is also comparable to shared psychotic disorder, which is called "delusional symptoms in partner of individual with delusional disorder" in *DSM-5.* In shared delusional disorder, one of the child's parents interacts with the child in a way that causes the child to adopt the parent's paranoid delusions, and the child then relates to other people in a paranoid manner. PA, RAD, and shared delusional disorder have similar etiologies: the child is subjected to a pathogenic relationship with a parent or other caregiver. PA, RAD, and shared delusional disorder have similar manifestations: the child has blatantly disturbed relationships with a parent, future caregivers, and other people in his or her world. It is, therefore, incorrect for the *DSM-5* Task Force to exclude PA as a mental disorder on the basis that the condition is not "located" in the child. Once the interactional pattern has occurred, the symptoms of PA do reside within the child and thus PA should not be excluded from *DSM-5* mental disorders for that reason.

Parental Alienation as a Relational Problem

After they excluded consideration of PA as a mental disorder, Task Force members repeatedly said they would consider including PA in the section of *DSM-5* that deals with relational problems. For example, Dr. Regier said, "The APA is . . . open to assessing the current *DSM-IV* V code of Parent-Child Relational Problem (That May Be a Focus of Clinical Attention) (v61.20) to revisions that would cover the issues raised by you and others related to the concept of parental alienation" (Regier, personal communication, January 24, 2012). Similarly, Dr. Daniel Pine commented at a *DSM-5* presentation at the May 2012 annual meeting of the American Psychiatric Association that there were "ongoing discussions" regarding including PA in the part of *DSM-5* pertaining to relational problems.

In September 2012, however, Dr. Regier was quoted in the national media (Crary, 2012) as saying that it was "very unlikely" that PA would be included in *DSM-5* as an example of a relational problem. Also, Dr. Regier summarized the position of the *DSM-5* Task Force regarding the proposal: "We consider [Parental Alienation Syndrome] primarily a relational problem covered under the V-codes in *ICD-9-CM* and Z-codes in *ICD-10-CM.* It is not a health related condition that resides with an individual. . . . Therefore, it does not meet our standard definition of a mental disorder. Since we do not have criteria for any of the V-codes in *ICD-9-CM* or for those selected for *DSM-IV,* there is no precedent for reviewing such proposals or for putting such criteria in place for *DSM-5*" (Regier, personal communication, October 12, 2012). To paraphrase, the *DSM-5* Task Force agreed that PA exists and is a type of relational problem, but they did not want to state that in the section of *DSM-5* pertaining to relational problems.

Parental Alienation Among "Criteria for Further Study"

Finally, between 2009 and 2012, the advocates of including PA in *DSM-5* repeatedly suggested that PA could be included in the part of *DSM-5* that discussed "Criteria for Further Study." We thought that if the Task Force concluded there was not enough systematic, quantitative research to include PA as a mental disorder or as a relational problem in *DSM-5,* surely they would agree that it should be listed among the proposed diagnoses that needed further study. Almost all the mental health and legal professionals who work with children of divorced parents agree that PA really exists (Baker, Jaffe, Bernet & Johnston, 2011) and that it damages many children. Almost every person involved in this debate–even those who oppose including PA in *DSM-5*–agree that there should be further study and research regarding PA. Other novel diagnoses were relegated to the chapter on mental conditions that need further study, so we could not understand why PA would not be placed there also.

Prior to sending the manuscript of this book to the publisher, the leadership of the *DSM-5* Task Force–specifically, Dr. David J. Kupfer, Dr. Darrel A. Regier, Dr. Daniel S. Pine, and Dr. David Shaffer–were notified that this chapter was being written. In order to ensure accuracy, they were invited to review this chapter prior to publication, but they did not express an interest in doing so.

THE WORKING GROUP ON RELATIONAL PROBLEMS

For about ten years, the Working Group on Relational Problems (WGRP) collected scientific evidence and wrote about the conceptual frameworks necessary to understand interpersonal relationships in clinical practice. The WGRP edited two books, *Relational Processes and DSM-V: Neuroscience, Assessment, Prevention, and Intervention* (Beach et al., 2006) and *Family Problems and Family Violence: Reliable Assessment and the ICD-11* (Foran, Beach, Slep, Heyman, & Wamboldt, 2012). The WGRP acted as consultants to the leadership of both *DSM-5* and *ICD-11* regarding relational problems and child maltreatment. They said, "Relational problems (intimate partner violence, partner relationship distress, child maltreatment, and parent-child relational problems) are major global concerns having vast impacts on psychological health, physical health, and economic well-being" (Foran et al., 2012, p. xi). Their books provided many specific recommendations for addressing those topics. Since the leadership at the American Psychiatric Association and at WHO repeatedly said they hoped to coordinate the psychiatric diagnoses in *DSM-5* and *ICD-11,* it made sense for the same committee of experts in relational problems to advise both organizations. For example, Marianne Wamboldt, M.D., a child and adolescent psychiatrist from Denver, Colorado, consulted with both *DSM* and *ICD* personnel regarding relational problems.

Dr. Wamboldt and the WGRP recommended that PA be included as an example of parent-child relational problem in *DSM-5* and caregiver-child relational problem in *ICD-11.* Specifically, in their proposed diagnostic criteria for caregiver-child relational problem, Wamboldt and Cordaro (2012, p. 219) included PA as defined in our proposals as an example of "caregiver-child relationship distress." Behavioral symptoms of that condition included "child's persistent rejection, denigration, and criticism of the alienated parent without cause."

During August to November 2012, a *DSM-5* committee chaired by William Narrow, M.D., considered how relational problems should be organized and discussed in *DSM-5.* Members of WGRP participated in Dr. Narrow's committee, which ultimately recommended that *the concept* of PA should be in *DSM-5,* but not the actual words parental alienation. For instance, the discussion of parent-child relational problem includes the example, "negative attributions of the other's intentions, hostility toward or scapegoating of the other, and unwarranted feelings of estrangement," which appears to be describing PA (American Psychiatric Association 2013, p. 715). Also, there are two new conditions in *DSM-5,* which can clearly be used as diagnoses in many cases of PA: child affected by parental relationship distress (p. 716) and child psychological abuse (p. 719). Both clinicians and forensic practitioners will find *DSM-5* very useful in classifying and diagnosing children and families that experience PA.

RESPONSE FROM ICD-11

Our primary contact at WHO was Geoffrey Reed, Ph.D., a staff member of the American Psychological Association who was on loan to the Department of Mental Health and Substance Abuse at WHO in Geneva. Dr. Reed was a senior project manager in charge of developing the psychiatric sections of *ICD-11.* There was fruitful communication between members of PASG and Dr. Reed and his colleagues at WHO. For instance, we arranged a conference call in September 2011 that included Dr. Reed, other professionals involved in writing *ICD-11,* and several members of PASG. Dr. Reed was clear that *ICD-11* personnel did not like the idea of PA becoming a distinct mental disorder with its own diagnostic code number. He cited an overall goal of simplifying the *ICD* by reducing the number of diagnoses. However, Dr. Reed and his colleagues said they would consider including PA as an example of diagnoses that were already in *ICD,* that is, caregiver-child relational problem, psychological abuse of child, and induced psychotic disorder. As this book was going to press, WHO had not yet announced proposed revisions of *ICD-10,* which should be published as *ICD-11* in 2015.

Editors' Note

- Although no one proposed PA or PAS for inclusion in *DSM-IV,* formal proposals were submitted that PA should be included in *DSM-5* and *ICD-11.*
- Regarding *DSM-5,* it was proposed that PA be included as *either* a mental disorder in the front part of the book *or* as a relational problem in the chapter of *DSM-5,* "Other Conditions That May Be of Clinical

Interest," *or* as a proposed diagnosis in the appendix of *DSM-5,* "Criteria Sets for Further Study."

- In recent years, PA has been featured at many national and international meetings for mental health and legal professionals, and many important books regarding PA have been published.
- An independent committee of experts, the Working Group on Relational Problems, recommended that PA be included as a type of relational problem in both *DSM-5* and *ICD-11.* In the end, the concept of PA was included in *DSM-5,* but not the actual words parental alienation.

REFERENCES

American Psychiatric Association. (2013). *Diagnostic and statistical manual of mental disorders,* Fifth Edition. Arlington, VA: American Psychiatric Association.

Andritzky, W. (2012). Parental Alienation: Keine geringfügige Störung [Parental alienation: No minor disturbance] [Review of the book *Parental Alienation, DSM-5, and ICD-11,* by William Bernet]. Deutsches Ärzteblatt, February 2012, p. 84.

Baker, A. J. L. (2011). *Figli divisi: Storie di manipolazione emotiva dei genitori nei confronti dei figli* [*Children divided: Stories of emotional manipulation of parents toward their children*]. Milan: Giunti Edizioni.

Baker, A. J. L., Jaffe, P. G., Bernet, W., & Johnston, J. R. (2011, May). Brief report on parental alienation survey. *Association of Family and Conciliation Courts eNEWS 30*(2).

Baker, A. J. L., & Sauber, S. R. (2013). *Working with alienated children and families: A clinical guidebook.* New York: Routledge.

Beach, S. R. H., Wamboldt., M. Z., Kaslow, N. J., Heyman, R. E., First, M.B., Underwood, L. G., & Reiss, D. (Eds.). (2006). *Relational processes and DSM-V: Neuroscience, assessment, prevention, and treatment.* Arlington, VA: American Psychiatric Publishing.

Bernet, W. (2008). Parental alienation disorder and DSM-V. *American Journal of Family Therapy 36,* 349–366.

Bernet, W. (Ed.) (2010). *Parental alienation, DSM-5, and ICD-11.* Springfield, IL: Charles C Thomas.

Bernet, W., & Baker, A. J. L. (2013). Parental alienation, DSM-5, and ICD-11: Response to critics. *J Am Acad Psychiatry Law, 41:* 98–104.

Bernet, W., Boch-Galhau, W. v., Baker, A. J. L., & Morrison, S. L. (2010). Parental alienation, DSM-V, and ICD-11. *American Journal of Family Therapy 38,* 76–187.

Boch-Galhau, W. v. (2012). *Parental Alienation und Parental Alienation Syndrome/D isorder: Eine ernst zu nehmende Form von psychischer Kindesmisshandlung. Mit Fallbeispielen* [*Parental alienation and parental alienation syndrome/disorder: A serious form of psychological child abuse–with case examples*]. Berlin: Verlag für Wissenschaft und Bildung.

Boch-Galhau, W. v., Kodjoe, U., Andritzky, W., & Koeppel, P. (Eds.). (2003). *Das Parental Alienation Syndrom: Eine interdisziplåre Herausforderung für scheidungsbegleitende Berufe* [*The parental alienation syndrome: An interdisciplinary challenge for professionals involved with divorce*]. Berlin: Verlag für Wissenschaft und Bildung.

Cavedon, A., & Magro, T. (2010). *Dalla separazione all'alienazione parentale: Come giungere a una valutazione peritale* [*Separation from parental alienation: Come giungere a una valutazione peritale: How to arrive at an expert evaluation*]. Milan, Italy: FrancoAngeli.

Clawar, S., & Rivlin, B. V. (1991). *Children held hostage: Dealing with programmed and brainwashed children.* Chicago, IL: American Bar Association.

Crary, D. (2012, September 21). Parental alienation not a mental disorder, American Psychiatric Association says. *Huffington Post* web site. Accessed at http://www.huffingtonpost.com.

Egizii, J., & Lowrance, M. (2012). *Parental alienation 911 workbook.* Accessed at www.parentalalienation911.net.

Evans, R. A., & Bone, J. M. (2011). *The essentials of parental alienation syndrome (PAS): It's real, it's here, and it hurts.* Palm Harbor, FL: Center for Human Potential of America.

Ferrari, J., & Zicavo, N. (2012). *Padres separados: Cómo criar juntos a sus hijos* [*Separated parents: How to raise your kids together*]. Mexico D.F.: Editorial Trillas.

Fidler, B. J., Bala, N., & Saini, M. A. (2012). *Children who resist postseparation parental contact: A differential approach for legal and mental health professionals.* New York: Oxford University Press.

Fink, P. J. (2010a). Fink! Still at large. *Clinical Psychiatry News.* March 6.

Fink, P. J. (2010b). Letter to the editor, Dr. Fink replies. *Clinical Psychiatry News,* May 10.

Foran, H. M., Beach, S. R. H., Slep, A. M. S., Heyman, R. E., & Wamboldt, M. Z. (Eds.). (2012). *Family problems and family violence: Reliable assessment and the ICD-11.* New York: Springer Publishing.

Gardner, R. A. (1985). Recent trends in divorce and custody litigation. *Academy Forum, 29*(2), 3–7.

Gardner, R. A., Sauber, S. R., & Lorandos, D. (Eds.). (2006). *The international handbook of parental alienation syndrome: Conceptual, clinical and legal considerations.* Springfield, IL: Charles C Thomas.

Gottlieb, L. J. (2012). *Parental alienation syndrome: A family therapy and collaborative systems approach to amelioration.* Springfield, IL: Charles C Thomas.

Gray, S. M. & Billick, S. B. (2011). *Review of: Parental Alienation Syndrome [sic], DSM-5, and ICD-11* [Review of the book, by William Bernet]. *Journal of Forensic Sciences 56,* 1079–1080.

Hellblom Sjögren, L. (2012). *Barnets rätt till familjeliv: 25 svenska fallstudier av föräldraalienation* [*The child's right to family life: 25 Swedish case studies of parental alienation*]. Lund, Sweden: Studentlitteratur.

Hirigoyen, M. (2012). *Abus de faiblesse et autres manipulations* [*Abuse of weakness and other manipulations*]. Paris: Éditions JC Lattès.

Houchin, T. M., Ranseen, J., Hash, P. A., & Bartnicki, D. J. (2012). The parental alienation debate belongs in the courtroom, not in DSM-5. *Journal of the Ameri-*

can Academy Psychiatry Law, 40(1), 127–131.

Johnston, J. R., Campbell, L. E. G., & Mayes, S. S. (1985). Latency children in post-separation and divorce disputes. *Journal of the American Academy of Child Psychiatry, 24,* 563–574.

Kaslow, F. W. (2011). [Review of the book *Parental Alienation, DSM-5, and ICD-11,* by William Bernet]. *American Journal of Family Therapy, 39,* 274–276.

Kloth-Zanard, J. (2012). *Where did I go wrong? How did I miss the signs? Dealing with hostile parenting and parental alienation.* Accessed at http://lulu.com.

Lowrance, M. (2010). *The good karma divorce: Avoid litigation, turn negative emotions into positive actions, and get on with the rest of your life.* New York: HarperCollins.

McBride, J. (2012). *Child less parent: "Snapshots" of parental alienation.* Seattle: CreateSpace Independent Publishing Platform.

O'Neill, T. (2010). [Letter to Daniel S. Pine, M.D.] National Organization for Women Foundation website. April, 2010. Retrieved from http://www.nowfoundation.org /issues/family/pad.html

Pepiton, M. B., Alvis, L. J., Allen, K., & Logid, G. (2012). Is parental alienation disorder a valid concept? Not according to scientic evidence. A review of Parental Alienation, DSM-5, and ICD-11 by William Bernet. *Journal of Child Sexual Abuse, 21*(2), 244–253.

Phélep, J. & Berger, M. (2012). *Divorce, séparation: les enfants sont-ils protégés [Divorce and separation: Are the children protected?]*. Paris: Dunod.

Rand, D. C. (2011). Parental alienation critics and the politics of science. *The American Journal of Family Therapy, 39*(1), 48–79.

Reay, K. (2011). *Toxic divorce: A workbook for alienated parents.* Penticton, British Columbia: Dr. Kathleen M. Reay, Inc.

Shapiro, G. (2011). [Review of the book *Parental Alienation, DSM-5, and ICD-11,* by William Bernet]. *Journal of the American Academy of Child and Adolescent Psychiatry, 50,* 1078–1079.

Steinbeck, J. T. (2011). *Brainwashing children.* Available at Amazon Digital Services.

Walker, L.E. & Shapiro, D. L. (2010). Parental alienation disorder: Why label children with a mental diagnosis? *Journal of Child Custody, 7*(4), 266–286.

Wallerstein, J. S., & Blakeslee, S. (1989). *Second chances: Men, women, and children a decade after divorce.* New York: Ticknor & Fields.

Wamboldt, M. Z. & Cordaro¸ A. R. (2012). Practical tools for assessing caregiver-child relationship problems. In H. M. Foran, S. R. H. Beach, A. M. S. Slep, R. E. Heyman, & M. Z. Wamboldt (Eds.), *Family problems and family violence: Reliable assessment and the ICD-11* (pp. 217–228). New York: Springer Publishing.

Warshak, R. A. (2012a). *Eromyrkky–kuinka suojella lasta avioerotilanteessa [Divorce poison: How to protect children in a divorce situation]*. Helsinki: Gummerus Kustannus.

Warshak, R. A. (2012b). ___ - __________ *[Divorce poison: Parental alienation and child abuse]* [Japanese, trans. by Satoshi Aoki]. Tokyo: Seishin Shobo K.K.

Warshak, R. A., & Otis, M. R. (2010). *Welcome back Pluto: Understanding, preventing, and overcoming parental alienation* [DVD]. Dallas, TX: WBP Media.

Zicavo Martínez, N. (2010). *Crianza compartida [Shared parenting]*. Mexico DF: Editorial Trillas.

Chapter 16

A JUDGE'S PERSPECTIVE ON PARENTAL ALIENATION

MICHELE LOWRANCE

I have been a judge in Domestic Relations Court in Chicago since 1995. For two decades prior to that I had sharpened my skills as a divorce attorney, but then I gave up being a warrior for the "right side." As an attorney I had to be an advocate only for my client, and my job was not designed to protect the children. Becoming a judge is one of the venues where that is, in fact, your job. Then, after years on the bench, I began to learn that there were many cases where even the judge, and certainly the parents had to really upgrade their skills and knowledge about parenting. In response to that observation, I wrote *The Good Karma Divorce* (Lowrance, 2010). A large part of that book was devoted to parenting skills that are not necessarily intuitive. *The Good Karma Divorce* is also in part about how to reduce anger and all of the difficult emotions that make parents so reactionary and frightened.

In more than seventeen years on the bench, the most disturbing thing I have witnessed is the corrosive legacy of parental alienation (PA) and visitation interference that can play out over decades. We have no statistics for measuring this group because the victims are too vast. The concentric circles include the children, their children, and the extended family as well. The declaration of war by one parent on another creates radioactive fallout that contaminates for generations.

It is very easy for a parent to malign another parent. It is tempting when you are angry. Even if it does not go to the level of full-out alienation, parents need to know that even the smallest act of maligning crushes the children's ability to feel good about themselves. I have witnessed impassioned declarations of love for a child by an alienating parent to mask the venom he or she feels for the other parent. I find that parents who do this are not interested in mere control. Their stakes are higher: total annihilation of the target parent's bond with the child. Little by little, alienation in a divorce case starts to take root. When it fully takes root, I see the child's boundaries collapse before my eyes. Soon the child forgets how to protect himself or herself and must align with the alienating parent as if life depends on it–because it does. From my perspective, destroying the child's loving attachment to one parent interrupts the child's intrinsic need to feel confident that he or she will be well taken care of by that parent.

WHY PARENTAL ALIENATION IS TROUBLESOME TO JUDGES

Here are some reasons these cases are so difficult, and why judges often have no love for them:

1. Professionals or litigants who do not really understand the full definition and qualities of PA often misuse the concept in court. They do not differentiate, for example, between oppositional disorder, anxiety disorder or even transitional anger at the parent versus actual PA. Judges often think that a parent may be claiming PA because they do not want to take responsibility for the breakdown of the parent-child relationship. In other words, the concept can be overused any time parents are having difficulties with their relationship with their children. It often gets far too inclusive, and when it really exists, often gets blurred because of the confusion.
2. Combative parents present conflicting stories of "he said, she said," and make it very difficult to determine who is telling the truth. Often an alienating parent comes to believe what he or she is saying, and his or her presentation seems authentic.
3. When target parents present their side of the case, they are often angry and frustrated and defensive, even when telling the truth–and as a result, they do not present very well in court. Sometimes judges consider *attitude* as influential as what is said in court.
4. The children often support the alienating parent by telling the judge, and their attorney and mental health professionals of their dislike for the target parent and how they have been treated badly. The reasoning skills of alienated children are often compromised, as is their ability to choose freely.
5. Alienated children often will not cooperate with traditional therapeutic intervention, and courts have difficulty enforcing these orders. Ultimately, judges like to believe that what they do works and that they have reached the right decision. When their decisions do not work, they often get exasperated with both parties.

Misperceptions Judges Often Have About Parental Alienation

Here are some of the misperceptions that the bench and bar too often believe, which results in their not taking adequate measures to either prevent or relieve PA.

1. PA is not in the *DSM-IV* so it cannot be real.
2. It is too confusing to tell the difference between alienation and estrangement.
3. It is too difficult to test the credibility of children's statements.
4. Traditional therapy is the answer for these alienated relationships.
5. There is no reason for these cases to be fast tracked.
6. Alienation usually resolves itself if the target parent does what he or she is supposed to do.
7. Supervised access is an appropriate tool to use to alleviate the fears of an anxiety-ridden parent.

Understanding that last perception is important. Alienators use fear. They say things like "The children are not safe [with the other parent]." They tell me the other parent is something the child should worry about. Supervised visitation, which is often requested by an alienating parent, reinforces the message that the target parent is too dangerous to be left alone with the child. When the court enters that order (unless you determine it is clearly warranted) it sends a message to the child that the court thinks the target parent is dangerous as well.

Alienators use this fear and treat the target parent like a disease in the child that must be removed. They make the child's survival contingent upon such removal. So the child, goaded by fear, must extricate herself or himself from the parent without the privilege of grieving the loss. These are crippling circumstances. The resultant high rate of serious anxiety, depression, withdrawal, delayed development and self-destructive behaviors has been aptly referred to as emotional abuse of a child, and we judges are the only ones who can stop this.

HOW THE COURT SYSTEM CAN CONTRIBUTE TO CREATING ALIENATION CASES

The adversarial model of our court system fosters a blame paradigm. This is true even though all of the states in the United States have adopted no-fault divorce. Many times parents think that if they do not fight, they are not being good parents. Sometimes parents believe that there will be an inference that they "didn't care enough" if they give up some of their custody time. Noncustodial or nonresidential parents, if they want more time with the children (standard visitation is generally alternating weekends and a weekday for dinner) to be really involved, have to hire a tough lawyer and dive into this adversarial model. The fear and anger born from the adversarial stance of the parents trickles down to the children and really damages them even in nonalienating cases. When one parent thinks dominating parenting time is the only way to have a secure relationship with her or his child, it can turn into an alienation case. For many parents, control over their children often feels like a win.

People cannot be blamed for their perception that divorce and custody is a blame-based system. Yes, we have no-fault divorce and no-fault divorce means blame does not count, but internally we have ourselves convinced that it does. Parents in this adversarial system think that they will get power if they can convince the judge that the other parent is at fault for any difficulties the child may be having. In the struggle for who is more wrong or right the focus is taken off the child.

Over the years in my courtroom, I began to see more and more that people were looking at divorce in a way that was damaging to them on three major levels. The first is that they believe the court system can provide emotional justice. That is not what the court does. That is not what the court is supposed to do. But parents in a highly charged battle, however, think they will get vindication and will feel better once it is over and the judge vindicates their position. To achieve this emotional justice parents give up power–power to the system and power to their lawyers. Looking for emotional justice, these parents forget that most of the power is still right in their hands.

The second basic error is that people believe they can behave in any kind of negative way emotionally, and ultimately, when the ordeal is over, they will go back to the way they were before. They believe to their detriment that these negative emotions will disappear. The fact is yes, they will dissipate for the parents but the children can be scarred forever.

The third major error I see is that parents believe that children are very resilient. Dr. Judith Wallerstein in her longitudinal study tells us that 50 percent of children from high-conflict cases do not want to ever get married and two thirds of them do not want to have children (Wallerstein, Lewis & Blakesley, 2000). That is a pretty potent statistic about children's resiliency. Yes, children can get over many things, but without upgraded parenting skills even in nonalienation cases, our children are at risk during any kind of battle between parents, let alone in a PA case.

PA or a similar type of acting out by divorcing parents has become a pervasive aspect of divorce in our society. A study done by Clawar and Rivlin (1991) found that PA was practiced to varying degrees by 80 percent of divorcing parents, with 20 percent engaging in such behaviors with their children at least once a day. Sometimes, it is as if the alienating parent does not even realize he or she is doing it. Sometimes, they do it right in front of me.

CASE EXAMPLES OF UNDIAGNOSED ALIENATION IN MY COURTROOM

Let me share an experience that many of you will recognize. I had a case in which for five years a child, Claire, did not want to see her father. Claire said her reason was that her father, Charles, did not come to see her when she was away at school. I was sure there was more to it than that. The mother, Susan, said she always told Claire, who was then fifteen, that she should see her father. Somehow, little progress had been made in changing Claire's mind, even with traditional therapy. I asked Susan if she had forgiven her former husband for the pain she felt he had caused her. She said, "Absolutely, but I will never forgive him for the pain he caused my child." She gave a righteous and even noble narrative about wanting to protect her child. She then broke down in tears that carried the quality of a fresh wound. Ever since the divorce thirteen years before, she had carried the weight of her fury strapped to her chest like a bomb. There it was, the smoldering fuse. Susan's refusal to forgive Charles had been causing her pain all this time, and she never realized it. She thought her anger had already been detonated and was over. It was the first time anyone could see that it was never over. Susan had passed on to her child her system of justice accounting. She said to me, and I think believed, it would be disloyal to her daughter if she forgave Charles. Deep down she knew the legacy she had passed on to her daughter, and she felt that to forgive Charles now would leave her child bound up in her own resentment. She had taught her daughter how to define her relationship with her father with this resentment and now she could not just leave her there alone by forgiving her former husband. Susan always told me how Claire was thriving as an A student until she became pregnant in her junior year of high school. Susan, the "perfect mother," was furious and embarrassed, so much so that Claire is now living with her father. All of this emotional heavy lifting for her Mom had prevented Claire from getting on fully with her life. All this time Susan thought she was nobly carrying the pain for her daughter, but in reality her daughter was carrying it for her.

Here is another example. One day in court, a mother was seeking an increase in child support from her former husband. The father testified that his income had declined dramatically. After the case was over, I was riding down the elevator with the mother and the parties' teenage daughter. They did not notice I was there or did not recognize me out of my black robe. The mother was sharing details of the case with the daughter, as I would not let the daughter come into the courtroom. The mother was telling her what a liar and manipulator her father was, fully expecting the daughter to agree. I doubted this child would ever be able to hear her father's side of the story. Even if the father was lying, I wondered why the mother could not share her frustration with her sister, her neighbor, or even the cashier at the corner store, anyone but the child. I was saddened because I knew that sharing this information with the daughter might forever affect the way the girl viewed her father and ultimately how she viewed men in general. Would they all be liars and manipulators to her? The daughter had no way to defend her trust in her father against this onslaught; she would certainly question it and probably cease to rely on it. Could the mother be sure the daughter would heal from believing her father is manipulative, uncaring, and a liar? I do not believe the mother considered the long-term effects. If she had, would she have intentionally hurt her daughter?

EMOTIONS AND ANGER IN THE COURTROOM

People come before me in court in deep pain, looking to the court to help them navigate and heal this pain. The couples I see in my courtroom are desperately searching for emotional release; they smuggle their pain into their testimony, even when it is not relevant to the topic. They do so at every opportunity, hoping that somehow the court will know how to lessen their agony. In the end, their desperate emotions remain unattended and unsatisfied. In an attempt to alleviate pain, even though the pain is transitory, they lash out and irreparable damage is done. The sight of couples who participate exuberantly in a demolition derby always disturbs me. The court system was not built to house these emotions, and attorneys are not trained to reduce this kind of suffering. Because they often feel disempowered, they use anger as an invigorating emotion. It feels more powerful to be angry than impotent.

I know from years in the courtroom that the most common way for alienated, or "target parents," to penetrate a situation in which they no longer feel relevant is through verbal warfare–words unleashed by both sides (perhaps via an attorney) that raise welts on the soul. The target parents I see are often anxious and emotionally exhausted. That is because often the single most important fear is losing access to your children. The maligning and alienating they endure is like invisible nerve gas that breaks down their resolve to control their pain. Raw, red and festering, they often release a torrent of accusations guaranteed to give the other parent a bad time. This torrent often sabotages their own best interests. Perhaps they feel it is justified because they have been so marginalized. Of course I see these tirades from alienators as well, but in many cases they appear more in control and present in court better. The core question I pose to both mom and dad is, what is more important, the children's happiness, or your being right? It really is a trick question but one that helps me flush out their motivations. I tell them they may be very right about every single thing, but it is going to affect the children in a way that is damaging. How do they intend to change their behavior? That is what judges want to know, even if they are talking to the party that has a right to be angry.

Sustained anger as a mode for managing fear always wears litigants out. The more they use anger to try to destroy the opposition, the more tired they become. I find that parents in these struggles are so occupied in this heightened state that eventually they find it difficult to remember how to get relief. Trying to break the anger cycle, I tell parents that well-practiced anger ignores other ways of responding. I have seen people self-destruct rather than risk letting anyone else "destroy them." Researchers at the University of North Carolina have found that people who have antagonistic hostility that is expressed angrily, either verbally or physically, are likely to have high levels of cholesterol. They found that men and women with higher levels of hostility also showed higher levels of homocysteine in the blood, which is strongly associated with heart disease (Williams et al., 2000). Targeted parents often are in too much pain to care, however.

HOW HAVE CHILDREN FAIRED IN OUR DIVORCING SYSTEM?

As we evaluate how children have fared in our system, we must consider some of the important studies. The result of long-term studies of children of divorce done by Dr. Judith Wallerstein and colleagues Julia Lewis and Sandra Blakeslee, authors of *The Unexpected Legacy of Divorce* (2000), have shown that two out of three children of divorce decide not to have children of their own. The reasons given range from that they would not want to be the kind of parent they had, to they would not know how to parent and thought they would have little talent for it, to if their marriage ended in divorce their children might go through the same horrible experience they had. Dr. Wallerstein reports that fights over custody and visitation give rise to a greater incidence of mental disorders in children. They often do not fare well in school and have a greater incidence of suicide, attempted suicide, clinical depression, and other disorders. Anxiety continues to be a theme in the children's lives well into adulthood. Dr. Wallerstein found that thirty years after divorce, many of them were still living with constant fear and were always waiting for disaster to strike without warning. This anxiety takes away joy from their childhood, but it also takes away the ability to feel sustained happiness in adulthood (Wallerstein et al., 2000).

Curiously, when Dr. Wallerstein interviewed children of divorce as adults, she noted that they could not remember much about their childhood playtime. They usually remembered worrying about arguments over which parent was going to pick them up or where they were going to go for the holidays. She found this troubling, because play is a vital part of a child's social and moral development. It is where children learn about loyalty, conflict resolution, and generally fitting into the world of their peers (Wallerstein et al., 2000). Children who worry about their parents, their parents' case, or taking care of their parents cannot be carefree. The chilling aspect of this research is that these were not necessarily high-conflict cases. Alienation cases are at the far end of the spectrum of damage to children.

After listening to hundreds of hours of psychological testimony about children and their parents, I have come to agree with Dr. Wallerstein that the results of PA do not necessarily show in childhood. They manifest themselves when the children are adults and move into romantic relationships. These adults unwittingly duplicate their parents' marriage when they are creating their own families. This is why experts say that PA is generational in effect.

SUGGESTIONS FOR PARENTS

When I wrote *The Good Karma Divorce,* I referred to what I called "wisdom building skills for heroic parenting." I attempted to help parents develop new skills in the trenches of adversity during the divorce. Parenting skills, when you're going through a divorce or alienation battle, are not the same skills that you use every day. You cannot always know them intuitively. Some of them are counterintuitive. They are not the regular garden-variety skills. When you are faced with PA, however, the upgrading of parenting skills becomes even more intense and your interaction with the court becomes more vital.

Despite these difficulties, there is plenty that target parents can do. Here are some suggestions for handling parental alienation that seem to help:

1. Parenting plan orders should be entered as soon as possible in a case. Oral agreements are not enforceable. Hoping to get cooperation from an alienating parent is not enough.

2. I recommend that parents get a court order for parenting therapy as soon as possible. I tell target parents you need to come to court, or you need to go right to mediation if there is a mediation requirement in your parenting order or state statute. Whatever mythology has been built against a parent, they will have a chance to respond to it in a neutral setting. In a family therapy context, the child has an opportunity to vent her or his misinformation and anger and resentment in a place where some healing, or confrontation by a therapist as to the truth of the child's beliefs, can take place.

3. If orders are violated, go to court on a *Rule To Show Cause* for violation of the order as soon as possible. When they cannot afford an attorney I tell them to do this themselves. I encourage parents to write their own petition for a ruling for visitation violation, for family therapy, or for makeup visitation. Go online and find form petitions for your jurisdiction. Some jurisdictions call it a Rule to Show Cause, Order to Show Cause, Adjudication of Contempt, or Violation of Court Order Petition. I know that is a terrifying thing to do, but if the alternative is to do nothing, you must educate yourself about how to get on the court calendar and how to file petitions. You might be surprised to find that many judges bend over backwards for an unrepresented parent who is not getting her or his visitation. Do not judge your experience in court as not worthwhile if you do not feel like you have "won." Winning is a very difficult thing to gauge in family court, it is more of a process. Sometimes it is two steps forward and then one step back; your child needs to know that you at least filed a petition, even if you do not feel satisfied with the result. They will know over the years that you never gave up.

4. I recommend that target parents create an alienation map or chart for the judge that shows him or her in five minutes what could not be said in five hours. This map should include a chart of all missed visits, and a list of all the denigrating phrases made by the alienating spouse to the children about the target parent, including the statements to friends and/or extended family of the target parent (if they are admissible in evidence). Also a graph can show the increase in missed visits in a very compelling and impactful way. This may show the judge how the situation is deteriorating.

5. Many judges are not warm to the phrase *parental alienation syndrome.* Instead, I tell parents to ask the judge to keep an eye open for *visitation interference* as the case progresses and describe the maligning behavior for the judge. Through education, judges are becoming more aware of the problem, but some still shut down when they hear the phrase PAS. I know things are getting better because I have been asked to speak on the topic to judges many times

this year, and the seminars were very well-attended by enthusiastic judges.

6. I also advise parents to keep a journal in detail. In their petitions they should itemize the interference. I tell them to be clear about itemizing the characteristics of alienation and showing the judge how it exists in their case. You may have to educate the court on what the red flags for alienation are. This is why target parents should really make the effort to itemize everything. Tell your lawyer to give you the assignment that you keep a journal so that it can be "work product" and not subject to discovery.

7. You may ask the judge to help you protect the children. Let the judge know what the initial red flags are and how they correspond to the characteristics of alienation. Remember in some courts they are still adverse to the words parental alienation. You might say, "I really need your help. I have had a good relationship with my child. Give us a way to keep it. If you do not take this case under your wing there is a good chance that our relationship will be destroyed."

SUGGESTED STRATEGIES FOR JUDGES AND ATTORNEYS

1. Never Base Your Strategy on "Getting Through" to the Alienating Parent

As judges we all develop a "speech" that we give parents who are interfering in the other parent's relationship or acting in other ways damaging to their children. We too often think that our speech is so good we could get through to a brick. In alienation cases, it is different. Never base your strategy or concentrate your efforts on getting through to the alienating parents. Not only are they committed to resisting change, but also they often believe in their perception. I have made this mistake myself and I can tell you that they have no epiphany. It is far more effective to attempt to change behavior by forcing them to fear consequences by the court. They do not recognize authority, especially once they have manipulated it. They only respond to a show of power. They will convincingly tell you how they view their own actions as being in the best interests of the children. They are cognitively blind to the effects on the children, or on the target parent and extended family.

2. Know the Difference Between Regular/Traditional Therapy and Reconciliation, Reunification, or Family Therapy

Naturally our first tool of choice is sending the parties to therapy, especially when the children do not want to visit with the target parent. This is very often a misinformed decision unless we understand the difference between traditional therapy and reconciliation therapy. Suffice it to say that with traditional therapy you get patients in touch with their issues and to feel their emotions. Because the child's perceptions and emotions may be distorted, traditional therapy can amplify the animosity and hatred. I have seen traditional therapists allow the child to determine how long it will be (if ever) before they agree to see the target parent. Because the child is aligned with the alienating parent, they are emotionally required to keep rejecting contact with the target parent. Remember, alienated children are often told that if they are nice to the target parent, it could be used "against" them in court.

Reconciliation therapy, in contrast to traditional therapy, activates old positive memories and challenges distorted thinking. Because of brain development and impressionability, it is very easy to implant false memories in a child. Whether a family is in traditional therapy or reunification therapy, a judge must be vigilant to determine if there is a therapeutic alliance between the therapist and the alienator. If there is extended therapy with little progress, this could be one of the reasons. Sadly, it has to be said that in severe alienation cases, the likelihood of a positive outcome for either kind of therapy is low, and other measures may need to be considered.

3. Appointing a Therapist or Expert Evaluator

Be on the lookout for a therapeutic alliance between alienator and therapist. Often the alienating parent will say to the court "my child's in therapy and we are working on this." In fact, the therapist may innocently be aligned with the alienating parent's point of view. You also want a strong therapist who is not afraid to take a stand against an intimidating alienating parent. In every jurisdiction, judges have the power to order psychological evaluations in custody cases. If you are not sure about the existence of alienation you might want to order a psychological assessment to find out what is going on. Choose an expert who knows about PA and perhaps will give you a road map or game plan.

4. Appointing Representatives for the Children

I recommend appointing a guardian ad litem to represent the interests of the children. The designation of Attorney for the Child can be problematic because too many child representatives feel they must advocate for the child's wishes. In these cases, the child's wishes are not in their best interest and in fact can be very damaging to the child. It is easy to see how an attorney for the child can unwittingly ally with an alienator. When considering whom to appoint, if necessary, also appoint a strong guardian or attorney for the child, who is not afraid to take a stand or oppose an alienating parent. Above all whatever designation you use, make sure they are very well-versed in PA.

5. Behavior Modification by Court Order

In my courtroom I use an exercise I created based on "Rules of Engagement," which are usually thought of as stated policies about the use of military force. This approach may be helpful in mild and some moderate alienation cases. The purpose of my Rules of Engagement, however, is to reduce fear and activate communication in the absence of the parties' ability to do so. If you can get communication going, no matter how minor, parents may become less terrified and may not feel as compelled to alienate. (This is not true in severe cases, especially with personality disorders.) I ask every parent to make a list of every nonfinancial fear they have about the custody process. I ask parents to include fears about how they perceive their spouse will behave and what damage they think the children will suffer from the process. I ask parents to make this list extensive but not to include financial issues at this time. The interesting thing about the Rules of Engagement is that it is difficult for people with children to say the words, "I refuse to enter into a process that will help my children," or, "I refuse to enter into a process that attempts civility." An interesting and effective tactic for the target parent may be to request an order on a temporary basis that protects the children from the other parent's behavior. The judge will notice who is more difficult during this negotiation.

6. Enter No Maligning Orders as Soon as Possible

Your order can make it clear that maligning is an immediate contempt of court. I have allowed the parent to record conversations if they are damaging at the time of pick-up for visitation. (The children should not see the recorder.) Sometimes I require that there is no discussion by one parent about the other about anything, not even what they are wearing. In my experience with alienation cases, parents tell me they're just being "truthful" to their children. In the name of truth, one parent erodes the child's positive attachment to the other parent. If the maligning parent is successful in grinding down the bond between the child and the other parent, it is viewed as a victory. Instead, what the maligning parent may have succeeded at is destroying that child's ability to have positive attachments later in life. This is why I always issue an order that says no maligning. I have had alienating parents object that my "no maligning" order interferes with their constitutional right to free speech. In the recent *International Handbook of Parental Alienation Syndrome,*

Dr. Lorandos described a Florida case in which an alienator objected to the judge's order to stop maligning and encourage the children to have a relationship with the target parent. The alienator took the case to the appeals court and then to the Florida Supreme Court. The courts supported the judge's no maligning order (Gardner, Sauber & Lorandos, 2006, p. 334).

7. Order Specific and Precise Parenting Times and Places and Resist Orders that Only State "Reasonable Visitation"

When judges are creating orders, they should hammer out a date- and time-specific visitation schedule, so that there are no ambiguities. You cannot get a contempt order for violation unless the dates of the order are specific. Judges may need to order a neutral location for visitation transfer if the parties are combative. One suggestion is that if your jurisdiction has parenting coordinators, they are valuable in facilitating transfers. Another idea might be a precisely worded authorization to all law enforcement officers to execute the transfer of the children. If both parents have the right to pick up the children from school, a judge should make the wording very clear and give the school authorities a copy of the order in advance of the pickup. In the same vein, a precise authorization and access instruction for all personnel involved in extracurricular activities is useful. The parenting orders should also specifically state that the custodial parent is not to schedule extracurricular activities that conflict with the visitation schedule.

8. Build the Sanctions into Your Court Order

There should be a clearly outlined set of consequences for missed visits or visitation interference. Perhaps the penalty could be monetary sanctions or double visits for each missed visit. If three visits are missed in a row, the order could state that the parties go right to therapy or to mediation. There can be provisions that all missed visits must be made up within fourteen days, or you can assess a monetary sanction for each missed visit or the payment of the injured party's legal fees. You might require all visits missed due to illness be verified by a doctor's report. The court, of course, should reserve the right to modify the orders or enforce them as it sees fit.

9. Limiting Telephone Calls

It is important to limit the alienator's phone calls to the child when the child is with the target parent. Many alienating parents insist on talking to the child every day. Every day is too much when the target parent is trying to reestablish his or her bond with the child; maybe every other day at most in the beginning is more appropriate. I have allowed the target parents to record the calls with the alienating parent if they believe the visit is being sabotaged. In more extreme cases, I have limited the topics the alienating parent can talk to the child about. For example, questions or statements such as: Do you miss me, or I am so lonely without you, are you safe?

10. These Cases Must Have Priority and Be Expedited

Perhaps my most important bit of advice for judges is not to let these cases drag out. Always set a time line to return to court. Absence does not make the heart grow fonder for these alienated children, and unfamiliarity breeds contempt. Time is on the side of the alienator. Conduct frequent case management sessions, and if necessary, use threats of the loss of custody to the alienating parent.

11. The Allegations of Sexual Abuse

When a parent comes to court with accusations of sexual abuse, it rightfully frightens judges. Nine times out of ten the judge says, "let's suspend visitation until we get to the bottom of this." Many times it is a grenade alienators throw into the courtroom. Everybody freezes and puts on their full metal vests. As judges, we must look at the context of the case. We must think about whether or not visitation has been obstructed in the past by the accusing parent. The lawyers must inform us of the prior pattern of visitation interference, because this goes to the accuser's credibility. Yes, it is a bomb thrown into the courtroom, but we must look at the total picture with the help of an expert who agrees to take the case immediately and follow the evidentiary and medical protocol. These cases should be top priority.

12. Crime Scene Investigation by Judges and Attorneys

I had the very important opportunity to meet Canadian family law attorney Brain Ludmer who has worked diligently in PA cases. I am devoting this section to the inspired ideas that he told me about flushing out the testimony and agenda of an alienating parent. I have adapted what he taught me to use as a judge. When the case is before you, a judge can subtly force the alienator to get involved in solving the problem of a child who does not want to visit. Expect that the alienating parent might come to court saying he or she is "supportive of the visits, I want her to love her father, it's not my fault she doesn't want to go. I always encourage her to go." If this happens three times, however, judges must say this support is not good enough or it is not happening. So, here are some covert, dare I say devious, ways I use to find out what is really going on. Here are some questions for the parents and sometimes it just may be the judges who have to ask these questions if the lawyers do not. It is not the questions that are the emphasis here, but how the parents respond will tell you a lot.

1. Ask the alienating parent: "Are you concerned about your child not going on visits?"
2. Ask the alienating parent: "How have you changed your conduct when you see your encouragement is not working?"
3. Ask the alienating parent: "What have you done differently to show your concern?
   The formula for the questions is: guidance-boundaries-incentives-consequences
   a. Guidance in your status calls on cases, ask the parents to tell the court (put this on the record) "What guidance do you give to your child about the other parent?"
   b. Boundaries . . . ask "What boundaries are in your household, what do you do when they are broken, what are the rules of the household?"
   c. Incentives . . . ask, "What incentives do you have for doing chores, and so on?" then ask "What incentives do you give your child to go on visits?"
   d. Consequences . . . ask, "What are the consequences in your household for low grades, not cleaning the room, and so on. What are consequences if you child does not go on the visits?"

Try to find out if they have used their best skill set, and it still does not work. What you want to look for: They are either lying about their good faith efforts to foster visitation or they are a completely ineffective parents. It may be that unless there is a transfer of custody, the situation cannot be turned around. Make sure you always have a court reporter for this questioning. I have ordered that these transcripts follow the case. It is important that the next judge see it before alienators have a chance to clean up their testimony. I had a recent case in which I transferred custody and then stayed the order if the child went on the visits. The older boy did because this got him off the hook with his mother at the same time he thought he was a hero for going because he was the one that made sure that his mom kept custody.

13. Interviewing the Children

If you do interview the children, you want to do it once alone and then again in the presence of the alienating parent. Notice if the children offer frivolous reasons for not wanting to see the target parent. Also look for commonality of phrasing that is similar to the alienating parent. The magic question that Brian Ludmer suggested and I have used is, "If this judge finds against you, what are you going to change about your parenting?" If they say nothing will change, you may be pretty sure you have made the right decision if you do transfer custody. Either way the alienating parent is not an appropriate trustee for the children's right to have a relationship with the other parent.

14. Contempt of Court Findings and Sanctions

When it comes to contempt, the better purpose is to secure compliance, not punish. You can suspend sentencing to see if there is compliance. You can make a purge of the contempt contingent upon compliance with visitation orders. In a study of more than 400 PA cases in which the court forced contact, it was effective 90 percent of the time (Clawar & Rivlin, 1991). Use behavioral compliance and conditions rather than jail. The risk of sending the alienator to jail is the risk that that parent might become a martyr to the child and be all the more angry at the target parent. If there is money available, I favor monetizing the sanctions. Then if you want to do jail it is easier when there is a money purge.

15. Change of Custody

When the circumstances warrant it or in some severe cases, changing custody may be the only effective option. Determining when it is warranted is the key. If the parent is just intractable, however, judges may order the children to live with the target parent. You will want to have evaluations to see what effect that transfer of custody may have on the child. You will also want to consult with an expert to find the most protective way to handle a transfer of custody. Sometimes the grandparents can be a halfway house for a few weeks when the child positively refuses to go with the target parent.

I had one case in which the son absolutely refused to see the father in a clear alienation case. I entered an order transferring custody to the father, and stayed the order pending the son's going on visits with the father. The son thought he was the mother's hero by making sure custody wasn't transferred. Eventually, he did repair his relationship with the father.

16. Joint Parenting and Expanded Visitation Time

I wrote visitation guidelines for the Cook County Courts in the early 1980s. At that time I thought that the best practice was alternating weekends; I was caught in the mass-hypnosis groupthink about what was best for the children. I am guilty. The protocols we used to order were usually alternating weekends and Wednesday for dinner, a week out of Christmas vacation, and two to four weeks of summer vacation. With these standard orders, studies have found that the visiting parent often gets marginalized and cannot handle the marginalization and too often detaches from the child. The divorcing culture needs to explore the science behind why both parents' active engagement with the children is crucial. Some judges will say if the parties cannot get along we cannot do a joint parenting order. I do not always agree with that. I think if the parties cannot get along, they may really need a joint parenting order. All the studies show that children of joint custody parental arrangements do much better than full custody arrangements.

CONCLUSION

In this chapter, I have tried to describe some of the methods I use to deal with PA. To do this I have used material from my book *The Good Karma Divorce,* from the *Family Matters* radio appearances I have been privileged to do with Alderwoman and PA Expert Jill Egizii, from my articles and lectures, as well as from my courtroom. The fear and anger that fuels PA is devastating to children, parents, and grandparents. When dealing with these difficult cases, I do everything I can to stop the alienation and to defuse the anger. My book was inspired by a Vietnamese Buddhist monk, Thich Nhat Hahn, who writes that children, like flowers, cannot survive independently. He explained that they are completely dependent upon the soil in which they are planted, the sunlight they receive, and the rain that waters them. Children in alienation struggles are often planted in soil contaminated by anger or depleted of vitality through depression; the sunlight they need may be occluded by a dark cloud that covers the hearts of their parents. The precipitation they receive may be tears of acid rain, carrying unfiltered chemical deposits from a sky polluted by the ashes of their parents' actions. Yes, I am concerned about the litigants before me, but the reason I do this job every day is the children.

REFERENCES

Clawar, S. S., & Rivlin, B. V. (1991). *Children held hostage: Dealing with programmed and brainwashed children.* Chicago, IL: American Bar Association Press.

Gardner, R., Sauber, R., & Lorandos, D. (Eds.). (2006). *The international handbook of parental alienation syndrome: Conceptual, clinical and legal considerations.* Springfield, IL: Charles C Thomas Publisher, Ltd.

Lowrance, M. (2010). *The good karma divorce: Avoid litigation, turn negative emotions into positive actions, and get on with the rest of your life.* New York: Harper One.

Wallerstein, J. S., Lewis, J. M., & Blakesley, S. (2000). *The unexpected legacy of divorce: A 25 year landmark study* (1st ed.). Hyperion.

Williams, J. E., Paton, C. C., Siegler, I. C., Eigenbrodt, M. L., Nieto, J., & Tyroler, H. A. (2000). Anger proneness predicts coronary heart disease risk. *Circulation, 101,* 2034–2039.

NAME INDEX

SUBJECT INDEX

ABOUT THE CD-ROM

This CD-ROM contains the *Supplemental Reference Guide for Parental Alienation: The Handbook for Mental Health and Legal Professionals*. In addition, there are separate Word files of each of the motions included in Part III. The reader may find it useful to use these files as templates in which to prepare their own motions. The three sections on the CD-ROM include the following:

- References in the Professional Literature
- Representative North American Legal Cases
- Sample Motions in Parental Alienation Cases